Kalaupapa Place Names

Kalaupapa
PLACE NAMES

Waikolu to Nihoa

JOHN R. K. CLARK

Translations by Iāsona Ellinwood and Keao NeSmith

UNIVERSITY OF HAWAI'I PRESS

HONOLULU

Library of Congress Cataloging-in-Publication Data

Names: Clark, John R. K., author. | Ellinwood, Iasona, translator. |
NeSmith, Keao, translator.
Title: Kalaupapa place names, Waikolu to Nihoa / John R.K. Clark ;
translations by Iasona Ellinwood and Keao NeSmith.
Description: Honolulu : University of Hawai'i Press, [2018] | Translations of
more than three hundred Hawaiian-language newspaper articles published by
residents of Kalaupapa between 1834 and 1948. | Includes bibliographical
references and index.
Identifiers: LCCN 2017055862 | ISBN 9780824872717 (cloth alk. paper) | ISBN
9780824872724 (pbk. alk. paper)
Subjects: LCSH: Leprosy—Patients—Hawaii—Kalaupapa—Social conditions. |
Kalaupapa (Hawaii)—History. | Kalaupapa (Hawaii)—Social conditions.
Classification: LCC RC154.5.H32 C53 2018 | DDC 362.196/99800996924—dc23
LC record available at https://lccn.loc.gov/2017055862

Front cover art: (Top) The gravestone of Kahalekumano (1855–1893)
on the summit of Kauhakō crater. Photo courtesy of Ann Marie Kirk.
(Bottom) Kalawao on the windward side of the Kalaupapa peninsula is
the site of the original settlement. Aerial photo courtesy of Brian Daniel.

Back cover art: Wai'ale'ia, the large valley inland of the original settlement
at Kalawao. The valley with its waterfall, Waimanu, was a popular hiking
destination for staff and patients. Photo courtesy of Ann Marie Kirk.

In memory of
my great-great-grandmother, Emele,
who was sent to Kalaupapa in 1884.

Contents

Acknowledgments

THIS BOOK WOULD not have been possible without the Office of Hawaiian Affairs' online archive of Hawaiian-language newspapers and the translations of the Hawaiian-language newspaper articles by Iāsona Ellinwood and Keao NeSmith.

Special thanks for their support to John Barker, Wendy Bolton, Ruben Boon, Drew Bryan, Stuart Ching, Jason Clark, Koji Clark, Sachi Clark, Brian Daniel, Barbara Dunn, Fern Duvall, George Engebretson, Ann Fagerroos, Kuupua Girod, Sandy Hall, Jennifer Higa, Shoko Hisayama, Takao Hojo, Masako Ikeda, Mie Inage, Robert Kekaianiani Irwin, Luana Kaaihue, Ann Marie Kirk, Shugen Komagata, Luella Kurkjian, Sister Alicia Damien Lau, Jeremy Lemarie, Nadine Little, Jill Matsui, Ka'ohulani McGuire, Valerie Monson, Alfred Morris, Nancy Morris, Yusuke Motohashi, Sidney Nakahara, Lolena Nicholas, Pua Niau-Puhipau, Naoko Nishiura, Puakea Nogelmeier, Yvonne Ono, Raul Ortega, Tom Penna, Mikiala Pescaia, Barbara Ritchie, Carol Rosa, Kau'i Sai-Dudoit, Naoe Sakai, Melissa Shimonishi, Chris Swenson, Julie Ushio, Grace Wen, Fred Woods, Elmer Wilson, and Barbara Wong.

Introduction

KALAUPAPA NATIONAL HISTORICAL PARK was established by Congress on December 22, 1980, to preserve the history of the Kalaupapa Leprosy Settlement and to honor the memory of the estimated eight thousand people who were sent there between 1866 and 1959. The story of the settlement, including the subsequent roles of Father Damien (Saint Damien since 2009) and Mother Marianne (Saint Marianne since 2012) has been told many times by many people. The most comprehensive history is *Kalaupapa: A Collective Memory* by Anwei Skinsnes Law, which was published by the University of Hawaiʻi Press in 2012. The culmination of forty years of research on the history of leprosy in Hawaiʻi, Law's magnum opus is a wealth of information, complete with archival documents, photographs, oral history interviews, and letters from the patients translated from Hawaiian.

Kalaupapa Place Names: Waikolu to Nihoa is also a history of the leprosy settlement, but it differs from the works of other authors by telling Kalaupapa's story almost exclusively from more than three hundred Hawaiian-language newspaper articles. From 1834 to 1948, approximately 125,000 pages of Hawaiian-language newspapers were printed in more than a hundred different papers. These newspapers are now an invaluable cultural and historical repository that document the history of the islands as Hawaiʻi moved from a kingdom to a constitutional monarchy to a republic and to a territory of the United States. When I discovered this amazing resource in 2005, I used it to research and write a book on traditional surfing, *Hawaiian Surfing: Traditions from the Past* (2011), and then again to research Oʻahu's North Shore, which resulted in *North Shore Place Names: Kahuku to Kaʻena* (2014). The Hawaiian-language newspaper archive is online and searchable in the Office of Hawaiian Affairs' Papakilo Database.

Like its two predecessors, *Kalaupapa Place Names: Waikolu to Nihoa* is a collection of original historical newspaper articles, most of which have not been translated previously. The translators for this book were Iāsona

KALAUPAPA
NATIONAL HISTORICAL PARK

Mōkapu

'Ōkala
Leinaopapio
Huelo

WAIKOLU

Makali'i

Ananāluawāhine

Kaupikiawa

Lae Ho'olehua

WAI'ALE'IA

KALAWAO

Lae o Kahio

Kauhakō

WAIHĀNAU

MAKANALUA

Lae o Kāhili

KALAUPAPA

Kalae'a
'Iliopi'i
Kalaemilo
Papaloa
Pauaka
Lenalena

Pūahi
Pikoone

Kukuiohāpu'u

N
W ⊕ E
S

Nihoa

Kalaupapa National Historical Park map

Ellinwood, a graduate of the University of Hawaiʻi at Mānoa with a master's degree in Hawaiian, and Keao NeSmith, an applied linguist and researcher who is fluent in Hawaiian. Keao also did the translations for *Hawaiian Surfing* and *North Shore Place Names*. In addition to Iāsona and Keao, Mikiala Pescaia translated several kanikau, and Puakea Nogelmeier assisted as a Hawaiian-language consultant. Articles in Japanese about Dr. Masanao Goto, which were from the National Hansen's Disease Museum in Tokyo, Japan, were translated by Shoko Hisayama.

Kalaupapa National Historical Park, the site of Hawaiʻi's historic leprosy settlement, is located on the Koʻolau, or windward, side of the island of Molokaʻi, one of the four islands in Maui County. Most of the island's seven thousand residents live on the Kona, or leeward, side of the island, while the Koʻolau side is uninhabited except for the patients and park staff who live in Kalaupapa National Historical Park. As of January 6, 2016, the 150th anniversary of the first patients taken to Kalaupapa, only fifteen patients remained, living either in the park or at Hale Mōhalu in Honolulu.

The geographical focal point of the park is a long, wide peninsula that extends into the ocean from the base of the Koʻolau sea cliffs. Although the Hawaiian language has a term for peninsula, ʻanemoku, Hawaiians did not use it for this wide point of land and instead called it ʻaina pālahalaha, or the "flat land"; kahi pālahalaha, or the "flat place"; kahua pālahalaha, or the "flat grounds"; and kula pālahalaha, or the "flat plain." While the peninsula is not completely level, it is flat in comparison to the high sea cliffs that stand behind it. In 1921, one writer called the peninsula ka ihu o ka moku, or "the bow of the ship," a poetic reference to the fact that it points due north from the island of Molokaʻi, which lies on an east-west axis.

Hawaiians divided the peninsula into three land divisions, which from east to west are Kalawao, Makanalua, and Kalaupapa. When the Board of Health, or Papa Ola, decided to isolate Hawaiʻi's leprosy patients, they selected Kalawao as the site of the first community on the peninsula. This is where the earliest homes and churches were built and where Father Damien lived and died. The settlement also included three coastal valleys: Waikolu to the east of the peninsula and Waiʻaleʻia and Waihānau, which are directly inland, and the shoreline and sea cliffs west of the peninsula to a small plateau called Nihoa. In 1894, the boundaries of the settlement were defined in a public notice published by the Board of Health in Hawaiian and English that was intended to evict the few remaining residents who were nonpatients.

Keena O Ka Papa Ola.
Hoolaha No Na Kamaaina
    Ke hoike ia aku nei i na poe apau e noho ana ma ke Kahua Maʻi Lepera ma Molokai, no lakou na Kuleana Aina i lawe ia e ke Aupuni no ka hooholo pono ana i na mea i kauoha ia ma ke Kanawai hookaawale no ke kinai ana i ka maʻi lepera, penei:
    Oiai ua hooko ia na mea a pau i koi ia na ke Aupuni e hana no ka uku ana aku i ka poe nona na kuleana ma ke Kahua Maʻi Lepera, nolaila, ke hoike ia aku nei mai a mahope aku o ka la 15 o Mei, 1894, ua lilo loa no ke Aupuni ia mau waiwai, a o na wahi apau ma ka Anemoku, na alanui, e komo ana iloko a puka

iwaho mai ia mau wahi aku mai ka Leina o Papio, Waikolu a ke awa o Kalau-
papa, a hiki loa aku i, a komo pu mai me, Nihoa, me na ala liilii a alanui apau e
pii ai iluna o ka pali a hiki i Kalae, e lilo a e hookaawale ia i Kahua Maʻi Lepera
ma ka Mokupuni o Molokai.

Ke hoike ia aku nei ma keia o na poe apau e loaa aku ana ma ke kauwahi
iloko oia Kahua Maʻi Lepera e like meia i hoike ia malunaʻe, me ka loaa ole aku
he palapala ae mai na luna Aupuni i kuleana e manao ia he poe komohewa, a e
hoopii ia e like me ke Kanawai, na Rula me na Kanawai hooponopono o ke Ka-
hua Maʻi Lepera e ku nei.

Ua haawi ia i na poe no lakou na Kuleana Aina mamua he kanaono (60) la
mai ka la 30 aku o Novemaba, 1894, no lakou e haalele iho ai ia mau wahi. E
hoolako aku ana ke Aupuni i mau mea kupono no ka lawe ana ia lakou me ko
lakou mau pono mai ia wahi aku, i ka manawa kupono, me ka uku ole a hiki i
Pukoo.

A ke kauoha pu ia aku nei lakou e hele ae ma ke Keena hana o R. W. Meyer,
iloko o na la he Kanaono (60) i uku ia aku na dala i hooholo ia e na Komisina oia
ka uku no na Kuleana o lakou, me ka loaa pu aku o na palapala sila mai ke Au-
puni aku no na Apana Aina ma ke Ahupuaa o Ualapue, Mokupuni o Molokai, ma
ke ano panai me na dala i olelo ia, me ka lilo hou ole aku o ka lakou mau dala.

O na poe i hooholo ia e uku ia aku no na mea kanu maluna o na Kuleana
a no na waiwai lewa e ae paha ke kauoha ia aku nei e hele koke ae iloko o elua
pule mai ka la i hoopuka ia ai keia hoolaha no ka uku ia mai i na dala e like me
ka mea i hooiaʻi e na Komisina.

William O. Smith, President Board of Health.
Aponoia: J. A. King, Kuhina Kalaiaina.
Honolulu, Nov. 30, 1894.

Office of the Board Of Health.
Notice To Kamaainas.

Notice is hereby given to all parties at the Leper Settlement, Molokai, whose kuleanas have been taken by the Government for the better carrying out of the Act of Segregation to prevent the spread of leprosy, to wit:

Whereas now all the conditions imposed upon the Government for the in-demnification of the owners of the kuleanas at the Leper Settlement have been complied with the said kuleanas are hereby declared from May 15, 1894, to be the property of the Government; and every portion of the peninsula, together with all the roads, through, in and out of the same from Leina Papio, Waikolu, to the Kalaupapa landing, to Nihoa and including the same, also all the trails or roads to the top of the mountain to Kalae, now comprise the Leper Settlement on the island of Molokai.

Notice is hereby given that all parties found on any portion within the limits of the Leper Settlement just described, without a permit from the authorities will be considered trespassers and subject to prosecution, according to law, rules and regulations now existing.

The former owners of the said kuleanas are granted sixty days from the 30th day of November, A.D. 1894 to evacuate the premises. Means of transport for themselves and effects will be provided them in due time by the Government free of charge to Pukoo.

And they are hereby requested to call at the office of R. W. Meyer, within sixty days, to receive the sums awarded them as indemnification for their kuleanas, together with a deed in fee simple from the Government for certain pieces of land in the Ahupuaa of Ualapue on the Island of Molokai in addition to the sums awarded and without further charge.

Parties who have received awards for indemnification of plantings on the said kuleanas or other personal property are hereby requested to call immediately within two weeks from date hereof to receive the sums awarded them by the Commissioners.

> William O. Smith, President, Board of Health.
> Approved: J. A. King, Interior Minister.
> Honolulu, Nov. 30, 1894.

» [The Board of Health printed copies of these notices as handbills for public distribution. The texts above are from original copies of the Hawaiian and English handbills that are on file at the Hawai'i State Archives.]

In the Hawaiian-language version of the notice, the Board of Health used the term kahua for "settlement," one of two words that writers in the Hawaiian-language newspapers also used to describe the community at Kalaupapa. The other is panala'au. Using the *Hawaiian Dictionary* by Pukui and Elbert as a guide, kahua is also translated as "settlement" in *Kalaupapa Place Names*, while panala'au is translated as "colony." The earliest newspaper article in *Kalaupapa Place Names* was written in 1836 and the latest in 1932, with many articles from every decade in between. While both kahua and panala'au are used as early as 1875, a survey of the articles shows that panala'au was used early in the history of Kalaupapa, most heavily from 1870 to 1900, while kahua began to replace it beginning in the early 1900s. In general, writers in English-language newspapers who referenced Kalaupapa almost always used the term "settlement," as did writers of other documents and texts. In a report to the Board of Health in 1886, which Dr. Arthur Mouritz included in his book *The Path of the Destroyer*, Father Damien, writing in English, used the term "Settlement" throughout his report.

To His Excellency Walter M. Gibson,
President of the Board of Health.

Dear Sir: I herewith enclose the report of my observations and action at the Leper Settlement during a residence of thirteen years, which Your Excellency requested me to prepare. Hoping that it will meet your views, I remain Your Excellency's most humble servant,

—J. Damien [Rev. Joseph Damien], Catholic Priest. Kalawao, MARCH 11, 1886.

The lands from Waikolu to Nihoa defined the lateral extent of the settlement and the areas that patients were permitted to go on their own. Eventually, however, patients and nonpatients alike simply referred to all these lands collectively as Kalaupapa. In *My Name Is Makia: A Memoir of Kalaupapa*, patient Elroy Makia Malo recalled that shortly after his arrival as a twelve-year-old in 1947, he was given a tour of the peninsula by Johnny Aruda, an older patient. At a stop where they could see the entire coast, Aruda explained,

"You see that spot way down there? That's what we call Nehoa [Nihoa]. Some guys call 'em The Flat. You see the two small islands on this side [Mōkapu and 'Ōkala]? You continue on to shore and you see that ridge. Well, that ends Kalaupapa on this side. So between Nehoa [Nihoa] and Wailolu [Waikolu] Point, this all Kalaupapa. This a pretty big place. We can go all this place. Anytime we like."

This broader sense of place in the name Kalaupapa is reflected in the name of the national historical park and in the title of this book, *Kalaupapa Place Names: Waikolu to Nihoa*. The boundaries of the national historical park today are the same as those of the original settlement.

Prior to the establishment of Kalaupapa National Historical Park, the Kalaupapa Leprosy Settlement was designated a National Historical Landmark on January 7, 1976. The NHL includes a marine boundary that extends 0.93 miles offshore from the NHP and includes Huelo, 'Ōkala, and Mōkapu islets.

To research the history of Kalaupapa I assembled a list of its Hawaiian place names and searched for them in the archive of Hawaiian-language newspapers. This approach turned up a wonderful cross section of information. The leprosy settlement was a unique community of Hawaiians from every island except uninhabited Kahoʻolawe. They spoke and wrote in their native language, and they brought their regional customs, skills, and traditions with them, including their love of place names. They learned the names of their new home, perpetuating the history and culture attached to them, and used the names in their everyday activities, in the letters they wrote to family and friends, and in the articles, announcements, obituaries, and letters to the editor they submitted to the Hawaiian-language newspapers. The articles show an active community with its members trying to live their lives as normally as possible in the face of a debilitating disease. They also contain a wealth of information about medical practices of the day, including medical terminology, and with death such a common occurrence they offer many descriptions of funeral services and burials, including the processions that often accompanied them.

In many of the translations, I included Hawaiian words and phrases from the original articles that I thought would be of interest to readers and researchers, such as medical terms. I placed them in brackets and copied them exactly as they appear in the original text, which occasionally includes an apostrophe where we would place a glottal stop today. Comments in the translations, including corrections of misspellings in the original articles, were added by me or the translator.

One of the best sources of place names in the Hawaiian-language newspapers are kanikau, which are dirges or poetic chants, that express deep emotions for someone who passed away. Prior to the introduction of the printed word, composing kanikau to honor the memory of a loved one was a common practice among Hawaiians. Composing them for publication in the 1800s offered a new way to express this important tradition, and many Hawaiians took advantage of the opportunity to create permanent memorials of family and friends. Today, kanikau are treasuries of language, history, genealogies, and cultural knowledge, especially place names.

Kanikau often take the form of a trip that goes past places familiar to the deceased and places famous throughout Hawai'i. In the example that follows the writer travels from mauka to makai, or from inland toward the sea, and identifies five place names, including Pua'o, a surf spot at 'Iliopi'i on the west side of the Kalaupapa peninsula.

Ke Aloha Aina. 19 AUGUST 1899. P. 3.
Kuu Opuu Rose Ua Mae. My Beloved Rose Bud Has Wilted.
Mr. Editor. Greetings to you:

Please insert into some available space of our newspaper the words placed above, and it will be the one to carry the news to the four corners of the land [kihi eha o ka aina], to be seen by all of the multitudes of my beloved rose bud that passed on the path of no return, while living in the Kanilehua Rain [Ua Kanilehua] of Hilo.

Mary Nohinohiana was born in Pu'u'eo-uka, Hilo, on January 13, 1883, from the loins of Mr. and Mrs. W. P. Kalohe. She entered the leprosy settlement [kahua ma'i lepera] on Moloka'i on May 9, 1889, and died on July 21, 1899, in Kalaupapa, Moloka'i. And because of how immense our love is, the two of us have composed a small chant [mele] for her.

> This is a dirge [kanikau], an expression of affection for you, Mary Nohino-
>   hiana,
> A wailing chant of remembrance [uwe helu] by me, Kealualu,
> Alas for my beloved daughter,
> My beloved friend of this unfamiliar land [aina malihini],
> My beloved companion in the sea spray of Pau'aka,
> From the breaking waves [nalu ha'i mai la] of Pua'o,
> Beloved are the broad plains of Papaloa,
> Beloved is that place where we would be together,
> We were close with the cold wind, a Ho'olehua,
> My beloved daughter from the crowds of Kalaupapa,
> My beloved daughter from the bow of the ship that is life,
> We survive on the uncommon food of the foreigner [haole],
> You are an adornment for the parent, a unique lei of mamo bird feathers,
> A wailing chant of remembrance by me, Mary,
> Alas for my beloved daughter,
> My beloved companion in following and carrying out the work of God,
> My beloved daughter from the shelter of the house called Homelani,
> Beloved is that home where I and my beloved daughter live,
> You go on the path of no return [ala hoi ole mai],
> I remain, mourning and grieving for you,
> My beloved daughter, my dear beloved has passed.

—Composed by Mrs. Kealualu, [and] Mrs. Mary Keaka.
» [This excerpt is from the kanikau section.]

INTRODUCTION

Hawaiian-Language Newspapers

The following are the Hawaiian-language newspapers that are cited in the text.

Ahailono a ka Lahui
Hawaii Holomua
Ka Elele
Ka Hae Hawaii
Ka Hoku Loa
Ka Hoku o ka Pakipika
Ka Lahui Hawaii
Ka Lama Hawaii
Ka Lanakila
Ka Leo o ka Lahui
Ka Makaainana
Ka Nonanona
Ka Nupepa Kuokoa
Ke Alaula
Ke Aloha Aina
Ke Au Okoa
Ke Kiai
Ke Kumu Hawaii
Ko Hawaii Pae Aina
Kuokoa Home Rula

Kalaupapa Place Names

THE PLACE NAMES in this section include many of the prominent names that appear in the Hawaiian-language newspaper articles about Kalaupapa. They are listed in alphabetical order. Each entry is followed by an English translation of one or more articles from a Hawaiian-language newspaper that includes the respective place name. Each translation is preceded by the name and date of the newspaper and the page number of the original article. The original articles in Hawaiian, which are exclusively from the Hawaiian-language newspapers of the 1800s and early 1900s, are online in the Office of Hawaiian Affairs' Papakilo Database.

Writers in the Hawaiian-language newspapers did not use the diacritical marks that are common now, the 'okina, or glottal stop, and the kahakō, or macron. Some of the early writers occasionally used an apostrophe, dash, or single open quote mark to represent the 'okina, but none of them used the kahakō. Hawaiian words in the English translations, including personal names and place names, are written with 'okina and kahakō that were provided by the translators, Iāsona Ellinwood and Keao NeSmith, and by the author.

In recognition of the Hawaiian language as an official language of the State of Hawai'i, Hawaiian words within the English texts are not regarded as foreign words and are therefore not italicized.

The articles in *Kalaupapa Place Names: Waikolu to Nihoa* were selected by the author and are representative of the information in the Hawaiian-language newspapers about Kalaupapa. Researchers looking for additional articles should visit the online newspaper archive in the Papakilo Database.

Words, phrases, sentences, and comments within the articles that are enclosed in parentheses are from the original articles, while those enclosed in brackets are comments by the author or the translator.

The articles include many lesser-known place names, which are listed in the index.

Alanui Pali. Literally, "cliff trail," a generic name for the cliff trails that were used to access the Kalaupapa peninsula. Although they were also described as narrow trails [alanui olowi] and winding trails [ala kikeekee], they had individual names, such as 'Ili'ilika'a and Kukuiohāpu'u.

Ka Hae Hawaii. 20 MAY 1857. P. 31.
Na Waiwai I Lawe Ia Aku Mai Ke Awa Aku O Kalaupapa A Me Ke Kumukuai. The Goods That Were Brought from the Harbor of Kalaupapa and the Prices.

Here is one more point: The commoners [Makaainana] of Kalaupapa are working on their cliff trail [**alanui pali**] since the government is taking so long.
—W. N. P. Pōhano, Kalaupapa, Moloka'i, MAY 11, 1857.

Ka Nupepa Kuokoa. 6 JUNE 1868. P. 1.
Waihoia i ke Komite o na Hana Hou. Presented to the Committee for Repairs.

Mr. Kalu read a decision granting $400 for the cliff trail [**alanui pali**] of Kalaupapa. Mr. Phillips [Pilipo] read that the time of the action of the House be set to eleven o'clock. This was submitted.

Awa o Kalaupapa. Literally, "harbor of Kalaupapa." The harbor was also called awa kumoku o Kalaupapa, or "anchorage of Kalaupapa," and awa pae ma Kalaupapa, or "harbor landing of Kalaupapa." The harbor is in the lee of the peninsula, which is on its west side.

Ka Makaainana. 7 DECEMBER 1896. P. 7.
Huakai No Molokai. Ka Ike Ana i na Maka o Kuu Aloha. Journey to Moloka'i. Seeing the Eyes of My Beloved.

Five o'clock, the chain was clanking with the anchor of the *'Iwalani* in the harbor of Kalaupapa [**awa o Kalaupapa**]. We gazed upon the shore [and] the limitless number of lights sparkling in the harbor, with the sweet murmuring sound of the brass horns of the boys of that place who practiced in that activity. It seemed as if, in my understanding, they probably had not slept at all during that joyful night of theirs, until they found us, wide awake, and they were probably filled with gaiety from seeing visitors. Yes, truly so.

Ka Nupepa Kuokoa. 16 AUGUST 1890. P. 4.
Hoike A Ke Komite A ka Ahahui Kula Sabati o ka Paeaina i ka Panalaau o Kalawao me Kalaupapa. Report of the Committee of the Sunday School Association of the Islands in the Colony of Kalawao and Kalaupapa.

The committee left Honolulu, going to the colony of Kalawao and Kalaupapa, on the evening of the Sabbath, July 27, 1890, on the steamship *Hawaii*, the ship that the majority of the legislative committee was on, and arrived on the morning of the 28th at the harbor of Kalaupapa [**awa kumoku o Kalaupapa**].

Ke Alakai o Hawaii. 30 JUNE 1888. P. 6.
Ka Huakai Noii A Na Komite Ahaolelo I Ke Panalaau O Kalawao, Iune 24, 1888. Exploratory Mission of the Legislative Committee to the Colony of Kalawao, June 24, 1888.

At 4:30 a.m. there were the towns of Kalawao and Kalaupapa as dawn approached through the darkness. Your correspondent scrambled for a way to reach the harbor of Kalaupapa [**awa pae ma Kalaupapa**] as quickly as possible.

» [This excerpt is from an article in chapter IV.]

Awa o Pauʻaka. Literally, "Harbor of Pauʻaka." A specific area near Kalaupapa Harbor that was used as a cattle landing.

Ka Nupepa Kuokoa. 9 MAY 1891. P. 1.
Ka Huakai a ke Alii ka Moiwahine Liliuokalani no ka Panalaau o Kalawao. The Journey of Her Majesty Queen Liliʻuokalani to the Colony at Kalawao.

Ka walohia [anguish] is the name of the harbor at Pauʻaka [**awa o Pauaka**], the harbor where cattle are unloaded, to the east of the harbor where the queen was returning to the ship.

Balawina Home or Balauwina Home. Balawina, or Balauwina, is Hawaiian for "Baldwin." The Baldwin Home for boys and single men in Kalawao opened in 1894, replacing a home built earlier by Father Damien. Brother Joseph Dutton, a Catholic lay volunteer who arrived in 1886 to assist Father Damien, managed the home with the help of several brothers of the Congregation of the Sacred Hearts of Jesus and Mary, who arrived later in 1895. Brother Dutton devoted the rest of his life to the care of its patients. The Board of Health relocated Baldwin Home from Kalawao to Kalaupapa in 1932 and finally closed it in 1950.

Ka Nupepa Kuokoa. 16 JUNE 1894. P. 4.
Kulu ka Waimaka Uwe ka Opua. The Tears Fall, the Billowy Cloud Weeps.
To Mr. J. U. Kawainui, Esq., Editor of the combined *Nupepa Kuokoa* and *Ko Hawaii Pae Aina.* Greetings to you.

I ask you and your typesetting boys of your printing shop to please insert the news from the leprosy colony [Panalaau Mai Lepera] here in Kalawao.

Monday, June 4, we left the family enclosure [pa ohana] called the Damien Home [Damiano Home], the place where the multitudes took shelter in days gone by and rested here in the sacred sleep of Niolopua [the god of sleep]. Love for this home where agony resided was permanently branded in the days as a newcomer [malihini] until becoming a local [kamaaina], and so tears fall due to memories of the home. Perhaps the constant use of its name will disappear from the letters of friends from now on, and thus, the new name of the family enclosure will appear in the newspapers of these days, Baldwin Home [**Balauwina Home**].

These new buildings stand with their beautiful features, and with true majesty, the diner, cookhouse, building for pounding taro [hale kui ai], storehouse for crackers, sugar, and rice, bathhouse, rest house for the children, doctor's office, and the dormitories, and a playground for the little children. It appears beautiful when looking all around; the breadth is like a race course; the sewing house of Mother Marianne [makuahine Marie Virigine] has adorned the stone walls. The work of the carpenters is not complete, they are cleaning, and here we are in the new buildings, where we live these days.

There is great calm here in Kalawao these days, the fields are parched, the crops are dry, and the rivers are dried by the sun. It is as if there is a mirage of Mānā [Kauaʻi] rippling in the fields, caused by the true calm. As for the quality of the life of the patients, some people have good health, while others have rotten and fragile skin. The effects of the disease are quite dreadful.

—Henry Kaʻauwai, Baldwin Home [**Balauwina Home**], Kalawao, Molokaʻi, JUNE 6, 1894.

Ka Nupepa Kuokoa. 28 SEPTEMBER 1895. P. 2.
Ka Aina a ka Ehaeha. The Land of Agony.

This past month, the number of leprosy patients [mai lepera] living in the colony [Panalaau] was 619 men and 451 women. The ethnicities [lahui] of these people were 21 Chinese, 7 Portuguese, 5 Americans, 4 Germans, 3 British, and 3 of other ethnicities, and the remainder that fills out the total of 1,070 are only Hawaiians.

Living here in the Baldwin Home [**Home Balauwina**] are 96 boys, and in the Pauahi Home [Home Pauahi] are 114 girls.

Also living in the colony are 92 locals [kamaaina] without the disease, who are the husbands and wives of those who wish to live with their loved ones. And also living with their parents are 42 children with leprosy.

Bay View Home. Established in 1901, this home in Kalaupapa was given the English name Bay View Home. It was for senior patients, both men and women, who were blind, disabled, or too weak physically to care for themselves. In the Hawaiian-language newspapers, the names of other homes at Kalaupapa were translated into Hawaiian, such as Bihopa Home for Bishop Home, but for Bay View Home the newspapers used only its English name.

Ka Nupepa Kuokoa. 13 JUNE 1913. P. 3.
Ekolu Pule I Ka Bay View Home. Three Weeks In the **Bay View Home**.

The infirm people [poe nawaliwali] constantly ask the caretakers [kahu mai] for what they want at every meal. The caretakers are pleasant and polite, but best of all is Huaʻā [sour], that old Palea [brushed aside]; there is no new Palea, it's a slip and slide in the heat, a pool of oil that makes the ship-towing path of Pauʻaka [deceit] slippery; Pauʻaka is the husband and ʻĀpiki [treachery] the wife; [when] they give birth, Hūkaʻaka [bubbling laughter] is the first born and Hoʻohauʻoli [source of joy] is the youngest.

The writer stands and confirms before the readers of the *Nupepa Kuokoa* that everything reported above and below is true. The writer also reports that this new supervisor is vigilant, as follows:

For the attendants to the patients who bring food, the supervisor examines the food before and after, and such is the case for the food of the strong folks [poe ikaika] in the dining room.

The writer has been told that the patients have just started drinking coffee. Before, the scent of coffee was not smelled, but with this new supervisor and father, the scent of coffee is smelled. The writer reports that this is completely true, Kona coffee [Kona kope] has finally been seen.

The writer was truly enraptured by the beauty of the things done at the **Bay View Home**. It is not just a home for the chronically infirm.

This pen tip invites the blind [poe makapo] and the infirm living out there to return to the aforementioned home, while the father is giving sight to his fellow men, and his motto is, "All are equal before him."

Yours truly, S. K. Nāhauowailē'ia. Kalaupapa, JUNE 6, 1913.

Ka Nupepa Kuokoa. 27 JUNE 1913. P. 3.
Mrs. Rose Kahananui Ua Hala. Mrs. Rose Kahananui Has Passed.

Mr. Editor of the *Nupepa Kuokoa* and your boys of the printing press, to you all.

Please insert in some available space of one of the compartments of the electric engine [enegini uwila] these letters placed above. You shall be the one to carry it and it shall be seen by the many friends of my dear beloved that live from Hawai'i, island of Keawe, to the sun that shimmers upon the surface of the ocean at Lehua. Here is a short story about my beloved wife who has traveled far:

Born in the Waipukaiki of Helani, Kahalu'u, North Kona, on August 23, 1881, from the loins of Mr. Kiliona Nākea and Mrs. Louisa Nākea. Left Kona at an unknown time, held in Kalihi on April 26, 1902; brought to the patient settlement [kahua ma'i] on May 16, 1902; lived in the Bishop Home [Bihopa Home], left the home and lived outside with relatives for two months; then we were joined in the covenant of marriage. We had from our loins two children, a female and a male. The girl already passed and accompanies the mother on her path. The boy is in Honolulu at the school for the children of patients [kula o na keiki a ka poe ma'i].

Burdened by a great amount of pain, she left the **Bay View Home** on May 26, 1913, and returned to the family for one week. Because the pains did not ease, she was returned to the Bishop Home on June 2, 1913. On June 8, at 6:00 p.m., she left me and returned to the roofless house. Alas for my beloved wife, my beloved companion in rain and shine, until your love arrives I shall weep!

My beloved wife from the ascent of Makanalua, this place where you and I lived with our children, until we became natives [kulaiwi] of this place. Alas for my beloved wife, traveling companion on the path to Kōloa, arriving at Pōhakuloa, you will no longer drink that cool water. My beloved wife, companion on the path going down to Māhulili, gazing upon the beauty of Kaukapua, the wide expanse of Pelekane. There is a climb up to Kawaluna, then a descent down to the Baldwin Home, that home where we admire how it is crowded by the verdant adornment of plants. Alas for my beloved wife! No longer will you see the beautiful things of this life, no longer will you experience the agonies, the hardships of this existence, alas for my beloved wife. And we arrive at Pu'uokapae, gazing upon the beauty of Waikakulu, that water trickling down the cliff, that water that I bathed in with my dear beloved, my beloved companion traveling with the hīnano flower, those lei perfumed with the fragrance of a sweet aroma. Never again will you wear as a lei those adornments of the land we lived in as strangers [aina i noho malihini], with only one native resident [kamaaina], the Board of Health. Alas for my beloved wife, my love for you is endless!

In Waikolu we wore lei of maile vines and lehua flowers. You are a lehua flower for me, and an unforgettable lei, my beloved wife who has traveled far, return so we are together. My beloved wife from the diving water [wai luupoo] of Waikolu, that water that pinched the skin of my beloved wife. Never again will you see the verdant beauty of Waikolu, on the headland that extends out into the sea, Pāpio. The light of the spirit has gone out. I search for you, where shall I find you? Perhaps you are with Hiku [Hikuikanahele], stringing a lei of 'āhihi flowers. Until your love arrives, I shall grieve.

We arrive at the point at Ho'olehua, on that day of enduring the ocean spray together. Never again will your ocean spray sprinkle upon the cheeks of my dear beloved. She has passed, she has left my bosom.

We go to the sands of 'Īliopi'i, those sands that my dear beloved traveled, and became familiar with, and became a native of. Beloved are the rough breaking waves of 'Īliopi'i [Aloha ka nalu haki kakala o Iliopii], those waves that my dear beloved surfed upon [oia nalu a kuu aloha i hee ai]. Alas for my beloved wife, my beloved companion! My beloved wife from the shelter of leafy trees of Kalaupapa, the confused hospitals of the Board of Health. Beloved is the gentle waft of the wind, a Malanai; no longer will you touch upon the cheeks of my dear beloved. Beloved is the palai fern of Waihau, that lei that my dear beloved wore, and what is this of yours that has caused me to turn away, the eyes of my dear beloved turn away, vanishing into the dark clouds of Kāne? Perhaps you have met with the host of angels, perhaps your spirit is in the bosom of the Almighty. Are you crying out, "Hosanna!" with the host of angels there? Alas for my endless love for you!

I give my deepest thanks to the mothers of the Bishop Home, the girls, everyone who came to mourn together with me in my hour of grief, and I also give thanks to those who gave flowers for my dear beloved.

Yours truly, Joseph Kahananui. **Bay View Home**, Kalaupapa, JUNE 14, 1913.

Beretania Hale. The Board of Health formally opened Beretania Hale, a social hall, on December 26, 1892. Beretania, which is also spelled Beritania, is the Hawaiian word for "Britannia," another name for Great Britain. The hall was named in recognition of the source of funding for its construction, which was money from England, provided by Sister Rose Gertrude, a former nurse at the Kalihi Hospital on O'ahu. She was from England, where people had donated money to her for the benefit of the leprosy patients at Kalaupapa. On January 10, 1893, the *Hawaiian Gazette* reported the following in an article called "Not Forgotten": "Our new building, the Beretania Hall, the money for which was donated by kind. friends in England to Sister Rose Gertrude for the benefit of the lepers, was formally opened on Dec. 26th." [Details of the grand opening festivities followed this acknowledgment.]

Ka Makaainana. 13 JANUARY 1896. P. 7.

Ka Hape Nu Ia ma ka Panalaau. The Happy New Year in the Colony.

From five o'clock the prior evening until noon on the 1st, there were various pigs being roasted from all across the patient settlement [kahua mai]. From the evening until daybreak, there was continuous singing by different singers with their melodious, pleasant, cherished voices until the approach of day that became drenched by the chilly water of the Nāulu [sudden rain shower]. The rumble of running horses and other conversing voices was constantly heard until the night turned to day. From eleven o'clock that night until three o'clock in the early morning, a commemorative church service for the past year and this one was held in the bethel of New Zion [Ziona Hou], belonging to those of Jesus's Congregation of Latter Days [Ekalesia o na La Hope], with light refreshments being freely provided before the massive crowd that assembled, so that everyone would go home with a large bundle. We ate until sated and drank coffee until we left. The writer was also one within that holy assembly, and to them I owe a great debt for elevating this writer to be a speaker on that night of joy.

At one o'clock in the morning a mass was held at the Roman Catholic church of Kalawao and Kalaupapa. At ten o'clock, a prayer service was held in the Protestant church of Kanaana Hou, which finished at noon. From noon until two o'clock, a baseball game was held on the field in Papaloa, between Kalawao's experts of that craft and Kalaupapa's heroes.

From 2:00 until 3:30 p.m., the horse racing was held under the careful administration of the writer for a prize that will bewilder the reader due to its limitless amount.

Because, it was two hundred cents ($2.00) for the first horse race, and fifty cents (50 cen.) was the prize for the second race. The writer has omitted the names of those who owned the horses that received this $2.50, as though they were nothing.

Perhaps if that great amount of money that was used to hold the concert at Kaumakapili Church was sent as cash to us, for a feast or entertainment, that would have been better than not having an answer about this great amount of cash. Where did it disappear to? And how about the money of the circus, might it be the same, lost to the wind, as some windswept scrap?

From 3:30 until 5:00 p.m., there was a free concert by Professor C. M. [N.] Kealakai and his hand-flicking boys of the band of the leprosy settlement [kahua ma'i lepera], in front of Beritania Hall [**Beritania Hale**].

A concert was held at six o'clock by some of the singing children of the patient settlement [kahua ma'i]. The activities undertaken by the intellect and skill of man were quite glorious. The crowd kept laughing until their ribs were numb. This was indeed the conclusion of the entertainments of this day of joy that was commemorated delightfully.

No prior holiday that the writer has seen was like this one, with a gathering on the broad field of Papaloa until the amount of people was as great as a body of water. From the morning the horses of the horse riders ran until night. The patients were filled with great joy on this day. The men held up their strength, the girls bowled [everyone] over [kulai] with their calm-bringing grace, but the thing most admired on this day was the peace without unrest, since there were hundreds of people leaning forward and back, and the taverns of the Chinese were like coffee houses, open publicly without regard for the pickaxes doing road work. And due to this money-wasting liquid, there were so many noses that were greeted for the first time [ua nui no na ihu i honi malihiniia] that they hurt from the wafting of the water-drinking Kiu wind of Lehua [ke kiu inu wai o Lehua].

Happy New Year greetings between us all! J. A. Kamanu. Kalaupapa, JAN. 2, 1896.

Bihopa Home. Bihopa is Hawaiian for "Bishop." Bishop Home for girls, which opened at Kalaupapa in 1888, was constructed with funds donated by Charles Reed Bishop, husband of Bernice Pauahi Bishop. Following her death in 1884, Bishop became president of the Board of Trustees that managed her vast estate and funded many charitable works, including Bishop Home.

Mother Marianne Cope and Sisters Leopoldina Burns and Vincentia McCormick of the Sisters of the Third Order of St. Francis arrived on November 14, 1888, to manage the new home and care for its patients. Mother Marianne remained there until her death in 1918.

Although the home was officially named Bishop Home, patients also called it Pauahi Home in honor of Bernice Pauahi Bishop. The first two articles that follow use the name Pauahi Home.

Ka Nupepa Kuokoa. 25 OCTOBER 1890. P. 3.
He Hoike Pololei. A True Report.

To the *Kuokoa:* In the *Elele* of October 4, J. H. K. Mapuhau was reporting in his editorial that the Committee of the Sunday School Association of the Islands [Ahahui Kula Sabati nui o ka Pae Aina] made a false report and truly maligned the Catholic religion existing in Kalawao and Kalaupapa; and that it was a terrible, lying voice.

In your issue of August 16, the committee was explaining about all of the children in the patient enclosure of Damien [pa mai o Damiano] and the **Pauahi Home**. Concerning all the children in the patient enclosure of Damien, they are all just Catholics. As for the majority of the girls in the **Pauahi Home**, they are Catholics, except for maybe ten of them who are within the Congregational [kalawina] religion.

For the majority of these children, before they arrive there, they are our children, but when they go in the Catholic priests strongly urge them to become children of that religion. These explanations by the committee concerning the boys and girls in these enclosures under their care are a completely correct report and an explanation of the truth.

When the children arrive and are taken into these patient enclosures, they are first asked about their faith, and if the children answer that they belong to the Congregational denomination, they urge them to become Catholic brethren and be baptized in that denomination. If the accuracy of this is questioned, the truth will be obtained from the children.

J. H. K. M. cannot report the truth, because that is his religion. It would just be a relief if it was believed by the committee that he was truly a liar. This clarification is brief, but if he appears again with his whining, then I will again uncover the truth.

—M. Kalepa.

Ka Nupepa Kuokoa. 4 APRIL 1891. P. 4.
Ka Maua Lei Aloha Ua Hala! Our Lei Has Passed!

> The flower that brought joy,
> Bloomed and then wilted,
> Immediately cut, it is gone,
> Alas for our hearts.

On March 9, the angel of death visited the **Pauahi Home** in Kalaupapa, Molokaʻi, and took the last breath of our beloved lei, our child, Miss Mary Timoteo, from among the crowd of her companions in agony, who struggle together with that ancient enemy of everyone on Earth. Death was victorious over the body! What sorrow!

Mary Timoteo was born in Puakea, North Kohala, on July 24, 1882, to Keaweʻōpala (male) and Nāholowaʻa (female). In the eleven children born from their loins, Mary Timoteo was the ninth, and among the four girls they had, Mary Timoteo was the third.

When three months of her nursing [omo] the milk of her mother had passed, she belonged to us from that moment until she just left us grieving for her on this edge of the river of death [muliwai o ka make]. She was with us, and we raised her into childhood, when we were ignorant about child rearing.

When she was four years old, we left the land of our birth and traveled here to Honolulu, in order to prepare for the ministry. When she was seven years old, she was sent to the girls school at Maunaʻolu, Maui. There she was educated. In the year 1883, she returned and lived with us here in Waialua; and due to suspicions about the family-separating disease [maʻi hookaawale ohana], she did not return to school, and lived with us. And on the first day of July, 1888, after she lay in bed with a strong fever for three months, she was taken to Kakaʻako. On November 14 she boarded the steamship *Lehua* going to Kalaupapa with a crowd of her companions in hardship, and the nuns [makuahine Virigini]. Due to the kindness of the Board of Health, her mother Mrs. Mary Timoteo traveled with her, and that was the last time she saw her, until she passed.

There were two times when I last met with her. The first was in the month of February 1889, the time when the steamship *Likelike* sailed under the generosity of the Hon. S. M. Damon [Damona]. However, that meeting was like a dream. The second was in the month of August 1890, due to the Sunday School Association of the Islands [Ahahui Kula Sabati Nui o ka Pae Aina] choosing a committee to go and present the resolution of the association before the friends who have been afflicted by agony. That meeting lasted a long time.

Mary Timoteo was a cordial, modest girl who listened to her parents. She was patient, had a great desire to clean the home, and liked all types of cleaning. She was a hospitable host. She was a parent for those of Waialua. No one would pass in front of our house without hearing her voice calling for them to visit our dwelling. She was a greatly beloved girl with many friends. She treated everyone she knew only with compassion.

She was truly devout and knew her beloved Lord. Because when she was little, while she was at school, she was stricken by an extremely strong illness,

Bihopa Home

9

and it was believed that she was in danger, but she was saved due to God's generosity. These are her words to her grandmother: "I almost died, but thanks to God I survived."

In all the letters she sent to us, there was no lack of her command to pray often to God for her, to prevent her soul from being stricken with the leprosy of sin. Maybe a week before she died, the Rev. Father H. H. Parker [Paleka] arrived at the side of the bed where she lay weakly. She laughed in front of the Father. The Father said, "Aren't you afraid of death?" She replied, "I am not at all afraid of death. When you return, give warm greetings to Papa and everyone, and do not sadden their thoughts about me."

Miss Mary Timoteo passed with her beloved Lord, and joined with the Sunday school crowds at Kanaana Hou. She was not with the students of the Sunday school class of the **Pauahi Home** in the quarterly convention of this past March. Her quarterly convention will be in New Jerusalem [Ierusalema Hou].

God's desire is just, his will be done. E. S. Timoteo.

Ka Nupepa Kuokoa. 9 APRIL 1909. P. 1.
Komite Ahaolelo No Molokai. Legislative Committee to Moloka'i.
The Meeting in Kalaupapa.

Before the time for lunch, the visitors returned to Kalaupapa, to the house of Superintendent McVeigh. A large meal was prepared in the yard, and there the honorable ones Coelho and Kealawa'a gave speeches. After lunch, a meeting was held right in front of the bandstand. There the many requests from the patients were heard, which were similar to the requests submitted in Kalawao.

VISITING THE BISHOP HOME [**BIHOPA HOME**].

After that meeting, most of the members went to the Bishop Home for girls, and there they saw the cruel symptoms of the disease among some of the little girls. Three of them sang the hymn, "We sing this merry lay and bid you hearty welcome here this day," and all of the members who had gone there were unable to suppress their feelings of pity and compassion. Because one of the honorable members was unable to endure his feelings, he immediately left that place and returned to the harbor. Those who went there expressed deep gratitude to Mother Marianne [Makuahine Mariame], just like their gratitude to Dutton, the father of the Baldwin Home.

» [This excerpt is from an article in chapter IV. A "lay," which is one of the words in the lyrics of the hymn, is a narrative poem meant to be sung. Joseph Dutton went to Kalaupapa in 1886 as a volunteer to assist Father Damien and remained there for forty-four years.]

Hale Ipukukui. The 138-foot lighthouse at the north end of Kalaupapa peninsula was completed in 1909 and officially named the Molokai Light Station, but writers in the Hawaiian-language newspapers called it Halekukui, Hale Kukui, and Hale Ipukukui, all of which mean "lighthouse." Today it is known as the Molokai Light.

Ka Nupepa Kuokoa. 17 JULY 1908. P. 7.
Na Meahou O Ka Aina O Kaehaeha. News From the Land of Agony.

To the swift Messenger of the People, the undying lamp [Ipukukui pio ole], *Ka Nupepa Kuokoa*. Greetings. The Lighthouse [**Hale Ipukukui**].

On June 27, the S.S. *Makee* arrived in the surging harbor of Kalaupapa with supplies for the lighthouse [hale Ipukukui], as well as workers. The houses of the workers are being built. The water pipe, with a length of approximately two miles, is being laid, to bring water for mixing the plaster, and the work is progressing.

—S. K. K. Nāhauowailēʻia. Kalawao, Molokaʻi, JULY 10, 1908.

Ka Nupepa Kuokoa. 29 APRIL 1921. P. 3.
Ka Huakaʻi A Na Komite Ola O Na Hale Kaukanawai No Kalaupapa. (Kakauia e J. K. Mokumaia. Hoopau ana.) The Journey by the Health Committees of the Legislative Chambers to Kalaupapa. (Written by J. K. Mokumaia. Conclusion.)

While I was on that site, I received a horse from a good friend. That one was already on horseback, so I quickly took that same position, and a gentleman assisted by guiding me all along the winding roads. Names are placed on the roads all around that site.

There is a School Street there, and many other names. The two of us entered the Bishop Home [Home Bihopa]. This home for girls is beautiful, and clean in appearance. I was shaking hands with the mothers of virtue [makuahine o ka pono] who were caring for them, and I met with that nun [makuahine Wilikina] who lived in the detention station [pa maʻi] of Kalihi before.

The two of us talked a lot about things that had happened, since she desired to find out the truth. I explained the things concerning her that would soon be known, while I was driving the bus running to Kalihi and Moanalua, and how I was hired to take the girls to go swimming in the ocean off of Waikīkī. Just then she found out about the marriage of a girl she had cared for to Mr. Chas. O'Sullivan.

She was quite pleased by our meeting, because she received clear information, while she was telling me about the condition of that home and the number of children, filled with the thing that makes their lives joyous, since everything is prepared.

There were many homes there, and some of these homes were not occupied. When we left that site, we went on to the Baldwin Home [Home Balawina], beautiful in appearance, which is the home for the patients with partial blindness. There were truly a lot of people that I knew, and just a greeting was given, since my pilot and I were on horseback. We went to the site of the little boys, handsome in appearance. Since my desire was to see more things, in order to make my journey upon the land that had only been heard of worthwhile, and since the path to go on had been shortened because the horse did the work, while time was moving forward, and so it was with what I always heard about the lighthouse [**hale ipukukui**] of Kalaupapa.

So your writer, Hon. R. Ahuna and Hon. Kaumeheiwa, thanks to the kindness of a helper who cares for the lighthouse [kokua malama halekukui], got into an automobile. The bow of this car-ship was pitching about in the wind. From what I saw, this was a truly knowledgeable pilot, because the bumps and ruts, what were those things to the knowledge and skill of this youngster? We arrived at his home and went to the place where the lighthouse [halekukui] stood, whose fame had only been heard of.

We admired the cleanliness and condition of this light, the neck breaking when looking up, while our leader went in the door and climbed up. There were stairs made in a curve, and while we were climbing with great effort, we were gasping for breath, but that desire to see in person, that was the thing that raised up the desire to climb to see in person. Once we arrived at the place that will be set down in my name song, this was a truly beautiful room, which was the fire that the caretaker of the light worships, and tends to some other work. After resting we climbed again to the place where the light shines.

There were many wondrous things that the eye saw, since everything was just glittering, the glass that was made curved and resembled shutters in appearance, and the machine that spun around, and the casting out of its shine for a distance of several miles. Its height from the ground up is 223 feet, and its strength in casting out its brilliance is 620,000.

While were looking at this wondrous thing and we were looking at the patient settlement [kahua mai], the ocean, the mountains, what we saw was just lovely. The wind blew forcefully, as if it was twisting down upon you. The blowing of the wind at this place where we were standing was truly unlike what is experienced on solid ground. A seagull [nene aukai: poetic name for a ship] was returning on the crest, returning south, bobbing up and down, while it anchored calmly, and I recalled these small kukui nuts, these words of light:

> Kalaupapa is glorious in my view,
> Due to the lighthouse set above,
> My sleep is startled with a shock,
> From the wondrous brilliance in the sky,
> The electricity uses its power,
> The *Mikahala* is clearly seen appearing,
> The *Enoka* is majestic when it appears,
> A skilled pilot in my view,
> And a query and a question is there,
> Who is this lighthouse?
> The lighthouse of Kalaupapa,
> Saving the lives of the ships,
> I only have what my ears have heard,
> I have just seen its glory in person,
> Seeing for myself its glory,
> With the magnetic wheel spinning,
> Light to the east and the west,
> Kalawao'and Kalaupapa are clearly seen,
> The refrain is told,
> Of the lighthouse of Kalaupapa.

Sorry, I slipped far away, but it is better to have a little garnish. I said to my friends that there are truly many blessings received by us this day, in having time to see these things that have only been heard of, and the true things were witnessed. I say in praise that this is the best in how clean it is kept, but not just at that place, also on the shores showing that on those shores are the things that supply this earthly life, and the same at the homes of those caring for this lighthouse, famous for its strength in casting out its brilliance. In what we saw we had great admiration for the one who piloted us up this lighthouse.

We returned and saw the boats carrying the visitors with continuous waving of handkerchiefs and calls of farewell to them as everyone boarded the ship and met with my good captain. Since everyone was on board, that little seagull departed at four o'clock, and moved forward.

While everyone was relaxing on board this little seagull, sea spray was constantly pelting my cheek. Since the body had become tired that day and curled up on a couch, I was lost with 'Ano'ipua [poetic for sweetheart] and was startled by a pan [being hit] to rouse us to fill up Hanalē [hunger]. Since we were at that time in the channel between Moloka'i and O'ahu, I met with my good captain and asked what time we would arrive in town. [He answered] at nine o'clock tonight.

I watched the expanse of the sea and the blinking of the light [kukui] of Makapu'u, and we passed by Hanauma. Diamond Head [Daimana Hila] was still and peaceful. The crests of the swells were at Māmala Bay. Smelling the līpoa seaweed-scented air of Waikīkī, you see the glory of the city, as the lights are shining, truly beautiful. Something that is most beautiful is the cross [ke'a] built on top of Punchbowl [Puowaina], standing in its glory, and the electric lights of the fort casting out all of their brilliance upon it, every place on this hill seen clearly.

Passing by Waikīkī and the sound of the bell buoy [boe bele] sounded sweetly, and a wayward buoy rested calmly. The lighthouse [hale kukui] of Kou Harbor [Honolulu Harbor] passed by. This little gull proceeded gently until doing a fine job of coming alongside the pier.

While everyone was disembarking to the pier, I warmly shook hands with my good captain, since the time that was told was exactly what he had said to me. At that time I met with my lady, whose heart had broken while waiting, and returned full of joy with no obstacles before returning home again.

I thank the health committees before God for how they graciously allowed me on this trip. I give my thanks to the superintendent who cares for Kalaupapa and Kalawao, and the friends I met with on that unforgettable day, and the things that supply this body. The prayer I ask is for God to watch over you, and over us all through his power.

Hale Kōkua. Literally, "House [for] Helpers." It is also known in English as the Kōkua House.

Ka Nupepa Kuokoa. 18 OCTOBER 1918. P. 8.
Kuu Pokii Aloha Ua Hala. My Beloved Younger Sibling Has Passed.

On June 1, 1916, the hands of the Board of Health seized and took away my beloved younger sister from my presence to the detention station [pama'i] of Kalihi, and there she lived for six months. After that time, she was taken away to the patient settlement [kahua ma'i] of Kalaupapa, and lived in the Bishop Home [Bihopa Home], under the care of the nuns [makuahine vilikina].

While she lived there, she became a brethren of the Protestant Congregation of Kalaupapa in the time of Rev. D. Ka'ai, the minister, and she appeared there until her death. On August 24, 1918, she left the Bishop Home with her infirmity and went to live with the older cousin of our mother, Mrs. K. Kala'au. Due to the immensity of my love for my dear younger sister, I sent a letter to [Superintendent] J. D. McVeigh to allow me to go there as a helper [kokua] for my dear younger sister. I received the response that I should go to see my dear younger sister at the house for helpers [**hale kokua**]. When I arrived and stayed at the house for helpers, I met with Dr. W. J. Goodhue and requested of his kindness to telegraph McVeigh for me to become a helper for my dear younger sister. He consented, and on the evening of Friday, Sept. 27, 1918, the response of the Board of Health was received, allowing me to go be a helper for my beloved younger sister.

Thus, I departed from the house for helpers and went to live with my dear younger sister for only three days, until she left me and her mother, living in grief and sorrow for her.

» [This excerpt is from an article in chapter IV.]

Halepa'ahao. Literally, iron-held house. Jail at Kalaupapa.

Ka Makaainana. 29 JUNE 1896. P. 1.

A written petition by several patients living in the jail [**halepaahao**] at Kalaupapa was read before the meeting of the Board of Health last Wednesday, asking President Dole to pardon them from their imprisonment. That petition was submitted to the superintendent of the patient settlement [kahua ma'i].

Haukapila o Goto. Literally, "Goto's Hospital." In the Hawaiian-language newspapers this name also appears as Haukapila o Kauka Goto, or "Dr. Goto's Hospital," and as Goto's Hospital in English. Dr. Masanao Goto (March 6, 1857–July 9, 1908) was a Japanese leprologist. He followed in the footsteps of his father, Dr. Shobun Goto, who in 1875 founded Kihai-byoin, a hospital in Kanda, Tokyo, dedicated to the treatment of leprosy patients. Both father and son believed leprosy could be cured through a combination of herbal medicine, nutritious food, moderate exercise, and medicinal baths. During a trip to Japan in 1881, King Kalākaua visited Kihai-byoin, where he discussed the leprosy situation in Hawai'i with the doctors and observed their treatments.

As word spread outside of Japan about Drs. Shobun and Masanao Goto, Kihai-byoin began attracting patients from other countries, including several from Hawai'i. One of these was Gilbert Waller, who, after two years of treatment from 1883 to 1885, returned to Hawai'i and proclaimed that he had been cured. With the possibility of a cure in mind, the Hawaiian government invited Dr. Shobun Goto to come to Hawai'i, but by then he felt he was too old to travel and instead sent his son.

Dr. Masanao Goto arrived in Hawai'i in 1885 and opened an office in Honolulu. He introduced new diets, medicines, and warm baths to treat leprosy. In a report to the Board of Health dated March 30, 1886, Dr. Goto provided a detailed description of his treatments for leprosy patients. The report, which he wrote in English, is included in the *Appendix to the Report on Leprosy of the President of the Board of Health to Legislative Assembly of 1886.*

When Father Damien learned about the baths, he visited Dr. Goto in Honolulu in July 1886. Impressed by the treatment he received, Father Damien constructed his own bathhouse at Kalawao.

In June 1887, Dr. Goto left Hawai'i to study abroad. He went to Cooper Medical College [Stanford University School of Medicine], and then returned to Japan. Many of the patients at Kalaupapa, however, wanted him back. They liked Dr. Goto's innovative therapies, especially the warm baths. The Board of Health eventually agreed and brought him back in March 1893. With the Board of Health's approval, Dr. Goto established Goto's Hospital in Kalawao on May 29, 1893, with thirty patients.

In 1894 the patients petitioned the Board of Health to appoint him their permanent resident physician, but their request was denied. When Dr. Goto's contract with the Board of Health ended on March 31, 1895, he returned to Japan, ending his devoted service to the leprosy patients of Hawai'i.

[Information about Dr. Masanao Goto, his father Dr. Shobun Goto, and King Kalākaua's visit in 1881 to their hospital in Tokyo was provided by the National Hansen's Disease Museum in Tokyo from reference materials in their archive.]

Ka Nupepa Kuokoa. 26 JANUARY 1878. P. 3.
Nu Hou Kuloko. Local News.

Leprosy. News came from Japan that leprosy is spreading in that nation, and a hospital has been opened in Naruko Machi, under the administration of a doctor named Goto Shobon [Shobun]. He has the means of suitable treatment for curing that disease, according to what was heard.

» [The article gives Dr. Goto's last name first.]

Ko Hawaii Pae Aina. 17 OCTOBER 1885. P. 2.
Na Nu Hou Hawaii. Hawai'i News.

We have heard that Doctor Goto has arrived here in Honolulu from Japan, amid the news that this government wanted him to come to treat the leprosy spreading in this nation, with assurances that he would receive a payment of $2,000 yearly from the government, with his expenses also being paid. The *Mariposa* arrived, and unless we were misinformed, the president of the Board of Health did not greet him in accordance with the assurances that invited him to journey here.

Ko Hawaii Pae Aina. 17 OCTOBER 1885. P. 2. [Advertisement]
Kauka Iapana M. Goto. Japanese Doctor M. [Masanao] Goto.

A doctor for leprosy, the illnesses related to the skin of man, syphilis [mai Kaokao] and so forth. Office: In Kapālama, right above the residence of the Hon. Jas. Keau.

Business Hours: Morning, nine o'clock to twelve o'clock. Afternoon, one o'clock to four o'clock.

Ka Nupepa Kuokoa. 17 OCTOBER 1885. P. 3.
Ke Kauka Iapana, M. Goto. The Japanese Doctor, M. [Masanao] Goto.

For many months past, some folks might have read a book printed in English about Doctor S. [Shobun] Goto's explanations of the path by which leprosy can be cured, and so on.

Some fine, uplifting words to the people about that doctor were published in a Hawaiian newspaper, and due to a suitable confirmation received by the president of the Board of Health, he ordered that doctor to voyage to Hawai'i, also reporting his annual payment when he came here. When this order was received by him, he immediately agreed, and he sent his doctor son, the aforementioned M. Goto.

He left his family this past month of September, and on the steamship *Mariposa* of last week he was brought all the way to Hawai'i.

When I met with him in the Hawaiian Hotel on Saturday of last week, I interrogated him about Doctor S. Goto, as I showed him the aforementioned book, and that one immediately replied to me that Doctor S. Goto was his own father, and he had traveled to Hawai'i due to the order of the president of the Board of Health.

This is a pleasant, young doctor, twenty-nine years old, and he could speak in English. He affirmed to me that he can certainly treat and cure leprosy, but only if the patient obeys and endures the rules of his treatment. He also told me that his nephew, the son of his younger brother, would be coming from Japan with the medical supplies.

He just met with the president of the Board of Health, and he took this doctor to visit the patients in Kaka'ako.

Last Monday he was permitted by the government to practice medicine, and these days he is preparing for his work.

This is perhaps the most excellent action by the government that has been seen, searching and finding the doctor who has confirmed and who has confirmations on his behalf that can be trusted, that he can truly treat and cure leprosy.

Doctor M. Goto told me that when the order of the president of the Board of Health came to him, he did not hesitate, and he traveled along this long path with faith in the order under his personal expense.

—T. K. N. [Thomas K. Nākana'ela]

Ka Nupepa Kuokoa. 24 OCTOBER 1885. P. 2.
Ke Kauka Iapana Hou. (Kakauia no ke Kuokoa.) The New Japanese Doctor. (Written for the *Kuokoa*.)

The Japanese doctor Goto arrived on the steamship *Mariposa*. This is a son of a Japanese doctor famous for curing the royal disease [mai alii: leprosy], and it has been said that the knowledge of the son is equal to that of the father. What we heard about the reason for him arriving here in Hawai'i is that it was caused by Mr. Waller [Wala] encouraging and writing to him to travel here, since he had clearly seen recovery in his personal treatment by this family of doctors. After he returned to Hawai'i, he told the president of the Board of Health about these doctors and their work, and his strong belief that the royal disease would be cured by them. The president gave spoken permission for Waller to give the order with some rather uncertain statements about the board giving assistance, but these tricky words were not put down on paper. With

Waller certain that the government would care for this man when he arrived, he immediately ordered the doctor to travel here, while also reporting the windy words of the president of the Board of Health. Once this doctor arrived, the president had completely forgotten his words of support. However, due to his great love for the wounded of the land, the president embraced with his chilly hands and his warm (like ice) heart. He arranged a visit to the patients in Kakaʻako, [but] released him right after the visit, not like what had been desired and believed. He was being stingy about the doctor trying his treatments. We see that the newspaper of Gibson [Kipikona: Walter Murray Gibson] is printing that the health of the people has not been mishandled. Waller was the one who ordered, and when the doctor arrived, because of the great love Gibson has for Dr. Webber [Weba], the Japanese was let go without being tested, and here he is working privately on his own, outside. So, in our understanding, Dr. Webber is quite cherished with all of his faults, more so than how Dr. Pika is admired by the people and how this famous Japanese doctor has been certified by Mr. Waller. We will all know in the future, if the Japanese doctor treats and cures a leprosy patient [mai alii], there will be no lack of immediate action by the president of the Board of Health in making him a favorite, with the call that he actually ordered him, not someone else, because of his love for the Hawaiian people. There will probably be no lack of support from the *Elele* if there is a cure from the Japanese doctor, in saying that it is a cure in a "Medical Book" translated from the medical books of foreign lands.

» [When Gilbert Waller, a Honolulu businessman, contracted leprosy in 1883, the Board of Health allowed him to travel to Japan for treatment in Dr. Shobun Goto's hospital. In 1885, he was declared cured. Waller died in San Francisco at age seventy-five on January 20, 1908.]

Ko Hawaii Pae Aina. 5 JUNE 1886. P. 1.
Ahaolelo O 1886. Legislature of 1886.
Session Day 26, MAY 31, 1886.
The House met at the usual time. The minutes were read and approved. Petitions. By Keau from Honolulu, requesting that Dr. Goto be assigned as doctor for Kalawao, Kakaʻako and the Medicine Dispensary of the government in Kīkīhale. Submitted to the Healthcare Committee.

Ko Hawaii Pae Aina. 24 JULY 1886. P. 4.
Ke Komite Ahaolelo ma Kalawao! The Legislative Committee in Kalawao!
The Mistakes of the Board of Health! One Shouting Voice!
W. M. Gibson [Kipikona: Walter Murray Gibson] Will Be Finished!
Wyllie [Waili] Will Be Chosen as President. The Wailing Voice Was Heard All
    Around!
—By several independent writers.
The main report by the party was that the patients had chosen to submit the complaints and their desires before the committee by N. B. Kamae.
Report by Kamae. 11. For Dr. M. Goto to be a permanent, resident doctor. That prior doctor, get rid of him because he did not reside permanently, only three days a month. Only in the first year he stayed, but afterwards that one left.

Ka Nupepa Kuokoa. 4 JUNE 1887. P. 3.
Kela Me Keia. This and That.
Dr. Goto will leave Honolulu for Europe and live there for perhaps two years. Dr. Iwai will take over his medical practice here. Take a look at the advertisements.

Ka Nupepa Kuokoa. 4 JUNE 1887. P. 2.
Hoolaha Hou. New Advertisements.
Doctor Iwai (Japanese)

Medical doctor and surgeon, in place of Dr. Goto, treating illnesses just as Dr. Goto does. Working hours in Kakaʻako from 9:00 until 11:00 a.m. every day except the Sabbath day. He will indeed go to the homes of those who are ill when called.

As for the other patients, go to his clinic, corner of Pūowaina and Beretania Streets, from 1:00 p.m. to 5:00 p.m. on weekdays and from 8:00 a.m. until 12:00 p.m. on Sabbaths. Bell Telephone number 387.

Ko Hawaii Pae Aina. 8 SEPTEMBER 1888. P. 4.
Mai A D. Keaweamahi. From D. Keaweamahi.
Chobachiku Motosushia Machi Sanchome No. 1 Tokyo, Japan. August 6, 1888.

To my dear friend: Hon. H. Waterhouse. Warm greetings to you and your family. I am living here in Japan without issue, and I am taking the medicine of Dr. M. [Masanao] Goto, with his observation that my illness is slight. He also said that if I properly maintain my taking of the medicine, then I will soon recover.

I am joyful at these words, but I did not see the result of his treatment. However, I am taking the medicine in keeping with what he said. I am immensely pleased by the recovery, and then we will be reunited, with my many friends, and my dear family. However, God is indeed the great benefactor for me and all of you. Give my greeting to all of our friends, to Rev. J. Waiʻamaʻu, and all of the brethren.

Forty-six is the number of patients [mai] staying in the Hospital of Goto [Haukipila o Goto] at this time, only leprosy patients [poe lepera], and over twenty people that regularly come from their own homes. Among these folks staying in the hospital, there is one white woman, Mrs. Gilley, and her daughter. She is familiar with Hawaiʻi and knows the Hawaiian language. She lived with Nāmilimili of Pauoa [in Honolulu], and when she contracted the disease she returned to Oakland, California, and from there to Japan. She has spent seven months taking the medicine and has improved somewhat.

This is a fine land and there are many people. I was told that just within Tokyo there are 1,552,457 people. This is the total from the census done in 1887 AD. The hands of the people are engaged in work, working from Monday to the Sabbath. There is no Sabbath here, except for those who have turned to virtue.

These people do much worshipping of the old things; for parents, there is bowing in front of images, with gifts of money. Amazing, but some people are not ashamed of these things. Everywhere in this city, there are many places of worship, called "Temples," and on the hills as well, some incredibly huge buildings.

Please tell me the news of the land, and the things concerning my family and their condition.

Yours truly in the Lord, D. Keaweamahi.

Ke Alakai O Hawaii. 15 SEPTEMBER 1888. P. 2.

It is true that the medicine of Japan that we had often heard of as a cure for leprosy was brought here, but here is the puzzling thing: no genuine success has been clearly observed from the applications of this practice in the days it was employed by Dr. Goto. Thus this lack of success has become something to again kill the hopes of this nation for the true healing of leprosy [mai lepera] resulting from the treatments from Japan.

And because of this, these questions arose. Is it true that leprosy is an incurable disease [maʻi hiki ole]? And because this disease truly could not be cured, is this what caused the failure of the treatments of Japan that were renowned as a treatment that can cure that disease?

And in our opinion, we can reply with the answers to these question, namely: (1) Leprosy is indeed a disease that can be cured in its suitable time, just like the other diseases that afflict man, under the scientific treatments that properly relate to the type of disease. (2) The Japanese treatment practiced here in Hawaiʻi by Dr. Goto did not fail because leprosy is incurable; instead, there was a different reason that stymied this treatment.

Regarding the statement that this disease cannot be cured, it is a statement of that darkly ignorant age gone by, since the truth is that this is indeed a curable disease, and the white doctors among us have seen this. However, perhaps it is true that if leprosy advances to the severe stages where the disease has engulfed the body, like some other diseases, then there will be no recovery.

As for the treatment performed by Dr. Goto without great success, we have heard rumors that the reason for this failure was the Board of Health not agreeing to all the things that the doctor wanted to employ, in accordance with what he had seen in the place he came to, being the things that would bring success to his work. However, the Board of Health squeezed his efforts firmly within the palm of its hand, not giving him free rein to do as he pleased in order to aid the progress of his undertakings. This is the reason that stymied his healing work, according to what we have heard, and it was this thing that compelled that doctor to depart from here and travel to England [Enelani].

Hawaii Holomua. 6 MARCH 1893. P. 2.

Mai lapana Mai. From Japan.

Upon the arrival of the Japanese steamship *Miiki Maru* last Monday, we received the news that five Hawaiians had returned from Japan, including D. Keaweamahi, and from him we heard about the wrecking of several whaling ships on the shores of Japan. Upon these whaling ships were four Hawaiian men, namely Kealakaʻa, Geo. Kanalu, Awana and Don. Wahine. They all boarded the steamship *Miiki Maru,* coming to Hawaiʻi, and here they all are in the harbor with their good health.

We also heard that the Japanese Dr. Goto has traveled here again by the order of several people. And here they all are being quarantined upon the ship for several days.

Ka Nupepa Kuokoa. 11 MARCH 1893. P. 4.

Ka Mokuahi Lawe Limahana Iapana. The Steamship Bringing Japanese Laborers.

The steamship transporting Japanese laborers, the *Miike Maru,* arrived in Honolulu on March 6, after thirteen and a half days voyaging from Yokohama. She brought 10 cabin passengers, 32 deck passengers, and 729 Japanese laborers, being 583 men and 146 [women]. Among the cabin passengers were Dr. Goto, Rev. D. Keaweamahi, and Dr. Foote. And it was said that among the deck passengers there were also several shipwrecked Hawaiians [olulo Hawaii] from aboard a whaling ship [moku okohola] that ran aground and wrecked on the shores of Japan some time recently. Meanwhile, no illness appeared among the laborers for seventeen days aboard the steamship, because the workers were already boarded upon the ship for three days before the voyage due to waiting for the new laborers wanting to travel to Hawai'i.

The Liberal. 11 MARCH 1893. P. 2.

Leprosy.

The arrival of Dr. Goto together with a Hawaiian patient apparently cured of leprosy ought to arouse a renewed interest in the question of the isolation and treatment of lepers.

» [This article was printed in English.]

Hawaii Holomua. 14 APRIL 1893. P. 2.

Kauka M. Goto. Doctor M. Goto.

Doctor Masanao Goto, the Japanese doctor treating leprosy [mai lepera], is preparing to travel again to the leprosy colony [panalaau lepera] on the island of Moloka'i. He will be leaving this city next Monday to spend one month living with Mr. David Dayton (Kewiki) in the name of the Board of Health of the government.

Our readers have probably not forgotten that Dr. Goto was ordered by the Hawaiian government to research everything related to the treatment of leprosy, and it is true that he has returned with this preparation. If his undertakings succeed here like in the hospitals in Japan, then he will be put in charge of the clinic for the leprosy patients [hale lapaau o na mai lepera] next year, by demonstrating before those of this world that the disease, said by some doctors to be an incurable misfortune, can simply be cured.

Ka Lei Momi. 28 AUGUST 1893. P. 8.

Ka Lapaau. The Treatment.

This is something that some people greatly desire, namely the folks who believe in the medicine of Dr. Goto.

Here are thirty patients being treated by Doctor Goto in **Goto's Hospital**, under the supervision of Mr. J. N. Travis.

I saw in another column of your *Lei* several things concerning the rules put out by the Board of Health saying that only the superintendent had written these rules and recently sent them to the Board of Health to approve. Perhaps he did not see the title saying, "An Old Law Administered many years ago."

Thus, I ask L. K. Makai to look at the title, and do not listen to the statements of no consequence.

Concerning the things about the folks who drank sweet potato liquor not being arrested: Here is what I say, some folks drank sweet potato liquor [inu uala] peacefully, without a disturbance giving cause for arrest.

That is probably enough between us, until another time when we meet again on the bright white of stationery. Here is A. K. Hutchson [Ambrose K. Hutchison] supervising the colony. Here being made is the house of the one who takes care of the new store under the leadership of B. Reid. To you my greeting, and to the typesetting boys my affection.

—Geo. Keli'imihihopeloa. Kalaupapa, AUGUST 24, 1893.

Ka Nupepa Kuokoa. 9 DECEMBER 1893. P. 3.
Na Anoai o ke Kahua Ma'i Lepera. News from the Leprosy Settlement.
Mr. Editor. Greetings to you:

I am always with you at all times, with the true, pure news from the leprosy settlement.

On November 20, the one who is admired, the Judge D. Kalauokalani, arrived in person at the Hospital of Dr. Goto [**Halemai o Dr. Goto**], with a purely gracious and kind appearance. He was introduced to the one of the boys of Dr. Goto, Thos. K. Nathaniel [Nakanaela], in the manner of gentlemanly rules. They met pleasantly, and he was the one to show the homes of the youths there. He was shown the bathhouse [hale auau], and there we gathered with joyous thoughts. Your writer was one at that place.

He spoke beautiful, flowing words before us, and the statements were embraced splendidly. Those artful words by him, we cherish that speech, and right after, he saw the boys, their body parts, as they were entering the tubs [kapuwai], and the fatherly judge was filled with admiration. In that clear examination of us, he had great admiration for Dr. Goto, and then he became a true witness on the side of the doctor, thank you very much!

On the 28th, the Independence Day of Hawai'i [la kuokoa o Hawaii], Mr. Kanui, a prosperous child of this colony [Panalaau], held a lū'au feast [paina luau], for his new castle [kakela hou] in Kalawao. At that place were the friends and boys of Dr. Goto, and the doctor was there as well. Also there was a small boy making entertainment, Palea his name, and that of the stove [kapuahi] was sent out, there was much of that [food]. Thos. K. Nathaniel [Nakanaela] recently became the postmaster for Kalawao, since he was approved by R. W. Meyer. He replaced William Clark.

—J. D. K. Nālehuao'āhina.

Ka Nupepa Kuokoa. 9 FEBRUARY 1895. P. 4.
Na Mea Hou Like Ole o na La Nui Ekolu ma ke Kahua Mai Lepera nei. Various News of the Three Holidays in the Leprosy Settlement.

On that wondrous night, the rascals [hueu] of Dr. Goto went to thank the friends enraptured by news of the day. Enjoyable songs were sung.

From Kalawao to Kalaupapa, with instruments: guitar, violin, autoharp, and mandolin under the leadership of Messer James and his attendants. They were glorious in this section of work, always playing merry tunes on the instruments each evening. The doctor was pleased by these entertainments. Here are the names of the rascals of Dr. Goto that take the honor of the day: Wm.

Kahoʻokaumaha, R. M. Pahau, Wm. H. Daniel, Wm. Taylor, Joe Keolanui, Jon. Kahaku, Kinney, Kealakai, Eddie, Kiaha, Solomon, Kalolo, Kāne Kaluakini, Kalepa, and Okaka. These folks gained the honor of the **Hospital of Dr. M. Goto**, the famous expert of Japan.

Ka Makaainana. 8 APRIL 1895. P. 8.
Kela A Me Keia. This and That.
     Doctor Goto is leaving us for Japan, his home, on the steamship *Coptic* [*Copetica*] on the 30th, since the time of his contract with the government [Aupuni] is finished.

Ka Leo o Ka Lahui. 1 MAY 1895. P. 2.
Nu Hou Kuloko. Local News
     Doctor Goto and his family returned to Japan on the steamship *Coptic* yesterday.

Ka Makaainana. 6 MAY 1895. P. 1.
Na Mokumahu Kuwaho. The Foreign Steamships.
     Doctor M. Goto returned to Japan on the steamship *Coptic* [*Kopetika*].

Ka Makaainana. 10 JUNE 1895. P. 8. [Advertisement]
Here with Dr. Ogawa (Japanese) is an excellent treatment for leprosy just arrived from Japan. There is no risk in trying it. Quite a low fee for two months at $10 for thirty days.
Office: Hotel Street, close to the long stream, Kīkīhale.
» [This ad ran weekly in *Ka Makaainana* from June 10, 1895, to July 15, 1895 (June 10, 17, 24, and July 1, 8, 15). The ads started one month after Dr. Goto returned to Japan, but after the sixth ad on July 15 Dr. Ogawa's name doesn't appear again in the Hawaiian-language newspapers.]

Ka Nupepa Kuokoa. 12 FEBRUARY 1897. P. 4.
Na Mea Hou O Ke Kahua Mai Lepera. News from the Leprosy Settlement.
     These days the patients are beginning to bathe in the new Japanese wooden bathhouse [hale auau laau Kepani] that the Board of Health just built for those in Kalaupapa. The bathtubs are beautiful, as well as the laying of the pipes that heat the medicinal bathing salts. The thing that is criticized and often complained about is that this bathhouse has no place to sit. When clothing is removed and when the bathing is done, there is no place to put clothes, hats and so forth within the walls of this bathhouse. People have often talked about this thing to me, and I have talked about this thing to the doctor, and it might be done.
     There are three days when the men bathe each week, and three for the women, until this day when the coal has completely crumbled and these days have nothing until the harbor stops being stormy, and then coal will be received on the *Mokoliʻi.*
» [This excerpt is from an article in chapter IV.]

Hoʻolehua. Shoreline area around the Kalaupapa lighthouse and the name of a point in the same area, which is variously called Laehoʻolehua, Kalaehoʻolehua, and Kalaeohoʻolehua.

Hoʻolehua includes a wide, sloping storm beach composed of white sand and coral rubble carried inland over the rocky shore by high surf. In the Hawaiian-language newspapers it is called one o Hoolehua, or "beach of Hoʻolehua," and oneloa o Hoolehua, or "long beach of Hoʻolehua."

For patients at the settlement, Hoʻolehua was known as the best place to gather paʻakai, sea salt, which forms when salt water evaporates in shallow depressions or kaheka in the shoreline boulders. Here at the end of the peninsula, the point is far enough away from the coastal valleys and sea cliffs to ensure the greatest exposure of the salt ponds to the sun and the least exposure to the diluting impact of rain. The west end of Hoʻolehua Beach includes a wide expanse of shallow pools in the rocky shore, the favorite place for residents of Kalaupapa to gather salt.

Prior to the arrival of electricity and refrigeration, salt was essential to everyday life. In addition to serving as a flavor enhancer in cooking, patients used it as a food preservative for salting meat and fish and as an ingredient in various medical potions and poultices. Salt was also used in processing a body for burial.

Gathering salt was primarily a summer activity with the longer days of sunlight and minimal days of rain. When a period of high surf filled the shallow depressions in the shoreline rocks, it took about a week for the water to evaporate, leaving a layer of salt. Patients would scoop salt from the depressions, put it in pillow cases, and hang the pillow cases at home, allowing the salt to drain. Then on a hot day they would spread the salt on a sheet to dry and later clean and bag it for future use.

Ka Nupepa Kuokoa. 12 NOVEMBER 1892. P. 2.
He Leta Hamama. An Open Letter.
To the *Nupepa Kuokoa.* To the people living in the colony of agony [Panalaau a ka ehaeha], from the line of mountains carrying mist on their backs. From the point of Kāhili [lae o Kahili] at Kalaupapa, obscured by ocean spray, to the point of Pāpio [lae o Papio] in the greatly beloved valley of Waikolu, how pitiful. Your father of days past, my wife and my children give our love to all of you. Greetings to you:

I left you on October 27, and at the final hour on the pier in Kalaupapa I boarded the skiff with my family, and right before that moment, as a portion of you were gathered before me, I uttered a portion of my affection before you, and it is this:

I am returning to the place I came from, and all that I request of you is that you all live quietly and preserve the peace of your way of life, with this peace being like the time of our living together for the past twenty-one months, while I was holding the paddle as a father for you. I will not forget the falling tears shared between us all on that unforgettable day.

We boarded the *Mokoliʻi* and the engines began operating to move the floating house forward, traveling at eight miles per hour. I saw you all, and Papaloa began to recede. I asked Capt. Alex. McGregor to please announce our final sight of you by sounding the bells three times. And thusly were three bells sounded while passing by ʻĪliopiʻi. When we reached **Hoʻolehua**, I saw those broad plains and those headlands, and it was quite emotional to see the broad expanse where you and I had searched together for a place to live in those hills, as those days of faintness passed in that land that love makes love to.

We passed by Kalaupapa, giving greetings to you with the bell. Tears fell caused by the warmth of the love for you all. I saw Waihānau, that mountain standing proud with its adornments of dark green forest, and I recalled these lines of affection:

> How lovely is the cliff of Kōloa,
> And the turning face at Waihānau,
> Give birth,
> Pity the father,
> Returning with nothing along that long place,
> Oh my, how pitiful.

We passed by the line of mountains in Waikolu, standing majestic like billowy clouds. I gazed briefly for a few short minutes, while that famous valley was completely open, with a breezy puff of wind gusting forth, bringing the sweet-smelling fragrance of that forest, drenched with the perfume that would adorn for the final time the father who has traveled to those arching lands, to the face of the cliffs, the valleys and the ridges and uttered these lines:

> O lofty uplands,
> Greetings to you:
> Misty clouds of the cliffs,
> Greetings to you:
> Forest made sweet by fragrance,
> Greetings to you:
> To the bud of the ginger flower,
> Greetings to you:
> Final Chant of Praise.

O Lehua flowers of ʻAhina, the chest of another will wear you as a lei. Maile vines of Pohākaʻa, you are done adorning his head. O chilly water of Waikolu, the lips of another will drink you. O gardenia flowers from the ridges of ʻĀkala, he will never again wear your fragrances upon your neck.

Yours truly, W. H. Tell. Kalihi, Honolulu, NOV. 8, 1892.

» [William Tell (Uilama Kele) was a superintendent at Kalaupapa for the Board of Health.]

Huelo. A small rock islet east of Waikolu that falls within the marine boundaries of the Kalaupapa National Historic Monument, Huelo is a sea stack, a remnant of the main shoreline that was isolated by erosion. It is 197 feet in elevation and approximately 1.8 acres.

Patients at Kalaupapa often mentioned it as one of the wahi pana, or famous places, when writing about the settlement along with Mōkapu and 'Ōkala, the two larger rock islets that are easily visible from the peninsula. A legend says Huelo was used for cliff jumping and that a man named Pāpio was the first to try it.

Huelo is known today for its biological diversity. As one of the few sites in the Main Hawaiian Islands that still has natural populations of rare lowland and coastal plant species, it is especially famous for its forest of loulu, or native palms (*Pritchardia*). The island is free of rats, which by eating palm hearts, seeds, and fruit have contributed to the destruction of loulu forests on the main islands. The only other loulu forest in the Hawaiian Archipelago is on the island of Nihoa, which is 130 miles northwest of Kaua'i.

Huelo is also a part of the Hawai'i State Seabird Sanctuary. A colony of shearwaters inhabits its summit. Public access to the island is prohibited.

Ke Au Okoa. 2 JUNE 1870. P. 4.
Kanikau Aloha no Kamakahukilani Kekeumuhinu. Loving Lament for Kamakahukilani Kekumuhinu.

Keomolewa, your brother, cries telling about you
My dear sister of the Ko'olau cliffs
My love for you is great as you have passed away
I live alone with the parent
You have cried out on the lonely path
There is only one great thing here within that I regard
The love and sadness for you, my younger sibling
How I love the plains of Kōloa
That lonely plain that was animated by you
Where many people were found with horses with Keki'inui leading the way
'Alae was above; I turned and looked
How I love the islets [puu] that swim in the sea
Huelo and 'Ōkala; I have love for Mōkapu
A lament, an expression of love for you, Kekumuhinu,
Kamakahukilani.
Keomolewa

» [This excerpt is from the kanikau section.]

'Ili'ilika'a. Also 'Ili'ilikā and Ka'ili'ilika'a. The name of a pali trail, ala pali o 'Ili'ilika'a, that was used to bring cattle to the settlement from Kala'e through Wai'ale'ia valley. It was not the main pali trail that is still in use today.

Ko Hawaii Pae Aina. 25 JANUARY 1879. P. 1.
Na Hunahuna O Ka Aina Mai Lepera. News Items from the Land of the Leprosy Patients.

25

Dear Editor. Greetings:

Please allow some space for me to report some bits of news of the country regarding those who have been separated who are afflicted with the leprosy disease that severs the connection between parents and children and spouses alike [aina i hookaawale ia no ka poe i loohia i ka mai lepera, e wehe ai i ka pili o na makua me na keiki, na kane hoi me na wahine], as with death, the bonds of matrimony are severed. Is that not so? Never to return to the family.

The way we saw it, we stood atop Kilohana and looked down, and afterward we trudged by foot down the cliff trail of 'Ili'ilika'a, breaking the joints and twisting knees, with our legs carrying us, breathing hard, which is why the place is called Kuliloli. But this cliff was not an issue for N. K. Nihipali, a good pilot for pioneers.

Description of the land. It is a very expansive land, very comfortable to live in.

Volcanic crater. The volcanic crater of Kauhakō is very beautiful to look at with its seawater pool [lua kai] of strange colors. On its north is the cliff of Koa with its winding pathway to Waihānau.

Wood-frame structures. These are beautiful to look at, a real town. It is estimated to be about a fifth of the size of the royal city of Honolulu.

The well-being of the patients. They are being well taken care of by the Board of Health, being provided with poi, beef, salmon, rice, bread, coffee; freely provisioned with tea cups and clothing for their bodies, with men handsomely dressed and women gorgeously adorned, with children talking giddily.

Some patients have run to the hills to hide, and in terror, they are overcome by a terrible death. This is ignorance. As Paul stated, "Brethren, I do not desire that you remain ignorant regarding our ancestors."

So, too, wherever the first sheep go, there also do the last sheep venture. This they find wonderful. I end here with aloha to the boys who work the typesetter of the *Ko Hawaii Pae Aina* newspaper.

—G. L. Kāne'aukai, Kalawao, Moloka'i.

Ka Leo o ka Lahui. 11 APRIL 1892. P. 2.
He Lele Pali Ma Molokai. A Fall From a Cliff on Moloka'i.

Last Monday, April 4, Pā'ele went up to daringly chase a goat upon the cliffs and without thinking that bad luck would be found along the way. He went straight along a path following the trail of the cliff-dwelling goats of these steep cliffs.

The place where Pā'ele fell off the cliff was on the trail, where cattle are brought down for Kalawao and Kalaupapa, called 'Ili'ilika'a.

His corpse was found by Kaluna and Kawahauila lying below the base of the cliff. The bones were broken to bits, pieces of the skull had shattered and bits had flown everywhere. Bits of brain had spattered everywhere, the ribs were broken, and one thigh and one arm were broken, while the torso was unchanged.

His appearance was quite dreadful and gruesome, bringing insomnia caused by memories of the one who died right before the eyes of the people living in that place. The chill rose over the base of the ears.

This is an example to teach to the people continuing in this disastrous activity. Do not be a daredevil on the cliff, lest the body tumble and fall off the cliff again, like Kaluna who passed away.

Last March this Kaluna and his wife were bonded in the precious covenant of marriage, and the joyous days of married life were soon wasted by an accidental disaster, since some people are happier chasing goats than being with their loving wives, who are companions to embrace and huddle together with in the cold of the mist.

So, friends, do not be dismissive of this disastrous event, lest you have no wives, and that is what those of old said, "To listen is life, and to ignore is death" [o ka lohe ke ola, a o ke kuli ka make], and you shall have no companion of the smokeless food where agony resides. What a pity.

Ka Leo o ka Lahui. 12 APRIL 1892. P. 4.
Killed by a Fall.

While a native was chasing goats on the Kalaupapa range of mountains, Molokai, the poor man fell and was dashed to a pulp some thousands of feet below. The unusual absence of the man caused a search and his discovery in the above condition, near the road leading out of the peninsula, called **Ka'ili'ilika'a** (Rolling Pebble). A state funeral being impossible under the circumstances, the remains were interred midst the wail of sincere sorrow without any ceremony other than the funeral sermon.

» [The title and brief summary of Pā'ele's death in *Ka Leo o ka Lahui* were written in English with the writer offering a translation of Ka'ili'ilika'a as "Rolling Pebble."]

Ka Nupepa Kuokoa. 16 APRIL 1892. P. 3.
Make Manaonao Ma Kalaupapa, Molokai. Gruesome Death In Kalaupapa, Moloka'i.

On Monday morning, April 4, Pā'ele (male) went up the cliff of **'Ili'ilika'a** [pali o Iliilikaa] to cut firewood, but when night fell he had not returned. His wife worried about him that night. On Tuesday morning, she, Wahineiki, got Kaluna and Kawahauwila to go up to look for Pā'ele, her husband.

These men went up to look, and Kaluna was the first to reach the top of the cliff where Pā'ele had cut firewood. He kept calling, but there was no answer. At that time he became fearful, but he continued to search, until he arrived at an extremely steep part of the cliff. He looked all around but did not see anything. When he looked down the cliff, suddenly there was Pā'ele lying below, dead. He went back to find Kawahauwila, and they went to the place where Pā'ele was lying. His appearance was gruesome. The head was shattered, a pupil had come out, the ribs were all broken, and an arm and a thigh were broken. Nākīlau arrived with a blanket and wrapped up the corpse of Pā'ele, which was taken to a suitable place and placed upon a stretcher. Aarona and some other people arrived to help and his body was returned home. Everyone went to see him.

At 8:30 that morning William Tell [Uilama Kele] arrived to determine the cause of death for Pā'ele. A coroner's inquest was called, which included S. K. Kahikina, J. Mokuhau, U. Inaina, Painamu, Kaulana, and J. Nākūkūlani. Dr. Swift also arrived at that place. The jury was sworn in, and then Dr. Swift went to fully examine the cause of death. When his investigation was complete,

the jury returned to the office of the Board of Health. There they gave this decision: "Pāʻele died due to an accident, falling off the cliff."

His body was interred that evening in the Papaloa cemetery [ilina o Pa-
paloa]. And here are his wife and children grieving for him in this realm.

—J. K. Kainuwai.

ʻĪliopiʻi . Beach, surf spot, shoreline area in Makanalua on the leeward side
of the peninsula. The most prominent feature in ʻĪliopiʻi is its crescent
white sand beach, which lies between two rocky points, Kalaemilo and
Kalaeʻā. The shallow reef fronting the beach produces the best surfing
waves at Kalaupapa at a spot called Puaʻō. In the Hawaiian-language
newspaper articles, people of all ages are mentioned as surfers at ʻĪliopiʻi,
such as: "the white-haired old men of Kalaupapa are surfing these days,
resembling white-feathered chickens in the sun" in the December 9,
1882, edition of *Ka Nupepa Kuokoa;* the "children who surf the rough
waves of ʻĪliopiʻi" in the December 28, 1907, edition of *Ke Aloha Aina;*
and "Beloved are the rough breaking waves of ʻĪliopiʻi, those waves that
my dear beloved [wife] surfed upon" in the June 27, 1913, edition of *Ka
Nupepa Kuokoa.*

In 1932, ʻĪliopiʻi was the site of a shipwreck when the interisland
steamship *Kaala* went aground at night on the shallow reef. Some of the
wreck still remains on the outer edge of the reef.

Ka Nupepa Kuokoa. 18 MARCH 1876. P. 3.

Let all men see, that I, Kahawai (male) previously of Kamoʻoloa, Kōloa,
Kauaʻi, and having contracted leprosy (mai lepera pake: Chinese disease) and
living in **ʻĪliopiʻi**, Makanalua, Molokaʻi, I state that my liquid assets and real
estate belonging to my elder brother, ʻAuana, who is deceased, and me, be left
and determined, being situated on the island of Kauaʻi; and as my brother is deceased and I as his next of kin, and being the one responsible for his remaining
property according to law, therefore, according to what we have by law, I decree
so that all may hear, that I have appointed Mrs. Maʻemaʻe Kahawai, as representative and executor of all of these properties of mine stated above, as I am
unavailable. She, along with whomever she chooses to assist, has the authority
over all of my possessions, and in my name to execute and publish as my representative according to the law; in my name, she has permission to determine
the fate of my liquid assets if she is to perform as executor over these properties
with the exercise of care, however, in the exercise of these duties, and with my
prior knowledge in writing. I perform this on this day, the 8th of March, 1876,
in my place of residence in **ʻĪliopiʻi**, Makanalua, Molokaʻi, before the witnesses,
S. N. Holokahiki, Kawaonāhele.

—Mr. Kahawai.

Ka Nupepa Kuokoa. 15 MARCH 1879. P. 2.

Ka Poi Palaoa. Flour Poi.

Dear *Ka Nupepa Kuokoa.* Greetings:

Here in the colony of the leprosy patients [panalaau o na mai lepera] in
Kalawao and Kalaupapa, flour poi is made, which is sort of like poi made of

breadfruit [ulu]. It is yellowish in color, it is really delicious, and it is sort of like poi made of taro [kalo]. It doesn't upset the stomach, and it fills you up when there has been a shortage of poi. We have not had taro here in the Koʻolau cliffs [pali Koolau] due to bad weather in recent months.

The new kind of poi was started in ʻIliopiʻi by a Hawaiian man who lived in California [Kaleponi] who is used to making flour poi there. That is how he started spreading this new kind of poi here, and its benefits are known here now. Now we have no more problems during this stormy season, and when the calm season returns, then the patients will have their taro poi.

Flour poi is good to eat during work hours, and it is filling and is interesting to make if you are used to eating this kind of staple. It's like mixing rice and bread together and you mix it in a pot. When it boils just enough and is cooked, it is filling to eat.

In my tour around, our superintendent [Luna Nui], Mr. N. B. Emerson, M.D., was quick to stock the warehouse with flour, rice, bread, bags of sugar, and salmon, and no one has any complaints.

Religions [Na Hoomana]. Religions are still present at this time, such as the Protestants, Mormons, and Catholics [Hoomana Hoole Pope, Moremona, a me ke Katolika]. Their church services are always full on the Sabbath and the lifestyle of the patients is peaceful at this time, not like it was before when Damien [Damiano] was here and W. K. Sumner served as superintendent. There were some riots from drinking moonshine [okolehao] made of tī, sweet potato, and so on.

Bell of the Church of Kalaupapa [Bele o ka Luakini o Kalaupapa]. On the 5th of Feb. last, the bell arrived on the *Warwick*. It is a very good bell and was a gift from the Sunday school of Central Union [Kaukeano] and the members of that church [in Honolulu]. It now hangs proudly in its honored steeple with its voice ringing in the cliff faces of Kalaupapa. The hands of its clock tell the time. The Sunday school of Kalaupapa is very appreciative for the gift of the Sunday school of Central Union.

—S. K. K. Kanohokula. Kalaupapa, FEB. 18, 1879.

» [In the absence of taro, flour poi (poi palaoa) was also substituted for taro poi (poi kalo) in other places, including the island of Niʻihau. Virginia Kananiokaleohoomana Nizo, one of the three authors of *Aloha Niihau,* describes the process of making poi palaoa in the chapter called "To Mama Kanani Hoomanao ana ia Niihau" (Mama Kanani's Recollection of Niihau).

Jonathan Nāpela established the first Mormon branch at Kalaupapa in 1873. A branch, which consists of fewer than one hundred members, is the smallest ecclesiastical unit in the church.]

Kaala. The *Kaala,* an interisland steamship, went aground on the reef at ʻIliopiʻi on January 5, 1932. The ship was never salvaged and its wreckage remains on the outer edge of the reef. Although different versions of the story behind the shipwreck surfaced over the years, one told often by the patients was that the crew had been guided by a red light they thought marked the harbor at Kalaupapa. On the night of the shipwreck, however, the red light turned out to be a porch light on one of the beach homes at ʻIliopiʻi. [See interviews for additional stories.]

On May 12, 1916, a similar "red light" incident occurred with the interisland steamer *Mikihala* when she went aground at Pūahi, near Kalaupapa harbor. During a heavy rainstorm in the middle of the night the crew had been guided by what they thought was the red light of the harbor [kukui ulaula o ke awa], but it turned out to be a red light at Pūahi hospital [kukui o ka haukapila oki]. The article describing this incident is in chapter IV.

Ke Alakai O Hawaii. 14 JANUARY 1932. P. 1.
Ae Ke Kapena O Ka Mokuahi Kaala No Kona Pili I Ka Hewa. The Captain of the Steamship **Kaala** Admits to His Fault.

By means of the meeting held by the inspector of steamships of the U.S. last Tuesday, Capt. S. Keawe Kopa admitted to his fault due to this ship wrecking at a place near Molokaʻi, being one of the steamships of the Inter-Island Steam Navigation Co.

And Captain Kopa was relieved from piloting ships within Hawaiian waters until the last day of March.

Ka Hoku o Hawaii. 19 JANUARY 1932. P. 3.
Aole Paha e Pakele Ana Ka Ukana. The Cargo Might Not Be Salvaged

It is assumed that the cargo of the ship **Kaala** [Moku Kaala] will not be possible to salvage following the understanding of its condition as it remains where it ran aground at an area near Molokaʻi.

There is a lot of cargo on the **Kaala**, but the cargo remaining on her can probably not be recovered.

The reason and manner of its stranding at that place is not clear today, and the owners of that ship are uncertain how it went aground on the lava rocks or whether there might have been a rocky outcrop [puu aa] in the sea.

Kāhili. Beach and point (Lae o Kāhili) near the north end of the peninsula. Kāhili Beach is a long, wide, steep strip of coral rubble and white sand seaward of the airport pavilion. Storm surf carries rubble and sand inland and deposits it inshore of the point.

Ka Nupepa Kuokoa. 8 SEPTEMBER 1877. P. 1.
He Makua I Aloha Nuiia. A Parent Greatly Loved.

My dear mother in the waters of the Nāulu breeze
In the patches of haokea taro in Kiʻikolu
There were three sharp points on the shore before God
The points of Hoʻolehua, **Kāhili**, and ʻĪliopiʻi.

Kahio. Point (Lae o Kahio) at the north end of the peninsula. In his memoir of fifty-three years at Kalaupapa (1879–1932), Ambrose Hutchison translated "Ka lae o ka hio" as "the hissing noise cape." He explained that the noise comes from a blow hole on the point. Hio in Hawaiian means "to blow in gusts."

Ke Au Okoa. 17 OCTOBER 1867. P. 4.

Kaahele Ma Molokai. Helu 5. No Ke Ano O Ka Waiho Ana O Molokai. A Tour of Molokaʻi. Chapter 5. Concerning the Geography of Molokaʻi.

Molokaʻi is to the northwest of Maui. To the north and the east is the Pacific Ocean; to the south is the Pailolo Channel, and Lānaʻi; to the west is Lāʻau Point and the Kaiwi Channel; to the north is **Kahio** Point [lae o Kahio]; to the east is Puʻuohaku [Puʻuohoku] Point; to the south is Kalaeloa Point. Molokaʻi is a long island, forty miles in length, and nine miles wide.

Kalaʻe. Land division near the top of the Kalaupapa pali trail. Kalaʻe was the home of Rudolph Wilhelm Meyer (1826–1897), who married High Chiefess Kalama Waha. When the Hawaiian government established the leprosy settlement at Kalaupapa in 1866, Meyer agreed to serve as its supply agent, a position he held for many years.

Ka Nupepa Kuokoa. 24 NOVEMBER 1877. P. 4.

Kaunakakai, Molokaʻi, Oct. 22

A meeting regarding saving and increasing the population [Hoola a Hooulu Lahui] was organized by the queen [Kapiʻolani] there. The amount that was raised was $36.50. That was the end of the activities there and the entourage of the queen continued from **Kalaʻe** to Puʻupāneʻeneʻe to look down upon Kalaupapa and Kalawao where Hawaiians were living. Such aloha. When the queen finished her sightseeing tour with her attendants at the cliff of Puʻupāneʻeneʻe, they returned to the home of R. W. Meyer, Kalaʻeʻs successful son. They ate there, and then the queen talked about her activities for which she was there. He agreed to them and gave $20.00 for the queen's campaign to save and increase the population (good boy). The queen, governor, and all attendants were also presented a three-pound bottle of sugar amounting to fourteen (pounds) in actual value, which was derived from a single [stalk of] sugar cane from a sugar cane patch of Meyer's in **Kalaʻe**. The sugar cane [stalk] was four feet long or more. The temperature of the water when he milled it with the grinder used by carpenters was thirty-two degrees at most. This was a lucky day.

» [The English words "good boy" were inserted in the Hawaiian text by the editor of the newspaper.]

Kalaeʻā. Also Kalaeʻaʻā. Point at the north end of ʻIliopiʻi Beach.

Ka Lahui Hawaii. 27 SEPTEMBER 1877. P. 1.

The [shoreline] points of Molokaʻi [Na lae o Molokai]. At Hālawa is the point of Puʻuohōkū and Kapuʻupoʻi is likely another name. At Hālawaiki is the point of Hīnalenale. At Puaʻahaunui is Hukaʻaʻano [Hākaʻaʻano] and Kīkīpua. In Wailau is the point of Malelewaʻa. There is a point to the east of Pelekunu near Oloʻupena. In Papapaiki at Waikolu is the point of Leinaopāpio. Surrounding Kalaupapa adjacent to Pōhakuloa is the point of Kaupokihawa [Kaupokiawa]. At Makanalua on the ocean side is the point of Kahiō [Kahi-o] where the spray of Kamakikī is and the point of Kōkīlae. At ʻIliopiʻi, **Kalaeʻaʻā** and Kamaemilo [Kalaemilo] are what could be little points that have been given names. At Kaluakoʻi is the point of Mōkio, the point of Kaʻīlio and Kalaeokalāʻau. At

Keawanui is the point of Kalaeloa. These are likely the points of Moloka‘i and Moloka‘i people can tell the rest.

Kalaupapa. One of three ahupua‘a, or land divisions, on the Kalaupapa peninsula.

The place name Kalaupapa is two words, ka, or "the," and laupapa, which the Pukui and Elbert *Hawaiian Dictionary* defines as "a broad flat, as of coral, lava, reef." The dictionary's authors selected Kalaupapa as an example of a place name that includes the word laupapa, and included this translation: "Kalaupapa (place on Molokai), the broad flat area." In his memoir of fifty-three years at Kalaupapa (1879–1932), Ambrose Hutchison offered a similar translation, but attached it specifically to the shoreline, explaining that "Kalaupapa derived its name from the many rock flats along its seacoast."

In 1978 while researching my book *Beaches of Maui County*, I visited Kalaupapa and interviewed John Cambra, a patient who had been sent to the settlement as a young boy in 1924. Several months later in 1979, I interviewed Elmer Wilson, a longtime administrator at Kalaupapa, at his home in Ho‘olehua, Moloka‘i. Both men told me the place name where the wharf is now is Laupapa, and that it referred to the shallow reef shelf there that edges the shore. Given this shoreline place name, an alternate definition of Kalaupapa would be "the reef flat."

The site of the wharf has always been an important destination for the Kalaupapa peninsula, first as a landing for canoes and later for sailing ships. It lies in the lee of the peninsula, where there is more protection from wind and waves than the landings on the windward side. Hawaiians called it awa o Kalaupapa, or "harbor of Kalaupapa." The harbor, however, is not always safe. During Hawai‘i's high surf season in the winter and spring, waves break in the bay outside the harbor, which often forced ships to anchor beyond the surf zone. When this happened, outrigger canoes or skiffs that were used to transfer passengers and cargo from ship to shore occasionally swamped in the surf. In October 1856 King Kamehameha IV visited Kalaupapa during a period of high winter surf. Although he and his party successfully returned to the ship, one of the canoes carrying cargo was caught in the waves. The December 3, 1856, issue of *Ka Hae Hawaii* reported, "The waves were really big that day, and one canoe broke in the big waves."

In the 1890s, the Board of Health began moving everyone in Kalawao to Kalaupapa. By 1932 all the patients were permanently relocated, and Kalaupapa is where everyone has lived ever since. The articles that follow offer miscellaneous information about Kalaupapa from 1866 to 1921.

Ka Nupepa Kuokoa. 31 MARCH 1866. P. 3.
Olelo Hoolaha. Announcement.

May all see that I, whose name appears below, make a restriction regarding my kuleana land situated in **Kalaupapa** on Moloka‘i that no animal should stray upon my kuleana, whether it be cattle, horses, donkeys, pigs, and other types of animals. Moreover, no person or persons should enter the kuleana to take anything therefrom. Those who ignore this and trespass and do not take care of their animals that are found by me on my kuleana land, I shall seize them and fine them $1.00 per head or I shall take them to the Government Yard [Pa Aupuni] according to the law. It is I, Ka'aihāpu'u. Honolulu, O'ahu, MARCH 29, 1866.

Ka Lahui Hawaii. 28 OCTOBER 1875. P. 1.
Auwe! Ua wela ka hale. Oh no! The house is burned.
Dear *Ka Lahui Hawaii.* Greetings:

Please print this sad burden quickly that appears above. The home of the royal [ke lii], Kekūokalani [Kekuaokalani], burned down here in **Kalaupapa** on the night of the 16th of October at four o'clock. The fire was not spotted. Perhaps it was set by some enemy and perhaps the fire started in the kitchen. Their lives were spared; however, some material items were lost.

With affection for the typesetter boys of the publisher. It is I with gratitude. D. M. Ka'aukai, Kalaupapa, Moloka'i, OCT. 18, 1875.

» [Peter Young Kaeo, a member of the House of Nobles and a cousin of Queen Emma, was sent to Kalaupapa on June 30, 1873. He used Kekuaokalani as a pen name. Discharged from Kalaupapa in 1876, he returned to Honolulu, where he died in 1880.]

Ka Lahui Hawaii. 28 OCTOBER 1875. P. 3.

We have received a letter from A. J. S. Ka'awa of **Kalaupapa**, Moloka'i, and here is what he said: "There is news here in recent days, on Friday, the 8th of October, the frigate ship *Britannia* [*Beritania*] arrived at our shores. The doctor disembarked and reviewed the sick among us and performed service with his own two hands. He told those obedient ones among us in English [olelo haole] that this disease is not leprosy [mai lebera], but that this disease was gonorrhea [pala] and syphilis [kaokao]. This was not a contagious disease and was curable with proper treatment by a doctor. Where is our doctor? We have no doctor. He then told us that we have been thrown out here only to die. The doctor also told us that, 'The leprosy that I have seen is in India, and that is the true leprosy,' according to this doctor."

Ka Lahui Hawaii. 25 NOVEMBER 1875. P. 3.

We have been given the "List of Names" ["Papa Inoa"] of all those who have died at the leprosy settlement [kahua mai lepera] on Moloka'i from the hands of Hon. S. G. Wilder, one of the members of the Board of Health. There were many who went before the Board of Health to inquire after their friends on Moloka'i, and there have been many letters from the other islands; and so that they may see and for the benefit of our readers, we publish these and will continue to publish the names of the dead from the month of November of the year 1873 up until this year.

Ka Nupepa Kuokoa. 22 JANUARY 1876. P. 2.
Ma Ke Kauoha. By Order.

We report what has been heard that the new warehouse [Hale Papaa] standing at **Kalaupapa**, Molokaʻi, has been designated as a place to cast ballots for legislators of this next session for that district. W. L. Moehonua.

—Minister of the Interior, Office of the Interior, JAN. 20, 1876.

Ka Lahui Hawaii. 19 JULY 1877. P. 1.

Dear Mr. Editor. Greetings:

On the 24th of June, which was Sunday, the sea gull [nene aukai: literally "ocean-going goose," but poetically a ship] pulled in here at **Kalaupapa** from Kaunakakai with a number of cattle, more than sixty, on that day. The cattle were offloaded on shore, and there was a man named ʻŌinoaʻole, a man afflicted with the family-splitting disease [mai hookaawale ohana: leprosy], who was going along, and suddenly he was chased by a cow. ʻŌinoaʻole jumped on a horse of another man, the horse bucked, and ʻŌinoaʻole fell over backwards. The cow that ran along saw this. Then the cowboys [paniolo] came and pushed the cow toward Kalawao. The cow reached the border of the rock wall near the stream [kahawai] of Wailua [Wailoa]. The cow knew the water [pipiwai] of that place and heard other cows. Kelaʻi, a man who had not contracted the family-splitting disease, went to get it and encouraged the cattle along. One bull came charging after Kelaʻi and he jumped off his horse. At that time, the bull chased Kelaʻi and gored him. Kelaʻi was holding onto the horns. The humpbacked bull tossed him away and the bull ran away. Someone came and got Kelaʻi, thinking his life was taken and that there was no hope. When his wounds were looked at, it was seen that he was wounded in the groin. Someone sent for the doctor. He came over, and when he looked him over, he saw that there was not much damage. This is where I rest my ink pen from lapping up the ink. The cliffs of Kalawao are being drenched and it is evening. I send my greetings to the typesetter boys.

—G. K. Kawaluna. Kalawao, Molokaʻi

Ka Nupepa Kuokoa. 15 JUNE 1878. P. 4.

Moolelo O Ka Ahahui O Na Mokupuni O Maui. Report of the Association of the Islands of Maui.

After lunch, we looked down over **Kalaupapa** and the way the houses were decorated and the lay of the expansive green plain [kula uliuli] and the round volcanic crater of Kauhakō [lua ponaha pele o Kauhako], and we were able to catch a glimpse of the pandanus trees of Kalawao just under the mountain. There we counted the number of buildings, large and small, in **Kalaupapa** and Kauhakō, which numbered 120, apart from Kalawao. This is where your correspondent ventured, and due to fright, my knees knocked and I had a hard time thinking, desiring to see the crashing of the waves at the bottom, but we did not see them because inside me it was as if I was going to fall into the deep ocean as my arms and legs descended. We climbed almost three miles to the village [kauhale] of **Kalaupapa** as one walks.

Ke Alakai O Hawaii. 24 NOVEMBER 1888. P. 3.

Make Iloko O Ke Kai. Death at Sea.

Because of the generosity of our good friend Mr. Kaoliko from upper Kauluwela [in Honolulu], he showed us a letter he received from **Kalaupapa** reporting some sad news, and this is it below:

On Friday, Nov. 9, Kale Kahuakaiula Palohau, son of Mr. G. B. Palohau of
Kaua'i, and Wailele attemped to escape from **Kalaupapa** on a canoe [waa]. No
one saw the escape of these men. As they began to sail away and got a little bit
outside of the harbor, the canoe flipped over [huli ka waa], but they recovered,
and bailed out all the water. They got back in the canoe and started sailing
again, but a short while later they flipped over again. So it went until they were
traveling right off of 'Īlio Point [lae o ka Ilio] when morning arrived. It was
Saturday. Palohau said to his companion, "Let us land on shore because the
canoe is filled with water and it will soon sink into the sea." Then Kahuakaiula
jumped into the ocean along with his companion and swam toward land. Perhaps a quarter mile from the canoe, his companion became weary. Kahuakaiula
told him to climb on top of him. That one climbed on and they began to swim.
When they reached the surf break [poina nalu], the waves began to pound
them, and they were separated from one another. Kahuakaiula landed safely
onshore, but his companion was never seen again.

Ka Nupepa Kuokoa. 8 APRIL 1921. P. 2.
He Mele No Kalaupapa. He mele he inoa no Kalaupapa. A Song For **Kalaupapa**. A song, a
name chant in honor of **Kalaupapa**.

Land famous around the world,
Hāpu'u [Kukuiohāpu'u] stands majestically,
Famous mountain, island of Hina,
Nihoa endures, extending out into the sea,
'Īlio Point [Ka lae o ka Ilio] extends out,
The desire appears for Ho'olehua,
For the kōnane board of Kaikilani,
The expanse of Wailē'ia is beautiful,
The close companion of Waihānau,
Love swells up for Kalawao,
Land at the mouth of Waikolu,
Three fragrant flowers,
Intensely piercing the heart,
Kala'e comes into my view,
On the Kīke'eke'e trail [ala] on the cliff,
Respond to your name,
O kōnane board of Kaikilani,
The refrain shall be told,
A name song for **Kalaupapa**.
Bay View Girl. **Kalaupapa**.

» [The phrase Ala Kike'eke'e means "winding trail." The references to the
"kōnane board of Kaikilani" were explained by historian Abraham Fornander
in the legend of Lonoikamakahiki. He noted that a large flat stone sits on the
beach of Pikoone, the black sand beach at the foot of the pali trail, where Lonoikamakahiki is said to have struck his wife, Kaikilani, with a kōnane board
for her infidelity. This story is also told in "Ka Moolelo o Lonoikamakahiki" in
the January 16, 1936, issue of *Ke Alakai o Hawaii*.]

Kalawao. One of three ahupuaʻa, or land divisions, on the Kalaupapa peninsula.

Hawaiians divided the peninsula into three land divisions, which from east to west are Kalawao, Makanalua, and Kalaupapa. When the Board of Health, or Papa Ola, decided to isolate Hawaiʻi's leprosy patients, they selected Kalawao as the site of the first settlement. This is where the earliest homes and churches were built. The first group of patients arrived on January 6, 1866, and this is where Father Damien made his home at St. Philomena Church in 1873.

By the time of Father Damien's death in 1889, Kalawao included hundreds of buildings, including a store, a hospital, and administrative offices. In the 1890s, the Board of Health began relocating the settlement from Kalawao on the windward side of the peninsula to Kalaupapa on the leeward side. This effort contined until 1932, when all the residents had moved to Kalaupapa and the only buildings left in Kalawao were the churches, St. Philomena and Siloama.

In 1905, the Territory of Hawaiʻi designated the entire settlement as a district independent of Maui County and gave it the name "Kalawao." This district, which is known as Kalawao County, is administered by the superintendent of the state Department of Health and therefore does not have an elected government.

The articles that follow offer miscellaneous information about Kalawao from 1861 to 1892.

Ka Hae Hawaii. 15 MAY 1861. P. 25.
He wahi Moolelo. Helu 5. A Story. Number 5.

These are the winds of Maui and Molokaʻi.
Kaʻupu, moa ʻula, [at] **Kalawao**
Makaluhau has the Kiliʻoʻopu wind
Kalaupapa has the Kōkī wind
which drinks up the waters born inland.

—S. K. K. [Samuel K. Kamakau]

Ka Lahui Hawaii. 3 JUNE 1875. P. 3.
Elemakule Naaupo a Make no iloko o kona Naaupo. An Ignorant Old Man Who Died in His Ignorance.
Dear *Ka Lahui Hawaii.* Greetings:

Please allow me to place a little of my baggage on your shoulders and please take it to the peaceful homes of those who would welcome you.

Here in **Kalawao** is an old man who is afflicted with leprosy [mai lepera] named Kāhinu of the Catholic faith.

In recent days his dog that he loved very much died and he weeped with laments [uwe kanikau] for some days. Being overcome with great love for the one without a soul in him, his face became distorted and his body became feeble and he went on the only road with the thing that he loved so much.

The coffin [pahu] was lined with a blanket [huluhulu], two sheets [kihei pili], and a quilt with appliquéd designs [kapa apana]. The body (of the dog) was wrapped in a Scottish cloak [kihei sekotia] with a calico dress [holoku kalako]. Around its neck was fastened a handkerchief [hainaka], and around its paws a handkerchief to clean it. Also left with it was one uku fish, a calabash [umeke], and a sauce dish [ipukai]. Before he buried his loving companion, he tried to get an orchestra to honor it in a funeral for the deceased, but since his [monetary] offering was too little, he was denied.

When the casket [pahu kupapau] reached the edge of the pit [lua], he said, "Go with our belongings and I will search for you. I will not eat anything and will not eat meat," and then the body disappeared into the dirt.

He fulfilled his words. He denied himself food and meat until the warmth of day left, as did the cool breezes of the motherland, the companionship of friends who gave likewise.

Dear readers, we see how ignorance has come from within the light of the early afternoon. Let us not give our affection to things that have no soul.

—It is I. S. A. Waikolu. **Kalawao**, Moloka'i, MAY 24, 1875.

» [While the writer was critical of Kāhinu, the article shows that dogs were valued companions to patients at Kalaupapa.]

Ka Lahui Hawaii. 3 JUNE 1875. P. 3.

The members of the Roman Catholic Church [in **Kalawao**] made a procession last week, as is usual, called the "Corpus Christi Procession" [huakai kaimalihini].

» [Huaka'ika'i malihini literally means "procession for the first time." The Corpus Christi Procession traditionally includes members of the church, such as children, who are receiving communion for the first time.]

Ka Lahui Hawaii. 17 JUNE 1875. P. 3.

We publish the report of the leprosy patients [poe ma'i lepera] in **Kalawao** to the Kawaiaha'o Church due to the request of the committee of patients, and here is the report:

To the Kawaiaha'o Church, the pastor, the directors and members of the Church:

Greetings to you: Your committee member of charity services, D. S. Mā'i'i, arrived among us here on the 23rd of May last. He brought olive branches and love filled with your generosity poured out upon your members here in **Kalawao** living in hardship. It is we with gratitude, with hearts filled with joy for your generosity in remembering us living in hardship; and as you do so, the respectful admonitions of the Bible are revealed, saying, "Weep with those who weep, and be joyous with those who are joyous." ["E uwe pu me ka poe e uwe ana, a e olioli pu hoi me ka poe e olioli ana."]

In keeping with our gratitude for these actions of yours over the course of this year, we understand the reason for your generosity. Should your actions motivate the churches from Hawai'i to Ni'ihau in assisting our fellow sufferers living here, then you will truly become the first to arrive and the rest to follow afterwards.

We welcomed with love and a handshake [lulu lima], D. S. Mā'i'i, and it is as if our receiving of him is our receiving with handshakes to all of you of Kawaiahaʻo with love. And as he sees us, so you, too, see us.

Let one copy of this document be published in the *Lahui Hawaii,* and let this copy be first read before the members of Kawaiahaʻo.

It is we with gratitude, the fellow members in Christ.

Committee members: H. Kamaka, K. ʻŌkuʻu, J. Paʻiʻāina, S. Kalepo, N. Kapawa.

Kalaupapa, Molokaʻi, JUNE 1, 1875.

Ka Lahui Hawaii. 24 JUNE 1875. P. 2.
Kauka Mai Lepera. Leprosy Doctor.

I have read with appreciation the explanations of the honorable minister of interior regarding the refusal of Mohabeer that he should not receive a license [palapala ae] as a medical expert [kahuna lapaau]. This is an appropriate action.

However, I have a question to pose to you. Does Dr. C. T. Akana possess a license? Since as I see it, this is something that absolutely should not be done. It is not right that a medical expert license should be granted to those who have no knowledge and who are not able to demonstrate their skills before the Board of Inquiry of the Board of Health to establish how to review the aptitude of those requesting to become doctors.

The president of the Board of Health needs to establish a Board of Inquiry regarding the aptitude of Dr. Akana in the field of medicine. I firmly believe that it will be seen that he does not possess any knowledge of the field of medicine. He often boasts that he can cure leprosy, so he was tested at this. It was seen that he was disappointed and was not able to cure the disease, so his boasting was rubbish [opala].

There were five leprosy patients [mai lepera] that the Board of Health gave to Akana to treat over the span of six months. His knowledge was tested, and he was disappointed as not one patient was cured. Dr. Akana was fortunate, however, as he received one dollar per day, and this is a large salary for those of his type.

Dr. Akana treated nearly fifteen people for leprosy [mai lepera] in Honolulu, but none has been cured. All these people have been sent here to Kalawao, Molokaʻi, according to these people. When Dr. Akana began to treat them, this is what he said: "I can cure this 'leprosy disease' [mai lepera]. In two months it will be over. Give me forty dollars, then buy the medicine, and this disease will be over." The people believed in him along with their friends. They gave their money and two months passed, but they ended up at Kalawao. There are a great many people living here in this leprosy colony [Panalaau Lepera] that was constructed for this purpose. These types of actions are nothing but bloodsucking [omo-koko], and his capacity as a doctor must be brought to an end for these reasons. And should the attorney general wish to inquire about these actions of Dr. Akana, there is a lot of evidence that can be shown to verify the truth of these words.

While he lived here in **Kalawao,** he went about and told some of the patients who are well-off that he could cure them if he was first paid forty or fifty dollars to purchase medicine. That is his clever deceit. Inquire after the truth of these things to the Hon. H. Kuihelani and Hon. N. Kepoʻikai of Wailuku, Maui.

Shall the king's Board of Health [Moi Papa Ola] allow people of this type to go among the people with lying tongues leading those of little knowledge astray, while they lose their money? I firmly believe this is not the intent of the Board of Health. Therefore, there should be an inquiry about the knowledge of this Chinese man [pake]. If it is determined that he has no knowledge, then the license he has been given should be revoked. May righteousness be done should the heavens fall [E hanaia ka pono ina e haule na lani].

With affection. Kauamoani'ala. Moloka'i. JUNE 7, 1875.

Ka Lahui Hawaii. 29 JULY 1875. P. 3.
Mahuka Mai Kalawao Mai. Escaped from **Kalawao**.

On the night of last Monday, a boat arrived at Kaka'ako with three escapees from **Kalawao** onboard. Their names were Kimo Kama'i, Anoho, and Nā'āka'akai. Kimo was apprehended by police just after disembarking onshore, but his companions ran off and disappeared. This is what Kimo said of himself and his companions:

"We left Kalaupapa on a skiff [waapa] on the evening of Sunday at 10:00 p.m. with a sail, and at 6:00 a.m. Monday morning next, we arrived at Hanauma [O'ahu]. We left there last evening, which was Monday evening, and from there we arrived at Kaka'ako the same night at 1:30 a.m. From there I was apprehended by the police, and Anoho and Nā'āka'akai disappeared up until this moment. There was no real reason for our departure. We met and discussed for days about running, and on the evening reported above, we left. There were no problems with living conditions, but we wanted to run and hide in the mountains here on O'ahu."

—Kimo Kama'i. One of the Escaped Patients [Kekahi o na Mai i mahuka mai].

Ka Lahui Hawaii. 24 FEBRUARY 1876. P. 2.
He Ia Pae. A Fish Washed Ashore.
Dear *Ka Lahui.* Greetings:

Please allow me to announce a bit of important news regarding our living. It is this: On the 13th of Sunday morning last of this year, a large fish, a porpoise [he ia nui he Nuao] washed up on our shore here at the leprosy colony [Panalaau lepera], but according to those who spear fish [poe holo o-ia], it was a Black Fish, and quite a large one when we saw it. It was almost twelve feet long and three feet in diameter, and since it washed ashore, the appetites of those who live near the area were satisfied. The fish was blind and that is why it washed up, but the all-powerful father provided us this fish. He was very generous and patient with us and may his name be praised. With great affection to the messenger and his director.

—Chas. W. **Kalawao**. Colony of Leprosy Patients [Panalaau o Na Lepera], FEB. 14, 1876.

» [The word nu'ao is used here for killer whales, which are also called Black Fish. The words "Black Fish" in the article were written in English.]

Ka Nupepa Kuokoa. 18 JANUARY 1890. P. 3.
Lilo I Ke Kai. Lost to the Sea.

On the seventh day of this month, three boys with leprosy went to the shore

Kalawao

from the fence of Damien [Kamiana]. At the shore they went to a point where they collected limpets [kui opihi]. One of them, Kuaʻana, jumped on a small cliff, and that was where he collected limpets. That was when a wave broke, and Kuaʻana was swept away. He called for his friends to come get him, but they could not. They immediately reported this crisis to Louis [Lui], their father who nourishes them with the food of the soul, and he ran down with some assistants. When they arrived at the point, Kuaʻana was not seen again. His body has sunk and disappeared completely, up until the time when this troubling news is being written. This loss to the ocean was in **Kalawao**, Molokaʻi.

—J. K. Kamakea.

Ka Nupepa Kuokoa. 19 NOVEMBER 1892. P. 4.
Kau ka Weli. Frightened.

It is being seen these days that the brewers of moonshine [poe puhi lama] here in **Kalawao** have gotten a chill of fear. It is the need for this fire burning in **Kalawao** to be extinguished. It has been overheard that Kānewaʻaliʻi is organizing the district that he will be in charge of, meaning that the policemen have been chosen for **Kalawao**. Thank you, Kānewaʻaliʻi, for your readiness to seek out the things that will bring peace. Yet there is this, do not choose a drinker [mea inu] as a policeman, or there will not be any peace. Look until you find someone who does not drink, and behaves properly, and then the land will be peaceful.

Also, do not get someone living with a mistress, and believe that the land will be made peaceful by them. The land will not be made peaceful by them because there is drinking and clear adultery. They are not the suitable ones who can complete the work. Look until a suitable one is found, and choose that one. The virtue and goodness will be greater if the various religions that are present in the colony of **Kalawao** [panalaau o Kalawao] become assistants in extinguishing these wicked deeds. It is necessary for you, the father, to go into the churches to encourage the leaders and the brethren to extinguish this fire that is burning. You have authority over the helpers [kokua]. They cannot ignore your command. They should agree to put out this fire, because the helpers, they are people who support this fire that is burning. They are people who break laws and go against the rules of the Board of Health. The helpers appeal to the followers and the stokers, people who have no love for the law and the land, those who adulterate and get drunk on the Sabbath day. They have no consideration for the peace. It [the fire] should be extinguished so that it goes out.

—J. K. Kawaluna. **Kalawao**, Molokaʻi, NOV. 10, 1892.

Kanaana Hou. A branch of Siloama Church in Kalawao that was established in Kalaupapa in 1878. On August 1, 1879, church elders named the Kalaupapa church Siloama Hou-Hale Aloha [New Siloama-House Beloved]. In October 1889, they gave it a new name, Kanaana Church [Canaan Church] and in May 1890 renamed it Kanaanahou Church [New Canaan Church]. In the meeting minutes of the church, Kanaanahou is spelled as one word into the early 1900s, but at the same time writers in the Hawaiian-language newspapers also spelled the name as two words, Kanaana Hou, which is the spelling used today.

In the *Hawaiian Dictionary* by Pukui and Elbert, Kanaana is spelled with a glottal stop, Kana'ana. Members of the church, however, have traditionally spelled the name without it, which is the spelling used here.

Canaan [Kanaana] is a biblical reference from Exodus, chapter 33 [Pukaana, Mokuna XXXIII], which tells the story of Moses [Mose] leading his people, the Israelites, out of slavery in Egypt to the promised land of Canaan. There, God [Iehova] had promised them, they would live in peace in a "land flowing with milk and honey" [aina e kahe ana o ka waiu a me ka meli]. This phrase appears in two *Ka Nupepa Kuokoa* articles in chapter IV: November 24, 1894, and October 15, 1915.

Ko Hawaii Pae Aina. 30 AUGUST 1879. P. 1.
Hoolaa Luakini Ma Kalaupapa. Church Dedication in Kalaupapa.
Dear *Ko Hawaii Pae Aina.* Greetings:

Please enter among your columns this heading that appears above, "Church Dedication in Kalaupapa." On the 3rd of August, 1879, which was the first Sunday of this month, all of the students [haumana] from Kalawao and Kalaupapa gathered together with the students of the Sunday School for their presentation that day.

I end here. This news is best. The chilling winds of Waihānau [makani huihui o Waihanau] are coming down. I leave my aloha with the editor and the typesetter boys. This is my final salutation.

—S. K. Lenalena.

Ka Nupepa Kuokoa. 16 AUGUST 1890. P. 4.
Hoike A Ke Komite A ka Ahahui Kula Sabati o ka Paeaina i ka Panalaau o Kalawao me Kalaupapa. Report of the Committee of the Sunday School Association of the [Hawaiian] Islands in the Colony of Kalawao and Kalaupapa.

The committee left Honolulu, going to the colony of Kalawao and Kalaupapa, on the evening of the Sabbath, July 27, 1890, on the steamship *Hawaii,* the ship that the majority of the legislative committee was on, and arrived on the morning of the 28th at the harbor in Kalaupapa.

The skiffs were released. We boarded and traveled to land, and when we reached land, there standing in a circle were the friends with hearts made sorrowful by longing for families and homelands. Upon jumping onto land, the friends immediately came and surrounded us. The friends whose hands did not have much affliction grasped our hands and shook them in greeting, while the friends whose hands were greatly afflicted spoke their greetings.

Right then we met with Mr. Kuala, the assistant Sunday school master of Kalaupapa. We discussed the convention of the Sunday schools on that day, and a decision was quickly made about the convention. (The story of that convention is on the fourth page of this newspaper, August 9.)

The activities of the convention proceeded well without impediment. The Resolution of the Sunday School Association of the [Hawaiian] Islands was presented before them, and it was accepted by them unanimously and with the same opinion. This resolution was also presented before the other religions, and they unanimously agreed to raise up that task together.

We had believed that our work would not go well because our committee would be confused with the legislative committee, since one member of that committee was the one who permanently branded the desire within the thoughts of the patients, due to a statement that came out of his mouth during the days before he was elected as a representative, saying, "If I am elected as a representative, then I will go to all of the patients in Kalawao and Kalaupapa and release them, and they will all return to their families."

However, God's glory was seen. Due to the business that was undertaken, the assembly was confined within the new church of **Kanaana Hou** from eleven in the morning until three in the afternoon, and then the business was settled with great joy.

Some things that were learned by the committee about Sunday school.

1. The youngsters: It is a thing of regret for the committee to report about the youngsters, since the total number of youngsters from Kalaupapa to Kalawao is only fourteen. Concerning the youngsters of Kalawao, there are only two in our denomination, and the rest are in the Mormon [Moremona] and Catholic [Kakolika] denominations. The Mormon children are released only for times of conventions and not at other times. As for the story of a little Catholic girl, this is how it goes.

This little girl was always passing outside of the Siloama church at the time when the Sunday school lessons were being taught to some youngsters. Because of her great joy at hearing the singing voices of those youngsters, she was constantly going there all the time, and due to her great desire to join with those youngsters, she actually went and asked the one who was leading, "Hey, would it be permitted for the Catholic children to learn the Sunday school activities together with your children?" The one who was leading replied,

"It would indeed be permitted, if you want, so come right in." That little girl replied, "My desire and the joy in my heart are great, but my parents would be extremely mad. I am not allowed to go to the Calvinist [Kalawina] Sunday school."

The leader gave hopeful thoughts to that little girl. After a discussion that little girl became a Sunday school student, and she was one of the students that presented before the committee.

The committee might be asked, what is the cause of the extremely small number of youngsters? Here is the answer:

All of our children are in the patient enclosure of Damien [pa mai o Damiano] and the Pauahi Home. Concerning the children in the patient enclosure of Damien, they are all Catholic. As for the majority of the girls at the Pauahi Home, they are Catholic, except for ten or so who are left in our denomination.

For the majority of these children, before they arrive there, they are our own children. But when they go there, the Catholic priests strongly urge them to become Catholics, since they are the authorities at that place. So our children agree to become Catholics.

(To be continued.)

Ke Aloha Aina. 5 FEBRUARY 1898. P. 6.
He Hoalohaloha Ia Mrs. Hattie Kamakahiki. Paumako Wale. A Letter of Condolence to Mrs. Hattie Kamakahiki. Simply Grieving.

Whereas, the hands of death heartlessly seized the living breath of your dearly beloved husband, Rev. S. K. Kamakahiki, at 9:00 p.m. last Tuesday, Jan.

25, at the residence of the Hawaiian ministers afflicted with leprosy [home noho o na Kahunapule Hawaii i loaa i ka maʻi lepera], that the Hawaiian Board [Papa Hawaii] prepared here in Kalaupapa.

While he was living, he was a kind and modest father in all of the spiritual activities of this congregation, and he was a constant member of the Congregational Association [Aha Ekalesia], and in accordance with the resolution approved by that association, at our meeting held at five o'clock yesterday evening, in the church of **Kanaana Hou**, as follows:

Resolved. We enter with you, the wife deprived of a husband, as well as the children greatly troubled by poverty and lack due to having no father, and the entire family. We bear with you all the sorrows and sadness of tragically remembering the one who passed, and

Resolved. We pray deeply to God's kindness to lighten our sorrows, within your unparalleled power, because we have no permanent dwelling here, and

Resolved. One copy of this resolution will be sent to the wife and the family and one copy each to the newspapers *Kuokoa, Ka Makaainana,* and the *Aloha Aina.*

We are with humility,

Committee. Jno. A. Kamanu. J. H. K. ʻImihia. J. K. Kainuwai. Kalaupapa, Molokaʻi, JANUARY 28, 1898.

Ka Nupepa Kuokoa. 25 JANUARY 1907. P. 5.
Mrs Lucy K. Makaena Ua Hala. Mrs. Lucy K. Makaʻena Has Passed.

Because, man goes to his eternal home,
And the mourners go about the streets,
While the silver chain is unbroken,
The golden cup is not cracked,
The bucket is not smashed at the spring,
The pulley is not broken at the well,
And then, the dust returns to the earth, like as before,
And as for the spirit, it returns to the God who gave it.

Because, it pleased Almighty God in his great kindness to separate what is his, the spirit, from the body of my wife, Mrs. Lucy K. Makaʻena, in Kalaupapa on the evening of the Sabbath, Dec. 2, 1906.

On the morning of Monday, Dec. 3, her funeral procession was held from our home to **Kanaanahou** Church [luakini o Kanaanahou]. The religious service was led by Rev. D. Kaʻai, and when the events there were finished, the procession went on to the graveyard in Papaloa [ilina ma Papaloa].

This procession was accompanied by the brethren, the Sunday school students, loved ones, the minister Rev. D. Kaʻai, and his wife, led by the band.

I give my thanks to those who accompanied the funeral procession of my beloved who passed, and to the students of the Sunday school class of young women for how you traveled with sincere compassion in the procession for your companion in equal labor, the school class that she belonged to for sixteen years.

Mrs. Lucy K. Makaʻena was born in Kuhua, Hilo, Hawaiʻi, on March 4, 1875. In Hālawa, Kohala was the place where she lived with her parents. She was edu-

Kanaana Hou

43

cated there at the Day School and from there to the Girls School of Waikupanaha [Kula Kaikamahine o Waikupanaha]. That schoolhouse was given the name by the students of that time, "Maunaoliva" [Mount of Olives, a biblical reference].

She stayed at that schoolhouse for several years in the period when E. W. Lyons was the teacher, until that schoolhouse was ended at that time. Afterwards, she lived with her parents, and because of the symptoms of the disease she had, she left her parents and came to Kalaupapa on November 2, 1890.

She spent sixteen years and one month living in this patient settlement [kahua mai], and it was thirty-one years, eight months, and twenty-eight days since her birth.

We were married by the late Rev. S. Waiwaiʻole in Kalaupapa, and that same father brought her into the brethren. We lived together and worked together in this congregation with ten ministers, and among them were the ministers sent by the Hawaiian Board to care for these parishes, who were the Rev. S. Waiwaiʻole, Rev. J. Hanaloa, Rev. M. C. Kealoha, Rev. D. Kaʻai, Rev. J. M. Naeʻole, Rev. E. M. Hānuna, until the time when Rev. D. Kaʻai returned for the second time to this parish, currently.

The ministers who were infirm, and came and lived here, were the Rev. J. Pahio, Rev. D. K. Pa, Rev. S. Kamakahiki, Rev. P. Keaupuni, and Rev. E. M. Hānuna.

Among these fathers of virtue who came to work in this parish, only two are still living and the majority have gone to rest. As for the majority of the old brethren, the Sunday school students, and the members of the society, they have died, and there are only a few of us, those who remain.

The congregation has been refilled at this time by the new folks coming in who came from within congregations outside. They have several fathers of this religious faith and are steadfast on the side of the fathers. That is where they stand.

Mrs. Lucy K. Makaʻena was a brethren, a Sunday school student, and a Sunday school teacher for several years, and a member of the Young People's Christian Endeavor Society [Ahahui Opiopio Imi Pono Kristiano] at that time, until the time it was changed to a Christian Endeavor Society [Ahahui Hooikaika Kristiano]. She often went to Sabbath meetings. Sometimes illness kept her at home.

We had children; five already went on the path she has taken, and four are living. She did not depart from this life because of the disease that made her come and live here, but due to a different illness. Educated treatments were attempted. The doctor strove to provide things that would bring ease, but the illness was greater than the thing that could control it.

She left me and our children, and her large family, a multitude living in her land of birth that grieve for her.

There is no permanent place here,
So those of the world weep,
But the good person has been saved,
She has respite above,
In the other realm, in the other realm,

—M. K. Makaʻena. Kalaupapa, JANUARY 4, 1907.

Kauhakō. A prominent volcanic crater in the land division of Makanalua. The interior of the crater contains a dryland forest, which includes ʻohe makai, one of the trees Hawaiians favored for surfboards.

According to *Volcanoes in the Sea: The Geology of Hawaii*, the Kalaupapa peninsula is a small volcanic shield that emerged late in the formation of Molokaʻi. The lava that formed the peninsula flowed principally from Kauhakō Crater and built against the inland sea cliff. The lowest point in the crater lies below sea level and contains a unique feature, a pool of brackish water. On the north face of the crater, a long trench runs seaward, which is the collapsed remnant of a lava tube.

According to Hawaiian legend, Kauhakō is a crater that was dug by the goddess of the volcano, Pele, while she was searching for a home in the Hawaiian Islands. She and her entourage arrived first on Niʻihau and then moved to Kauaʻi and Oʻahu. On each island she dug a crater, but struck salt water. She tried again on Molokaʻi, where the same effort produced Kauhakō Crater with it brackish water pond. This story, which is told many times in the Hawaiian-language newspapers, celebrates Kauhakō as a wahi pana, a famous place, on the Kalaupapa peninsula and throughout Hawaiʻi.

The Hawaiian word lua, which is usually translated as "hole" or "pit," also means "crater" and is the term that was commonly used to describe Kauhakō. Some writers also called it Puʻu Kauhakō, or Kauhakō Hill. The following are descriptions of the crater that appear in the Hawaiian-language newspapers.

Lua o Kauhako, crater of Kauhakō
Lua kai o Kauhako or Luakai o Kauhako, sea crater of Kauhakō
Lua kai hohonu o Kauhako, deep sea crater of Kauhakō
Lua kai uliuli a lipolipo, deep dark pool of sea water
Lua pele o Kauhako, volcanic crater of Kauhakō
Luapele kai o Kauhako, volcanic sea crater of Kauhakō
Lua ponaha pele o Kauhako, circular volcanic sea crater of Kauhakō

The brackish water pond in the bottom of the crater was most commonly described as a loko, a "pond" or "pool." The following are descriptions of the pond that appear in the Hawaiian-language newspapers.

Kiokai nui, large pool
Kukai o Kauhako, dip in the sea of Kauhakō
Loko, pond
Loko kai o Kauhako, sea pond of Kauhakō
Loko kai hohonu o Kauhako, deep sea pond of Kauhakō
Wai a ka pele, water of the volcano
Wai kamahao o Kauhako, amazing water of Kauhakō

Kauhakō is also known as Puʻu ʻUaʻu, or Petrel Hill. ʻUaʻu, which is also spelled ʻuwaʻu, are Hawaiian petrels, sea birds that nest in burrows on land [lua manu uwau]. [See Pu'u 'Ua'u in this section.] In the Hawaiian-language newspapers, however, the hill is rarely called Pu'u 'Ua'u and almost always called Kauhakō.

Ka Nupepa Kuokoa. 2 FEBRUARY 1865. P. 2.
Ka Moolelo No Pele; Kana Hana Kona Mana, A Me Kona Noho Ana: Kona Hiki Mua Ana I Hawaii Nei, a Me Kona Noho Ana. The Account of Pele, Her Actions, Her Power, and Her Lifestyle: Her First Arrival Here to Hawai'i, and Her Manner of Living.

Pele first arrived at Ni'ihau and that is where she first struck the land, and since it was shallow, and since she quickly struck ocean, she left Ni'ihau. She entered Kaua'iomanōkalanipō at Pu'uopāpa'i, where she dug, and since that land was shallow, and since the ocean entered it, that is why she abandoned Kaua'i. She went and lived on O'ahu and struck a crater there called Āliapa'akai, and since it was shallow, she abandoned O'ahu and came to Moloka'i at Kalaupapa. The name of the place where she dug was **Kauhakō** and Kaholoapele, and she abandoned Moloka'i. She came to Maui and struck at Keōihuihu near Lāhainaluna, and since that place was shallow, she left that place and and dwelt on Haleakalā, and since that mountain was shallow, she left that place and went to live on Maunaloa, Hawai'i, and Kīlauea is where she lives. That is her permanent dwelling until today.

Ko Hawaii Ponoi. 24 SEPTEMBER 1873. P. 2.
Na Lilo O Ke Aupuni No Ka Malama Ana I Na Lepera Ma Kalawao Nei. The Expenses of the Government for Caring for the Leprosy Patients Here in Kalawao.
Dear *Ko Hawaii Ponoi,* the announcer of these days. Greetings:

Captains of ships in these days, please place this cargo without hesitation on the flat decks of *Ko Hawaii Ponoi.* The people of the "Secret Societies" [Hui Malu] here in Kalawao met on the 8th of Sept. last under the shade of the kukui trees of **Kauhakō.** They discussed with great expertise the expenditures of the government. The extent of these is known as far as what the government has set aside for these two years going on. Here are the expenditures: [The table is not included here, but the expenditures total $47,587.00.]

This is the amount of the monies being expended for the livelihood of this people in almost the past two years. The livelihood of this people set aside for two years is $30,000. The estimated expenses are $47,587, expected loans are $17,587, so the government is in debt at this time. Therefore, at the end of the two-year period, the debt of the people will reach $20,000.

For this reason, we lay before you, Hawai'i, the estimations, and may the entire country filter out what is needed.

We, the patients, are living in these days, without food, rice, bread, molasses, and so on.

Therefore, the patients live constantly speculating [that they are] on the verge of a riot these days.

One reason the patients constantly speculate is due to the constant influx of aid. Some bring financial assistance and some have no money. This is it with appreciation.

—Secret Society Members [Poe Hui Malu]. Kalawao, SEPT. 15, 1873.

Ko Hawaii Ponoi. 8 APRIL 1874. P. 1.
Kekahi mau ano nui o ka aina o na Mai Lepera. Some important issues about the land of the leprosy patients.

In the land where the patients are living, there are eight ahupuaʻa: Waikolu, Kalawao, Kawaluna, Polapola, Māhulili, Makanalua, and Kalaupapa. Waikolu is the border on the east, and Kalaupapa on the western border, with a steep series of cliffs [kakai pali nihinihi] on the southern flank with the deep, blue ocean [moana kai lipolipo] on the northern shore. There are three large valleys and one deep saltwater pond [loko kai hohonu] in the middle of the land called **Kauhakō**.

» [The article says there are eight ahupuaʻa, but lists only seven. The missing ahupuaʻa is Pōhakuloa.]

Ke Alakai o Hawaii. 30 JUNE 1888. P. 6.
Ka Huakai Noii A Na Komite Ahaolelo I Ke Panalaau O Kalawao, Iune 24, 1888. Exploratory Journey of the Legislative Committee to the Colony of Kalawao, June 24, 1888.

At this time, the company progressed toward the coast of Kalaupapa, where they visited the cliff of **Kauhakō** [pali o Kauhako] where Pele had dug a home out for herself. As she found it too shallow, she left that spot and moved on to Hawaiʻi.

On this hill [puu] is the grave [kupapau] of J. W. Nākuʻina and two others situated next to him. This is a beautiful spot to view for visitors since it [Kalaupapa] is laid out clearly and splendidly with a good view of the farms of the patients to the southeast of the road with patches of clearings, [which are] the kuleana lands that had not become those of the government.

» [This excerpt is from an article in chapter IV.]

Ka Leo o ka Lahui. 9 JANUARY 1893. P. 1.
Ka Moolelo O Hiiakaikapoliopele. The Epic Tale of Hiʻiakaikapoliopele.
Edited From the People of Old and the People Who Have Retained the Stories and Ancient Tales of Hawaiʻi by Jno. E. Bush and S. Paʻaluhi.

INTRODUCTION.

When the chiefly flowers [pua alii: royal children] of Haumea first arrived, Pele immediately urged her multitudes to dig out a home where they could live in the Koʻolau [windward] districts of that island, at Kīlauea.

They walked upon the ocean floor of this group of islands [Paeaina], until proceeding onto dry land on the little islands in the west, where Kūhaimoana, a brother of that chiefess, was placed.

The rest of the brothers and the younger Hiʻiaka sisters continued on their journey until reaching the place we mentioned earlier where they began to dig out a home to live in. They stayed on Kauaʻi, and Pele began to dig out a crater at Kīlauea, but because of the shallowness of that place, she quit digging a crater home for them to live in, and went on the path to Oʻahu. Another brother of Pele, who is Kalaeokaʻena, stayed there, and that name remains to this day.

There are many signs in the places where Pele stayed, and because they were shallow, she moved on. After that, Pele and company left Oʻahu, journeyed to Molokaʻi and stayed on the Koʻolau side in the land of Kalaupapa. Pele again dug out a crater [lua], which was **Kauhakō**, but because it was quite shallow, she quit digging that crater.

Ka Nupepa Kuokoa. 5 NOVEMBER 1915. P. 3.
Pau Elua Waa i ka Nohaha. Two Boats Completely Smashed.

On the night of October 26, 1915, there were high seas, reaching a place where the sea does not usually rise. At the wharf [uwapo] of Kalaupapa, a skiff [waapa] belonging to Uha was taken by the sea. Not a piece was found, and in the boat harbor [awa pae waa] of the B. [Bishop] Home, a boat [waapapa] belonging to Mr. Kaiwi [was taken]. There was no piece taken from the skiffs in that same place, which were almost lost to the sea.

HIGH SEAS.

On the night mentioned above, while the writer was sleeping in his sleeping place, it was as if the bed was being lifted up, and in the understanding of the writer it was like the bottom of the patient settlement [kahua mai] was raised by the sea, something that was confirmed like so:

At **Kauhakō** Hill [puu o Kauhako], a hill [puu] between Kalawao and Kalaupapa, there is a large pool [kiokai nui] with no fish living in it, except for shrimp [opae]. In the understanding of the writer, the height above sea level of this crater is between 600 and 900 feet, and the home of the writer is about an eighth of a mile away from the ocean. At daybreak on the 19th the ocean was extremely calm, but the sea was a bounty for the birds, double the usual.

Kaupokiawa. Point on the shore of Pōhakuloa, which is on the east coast of the peninsula. The article that follows identifies several areas of Kalaupapa that were important gathering sites for natural resources, including food from the sea. Kaupokiawa is noted for its limu līpoa ʻaʻala, or "fragrant līpoa seaweed."

Ka Nupepa Kuokoa. 12 JULY 1912. P. 6.
Paina Hoomanao Ma Ka Aina O Ka Ehaeha. Remembrance Feast in the Land of Agony.

On June 28, 1:00 p.m., Mrs. Ellen Noholoa began a feast of remembrance for her beloved to mark a year passing since their separation, and since they have not had anything to eat or drink together at their dining table.

The wife who loved her husband laid out a feast completely filled with the rich foods of Kapuʻukolu [a place famous for abundance] for her to eat and drink with the loved ones of her husband, the grandchildren, the children, the sisters and all the friends.

Before the aforementioned hour, the dining table and the room were covered with the adornments of the upland forest [wehi o ka waokele], the cool misty palai fern of Waihānau, the fine-leafed kupukupu fern, and the dining table was filled with various delicacies: sticky poi that settles nicely down the throat [poi kalo uouo kaohi puu] from Kalawao; poi ʻuala [sweet potato poi] that was made sour [hoawaawaia]; chicken [moa] mixed with long rice [laiki loloa]; octopus [hee] mixed with seaweed [alaalaula, which is also known as wawaeiole]; limpets [opihi] mixed with seaweed [limu] from the headland extending into the sea of Hoʻolehua; shellfish [pupu] found on the cliffs; the māhikihiki shrimp [opae mahikihiki] of Waikolu; the fragrant seaweed [lipoa aala] of **Kaupokiawa**; the famous kukui nuts of Kauhakō Crater [lua o Kauhakō]; the bonefish [oio] that lie on the sands of Pūahi; the convict fish [manini] that lie in pools in ʻĪliopiʻi; the sweet beverages; the soft pastries skillfully made by Willie Kaleiheana; sweet potatoes baked with pig; sea urchin roe [iʻo wana]; seaweed [limu kohu]; and so on.

In the count by the writer of the number of plates filled with each and every thing, except for the sweet beverages and the sweet potato, there were 156 plates, from big to small. The dining table was decked out.

When everything was ready, the diners were called and the writer was invited to appeal to the heavenly powers. When the prayer was finished, the forks went down, the spoons went up, John Bull [Keonipulu: a pun on "full"] arrived and Paohaka [empty-cavern] departed. The feast was continued until 7:00 p.m. It was peaceful, without any rising seas [no one got angry].

—Nāhauowailēʻia. Kalawao, Molokaʻi, JULY 1, 1912.

Kawailoa. Stream, Waikolu. Also called Wailoa.

Ka Leo o ka Lahui. 20 JUNE 1895. P. 2.
Na Mea Hou O Ka Panalaau. News From the Colony.
Mr. Editor. Greetings to you:

Here I am with heart-stirring bits of material from these current days. There is a great amount of news that I report before your glory.

In these recent days someone died here in Kalawao, Solomona Kekipi, last month, with the Board of Health wanting to take away the food allotment belonging to this one who died. However, this cooked taro [pai ai] had already been eaten by the family of the deceased. If anything remained, then Makaliʻi would have taken it, to be placed up with Lonomuku. So we must remain in the human realm, since that might be the Board of Health's privilege, or maybe not. [Makaliʻi, a supernatural chief, was a selfish ruler who kept all of the food plants for himself, leaving his people to starve. Lonomuku was his wife who escaped to the moon.]

In my understanding, these actions on the part of the superintendent were not at all correct, since this privilege had gone to the patient. However, this action was already unfair.

CONCERNING THE VOUCHERS. [NO NA BILA ALUALU.]

Here is this new deceit, the vouchers at the store: if a patient is about to die, then the remainder of the voucher is fetched to collect the full value, since the one who cares for the patient knew that his patient was going to die. However, there is nothing that day. You would be better off pulling up the Ahuʻawa sedge at Hamohamo (Waikīkī), the place where there is a lot of that thing. This is the second hunger [Ka Haka elua] on the side of the patients.

CONCERNING THE TRAVELERS OF WAIKOLU. [NO NA POE HELE O WAIKOLU.]

Here at Waikolu is the place often visited by the patients with permits from the superintendent. In recent days, some people went to upper **Kawailoa** to sightsee and fish for ʻOʻopu fish. After these people, I saw some others doing a different activity (Kahuna) [practicing the ancient religion]. A girl returned and talked about these activities with the government policeman Ka'aikauna.

This policeman went to make an official complaint to the sheriff of the patient settlement [kahua mai]. These people were fetched and brought to be questioned by our Father, but there was not sufficient evidence on the part of the government, so they were simply let go. The work of the police wanders lost in the fields. "Yet here is this pen getting revenge." Do not do it again, examine carefully and see clearly with correctness, and then it will be admired. "The canoe fleet without a compass wanders lost in the fields [Hu i kula ka Auwaa Panana ole.]."

CONCERNING THE SCHOOLING FISH. [NO KA I-AKU.]

In these recent days, schooling fish were seen in Waikolu. A great number of men and women went to that place with strong desire in their minds to catch fish, but there was nothing. They returned empty-handed to the fields of Kalawao. Here are the words that came out of the mouth of the one who owned the net: "If we get fish, those who pulled the net get none."

Friends of this land of agony [aina nei o ka ehaeha], do not go there again or else be stabbed by the a'u fish [marlin], a fish with a sharp nose [bill], and such is the case with this one. Those actions are shameful, that the name of the person makes receiving possible. This is finished.

THE DAY OF THE CONQUEROR OF THE NATION [KA LA O KA NAIAUPUNI: KAMEHAMEHA DAY, JUNE 11].

On the 11th, the patients made a display for the day of the conqueror of the Pacific [naiaupuni o ka Pakipika], Kamehameha I, with the way the days are observed here in the patient colony. The patients arose in unity and that day became a joyous day for us, in accordance with the declaration by the interior minister of the republic.

On that day the patients had fun peacefully riding horses. On that same day our superintendent had a feast in Waikolu (**Kawailoa**). There were several foreign foods as well as Hawaiian, and there were a multitude of friends there, gentlemen and ladies of the weaker sex [aoao palupalu]. "That was beautiful, the bay sparkled." To be continued.

» [On December 22, 1871 King Kamehameha V proclaimed June 11 a national holiday to honor Kamehameha I, the king who united the islands and established the Hawaiian nation. Hawai'i celebrated its first Kamehameha Day in 1872, and today June 11 is a state holiday.]

Kawaluna. Land division in Kalawao.

Ka Hae Hawaii. 20 MAY 1857. P. 31.
Dear *Hae Hawaii:*

In the early morning hours of the 8th of May, a man died in **Kawaluna** by the name of Nāhau. This is how he died: he had been experiencing mental disorders for four years. It was a chronic affliction. In the fifth year of his affliction, he encountered episodes of mental fits [mai pupule]. He had experienced a one-week bout of fits and jumped into the sea and died. He was at sea for two nights and on the 10th of May on the Sabbath, he washed up onshore and was discovered by acquaintances who took him to his home where he was buried. Nāhau was a church member before and later fell out of favor. He was in his forties.

—W. N. P. 'Ikepono. Kalaupapa, Moloka'i, MAY 11, 1857.

Kilohana. Lookout at the top of the cliff trail [alanui pali].

Ka Nupepa Kuokoa. 12 MARCH 1892. P. 3.
Ka Misiona a ke Kuhina Kalaiaina no Kalaupapa me Kalawao. The Mission of the Interior Minister to Kalaupapa and Kalawao.

Mr. Editor. Greetings to you:

The *Kilauea Hou* arrived on the morning of February 18, with the interior minister and his traveling companions. They went up and stayed at the house of the head supervisor until the eighth hour had passed. Then the party went all the way up to Kalawao and arrived at the famous small waterways [makawai] of Waikolu. At the end of the pipe running to the stream in Waikolu, the party sat down to have a meal upon a flat stone. After the meal, they went up to the place that has been excavated, which is the edge of the place being cultivated with several taro patches. And from there to the old storehouse [halepapaa kahiko] in Waikolu. From there they entered the patient homes. The home for children was the first, going everywhere with Father Louis [Lui] and Mother Marianne [Maria]. After that, they entered the settlement of old patient homes standing in Polapola and went to the place of Dr. Swift, but he was not in his home. They went to the house of the president of the Board of Health, and from there to the pharmacy, where the doctor was found. From there they went to the house of a deaf Caucasian [haole kuli], and there the party stopped a bit to take a good look around. From there to the Bishop [Bihopa] Home, where they met with Mother Marianne [Mariana]. They stayed there for a bit to watch the activities of the children. After that, the party returned to the home of W. H. Tell.

The visiting party rested there that night, and they were entertained by musicians. The interior minister stood and gave these simple words: "Greetings to you." Here are some more words: "The queen sends her greetings to all of you." When that was over, an excellent song was presented, and the activities continued in that way until three hours had passed.

On the morning of the 19th, the steamship *Waimanalo* arrived with food for the patients. The minister went to observe the cooked taro [paiai] and the work of the helpers [kokua ma'i]. At 10:00 a.m., they left the place of the head supervisor and went to the cliffs, although the president and the bishop of Honolulu stayed. The head supervisor and two policemen also went on this journey, and at the base of the cliff, warm farewells were exchanged between the minister and the head supervisor. The minister had great fortitude in going up the cliff, and he said how great his fatigue was. And he went to see this problem. We got up to **Kilohana**. There were horses belonging to the children of Māea, and we mounted the horses. We arrived at Wai'alalā, dipped the water pitcher and praised God, and drank to the health of William Tell [Uilama Kele] and all of the patients. And then, we traveled to the home of Mr. Māea.

—S. Keanu. Kalaupapa. FEB. 26, 1892.

Kōloa. Cemetery, plain in front of Waihānau, Makanalua.

Ka Lahui Hawaii. 6 DECEMBER 1877. P. 3.
Na hiona walohia o ke Aupuni Poepoe. The Sad State of the Round World
Dear *Ka Lahui Hawaii.* Greetings:

While the mountain mists blanket the base of the Koʻolau cliffs, with its furrows [oawa] eternally drenched with the droplets of misty rain of the forest, and as the chill stabs at the skin as it gently moves about me, my eyes gaze down upon the earth and I contemplate, saying to myself, "The cold is the cold of the land, but it has passed on and disappeared from view. It is true that the country is round, where I and we live is narrow, and so I report what appears above, from Kalaupapa to Waikolu, since the entire length of the land from Hoʻolehua to the sea and all the way to Waihānau is full of the great attractions of the land that are great to visit.

Kalaupapa. This is where the harbor [awa ku o na moku] is. There are buoys [mouo] like buoys in the channel of Māmala [nuku o Mamala: entrance channel to Honolulu Harbor], where good word arrives ashore that we consider good, along with well-to-do children from around the world. There are lots of houses there, wood-frame houses large and small, along with pili grass houses [hale pili], churches for Catholics as well, with Protestants secondly. There are many people living there with a primary school in the middle of that Protestant town.

Makanalua. This is half of the land from Kalaupapa. It is said that it rises up as a slope from the sea, and this is where I live. There are not many houses in this place, and this is where my biological father [luaui], J. S. Kaʻawa Nāpela, lives, where Kuaokalani [Kekuaokalani] returned to. Wm. Keolaloa is there, Mrs. Hila formerly of the white man, Kalani, of Wailuku, and at the back of our homes there is a deep sea pool [lua kai hohonu] formed out of lava. It is called the pool of Kauhakō [lua o Kauhako]. This is a moʻo name. [He moo ke ano oia inoa.]

Kōloa. This is an uninhabited plain, where cattle and horses live. It is a pleasant-looking plain and reminds me of the plain of Pāwaʻa in Honolulu. There is a story of this plain that I've heard of about Kāneiakama. He was a man of Kona here [on Molokaʻi] who gambled with the nobles here in Koʻolau until he lost all of his wealth on this side. The plain here is slick with pili grass, where they would have fun until all was gone, and since everything was gone, he would return empty-handed to Kona. I, therefore, bring up this mele:

How I love the cliff of **Kōloa**
With its face turning toward Waihānau, etc.

And with this lament, he had an amazing ghostly encounter, where Kālaipāhoa was first discovered by Kāneiakama at the top of Mauna Loa [Maunaloa, Molokaʻi]. This is when all of his horses came back to him and he beat Koʻolau.

Polapola. Here are the hospitals, the store, the manager's residence, like the market area of Honolulu where people would hang out, and this is where you would see the horrible end of the nearly dead masses [kini aneane make]. So sad and pathetic. This is where the sacred heiau of Kapo [heiau kapu a Kapo] is until today. Women do not go on it, only men go on that place. This place is nearly facing the base of the cliff. It is a good place.

About Kalawao. This is a place name [wahi inoa] that causes people to fear from the talk outside this land. It looks like Kaināliu in Kona, Hawai'i. It has a pleasant smell, with the scent of the foliage wafting down. There are many things that please the soul, planted crops, such as bananas, sugar cane, sweet potatoes, and so forth. There are two churches there. Siloama Church [Hale-pule Siloama] is a beautiful building with an attractive pulpit, a piano, and its choir, a pastor, W. P. Ka'awa. To look at those who live there, they are people who would not agree to see their homelands since this place is well-supplied at the back in appearance.

Waikolu. This is a very high cliff like Waipi'o in Hawai'i [island]. Where that [Waipi'o] is very wide, this is small, with streams flowing out to the sea from the base of the verdant and cool cliffs. The trail we take to get there is below the cliffs on horseback as well as on foot. We are always at the bottom of those cliffs going every Wednesday to get our rations of poi. When I first went below the cliff, I was completely scared of rocks falling down on us because as you go and look up, the cliff towers above you as if you are traveling in a cave, enduring the journey, but that is where our warehouse [hale papaa] is located.

The people above [Na kanaka maluna iho]. There are three types of people seen here: (1) Hawaiians and part Hawaiians [Kanaka Hawaii a hapa Hawaii], (2) Full Chinese [Pake maoli], (3) Whites [Haole]. I did not see any black people [Nika] among these people. I asked the locals here about there being no black people [haole eleele] among them, and they said no, that there were none. These are all the people here. The types of characters you find here are highly educated, people who are bilingual or trilingual, good people and peaceful people too. One part of the population consists of some who are ignorant and very difficult. The religious sects found here are busily doing good works. Also among these people are commoners and nobles [makaainana a ke lii] alike, and here is where the deceased body of the ali'i, C. Ke'eaumoku [William Charles Ke'eaumoku], is found. Pika [Peter Young Kaeo] went home [to Honolulu], it is hoped. If there is no way for the people to leave, then everyone from outside would come here, as we have seen before. The one who proposed this law was brought here to eat the fruit of his actions. He is found here.

Restrictions here [Na Kapu oonei]. The inland part is surrounded by cliffs and the other side is wide-open ocean. It is restricted to climb up to the land, and so too to go out. It is not allowed to step one foot on the seashore [kapakai] here. There is a jail [halepaahao] like there is outside. There are strict laws established upon these people. The people now consider the laws that have been established, when we do wrong before you. All are left here to be buried. I finish here. The [sea] birds are going home as it is evening.

—D. Puna. Makanalua, M. NOV. 26, 1877.

Ko'olau. Windward side of Moloka'i, which includes Kalaupapa. The same name is used for the windward districts on Maui, O'ahu, and Kaua'i. Many districts in Hawai'i have well-known epithets, or poetic phrases that describe a representative feature of the district. The epithet for Ko'olau, Moloka'i is Pali hāuliuli, or "dark green cliffs," which is the same epithet for the Ko'olau districts of O'ahu.

Ka Hoku O Ka Pakipika. 18 SEPTEMBER 1862. P. 4.
Kanikau Aloha No Luka Maioholani. A loving lament for Luka Maioholani.

> My wife of the leaf-wrapped trumpet fish of the land,
> Of the branch-splitting wind [makani koo laau] of Molokaʻi,
> My wife of the dark green cliffs of **Koʻolau** [pali hauliuli la e Koolau]

» [This exerpt from a kanikau for Luka Maioholani includes many place names on Molokaʻi outside of the Koʻolau district.]

Kukuiohāpuʻu. Also Kukuihāpuʻu. Name of the Kalaupapa cliff trail [alanui pali] in use today.

Ke Aloha Aina. 5 DECEMBER 1896. P. 3.
Mai Molokai Mai. From Molokaʻi.
Mr. Editor. Greetings to you:

At 7:30 this morning was the arrival of the president and the gentlemen of the Board of Health [at Kaunakakai], and a great multitude of other people. Right at nine o'clock, the party headed straight for Kalaupapa, arriving at twelve o'clock. Right after lunch, the president and the members of the board sat to hear the petitions of the leprosy patients [mai lepera]. After the president viewed the petitioned requests, he said that he would submit these petitioned requests before the meeting of the board to be considered individually. Here are these petitions:

1. The beef distribution center [hale haawi bipi] in Kalaupapa should be expanded, and a covered veranda [lanai] should be built in front, as well as a gable on the ocean side.
2. A Board of Health agent should be placed at every judicial district all across the islands, besides the island of Oʻahu, so that the friends of each leprosy patient [maʻi lepera] have a place to get permits for cargo without charge.
3. The little outhouse pits [lua liilii] everyone has dug should immediately be worked upon by the Board of Health until their pits are deep.
4. The Board of Health should pay Mano (male) 250 dollars for his labor and his part of the creation and cultivation of eighty-four taro patches [loi kalo] in Waikolu.
5. The Board of Health should order C. Kopena to leave this leprosy settlement [Kahua mai lepera] for these reasons:
   1. He is not a leprosy helper [kokua mai lepera]. 2. He is a man of public intoxication. 3. He assaults the leprosy patients [mai lepera] without cause. 4. He is a man who blasphemes and swears.
6. The patients [mai] taking food allotments of rice, crackers, and bread should be given two pounds of sugar each week, not just one pound.
7. The sale of food allotments [ai hanai] should be allowed.
8. Water pipes [paipu wai] should be laid for those lacking them.
9. A cookhouse [hale kuke] should be built for those lacking cookhouses.
10. Six packs of matches [ahi kukaepele] should be given to each leprosy pa-

Kukuiohāpuʻu

tient [mai lepera] monthly, rather than what is being regularly received, only four.

11. The band boys [keiki puhiohe] of Kalaupapa should be paid two dollars per boy monthly.
12. Leprosy patients [mai lepera] should be allowed to cut firewood from and between the ʻIliʻilikaʻa and **Kukuiohāpuʻu** trails [alanui o Iliilikaa a Kukuiohapuu].
13. The district judge of Molokaʻi should not be allowed to stay at another house [hale okoa] besides the guest house [hale hookipa malihini] at Kalaupapa, while he is in the leprosy settlement [kahua mai lepera].
14. Leprosy prisoners [paahao mai lepera] should receive supplies of clothing and food like those given to Honolulu's prisoners.
15. The superintendent of this leprosy settlement [Kahua Mai Lepera] and his assistant should not be allowed to work in law enforcement in the position of supervisor or police captain.
16. The one who cares for the cemetery in Kōloa [Ilina kupapau ma Koloa] should be permanently banned from releasing his horses within that enclosure [pa], and that enclosure needs to be cleaned immediately.
17. Pills like the medicinal tea from Dr. Goto should be supplied.
18. [unreadable text]

PETITIONS FROM THE BALDWIN HOME.
[NA NOI HOOPII MAI BALDWIN HOME MAI.]

1. Infected boys with rotten and fragile skin should not be put to work.
2. New clothes should simply be given without the old clothes being returned.
3. Clothes of the deceased should not be given to the living.
4. Food should be prepared cleanly.
5. Everyone who wants to should be allowed to go to Kalaupapa twice a week.
6. Supplies of clothes that are provided should not be retrieved from anyone leaving the home.

We are humbly, Committee: W. K. Makakoa, T. K. Nākanaʻela, D. C. Kahalehili.
Kalaupapa, Molokaʻi, NOV. 22, 1896.

Ka Nupepa Kuokoa. 16 OCTOBER 1924. P. 5.
Kuu Wahine Aloha Ua Hala. My Beloved Wife Has Passed.
    Beloved is the cliff trail [ala pali] of **Kukuiohāpuʻu**, that place where you trudged along, the rain and wind above, you marching below. Beloved is the plain of Kalaʻe red with dirt, the water of Waiʻalalā, that lofty water with the acidic soil.
» [This excerpt is from the kanikau section.]

Leinaopāpio. Also Leina o Pāpio and Leinapāpio. This point extends into the ocean on the east side of Waikolu valley. Leina o Pāpio means "Leap of Pāpio," a reference to the sport of lele pali, or "cliff jumping," into the ocean from the summit of nearby Huelo islet. Pāpio is said to be the name of the man who made the first jump.

Ko Hawaii Pae Aina. 20 APRIL 1878. P. 4.

Ola i ka hua Pioi! Ka moolelo walohia o ka Panalaau mai lepera o Kalawao, i ke Au o ka Luna Hou. Helu 2. Saved by Yams! The sad story of the leprosy colony of Kalawao in the era of the new manager. Vol. 2.

The sad dangers of the patients. One day last week, our feeble father, the interim supervisor, Mr. W. K. Sumner [and] Keolaloa went to the valley of Pele-kunu to cook with the farmers of that place to help those people. Right when the boat passed that area [Kalawao], the horses of the leprosy patients for hauling the supply of poi arrived. They waited from the morning until Lehua nearly captured the sun [Lehua e kailiaku i ka la: sunset], and the boat came back with a hundred or more orders of poi. Since the bay of Waikolu was rough, the boat tied up at the point of Linopapio [**Leinaopāpio**] and that is where the poi was unloaded. This is when the voice of the manager was heard announcing that the patients should go and get the poi and carry it over to the storage house [hale papaa]. That is when the patients quickly made their way over. They could not hear.

Ka Nupepa Kuokoa. 13 MARCH 1903. P. 5.

Mea Hou O Ka Hale Ahaolelo. Hale O Na Lunamakaainana. News from the Legislature. House of Representatives.

From Nakaleka these [items] below: trail [alanui] from **Leinapāpio** to Kalawao, $2,000; plank bridges [alahaka] of Moloka'i, $100; cargo crane [mikini hapai ukana] in the harbor [awa kumoku] of Wailau, $2,000.

Ka Nupepa Kuokoa. 6 JULY 1922. P. 3.

Ka Huakai Makaikai Ia Molokai. The Journey Visiting Moloka'i.

The cliffs were quite beautiful. Hā'upu was clearly seen, the place where Hina lived. Huelo stands with its loulu palm grove right below **Leinapāpio**.

This place was the famous place [kahi kaulana] for those who did cliff jumping [poe lele pali] in the days of old. From Huelo is the loulu that is used to make hammocks [ahamaka] that resemble floor mats [palau moena]. A person gets on top and is launched [hooleleia] into the ocean. This game is like how children slide on pieces of cardboard. The first Hawaiian man who started this cliff jumping activity, like an airplane, was Pāpio. And, due to how very enjoyable this game was, that cliff was called **Leinapāpio**, which is, "the jumping of Pāpio," a jumping place for Pāpio [he wahi lele na Papio].

Before we arrived at this place, I pointed out the place where the shark lived, Keanapuhi [the Eel Cave]. When he went to Kahiki and returned, his cave was occupied by an eel [puhi]. He covered up the mouth of the cave with rocks. But when he thought that the eel would just die, in fact, the eel was digging and came out the other side. When the shark saw the eel appear on the other side, he followed it. The two of them fought until the eel fled and climbed up the cliff to Kalawao and escaped. That is the hole in that place to this day. It can be clearly seen from a ship.

While we were nearing Lae-o-ka-Hi'u [Lae-o-ka-Hio], we saw the horses running on shore with the automobiles. As we went around right off of the point, we saw a line of horses with people dressed uniformly standing together like a cavalry, and one automobile covered with a flag. When we went around right below them, they gave us a greeting with the flags.

We gave our greeting with handkerchiefs and also the [ship's] bell. While we were voyaging from there to Kalaupapa, that cavalry traveled with us on shore.

Upon arriving at Kalaupapa, the sweet, loving sound of the band quietly played the National Anthem [Mele Lahui], "Hawaiʻi Ponoʻī." There was great affection for the people of that place. While the band was playing, there was a procession of automobiles with American flags, perhaps ten automobiles with people in them, with the cavalry behind them, and behind them was the Military Officers' Association [ahahui Pukaua]. When the crowd saw the beauty of all these people, the tears of the crowd fell due to being truly filled with love for these honorific and affectionate actions by the patients.

Personally, I was unable to repress the pangs of emotion within me, since Kalaupapa had raised me up so that I became a representative and even a senator. While I was conversing with some visitors, I was called, since those of the ship could indeed hear my name being called by those on shore. When I heard my name being yelled, I went up to a place close to the captain's deck, and with the loudspeaker I gave my greeting to those on shore. And they gave their greeting. I reciprocated with thanks full of affection from everyone aboard the ship to the patients and everyone of Kalaupapa. And they also gave thanks.

Oh, my dear unloving people! For you, the people, those there are family, residing there. Why did you not go too? To perhaps just see Kalaupapa is a big thing. The falling of compassionate tears for those folks goes to the visiting foreigners, but we who are the closest, our own flesh and blood, what about us?

I praise God, because the thing that I spoke of in Kalaupapa in 1905, 1907, and 1909 has come to pass. Leprosy is being healed, and the place where it is being done is within the large schoolhouse that I strove for until it appeared. Kalaupapa and Maui chose me to win, and this is the fruit that is gained, health.

While we were departing from Kalaupapa, a letter for me was given from my dear friend, Mr. Jack McVeigh, the superintendent of the patient settlement [Luna Nui o ke Kahua maʻi], requesting that I help in giving some brief words to the visitors in order that he receive some money for buying instruments and his new songs for the band.

I carried this out, and the visitors were quite pleased, from the Caucasians [haole] to the Hawaiians. The gain from this fundraiser was $104.30. This money will be sent today to the superintendent of Kalaupapa. Here is this money in the hand of the purser of the steamship company. If there are other Hawaiians who also wish to give their assistance for this issue, it should be given to the secretary of the Board of Health.

As we neared this land, a Caucasian woman of significant status, a local visitor, came over, and this is what she said to me: "I am quite pleased to arrive in Hawaiʻi and see this famous place. I have great love for those people of Kalaupapa. The actions by which they rewarded us visitors were beautiful. The music that the band played for us was beautiful. Here is what I say to you: I will return to my home. I will encourage our organization to agree that a sum of money will be sent at all times for activities bringing joy to the people of Kalaupapa. Here are the organizations of us Caucasians thinking about and greatly aiding animals. Compassion goes to the animals, without considering the people experiencing disfiguring and agonizing symptoms, like these people. So I will return and give my strength to compassion for these people." I thanked her for her compassionate thoughts.

Before we landed here, most of the Caucasians came and gave their thanks for what the patients had done for us. They asked me to give those of Kalaupapa their affection and full gratitude. According to them, in the places they came from, they have never seen an observance of the national holiday, Fourth of July, like this. There are only Hawaiians in Kalaupapa, yet this day became a holiday for them personally. Showing their status as true Americans, all of America can be proud to have a truly loyal people like the Hawaiians.

So, to Kalaupapa and Kalawao, on behalf of the 327 visitors on the touring voyage of the Fourth of July, I reply with greetings to all of you. In the near future, you will receive their gifts of compassion in accordance with what I was told.

With haste and with affection. W. J. Coelho.

» [In addition to supporting the residents at Kalaupapa, Sen. William Joseph Coelho was also known for introducing the legislation in 1907 that led to the founding of the University of Hawai'i.]

Lenalena. A famous spring near the Kalaupapa landing. Its waters flowed into the ocean and mixed with the salt water [kahi wai awili kai].

Ka Nupepa Kuokoa. 2 MAY 1891. P. 3.
Ka Huakai a ke Alii ka Moiwahine Liliuokalani no ka Panalaau o Kalawao. I ka Luna Hooponopono o ka "Pae Aina Puka La" J. U. Kawainui. The Journey of Her Majesty Queen Lili'uokalani to the Colony at Kalawao. To the Editor of the *Pae Aina Puka La,* J. U. Kawainui.

And when the queen came up and stepped ashore, the national anthem [mele lahui] was played by six musicians with two drummers from the United Heart Association of Kalawao [Hui Puuwai Lokahi o Kalawao], in a round building standing above the spring [punawai] called **Lenalena** (which is the spring where the friends lay bones to rest in the dirt of that unfamiliar land [aina malihini] with pity caused by the stories of that time when heard), under the direction of Chas. Manua Jr. There was a helper and five boys stricken with this pitiful affliction, along with the loud, joyful voices of the land, and with the skiffs escorting the passengers to land.

» [This excerpt is from an article in chapter IV.]

Māhulili. Also abbreviated as Māulili. Land division in Kalawao.

Ka Nupepa Kuokoa. 9 FEBRUARY 1889. P. 3.
He Mau Hunahuna No Ke Kahua Mai Lepera O Kalawao A Me Kalaupapa. Some Tidbits about the Leprosy Settlement of Kalawao and Kalaupapa.

If you, the sightseer, desire to see clearly the majesty of the two towns, climb up to the western edge of Kauhakō Crater [lua o puu Kauhako] and turn out and view the buildings of lower Kalaupapa like kōnane pebbles lined up on the kōnane board that Kamalālāwalu left from his days living here. Then turn toward O'ahu of Kākuhihewa, which you, the reader of this story, will be stirred to express affection for:

"Like a white tapa cloth is the pili grass of Kohala
Small red Kaulu shrubs in the pili grass
The white buoy at the water's edge."

Then move up on the left edge of this crater and turn to the coming of the sun [east], and your gaze will first meet with the buildings of **Māhulili**, Polapola, Kawaluna, and Kalawao.

» [This excerpt is from an article in chapter III.]

Makanalua. One of three ahupuaʻa, or land divisions, on the Kalaupapa peninsula.

Hawaiians divided the peninsula into three land divisions, which from east to west are Kalawao, Makanalua, and Kalaupapa. The Board of Health established the first leprosy settlement in Kalawao, which is where the earliest homes and churches were built and where Father Damien lived and died. As the patient population increased in Kalawao, the settlement expanded into Makanalua, which includes the following places: Waihānau, Kōloa, Kahaloko, Lahupuʻu, Papakailoi, Kanomanu, Kauhakō, Puʻu ʻUaʻu, Kahinahina, Kaluaokahealiʻi, Puʻu Moehewa, Anakahalelo, Makapulapai, Kapapakikane, and Kiʻikolu.

The first four articles that follow were written before the arrival of the first patients in 1866.

Ka Hae Hawaii. 3 AUGUST 1859. P. 71.
Olelo Hoolaha. Announcement.

May all people know that from Kalaupapa to Waikolu, if you pay attention, we are the commoners [Makaainana] of **Makanalua** and we forbid horses, cattle, donkeys, mules, sheep, goats, and pigs from trespassing on the plains of **Makanalua**. Should any horses, cattle, donkeys, or mules stray onto the property, they must pay $1.00 per head. Should any sheep, goat, or pig stray onto the property, it is half a dollar a head. The fee is different if any of the crops are damaged. The animals will be kept along with the animals of **Makanalua** should crops be damaged and payment shall be made according to the damage done. The day this announcement is published in the *Hae* [*Ka Hae Hawaii*] is when this law shall take effect. Should anyone refuse to pay the required penalty, his animal shall be taken to the government yard [Pa Aupuni]. To attest to the truth of this, we affix our names on this day, the 12th of July 1859.

The Commoners Association of **Makanalua** [Makaainana hui o Makanalua]. **Makanalua**, Molokaʻi, JULY 12, 1859.

Ka Hae Hawaii. 24 JULY 1861. P. 67.

June 30, in **Makanalua**, Molokaʻi, Nākaipuni (female) died of a lingering sickness.

July 3, in Waikolu, Molokaʻi, Ziona (male) died as a result of venereal disease [kaokao] and vomiting blood [luaiakoko].

Ka Nupepa Kuokoa. 27 SEPTEMBER 1862. P. 3.
Olelo Hoolaha. Announcement.

May all people know on Moloka'i who pay attention that I am the one whose name appears below. I am placing a restriction on my kuleana land in Puhi'ula, **Makanalua**, Moloka'i that no one who has a horse shall ride their horse on my land. I do not restrict those who travel on foot [poe hele wawae]; only those who travel on horseback [poe hele pu me ka Lio] are restricted. If I and my supervisors should see those violating this announcement of mine, I will sue them according to the law of the land.

—By Maka'imi, Waikolu, Moloka'i, SEPT. 22, 1862.

Ka Nupepa Kuokoa. 1 AUGUST 1863. P. 4.

The birthplace [aina hanau] of this woman and her father and brother is the ahupua'a of **Makanalua**, which is situated among the windward cliffs [pali koolau] of Moloka'i, adjacent to the ahupua'a of Kalaupapa. I will await a reply then I will provide a response. This child of the windward cliffs of Moloka'i is returning home to drink the water of Waihānau [inu i ka wai o Waihanau].

—W. K. Keli'ihananui. Makanalua, Moloka'i, JULY 18, 1863.

Ka Nupepa Kuokoa. 4 JUNE 1915. P. 2.
Ka Nani O Ka Home Ua Hala. The Beauty of the Home Passed Away.

The land of agony [aina o ka ehaeha] was connected with the lei, a child, from the rippling waters of Waimanu, to the leaf of the 'ama'u fern, to the slope of the cliff, to the waters thick with the fragrance of the hīnano flower of Wailē'ia, to the sea spray of Kauō. Quite beloved are the plains of Waikolupa, the smooth mound of the Baldwin Home buildings, the sweetly ringing bell of Pilemona [St. Philomena], the bathing waters of Siloama [wai auau o Siloama], Kawaluna, the incline of Maulili [Mahulili], the hala trees of Kōloa, the wide plain of Pōhakuloa, the cliffs of Kōloa in the turning face of Waihānau, the pleasant descent of **Makanalua**, resting in the pleasant home of the father of Britannia Hall [Beretania Hale].

» [This excerpt is from a letter regarding the death of Esther Keakaokalani Imihia Kealoha, who was born in Kalaupapa on March 8, 1901.]

Mōkapu. The largest of three islets off Waikolu, Mōkapu has an elevation of 360 feet and is approximately 14.8 acres. The three islets, Mōkapu, 'Ōkala, and Huelo, are sea stacks, remnants of the main shoreline that were isolated by erosion. Hawaiians regarded all three islets as wahi pana, or famous places.

Mōkapu, along with 'Ōkala and Huelo, is one of the most botanically diverse islets in Hawai'i. Although it lies outside the marine boundaries of the Kalaupapa National Historic Monument, Mōkapu is part of the Hawai'i State Seabird Sanctuary. Seabirds found on the island include: 'akē'akē (band-rumped storm petrels), 'iwa (great frigate birds), koa'e kea (white-tailed tropic birds), koa'e 'ula (red-tailed tropic birds), noio (black noddies), 'ou (Bulwer's petrels), and 'ua'u kani (wedge-tailed shearwaters). Public access to Mōkapu is prohibited.

Ka Nupepa Kuokoa. 8 JUNE 1878. P. 1.
Huakai A Ke Komite 13 O Ka Ahaolelo I Ka Panalaau O Na Mai Lepera Ma Kalawao. (Mai ka mea Kakau mai o ke Kuokoa.) Journey of the Legislative Committee of 13 to the Colony of the Leprosy Patients at Kalawao. (By a writer from the *Kuokoa*)

At five o'clock on Tuesday morning, I went up to the deck and saw Kalaupapa below us and the flat platform of Kalawao before us.

Mōkapu was out before us on the sea and ʻŌkala passed by to the side. The steep slope of Huelo was there in the calm and the falls of Waiehu [in Waikolu] tumbled down the cliffs. That is where a loving memory came up in me as I remembered the waterfalls of Waiānuenue and Akāka in Hilo.

» [This excerpt is from an article in chapter III.]

Nihoa. A small plateau at the base of the sea cliffs west of Kalaupapa that marks the boundary of the settlement. An old cliff trail ended here. Patients were not allowed to go beyond Nihoa.

Ka Nonanona. 29 MARCH 1842. P. 94.
Kīpū is the name of the cliff and **Nihoa** is below it. It is a cliff that turns toward Kalaupapa.

Ka Nupepa Kuokoa. 3 JULY 1875. P. 2.
There is no death that is more heartfelt that the death of Mrs. ʻEmelia Nāmaʻiʻelua Kalāuli, female schoolteacher of Kawaiahaʻo, at 10:30 p.m. on the 25th of June 1875. Her school will have its program on the 2nd, but at three o'clock in the morning of the 24th, she fell seriously ill so that she was not able to fulfill her duties at her school, and it was not twenty hours later with the affliction that she died. She was provided various treatments, but was not able to be cured. She was born in Kalaupapa on Molokaʻi on the 17th of October 1837, and on the 19th of April 1857, she got married to A. Kalāuli. She had lived in Honolulu for thirteen years, and in that time she served as a teacher for twelve years. Among all women that we have seen, we attest that there is not a handful of women like her in kindness, patience, graciousness in hosting, and love for all who call into their home. If there was a visitor passing in front of her home, they would be called as if they were an acquaintance. If friends of her associates in the household passed, they would be welcomed. At her funeral, her procession was attended by a steady and long ebb and flow of friends and acquaintances, and her body was laid to rest on the eastern side of Kawaiahaʻo. A. Kalāuli and we, the friends, would be fortunate should there be another Nāmaʻiʻelua like the one who passed. We mourn together, however, for the man who was left without his wife. It is true that her days in this world have passed and she has arrived at the goal of life of all people, "Dust to dust," as usual. We will miss her spot in the choir at Kawaiahaʻo. We all will cry knowingly as the roadway that she will travel is a trench that we all can lay at Muliwaʻa. And here we leave our tears of love on the side of her husband.

My dear wife from the single path of Molokaʻi,
From the cold rain of Kalaupapa,

Nihoa

That drenches the pandanus blossoms of **Nihoa**,
My dear companion living as strangers in Honolulu,
We know the occupation of teachers,
Oh my dear love, my dear wife.

Ka Nupepa Kuokoa. 27 AUGUST 1887. P. 1.
He Moolelo No Lonoikamakahiki. A Story about Lonoikamakahiki.

There are two old trails [alanui kahiko] on that windward side [Koolau] of
Moloka'i. One trail comes down at Kīpū and reaches the pandanus [hala] grove
of **Nihoa** below.

Ka Makaainana. 17 JUNE 1895. P. 6.
Apiki ka Noonoo o ka Lunakanawai Apana. The Deliberations of the District Judge Are
Unfair.

For several days of the weeks of this past May, Kukamana, a district judge
[Lunakanawai Apana] here on Moloka'i, came down to try several cases [of
those] charged with leaving the leprosy settlement [haalele no i ke kahua ma'i
lepera], and many other cases. However, while the court sat to hear that case
of the group of girls, Rose, Kamala, and Kamakele, Keawe was arrested for doing the same thing, for leaving the patient settlement [kahua mai]. When the
court listened to the testimony of the witnesses, no witness said that they had
gone outside of the boundaries of the patient colony, and such was also the case
with the policemen that are trusted by the government. The girls were found
by them in **Nihoa**, fishing, at the place that is said to be owned by the Board
of Health. When the court sat and examined these fine witnesses, this Kukamana issued the sentence, "You are charged with leaving the patient settlement,
$10,475 fine." Right afterwards Keawe's trial was held, just like it, and he was let
go. I report publicly from Hawai'i to Ni'ihau, this is a foolish government that I
elected, and it is also foolish with Kukamana. Its Judge Kukamana was probably
not educated. Here is my question before you, O friends and an ignorant judge
[Lunakanawai hupo] of Moloka'i: Which part of the patient settlement is the
one that has not been transferred to the Board of Health? Perhaps you will say
that it all has. Then how indeed did this Kukamana foolishly punish that group
of girls?

And here is that group of girls digging the road. The ardor of the work is
like that of healthy people. Some folks have no hands, yet they are forced to
work by the superintendent. There are many problems for the patients caused
by this superintendent.
—K. Samuela. Kalaupapa, Moloka'i.

Ka Makaainana. 24 MAY 1897. P. 2.
Pahoa [Pahoe] Malolo ma Molokai. Beating Flying Fish on Moloka'i.

These are calm days here in Ko'olau [windward district], Moloka'i. The
paddle strokes of the children of Kalaupapa who beat the surface of the ocean
to scare flying fish into nets [keiki lawaia pahoe malolo] are striking forcefully
in these early mornings.

It is crowded out in the deep sea, from the cliff face of **Nihoa**, all around
the sea to the windy point of Kahio [lae makani o Kahio], kissing [honi aku]

Ho'olehua, turning to outside of Kalawao, and returning to the harbors [awa-pae] of 'Iliopi'i and Kalaupapa. The assistant superintendent is one who is beating flying fish, and he has eaten and survived. The quarters sound by fours.

Saturday, May 8, the glistening mouth of the net turned with flying fish inside, and John Paumano arrived to have a small meal in his morning, and with incredible speed the people of that canoe [waa] boarded other canoes. Was something wrong in the household of the fishermen?

From those days until Monday, there has been one flying fish for a quarter. Last Tuesday was two flying fish for a quarter. And at Kalawao, four flying fish for a quarter, and five. Where it is a great labor to bring them, there are many flying fish for a quarter, and where there is little effort to peddle them, the breath is held. Good for you, peddling children of Kalaupapa, such vast wisdom! Hooray [Hai lo]!

—Sam Kalei. Kalaupapa, MAY 13, 1897.

'Ōkala. One of three rock islets off Waikolu that are sea stacks, remnants of the main shoreline that were isolated by erosion, 'Ōkala is the highest with an elevation of 394 feet. It is approximately 7.4 acres and prominently visible from the Kalaupapa peninsula along with Mōkapu, the largest of the three islands. 'Ōkala, along with Huelo and Mōkapu, is one of the most botanically diverse islets in Hawai'i. Hawaiians regarded all three islets as wahi pana, or famous places. As part of the Hawai'i State Seabird Sanctuary, public access to 'Ōkala is prohibited.

Ka Nupepa Kuokoa. 10 AUGUST 1922. P. 3.
Ike Wale Ke Kilauea Ia Molokai. The *Kilauea* Only Sees Moloka'i.

In accordance with the advertisement by the Inter-Island Steamship Company of recent weeks, due to the large amount of people wanting to see the Great island of Hina in the calm of the Ko'olau cliffs [Moku-nui-a-Hina i noho la'i ai i na pali Koolau], thusly was the *Kilauea* filled again last Sunday morning with those going sightseeing. The number of those traveling was 249, not counting the ship's officers and sailors.

There were many visiting Caucasians [haole malihini] on this journey and also many locals [kamaaina]. There were many folks who had gone before, who went again on this ship. The thing that gladdened the heart was seeing that there were many native Hawaiians [oiwi Hawaii] among this group of Caucasians. The Hawaiians met with the Caucasians, and it was as though "similarities flowed together like water" for all. If descending to gibberish [namu: English], it was the epitome of smooth, and when our language arose, the Caucasians were quite delighted by the deftness of the language.

This journey was honored by Hon. Oscar P. Cox, the American marshal; Senator W. J. Coelho; the Hon. J. M. Dowsett, former senator of O'ahu; Professor Major Kealakai; J. K. Mokumaia; Chas. Lake; Mrs. Capt. Louis Self; Mr. and Mrs. J. Asing; Mr. and Mrs. Alex Bishaw; Wm. J. Kuniakea Coelho Jr.; and many other Hawaiians.

The ocean was blustery on this stumbling journey, and there were many folks whose heads were on pillows during the voyage through the Kaiwi channel [kai o Kaiwi]. However, upon reaching land, everyone got moving together, entering the lee. The land was quite calm; every place was seen, a clear expanse.

Upon nearing Lāʻau Point [Lae o ka Laau], the "pilot" [pailaka: used here to mean a tour guide], the local of the journey [kamaaina o ka huakai], began his part of the work. Stories were listed from various places, from Lāʻau Point to the Koʻolau [windward] districts, and all the way to ʻĪlio Point [Lae o ka Ilio], blow out the light, sprinkled, the tale runs [the end]!

The visitors were greatly entertained by Senator Coelho acting out different stories of Molokaʻi. The laughter of the Caucasians erupted as Coelho [Kuelo] explained how people from Molokaʻi weigh the corn they plant. What is done on Molokaʻi is just like what is done in foreign lands, measuring weight by the "peka" (peck), "kuaka" (quart), "pukela" (bushel), and "kana" (ton). And in his land of birth, Maui, it is quite different. The folks there (those up in Kula) do it by the "paina" (pint), "kuaka" (quart), "galani" (gallon), and "palela" (barrel). For several minutes, the Caucasians were puzzled, and upon understanding laughter burst forth, until drooling at the mouth, because of that yearning for the "liquid corn" [kulina wai] of Maui.

As the ship was passing off of Hālawa, several Caucasian women were heard calling to Coelho [Kuelo] and pointing up at the cliff of Lamaloa. These women saw goats standing together, and a goat that looked just like a person, standing beside a donkey. These women insisted that it was a man with a horse. Coelho explained, "No person can go there with a horse. However, that which we see are goats. The Koʻolau cliffs [Pali Koolau] are only a place for goats."

The cliffs were quite beautiful in the calm. We just hungered for the limpets [opihi] clinging to the stone cliffs, the makaiauli and kōʻele varieties. So it was when passing off of Wailau. The shore was clearly visible, but there were no people in the village [kauhale]. The delicious things of that place were simply recalled: the fresh water snails [hihiwai], and the goby fish [oopu], the shrimp [opae], and the young goby fish [hinana].

According to our local: at these places, from Hālawa and going down to Kalaupapa, these were places for fishing with kāʻili nets for Nāʻōpala and [his] company and the other Hawaiian captains [kapena Hawaii], at the times when ships sailed in these waters. When all the cargo was unloaded at Kalaupapa, they returned to these cliffs, the ship lying off. Then fishing was the work of some folks, and some children traveled to the cliff on a skiff [waapa], picking limpets [kui opihi] until the gunny sacks [eke huluhulu] were full, and then returned to the ship. Upon returning to Honolulu, everyone went home with the same bundle. And if goats were seen on the lands of Kikipua and [his] company, then people went ashore to shoot. After getting the goats, they returned to the ship. The ocean fish were hung up to dry. Quite delicious. [Nui ka ono.]

While nearing Pelekunu, Coelho [Kuelo] told a story that was greatly appreciated about Kini Wilson, the wife of Mayor [John] Wilson [of Honolulu]. According to Coelho: "When the Wilsons were living in Pelekunu, the two of them worked a lot. If Wilson went to his road work contracts on Maui or Oʻahu, Kini stayed in Pelekunu, farming. They had many taro patches [kaupapaloʻi] always filled with taro. Due to Kini's farming, the people there were toiling. When some folks were lazy, they were persistently urged by Kini

to go independently to farm a living for themselves. When Kini went away to
O'ahu, all of Pelekunu's people went to Honolulu, to the place without the labor
of farming. The land that simply has water is to be prized. The Chinese are the
ones living there [now]!"

When the *Kilauea* neared the sea of Kuka'ipa'a [Kuka'iwa'a], the voyage of
the ship was stopped, and some boats were released with a Caucasian film-
maker [haole pa'ikii onioni], to record the *Kilauea* and the passengers in the
channel between 'Ōkala [island] and Kiloi'a Point [Ka Lae o Kiloi'a].

As we entered the channel, our local told the beloved story about the very
first superintendent of the patient settlement [lunanui mua loa o ke kahua
ma'i], William Ragsdale. He was a true Caucasian [haole maoli]. He married a
Hawaiian woman and had several children. There is a son living in Hilo today.

In AD 1866 the patient colony was started in Kalawao, and the number
of patients confined there was 115. Wm. Ragsdale was the very first superintendent. Because of the kindness of that Caucasian and his wife, they did not
scorn the patients, and they were greatly beloved. When that Caucasian went
to Wailau or to Pelekunu by canoe, the helpers [kokua] did not allow Bill [Bila]
Ragsdale's feet to get wet in the sea.

The people carried him on their backs [e kua ana], like how the chiefs [of
old] were carried on backs. And when Bill [Bila] Ragsdale died, the people
worried that his bones would be moved by those without compassionate hands,
and so they took his body and buried it directly atop the summit of the island
of 'Ōkala.

The ship stopped at Kalaupapa for half an hour for the Caucasian film-
maker to get off.

There was great compassion for the patients, and the heart was pained at
hearing of some unsuitable, unjust actions by Superintendent McVeigh. The
tourists had hoped to hear the sweet melody of the famous band of Kalaupapa
and were prepared to donate a [monetary] gift for the band. However, upon
arriving there, the whistle of the wind was heard, no band. Our guide and local
was questioned. He said that maybe the superintendent of the patient settlement [Lunanui o ke Kahua ma'i] was sulking.

The reason for the sulking and the contempt for the visitors was a trifling
personal thing between him and the head of the steamship company. However,
he thought by doing that then the steamship company would lose out. He was
quite mistaken, if that was truly the case. Because it was not for the visitors.
Money is the thing that pleases the steamship company. Having something
that increases compassion within the visitors is the thing that strengthens the
boldness of the friends in asking for money for a gift and bringing joy to those
living in the land of agony [aina o ka ehaeha].

On that recent journey on the 4th, according to Coelho, because the band
played and the visitors listened, then when the letter from McVeigh asking for
the visitors to donate to the band was received by Coelho, it was carried out,
and $104.30 was received. On this voyage, no one could be so forward because
McVeigh has deprived those who could provide compassion for the patients.
Therefore, you went without [a donation] on this journey, Kalaupapa, due to
the childish action of your superintendent.

Upon returning, the unparalleled beauty of the Ko'olau cliffs [pali Koolau] of Moloka'i became a main topic of conversation among the Caucasian visitors. Everyone felt the same delight.

It was discussed that once the new steamship arrives in December, then the travel times to Maui and Moloka'i will be known, and the *Maunakea* will be the ship. If there are no obstacles, and if there are confirmations for the amount of people going sightseeing, then there will be another trip to Moloka'i in the near future. It would be good if many of us Hawaiians go too, to make the journey enjoyable.

—Mea Māka'ika'i [Sightseer: a pen name].

» [During the Kalaupapa part of this trip around Moloka'i, the guide provides some conflicting information about William Ragsdale. He says Ragsdale was a true Caucasian (He haole maoli oia), when he was actually half Caucasian and half Hawaiian (hapa haole). The guide says Ragsdale was the first superintendent of the colony, but Ragsdale arrived on June 14, 1873, more than seven years after the arrival of the first leprosy patients in 1866. The guide says when Ragsdale died, which was November 27, 1877, the patients buried him on the summit of 'Ōkala islet. Other sources say he was buried in the field next to Father Damien's church in Kalawao.]

Pali Hāuliuli. Literally, "dark green cliffs." This epithet, or poetic phrase, is used to describe the Ko'olau district of Moloka'i, which includes Kalaupapa. The same phrase is used for the two Ko'olau districts of O'ahu.

Ke Aloha Aina. 30 APRIL 1898. P. 1.
Na Anoai O Kahua Ma'i. News of [the] Patient Settlement.
Mr. Editor. Greetings to you:

When the steamship *Mokolii* arrived on Wednesday, April 20, it carried in an embrace on its deck three hundred portions of cooked taro [pa'i ai] for the patient settlement [kahua ma'i], an amount of cooked taro that could not adequately supply the patients here in the patient settlement, perhaps with the belief that the farmers [kanaka mahiai] of Waikolu would supply the remainder. However, upon examination, there was nothing on the blind hill [puu balaiana] and so it was that some folks took their ration [helu] in bread, rice, and crackers. The Hawaiian cannot persist in eating those things, since the sticky poi that settles nicely down the throat is the food that they are used to, like the song:

And quite delicious, and gulped down [A he onoono la, a he monimoni la].

And your writer thinks that Hon. W. L. Wilcox [Wilikoki] & Co. might not be able to fully supply the cooked taro for this patient settlement in the future, since the shortage has already been seen in these current weeks.

On Friday, April 15, Henry [Henery] Mahi was chasing cattle with some cowboys [paniolo] on the plains of Kaupokiawa (he is a cowboy [paniolo bipi] for the Board of Health), and while he was continuing to chase, he fell together with his horse. When someone else named Nā'ilima rode over, he saw that Henry Mahi had fallen together with his horse. When he arrived there, he (Nā'ilima) saw that the injuries that Mahi had were quite serious, and in fact he could not see and could not hear. He was supported by two others for several miles to his home, and in this state of injury he was left. Between the hours 8:00 and 9:00 a.m. on Sunday, April 17, his final breath flew away, and dust returned to dust.

He was a young man, and a helper [kokua maʻi], who came after his loved ones, a wife and child. He was a native son of Nāpoʻopoʻo, S. Kona, Hawaiʻi. Alas for him.

On Monday, April 18, his funeral was held by the Compassionate Societies, Knights and Angels [Hui Aloha, Naita a me Anela]. His earthly body was laid down in the sand of Papaloa [one o Papaloa]. Alas! Simply sorrowful.

These are extremely hot, dry days here in the patient settlement [kahua mai], and the row of cliffs, the dark green cliffs of Koʻolau [kakai pali o na **pali hauliuli** o na Koolau], have been seen quite clearly.

All the buildings here in the patient settlement are being cleaned again, and such is also true of the roads, under the management of the new superintendents, W. J. Feary and J. K. Waiʻamaʻu, his assistant. It appears quite beautiful and excellent, a condition that has not been seen before.

In these current days, there are not many deaths among the patients.

Here I stop my pen from drinking the water of ink with the hope that it will flash again.

With you, Mr. Editor, my greeting, and with your typesetting boys my adieu.

With thanks, Wm. N. Kuaana. Pūahi, Kalaupapa, APR. 21, 1898.

Pali Koʻolau. Literally, "windward cliffs." A poetic name for the Koʻolau district of Molokaʻi, which includes Kalaupapa, and its spectacular sea cliffs.

Ka Hae Hawaii. 19 JUNE 1861. P. 47.
Olelo Hoolaha. Announcement.
    May all people know that those of us living in **Pali Koʻolau** on the island of Molokaʻi strictly forbid horses, cattle, donkeys, mules, sheep, goats, pigs, and all other animals from being raised and kept, nor should any of these animals described above be released in the ahupuaʻa of Kalaupapa. This is strictly forbidden. Should anyone refuse to heed this and do these things and if they are found by the supervisor, the owners of the animals shall pay a fee of half a dollar for each animal for each day, and they can be expelled from living on our land as we are the ones raising the animals. With regards to farmers, cotton growers, and businessmen, these are the only ones allowed to lease on our lands.
    —W. L. Moehonua. E. P. Kamaʻipelekāne. Honolulu, JUNE 18, 1861.

Ka Nupepa Kuokoa. 17 MAY 1879. P. 3.
Ko Kalaupapa mau mea Hou. News from Kalaupapa.
    In January and February of this year, 1879, I finally got to witness a year of great productivity. The rain is doing its job falling on the surface of the earth. Water is falling off the cliffs, along with rocks. The wind is doing its job carrying off the bad air of the land, and the ocean is doing its job.
    These three things are constant powerful guardians [kiai ikaika loa] of the Koʻolau cliffs [**Pali Koolau**] of ours here and shut off the streams of food that arrive for us. There will be no food from outside, such as the amazing food from China that our ancestors had never seen before. But our troubles have

been taken away, meaning the days of want, and I have great appreciation for the Board of Health for keeping some of our traditional Hawaiian foods [ai kupa Hawaii] and some foreign foods [ai a ka malihini]. I have not forgotten the graciousness of God, since "The heavens reveal the glory of God, and the universe tells of his true works," telling about his love for all people by providing three doctors for us: one Hawaiian doctor [Kauka kanaka] and two Caucasian doctors [Kauka haole].

Yours truly. Kanaka'ole.

Ko Hawaii Pae Aina. 4 DECEMBER 1880. P. 4.
[*Kanikau no Alice Keanuenue Kahaulelio.* A lament for Alice Keānuenue Kahāʻulelio.]

Answer me, Keānuenue, the woman whose name this is
How beautiful are the Koʻolau cliffs [**Pali Koolau**] that stand proudly in the calm
Spreading out across Kalaupapa
Carrying on a conversation with Nihoa in the sea
How I love the plains of Kōloa facing Waihānau
Love is born and I realize what I desire
Gazing upon the beauty of the lehua flower
Blossoming atop Kaunuʻōhua
Relaxing in the mist of Kaulanakaʻōpua
Adorning the top of Ahumāuna
Wailau and Hālawa come together
Satisfying the desire for love and affection
It is my burden of love
Offered with a fragrance.

—Mrs. J. H. Leialoha.

I saw Molokaʻi Nui a Hina
The woman beautifully adorned with the Koʻolau cliffs [**Pali Koolau**]
There can be no other in comparison
It is the name of your mother
To whom this beautiful flower [Pua Nani] belongs
It is the name, Keānuenue
So calm
In Waiʻeleʻia [Waiʻaleʻia], where love is found
At Hālaulani.

—Mrs. M. Lelekahuna.

Papaloa. Section of the Kalaupapa peninsula that lies between the wharf and Kalaemilo Point.

The shoreline of Papaloa is a white sand beach, Papaloa Beach. Vegetated sand dunes line the backshore and extend inland, and a shallow reef shelf fronts the foreshore. A common Hawaiian word for reef shelf is papa, an abbreviation of ʻāpapa, so one definition of Papaloa is "long reef shelf," like the one that fronts the beach. *Place Names of Hawaii* offers another definition, which is "long flat."

The inland section of Papaloa and its sandy soil once produced sweet potatoes and watermelons, but as the original patient settlement in Kalawao grew and eventually moved to Kalaupapa, Papaloa was designated as the site of a cemetery [Ilina o Papaloa]. Eventually it became the largest cemetery on the peninsula.

The following are phrases in the Hawaiian-language newspapers that were used to describe Papaloa and Papaloa Cemetery.

Kahua o Papaloa, grounds of Papaloa
Kai o Papaloa, sea of Papaloa
Kula o Papaloa, plain of Papaloa
Kula laula o Papaloa, wide plain of Papaloa
One o Papaloa, beach of Papaloa
Oneloa o Papaloa, long beach of Papaloa
One puni hele o Papaloa, traveling beach of Papaloa
Puuone o Papaloa, sand dunes of Papaloa
Puuone kinikini o Papaloa, numerous sand dunes of Papaloa
Ilina o Kanuola ma Papaloa, buried alive cemetery of Papaloa. [Kanu-
    ola, literally "buried alive," was a phrase some patients used to de-
    scribe themselves when they were sent to Kalaupapa.]
Ilina o Papaloa, cemetery of Papaloa
Ilina Kakolika ma Papaloa, Catholic cemetery of Papaloa
Ilina kaulana o Papaloa, famous cemetery of Papaloa
Ilina one puakea o Papaloa, white sand cemetery of Papaloa
Pa ilina o ka L. D. S., cemetery of the Latter-day Saints
Pa ilina o Papaloa, cemetery of Papaloa

As the population of the settlement increased dramatically, so did the number of deaths, sometimes to the point where several patients died per day. [See "death statistics" in the index.] Father Damien and others established funeral associations [hui hoolewa kupapau] to help with funeral arrangements, which included providing services for the deceased and attending to the logistics of burials. One of the earliest references to Papaloa Cemetery in the Hawaiian-language newspapers is in an article published in 1885.

Ko Hawaii Pae Aina. 7 NOVEMBER 1885. P. 2.
Hou Pahi Mainoino Ma Kalaupapa. Vicious Knife Stabbing in Kalaupapa.
    Kanohooʻahu (male), Kaunulau and Mahiki were stabbed with a knife by Momona between the hours of five and six on Thursday evening, October 26. For the first names reported above, their stomachs were cut by the knife, and what was inside came out. The two of them died on Saturday, October 31, and their bodies were buried on the first day of this month at **Papaloa** Cemetery [ilina o Papaloa] in Kalaupapa.

In other articles in the Hawaiian-language newspapers that reference burials at Papaloa, writers used various sayings about death and life after death. The first two that follow show Christian influence, while the rest are traditional Hawaiian.

1. E hoi ka lepo i ka lepo. This saying is from Genesis 3:19 in the Holy Bible: "You are dust, and to dust you shall return."
2. Ipukukui pio ole. This poetic phrase for everlasting life, "never ending light," uses the word ipukukui, the traditional candlenut lamp, as a symbol for light.
3. Ke ala hoi ole mai: the road of no return.
4. Ke alaula o Kane and ke alaula o Kanaloa. The word "alaula" means "scarlet road," a poetic description of the light at either sunrise, ke alaula o Kane, or sunset, ke alaula o Kanaloa. In Hawaiian culture, as in many others, the western sky and the setting sun were used to represent the end of life on earth. Kāne and Kanaloa are two of the four main Hawaiian gods. Other similar sayings are:

   Ke ala koiula a Kane: the rainbow-hued trail of Kāne.
   Ke ala muku a Kanaloa: the road cut short of Kanaloa.
   Ke ala polikapu a Kane: the path of the sacred heart of Kāne.
   Ke ala polikua a Kane: the invisible dark road of Kāne.
   Ke ao polikua a Kane: the invisible dark cloud of Kāne.

5. Waiho iho la i Kaea na iwi o kamahele: the bones of the traveler are left in Kaea. Said of one who dies away from his homeland. [The story that explains this saying is in 'Ōlelo No'eau: Hawaiian Proverbs and Poetical Sayings.]

The following are some of the phrases writers used to show the final separation of death:

1. Ala hoi ole mai: path of no return.
2. Na pali hulilua o Kalaupapa: the cliffs that turn in two directions of Kalaupapa. The term hulilua, which means "turn in two directions," is often used to describe the separation at death, where the deceased and the living go in different directions.
3. Kai okia: sea that separates.
4. Ma keia aoao aku ka muliwai eleele o ka Make: on the other side of the black river of death.
5. Ma ke alanui poeleele: on the dark road.
6. Kahikimoe, the horizon, and Kahikiku, the sky just above the horizon: places where spirits departed earth to reach the afterlife.

Graves were decorated with:

1. Makana lei: gifts of flower lei.
2. Poke pua (also bo-ke pua): flower bouquets.
3. Pupuweuweu: greenery arrangements.

Ka Leo o ka Lahui. 29 JUNE 1892. P. 4.
Ua Muumuu Anei Ka Papa Ola? Has the Board of Health Been Amputated?
Submitted. JUNE 22, 1892.

O Cannon [Pukuniahi]. Greetings to you:

Please endure to absorb this news in some empty space of your offices, so that it is seen by our friends. On one of those recent days, your spy [kiu] saw two female helpers [wahine kokua] riding gracefully with patients upon horses in **Papaloa**, here in Kalaupapa, on the straight road heading to Kalawao. When I tracked down the true end of their journey, it was reported to me that the two of them had entered the home of the patients without a permit allowing them to do that in a place under the authority of the Board of Health. In my understanding, the thing that was done by these tender parties was greater than the crime committed by Nāhinu, but he was charged, and that is what I am astonished at. Perhaps the hands of the Board of Health have been amputated, or perhaps that was for a man and these are women, so the law can just be massaged [ke kanawai ke lomi ia]. For many days have I waited for a result to arise for this thing that was done, but the plain [kula] is completely silent with no movement. With the hope that justice will be done, it is necessary for those women to be warned not to do that again, or else they might get used to doing that, and then the time when the law had a bite will be over. That is significant.

For your editor my greeting, and to your typesetting boys my salutation.

Sincerely, K. K. Kauamoe. Kalaupapa. JUNE 22, 1892.

Ka Nupepa Kuokoa. 6 AUGUST 1892. P. 3.
Ua Hala ka Makua Rev. S. Waiwaiole. The Rev. Father S. Waiwaiʻole Has Passed.

On Thursday, July 21, 1892, at eleven oʻclock that morning, it pleased the Almighty to take the life breath of the Rev. S. Waiwaiʻole from his residence in Kalaupapa, Molokaʻi, and leave the earthly body for the family and friends who are grieving in this world. He left behind a wife, two sons and two daughters, many grandchildren, and a great many friends. At three in the afternoon on Friday, his body was carried to the cemetery in **Papaloa** [ilina ma Papaloa], escorted by family and many friends, and placed into the immeasurable belly of the earth; and "dust returns to dust, and the soul to the one who made it." The Revs. J. H. Pahio and D. K. Pa led the funeral service.

The Rev. S. Waiwaiʻole was born in Lāʻie, Koʻolauloa, Oʻahu, to Kamano (male) and Keala (female), on May 21, 1832, and sixty years and two months of his life in this world had passed. He has a living younger brother, W. B. Kapu, living in Tabiteuea, Islands of Kiribati. In September of 1849, S. Waiwaiʻole was chosen as a policeman [makai], and he held that post for six months. On August 27, 1850, he was married to Miss Haliaka Kaehu by Rev. J. S. Emerson [Emekona], and almost forty-two years of them being in the covenant of marriage had passed. They had fourteen children and many grandchildren. In September of that same year, he became assistant tax supervisor for G. B. Ukeke for two years. January 1851, he was chosen by P. Naue as a schoolteacher for Lāʻie, while P. Naue was serving as schoolmaster at that time. Ten years passed in that job, and then he left work due to infirmity. In 1862, he entered the seminary of Rev. A. Bishop [Bihopa] in Nuʻuanu, but after six months that school shut down. In 1864, Rev. B. W. Parker [Pareka] created another seminary in

Kāneʻohe, and he re-enrolled at that school. February 13, 1865, he received the preaching certificate [palapala haiolelo] for Waimānalo. October 16 of that same year, he was ordained as a minister for that congregation. In 1872, he was chosen as vice president for the Sunday Schools of the Islands [Kula Sabati o ka Pae Aina].

From the start of construction of the new Kaumakapili Church in 1881 until it was completed, he strived in every way to advance the work. On June 30, 1882, he was sent by the Congregational Association of Oʻahu to the island of Kauaʻi as a committee member requesting money for Kaumakapili Church. November 5, he traveled to Kohala, Hawaiʻi, on this same mission in that same year.

In June of 1884, he was again chosen as vice president for the Sunday Schools of the Islands, and as a Sunday school master for the Island of Oʻahu. He left that work in June of 1889, due to infirmity. April 1887, he left the congregation where he had been minister for twenty-two years, which was Waimānalo.

In December of 1888, he was sent by the Hawaiian Board as a committee member to go and examine the state of the leprosy patients [maʻi lepera] in the colony [Panalaau]. On April 21, 1889, he was again sent by the Hawaiian Board to return and serve as minister for the flock in the colony and left his children and grandchildren behind for the good of the souls of the people in the agony of leprosy. There he lived and worked until he slept to awaken anew in that realm.

He served in the capacity of committee member for the congregations of Kāneʻohe, Waikāne, Hauʻula, Kahuku and ʻEwa for several years.

Ka Nupepa Kuokoa. 13 JULY 1895. P. 4.
Kuu Pokii ua Hala Ma-o. My Dear Little Brother Passed Away to Over There.
To my dear Combined *Nupepa Kuokoa* and *Paeaina.* Greetings to you:

On Monday, June 3, at 6:00 p.m., Mr. Sam. Maʻalo Kalawaiʻaopuna left this life and returned to the eternal place of all things.

He was born in Hōlualoa, North Kona, Hawaiʻi, June 4, 1835, from the loins of Mrs. Sipa Mokuola and Samuela Kalawaiʻakanoa. The people of Kona named him "The-fisherman-of-Puna" [Kalawaiaopuna] because he was from Puna. In AD 1889, June 12, he was brought here to Kalaupapa.

The illness that he died from was a tumor [puu] on the right side, as well as the left side. He left behind a wife and children, an older brother and younger brothers, and several grandchildren living in Honolulu and in Wainiha, Kauaʻi, and all the friends living in the land of birth.

The amount of children the parents had was seventeen, and this one was the seventh of their children. He was sixty years old when he passed away to over there. Alas, how pitiful!

My dear younger brother in the diving water [wai luu poo] of Puʻu.
My dear younger brother at the long beach of **Papaloa** [one loa o Papaloa].

God be praised, the one who creates and the one who takes, Amen.
Yours truly, S. H. P. Kalawaiʻaopuna. Kalaupapa, JULY 4, 1895.

Ka Nupepa Kuokoa. 16 NOVEMBER 1895. P. 3.
Ua Hala o G. K. Koieamo. G. K. Kōʻieamo Has Passed.

Mr. Editor. Greetings to you:

Please allow me to report to you about the death of Mr. G. K. Kōʻieamo, and then you will set it down upon smooth deck of the firmament, "The Great Prize of the Hawaiian People" [slogan of *Ka Nupepa Kuokoa*], and it will travel like lightning among the multitude of friends from Hawaiʻi to Niʻihau.

Mr. Kōʻieamo left this life at 7:00 a.m. on Saturday, October 26, here in Kalaupapa, after the long, relentless emaciation of illness upon the rotten and feeble body that God provided, with great effort by the doctor's skill to find respite. However, the skilled learning of this world turned to ignorance due to he who created the heavens and the earth.

Mr. Kōʻieamo was born in Kealakomo, Puna, Hawaiʻi, in the month of March, AD 1823, to Nahakuelu (male) and Kaulapaʻa (female), and he was educated in the days of his youth at the district schools of Puna. He was a native of the forest bower fragrant with pandanus [Paia ala i ka Hala: a poetic name for Puna], from Māwae to Okiokiaho, and also a native resident of the famous Rain of Mokaulele [a reference to the Ua Kanilehua rain of Hilo].

He married his wife, Mrs. Kaunuahana Keaka, and she is living to this day, in poor health. She was blinded, and they did not produce children from their loins.

Mr. Kōʻieamo was a member of the combined congregations of Kalapana and ʻOpihikao. On Sept. 9, 1891, he was brought here to Molokaʻi due to being afflicted with the horrible disease of leprosy, and departed from the beloved heroine, his wife.

He arrived here on Molokaʻi on Oct. 27, 1891, and he was chosen as an elder for the congregation of Kalaupapa in the month of Feb. 1892. He held that position until he was removed due to the recent bias [hoopaewaewa nihoniho] imposed on the congregation of Kalaupapa by Rev. M. C. Kealoha.

He was a steadfast man in all Christian works, pleasant and modest, and knew everything. All of these things remain as a monument that the multitudes will not forget.

At 4:00 p.m. on the day he died, a prayer service was held over his body in the church of Kanaana Hou by Rev. M. C. Kealoha. After the prayers were finished, his earthly body was carried to Kanuola Cemetery in **Papaloa** [Ilina o Kanuola ma Papaloa] with a funeral held by the band [Puali Puhiohe] of this patient settlement [Kahua Maʻi], under the direction of C. N. Kealakai, the professor of all of Molokaʻi.

Thusly did Mr. Kōʻieamo pass gently on the path of no return [ala hoi ole mai], and the words of the Holy Scriptures were fulfilled:

"From dust comes man, and so shall he return to dust." And so it is for all who are deprived of seeing again the beloved features of everyone of this quite toilsome world. However, we must all go near to him, the wretched people, and he will ease us.

To you, Mr. Editor, goes the great affection of the writer, and also to the deft-handed boys of the lightning press of the *Kuokoa* goes my great grief.

—J. A. Kamanu. Kalaupapa, OCT. 30, 1895.

Ke Aloha Aina. 5 FEBRUARY 1898. P. 6.

Make Hikiwawe. Sudden Death.

Rev. S. K. Kamakahiki died here in the leprosy settlement [kahua ma'i lepera], on the night of the 25th, 9:00 p.m., Tuesday. He disappeared at 4:00 p.m. on Wednesday in the cemetery of the Society of the Knights of the Red Cape [Naita o ka aahu ula: Knights of Columbus] in **Papaloa**. His final funeral procession was accompanied by Rev. D. Ka'ai, the band of Kalaupapa led by Prof. C. N. Kealakai, the members of Society of Knights pulling the hearse led by the vice president S. K. Kainuwai, the family, the members of the Society of Knights, the Youth Organization of Kalaupapa led by Wm. Notley, the president, and members. The Angel Society under J. H. Imihia refused [to join the procession] for this reason: [they participate] only when they are hired.

The flagpoles of the organizations here gave their salutes by lowering the flags to half-staff [ma ka hoohapa ia ana o na hae], and the colors were various, red, white, and the Hawaiian flag. They showed his status. He had a distinguished status, and so it was with the heavens, they overflowed with tears that caused a drizzling rain, and a rainbow was arching, and the wind was twisting. All that was missing was thunder.

Thus, he left us, his companions in service, and his soul passed on, alone, to the other side of the black river of death [muliwai eleele o ka make], the single path of all things on this earth. Simply tragic.

—John Like

» [The official regalia dress for members of the Knights of Columbus included a red cape. In the next to the last paragraph, the writer identities three hō'ailona, signs from nature, that occurred during the funeral service: rain (ua), a rainbow (ānuenue), and wind (makani). He notes that only thunder (hekili) was missing. The appearance of hō'ailona during a funeral service was believed to come from a greater power in recognition of the deceased.]

Ke Aloha Aina. 25 JUNE 1898. P. 8.

Ua Hala I Ke Ala Hoi Ole Mai. Passed on the Path of No Return.

Mr. Editor. Greetings to you:

Please insert [this] into some available section of our mouthpiece, and it shall carry the news to the islands [Paeaina] all around Hawai'i.

At 5:00 a.m. last Monday, the quiet hands of death carried John T. Unea Jr. to the other side, leaving his family welling up with tears of love. Alas. How pitiful.

He was born on March 21, 1877, from the loins of Mrs. Kaenaku and Mr. John T. Unea Sr., in Lāwa'i, Kōloa, Kaua'i. When he was three, he left his land of birth and went to Hilo.

There he was educated until he was fifteen, when he contracted the family-separating disease [ma'i hookaawale ohana: leprosy]. On June 25, 1893, he was taken with his father to the land of agony [aina o ka ehaeha], and in this land he lived in hardship and the agonies of this life.

He was known to strive in Christian works, and he had many friends in all of his good works. On June 13, 1898, he departed from this life. There were twenty-one years, two months and twenty-two days of his breathing air until his burden was released.

At 4:00 p.m. in the afternoon he was borne to the Protestant church here in Kalaupapa. After his earthly body was blessed, he was taken all the way to the graveyard in **Papaloa** [pa ilina ma Papaloa]. His hearse was pulled by his organization, the "Knights of the Red Cape [Naita o ka aahu ula: Knights of Columbus] of Kalaupapa," accompanied by his father, his older male cousin and his friends, and also accompanied by the Angel Society [Ahahui Anela].

Thus, we, his friends, join with his family in remembering him.

We are with humility, J. M. K., H. K. P. Kalaupapa, Moloka'i, JUNE 15, 1898.

» [The official regalia dress for members of the Knights of Columbus included a red cape.]

Ka Nupepa Kuokoa. 28 MARCH 1902. P. 4.
Moe Ke Kini O Lalo Ua Ahiahi. The Multitudes Below Rest, Evening Has Come.
Mr. Editor. Greetings to you:

At 2:00 p.m. on Saturday, Mar. 15, 1902, Mr. Pilipo Miguell left this life in Pūahi, Kalaupapa.

In the late afternoon of the following Sabbath his body received a funeral. His final journey was accompanied by his friends and the loved ones of this land. He was laid to rest in the sand dunes of **Papaloa** [puuone o Papaloa]. "The bones of the traveler are left in Kaea" [Waiho iho la i Kaea na iwi o kamahele: said of one who dies away from his homeland]. Thusly shall I say: The multitudes below rest, evening has come.

M. Pilipo Miguell was the mistreated prisoner [paahao] from the days when the government harvested sea cucumbers [luu loli], who waited to be tried within the hardship and agonies of his life for the majority of his time within the prison. He was returned with his feeble body to his home due to the request by the Society of the Knights of the Red Cape [Ahahui o na Naita o ka Aahu Ula: Knights of Columbus] here in Kalaupapa that he be released under their care and their personal expenditures. That was the society he was a member of. In his home he passed the final hours of his life from Wednesday evening until 2:00 p.m. on Saturday the 15th, and then his burdens were eased. The messenger of death carried him off and prevented his trial by the high priests [kahuna nui], because the government of Rome had the authority.

He was from Anahola, Kaua'i. He has living relatives: a father whose name was passed down to him, and several older brothers, younger brothers, and sisters.

My pen tip concludes with affectionate greetings to the fans of the *Kuokoa* and the boys of the printing press.

—Mea Kākau [Writer: a pseudonym]. Kalaupapa, Moloka'i, T. H. [Territory of Hawai'i] MAR. 19, 1902.

» [The official regalia dress for members of the Knights of Columbus included a red cape.]

Ka Nupepa Kuokoa. 17 APRIL 1908. P. 4.
Mrs. Julia Lawelawe Ua Hala! Ua Nalo Ma Ke Ala Polikapu A Kane. Mrs. Julia Lawelawe Has Passed! [She] Has Vanished on the Path to the Sacred Heart of Kāne.
Mr. Editor of the *Kuokoa:* Affectionate greetings between us:

Please be patient with my small bundle placed above and allow me some small, available space in your columns, and you will carry it out like lightning all across the islands of beloved Hawai'i [Paeaina o Hawaii aloha], to be seen by the many relatives of the deceased who reside from the rising sun at Kumukahi to the setting of the sun at Lehua [mai i ka La hiki mai ma Kumukahi a i ka welona a ka la i ka Lehua].

On the night of March 29, 1908, after two o'clock, Mrs. Julia Lawelawe departed from this life, and quietly passed on the path to the invisible beyond of Kāne and Kanaloa [ala polikua a Kane me Kanaloa]. Thus was it written in the Bible, "You are dust, and you will return to dust, and the spirit returns to the one who gave it. Praised be the name of Jehovah in the highest heavens. Peace on earth, love for man."

Mrs. Julia Lawelawe was born in Hilo, Hawai'i, from the loins of Mrs. Kahau and Mr. Lawelawe. She was educated at the girls school in Kohala, Hawai'i. From there she moved to Wiluku [Wailuku], Maui, and there she lived with the family of her father for a long time.

She married a husband, Mr. Haole, and then that marriage was simply ended. She returned to Kohala, Hawai'i, and lived there for many long years until she was seized for having a suspicious illness. From there she was taken to the leprosy settlement on Moloka'i, the place called "the grave where one is buried alive forever" [Kahua ma'i lepera ma Molokai, kahi hoi i kapaia ka lua kupapau kanu ola no ka wa mau loa].

She spent over three years enduring this land of agony [aina o ka ehaeha], until she passed on the path of all things. She had not lived here in the patient settlement for long when she took me as her husband, and we spent over two years together. Our marriage was pleasant for us, modest and lacking disagreement, up until she left me to bear the agonies and sorrow of this dispirited world in solitude. The wasting of disease upon her body began in the month of June, 1907, and went until the month of March, 1908. It was about nine months that the illness besieged her until she passed. The problems with her feet began to grow and increase until she could not walk. Dr. Goodhue tried amputating [oki] them. This action brought relief, but the rot began to appear on her whole body. There were many attempts made to recover her health, but there was no period of relief until she passed on the path of no return [ala hoi ole mai]. Her age was between thirty and forty years.

She was a skilled and tidy mother in keeping a home, prosperous in living; her nature was enriching, kind, and hospitable to her friends. Thus, on March 30 her earthly body was borne to her burial home in the Catholic graveyard in **Papaloa** [ilina Kakolika ma Papaloa]. Thus, with grief I issue this small remembrance for my dear, beloved, unforgettable lei, my beloved companion in the small rain of Kalaupapa [ua liilii o Kalaupapa], beloved is that place where we were together, but his will be done until the heavens fall.

I am the husband lacking the wife.

Yours truly, S. K. Ho'opi'i. Kalaupapa, APRIL 3, 1908.

Pauahi Home. See Bihopa [Bishop] Home.

Pikoone. Black sand beach at the foot of the pali trail. This beach has been known by many names, including Awahua Beach, Pūahi Beach, and during the twentieth century as Black Sands Beach in English, but Pikoone is the name used most often in the Hawaiian-language newspapers. The story, or moʻolelo, behind the name is in the July 30, 1887, article that follows.

Ka Nupepa Kuokoa. 8 SEPTEMBER 1877. P. 1.
He Makua I Aloha Nuiia. A Parent Greatly Loved.

> How I love Lenalena, the waters enjoyed by visitors
> How I love Puʻuhahi in the sands of **Pikoone**
> How I love the ʻōhiʻa trees of Kiʻokiʻo and ʻŌhiʻa.

» [This excerpt is from the kanikau section. The kanikau was written for a woman named Kaumiokalani, who was born on Molokaʻi and lived in Kalaupapa before it became a leprosy settlement. The writer mentions several places in Kalaupapa, including one o Pikoone, or the "sands of Pikoone."]

Ka Lahui Hawaii. 11 OCTOBER 1877. P. 1.
Na Kaikuono. The Bays.

The bays of Waiākea, Kawaihae, and Kaʻawaloa are on Hawaiʻi [island]. The bays of Kahului, Maʻalaea are of Maui. The bays of Waikolu and **Pikoone** are of Molokaʻi. The bays of Maunalua, Puʻuloa, Māeaea, Kahana, and between Kualoa and Mōkapu are of Oʻahu. Hanalei and Nāwiliwili are of Kauaʻi. These are areas where the ocean enters into the land, and this is called a bay. To be continued.

Ka Nupepa Kuokoa. 30 JULY 1887. P. 4.
He Moolelo No Lonoikamakahiki Ka Pua Alii Kiekie Na Kalani. Ke Alii Nui o Hawaii. A Story about Lonoikamakahiki, the High-Ranking Royal Descendant of Kalani, the Paramount Chief of Hawaiʻi.

They voyaged and landed at the place called **Pikoone**. That is where they went ashore. As for the nature of this name **"Pikoone,"** that is where the umbilical cords [piko] of newborn children are left.

Ka Nupepa Kuokoa. 23 SEPTEMBER 1921. P. 3.
Hoomaha I Ka Ikiiki Wela O Ke Kaona. Taking a Break From the Stifling Heat of the City.

Everyone passed along the sides of the path, until reaching the home of the local. A few days were spent resting before the dear friend made stirrings to travel. That is my usual thing, importuning to see in person.

The woman urged, "If it is you and me, let us see Kalaupapa, the land that is beloved."

> Kalaupapa is beautiful,
> On the bow of the ship,
> Made majestic by what is above,
> The Koʻolau cliffs.

We got in the car, and the machine did the work. The length of the road was sixteen miles to Kaunakakai, and from there to the cliffs of Kalaupapa was who knows how many miles. The dear friend said the names of these places until reaching Kamalō. From that place on, the road was in the kiawe trees until reaching Kawela. Below Kawela are the homestead lands that are desired. To Kaunakakai, you go up to the hot plain of Kalaʻe and enter the comfort of Kaulu-wai. From there you go to the top of the lookout [kilohana] of Kalaupapa to Kukuiohāpuʻu, where the cliff trail [alanui pali] lays winding down to **Pikoone**.

We stopped and looked at the town of Kalaupapa, spread out, and the home of leprosy, which has caused the Hawaiian people to grieve, from the beginning of this law, and perhaps to this day, when I write this.

Here are several lines of song composed about this disease. You will be the one to see the hidden meaning [kaona] and the answer of the dream [puana a ka moe: the result].

> What will be done to Hawaiʻi,
> By this disease of leprosy,
> Scorned disease, scorned of the multitudes,
> Of the red-skinned, of the white-skinned,
> Associates act strangely,
> The relationship is not the same as before,
> Wild when they see,
> Moving to be somewhere else,
> The hands point,
> And "That one has leprosy [maʻi Pake],"
> I bow my head and run,
> Shame enters the heart,
> The doctors of the government hear,
> The police soldiers are sent,
> Grabbed like a chicken,
> Led down the road like cattle,
> Standing before the Board of Health,
> Board of no health for this disease,
> The doctors simply look down,
> Peering here and there,
> The hand points to Diamond Head [Leahi],
> "You will go to Kalawao,"
> The government soldiers seize,
> Carry you down to the pier,
> All of the prisoners are tossed,
> Into the fiery pit of leprosy [luahi a ka maʻi lepera].

Now, my eyes see the place called the "grave where the Hawaiian people are buried alive [luakupapau kanu ola o ka lahui Hawaii]," but in the journey as a visitor desiring to see, and seeing in person, I am not wrong in saying, Kalaupapa is beautiful, on the bow of the ship [nani o Kalaupapa, i ka ihu o ka moku]; made majestic by what is above [hanohano i ka luna], the Koʻolau cliffs [na pali Koolau].

Ka Nupepa Kuokoa. 22 JUNE 1922. P. 7.
Ka Halawai Ana, A Ike Aku A Ike Mai Me Kuu Mea Aloha. Meeting, and Seeing, and Being Seen With My Dear Beloved. (Written by A. G. Kannegiesser)

The fisher folk [kanaka lawaiʻa] of Kalaupapa met with some terrible luck [pakalaki loa]. The big-eyed scad fish [akule] that were caught by them during the net fishing on Monday were left in the net that night in the ocean with the idea by someone to get it [in the morning] and bring it on shore, but, while they were pulling the fish ashore, the nets ripped and the fish were all returned to the depths, to their place.

» [At certain times of the year, large schools of akule come into the nearshore waters of Kalaupapa off **Pikoone**. Fishermen using canoes or skiffs would surround a school with a long net, then pull the net onshore. In this brief article, the net ripped, perhaps on submerged rocks, and the fish escaped.]

Polapola. Place, Kalawao. Named for Borabora [Polapola in Hawaiian] in the Society Islands. The September 8, 1877, article that follows explains the origin of this name on the peninsula.

Ka Nupepa Kuokoa. 8 SEPTEMBER 1877. P. 1.
He Makua I Aloha Nuiia. A Parent Greatly Loved.

It pleased the heavens to take our mother who was greatly loved in the early morning of the 13th of July 1877 here in Waihoʻolana in Mānoa. We miss her dearly, and so we warded off the final enemy of the world with strong medicine [lapaau kupaoa], but such was not the plan of the creator.

Kaumiokalani was born at the time of the first great plague [Okuu mua] in Kapuna in Kalamaʻula, Kona, Molokaʻi. Her father was Malamakūhiʻona, a man of ʻEwa, and her mother was Nāwai of Maui and Molokaʻi, where her family hails from. She was a descendant of Haʻehaʻeahuakākaʻalaneo, and a descendant of Borabora on the other side. It is after her Borabora ancestor that the name of the place in Kalawao is called "Borabora," which is its name until this very day, and so she is a daughter of royal lineage of all these places. Kalamaʻula is where they lived mostly until she got married to the descendant of ʻEwanuiʻalaakona, Malamakūhiʻona, and they had a child named Kupihea Kaumiokalani.

However, in her childhood days, she was taught the duties of women, and when she blossomed, she married H. Hukilani. They lived together well. They had two children during the time of Liholiho Kamehameha II. At that time she was taught literacy, and since she did so well, she was made a schoolteacher. At the time of Kamehameha III is when the last of her children was born. She had seven children in Kalamaʻula, and she went to live in Koʻolau in Kalaupapa. She had seven more children there, and so she had fourteen children altogether. Ten of these were boys and four were girls. The strength of her health was rather amazing, and the world would be so beautiful if all women were like that. Of greatest importance to this woman was that her children be knowledgeable, so she sent some of her children to the college [Kulanui] at Lāhainaluna.

In 1860, her husband left her to live as a single mother with children. In that year she left Molokaʻi and came back to the sands of Kākuhihewa [one o Kakuhihewa: Oʻahu]. She lived for a little while in the city and then returned to "The beauty of Mānoa" [Ka ui o Manoa], where she lived for many years.

Polapola

79

She passed some of the time in Lāhaina and in Hawai'i [island] with the royal, 'Akahi. Here in Mānoa is where she last lived until her body recovered. In her eightieth year of life on this earth, she left us to live parentless.

She was a woman who was taught the songs and chants of the royals of the old days and she had memorized the days, years, and months according to the Western system and the Hawaiian system. She was a calendar for those who inquired of her. She did not forget those things. For these reasons she invoked tears to fall on our cheeks, and because of our great love for her, we composed a lament [kanikau] for her.

» [This excerpt is from the kanikau section. The place name "Borabora" is spelled in the translation as it is spelled in the original Hawaiian text.]

Ka Makaainana. 9 DECEMBER 1895. P. 5.
Haki ke Ku'e o Mokolii. The Piston of the *Mokolii* Broke.

On Wednesday evening, the 4th, the *Mokolii* arrived at Waikolu, Moloka'i, to unload the live cattle for the patients. After the cattle were unloaded, it left that harbor for Kalaupapa. As the ship passed outside of **Polapola**, the rod that was keeping an intense rhythm broke, and then the ship stayed still without moving forward. At that time the sails were hoisted and they sailed with difficulty, arriving at Kalaupapa at 8:30 that night. Thursday morning, the food of the patients and some other cargo were unloaded, though some was left due to the extremely rough nature [ano okaikai loa] of the harbor. Because of the damage to the piston of the ship, the *Mokolii* left Kalaupapa at 3:15 p.m. that day and returned here to Honolulu. As it passed off of Diamond Head [Laeahi], it gave a distress signal to the land on Saturday, and the *Hawaii* was quickly sent to give aid. It towed [the *Mokolii*] until reaching the wharf at 10:50. About fifty-five hours were spent going in circles in the ocean.

Pūahi. See Pu'uhahi.

Pua'ō. Surf spot, 'Īliopi'i. In the January 26, 1871, edition of the Hawaiian-language newspaper *Ke Au Okoa,* historian Samuel Kamakau wrote in his column *Ka Moolelo Hawaii* that the chiefs of Moloka'i considered the surf spot at Kalaupapa to be one of the best places to surf on the island. Pua'ō at 'Īliopi'i, the spot he was referring to, is also mentioned in other newspaper articles about Kalaupapa.

Ka Nupepa Kuokoa. 2 APRIL 1864. P. 3.

Therefore, dear editor of the *Nupepa Kuokoa,* may your kind and patient heart be displayed before the public so that parents with children may see and not presume that you are small and hardhearted. This is not the case. You carry on casually holding a cup of cold water, smooth to the throat as water carried by the Nāulu rain, and if this is the case, this child of Kalaupapa can return home to catch the curling waves [nalu hai-muku] of **Pua'ō**, since the trade wind [makani kaomi] is ideal as it battles upon the swelling waves [nalu opuu]. They hurry to bathe in the fresh water mixing with the sea [wai awilipu me ke kai] of Pau'aka.

With great affection to all surfing friends [hoa heenalu] who understand.
D. W. P. Kahananui.

Ka Au Okoa. 17 OCTOBER 1867. P. 4.

The waves are fearful [weliweli], but fun [lealea] for the children of Kalaupapa who know how to surf these waves that are well-known around the world.
—J. H. Kānepuʻu. Pālolo [Oahu]. OCTOBER 8, 1867.

» [This excerpt is from an article in chapter II.]

Ka Nupepa Kuokoa. 8 SEPTEMBER 1877. P. 1.
He Makua I Aloha Nuiia. A Parent Greatly Loved.

Love is a continuous chief [alii] of mine
How I love the waves of Kaiʻa and Kanaloa
Pūōhāhā and **Puaʻō** are joined together.

» [This excerpt is from the kanikau section. In addition to Puaʻō the writer names three other surf spots at Kalaupapa.]

Puʻuhahi. Land division [apana], plain [kula loa], Kalaupapa. The place name Puʻuhahi, sometimes spelled Pūhahi, appears in Hawaiian-language newspaper articles from 1862 to 1897. In the 1890s, however, writers began to spell it Pūahi. This variant spelling probably reflected its abbreviated pronounciation in everyday conversation, which also occurred in other Kalaupapa place names, such as Māulili for Māhulili and Wailēʻia for Waiʻaleʻia.

Beginning in the 1900s only Pūahi, sometimes spelled Pūwahi, appears in the newspaper articles. About the same time residents also started using Pūahi as the name of the black sand beach at the foot of the pali trail instead of Pikoone, its former name.

Ka Nupepa Kuokoa. 23 AUGUST 1862. P. 3.
Aug. 13, in **Puʻuhahi**, Kalaupapa, Molokaʻi, R. Kaikū was born to Kanakaʻole and Kainaina.

Ka Nupepa Kuokoa. 8 SEPTEMBER 1877. P. 1.
He Makua I Aloha Nuiia. A Parent Greatly Loved.

How I love Lenalena, the waters enjoyed by visitors
How I love **Puʻuhahi** in the sands of Pikoone
How I love the ʻōhiʻa trees of Kiʻokiʻo and ʻŌhiʻa.

» [This excerpt is from the kanikau section. The kanikau was written for a woman named Kaumiokalani, who was born on Molokaʻi and lived in Kalaupapa before the first patients arrived.]

Ka Nupepa Kuokoa. 9 DECEMBER 1882. P. 3.
Na Mea Hou O Molokai. News from Molokaʻi.
The greatest prize of the Hawaiian nation, the lightning that flashes over the cliff tops of the islands: greetings between us:

In the district of **Puʻuhahi**, Kalaupapa, Molokaʻi, there were some deplorable incidences, and one was this: There was sweet potato being fermented in bowls, and the dormitory was turned into a place of fighting due to drunkenness, along with the speaking of these words:

"Goddamn you bloody Hawaiian! You wanna fight? I am strong, me give you good blow, me Englishman" [Kokami iu palali kanaka! Iu anu faita, ai am solon, mi kivi iu kut polo, mi inilis man], while he punched the wall of the building.

These are people who were appointed with positions from the Board of Health with the belief that it was the correct action to take. Then this reprehensible activity erupted between the locals [kamaaina] and the leprosy patients [mai lepera].

The white-haired old men of Kalaupapa are surfing these days [Ke hee nalu nei na elemakule poohina o Kalaupapa nei i keia mau la], resembling white-feathered chickens in the sun [ke hele la a mauakea i ka la].

To the typesetting boys my affectionate greeting.

—W. S. Kekuni. **Pūhahi**, Moloka'i, NOV. 18, 1882.

» [The challenge to fight in the third paragraph is an example of pidgin English that was in use at the time.]

Ka Nupepa Kuokoa. 10 SEPTEMBER 1892. P. 2.
Malihini Kipa. Unusual Visitors.

It is this: on August 30th, Tuesday, the anchovies [nehu] were seen. On the 31st they were caught, and when they were caught, a great number of anchovies were obtained. These anchovies are being caught with mosquito nets and small bag nets. The anchovies that are swimming in pools and cracks in the rocks are being caught in small bag nets. These anchovies appear from **Pūahi** to the harbor at Kalaupapa. Anchovies are not the only fish, but in fact mackerel scad [opelu] and skipjack tuna [aku] are other fish being seen. We might eat skipjack tuna or we might not. There is eating, feasting, selling, and the desire is completely fulfilled. On this 31st day of August, the anchovies were seen, and the little tunny [kawakawa], skipjack tuna, and mackerel scad. In Waikolu, little tunny have been caught by polefishing from the shore at the headlands and the edge of the cliffs. They are being sold, three little tunny for one dollar. This is a rather significant new thing seen in this colony [panalaau]. Praise be to the generosity of the one who made all things.

—S. Hāla'i. Kawaluna, Kalawao, Moloka'i.

Ka Leo O Ka Lahui. 15 AUGUST 1894. P. 2.
Ua Hala O Mrs. Akiu Kealakai. Mrs. Akiu Kealakai Has Passed.

Mr. Editor. Greetings to you:

Mrs. Akiu Kealakai was born in Hilo Hanakahi from the loins of Mr. Palapala Hā'upu and Mrs. Nāki'owai Palapala on October 17, AD 1871, and on November 14, AD 1885, she was married to Mr. Major Kealakai. And on Thursday, August 9, at 4:35 P.M., here in **Pu'uhahi**, Kalaupapa, she left this dispirited world and released her burden.

She left a husband and several brothers, as well as a family mourning and lamenting for her. Mrs. Akiu Mekia has given her final expression of love for all of you.

Good bye. [In English] C. N. Kealakai. Kalaupapa, AUG. 10, 1894.

Ka Nupepa Kuokoa. 15 OCTOBER 1897. P. 3.

Walohia Wale. Simply Tragic.

Mr. Editor, with thanks.

Please allow me some available place in your famous newspaper to insert those few words above, so that they may be seen by the multitudes and friends of my dear beloved lei.

On Monday, Sept. 13, 11:45 p.m., in **Puʻuhahi**, Kalaupapa, it pleased Almighty God to take the soul of my dear beloved, Mrs. Eliza Hakuaikawai Kahula Kalua.

It had been almost two years of tuberculosis [maʻi hokii] emaciating her. Many attempts at medical treatment had been made for her but had not succeeded, until she simply passed away to the eternal side of the world. Yes! Alas!!

She was born in Puakō, Waimea, S. Kohala, Hawaiʻi, to Mr. B. Kauwewahine and Mrs. Kahele Kauwewahine on April 8, AD 1864, and so the amount of her days on this earth was thirty-three years, five months, and five days, until her burden was released. "We have no city that will endure here, we seek what comes after." And also in that way: "You come from dust, and you shall return to dust." Alas! How sorrowful!

On April 8, AD 1884, we were married. We had six children, three living and three that died before her. Alas! How heartbreaking! The amount of days in which we together bore the agonies of this life was thirteen years, five months, and five days.

She was a humble, gentle, gracious and hospitable mother, and she had many friends.

She was educated in her land of birth, taught by her older brother, S. H. Mahuka, Esq., who is a judge. She spent time with the famous songwriting father of Hawaiʻi, the one known as, "The sound of the calls of the birds in the mountains of Kaʻala will not cease" [Aole e pau ke kani ana o ka leo oia manu ma na kuahiwi o Kaala], who is Rev. L. [Lorenzo] Lyons. He gave her the name that endures, Elizabeth.

She served as schoolteacher for Puakō, Waimea, for three years, she was a member of that congregation, and a president for the Youth Association and the Temperance League of that district.

And because I was afflicted with the disease that separates families [maʻi hookaawale ohana: leprosy], and was taken to this land, she was steadfast in requesting the kindness of the Board of Health in giving a permit to become a helper [kokua] for me. That desire of hers was fulfilled, for on January 12, AD 1895, she received her permission to become a helper for me. The amount of our days enduring the agonies of this land [ehaeha o keia aina] was two years, eight months, and one day, until her body rested in the soil of this unfamiliar land [aina malihini]. Simply tragic!

> O Haleola! The one carried in your arms has vanished, has passed along the path of no return! Simply sorrowful.
>
> O great breadfruit trees of Lālāmilo and Keakahiwa! Elizabeth Hakuaikawaiʻs strolling under your shade has ended.
>
> O short-breaking waves of Kapuaʻilima in the Kaihāwanawana! Your sea spray will not again pelt the skin of Hakuaikawai.

Puʻuhahi

O ʻŌlauniu wind! and the ʻEka wind that gently blows! The two of you will
   not see her again.

Ah! O Kīpuʻupuʻu Rain of Waimea and the Nāulu Rain that pours upon
   the pili grass of Paiʻea! You will not again dampen the beloved cheeks of
   Hakuaikawai. And for her I express affection with a pitiful call, for my
   dear unforgettable lei [kuu lei poina ole].

1. O Kīpuʻupuʻu Rain,
    With the Nāulu Rain in the forest,
    No more shall you pelt,
    The skin of Hakuaikawai.
    Cho. How sorrowful,
      My beloved adornment, my dear unforgettable lei;
      How sorrowful,
      My beloved adornment, my dear unforgettable lei.
2. O ʻŌlauniu wind,
    With the ʻEka wind that gently blows,
    Your soft voices are silent,
    And Hakuaikawai has passed.
3. O rustling sea of Kawaihae,
    Sea whispering softly in the calm,
    And here is your cherished one,
    And Hakuaikawai has passed.

I am with endless sorrow, Wm. Kalikokalani Kalua.

—Huʻilani Home, Kalaupapa, Molokaʻi, SEPT. 20, 1897.

Ka Nupepa Kuokoa. 17 JULY 1914. P. 5.
Ua Haalele Mai Ko Makou Mau Makua. Our Parents Have Departed.
Mr. Editor of the Excellence [nickname for *Ka Nupepa Kuokoa*]. Warmest
greetings between us: Please insert into some available space of the People's
Favorite my sorrowful thoughts for our beloved Mama, Mrs. Kahuilaokalani
S. W. Waiau, who left us, her children, grandchildren, and our greatly beloved
Papa, Sam W. Waiau.

    My beloved Mama, alas for my sorrow for you. I did not see you again, and
I never again heard your voice for over fifteen years, because of the disease that
separates families [maʻi hookaawale ohana: leprosy]. I did not witness your
final breath, alas for my grief for you, when you departed from us. Someone
else may soon be made into a mother, one who is not familiar with us.

    I suppose that you know my sad news, about Liwai Haʻalelea departing from
this earthly life, on June 29, 1914, in the hospital of **Pūahi** [haukapila o Puahi],
Kalaupapa, Molokaʻi. However, the two of you departed together from this
earthly life, in the same month with your younger brother, who emerged from
the same loins, Haʻalelea (male) and Haʻalou (female).

    My beloved Mama, we were an important thing to you, your children, and
our greatly beloved Papa, and we felt safe with you; but we will not mingle

together, we have been obstructed by the billowy cloud; we were separated, Mama, and I did not witness your final breath.

Therefore, I ask the powers of the Trinity [na mana Kahi Kolu] to receive the spirit of my beloved Mama, and my beloved Papa who also departed from this earthly life, in that glorious home over there, and for the numbing thoughts of my dear beloved Papa, and the family, to be eased.

Thusly we, her children, give many thanks to those who joined together in the hours of grief of our beloved Papa, who lost a Mama. And above all things is that of the highest God, easing the sorrowful thoughts of us all, through Jesus Christ, our Lord.

With you are our warmest greetings, Mr. Editor, and with the boys of the printing press as well.

We are with sorrow, Mrs. Emma Waiau Kalauao, Mr. William Kalauao. Kalawao, Moloka'i, JULY 8, 1914.

Ka Nupepa Kuokoa. 12 MAY 1916. P. 5.
Iliia o Mikahala I Ka Hapapa O Kalaupapa. The *Mikahala* Ran Aground in the Shallows of Kalaupapa.

Between 3:00 and 4:00 a.m. on April 26, 1916, the steamship [mokuahi] *Mikahala* ran aground offshore of **Pūahi**, right off of the point where locals jump into the water [kawa o na kamaaina]. It was seen from Kalaupapa, and here is a short story provided to the writer by the spy who sniffs out news [kiu hanu meahou]:

Between the aforementioned times, the rain and wind were pelting from the west, the land was darkened by rain, and the red light of the harbor [kukui ulaula o ke awa] was hazy, since the light was on the porch of the store of the Board of Health, and due to the force of the wind, the rain blew and misted the glass.

The navigation of the ship followed the light of the surgical hospital [kukui o ka haukapila oki], and the nursery [home bebe], standing in **Pūahi**. As for the night watchman on land, when he saw the ship sailing inwards, he ran down with his lantern swinging about, but the proper time had passed and the ship went onto the shallows and sand [hapapa me ke one]. It was the watch of the ship's mate, and that was when the captain was roused and the resting anchor [heleuma haka] was taken out. The flag showing they had run aground was raised, and the tugboat [moku kukui] was far out. Upon seeing the distress signal, since the sailors had climbed up the mast to swing the lantern, the tugboat sailed at full speed. The line was made fast to the distressed ship, while the tugboat was continually pulling until it came loose after four or five hours of being stuck.

If this grounding had occurred in the days of [high] tide, then it would probably have been completely stuck, lifted by a wave and placed all the way on shore, and then the bones would have been left in Kalaupapa.

Upon determining that there was no damage to the ship, the ship returned safely to the harbor and unloaded all of the cargo, and sailed again for its ports. Honolulu was told via telegraph that there was no damage to the ship. The ship's mate was someone new. The regular ship's mate had stayed, and if it had been him then they would not have run aground, since he is familiar with the lights of the land.

Yours truly, Nāhauowailēʻia. Kalawao, APRIL 29, 1916.

Ka Leo o Molokai. 22 DECEMBER 1950. P. 5. [Newsletter published in English.]
Phone Call from Kalaupapa.
Oio [bonefish] are running wild at **Puahi** black sand beach. Sheriff Malo caught six big ones in one hour.

Puʻupāneʻenʻe. Steep hill that is the site of the Kalaupapa cliff trail. The name of the trail is Kukuiohāpuʻu.

Ka Nupepa Kuokoa. 21 AUGUST 1875. P. 2.
We arrived at Moʻomomi at 12:30 and left there at that hour for **Puʻupāneʻenʻe**, overlooking the cliff of the land of my birth, reaching there at 3:00 p.m. From there we went to look at Kalaupapa, and then I paid my respects to Māmālua gazing at the homeland of the two of us, and my thoughts turned back to the one and I cried with love as if I was in Honolulu at that time. We left **Puʻupāneʻenʻe** at 3:30 p.m. for the home of R. W. Meyer, and arrived there at 4:00 p.m. There we rested, where a lunch was made ready, along with dinner. After our meal, we left that place for Kaunakakai at 6:00 p.m. and we arrived at Kaunakakai at 8:00 p.m. You can probably see that the people were not used to horseback riding. The two rode in carriages. They arrived at Kaunakakai and disembarked without injury except for the pains of the thighs of the horses on this journey.

» [This exerpt is from an article written by A. Kalauli that describes a sightseeing trip of Molokaʻi on horseback. Part of the trip included a stop at Puʻupāneʻenʻe to look down at the Kalaupapa peninsula.]

Ka Nupepa Kuokoa. 8 SEPTEMBER 1877. P. 1.
He Makua I Aloha Nuiia. A parent greatly loved.
(A true lament of Kaumiokalani)

> This is a lament for you, Kaumiokalani
> My dear mother from the land of your birth at Kalaupapa
> Where the waves are is where we would fish by net at ʻIliopiʻi
> From the long slopes of **Puʻupāneʻeneʻe**
> There is nowhere on that cliff that you and I did not travel
> We drank the water of Waiʻalalā
> The water that our ancestors drank
> The soul drank the water of Kāne
> In your lifetime you lived with the Powerful Father above
> With Jesus Christ the savior of all
> Our lives are from him along with our blessings
> The one who lengthens our lives
> Our loftiness and our eternal victory
> This is a memory of love for you.

—N. H. Poʻookalani

» [This excerpt is from the kanikau section. It was written for a woman named Kaumiokalani, who was born on Moloka'i and lived in Kalaupapa before the first patients arrived.]

Pu'u 'Ua'u. This prominent hill lies along the road between Kalawao and Kalaupapa where it has an elevation of 405 feet. Pu'u 'Ua'u, or "Petrel Hill," was named for Hawaiian petrels, ground-nesting sea birds that dig burrows on the windward sides of the main islands and offshore islets. In the May 16, 1863, article that follows, the writer, G. W. Kahiolo, gives a detailed description of the birds, their habits, and how they were caught by bird catchers.

When Hawaiians named the hill at Kalaupapa, Hawaiian petrels probably lived there, but as a prized food item, the colony would have fallen victim to predation by man and his domestic animals. In the December 7, 1896, article that follows, the writer lists burrow-dwelling petrel birds [uwa'u noho-lua] as a menu item that was served for lunch in Kalaupapa, but does not say if the birds came from Kalaupapa or elsewhere on the Ko'olau coast.

While 'ua'u is the preferred spelling for Hawaiian petrels today, 'uwa'u with a "w-glide" is the common variant spelling for them in the Hawaiian-language newspapers. In the September 8, 1877, article that follows, the writer calls the hill Puuwau, which in today's ornithography would be Pū'uwa'u, or Petrel Hill.

In addition to being a hill, Pu'u 'Ua'u is also a volcanic crater, and the crater has its own name, Kauhakō. In the Hawaiian-language newspapers Kauhakō is almost always used for both the hill and the crater.

Ka Nupepa Kuokoa. 16 MAY 1863. P. 1.
Ka Moolelo o Na Manu o Hawaii nei. Helu 3. The Story of the Birds of Hawai'i. Number 3. The 'Uwa'u Bird.

The 'uwa'u is the tastiest of all birds. There are two qualities in eating it: its taste is like a piece of fish and like a bird. The tastiness and sweetness of the 'uwa'u cannot be debated. The tastiness of other birds and the tastiness of the fish of the sea are nothing. Due to its great sweetness, it has been named "the best of the tasty birds" [ka oi o na manu ono].

The 'uwa'u is the same size as the chicken. Its head is small like that of the pigeon, and such is the case for its feathers, and all of its qualities. However, its feet are yellow, and its feet are wide. Its footprints are wide like that of the duck, and its talons are not long. Its eyes are reddish purple like those of the pigeon.

During the day the 'uwa'u searches for its food, which is the fish of the ocean, the aku [skipjack tuna], the mālolo [flying fish], the iheihe [halfbeak], and the such-and-such fish and so on, that it finds in the ocean. It will not eat the things on land.

The 'uwa'u is a flocking bird, staying with his female 'uwa'u companion. The two of them fly together to search for fish in the sea, and they return together in the evening. The male 'uwa'u bird does not abandon the female 'uwa'u bird, and it is the same for the female 'uwa'u with the male 'uwa'u. They are equal in work and labor.

The 'uwa'u is a bird that works, and stays a little vigilant when it sleeps. It spends a lot of time working, and the 'uwa'u has been praised, like so: "The bird of the day gathers [Ohi ka manu o ke ao]." Here is its nature: 1. The birds have already crouched, due to knowing that it is almost time to work; 2. The fish [Milky Way] has turned [midnight has passed]; 3. The predawn darkness has almost broken; 4. The birds have already stirred; 5. The birds have perched aloft; 6. The bird has almost seen the deep ocean.

The mountains are the place they really like. That is where they live, in burrows [ana], that is their house. The hollow crevices in the burrows are their rooms, and that is where they lay their eggs.

If the female 'uwa'u lays eggs, then she stops flying with the male 'uwa'u. He is the one that flies to fish in the ocean and returns with the fish in his mouth. He returns and spits the chewed fish into the mouth of his female, like how a bird feeds its children.

When they sit on their eggs, they divide the time of sitting as follows: If sitting on the eggs is the job of the female bird, then the male bird flies out to fish for sustenance for his female, and such is what the female bird does, if sitting is the job of the male bird. So they do it equally until the time when the eggs hatch.

When the eggs hatch, then the two of them go fishing together, and return with fish in their beaks, and feed their children by spitting chewed food. That is what they do until the children are feathered out.

When their children are feathered out, then they bring back whole fish and place them before the children. The two of them peck, and the children see and act like the parents are acting, as if they are learning to act that way. Due to these qualities of the 'uwa'u, living and working equally, striving equally in labor, and properly caring for children, "The people of Hawai'i are blessed if the working and living together is in that manner, as well as the proper care of children."

And here are the words in the Bible of God: "In this thing man leaves his father, and his mother, and he joins with his wife, and the two of them become one, until dying, and then are separated."

The name " 'uwa'u" is taken from within its call, and its call is "tegue," and "tegue, gue gue gue."

In order for the 'uwa'u to be caught by bird catchers [poe kono manu], they make the snare [kono], which is an 'ie'ie vine that has been extended to be long, the length being five or six fathoms, or more, joined with a completely straight wooden rod. The reason that the 'ie'ie is used before the rod is that the 'ie'ie can move in a crooked kind of burrow, twisting here and there, along with the crooked path of the burrow of the 'uwa'u.

The bird catcher utilizes gum to smear on the top of the rod. The bird catcher goes with these things to the 'uwa'u burrow [lua Uwau], and then goes down flat and lies at the entrance of the burrow. Then the bird catcher calls, his call the same as a call of the 'uwa'u, in order to be clear to the bird in the burrow that the bird catcher is calling "tetegue" too. It is not good to go all the way down and touch the edge of the burrow, lest the eyes get powder in them, making one blind.

When the 'uwa'u hear the "tetegue" call of the bird catcher, the 'uwa'u fledglings wrongly assume that this is their parents calling "gue" outside, and then they "gue" with misplaced joy, making a great stir, and disperse the powder from their feathers, something rather like ash.

At that time, the bird catcher inserts his rod with gum smeared on the top of the 'ie'ie, crouching in silence until the bird touches. When the bird catcher twirls the rod to stick to the feathers of the bird, he then carefully pulls it out with that one simply following.

The bird catcher does not take all of the birds from the burrows, only one to three, not more than these numbers, so that the birds continue to live in that burrow. He does not take all of the parents, lest that burrow become uninhabited.

The 'uwa'u who have produced young are called "kaini." The tasty birds are the larger birds. If the kaini laid eggs, there are two or three eggs, but if the young birds [Ouo] laid, there is only one egg, and thus that saying, an "egg of the 'uwa'u, a single egg [hua na ka Uwau, he hua kahi]."

» [This article is the third in a series of six articles on birds by G. W. Kahiolo.]

Ka Nupepa Kuokoa. 8 SEPTEMBER 1877. P. 1.
He Makua I Aloha Nuiia. A Parent Greatly Loved.

> My dear mother in the waters of Waikolu
> From the high cliffs of Keanakua
> From the rain that creeps over the cliff at Kalawao
> From the steep face of Polapola [Borabora]
> The land where our ancestors lived
> Where we loved the inland of Māulili [Māhulili]
> I ache in my heart, and I am filled with your love
> How I love Kōloa in the face that turns at Waihānau
> You were born in the month of Ka'elo
> The parent passes by and is atop **Pū'uwa'u**
> Watching the mirage of the land
> You saw the amazing waters of Kauhakō
> I am dragged, being tugged by love
> How I love Kanomanō in the pathway on the plains
> Those plains where we lived
> Where we relaxed in the comfort of the bowl,

» [In this excerpt from the kanikau section, the writer mentions several places in Kalaupapa, including Pū'uwa'u.]

Ka Makaainana. 7 DECEMBER 1896. P. 7.
Huakai No Molokai. Ka Ike Ana i na Maka o Kuu Aloha. Journey to Moloka'i. Seeing the Eyes of My Beloved.
To the Editor.

Due to the kindness of the president of the Board of Health, William O. Smith [Wiliama O. Kamika], I received permission to travel to Kalaupapa, Moloka'i, on Saturday, November 21. Upon arriving at nine o'clock or so, the lines of the *Iwalani* were undone from the wharf.

When we were outside the [harbor] entrance [nuku], I counted the number of people going on this sea voyage to Moloka'i. The number was forty, counting the men and women and the Caucasians [haole]. The sea had a fine calm on this ocean journey, and the queen of the night shone finely upon the surface of the ocean. The gust of the travel of the *Iwalani* provided a gentle breeze up to the people on the deck of the ship.

Two o'clock or so, we passed by 'Īlio Point [Lae-o-ka-Ilio: west end of Moloka'i], and those on the ship simply gazed at the place where the clipper *Wilikoki* [Wilcox] was lying at ease in the depths right below the tall cliff.

Four o'clock in the early morning, we passed outside of the bay of Mo'omomi, and only the dark lava rock was seen, along with the foam bleaching the headland rocks.

Five o'clock, the chain was clanking with the anchor of the *Iwalani* in the harbor of Kalaupapa [awa o Kalaupapa]. We gazed upon the shore, [where] the limitless number of lights were sparkling in the harbor with the sweet murmuring sound of the brass horns of the boys of that place who practiced in that activity. It seemed as if, in my understanding, they probably had not slept at all during that joyful night of theirs, until they found us, wide awake. They were probably filled with gaiety from seeing visitors. Yes, truly so.

Seven o'clock, we disembarked to the wharf, and mingled with the friends in agony at that time; and it was a time of tears and pitiful voices echoing to the heavens.

Alas! A person filled with hardness who was standing at that place could not keep his heart hard like a stone. His heart would immediately be induced to feel agonizing anguish and to pour forth from his eyes tears of pity.

Eight o'clock, everyone just moved from the wharf to the site of the hospitals of Kalaupapa, the homes and all the small communities [kauhale]. There were many people with good health as well as many with greater agony.

Ten o'clock, we traveled to Kalawao, and we quickly visited those places, the small communities, the home of that place [Baldwin Home], and the other places. Some people of that place were in fine health, but the majority are ones who bring pain to the heart due to pity. Give compassion to the people there.

Twelve o'clock or so, we arrived back in Kalaupapa, and a meal had been laid out by the patients. Some people began to eat heartily of the baked pig, baked beef, steamed chicken, fish cooked in ti leaves, burrow-dwelling **'uwa'u** birds [uwa'u noho-lua], watermelons, sugar cane sections, overripe banana, and a great amount of food that was supplied, accompanied by the "waters of Makapala."

Mr. Editor, I am greatly indebted to your generosity due to this report by me to your readers. On this journey I also met with my wife in that settlement of agony [kahua o ka ehaeha]. She had been separated from me for almost one year, due to the suspicion that she was afflicted with the "separating disease" [ma'i hookaawale: leprosy], but when I met with her, she was the same as from the time I left her until I met with her again on this journey. Her state of health had changed from infirmity to a plump, affable health, and the old sign that had caused her to be taken has changed into lasting health.

She wailed a list of her friends of the Kūkalahale Rain [Honolulu], the friends of the same heartbeat in the confusion of this town. Yes, Sela Ringer gave an affectionate greeting to her friends here in Honolulu, from the Kiʻowao Rain of Luakaha that drenches lehua flowers to the crab-catching girl of Kapuʻukolo, to the body surfing boy of ʻUlakua, and from Moanalua to the lily flowers of Kapiʻolani Park, she cried for you all and the places where you stroll about.

Mrs. Sela Ringer sent greetings to her girlfriends, friends, and loved ones, from the rising sun at Haʻehaʻe to the setting of the sun at the Garden Isle [mokupuni kihapai: Kauaʻi] below. She gave her great call to all of you without leaving one out. "What I covet," said Solomon the king, "I see, and it is mine." However, the murderous law entered by force and separated us from our fulfillment of the last part of our oath, "to care for in sickness and in health." And thus was she separated from our relationship.

Four oʻclock, emotional tears were again given with echoing calls of affectionate farewells between us and those on shore. This was a time that increased the agony between the parent and child, the husband and wife, the loved one and friend, since they would be separated. During the crying of voices, the fluttering of handkerchiefs, and the waving of hands, the skiffs carried us to the ship.

Four-thirty, we set off back to Honolulu, while those on shore were waving pieces of white cloth upon sticks. I stayed at the rear of the ship and turned to look back at my beloved. The nighttime moon rose, and that was what startled me, as if it were my beloved, and I began the song,

"When Māhealani [the full moon] rises,
It appears together with my beloved."

With sorrowful and grieving thoughts about my wife, that return was made.

Nine oʻclock Sunday night, we arrived back in Honolulu.

With great affection to you, Mr. Editor, and your workers, and also my thanks to President W. O. Kamika of the Board of Health, for kindly permitting me to go.

—Willie Ringer, one of your subscribers. Honolulu, NOVEMBER 27, 1896.

St. Philomena. This Catholic church in Kalawao was built in 1872 by Brother Victorin Bertrand, a member of the Congregation of the Sacred Hearts of Jesus and Mary, and dedicated on May 30, 1872, by Father Raymond Delelande.

The church was named for Philomena, a young Christian who was martyred about AD 300. Her name, which is Filumina in Italian, Philomene in French, and Philomena in English, means "daughter of light." While almost nothing is known about her personal life, she became famous after her tomb was discovered in a catacomb in 1802. When the Catholic Church removed her remains and enshrined them in a church in Mugnano, Rome, in 1805, people visiting the church began to report that praying to Philomena resulted in miraculous cures. As miracles continued to occur, veneration of her ran high. In 1837, in recognition of the cures attributed to Philomena, Pope Gregory XVI proclaimed her a saint in the Catholic Church. Given the history of her veneration in the 1800s as someone who could cure disease, it was appropriate that the Catholic Mission in Hawai'i named its church at Kalawao St. Philomena.

A pamphlet published by the Catholic Mission Press in 1875 titled *Mission Catholique des Iles Sandwich, Eglises, chapelles, du Vacariat Apostolique des Iles Sandwich* [Catholic Missions in the Sandwich Islands: Churches, Chapels of the Apostolic Vicariate of the Sandwich Islands] offered the following information: "Besides the first chapel under the protection of St. Philomena [in Rome], we built a second one at Kalaupapa." [Outre la premiere chapelle mise sous la protection de Ste. Philomene, on en a construit une seconde a Kalaupapa.]

In the *Hawaiian Dictionary* Philomena is spelled Pilomena, but writers in the Hawaiian-language newspapers also used variant spellings, including Pilemena, Pilemeno, Pilemona, and Pilemone.

Father Damien arrived at St. Philomena on May 10, 1873, and served as its priest until his death on April 15, 1889. During his tenure he enlarged the original structure twice.

Ka Nupepa Kuokoa. 15 OCTOBER 1881. P. 4.
Haina O Na Ninau Hauoli A L S Keaniani. Answer for the Enjoyable Questions of L. S. Keaniani.

I end here, since the fronds of the palai fern are beckoning for me to return. Evening has come, and the bell of **St. Philomena** [Pilemena] is ringing sweetly. The windward [Ko'olau] cliffs are chilly.

With thanks, Peter N. Mailou. Kalaupapa, Moloka'i, OCT. 5, 1881.
» [This exerpt is the conclusion of a letter to the editor.]

Ko Hawaii Pae Aina. 14 OCTOBER 1882. P. 4.
He Niua I Ke Aloha Welawela I Kuu Lei Momi Ua Hala. Dizzy With Heated Love for my Pearl Necklace Who Has Passed.

> A loving lament for you, Luka
> My dear wife from the hot plains of Kawaluna
> That place where she and I were together in love.
> I send out my love for my wife of the Wai'ōpua wind
> Carrying the sweet fragrance of the nēnē grass down to **St. Philomena**
>   [Pilemona]
> The soul is hot, my dear wife living in the mountains
> Cavorting with Lā'ieikawai
> With the woman who strings lehua flower lei at Paliuli
> I am dark inside me, bitten by love
> My heart shakes within me like an affliction
> Oh, my wife, my dear companion.

» [This excerpt is from the kanikau section.]

Siloama. This Protestant church in Kalawao was founded in June 1866, the year the first patients arrived, and was given the name Siloama on December 23, 1866. Siloama is Hawaiian for "Siloam," a pool of spring water mentioned in the Holy Bible.

One of the earliest references to Siloama in the Hawaiian-language newspapers is in the November 25, 1835, issue of *Ke Kumu Hawaii*. In an article that lists several historical sites in Jerusalem, the writer included "the spring and watchtower of Siloam" [Ka punawai a me ka hale kiai o Siloama]. When early translators, such as the staff of *Ke Kumu Hawaii,* converted English words into Hawaiian, they usually substituted the letter "k" for "s," but in the case of Siloama, the "S" was not changed.

The historical significance of the pool is found in the Holy Bible [Baibala Hemolele], which was translated and published in 1839 by the early Prostestant missionaries in Hawai'i. It appears in the Gospel of John [Ka Euanelio I Kakauia'i E Ioane], where it is found in chapter 9, verse 7 [Mokuna IX, Pauku 7] as "ka wai auau o Siloama," or "the bathing pool of Siloam." In verses 1–12 John tells the story of a miracle that Jesus performed when he cured a man who was blind from birth [kekahi kanaka i makapo mai ka hanau ana mai]. Jesus spat [kuka] on the ground, mixed his saliva in the dirt, and dabbed [hoopala] some of the mixture on the eyes of the blind man. He then told the man to wash his eyes with water from the pool of Siloam [E hele oe, e holoi ma ka wai auau o Siloama]. When this was done, the man could see. For Christian patients at Kalaupapa the pool of Siloam was a symbol of hope and healing. They called their church "Siloama, Church of the Healing Spring."

Ka Nupepa Kuokoa. 2 FEBRUARY 1867. P. 3.
Ekalesia No Na Lepera. A Church for the Leprosy Patients.

In the month of December last, Rev. A. O. Forbes [Porebe] went among the leprosy patients [mai lepera] at Kalaupapa and established a church for those people according to the decision of the Assembly of the Islands [Ahahui o ka Pae aina] in June. The number of members of that church who were admitted was fifty-three [53], and from among those people, three leaders were chosen, those being Hae from Kāne'ohe, Kahulanui from Lāhaina, and the third was from Moloka'i. The church was given the name "**Siloama**," where the leprosy patients [mai lepera] were cleansed in the Bible.

» [The Ahahui o ka Pae aina was the annual meeting of Congregational churches in Honolulu. There were thirty-five members at this meeting, not fifty-three.]

Ka Nupepa Kuokoa. 27 FEBRUARY 1869. P. 4.
Mai Molokai Mai. From Moloka'i.

You probably do not think that we have been completely engaged in maintaining virtue, while entirely avoiding sin. That is not the case. However, we request of his patience, to make real our desires, for a monument to him to stand in this part of our islands. And this monument is perhaps like the bathing pool of Siloam [ka wai auau o **Siloama**] in days past, when the Lord had a body upon this wretched world. Therefore, we decided unanimously to build a church for ourselves, to be named "The bathing pool of Siloam" [Ka wai auau o **Siloama**]. In our past meeting on the third Sabbath of January, each of us reported our own contribution. It will be collected into the hand of Muolo, the head of our congregation, on the first Sabbath of March, this same year, to be quickly secured for emerging out of this winter. However, upon careful examination of each person's contribution, it was immediately understood that there would not be enough for the building that has been planned.

» [This excerpt is from a letter to *Ka Nupepa Kuokoa* that was signed: W. H. Uwēleʻaleʻa. Place of the leprosy patients (Wahi o na Lepera). Feb. 3, 1869. William Humphreys Uwēleʻaleʻa was an early member of Siloama Church.]

Ka Nupepa Kuokoa. 12 AUGUST 1871. P. 1.
E kokua! E kokua! Help! Help!
Dear *Nupepa Kuokoa.* Greetings.

Due to the order of **Siloama** Church [Ekalesia Siloama], the church of the leprosy patients [ekalesia o na mai lepera] here at Kalawao, Molokaʻi, the two of us have been chosen as committee members to publish in the newspaper *Kuokoa* the troubles regarding the remainder of the debt pertaining to our church building according to what has already been published in previous newspapers.

The church [Halepule] continues to stand majestically between Kawaluna and Kalawao and will become an anchor in our tribulations. However, its debts are mounting and increasing as they are established. This is why you, those who love their fellow men, who love the spirit, love the nation, assist us with our debts regarding our church [luakini] of the Lord here in Kalawao.

Committee members: J. H. Haʻo, W. N. Pualewa. Māhulili, Molokaʻi. JULY 24, 1871.

Ka Lahui Hawaii. 6 APRIL 1876. P. 2.
E huli ana i ka Palapala Hemolele. Searching the Holy Scriptures.
Dear *Ka Lahui Hawaii.* Greetings.

In keeping with the commandment of the Lord in John 5:39, some of the Protestant faith in Kalawao, Molokaʻi, have fulfilled the commandment, whose names appear below:

A. W. Pupulenui, Timoteo Kaʻāhui, W. K. Kanalu, W. H. Kanakaʻole, D. W. Malo, Pilipo Kaʻōkuʻu, G. Pelekāne, S. N. H. Kapeʻa, D. W. Keukahi, S. Malule, B. Kaʻāhaʻihanu, J. Kalohi, Noa Kapua.

On Thursdays and Saturdays of each week are the days when they search the New Testament and read the topical lessons guided by their reflections and testify before the gathering on Thursday meetings. The Bible is their guide. The Holy Trinity [Kahikolu Mana Loa] is their aide. Leprosy ravages their bodies, and the precious blood of Christ cleanses them. Blessed are those who trust in him.

With appreciation, **Siloama** Churches, Kalawao, Molokaʻi. MARCH 28, 1876.

Ka Lahui Hawaii. 22 FEBRUARY 1877. P. 3.
Hoike Kula Sabati o Siloama. Report of the Sunday Schools of **Siloama**.
Dear *Ka Lahui Hawaii.* Greetings.

I have the full honor to report on all the activities and love of the Sunday School Society [Aha Kula Sabati] by the name that appears above on the 29th of December 1876. What was decided was carried out. In the morning of that day at ten o'clock, the students and teachers gathered together outside of the courtyard of the hospital. When everything was ready, the procession marched to the beautiful sound of one of our horn bands under the direction of the Sunday school master.

The procession proceeded and went into the Protestant church called "**Siloama**" [luakini hoole pope, i kapa ia o "Siloama"]. The select committees went up, including G. H. E. Keaui'a'ole and Rev. N. Pali, and the two oversaw all that took place. When the school classes took their seats, people came in who wanted to see and hear what was taking place among the members. When all took their places, Keaui'a'ole stood and provided the explanation for all, and everyone was settled. The pastor of the Sunday Schools stood and gave an order to the choir and the audience to sing hymn #343, which has the following lines:

"All are quiet here on earth at the sound of the horn
Encouraging all to wake up."

After the singing was over, Rev. Pali offered the invocation. When that was done, the business of the day was started, which was organized in the following way: The children's class, under the direction of J. Europa; their first lesson began with a hymn, "Here Is the Glorious Day." Next was the inquiry lesson regarding the miracles of Jesus, followed by another hymn, "Love One Another," then a debate between a student and the assistant teacher. This was followed up with a lesson on the pharaohs, followed by a hymn, "Don't Give Up." Next was the mothers' class led by W. S. Kipi. The first lesson, followed by a hymn, "Meet at **Siloama**." Questions on Eve, the first mother, followed by a hymn, "My Home in Heaven." Lesson two, followed by a hymn, "Jesus Is the Moving Ship." Two questions on Eve, followed by a hymn, "We All Love." Lesson three, with a hymn afterwards, "The Good Crown of Roses." Three questions on Eve, rote scriptures by individuals, followed with a hymn, "Let Us All Hearken."

The fathers' class is under the direction of N. Kawe'awe'a (but due to a terrible accident that came upon him, some sort of physical weakness, he dropped out and his spot was assisted by the Sunday school pastor). Lesson one, followed by a hymn, "Ho, Ho, Ho, There Are Bells." Lesson two, a hymn, "Zion Hill." Verses on Job, Job chapter 6, verses 1–9, followed by a hymn, "Straying Men Turn Again." Lesson three, followed by a hymn, "The Peaceful Summit of **Siloama**," followed by a presentation on angels descending from heaven to bind Satan, the dragon, the ancient lizard, Revelations, chapter 20, verse 1, followed by a hymn, "My Heavenly Home."

The young boys and young girls class of Kalaupapa and 'Īliopi'i, led by J. Hūmelekoa. Lesson one, followed by a hymn, "Barn Boy," verses from the Bible, a hymn, "I Am a Child Who Resists Strong Drink," followed by the second lesson and a hymn, "For Those Who Drink 'Awa." Bible lessons from the small book, followed by a hymn, "Jesus Is the Moving Ship," a talk on Matthew, chapter 5, verses 1–4, followed by a combined hymn in Tahitian, "Jesus Is the High King" [Iesu te Arii Teitei]. Lesson three, question and answer based on the reading, followed by a hymn, "Who Shall Testify," followed by questions on the nature of God.

The class of mothers of Kalaupapa and 'Īliopi'i under the direction of Mrs. Mīleka. Hymn, "Glorious Father," Bible lesson in Matthew 5, verses 1–3; lesson 2, followed by a hymn, "Remember Him," followed by a lesson from John, chapter 1, verse 14; lesson three, a hymn, "Zion Hill Is Sacred," lesson from John, chapter 1, verses 2–4, followed by a hymn, "Somewhat Stranded."

Parents' class (of those places), lesson one, a hymn, "A Perfect God," rote lessons, Acts chapter 1; lesson two, a hymn, "How Great the Power of Jehovah," reading lesson in Luke, chapter 1, verses 1–9. Lesson three, a hymn, "Lead Me Jehovah." Alphabet lesson, etc., a talk by two parents of the class, followed by a hymn, "Done Together in the Daylight."

Children's class, under the direction of their female teacher, Mrs. Makaleka Kahāʻulelio. Lesson one in John, chapter 1, verses 1–7, a hymn, "If You Have Joy," lesson two in Matthew 26, verses 1–7, a hymn, "Jesus Is Brave." Lesson three in Matthew 22, verses 17–23, a hymn, "The Waters of Life Come From Jesus." Three rounds as announced under the direction of the pastor of the Sunday schools. After the activities of the day, one of the committee members, Rev. N. Pali, spoke on his message, saying the Sunday school is like a tree that produces fruit and is eaten by each and every one with gratitude. When his talk was done, the second committee member, G. H. E. Keauiʻaʻole, stood and gave his appreciation to two-thirds of the activities of the Sunday school, but did not give appreciation to one-third. After that, the entire congregation sang hymn 598, which begins:

"Dear ever powerful King
Help us, etc."

After the hymn, Keauiʻaʻole offered the benediction, and the festivities were ended. With appreciation, J. Keʻeaumoku. Sunday School Pastor. Kalawao, Molokaʻi, Jan. 1877.

Ka Lahui Hawaii. 5 APRIL 1877. P. 2.
Kokua ikaika no Parigama Iana. Strong support for Brigham Young.

Here in Kalaupapa on Molokaʻi, there is great and strong support for the Mormon faith, encouraging and inspiring faith, converting members, and rais-ing up and building one chapel for two religions, true Christians and Mormons.

Over the span of a few days, P. W. Kaʻawa, the pastor of the Christian reli-gion, had a conversation with J. H. Nāpela, the teacher of the Mormon religion, and here is how their conversation proceeded:

Mr. Nāpela: I would like you and me to meet and raise up a church here in Kalaupapa for your members and my members, so we have one chapel where you all pray on one side and we on the other side, or we meet in the morning and you meet in the evening.

Mr. Kaʻawa: Yes, we can do that, that's great. What you are suggesting is what I think as well. What will be wrong with that? However, let us name the chapel "The Savior of the Nation [Ka Hoola Lahui]," so that my name as pastor vanishes beneath it and the brethren of my faith mistakenly think it is some-thing that will cure leprosy. Then they will agree, because I will have a stubborn faction.

Mr. Nāpela: Yes, that will be the name of our chapel. That is a good name.

Mr. Kaʻawa: Yes, that name has the same theme as the king of our country, which is to increase the nation [Hoola Lahui], and ours is to heal the nation; so that is how the members of my side misjudge me, and then I try to change their minds.

When they were done talking, the Rev. Kaʻawa went to each house convincing the firm minds of each person under the influence of instability and great slickness of his words like a lion seeking to swallow his prey. And when each member heard this, the roof of his house slanted that he raised over his true platform, and he was beguiled like Eve and Adam who followed after Satan, the two falling to tribulation, and so too likely these people who agreed to the slick words of Kaʻawa misguidedly. And when he got what he wanted, his support increased among those who were convinced by him. They called together a large meeting in the school at Kalaupapa, and what was decided at that meeting was that there would be committees set up as directors, secretaries, and for thinking about the idea to construct a chapel. It was also decided by them to ask the tribunal of **Siloama** [Ahaluna o Siloama] at Kalawao to accede to their desire. When the tribunal sat to consider the request, they quickly decided against this action. But they chose a time to have the committees consider further.

On Monday, the 19th of February last, the committees met together at the school at Kalaupapa between the hours of two and three o'clock. When the activities began, it was clear that there were many committee members who wanted to construct a chapel for the two religions, and there were only three committee members on the opposition side, namely G. E. Keauiʻaʻole, W. S. Kipi, and C. Keʻeaumoku. After the opening exercises and some discussion about the benefits of the two sides, their desire and hope and great desire to build one chapel for the two religions fell apart.

Therefore, the board of committees decided not to allow the building of one chapel for the two religions, that each should build their own chapels.

So, their hope had come together like the chirping of a bird that calls out: "Unele! Unele!" [Deprived! Deprived!]

Oh, parents of the rights of Christians, and to all who read this, would you allow for these actions of the Rev. P. W. Kaʻawa, who leads these people astray in pathways of darkness?

With appreciation. S. W. [W. S.] Kipi. Kalawao, Molokaʻi, FEB. 20, 1876 [1877].

Ka Lahui Hawaii. 20 SEPTEMBER 1877. P. 1.
Olelo Hoolaha. Announcement.

We, in the name of the Church of **Siloama** [Ekalesia o Siloama], Kalawao, Molokaʻi, with Mr. John Kaʻāhaʻihana being approved as committee member of the records committee and the fundraising committee outside the parameters of the law that set us apart for the building of a new Protestant church [Halepule Hoole Pope hou] for the leprosy patients [mai lepera], we proclaim that all churches of the same confederation may hear, may you accept him with aloha. By order of the Administration of **Siloama** Church [Ekalesia Siloama].

—Rev. P. W. Kaʻawa, W. S. Kipi, secretary of **Siloama** Church. Adam Kalua, treasurer of **Siloama** Church. Kalawao, Molokaʻi, SEPT. 8, 1877.

Ka Lahui Hawaii. 4 OCTOBER 1877. P. 3.
Hoike Kula Sabati o Siloama. Sunday School Report of **Siloama**.

Mr. Editor. Greetings.

On Sunday, August 26th, the quarterly presentation activities of the Sunday school of **Siloama** were opened at Kalawao. All students gathered, the children, the youth, and the adults, at 10:00 a.m. and the exercises were started right at 11:00. These were the activities of the day:

1. Combined hymn, "Ka'i a Naue i ka Nani."
2. Invocation by Rev. P. W. Ka'awa and Bible reading.
3. Inspiring talk by the Sunday school director. Combined hymn, "Hui mai a Naue a'e."
4. Rote verses by each class of the Sunday school and collection plate of the Sunday school when the rote verses of each class were done.
5. Combined hymn, "Inā he Hau'oli Kou."
6. Lessons by the teachers to the classes starting with the class of the fathers led by P. W. Ka'awa. Various lessons from the Bible.
7. Women's class led by Mrs. Mary Kalehua. Lesson: Christian acts and Bible questions.
8. Men's class led by Ephraim Kanoe. Lesson: Jesus is the Messiah.
9. Children's class led by Charles Richardson. Lesson: Christian teachings.
10. Boy's class led by W. K. Kawalu. Reading lesson: Matthew 7:1–12.
11. Story class led by J. N. Kamaka. Lesson on 'Ōpūkaha'ia.
12. Stray kids' class led by Ephraim Kanoe. Lesson: In our youth. Combined hymn, "Mele anei ma ka Lani."
13. Bible questions from outside.

1: What is the commandment? What is the law? Mrs. Ruth Ha'o provided the answers to these questions. Proverbs 6:23.

2: The kingdom of heaven is likened unto a woman who took leaven and mixed with three measures of meal and the whole became leavened. These are the questions: Who is the woman? Who is the leaven? What are the three measures of meal? The answers were provided by all those of the congregation of the Sunday school, but the ideas were not like those of D. Puna, who raised the questions, and so the one who posed the questions provided the answers, but these were not like those of anyone else, but they were good answers. This was the last activity of the day. Closing hymn 595 in the new book. Benediction by Rev. P. W. Ka'awa.

This was the end of the activities of this presentation day. The skill of the students in their lessons was evident, as well as the skill of the teachers. The best class was that of Mrs. Mary Kalehua, the second best was the class of Charles Richardson, and the third best was the class of Ephraim Kanoe. The other classes came afterwards. This was the first of the presentations done that Sunday. This place was accustomed to weekday activities, and in this presentation the peace of the Sabbath was demonstrated.

—W. S. Kipi. Kawaluna, Kalawao, AUG. 29, 1877.

Ka Lahui Hawaii. 4 OCTOBER 1877. P. 3.
Ka Poka-pahu o Siloama. The Bomb of **Siloama**.

At the close of the activities of the Sunday school presentation here at **Si-**

Ioama on Sunday, Aug. 26th, the director of the Sunday school (W. S. Kipi) left two Bible questions raised the previous Sunday. One of the questions was by D. Puna. Bible verse: Matt. 12:33: "Another parable spake he unto them; The kingdom of heaven is like unto leaven, which a woman took, and hid in three measures of meal, till the whole was leavened."

THE ANSWERS OF SOME PEOPLE

Mrs. R. K. Haʻo. 1. Jesus is the woman and the word of God is the leaven, and repentance, prayer, and faith are the measures of meal. 2. The Church is the woman, the word of God is the leaven, and the meal is what St. Paul revealed in 1 Cor. 13:13: "And now abideth faith, hope charity, these three; but the greatest of these is charity." Rev. P. W. Kaʻawa. The Church is the woman and the word of God is the leaven. The Bible, the pious, our place in heaven, these are the measures of meal. W. H. Kanalu. The Church is the woman, the word of God is the leaven, the father, the son, and the holy ghost are the three measures of meal. What I say is that God is the woman and the word is the leaven and the world is the loaf of bread, which has three measures of meal: the king, the nobles, and the commoners. Answer provided by the one who raised the question (D. Puna)—God is the maker of the bread (the woman), and Adam is the red dirt, who is the first loaf of bread made, and the breath of Jehovah that he breathed is the leaven and became a good loaf of bread and baked in the oven until the time of Noah, at which time this loaf of bread became leavened in full measure, three measures of meal; these are the children of Noah's loins, namely Shem, Ham, and Japheth. It leavened in various forms of the flesh—brown, black, white—and these three types are leavened and have spread profusely until there have become a great multitude on the face of the earth. This parable of Jesus is in regards to the past, and this is the reason for the variety of answers from the one who raised the questions, and this is how I leave this before you.

Aloha to all. E. Kanoe. Kawaluna, SEPT. 3, 1877.

Waiʻalalā. A famous spring near the top of the Kalaupapa cliff trail.

Ka Nupepa Kuokoa. 8 SEPTEMBER 1877. P. 1.
He Makua I Aloha Nuiia. A parent greatly loved.

(A true lament of Kaumiokalani)
This is a lament for you, Kaumiokalani
My dear mother from the land of your birth at Kalaupapa
Where the waves are is where we would fish by net at ʻIliopiʻi
From the long slopes of Puʻupāneʻeneʻe
There is nowhere on that cliff that you and I did not travel
We drank the water of **Waiʻalalā**
The water that our ancestors drank
The soul drank the water of Kāne
In your lifetime you lived with the Powerful Father above
With Jesus Christ the savior of all
Our lives are from him along with our blessings

The one who lengthens our lives
Our loftiness and our eternal victory
This is a memory of love for you

—N. H. Poʻookalani
» [This excerpt is from the kanikau section.]

Ka Oiaio. 26 JANUARY 1894. P. 4. [reprinted 10 JANUARY 1896.]
He Moolelo Kaao Hawaii No Laukaieie. A Legendary Hawaiian Story about Laukaieie.
When Makanikeoe left the top of Maunaloa, he traveled to Kaluakoʻi; he turned to look at Kalaʻe, and his desire grew to go to that place, so he arrived at that spring given the name **Waiʻalalā**. And he then arrived right on top of the cliffs of Kalaupapa and Kalawao and he turned to look at the broad plains and the seawater pool [luakai] of Kauhakō that Pele dug.

On this journey of Makanikeoe, he reached the Koʻolau cliffs [pali Koolau] of Molokaʻi, and arrived atop Koki, Wailau, and Malelewaʻa; he was gazing upon Hāʻupu and the bird children of Keōlewa, and Huelo appeared in the sea, with the peak of Kaunuhoa at Pelekunu.

Waiʻaleʻia. One of two large valleys, along with Waihānau, inland of the Kalaupapa peninsula. In the Hawaiian-language newspapers the valley's name is almost invariably spelled Wailēʻia and in everyday conversation is almost always pronounced the same way. The valley was a popular hiking destination for patients and at one time supplied water for the settlement in Kalawao.

Ka Nupepa Kuokoa. 31 MAY 1862. P. 3.
Olelo Hoolaha. Announcement.
I, whose name appears below, make a restriction regarding my kuleana land in **Wailēʻia** in Kalawao on Molokaʻi. Taking pandanus leaves [lauhala] and roots [aahala] and cutting firewood [wahie] is strictly forbidden. Should anyone contest this order, they shall pay ($1.00), and so, too, for straying animals, cattle, horses, mules, donkeys, they shall pay ($1.00)
—K. Kapika. Kalawao, MAY 26, 1862.

Ka Nupepa Kuokoa. 8 JUNE 1878. P. 1.
Huakai A Ke Komite 13 O Ka Ahaolelo I Ka Panalaau O Na Mai Lepera Ma Kalawao. Journey of the Legislative Committee of Thirteen to the Colony of the Leprosy Patients at Kalawao.
Before starting their activities, a few delegates of the committee went on a tour of the flat settlement [kahua palahalaha] of Kalawao, and the Hons. J. Nāwahī, J. N. Kaiʻaikawa, and I went up to the source of the water line [kumu o waipiula] at **Wailēʻia**, and from this pond [kiowai] is where the water enters the line [paipu] up against the cliff, where it is placed on posts until it reaches the flats of the land, and from there it goes underground until the square of the hospital at Kalawao. In my estimation it is almost a full mile in length.
» [This excerpt is from an article in chapter III.]

Ka Makaainana. 22 OCTOBER 1894. P. 6.
Na Lono Hoohialaai mai ka Panalaau mai o ka Ehaeha. Delightful News from the Colony of Agony.

On September 12, the rose buds [opuu pua rose: poetic for girls] were released from the Pauahi Home [Home Pauahi] to head along their path to the forested uplands of the waterfall [wailele] of **Wailēʻia**, in upper Kalawao. At 9:00 a.m. they left the Pauahi Home and marched along the path to the place mentioned above. The nuns [Makuahine Virigine: Virgin Mothers] were also with them, from the young to the elderly. In the count by the experts of Dr. Goto, it seemed that there were approximately sixty of them. The distance from Kalaupapa to Kalawao is a little more than three miles. The nuns and the older women had great speed. They arrived at the Baldwin Home [Balauwina Home]. The travelers caught their breath, and there they rested for a time until they went up to **Wailēʻia**.

This place is upland, a valley like Pauoa [in Honolulu] and such. The ʻiwa birds [poetic for the girls] safely arrived at that upland where fragrance resides, and there they smelled the chilly air and the pandanus [hala] trees wafting their fragrance to the youths of the pleasant home of Pauahi. They strung some pandanus flowers, since Kahalaopuna had seen her descendants, and such was the case with Mailelauliʻi and company. They had given their affectionate greeting to these ones, and the various leaves of the forest. While they were relaxing with these ones, the demigod [kupua] Kūlanihākoʻi saw that it was hot, so that one released a fine mist of rain. Those youngsters as well as the mothers were completely overcome by the heavy raindrops of the sudden shower. This small expression of affection was found:

> "Mana overflows with water from billowy clouds [Hoohanini Mana i ka wai opua],
> Rippling in the uplands of **Wailēʻia** [Hoaleale i ka uka o Waileia]."

When the girls returned from the upland, they had been completely drenched by the misty droplets of that upland, but this had not been grieved over by those pretty ones; those small drizzles of rain were nothing to the uplifted hearts.

On this same day, the youngsters [boys] of the Baldwin Home set out. Their sightseeing trip was to Waikolu, and they always returned with Father Conrardy [Conorade: Father Lambert Louis Conrardy]. They set out before the nuns [Virigine] returned. One small youngster grumbled about his little pail being stepped on. Here was my joke, "Maybe it was the big, fat ulua fish that did it," and laughter erupted.

On the 15th of the month, the doctor invited [his young patients], at the pleasure of the hospital, to travel with him to this place where the girls of the Pauahi Home had gone up to. His rascals accepted, since it was their pleasure, and your writer was another one on this journey. When lunch was over, we headed straight to that solitary upland. We met with the locals [kamaaina] of that upland, Mr. Kamakau and Manua, and took a little break for a time. These locals provided bunches of ripe bananas for Dr. Goto, and we gave thanks. We reached the place where the girls had been and that place passed behind us. We

Waiʻalalā

101

traveled far upland. The boys went to climb mountain apple trees [ohia] by the order of the doctor. We obtained many mountain apples [hua ohia], as well as candlenuts [hua kukui]. There was great admiration in seeing the forest leaves of the uplands, a pleasure to smell. We returned with fern [palapalai] leaves and ginger [awapuhi]. We smelled the chilly air of that upland, the place where the patients pass the time pleasurably. It is a place often visited these days. The youngsters of the home of health returned to see the heart-snatching water of Japan [wai kaili puuwai o Iapana].

» [This excerpt is from an article in chapter IV.]

Waiehu. A waterfall in Waikolu valley.

Ka Nupepa Kuokoa. 3 SEPTEMBER 1864. P. 4.
He Inoa No H. [Heneri] W. Auld. A Name Chant For H. [Henry] W. Auld.

The waters of **Waiehu** hang, hanging against the cliff [lewa i na pali],
Continuously swirled around by the Kiliʻoʻopu wind.

» [This excerpt, which is from the kanikau section, describes Waiehu as a hanging waterfall, which is also known as an "upside-down" falls. These waterfalls occur when water flow in the falls is light and wind gusting up the face of the cliff is strong enough to suspend the falling water and turn it into mist.]

Waihānau. One of two large valleys, along with Wailēʻia, inland of the Kalaupapa peninsula. A large natural reservoir in the back of the valley was once used as a source of fresh water for the settlement.

Ke Au Okoa. 17 OCTOBER 1867. P. 4.
Kaahele Ma Molokai. Helu 5. No Na Makani O Molokai & Ke Kai Koo. Tour of Molokaʻi. Number 5. The Winds of Molokaʻi and the High Seas.
The Mountains of Molokaʻi. [Na Kuahiwi Hui O Molokai.]
These are the high mountains [kuahiwi kiekie] of Molokaʻi as called by name. Maunaloa at Kaluakoʻi, where Kalapahoa [Kalaipāhoa] is found. It is probably gone now as a result of harvesting and quarrying as a sorcery god or a god to kill people when inserted into food. (This is why Molokaʻi is called Molokaʻi of the potent prayers [Molokai i ka pule-oo], from when the chiefs of Hawaiʻi came to war with the people of these islands all the way here to Oʻahu, and with Kauaʻi being joined in.) Keōlewa is located between Kalaupapa and **Waihānau** in Makanalua. Kameʻekū is the mountain on the leeward side, where the spring, Keālia, is found. This is a spring that Pele dug, whose water travels all the way to Maui. ʻAlae is located between Makanalua and Kalawao, Moaʻula is located between Kalawao and Waikolu, Ahumāuna is located between Waikolu and Pelekunu, ʻOlokuʻi is located between Pelekunu and Wailau, and inland of Pelekunu is Kaunuʻōhua. Kawainui is located between Wailua [Waialua] and Pāpala; Kaʻahakualua is located between Pāpala, Hakaʻaʻano, Puaʻahaunui, and Hālawa.

» [This excerpt is from an article in chapter II.]

Ka Lahui Hawaii. 20 SEPTEMBER 1877. P. 1.
Ka Honua Nei A Me Na Mea A Pau Maluna Iho. The World and All Things Thereon.
(Written by J. H. Kānepuʻu)

In Kalawao is a place called ʻAimanu [Waimanu], where water disappears in the autumn months until winter, when there is more water. It is from this water source that the water lines are laid all the way to the Chinese hospital two or more miles away. There is a waterfall inland of **Waihānau** where water gradually disappears until it is dry in the autumn months. That is the season. If the water flow of this waterfall continued, Makanalua and Kalaupapa would become a land of taro patches. Molokaʻi people can tell the rest.

Ka Nupepa Kuokoa. 10 APRIL 1886. P. 3.
Nuhou o Kalawao. News of Kalawao.
Dear *Kuokoa.* Greetings. Below are remembrances of Kalawao. Just a few, but perhaps this is enough like Paul said.

Tobacco [No ka paka]. Tobacco planting [kanu paka] is the biggest industry among the patients at this time, and as they work hard, the leaves are budding, and all they need to do is put it in their mouths. If the tobacco of this colony [panalaau] is allowed to go out, then this is income for large-scale planters. Some squash seeds are growing as well.

Calm [Malie]. Calm is returning these days, and the rumble of the sea has ended. It is really beautiful at this time with the feathers not being ruffled.

Sheep ship [Moku hipa]. On Friday last week, the schooner, *Mile,* captained by Capt. J. Mose, came rumbling into Kalaupapa Harbor, and became heavily laden with a hundred or more sheep from this colony.

Water pipe [Paipu wai]. Our new water pipeline is being installed, slightly increasing the volume of the old pipe, but in the future we will drink its sweet water. It has been heard that the water of **Waihānau**, Kalaupapa was going to be tapped. It has already been measured.

Life spared [Pakele ke ola]. On Mar. 20, at two oʻclock or later, two little children were involved in an explosion while fishing with dynamite [kukaepele hoopahu], and the hand of one was cut and the other had only his fingers cut. What was most fortunate is that no life was in danger. This tragedy was a case of incompetent parents. Such pity.

Bill introduction [Haawina bila]. The bill book of the patients was obtained, and all that is left to do is apply the pen of the bookkeepers. The book was obtained for April.

Regarding the patients, they are well and lively. They are also cold.
—J. J. Kawehena.

Waikakulu. A freshwater pool in Waiʻaleʻia valley.

Ko Hawaii Pae Aina. 14 OCTOBER 1882. P. 4.
He Niua I Ke Aloha Welawela I Kuu Lei Momi Ua Hala. Dizzy With Heated Love for my Pearl Necklace Who Has Passed.

My dear wife at the source of the faucet water [kumu o ka waipiula]
From the fragrant hala grove of Wailēʻia

How I love that place where you and I went
Where we dove headfirst [luu poo] into the water of **Waikakulu**
That water of my dear love that I shall never forget.

» [This excerpt is from the kanikau section.]

Ka Nupepa Kuokoa. 16 OCTOBER 1924. P. 5.
Kuu Wahine Aloha Ua Hala. My Beloved Wife Has Passed.
 Beloved are the lines of cliffs of that homeland of ours. Beloved also are the three waters [na wai ekolu], Wailēʻia, **Waikakulu**, and Waihānau. Beloved are those waters where you bathe.

» [This excerpt is from the kanikau section.]

Waikolu. This coastal valley east of the Kalaupapa peninsula was home to a fishing and taro farming community before the leprosy settlement was established. Although the Board of Health included Waikolu within the boundaries of the settlement, some of the valley residents continued to live there after the first patients arrived in 1866. They and other residents who remained on the peninsula helped to support the early arrivals. Several of the articles that follow predate the settlement and refer to the original residents in the valley and elsewhere.

 In later years when the patient population increased at Kalawao, the Board of Health tapped the stream in Waikolu to provide drinking water for the patients via a pipeline over the boulder beach at the base of the sea cliff between the valley and the peninsula.

Ka Hae Hawaii. 1 FEBRUARY 1860. P. 176.
On December 25, in **Waikolu**, Molokaʻi, Kanalu (male) died of a disease known as ʻaʻahu mau [unknown].
On January 25, in Kalaupapa, Molokaʻi, Hākalia (female) died as a result of syphylis [kaokao].

Ka Hae Hawaii. 7 AUGUST 1861.
Olelo Hoolaha. Announcement.
 May all people who see this announcement know that I am issuing an order restricting those who are related by blood to Kanalu, my husband of **Waikolu**, Molokaʻi, who died recently without a will, from seizing the liquid assets and real estate. These shall remain under my control until such time as an executor judge issues an order from the one whose name appears below or by those who are blood relatives of the deceased mentioned above. Should anyone contest this announcement, they shall be sued immediately according to the law.
 —Mrs. S. Kawaiola. Honolulu, JULY 30, 1861.

Ka Nupepa Kuokoa. 12 APRIL 1862. P. 3.
ʻŌpiopio. March 11, in **Waikolu**, Molokaʻi, ʻŌpiopio (female) died.
Wāhia. March 16, in Makanalua, Molokaʻi, Wāhia died.
Mauikoale. March 24, in ʻĪliopiʻi, Molokaʻi, Mauikoale died.
Kaʻōhā. March 28, in Kalaupapa, Molokaʻi, Kaʻōhā (female) died.

Ka Nupepa Kuokoa. 23 AUGUST 1862. P. 3.
Aug. 12, in **Waikolu**, Moloka'i, Kanuku (female) died.

Ka Nupepa Kuokoa. 20 SEPTEMBER 1862. P. 3.
Sept. 4, in **Waikolu**, Moloka'i, Kawahineuē died (female).

Ka Nupepa Kuokoa. 6 OCTOBER 1888. P. 2.
Leta a na Makamaka. Ua Ola E Ka Lehulehu A Pau. Letter from the Friends. The Populace Is Saved.

From the leprosy settlement of Kalawao [kahua mai lepera o Kalawao], from the day the piped water properly flowed out at the shore of Kalaupapa up to this day as I write, the disastrous predictions of those outside and in this community have been dashed, and everyone is uttering those words placed above. And because of great interest in the teasing gurgle of the lighthearted faucet [piula], I composed these lines of praise that just welled up. They should be sung along with a cigar [ciga]:

1. One new thing at Kalawao
   Is the bubbling of the faucet water
   It gushes forth at Wailē'ia
   Roaring to the shore of Kalaupapa
   The entire populace is saved
   By the cold waters of **Waikolu**.

2. Kawailoa is chilled
   With water for the public to drink
   Gained through the power of the government
   It is that water that dwells in the heights
   The entire populace is saved
   By the cold waters of **Waikolu**.

3. Fifty or sixty degrees
   Whizzing into the bucket
   When you look, it's like milk
   As it streams into the surface
   The entire populace is saved
   By those cold waters of **Waikolu**.

4. One unusual thing in Kalawao
   Is the rain sprinkling down on the cliffs
   Creeping along to the Waikolu yard
   Spreading out over the ocean
   The entire populace is saved
   By the cold waters of **Waikolu**.

5. The birds bring a proud beauty
   As they circle up above
   Like the cape of Kalā'au Point

As it emerges grandly out, rising up
At its summit so very rich
The pulsing waters of **Waikolu**.

Ke Alakai O Hawaii. 24 NOVEMBER 1888. P. 2.
Ko Kalawao Mau Anoai. News From Kalawao.
Mr. Editor. Greetings to you:

On Thursday the 8th at four o'clock the rain began to drizzle, then from five o'clock on the rain became much heavier, with thunder and lightning, as the Nāulu showers encircled the face of the cliffs. When it neared seven o'clock that evening, as was told by Kopena, the one farming in **Waikolu,** there was a great and powerful flood [waikahe nui ikaika]. Neither the residents [kupa] who came to this strange land [aina malihini] ten to eighteen years ago or the locals [kamaaina] have seen a remarkable flood like this before.

Driftwood was carried out to sea, and part of the land farmed by Kopena in **Waikolu** was scattered out to sea, causing $600 in losses for Kopena. As for the source of drinking water for Kalawao and Kalaupapa, the pipe was broken and carried away, and the bridge that the pipe was on was smashed and completely washed out to sea.

Kalaupapa is greatly troubled by the lack of water these days, but Kalawao does have drinking water. Our water is not from **Waikolu**. Instead, Kalawao's drinking water comes from Wailēʻia. The firewood scattered about is the water's blessing to the troubled people. The shores of Kalawao are crowded with patients gathering firewood these days.

W. E. Rowell, the supervisor of new works [Luna o na Hana Hou], came to us, and he is planning the things that will bring water to this colony [Panalaau]. According to him, it will not take much work. After two weeks the problem will be gone, starting from Tuesday the 13th.

Three nuns [Virigine] and twenty-two girls have come to us. There were forty-eight patients on this trip, and now there are over a thousand patients. Father Matia also came to us, and the chair of the Board of Health is here wasting time with the shacks brought over from Kakaʻako. He is the chair in place of Myer [Meyer].

Wailele has met with disaster, or else he wandered off to some other place. [He was one of the] patients who ran away on Thursday the 8th. Palohau and Wailele tried to escape on the harbor duty skiff [waa papa o ke kuke awa]. At the point of Nihoa, they were swamped, and that was when the patient Palohau returned. But Wailele, because he was obstinate due to his love for a woman, swam off in the ocean. Maybe he is dead, maybe not.

Two female helpers [wahine kokua] returned to Honolulu on the *Mokolii*, one being Mrs. C. Graves, the wife of Jno. Hakau, and another woman. How lovely for them to again see the sun of Honolulu, the city adorned with fragrance and perfume.

The new Catholic church [halepule Katolika hou] that Damien [Damiano] is building is coming together nicely, and looking good. Give greetings to our busy friends.

Yours Truly, W. H. Kahumoku, Kalawao, Molokaʻi, NOV. 15, 1888.

Ka Leo o Ka Lahui. 6 JULY 1891. P. 2.

Hunahuna Materia O Ka Aina O Ka Ehaeha. Bits of Material from the Land of Agony.

Mr. Editor. Greetings between us:

Have patience, O brilliant electric lamp, the alabaster lamp filled with wise thoughts, to report my small bits of material to the shores of our beloved land.

The state of the colony [panalaau] progresses during these current days. The time of toil and gnashing teeth has passed, and here is this time in peace and calm. There are no dissenting riots these days. Taro was eaten in **Waikolu** in the seasons before the patients lived here, and now at this time the patients [maʻi] and the helpers [kokua] farm taro, although it was not the same kind as this.

These good works were not spread by the first supervisors. They had no famous accomplishments in the past. From T. Evans and his assistant, Pila Kilonue, a great amount of farming was begun in **Waikolu,** and now the mouths of the patients will soon be fed, the mouth-to-mouth feeding that the wise skull [poetic for intellect] of this supervisor has been accomplished.

This is a vast land where taro grows, filled with taro patches [kaupapaloi] from the shore to the uplands. Makaluahau is the first of the taro patches, Pōʻaiwa is the second place where taro is planted, ʻĀlina is the third of the places where it is planted, Halemauʻu, the two ʻOpihi, Pohākaʻakaʻa, and those are all of the places where taro is planted. And here is the taro growing with fine health. You see only green from the shore to the mountain [mai kai a uka].

This is a quite famous project done in the time of Evans while he was acting as a father for this patient colony [makua no keia panalaau maʻi]. When he left this job, and a successor was sought who would act as a father for this colony, W. Tell was chosen as a father who would look after the needs of the patients living in this colony. In the days when he stepped onto the dirt of Kalaupapa, there were many people who strongly repudiated him because they knew about his wrongdoing while he was working as a police captain [kapena makai] for Honolulu.

In the first days when he began to carry out the work he had been sent here to do, the work was excellent, with it being assumed that the good would continue, but in fact it continued like a bottle, shiny on the outside but sharp on the inside [eia ka e oi mai ona kohu omole, hinuhinu mawaho he oi maloko: a bottle is sharp when itʻs broken. (This is a shortened version of a longer saying.)].

Concerning this supervisor of ours that is in place: he continues to limit the rights of the patients living in this colony.

Because of this supervisor, the patients and the helpers [na maʻi a me na kokua] have been forbidden from collecting firewood at the cliffs without being permitted by him. If a patient wants to collect cooking firewood for himself, then he first goes to get a permit, and then collects firewood. If you just collect firewood without permission, then he will fine you.

The second of the improper actions by this supervisor is the following statement: If a patient dies and there is some property (a house, a horse, etc.), then all of this property will go to the Board of Health. It is not allowed to go to the people who cared for the patient until death. This is an action that is extremely foolish and truly unjust.

This is a great restriction on the right of the patients. If I care for my patient until he dies, then I have no claim to the property of the deceased, and the Board of Health is the one with the claim to that property. This is an extremely terrible idea, and the labor will be in vain for the people providing care without this supervisor assisting the care.

Look, my multitudes [kini], at the improper work that W. H. Tell is doing, a reason for him to step out of office. With gratitude to the editor and with the typesetting boys my endless greeting.

I am sincerely, E. M. Kaila. Kalaupapa, JULY 6, 1891.

Waimanu. A waterfall in Waiʻaleʻia valley.

Ka Nupepa Kuokoa. 29 NOVEMBER 1918. P. 4.
He Hoalohaloha No Mrs. Hokela Holt. A Condolence concerning Mrs. Hokela Holt.
O fog of Waikolu, your dampening of the lovely cheeks of Mrs. H. Holt has ended. O waterfall [wailele] of **Waimanu**, her gazing upon your hidden cascades is over; O pandanus [hala] trees of Wailēʻia, she will never wear your lei again.
» [This excerpt is from the kanikau section.]

Wilikoki Hale. Wilcox Hall. Meeting hall for youth in Kalaupapa.

Ka Makaainana. 29 JULY 1895. P. 8.
Kela A Me Keia. This and That.
On Thursday, the 18th, was the dedication of the meeting hall [hale halawai] of the Youth Association of Kalaupapa [Ahahui Opiopio o Kalaupapa], Molokaʻi, a gift from George Wilcox [Keoki Wilikoki] of Kauaʻi. It was given the name "Wilcox Hall" [**Wilikoki Hale**].

Kalaupapa History

MY SEARCH FOR INFORMATION about Kalaupapa by looking for its place names in the Hawaiian-language newspapers turned up a wealth of articles, far more than I ever expected. They told such a unique and compelling story of everyday life there that I decided to include almost all of them in *Kalaupapa Place Names*. The articles, which are listed chronologically in the four chapters that follow, offer an insider's look at the activities that took place in Kalaupapa before and after the establishment of the leprosy settlement. The chapters are:

   I. Kalaupapa Before 1866
  II. Kalaupapa, the Early Years: 1866 to 1873
       Establishing a Leprosy Settlement
       Schooner *Warwick*: Kuna Wawiki
       Leprosy Patients: Nā Maʻi Lepera
       Patient Helpers: Nā Kōkua o Nā Maʻi
  III. Father Damien (Makua Damiano) in Hawaiʻi: 1873 to 1889
  IV. Mother Marianne (Makuahine Mariana) in Hawaiʻi: 1888 to 1918

The canonizations of Father Damien and Mother Marianne as saints in the Catholic Church in 2011 and 2012, respectively, focused worldwide attention on their lives at Kalaupapa. The Hawaiian-language newspaper articles written during their years there, 1873 to 1889 for Father Damien and 1888 to 1918 for Mother Marianne, may or may not mention their names, but they describe what life was like while they lived there.

Many of the articles read like short stories, each adding insight to the history of Kalaupapa. The poetry in the Hawaiian language is evident throughout the texts, especially in the kanikau, or dirges. The articles also show the human side of everyday life in the settlement. Patients at Kalaupapa had no reservations about voicing their opinions about anyone or anything that impacted their way of life. Their letters to the editor are just as critical, complimentary, humorous, and informative as those we read today.

The articles in each chapter also contain many personal names and place names. The index lists all of them, including the names featured in the Kalaupapa Place Names section.

I. KALAUPAPA BEFORE 1866

HAWAIIANS INHABITED the Koʻolau side of Molokaʻi for hundreds of years prior to the arrival of the first leprosy patients in 1866. Fishing and farming communities were well established in the coastal valleys of Hālawa, Wailau, Pelekunu, and Waikolu, and on the Kalaupapa peninsula. Protestant missionaries were among the first non-Hawaiians to visit the area, some of them describing their adventures in the early Hawaiian-language newspapers. They established a mission at Kaluaʻaha on the Kona side of the island and began preaching and organizing schools. Catholic missionaries followed the Protestants, creating tension between the two groups and their converts. During the 1830s, Kalaupapa residents began growing sweet potatoes and other produce commercially, supplying the whaling industry in the Pacific and later the gold rush in California, which one newspaper described as "aina eli gula o Kalefonia," or the "gold-digging land of California." Some of the highlights of Kalaupapa from the Hawaiian-language newspaper articles before 1866 are listed below.

1. 1836. Reverend Harvey Hitchcock travels by canoe to Kalaupapa and describes the peninsula as populated with a good harbor. He returns to the Kona side of the island by taking off his shoes and hiking up the slippery pali trail barefooted in the rain.
2. 1842. In a letter titled "The Amazing Acts of the Catholics on Molokaʻi," the writer criticizes activities of the Catholics.
3. 1843. Two letters describe a new chapel built at Kalaʻe, which is at the top of the Kalaupapa pali trail. The chapel was intended to serve the communities of Kalaʻe and Kalaupapa, requiring the residents of Kalaupapa to hike the pali trail to attend services.
4. 1848. In a letter about vacant lands at Kalaupapa that were being farmed by teachers and students, the writer complains that the agents of the landowners have demanded that they stop farming.

5. 1856. In August, Kamehameha IV does a Kaapuni Ana O Ke Alii, or a "King's Tour," from Ni'ihau to Hawai'i island. Back in Honolulu after the tour, the king writes a letter to the editor in November that describes his stop at Kalaupapa and its sweet potato industry. In December a resident of Kalaupapa writes a letter to the editor, recalling a brief speech the king made there before his departure to Honolulu.

6. 1857. These articles appeared in *Ka Hae Hawaii*.
   a. March. A detailed letter about the sweet potato industry at Kalaupapa, including the names of the varieties grown there, written by one of the residents.
   b. May. A report titled the "Goods Exported from Kalaupapa Harbor and Their Prices."
   c. July. A report written about the students at Kalaupapa.

7. 1859. A note describes commercial taro farming on Moloka'i, including in Waikolu valley.

8. 1860.
   a. "Names of Sweet Potatoes" is a list of the sweet potato varieties in Hawai'i.
   b. A report from the Farmers Association of Moloka'i explains how profitable the sweet potato industry has been for their association's chapter at Kalaupapa.

9. 1861. A letter to the editor notes the delays in newspaper and mail delivery to remote areas like Kalaupapa and makes a suggestion for greater efficiency.

10. 1864. An article on churches notes that there are three on Moloka'i, but only two, Kalua'aha and Hālawa, have pastors. The third church at Kalaupapa has a lecturer, but not a pastor.

11. 1865.
    a. June. An article says that a Hawaiian pastor was found for Kalaupapa, but was reassigned to Lana'i, the island of his birth.
    b. November. In a brief comment a visitor to Kalaupapa says that he observed members of a church congregation who from the looks of their physical appearance seemed to be chronic awa drinkers.

Ke Kumu Hawaii. 8 JUNE 1836. P. 46.
No Ko Makou Pii Ana I Ka Pali A Me Ka Hoi Ana I Kaluaaha. Our Ascent Up the Cliff and Return to Kalua'aha.

There were lots of amazing things that were seen by us on this trip and not all of it can be accounted for in this report at this time. We slept that night in Kalaupapa, a place inhabited by people, with a good harbor. That is probably where the new missionaries will arrive. We awoke in the morning and looked out and saw that it was windy! It was decided that it was not good for me to travel again by canoe [waa], so I left the canoe and climbed the cliff with three men with me. The path was in bad shape being slippery in the rain. I took off my shoes and climbed. I did not look back for fear of becoming dizzy and falling. We climbed until we reached a rock that stood up. The space to stand was very narrow and there wasn't much space for the hands to grab hold. I could not make it alone and I relied on the others who were familiar with the way.

As I climbed, a thought came to me. I was like the one who desired to climb to heaven. If he thought that he could do it alone, he surely would fall in the darkness, but if he thought that he could not do it except by relying on Jesus, he surely would make it. I made it up to the top and quickly made my way down to Kalama'ula with tired muscles and slept there. In the morning I reached here at Kalua'aha.

—Aloha. H. R. H. [Rev. Harvey R. Hitchcock]

Ka Nonanona. 13 SEPTEMBER 1842. P. 39.
Na Mea A Kupanaha O Ka Poe Pope Ma Molokai. The Amazing Acts of the Catholics on Moloka'i.

Dear *Ka Nonanona.* I am reporting to you some of the amazing things about the Catholics here on Moloka'i.

This is the first thing. They desire to do wrong and this is well-known about the Catholics here. They do not desire to do good. This is what we know. The Catholic woman who first became involved in the work left Honolulu. Here is what she said: "I went to Honolulu and heard the word of the French teacher. And when I heard it, I learned that they have a kind way about them, but that smoking tobacco was not restricted among them, nor was drinking or lasciviousness. I liked this and immediately followed after the Catholics." This Catholic woman came back to Kalaupapa and met with a friend of hers and told her of the Catholic ways. When she learned that tobacco smoking was not restricted by the Catholics, nor was drinking or lasciviousness, she quickly became a disciple. Afterwards, these women went about committing sins without fear since, according to that religion, drunkenness does not cause one to fall, neither does sleeping around and lasciviousness. That is how those two lived until this year in about the month of July. Then God showed them the error of their ways, and then they saw how wrong their behavior was. The two left the Catholic Church and they live repentantly. They said that they did not follow after the Catholic Church because they thought it was right, but because sin was not restricted. This is why they converted. So it is clear that it is due to a desire for sin that the Catholic religion has spread on Moloka'i and not for a desire for righteousness.

This is another thing. The Catholic teacher at Kalaupapa is amazing. He is a hard-working man but he became lazy about attending church. He resented it and turned to the Catholic Church. He is the lead teacher of the Catholics there. He is very ignorant and does not read well. He does not know how to write and does not know his numbers.

Here is another thing. After becoming a Catholic along with his wife, some church members met with these two and investigated their reason for abandoning what they had previously sought. The two were asked whether this new religion that they were adhering to was the right thing. His wife denied it, saying it was wrong. They were asked again, "Won't you leave it then?" She agreed, saying, "I will leave it and will not do that again." She had lied in saying this since she did not leave the Catholic religion. The two continue doing the things they had called evil and unrighteous. So it is clear that their becoming Catholics was wrong and is not something they did because they thought it was right.

This is another amazing thing about Moloka'i Catholic residents. They do not observe the laws of the land. It is only with patience that leaders suffer the children to go to school. They refuse to observe or do according to the laws of the government.

Another thing that is amazing is that those who follow after that religion will not convert. Those who know how to read well, the educated, thinkers or important people do not follow after the Catholic religion. Only the ignorant, those who prefer lasciviousness, the stiff-necked and the little children are the ones who do not desire to go to school. The people of this place who fear sin, repentance, seriousness, and piety are the ones who do not convert to that religion.

One more thing is that a Catholic priest arrived here. Not many people like him. What's amazing about him is that he refuses to worship idols, he does not pray to Mary or this or that dead person. We have just heard about the Catholic priest who does not pray to Mary. Is that what Catholic priests do in Honolulu? Perhaps this is a redeeming quality of this priest that he abandoned praying to Mary and worshiping idols. If a Catholic follower quits praying to Mary, would the Catholic priests be pleased?

Does anyone have any quandaries [manao ninau]? How about the treaty between Kauikeaouli and L. Place? Was it ratified by the king of France? Let *Ka Nonanona* reply to that because I don't know. I have heard it said often by Catholics, "The treaty was broken." [Ua hai ke kuikahi.]

Ka Nonanona. 4 JULY 1843. P. 11.
Kaluaaha, Iune 13, 1843. Kalua'aha, June 13, 1843
Greetings Armstrong:

Here I'll explain about our stay at Kala'e last week. We all went with the women and the children. On Thursday we left by canoe [waa] and in two and a half hours, we landed at Kalama'ula, where you and I went while you both were staying with us. We reached there, but there was no lodging. So we set up a screen at the gable of the church and that is where we slept until daylight. The next morning we awoke, and after church services, Mrs. Hitchcock [Hikikoki wahine] sat on a chair [noho] and she was carried [amo] by two men, with six other men assisting in this effort. Our children walked and Mr. Brown [Balauna] rode with me on horseback. We climbed inland seven miles to the new chapel [luakini hou] that was made for the people of Kalaupapa and Kala'e. The building had not yet been entered. It's a very good building: twelve fathoms long and four wide. There was carpeting as well. There was only one problem, but otherwise, it was a magnificent building. The doorways had no doors. But the people were preparing to close them up.

The people were very happy when we arrived. They gave us food and fish in great amounts and we had nothing lacking. However, with regards to lodging, we had none, and so we set up a screen in the new chapel and that is where we stayed. It was a magnificent place. The cold is like our country. It's about two thousand and a few hundred feet high? It was cold. Two thousand and a few hundred feet high, perhaps five, above sea level. This is a very good place for people who are not able to endure living on the coast in the heat.

This is what I did there: I went searching out the sheep of God [hipa o ke

Akua], those who converted from the dark last year, but as a result of the troubles I was experiencing and my sickness, they were not interviewed. We had four interviews, but I had not met with those who were known. On the Sabbath it was said that there were thirty men and women.

When a cottage is built, then I will go there again to seek out the sheep. After that we will observe a holy communion [ahaaina a ka Haku] on that mountain in the new chapel. Then we will divide the congregation into new parishes and the Church will be established in Kalaʻe and Kalaupapa. Then at that time, the people will no longer have to endure climbing the cliff to get to the place thirty miles in distance or twenty to hear the word of God.

I was happy to hear that Gulick [Gulika] was appointed here because I am now able to go here and there to preach the word of God.

On the Sabbath, the large hall was filled and the house of God was dedicated and it was my prayer to him that the building become a place where many people could be born again.

I remain your brother and loving fellow laborer of the Lord.

Do not trouble yourself searching through this epistle. My problem is that night has fallen quickly and I have been burdened and cannot seek out the sinners.

» [Reverend Richard Armstrong was the editor of *Ka Nonanona* (The Ant). Hawaiians called him Limaikaika, which literally means "arm (lima) strong (ikaika)."]

Ka Elele. 8 JUNE 1848. P. 2.
He hoopaapaa no na Komohiki [Konohiki] me na Kumukula ma Kalaupapa nei, no ka mahiai ana o na kumu me na haumana ma na aina kaawale. Kalaupapa, Molokai, Maraki 22, 1848. An argument concerning the land stewards and the schoolteachers here in Kalaupapa, about farming by the teachers and students on available lands. Kalaupapa, Molokaʻi, March 22, 1848.

Dear editor of *Ka Elele* and the lead instructor, the political minister [Kuhina Kalaiaina]. With you both remains the peace and with us, the blessings and success.

I have something that I'd like to explain to you both regarding a problem that has arrived here in Kalaupapa. This is the problem. In the month of January on the 3rd in 1848, Armstrong [Limaikaika] spoke at a teachers' meeting of ours. This is what he said: "John Young [Keoni Ana] ordered us to work with the teachers and students on the vacant lands and small, unused, public farming parcels." When we heard this, we did not follow through on the idea. Not long after that, we received word from John Young in paper 18 of the *Elele* repeating the same message as above. Then I took some pigs and went to Makanalua and Pāʻōʻōole, the names of these two ʻili parcels. And when I did this I planted a garden. My plants grew, which consisted of melons [ipuhaole]. Later we planted a patch of sugar cane [ko], and the land managers [konohiki] did not come and forbid us from planting on that spot. But when we planted our sweet potatoes [uwala], this is how they came: they spent part of Friday in our sweet potato patch and were angry at us and our students and gave us trouble.

They came before me, W. N. Pualewa, and said to me in a stern voice, "Who

gave this land to you?" I told them to look in the *Elele*, paper number 18, and
that is where it was given to us since no one was in any of these 'ili parcels.
I also said if you would like to make an issue of this with your landowner
[hakuaina], it was up to you. They told me, "Do not work any more on my land
because Kekauʻōnohi ordered that none of the teachers or students were to
work his lands." Then I said to them that they were perhaps mistaken and that
this land had fallen to me, but I was not allowed that. I was allowed, however,
to finish growing what we had planted, but the dirt was to remain.

Here is the point: This 'ili parcel of Pāʻōʻōʻole was vacant of any people. It
was vacant land from the years when it was wild brush here in Kalaupapa until
1848. I was not aware of this land being farmed; not at all. But when we took
the land to farm, the land managers came and forbade us. I think this amounts
to obstruction and relates to a clause in the law regarding dividing out the land.
What I'd like to ask you two is, is it true that Kekauʻōnohi forbade his lands
from being farmed by the teachers and students? If this is true, then the land
managers have truly restricted their lands from being farmed by us and the
students.

So what I'd like to ask is that you both set up a pot of boiling water [ipuhao
paila wai wela] in the *Elele* to warm up the coldness of the land managers due
the coldness of their lips and therefore misspeaking. Here are the names of
these people who have caused us trouble: Kamakeʻe, who caused trouble with
Koa, a teacher at Kalawao; Kaʻōhā and Kalāhili, who caused trouble with us and
our toddlers [keiki omo waiu] here in Kalaupapa. This is all I have to say.
—W. N. Pualewa.

Ka Hae Hawaii. 5 NOVEMBER 1856. P. 142.
Hale Alii, Honolulu, 1 Novemaba, 1856. Hale Aliʻi [Royal Palace], Honolulu, November
1, 1856.
Dear *Ka Hae Hawaii.*

I would like to let you know publicly about some things that transpired
on Molokaʻi between me and some subjects [makaainana] and members [ho-
ahanau] at Kalaupapa. Please let the public know since some have not been
ashamed, and these things, that if likened unto the entire nation, would benefit
everyone.

When I arrived at Kalaupapa, I saw a ship docked there and asked, "Whose
ship is that?" I was answered, "It belongs to Kawana, a Hawaiian, who came to
buy sweet potatoes [uala] from the people." So I decided that I would buy sweet
potatoes as well. As a result, I immediately inquired about the price of a box
[pahu]. I was told that it was three-quarters of a dollar to a dollar. At that time,
the word got around about buying sweet potatoes among those who had them.
Upon hearing this, it was decided to go the next morning to unload crops.

The next morning, one of my friends came to me and said, "We discussed
selling our sweet potatoes and we think we should just give you as much as
you'd like." I was very reluctant about this because I had two ships docked there
at the time and thought about how much they would lose out. So I refused,
saying, "I have money and you have sweet potatoes. I'll take the sweet potatoes
and you take the money." They said to me, "The sweet potatoes are yours and
whoever brings in any money, we will take those dollars and throw them into

the ocean." After this, I agreed to their idea. I have the sweet potatoes in my possession now and I leave my aloha here for you to pass on to those who were so generous to me. However, I did not set out when I started this message to admire my success as a result of their generosity toward me. Rather what I wish to admire is that they have what it takes to give according to their generosity as a result of their labor, working hard and with sweat of their brow according to the order. This is what I appreciated: seeing the fruit of their labor and their farming. This is what I admired and my heart was filled with joy. How can one buy if there is no one to sell? And how is it (for these people in Kaluaʻaha) that they can give according to their generosity if it was lacking? It is because of the yield that they were able to sell, and since they had much, they were able to give. This is what I wanted to share with all so that they may see: "There is no labor for which there is no reward. There is no reward from lack of labor." [Aohe hana i loaa ole mai kekahi pomaikai ; aole hoi he pomaikai i loaa mai ke hana ole.]

—Kamehameha. [IV]

Ka Hae Hawaii. 3 DECEMBER 1856. P. 159.
Ka Ike Ana I Ka Moi. Seeing the King.
Dear *Ka Hae Hawaii.* Greetings.

On the evening of the 28th of October, King Kamehameha IV [Moi Kamehameha IV] arrived here in Kalaupapa and we saw him. On the morning of the 29th, we met again. Some pigs, chickens, and sweet potatoes were brought. On that day, the king began his journey back to Honolulu. It was a rough day at sea and one canoe was broken in the big waves [nahaha kekahi waa ia la i ka nui o ka nalu]. The passengers and their gear were brought on the ship with the royals boarding later. At that time, the king stood and said, "Dear people, aloha [E na makaainana, aloha oukou]. I did not expect that we would meet, but here we are meeting. I had not thought to speak to you, but here we are meeting. I did not bring anything more of benefit, except for the benefits enjoyed from the past among our ancestors who have passed on long ago. Therefore, let us continue to enjoy these benefits from the past. There is nothing more to rely on at this time other than those old benefits. I have nothing new at this time to offer that could be considered a new benefit as there are reasons for you to be wary of me: 1. My youth. 2. The newness of my taking up of office. 3. Not seeing much in the way of results. Therefore, I hope to impress upon you to continue in the goodness that we have known of our ancestors [kupuna]. You have not come here today to show your affection to me for my good works, but for the good works of your ancestors and mine. So as your aloha for me has swelled, I leave, in turn, my money with you today. Here I say, the righteous man and righteous woman are my people [Eia keia, o ke kanaka pono, wahine pono, o koʻu kanaka ia]."

When he was done speaking, the king and P. Nahāʻolelua boarded the canoe [waa] and returned to the ship [moku].

—W. N. Pualewa, Kalaupapa, OCT. 30, 1856.

Ka Hae Hawaii. 4 MARCH 1857. P. 1.
Uala! Uala! Sweet potatoes! Sweet potatoes!

"The following is the announcement by the president of the Board of Education." Greetings. Volume 40, page 158, explains that we need to reveal some types of ancient sweet potatoes [uala kahiko] of the island or district where they live.

South American Sweet Potatoes [Uala Amerika Hema]. These are the new sweet potatoes [uala hou]. Kamaʻipelekāne brought this sweet potato after the Civic Association [Ahahui Makaainana] ended its session. The area where he first distributed this sweet potato was the district of Kalaupapa since it is where he first arrived.

This sweet potato spread here at Kalaupapa, and it has been seen in many forms. But these varieties of sweet potato are new ones. People are saying that they hear that these are Japanese sweet potatoes [uala Iapana] or Californian sweet potatoes [uala Kaleponi]. The amount of sweet potatoes being spread about by some are by the mound or by rows and so on. But perhaps after we see the result of this activity, God would spare their lives and not allow the land to be dug up all over the place like it had been in the past.

Kalaupapa Sweet Potatoes [Uala Kalaupapa]. These are the old varieties of sweet potatoes. The number of varieties of sweet potato I've seen here in Kalaupapa is nineteen: nine varieties of black sweet potatoes [uala eleele] and ten varieties of white sweet potatoes [uala keokeo]. Only three of these varieties are any good. They are the ʻapo, likolehua, and hālonaipu varieties. Those are likely the names of these varieties of sweet potato that have spread on some of the islands. They probably go by different names in some places. I have heard that on Kauaʻi, the hālonaipu variety is called mōhihi. These three varieties of sweet potato explained above are what are normally sold in Kalaupapa, and some varieties of white and black are included. But the likolehua and hālonaipu are stored up at the harbor when it's time to sell. The beach became darkened on all parts by the number of people who showed up to buy the products of the farmers.

As a result of the announcement of the president of the Board of Education saying the sweet potatoes that are not wanted are the rotten and mosquito-infested ones, the white sweet potatoes [were identified as the ones that] are rotten and mosquito-infested. But due to the order, all unsatisfactory sweet potatoes need to be destroyed. Before that happens, we need to separate the sweet potatoes that are not wanted for the families and animals. We know that Hawaiian families have big stomachs [opu nui]. As soon as they touch food, they eat, and that is how they get fat when they eat vegetables. So we need to separate the old black varieties of sweet potato from the South American varieties to sell to the ships.

Kalaupapa is a good place for plants. Things grow when planted and it is very bountiful. The crops are not destroyed by caterpillars [enuhe] and cutworms [poko]. There is only one type of large caterpillar and that is the large-mouth animals in Kalaupapa. When you reach Waikolu, there are a hundred or more animals: cattle, horses, mules, donkeys, and they are insatiable, eating everything, and this continues. The people wrongly believe that they would expand on the land, but it's the animals that are expanding. They are loaded upon and our gardens have become like storage units where the riggings are stored outside the breakwater where the whale ships [moku okohola] head out to sea without regard for deluge.

Lots of varieties of sweet potato are being planted now. Each person has about three or four gardens, but the biggest crop is watermelon [ipu haole]. Two types of beans are being planted: pāpapa hiki and pāpapa ʻauka, as well as onions [akaakai]. Vendors should be aware that Kalaupapa has the best the island has to offer with regard to price and the progress in industry. Here in Kalaupapa is where all ships from California arrive. It is also the place I think of the most with affection.

—By M. L. Nāpihelua, Kalaupapa, Molokaʻi, JAN. 31, 1857.

Ka Hae Hawaii. 20 MAY 1857. P. 31.
Na Waiwai I Lawe Ia Aku Mai Ke Awa Aku O Kalaupapa, A Me Ke Kumukuai. Goods Exported from Kalaupapa Harbor and Their Prices.

April 11. Two-masted ship [moku kialoa], Piʻikoi.
    Shipped out 400 watermelons, $15.00
    Shipped out 15 boxes [pahu] of sweet potatos, $15.00
    Shipped out 16 chickens, $4.00
April 13. Two-masted ship, Lapaʻula.
    Shipped out 546 watermelons, $25.87
April 16. Two-masted ship, Piʻikoi.
    Shipped out 521 watermelons, $20.00
    Shipped out 15 boxes of sweet potatoes, $15.00
    Shipped out 16 chickens, $4.00
April 25. One-masted ship [moku kiakahi], Lapaʻula.
    Shipped out 100 watermelons, $4.00
May 3. Two-masted ship, Piʻikoi.
    Shipped out 678 watermelons, $27.00
    Shipped out 9 chickens, $1.12
Total, $131.00

Ka Hae Hawaii. 29 JULY 1857. P. 70.
    The school at Kalaupapa was the best at reading and writing. The students at that school excel at reading and their writing skills are great. That was not the case before, but since they have a clever, educated teacher there, there has been improvement in their performance now.
    —D. W. Kaiuē

Ka Hae Hawaii. 29 JUNE 1859. P. 50.
    Kahananui wrote saying, "Here in some places on Molokaʻi, taro farmers [poe mahiai kalo] are very blessed at this time. In Waikolu and Pelekunu and Wailua [Waialua] and Hālawa, a lot of money was given for their pounded taro [paikalo], and so farmers of these places are very rich. Some of the revenue derives from two-masted ships [Moku kialua] and some derives from vendors, and the income of the farmers of these places has increased. This was not the case in old times, but is rather a new phenomenon."

Ka Hae Hawaii. 28 MARCH 1860. P. 201.
Inoa a na Uala. Names of Sweet Potatoes.

Dear *Hae Hawaii*. Greetings. Below is a list of sweet potatoes from olden times [uala kahiko] and new sweet potatoes [uala hou] here in Hawai'i.

'Āliolio, Kokoko'okeuhi
'Alalā, Ka'eumu
'Alamea, Kawelo
'Au'ono, Ki'ihekeke
'Apo, Kihilauli'ili'i
'Apanakeoe, Kepoe
'Aumahiki, Likolehua
'E'epu'u, Lapa
'Eu'au, Lihilihimōlina
Ihuma'i, Lau'oloa
Unahiuhu, Mahina
'Ualahelele'i, Māio
Hālonaipu, Malihini'akawai
Ho'okano, Makeawe
Haole, Nukulehu
Hā'ulelani, Nau
Huamoa, Nukukau
Hilo, Ne'ene'emai
Hōkeo, Nika
Hua'ono, Pehu
Hōlei, Piapia
Ha'alelelepo, Panikohe
Hāwa'e, Pala
Kipawale, Pālamahiki
Kala, Pa'apa'a'ina
Ki'oki'o, Pā'elehilimānoanoa
Kupa, Puakawaihae
Kihilaunui, Paniolo
Kakake'ilipōhole, Pilimai
Kakakaokeawe, Wehiwa
Kō'ume

—J. W. K. Ka'ai'ē. Waikīkīwaena, MARCH 17, 1860.

Ka Hae Hawaii. 8 AUGUST 1860. P. 80.
Ahahui Mahiai ma Molokai. Farmers' Association of Moloka'i.
I am announcing this message to proclaim my great appreciation to the people of Moloka'i and their new supervisor, E. G. Hitchcock [Hikikoke]. Subscribers to the *Hae* have increased greatly there as a result of the great work of this supervisor. There were only 50 people who took Book IV there, and 183 who took Book V on Moloka'i!

In the month of March, the Farmers' Association in Kalaupapa, Moloka'i, was started. This is what happens: Everything is planted, sweet potatoes, watermelons, and corn, and pigs, sheep, goats, birds, etc., are raised. They have much as a result of this gathering, [including] lots of sweet potatoes. That is how it was in 1850 and 1851. They did a lot of work. Thousands of barrels of sweet potatoes were sold to the two-masted ships, three-masted ships, and they were very profitable in those years. Like the many thousands of barrels that were sold, so too were there thousands of dollars in income. But these years, the income was greater than in those years mentioned above. When it is published in the *Hae Hawaii,* then the profits of the land are revealed, as well as the earnings of each person. In these announcements in the *Hae Hawaii,* the names of these people who are doing such a great job are revealed so that all can see how well they work. This is so that all may see and honor the merchants and ship owners in the town of Honolulu.

From us, the leaders of the Farmers' Association. D. N. Mokuhïʻai. J. Kaihelua. A. Kalāuli.

Ka Hae Hawaii. 13 MARCH 1861. P. 204.
Hoohalahala. Accusation.

Someone of Kalaupapa, Molokaʻi, wrote to ask, "What is the reason the *Hae Hawaii* is so late to arrive?" This is my idea about why it is so late.

Kalaupapa is such a remote place. They have to wait for letter carriers who don't go there. So this is why the *Hae* does not get there. But this is not the fault of the editor. He cannot carry the *Hae* to each of the islands and each of the districts and to each and every valley each and every morning to each and every person. This is true also for the supervisors. They cannot take the *Hae* to all places where people are found. So this is probably how the situation can be fixed: People need to band together in remote places far from post offices so that they can become *Hae* carrier groups and choose leaders among them and forward the monies to us and account for the number of subscriptions, and I will forward them the batch of *Hae* each week. They can then go and get the batch and take them to the homes in their districts. One week, Mr. A can be the courier and Mr. B can do it the next, and the same for Mr. K. and so on until all have been picked up. Then Messrs. A, B, and K do it over again. If they do this, things will run quickly, and people will obtain their *Hae* happily and there won't be any problems any more with late deliveries of the *Hae* as seen before. Try it [E hoao]! Try it!

Ka Hoku Loa. JUNE 1864 [MONTHLY]. P. 24.
Na Ekalesia ma Maui a me Molokai. The churches on Maui and Molokaʻi.

"The garden is big and there are few workers" [He nui ke kihapai, he uuku na paahana]. Ten various churches have been established on Maui and three on Molokaʻi.

On Maui in Lāhaina, Lāhainaluna, in Kāʻanapali, Wailuku, Honuaʻula, Kaupō, Hāna, Koʻolau, Makawao, and Keōkea.

On Molokaʻi in Kaluaʻaha, Kalaupapa, and Hālawa.

Only five of these churches on Maui are furnished with pastors: the ones in Lāhaina, Wailuku, Makawao, and Hāna. Two on Molokaʻi are furnished with pastors: Kaluaʻaha and Hālawa.

There are two other places on Maui that are appropriate places to establish another church. They are Huelo and Kīpahulu. One [also] on Molokaʻi in Kaunakahakai [Kaunakakai] and one on Lānaʻi. So there are nine pastors

[kahu] needed in order for the churches on Maui, Moloka'i, and Lāna'i to be fully staffed. There are four lecturers [haiolelo] at Kalaupapa, Kā'anapali, Ko'olau, and Kaupō, with six vacancies remaining. This is probably the problem seen from Hawai'i to Ni'ihau, and if this is the case, we need to beseech the Lord whose gardens these are to alert the workers and to prepare them.

—W. P. Alexander. Wailuku, APRIL 12, 1864.

Ka Nupepa Kuokoa. 1 JUNE 1865. P. 1.

Noa Pali of Lāna'i lived in Wailuku before the start of the pastor's school, and later he asked Rev. W. P. Alexander saying that he wanted to be taught at this school, not intending to become a pastor, but instead intending to become an aide to him in studying the Bible. In the month of October of the year 1864, the Elders Association [Ahahui Luna-kahiko] of Maui and Moloka'i met in Hāna. At that time, the association appointed Noa Pali to Kalaupapa to preach to those people. In the month of January, the association met again at Kā'anapali and the people of Lāna'i requested that N. P. come back as a pastor for them. Their request was granted.

Ka Nupepa Kuokoa. 25 NOVEMBER 1865. P. 2.
Mahuna I Ka Awa. Scaly Skin as a Result of 'Awa.

One colleague of ours who traveled to Moloka'i and returned told us of the bizarre nature of the people of Kalaupapa. In one church congregation [anaina pule] of that place was a strange thing about the people, as if they were foreigners. It was as if they were smeared with poi that was allowed to dry. The skin was cracked and craggly like scales. The eyes were full of dried mucus. Those people abandoned farming, which is a great fruit. Drunkenness is the father of laziness [He makua ka ona no ka palaualelo].

II. KALAUPAPA, THE EARLY YEARS: 1866 TO 1873

LEPROSY WAS IDENTIFIED in Hawaiʻi as early as 1835 and began to spread slowly through the islands. Hawaiians called it maʻi pake, or "Chinese disease," from a common belief that it was introduced by Chinese immigrants. By the early 1860s Hawaiʻi residents considered it a serious health problem and looked to the government for help. In December 1864 the legislature passed an Act to Prevent the Spread of Leprosy, and on January 3, 1865, King Kamehameha V signed it into law. In the months that followed, the Board of Health developed a plan of action to implement the new law. The basic strategy was simple: identify everyone who had leprosy and isolate them from the general population.

The Board of Health selected Kalihi Kai as the site for a hospital on Oʻahu for those in early stages of the disease and the Kalaupapa peninsula on Molokaʻi for those in the advanced stages. The hospital also included a detention station, where patients were evaluated and processed. During the late 1800s the hospital/detention station moved several times. The Kalihi facility closed in 1875 and temporary buildings were constructed on King Street in Honolulu near the police station. The Board of Health opened a new facility on the shoreline of Kakaʻako on December 12, 1881, but when the site proved unsuitable, they moved their hospital/detention operations back to their original location in Kalihi in 1889. These changes are reflected in the newspaper articles that follow. The place names Kalihi, sometimes Kalihi Kai, and Kakaʻako appear at different times, depending on the years the articles were published.

In the Hawaiian-language newspapers the Kalihi and Kakaʻako detention stations are often called pa maʻi, which means "patient enclosure." The receiving area that was established with the first Kalihi hospital in 1865 was originally a pa nui or "large enclosure." The term pa nui later became pa maʻi and was used for the various detention stations. During the late 1800s two other terms, kahua hoʻomalu and kahua hoʻomalu lepera, were used respectively for "quarantine station" and leprosy quarantine station."

The Hawaiian-language newspaper articles in this section describe the early years of the settlement, prior to the arrival of Father Damien in 1873. They are listed chronologically under the following headings:

Establishing a Leprosy Settlement
Schooner *Warwick:* Kuna Wawiki
Leprosy Patients: Nā Maʻi Lepera
Patient Helpers: Nā Kōkua o Nā Maʻi
Additional Early History

Establishing a Leprosy Settlement

In the two letters that follow, both written in 1865, the writers voice the fears of the general public and add their support to the solution recommended by the Board of Health: remove those with leprosy from their homes and isolate them, either at Kalihi hospital on Oʻahu or at Kalaupapa on Molokaʻi.

Ka Nupepa Kuokoa. 2 FEBRUARY 1865. P. 2.
Mai Pake ino ma Honouliuli i Ewa. Serious Case of Leprosy in Honouliuli in ʻEwa.
Dear *Nupepa Kuokoa.* Greetings.

The number of Chinese here in Honouliuli has swelled, and they are known by name, four men and one woman. Kuahihine, Hinaʻā, Kalei, and ʻŌʻino are the men, and Paewahine is the one woman. And because of this, I have great hope to clarify in the *Nupepa* that perhaps some people have been designated from the Board of Health as sanitizers to extract the bad foliage from the earth as this terrible plant has been growing among us here.

I have been living in the district [moku aina] of ʻEwa here for six months now, from June of 1864 to this November. I can see well these people who have been afflicted with leprosy [mai Pake]. They live mixed together with those who have not been afflicted with this disease; and they freely go here and there and they go around defiling the doorways of the people; and they bathe themselves in our headwaters [poo wai] because their houses are near the water flowing down to where we are. That is how my thoughts have become so saddened as we eat well on the oceanside of this place, and it is as if the poison of the ʻauhuhu plant has entered the mouths of all the people here. This is my opinion.

So, I ask the Board of Health, who takes care of the health of these people? Who watches over them so that they do not live among all the people? I think it should probably be the Queen's Hospital [Halemai o ka Moi Wahine: Hospital of the Queen] or the Board of Health [Papa Ola]. I think that the board should come and seize them and take them into its hands so that the terrible disease does not spread here in Honouliuli.

In my opinion, Hawaiʻi is nearly full of leprosy patients [mai Pake], and they are almost more than a hundred in number, if they were to be counted properly. Regarding this point, I ask myself, "Where did this disease come from?" Some people say, "It has come from within those afflicted with leprosy [mai Lebera] and from the ground, entering into the people and afflicting them."

Perhaps it is true or not; however, this much is known: there has not been a leprosy ship [moku mai Pake] that has arrived among us, so we should not assume that is the origin of this terrible sickness. If there has been a ship that has arrived, I am not aware of it.

Ka Nupepa Kuokoa. 7 OCTOBER 1865. P. 3.
Hanaio Ka Mai Pake Ma Hawaii Nei. Leprosy Takes Hold Here in Hawai'i.
Dear Captains of the *Nupepa Kuokoa*, H. H. P. and L. H. K. Greetings with my hopes to tell the public about these words found above regarding the seriousness of leprosy [mai pake] here in Hawai'i.

This disease is serious and has spread here in these islands. Its spread has not ceased in this nation, as among the people of Canaan [Kanaana] in days past, who worked to isolate those families afflicted with this disease, as seen in the Holy Bible in Deuteronomy [Buke Baibala ma Oihanakahuna]. This is what is seen among the Chinese. They have tossed those who have been afflicted with this disease into the sea, whether they are men who have been afflicted or women. They all have been tossed into the sea, and this is the only reason it has not spread among the people. Oh no! Oh no! How tragic for us that there have been so many who have come down with this sickness, not quite a hundred if counting from Hawai'i to Ni'ihau, and those who are afflicted live miserably and their countenances have become deformed.

This disease is spreading among those with white skin, the Caucasian locals [haole kamaaina]. Last week Monday, I saw a white person of 'Ulupalakua [Maui] who came down with this disease. I saw him from my veranda at Kaluaihākōkō [in Kīhei, Maui]. Oh, my goodness! We should be doubly concerned for the Hawaiian race [lahui Hawaii] and the white race of America [lahui ili keokeo o Maleka]. These are my thoughts for you all. Let us look to the words of the *Au Okoa* where I have seen that the succeeding King Kamehameha V has set aside Kalaupapa and Kalawao and Waikolu on Moloka'i as the places for these diseased people to live.

There is also a large walled yard [kahua pa nui] in Kalihi on O'ahu, where those afflicted with this disease reside. These words in the *Au Okoa* are appropriate so that there can be a cessation of the disease so that the Hawaiian race can benefit. Upon hearing these words, this white man referred to above encourages those who are indebted to him, myself being one who is indebted to him at his store, that his days have also come. How terrible for this resident of the place that the day of trouble has passed over him.

However, according to some people, this encouragement is not needed as he had already known of his problem, and has granted loans to people without declaring a due date for these to be paid off and having signed off on them too. So, all of you of Lāhaina, let us be aware that these two months are term of the loans.

To the King Kamehameha V, the Successor of the Hawaiian Islands [Hawaii Pae Moku]. Be aware and call upon your guards to stand and take these people to those places that you have seen in the *Au Okoa* so that your people may be spared in this blazing fire [ahi lapulapu].

With great affection to the Successor King of Hawai'i. D. H. L. Haku'ole. Polonuiuka, Lāhaina, Maui, SEPT. 29, 1865.

Ke Au Okoa. 26 SEPTEMBER 1867. P. 2.
Kaahele Ma Molokai. Helu 2. Ka Apana O Honomuni. Tour of Moloka'i. Number 2. The District of Honomuni.

This district of Honomuni is a good district, extending from Kainalu to 'Aha'inoiki, with seven areas in it: 1. Kainalu, 2. Kawaikapu, 3. Kamanoni, 4. Honomuni, 5. Kūli'ulā, 6. 'Aha'ino 1, 7. 'Aha'ino 2. Regarding Kainalu: This was a very famous place in ancient times. It was said that Haku A. Pākī was born here in recent years, and that it was desolate with no inhabitants. When the locals of Waikolu, Kalawao, Kawaluna, Polapola, Māhulili, and Pōhakuloa relocated and becames residents of Kainalu, the district of Honomuni became almost full with people and the place they had known became a home for leprosy patients (the Chinese disease) [home no na Lepela (mai Pake)]. Kainalu became greatly inhabited, a good place, and in this district of Honomuni was found a good place with the lifestyle being more like whites [haole] with homes adorned with plants. And in this place of Kainalu, there is a good school and a good lifestyle, where the people live rightly as those in Poni'ōhua. The same also for those in Kawaikapu, very good with fertile soil, as in Kamanoni and Honomuni, which has the most fertile land of the district. It was a famous place in ancient times as a favorite spot of some chiefs and kings of Moloka'i, such as Ha'alo'u, the father of L. Ha'alelea and T. Ha'alilio, the famous ones admired who recently passed. Ha'alo'u is survived by Nā'ea. In this land is a large taro field [loi] belonging to Ha'alo'u, with an announcement put out to all the people of Moloka'i to come and work. Pu'ikuhawai is the name of the taro field, in which lots of people who love the land work, such as Kanakaokai and others who have leased the land. I have heard it was not yet expired when the tax collector, Ilae Nāpōhaku, was there. There is a pond on the land and the meeting house is filled there with people who love God and who always meet in the morning on Wednesdays and Fridays. One big event that occurs there is the Bible school to expound on its content, with Kanakaokai as the leader.

» [Before the arrival of the first patients on the Kalaupapa peninsula, the Board of Health offered to relocate the local residents, or kama'aina, who wanted to move. This article, which was written in 1867, details the relocation of Kalaupapa residents to the Kona side of the island. Most of them went to the land division of Kainalu. Although the article doesn't mention it, the Board of Health initially did not require all of the original residents to move and a number of them remained in their homes.]

When the Board of Health decided to establish a leprosy settlement, they looked for a site that was not only isolated, but one that had the natural resources to support a Hawaiian community. The board expected the patients to be self-sufficient. They wanted them to practice the subsistence activities that took place throughout the Hawaiian Islands. The Kalaupapa peninsula and its coastal valleys were not only remote, but already home to thriving fishing and farming communities. A freshwater stream flowed into the ocean year-round through Waikolu valley on the windward side of the peninsula. Residents there farmed taro, or kalo, while sweet potatoes, or 'uala, were grown on the leeward side of the peninsula. Like taro, sweet potatoes were a staple in the Hawaiian diet, but unlike taro, which needs flowing fresh water, sweet potatoes thrive in dry sandy soil.

When the whaling industry escalated in the Pacific in the 1840s, the whaling fleet used the Hawaiian Islands as a supply depot for fresh food. Their preference for starch was Irish potatoes, 'uala kahiko, which were soon a major export crop, especially on Maui, but they also bought sweet potatoes. Kalaupapa was one of the major producers. Demand for sweet potatoes increased substantially during the gold rush of 1849, when California markets were overwhelmed with the demand for food supplies. The export market at Kalaupapa was strong until 1851 when California potato production caught up with demand. Commercial sales of sweet potatoes and other produce declined, but Kalaupapa had demonstrated it was a viable venue for large-scale farming.

The Kalaupapa peninsula extends approximately two miles into the ocean, a unique geographical feature on Moloka'i. Its windward side is rocky and exposed to the trade winds, while its leeward side is more protected, encouraging the growth of coral reefs and the development of white sand beaches. Each of these environments attracts different types of marine life, most of which were sources of food for Hawaiians, so fishing was excellent around the entire peninsula. Residents fished from rocky points for giant trevally (ulua), used their canoes to net schools of big-eyed scad (akule), hooked bonefish ('ōi'o) near the black sand beach at the bottom of the cliff trail, and speared octopus (he'e) and many species of reef fish off the white sand beaches. They picked limpets ('opihi) off the rocks, gathered edible seaweed (limu), and caught spiny lobsters (ula) and slipper lobsters (ula papa). They also gathered salt (pa'akai) from Ho'olehua at the tip of the peninsula, where salt water in rocky depressions (kaheka) evaporates in the hot summer sun. Salt was a vital component for preserving food, and Kalaupapa was the only place on the Ko'olau coast that produced it in quantity. All things considered, the Board of Health believed the opportunity for the patients to be as self-sufficient as the original residents was good. On Saturday, January 6, 1866, they sent the first group of twelve leprosy patients to Kalaupapa.

In their report to the legislature in May of 1866, the Board of Health identified the attractive features of the Kalaupapa peninsula and its coastal valleys and summarized the actions they had taken prior to the first landing and during the four months that followed.

Ka Nupepa Kuokoa. 12 MAY 1866. P. 4.

Palapala Hoike O Ka Papa Ola, I Ka Ahaolelo o Ka Makahiki 1866. E na 'Lii a me ka Poeiko-hoia. Report of the Board of Health, in the Legislature of the Year 1866. To all Nobles and Representatives.

According to the law passed in the last legislative session called A Law to Prevent the Spread of Leprosy [He Kanawai e Kaohi ai ka laha ana o ka Mai Lepera], the Board of Health reports as follows:

After having decided on the aforementioned law, the board was convened by the political minister of that time to consider the important matters taken up by the board. After a thorough discussion, it was decided to purchase a parcel of land situated in Pālolo on the island of Oʻahu to build a hospital according to Article 4 of the law. But when the board took up this item of business, the landowners on the ocean side of Pālolo whose lands are adjacent to the river flowing down from Pālolo raised objections as, according to them, the water would become polluted, which would cause problems to the health of the people. The board was of the opinion that this was reasonable, so they searched for another location where nearby landowners could not make accusations. But a suitable land was not quickly found as fresh water was the most important factor in consideration. After a long search, a site was found in Kalihi adjacent to the stream, and buildings were built there suitable for accommodating sixty leprosy patients [mai Lepera], in addition to other facilities, such as the kitchen, showers, and the cottage for the manager. It was clear that this place was suitable for this venture since these facilities were far off from the homes of other people and it was near Honolulu. The breezes of the area are fine and the members of the board do not have a long way to go with the supervisors and doctors, those who take care of the health of the patients.

As the board had organized this facility for leprosy patients [mai Lepera] to keep watch over them to attempt to treat those who had just contracted the disease, the board began to build living quarters for leprosy patients [poe Lepera] on the north side [aoao akau] of the island of Molokaʻi. The current president of the board made two trips there and purchased two kuleana parcels in the valleys of Waikolu and Wainiha [Wailēʻia], and these were converted to kuleana parcels for the board. The government owns most of the land, which was first leased to a number of businesses, and presently these have fallen to the ownership of the board.

That land is suitable for the planned activities. It took some time to land from out to sea due to the surf, and there are no roads leading out to the other areas. There are two streams that flow continuously, the taro fields are large, and the local breezes are constant there. There are lots of wide open spaces for raising animals, and the soil is good for raising crops of all types. These lands are situated at a point [lae] surrounded by the ocean on three sides and on the south side are high cliffs [pali kiekie] with one trail [ala] heading down to this place on a 1,800-foot-high cliff.

When the kuleana lands were purchased at this place, the board appointed Mr. R. W. [Rudolph William] Meyer as supervisor [luna] over the business, and they appreciate him for his efforts in carrying out the work envisaged. Some of the lands have been paid for in cash (and the expenditures have been reported in the budget attached to this report), and some lands were swapped for government lands. In recent days, the board purchased and came into ownership of a large tract of land called Makanalua, which is land belonging to L. Haʻalelea, who died recently. This land is adjacent to the land acquired for the leprosy patients [mai Lepera]. When the lands were purchased, the government acquired the majority of the lands on that point [lae], and the few people who are situated at the harbor of Kalaupapa are far from where the leprosy patients [lepera] reside, so there should be no reason to come into contact with them. Those who do so can be blamed for that.

A supervisor [luna] was obtained to oversee the planned work to provide rest for these people who are pitied. He is located on that land, where he lives, and it is through him that the board is made aware of the conditions of the leprosy patients [Lopera: Lepera].

By order of the treasury minister, the accountants of each district from Hawai'i to Ni'ihau reported the number of people who are thought to have contracted leprosy, and here it is:

Hawai'i	75
Maui, Moloka'i, and Lāna'i	112
O'ahu	80
Kaua'i and Ni'ihau	7
Total	274

As the hospital in Kalihi was prepared and furnished, the board began the great job of selecting and transporting those who are said to have come down with leprosy [mai Lepera] to that location. The leprosy patients [Lepera] were ordered to stay on the island of O'ahu to wait for the hospital. Earlier it was thought that the people would resist this law, but they did not do so, as if those who were branded as leprosy patients [Lepera] wanted to be subjected to this law. There were more people who came forward than those who were ordered and greater in number than what the accountants [Luna Helu] of the districts [Apana] reported. Most of them will be seen on the island of O'ahu. Those who showed up at the leprosy hospital [Halemai Lepera] were attended to by the doctor, and according to these words copied from his report to the board on the 2nd of March 1866, and here it is:

"Since the beginning of the hospital in the month of November last, 165 people have come and have been seen by me; 68 of them were released as they were seen to have come down with some disease other than leprosy and 104 were remanded for treatment. Among this 104, 47 were taken to Moloka'i according to the order. Twenty-eight [28] had skin blight [kakani (kakane) o ka ili] that had the appearance of leprosy, but this was not really leprosy, so according to your order, they had been remanded to the hospital and treated. They are in good health at present and returned to their own places with medicine. Twenty-six [26] remain and are being treated at the hospital. The remainder are from the island of O'ahu."

All leprosy patients [Lepera] seen on the island of O'ahu have been seen and treated, but it is thought that some went into hiding and are being hidden by friends. They are currently being searched for.

There are 69 leprosy patients [mai Lepera] from Maui who are thought to have died from leprosy in West Maui, but those on the east side are being brought in. When Maui is done, then they take on Hawai'i residents. It is the hope of the board that this job will be done within the next four to five months.

The total number of people who have been tended to by the doctor in Kalihi up until now is 234, 79 of whom have been released, not having contracted leprosy, and 57 have been sent to live on Moloka'i. Others are known to have contracted a strange sickness not leprosy. The rest are at Kalihi Hospital [Halemai o Kalihi] where they are being treated.

As a result of careful consideration by the board, they purchased some cattle, sheep, goats, and other things for the superintendent at Moloka'i so that the funds would not be lost afterward.

We are happy to report that indeed these people are greatly blessed by being remanded to the care of the government. They are in good health and they live comfortably as previously they had been living in small shelters and not attended to, and were ashamed to go out. But at this time, they go out in the open in town. We have been told that those who have gone to Moloka'i are comfortable with the idea. Those who are in good health and are building dwellings and have begun to farm with the intention to remain, they say that they are comfortable with the idea of staying there, and so it appears. Some parents [makua] have been allowed to go and stay with their children [keiki], and so, too, wives and husbands to stay with their partners [kokoolua].

Doctor Hillebrand [Kauka Hilebarani: Dr. William Hillebrand], the commissioner of the king in China [Komisina a ka Moi ma Kina], was ordered to go and inspect the leprosy hospitals in all places that he could go to and report back to the board regarding their activities and treatment of the disease in those places. One thousand dollars [$1,000] was set aside to pay the expenses of the doctor. He also stated in his report the things he had witnessed, and there was nothing out of the ordinary. It was just as we had seen regarding this disease as at these places, the leprosy patients [mai Lepera] had not been attended to and cared for.

The board wanted to purchase or lease a ship to transport patients, but none was acquired. Later, the two-masted ship [moku kialua] *Warwick* was leased in the amount of $250 a month, but as transport under the lease is slow, it was purchased. The board took ownership of that ship at the cost of $800. It is hoped that the work will go smoothly from here on out.

The land that was purchased in Pālolo belongs to the board, but will be used for other functions of the government.

It is not yet clear regarding this disease if it is contagious or not. Here are the words of the doctor regarding this:

"It is not totally clear to me whether leprosy patients [mai Lepera] can be cured since they have been taken to Moloka'i to be quarantined from the public, but some of them need to be left in Kalihi for this to be determined. The nature of the sickness is not yet totally clear, whether it is contagious or not. Among those who have come in Kalihi Hospital, only three of them admitted that the leprosy disease was found among their family. I believe that this disease is not contagious as long as people do not come into close contact with the leprosy patient."

In these two years, there has been no plague in the country. Some have come forward to report that they had little bumps on them, but upon observation it was found not to be the case. Vaccinations were held and the best people in each place were selected to carry out this job. There are only a few people who were not vaccinated on the island of O'ahu as that job was done by Mr. Doiron (Alfred) [Apale], the vaccination supervisor of the island.

The medicines that were ordered were obtained in each location by the hands of those who had agreed to give these to the poor. It was thought that lives were saved and that some were comforted by this action.

In the reports of the doctor who oversees the storage of medicines in Honolulu, where the women who are said by law to "reduce the damage" and the like, it is known that a number of women have come forward in the last two years from the time the law was decided and enforced regarding passports. There are fewer girls who have come to Honolulu to conduct prostitution [hooka-makama]. Some women of that type have been treated in prison and a separate hospital needs to be constructed for those people.

The construction of an insane asylum [Hale Malama Pupule] is another matter of business pertaining to the health of the public. According to the law, these things have been charged to the political minister, but due to his own views, he consulted with the members of the board. They report with great interest that a large piece of land has been obtained that is suitable, where this facility will be built far off, and it is presently being built. It is hoped that in no time the facility will be completed and that it will be organized to house the insane. At this time, they are being accommodated at the jail [Halewai] and the prison [Halepaahao], places that are not well-suited to take care of these people who have been afflicted with the dreadful disease of insanity [pupule]. It is where they become more insane. It is hoped by the board that the legislature will set aside funding for the insane asylum based on good, Christian generosity.

God Save the King [E Ola Ka Moi I Ke Akua]

For the Board, F. W. Hutchison, President of the Board of Health.

EXPENSES OF THE BOARD OF HEALTH IN THE PAST TWO YEARS ENDING ON MARCH 31, 1866.

In order to reduce the spread of leprosy [mai Lepera]:

Land in Pālolo	$1,002.50
Expenses of Dr. Hillebrand	1,000.00
Land on Moloka'i	3,471.75
Kalihi, O'ahu	665.00
The enclosed facilities, etc., Kalihi	3,702.03
Furnishings for the facility in Kalihi	764.50
Various expenses of the hospital in Kalihi, to pay the doctor, the supervisor, medicine, the workers, etc., from the 12th of Nov. 1865 until March 31, 1866	282.75
Expenses for food and clothing in Kalihi	1,039.15
Expenses for food, clothes, medicine, farm hands, canoes, nets, carriages, cattle, etc., for those residing on Moloka'i	1,801.43
Expenses for animals kept on Moloka'i—cattle, sheep, goats, etc.	450.00
Salary of the supervisor on Moloka'i, four months	133.37
To lease the ship *Warwick*	1,000.00
[Total]	$16,012.48

Schooner *Warwick:* Kuna Wawiki

In their report of the Board of Health for the Legislature of 1866, the board noted that it had first leased, then purchased the schooner *Warwick* to transport passengers and cargo between Honolulu and the Kalaupapa peninsula. The *Warwick* was one of many packet schooners in Hawai'i, sailing ships that traveled regular routes between ports and landings, carrying passengers, freight, and mail. In Hawaiian the *Warwick* was variously called ka moku kialua o Wawiki, or "the two-masted ship *Warwick*," ka moku kuna Wawiki, or "the schooner ship *Warwick*," and ke kuna Wawiki, or "the schooner *Warwick*."

Schooners like the *Warwick* were also called coasters. As one of a large fleet of interisland coasters, the *Warwick* picked up livestock, produce, and other provisions and transported them to the major harbors in Honolulu, Lāhaina, Hilo, and Kōloa (Kaua'i). These supplies supported the whaling industry and were also transshipped to other countries, including the United States. In its July 2, 1857, edition, the *Pacific Commercial Advertiser*, which was published in English, featured an article called "Our Coasting Fleet," and offered the following observation about the *Warwick*.

"The little *Warwick* is as smart for her inches as the best of them; and the *Maui Hikina* is a fine vessel for one 'built in the woods.' They are both well-managed craft, and often available in times of need, in running to and from Honolulu and Lahaina. The above are the regular packet schooners that can be depended upon as touching Lahaina."

With dozens of schooners plying Hawaiian waters in the mid-1800s, it was happenstance that the *Warwick* sailed into history by delivering the first patients to the Kalaupapa peninsula. She continued to service the leprosy settlement until September 3, 1867, when she sank off Lāna'i. The articles that follow tell the saga of the *Warwick*, beginning in 1865 with an item in a shipping column called *Honolulu Harbor* and ending in 1881.

Ka Nupepa Kuokoa. 9 FEBRUARY 1865. P. 3.
Awa o Honolulu. Honolulu Harbor.
    Jan. 28. The *Warwick* returned from Moloka'i with forty-five sheep, six pigs, ten containers of butter, and ten passengers with their belongings.

Ka Nupepa Kuokoa. 10 MARCH 1866. P. 2.
Hunahuna Mea Hou O Hawaii Nei. No Ka Mai Pake. News Items from around Hawai'i. Regarding Leprosy.
    Last week we heard about the restarting of the schooner [moku kuna] *Warwick* [Wawiki], which was bringing back leprosy patients [mai Pake] to the leprosy hospital [hale mai lepera] in Kalihi.

Ka Nupepa Kuokoa. 5 JANUARY 1867. P. 3.
Moku Kuna Wawiki!! The Schooner *Warwick!!*
    This ship goes regularly each and every week to Moloka'i from Honolulu. And if anyone has cargo or is a passenger, then ask for the captain [Kapena], Kahalemake.

Ke Au Okoa. 12 SEPTEMBER 1867. P. 3.
No Ka Ili Ana O Ke Kuna Warwick. Concerning the Wreck of the Schooner *Warwick*.
    When the steamship [mokuahi] *Kilauea* arrived last Saturday morning,

the news came about the wreck of the schooner *Warwick*. This schooner was wrecked, according to what we heard, on Tuesday of last week, at Mānele, Lāna'i. In recent days this schooner traveled regularly between this town [Honolulu] and Moloka'i, under the command of Kahalemake; and it regularly escorted those afflicted by leprosy to Kalaupapa. But there it is. Its plowing [palau ana] through the waves of our local seas has ended.

Pacific Commercial Advertiser. 14 SEPTEMBER 1867. P. 2.
    Coaster Lost. The schooner *Warwick*, of about 20 tons burthen, ran ashore on the southwest point of Lanai, on the night of September 3, while bound from Molokai to Honolulu. The native captain was asleep below at the time, having left the vessel in charge of the mate. It is supposed that the latter as well as the sailors also went to sleep, which is sufficient cause for the accident. The vessel belonged to Capt. J. Brown, of the tug *Pele*, and will be a total loss, as she drifted to sea and sank in deep water.
» [The *Pacific Commercial Advertiser* was published in English.]

Ka Nupepa Kuokoa. 14 SEPTEMBER 1867. P. 3.
    The schooner [Kuna] *Warwick* ran aground at Keaea at Lāna'i one day last week, on September 3, and the Captain Kahalemake came back to Honolulu to report about his encounter last Saturday. It was probably due to the eruption of his leprosy [mai pake] condition. It is a pity, however, that our dear old schooner is now gone from before us.
» [With the loss of the *Warwick*, the Board of Health used other schooners to service Kalaupapa while a new boat was built. Shipwright [kamana kapili moku] Daniel Foster of Foster and Company in Honolulu was contracted for the job. When he completed the twenty-three-ton *Warwick II*, she sailed to Moloka'i on April 15, 1868, and continued making regular runs to Kalaupapa.]

Ke Au Okoa. 16 APRIL 1868. P. 3.
Ke Kuna Warwick. The Schooner *Warwick*.
    We have heard the name of a schooner [Kuna] recently built by Foster and Co. [Foster ma] for Capt. Jake Brown, aboard the steamship [mokuahi] *Pele*. Its construction was deft and fine. We have also been told that it will be sailed to all of the ports that the first *Warwick* regularly traveled to during its days.

Ka Nupepa Kuokoa. 2 MAY 1868. P. 3
Paapu I Ka Uahi. Covered With Smoke.
    In these recent days, the days when the volcanic smoke [uahi pele] was rising, the *Warwick* sailed from Honolulu on Monday, April 20. Due to the extreme density of the smoke, Moloka'i was not seen, and they simply drifted quietly for a time on the surface of the ocean with the belief that they were below Lāna'i. For Tuesday and Wednesday they were at sea without sight of land. On Thursday morning they met with another ship, *Hawaii Mauna Loa*, forty or more miles north of Moloka'i. They asked that ship about the land and were told, "You almost passed into the deep ocean." However, the bow was guided to return to Moloka'i. Early Friday morning they arrived at Pūko'o. There was no trouble with food, but if they had spent another night at sea, they would have

run out of oil. Rev. A. O. Forbes [Forebe] was the only passenger aboard. According to him, they barely survived, but he was grateful for the fine quality of the ship. Perhaps the captain, or maybe the compass [panana], was responsible for the blunder.

Ka Nupepa Kuokoa. 19 SEPTEMBER 1868. P. 2.
Ka Moku Kuna Hou. The New Schooner.

D. Foster and Co. [D. Poka ma] has completed their newly built schooner. The masts are up now, and here they are standing tall. The sails go in, the rudder appears, and then what will be the port? The ship is an image of excellence in appearance, short and stout, but it is the younger sibling of the *Helena* that broke and also the likeness of the *Warwick* that is sailing now. They were built together, but that one [the *Warwick*] was completed earlier and already pushed into voyaging upon the waves of Pailolo Channel. That one has been admired for its excellence at sea, and such will soon be the case for this one, because there is nothing irregular about it. It is all as one.

Ke Au Okoa. 6 MAY 1869. P. 2.
Ke Kuna Warwick. The Schooner *Warwick.*

It was heard earlier that the schooner *Warwick* had wrecked by Lānaʻi. On the last schooners that arrived, the news came that it has been hauled ashore for the damaged parts to be worked on. This is second of the schooners with this same name that wrecked, almost at the same place, and it was under the very same captain.

Ke Au Okoa. 12 MAY 1870. P. 2.
Hoao E Lawe Aihue I Ke Kuna "Warwick." Attempt to Steal the Schooner *Warwick.*

Last Monday night, just before two oʻclock at night, an attempt was made to steal the schooner *Warwick* by three men, with the plan to sail it away. The schooner was moored at the wharf at ʻĀinahou [in Honolulu Harbor], between the *Pele* and the bark [moku kiapa] *Agate.* The captain, John Bull [Keoni Bulu], his wife, and the two sailors were all deeply asleep in the cabin of the ship. These people who took the schooner, they stole a skiff from the brig *Francisco*, and right after, they cut the lines tying the ship to the wharf. Two sat in the skiff to tow the ship, and one was on the ship to steer it. When they reached the lighthouse [hale kukui] outside [of the harbor], the rolling of the ship woke the captain from his sleep. He went up to the deck, but when he got to the door, he was surprised to find that it was locked. He grabbed a piece of iron lying in the rear cabin of the ship, and with it he broke through the door. Perhaps because these wrongdoers were afraid of the people within the ship, they left the ship and sailed away on their skiff. As for John Bull, the captain, he quickly released the anchor, and then he set down his own skiff to follow after the wrongdoers, but he did not catch them. So he did not find out who had stolen his ship. The ship was full of squash [ipupu] and cooked taro [pai ai], and some other things, so if the deed of the wrongdoers had succeeded, then they would have had enough food for a long voyage. However, there was no water. It has been surmised that foreign sailors [poe luina haole] aboard another ship in port were the ones who attempted this robbery. It is believed that they will indeed be found, and they will be punished in accordance with the fine for their wrong-doing.

Ka Lahui Hawaii. 6 SEPTEMBER 1877. P. 3.
Halia mau ke aloha. (He Leta Walohia.) Love is remembered. (A Sad Letter)
Dear *Ka Lahui Hawaii.* Greetings.

While I was listening to the gentle rustling of the misty breezes of the Koʻolau cliffs, moving along with the ocean winds, the ocean provided no invitation of love calling me to come back. This is the reason why I utter these words:

> "Let us come back together
> While love is still here
> My companion that I hold hands with is love
> My partner of the evening."

While the tears were continually welling up in me like a spring, these eyelashes became drenched, completely soaked in water and my heart began to boil, pained as the blood was pumped an ounce at a time throughout my whole body, and the point of my pen spilled out its black ink all over the writing pad without stopping. In correspondences, we exchange thoughts in sad columns, which causes me once again to utter:

> "Love is dark, oh Kānehoa
> The cold does not overcome the heat"

I am cold with love that lingers for you all, the multitudes reading this. I send my love to my birthplace: Kohala-iki, Kohalanui, Kohala in the ʻĀpaʻapaʻa Rain [Ia Kohala-iki, Kohalanui, Kohala ua apaapaa], to Pili and Kalāhikiola, the two mountains that go together. There are two problems that linger here: Separation and returning. My birthplace: From the borders of Keahualono, listening to the rustling of the ʻŌlauniu wind of Kekaha all the way to Honokeā at the border of Honopuʻe. I am hunched over with love that comes to me, save me.

It is Kohala in the day of my pride, of which it is said, "There is no handsome one that just goes alone in Kohala [Aohe ui hele wale o Kohala]." My birthplace in the whispering sea [kai hawanawana] of Kawaihae, love tears at me on the inside like a dog from the coconut grove at Waikuʻi, where my love that lingers is satiated, all the way to the kou tree grove of Onouli. The house of love is dark and obscure where my love dwells at my birthplace, and this is why I utter the words:

> "The land of my birth
> It is for you that I sing
> A good land, etc."

I send out my love to my friends. I shall not forget my love for you all, my friends, from the sun's rising at Kumukahi, all the way to the hanging ladder [haka lewa] at Nuʻalolo. [Nuʻalolo was famous for a rope ladder that hung over a sea cliff.] Come back, my parents of righteousness, along with my teachers who raised me, as well as those who endured the rains of summer with me, bundling together in the Kūkalahale Rain of Honolulu where my love and I traveled, along with our son. It is there where I rested comfortably with all those who came and visited my home until Pāmanō and I were taken to the temple (hospital). [The word heiau, or "temple," was used here and was followed by the word halemai, or "hospital," in parentheses.] As I was resting at the hospital [halemai], the doctor came and looked me over and pointed at Diamond Head [Leahi] and said, "You go to Kalawao." [E hele oe ma Kalawao.] At that time a terrible dread came over me called Ichabod whose beauty had left him! [Ichabod in the Bible is associated with loss.] There was nothing else to do. We were all left standing at the pier by the sea, exchanging farewells with the crowd while wiping our noses and tears, which causes me to say,

> "The tears spill over
> The clouds cry"

I stepped onboard with great pain, bearing down as I made my way onto the deck of the slithering eel of Kalawao [ka puhi olali o Kalawao], the schooner, the *Warwick*, the object of fear and agony for those who are being segregated, and that is when the ship made its way out gently, with sails unfurled, disappearing as if on its way to America, with [Captain] John Bull [Keonipulu] at the helm [ma ka hoe]. I turned inland to look at the capital [Honolulu] disappearing, and I cried! Offshore winds blew our way and the sails filled, and I remembered these lines of a mele:

> "The wind blows
> Blows, blows, blows
> Changing the sails
> And the ship has gone."

There is love of the family that never ends, and if there are prophecies, they shall end. For you, my father who has two children, here I am, your loving son, about whom it is said, "the glory of youth is have a first born son," and as James says, "If my son is not returned to me, my gray hair shall go with him to the grave." I ask the heavens that your days be lengthened on the land, until the heavens open the doors and open the pathway for his people to return home, which causes me to utter:

> "Chant to Jehovah
> Victorious blessing
> A powerful general
> The enemies are vanquished"

There is love of children, a very heavy burden of love, that has been placed on me, which I carry everywhere desiring to have this burden taken from me, for which I utter the words:

"I am troubled inside with love
When it comes my body runs cold
I presume it to be the pains of thought
I am troubled because of your voice"

And for the past few days, I have shaken hands and met pleasantly with my dear friends, Ephraim Kanoe, P. W. Kaʻawa, and all friends. And those of us living here in this Koʻolau home, we cry aloud for our love for our place of birth [one oiwi], our friends, the family and everyone. So it is I with a heart pained severely.

—D. Puna. Makanalua, Kalaupapa, AUG. 22, 1877.

Ka Nupepa Kuokoa. 31 AUGUST 1878. P. 2.
Na Mea Hou o ka Panalaau o Kalawao. News from the Colony at Kalawao.

This has been something that your correspondent has been scrutinizing in the far reaches of all that is new, and so it is to this extent that I apply my pen and report to the general public.

The total number of patients from the 7th of July 1878 who have been brought to this shore, gentlemen and ladies alike, from the last time up to the 23rd of August last, is thirty-three patients. This causes me to recount the words, "As the torrents of floods flow, no debris is left."

Sailed away. Since Oct. 1877 with winter raging. This causes me to remember:

Who could not have compassion
We two were drenched there
Pained and tormented in the heart
In the Kilihune rain of the uplands

Sower Boys: The hands of the boys are fertile, reaping the rewards of their labor in planting tobacco [paka]. There is lots of tobacco, but these boys are not infected with disease. The best is Mr. E. Kahului, one who is infected, who has earned $100 or more planting watermelons [ipu ai] in the past four months. It is not for me to praise, but for the turkeys to say let them continue to grow until they are plump.

Total Number of Ladies Transported: When the schooner, the *Warwick,* returned, our documents were loaded on that return voyage, with 184 letters for our families on the 15th of August last.

Yearning: In recent days a man was overcome with hysterics and ran off and jumped over the cliff as a result of someone having worn his blue dress. He escaped injury, however. How everyone laughed all around Hawaiʻi.

A Pillar of Fire to the Clouds. The church here in Kalaupapa was recently completed, with its beautiful spire, expertly made by J. S. Kanakaʻole, one of the colleagues in trouble. It has not yet been dedicated.

Arrived: On this arrival of the schooner, the *Warwick,* Mr. Loke was also aboard to take care of the affairs of the Board of Health, along with his wife. They arrived in good health. The sea was a bit rough with lots of sea spray, with the trade wind [moae] trampled waves of the Kaiwi Channel, with our deceased colleague of this land, Kopena. It is better than nothing, otherwise our windward [Koolau] home would be lacking any news.

—Kauhakō, Kalaupapa, AUGUST 23, 1878.

Ka Nupepa Kuokoa. 31 AUGUST 1878. P. 2.
Ka Mai Lepera. The Leprosy Disease.

It is so pitiful and saddens the heart, the activities of the leprosy disease that is spreading all across our country. There perhaps is no disease as powerful at suppressing the majority of us in the pit of sorrow like this disease. It is rare or perhaps there is no one who has been delivered from this dreadful disease. This disease has not yet reached the proportions of the measles epidemic [mai puupuu Ulalii lua] in 1848, however, or the smallpox epidemic [mai Hebela: literally, Hebrew disease] of 1853 in its speed because it is a disease that moves slowly and stays idle in the body of people. This disease can stay in the body of people for two or three years or more and does not emerge on the outside quickly.

Many years ago the leprosy disease started its spread and in 1864 it really caught on and spread among the people. As a result of realizing this problem the legislature enacted the law of well-known John [Jno.] Wāhiawā, Haleakalā, and Kauwahi, which they promoted before it was ratified, "A Coffin Law for Hawai'i" [He Kanawai Pahu Kupapau no Hawaii nei]. In 1868, the legislature of that session created the "Addendum to Section 1828 of the Civil Code, in which it is stated that a husband or wife being afflicted with leprosy can be cause for divorce if it is seen that it cannot be cured."

In the legislative session of 1870, the law that was passed on the 3rd of January in 1865 was amended by adding a few more sections as rules of the Board of Health.

It was the legislature, too, of 1874 that completed Section 6 of the law that was passed on the 3rd of January 1865.

In the legislative session of 1876 a law was created, "to allow Hawaiian doctors without a license to treat those afflicted with the leprosy disease [E ae ai i na kauka Hawaii e lapaau i ka poe i loohia i ka mai lepera me ka laikini ole]."

In the last legislative session of 1878, the Honorables J. W. Moanauli Jr. and G. B. Palehau introduced bills for acts to return leprosy patients [mai lepera] to their various districts, but these were not passed.

Underlying the things explained above are the rationale and platform that our government officials are fulfilling what was ratified in numerous legislative sessions in the past.

However, we have not yet discussed this matter with the intent to lay blame with the servants of the government in enforcing the law that ordered them to act accordingly. Instead, we express appreciation for the action, since as Paul stated, "Love fulfills the law."

However, what we are talking about is this, that all actions pertaining to our fellow men afflicted with this debilitating disease be done with aloha, with compassion, and with care and not in haste, as if they had committed a high crime worthy of the death penalty, but as patients, separating those who have confirmed cases of the disease from among the masses in quarantine quarters before removing them elsewhere, to segregate them so that we do not "mix the wild taro with the domestic and the white taro with the black [hui kalo i ka nawao a hapala ke kea na ka ele ka ai]." We must also take care of them properly onboard the ship so that their sickness does not spread further with the bitter cold on the harsh waves of the open ocean.

We write these thoughts in agony and sadness, and we join together with the families of those afflicted with this disease in deep affection.

Perhaps there is no one who has not heard this voice of mourning from Hawai'i to Kaua'i over being separated from each other.

It is painful for us to witness on the ocean side of 'Āinahou all the time, the schooner, *Warwick,* making preparations to transport patients. Parents give their last embrace to their children, and children to their parents, husbands to their wives, and wives to their husbands, siblings to siblings, friends to friends, voices of lament and mourning are witnessed as if to tear apart the heavens above.

The legislature of 1878 ratified a grant of $10,000 for doctors permanently residing in Kalawao to treat patients. Therefore, what we are advising is that there must be a kindhearted doctor, a true patriot of Hawai'i, and intelligent man prepared to offer treatment to leprosy patients [poe mai lepera] who double over in the cold of the Mālualua wind of the Ko'olau cliffs of Kalawao and Kalaupapa. Someone who can persevere and desires to obtain what is necessary to deliver people from the disease pit [lua mai].

And may the heavenly power protect and take care of them in the days of pain and sadness while living in that unfamiliar place [aina malihini].

And may that same heavenly power also provide rest in the hearts of the families who sit and mourn for compassion for their families who have been separated. There are many things that we thought to discuss on this platform, but this is probably enough for now.

» [In the paragraph about the *Warwick* the place name 'Āinahou, or "new land," refers to the landfill project on the shore of Honolulu Harbor that created Irwin Park and Piers 8, 9, and 10, where the Aloha Tower stands today. In articles about Kalaupapa, 'Āinahou is often mentioned as the departure point for the *Warwick* and other ships that carried patients to the settlement.]

Ka Nupepa Kuokoa. 17 SEPTEMBER 1881. P. 3.

Over ten leprosy patients [mai lepera] were taken to Kalawao aboard the *Warwick* last Monday. Here are their names: Kealoha, Kaua, Kānehoa, Kamuela, Kela, Kealiko, Kuina, Wili, M. Nāukana, 'Iopa, Paku, Mileka, Uluo'a.

Ko Hawaii Pae Aina. 24 DECEMBER 1881. P. 3.

We are wondering about the schooner *Warwick.* It disappeared and never returned to Honolulu. It left here on November 25. Where is it now?

Leprosy Patients: Nā Ma'i Lepera

The Hawaiian word ma'i has several meanings. One is "disease" and another is "patient," someone receiving medical care. The Hawaiian word for leprosy and leper is lēpela, a loan word from English, but in the Hawaiian-language newspapers lēpela is more commonly spelled lepera and sometimes lebera.

Ma'i lepera, then, means either "leprosy" or "leprosy patient." Writers in the Hawaiian-language newspapers used a variety of terms to refer to leprosy. These are listed below. They also used a variety of terms to refer to leprosy patients, including lepera, ma'i, ma'i ali'i, ma'i lebera, ma'i lepera, ma'i pake, mea ma'i lepera, poe lepera, poe ma'i, poe ma'i lepera, and poe ma'i pake. Throughout the text I used the phrase "leprosy patients" as the translation for all of these terms, but readers interested in the original terms will find them in brackets after each use of "leprosy patients."

The name Hansen's Disease as an alternate term for leprosy does not appear in the Hawaiian-language newspapers and is, therefore, not used in this book. Hansen's Disease, which recognizes Dr. Gerhard Henrik Armauer Hansen, who in 1873 identified *Mycobacterium leprae* as the bacillus that causes leprosy, was not coined until late in the twentieth century.

The pain of a life sentence to Kalaupapa resulted in many descriptive names for leprosy and the settlement, all of which are found in the Hawaiian-language newspapers. In addition to ma'i lepera, Hawaiians coined the following names for leprosy:

1. Enemi kahiko o ko ka honua a pau. Ancient enemy of everyone on Earth.
2. Ka pilikia. The trouble.
3. Kupueu hoopio lahui o Hawaii nei. Nation-extinguishing scamp of Hawai'i.
4. Mai aai. Disease that eats the body.
5. Mai alii. Royal disease, because it spared no one, including royalty.
6. Mai aloha ole. Disease without love.
7. Mai ehaeha o ka lepera. Agonizing disease of leprosy.
8. Mai e kau nuiia nei ka weli e ko ke ao holookoa. Disease that is feared by the rest of the world.
9. Mai e makau loa ia. Disease that is greatly feared.
10. Mai e makau nui ia. Disease that is greatly feared.
11. Mai hoehaeha kino. Disease that agonizes the body.
12. Mai hoehaeha puuwai. Disease that agonizes the heart.
13. Mai hookaawale ohana. Disease that separates families.
14. Mai hookae a ka lehulehu. Disease that destroys so many people.
15. Mai kupua he lepera. Supernatural disease known as leprosy. [Kupua were supernatural beings who could assume more than one form. Perhaps a reference to the change that leprosy inflicts on the body.]
16. Mai lepera hana lokoino. Merciless leprosy.
17. Mai lepera hookae a ka lehulehu. Leprosy disease that destroys so many people.
18. Mai luku weliweli a hookaawale ohana ana. Terribly destructive disease that splits the family apart.
19. Mai mainoino. Dreadful disease.
20. Mai makamaka ole. Disease that leaves you without friends.
21. Mai pake. Chinese disease, from the widespread belief that Chinese immigrants introduced leprosy to Hawai'i.
22. Mai weliweli. Terrifying disease.
23. Mai weliweli loa. Extremely terrifying disease.

Hawaiians also coined the following names for the leprosy settlement.

1. Aina a ka ehaeha, aina o ka ehaeha, aina nei o ka ehaeha. Land of agony.
2. Aina a ka ehaeha e hoopoluluhi mai ana. Land overcast by agony.
3. Aina a ka luuluu. Land of sorrow.
4. Aina hoolaukanaka i na hoa o ka ehaeha. Land where loneliness is dispelled by the friends in agony.
5. Aina hooluhi. Burdensome land.
6. Aina i kau nui ia ka weli. Land that is greatly feared.
7. Aina i noho malihini. Land where strangers live.
8. Aina i weli ia e kakou. Land feared by all of us.
9. Aina i weli nuiia. Land that is greatly feared.
10. Aina kaulana o Kalaupapa. Famous land of Kalaupapa.
11. Aina makamaka ole. Land that leaves you without friends.
12. Aina malihini. Unfamiliar land.
13. Aina no ke aho hope loa o keia ola ana. Land for the final breath of this life.
14. Aina o ka mai lepera or aina o na mai lepera. Land of the leprosy patients.
15. Aina pahaohao. Iron fence (prison) land.
16. Aina pilikia. Troubled land.
17. Aupuni poepoe. Enclosed nation.
18. Awaawa malu o ka make. Shady valley of death.
19. Home kaukaweli o na lepera. Terrifying home of the leprosy patients.
20. Kahua i kau ia ka weli. Settlement that is feared.
21. Kahua mai. Disease settlement
22. Kahua mai lepera. Leprosy settlement.
23. Kahua mai lepera i kau ia ka weli. Leprosy settlement that is feared.
24. Kahua o na mai. Settlement of the patients.
25. Lahui i hoehaeha. Nation of great agony.
26. Luahi o ka make mau loa. Fiery pit [hell] of endless death.
27. Luakupapau hope loa o na kanaka Hawaii. Final grave [corpse pit] of the Hawaiian people.
28. Luakupapau. Literally, "corpse pit," a figurative term for grave. This is a reference to the high number of deaths that occurred almost daily in the settlement.
29. Lua kupapau o ke ola. Grave [corpse pit] of the living.
30. Lua Kupapau hoi e kanu ola ia ai na kanaka Hawaii. Grave [corpse pit] where Native Hawaiians are buried alive.
31. Luakupapau o ka Panalaau. Grave [corpse pit] of the colony.
32. Lua mai o ka make. Patient pit of death.
33. Lua-pihawelu a ke aloha ole. Rag-filled pit without love.
34. Lua puhi o ka ehaeha. Blow hole of agony.
35. Panalaau Lepera. Leprosy colony.
36. Panalaau Mai Lepera. Leprosy patient colony.
37. Wahi a ehaeha i noho ai. Place where agony resides.
38. Wahi malihini. Unfamiliar place.

Patient Helpers: Nā Kōkua o Nā Maʻi

The Board of Health's assumption that patients at Kalaupapa would be self-sufficient proved to be true only for those who were still strong and healthy when they arrived. Leprosy is a debilitating disease that attacks the human body as a chronic bacterial infection. It destroys the body's nerves, slowly causing numbness, which may result in serious injuries because the patient does not feel pain. Disfigurement, the loss of fingers and toes from infection and injuries, and sores are among the deformities for which the disease is so well known. Depending on how advanced the disease was, patients sometimes referred to themselves as poe ikaika, or "strong people," those strong enough to care for themselves, or poe nāwaliwali, or "weak people," those too weak to care for themselves.

When the first patients arrived on January 6, 1866, they were met by Louis Lepart, the first supervisor and at that time the only government employee at the settlement. With no one else there to assist them, the Board of Health allowed helpers who were family members and spouses to accompany the patients. This concession was mentioned briefly in their May 12, 1866, report.

"Some parents [makua] have been allowed to go and stay with their children, and so, too, wives and husbands to stay with their partners [kokoolua]."

Family members and spouses who did not have leprosy but who volunteered to accompany their loved ones were called kōkua, or "helpers." Although other terms, such as ʻōhua, or "attendants," were used for the volunteer helpers, kōkua was most common, a term that is still used today.

Ka Nupepa Kuokoa. 16 MAY 1868. P. 4.

These are the helpers of the patients [kokua o na mai] who have also come by ships 1–22, forty or more, but four have died and their names have been added to the list of patients as was reported in the ninth issue of last 29th of February, with some returning permanently leaving twenty-three, the total number of those residing. The patients live with hardship lacking food. It is almost this entire month that they have gone without eating [ai ole].

» [This excerpt is from an article in chapter II.]

Ka Nupepa Kuokoa. 28 MARCH 1919. P. 8.

He Maʻi Lele Iʻo Anei Ka Maʻi Lepera? Is Leprosy Truly a Contagious Disease?

Mr. Solomon Hanohano. Greetings to you:

Please provide a small space of our "Excellence [Kilohana]," for submitting before your readers and the people my answer and explanations for this question placed above, the question that disturbs the thoughts of the people, and most of all us, the citizens residing in this land of agony [aina o ka ehaeha].

We know the answer of the wise and the scientists [poe naauao ame ka poe akeakamai] concerning this question, which is, "Leprosy is a contagious disease [he maʻi lele ka maʻi lepera]," as supported by the principles and paths of science. However, the answer and explanation that I will submit before you, the public, have been built upon things that actually happened and were witnessed.

My answer is this: Leprosy is not a contagious disease [Aole ka maʻi lepera he maʻi lele] like the flu, smallpox, the bubonic plague [flu, kamola poki, bubonika], etc. They are diseases with germs [anoano maʻi] that can live outside of the human body, constantly scattering as the disease is transported and quickly spread along its path.

Leprosy has a bacillus [O ka maʻi lepera he iloilo kona (bacillus)] that cannot live outside the human body. Only when it is nourished and warmed by the blood and warmth of the body, then it lives. Therefore, the leprosy bacilli [iloilo a ka maʻi lepera] do not constantly scatter to spread the disease quickly, like the other contagious diseases.

The only path by which leprosy can be contracted is by the leprous fluid or pus entering the body of a healthy person, perhaps due to a sore, or due to actually being inserted, like so: If you have a sore on your hand and you shake hands with a leprosy patient who has an sore on his hand, then when his sore connects with yours at the same spot and the infected fluid or pus enters, you will contract leprosy. You cannot escape it. However, if there is no sore on your hand, you can shake hands with all of the patients here in the colony and you will not catch the disease.

This is the path by which Father Damien [Makua Damiano] contracted leprosy, because he did not know there were sores on his hand. With these sores on his hand, he held the pus-covered hands of his injured children, and through this act their infected pus entered his sores, and therefore he contracted leprosy [nolaila ua loaa oia i ka maʻi lepera]. This is not just a guess, but something witnessed. [Aole keia he koho wale, aka, he ikemaka.]

Another path for contracting leprosy is that if you eat or drink something bitten or chewed by a leprosy patient, then that thing will have leprosy, like this: If a mother with leprosy chews starch or meat and spits it into the mouth of a child, then that child will contract leprosy because the saliva from the mouth of the infected one is the thing that inserts the bacilli of the illness into the uninfected one.

At this point, allow me to submit the explanations through which we see whether the disease is contagious or not. The third time patients were brought to Kalawao, right after the decision by the legislature to quarantine Kalawao as a leprosy colony [panalaau lepera], the husband of Hoʻolemakani, a leprosy patient [maʻi lepera], was brought [to Kalawao]. When he was brought, Hoʻolemakani came, too, as a helper [kokua] for her husband. She lived together, ate together, and slept together with her husband until that husband died. She married again to a helper [kokua], and they lived together for two years until that husband died. She married again to a leprosy patient [kanaka maʻi lepera], and for three years they lived together until that husband died. She lived without a husband until she died in the year 1917. Until she died, there was no spot or appearance of leprosy upon her, yet she lived in this colony for forty-nine years.

Mrs. Hokela Holt came with her parents when she was nine years old. The father was brought as a leprosy patient, and the mother and Hokela came, too, in the year 1872. Hokela married two male leprosy patients [kane maʻi lepera], and she spent forty-six years living within this colony [Panalaau]. Hokela was a beautiful woman until her death this past year, and her beauty as a woman persisted without a spot or appearance of leprosy upon her, and yet she had met with, lived with, eaten with, and slept with leprosy within these long forty-six years.

Poʻokela (female) came as a helper [kokua] for Kukaʻuahi, her husband, in the year 1879, and they lived together until her husband died. She married again to Puna, a leprosy patient [maʻi lepera], and they lived together until that husband died. Her husbands afterwards were helpers [kokua]. To this day, she has spent forty years living with, eating with, and sleeping with leprosy, without any appearance of leprosy upon her.

Charles Manua entered this colony in the year 1880, when he was ten years old. His foster mother [kahuhanai wahine] was the one who had leprosy. He married two female leprosy patients [wahine maʻi lepera], and lived with, ate with, and slept with leprosy for thirty-nine years, and to this day no appearance of leprosy has befallen him.

Henry Ma came into this colony as a helper [kokua] for his wife in the year 1881. They lived together until that leprosy patient wife died, and Henry Ma spent thirty-eight years meeting with, living with, eating with, and sleeping with leprosy, without any appearance of this disease upon him.

Kinoʻole (female) entered this colony as a helper [kokua] for her husband and their son in the year 1888. She lived with and cared for the two of them until they died, and then she married again to a male leprosy patient [kane maʻi lepera]. To this day, she has spent over thirty years meeting with, living with, eating with, and sleeping with leprosy, yet absolutely no appearance of leprosy is on her.

Pahia entered this colony in the year 1879 as a helper [kokua] for his daughter. He married Rebecca, a female leprosy patient [wahine maʻi lepera]. He spent forty years meeting with, living with, eating with, and sleeping with leprosy. He is elderly and frail now, but absolutely no aspect of the disease has appeared upon him.

These are the helpers [kokua] who have lived here for a long time and profoundly entered into leprosy. There are many other helpers who have lived in this colony for around fifteen years or less, but I think this is enough to show before you, the public.

Here I will report on those who did not enter profoundly, and yet have been in the heat of this red-hot, fiery oven [iloko o ka wela o keia imuahi enaena]. The Sisters of Mercy [Na Kaikuahine o ke Aloha], here they are living in this colony, mixing with, meeting with, and living with the leprosy patients [poe maʻi lepera], tending to their wounds and everything that eases those who have this terrible affliction, entering the rooms where the ill one is laying, surrounded by unsuitable smells. The oldest among them has spent thirty-five years living among the leprosy patients [maʻi lepera], from the quarantine center [pa hoomalu] in Kakaʻako to here in the colony. To this day, not one of them has the symptoms of this illness.

The brothers [Kaikunane] living in the Baldwin Home [Balauwina Home], their work is like that of the Sisters of Mercy, and to this day, no feature of this disease has appeared upon them. Our Maxime [Makimo] has spent seventeen years living with, meeting with, and mixing with the leprosy patients [maʻi lepera], entering the dwellings of the ill to watch over and tend to his sheep.

Whenever he is told that one of his sheep is infirm, be it day or night, he immediately goes to see that infirmed one, among the unsuitable smells surrounding
the room of the ill one, as he sits beside the bed of the ill one, and hears his
confession [penikenia], giving the holy sacrament [sakarema hemolele], the
Extreme Unction [Ukiona], to him, preparing his sheep for his heavenly journey. To this day, absolutely no aspect of this disease has appeared upon him.

At this point, I submit these questions before you, the reader, and before
you all, the public, and you shall reply with your answers:

One. If leprosy was not contracted by healthy people who have met with,
lived with, eaten with, and slept with leprosy for years, at least seventeen and at
most forty-nine, is leprosy a contagious disease?

Two. If leprosy was not contracted by people in good health who met with,
ate with, and slept with leprosy, how is it contracted by those who did not meet
with, live with, eat with, or sleep with leprosy?

Over thirty years ago, Germany sent Prof. [Eduard] Arning, a German doctor [kauka Kelemania], to investigate and thoroughly research the nature of the
leprosy spreading in Hawai'i. When he arrived, he made the patient quarantine
center [pa hoomalu ma'i] in Kaka'ako his site of work. There he performed his
unshrinking work upon the leprosy patients [ma'i lepera]. Among the animals
he injected with leprous pus were two monkeys and two female pigs. One
monkey showed that it had contracted leprosy, because the ear was pimply and
bumpy, and the features became wrinkled, resembling an extremely old man.

For one pig, her body hair fell out and her body was covered in mange, and
a layman could see that these animals had leprosy. The work of this foreigner
[haole] did not end here, but instead he wanted to try upon a human body. So
when he heard that Keanu had been sentenced to die on the gallows [amana
li kanaka] for the crime of murder, he immediately asked the government for
Keanu to be granted life if he agreed to have the leprous pus inserted into him.
Keanu agreed, and so he escaped the gallows.

A girl named Emily [Emale], whose hands and face were disfigured [palahe],
was brought from the detention station [pa ma'i] of Kaka'ako to Kāwā Prison.
Keanu was injected in the arm and the pus of this girl was inserted. He contracted leprosy and was taken to Kalawao in the year 1888 and died that year.

Therefore, if leprosy was not contracted by people in good health who met
with, lived with, ate with, and slept with leprosy, and it was contracted by Keanu because the pus was inserted, then this is proof of the answer shown above,
that this is not a contagious disease; but only when the infected pus enters or is
inserted into a body in good health, then it will contract leprosy.

If I am not mistaken, Dr. Jenner was the one who clarified the nature of this
thing called an injection [o: the word 'ō means to pierce or vaccinate], as follows: The injection is a fine thing, if done properly, but a terrible thing if done
improperly. Thus, if that is the nature of this thing called an injection, is it not
necessary to clean up the law requiring injections that is held within our law
book for the benefit and the protection of the people?

I give my thanks to you, Mr. Editor, and your typesetting boys.

—Ma'i Lepera [Leprosy patient: a pen name]. Kalaupapa, MAR. 19, 1919.

» [The writer, an unidentified patient at Kalaupapa, believed that leprosy was not
a contagious disease. Although he gives many examples of kōkua who never

contracted leprosy, the isolationist law was not rescinded until 1969. In the early years of Mother Marianne's Catholic order the sisters who worked at caring for the sick were called Sisters of Mercy.]

Additional Early History

The Hawaiian-language newspaper articles that follow are from many people: government officials, visitors, including Hawaiian royalty, and the patients themselves. They span the seven years from January 6, 1866, when the first patients were transported to Kalaupapa, to May 10, 1873, when Father Damien arrived. The articles, which are in chronological order, help to tell the story of the early years of the settlement and describe the challenges the Hawaiian government faced in establishing an isolated community for people afflicted with a debilitating disease.

> *Ka Nupepa Kuokoa.* 21 APRIL 1866. P. 4.
> *Ka noho ana o na mai Lepera ma Kalaupapa, o Molokai.* The Lifestyle of the Leprosy Patients in Kalaupapa on Moloka'i.
> Dear *Nupepa Kuokoa.* Greetings.
>
> I have three things that I'd like to share with the public. The first is that it is good that the leprosy patients [mai lepera] live in Waikolu, Kalawao, and Kawaluna here on Moloka'i these days from the month of January this year up until this month. Not one of these patients has passed away or become terribly weak. But the situation remains as from the first ship to the last ship. It is as comfortable as when they were living in Kalihikai [on O'ahu] and came here. Our number in total, taking into account the attendants [ohua] who have arrived after the afflicted patients is seventy-six. That is, fifty-nine leprosy patients [mai lepera] and seventeen attendants who tend to the patients. There have been no arguments among these residents. They are comfortable in their living. So what I'd like to leave with the public is that as some people have thought misguidedly that the lifestyle of the leprosy patients is plagued with trouble in these lands designated by the government for those who have been afflicted with this lesson from God. I have heard some people saying that if the leprosy patients [poe mai pake] should be taken to Kalaupapa, that there would be a lot of trouble, that they would not be taken care of and should not see their friends or any other people. And so, some person or people residing in Kalihi Kai live in fear of the doctor saying, "You will go to Moloka'i." And then the one who has been told to travel to Moloka'i is struck with terror, due to truly believing that this will be trouble, having already heard something like what I heard, as I mentioned above, if I am not mistaken in hearing as I did. What he heard is like what I heard; and at this point, I will leave off discussing this, and report on the second topic.
>
> THE GOVERNMENT SHOULD BE VIGILANT [MAKAALA MAOLI KE AUPUNI]
>
> This is the second of the ideas of mine that I have reported above, that the government should truly take care of the people. This is what I have informed regarding "The Government Should Be Vigilant." Since the beginning of the importing of the patients here, I was among those who lived on lands desig-

nated by the government whose names appear above. This is what I understand to be the case up until this past April. It was almost three months or more that I witnessed the generosity of the government to its people. There were six trips by the ship that brought the patients, and it is not done bringing them.

However, the first thing that I witnessed and discovered when I first arrived is the great number of taro patches [loi kalo] filled with taro, and so too for sweet potatoes [uwala], bananas, sugar cane, and house furnishings and houses, too. All these things were prepared by the government and all had been supplied accordingly. There was nothing more that could have been done. All this was done at once and this reminds me of the word of the Holy Bible, which states, "You have built a house, but have not lived as keepers of the well you have dug. You shall not drink the water. You have labored in the vineyard, but you shall not eat of the fruit of the vineyard." So some people might say that you just eat, but there is not fish. If it is only a question, I shall answer. When this ship comes, there will always be the containers of cattle and fish from other lands made by foreigners [haole] and filled with camphor. Not only that but also clothes: men's clothes and women's clothes of all kinds; and not only these things but also foreign foods, such as sugar, tea, biscuits, tea pots, large pots, small pots, knives, spoons, and all types of foreign food items that you see. These are all here. As I understand it, there are two houses that are filled with these types of goods mentioned above. A part of these types of goods are used by the patients for appearances, and it is said that there is a store in which carpenters' tools are kept as well as farming tools. I have two things to ask to some of the locals [kamaaina] of Kalaupapa first as I believe that I have a quarter left in my pocket; an eighth [hapawalu: one eighth of a dollar] for a fishhook [maka'u lawaia] and another eighth for the *Nupepa Kuokoa*. I ask first, "Is there not a store in this place?" This locale does not have a place. Is there not a postal bag brought here with the newspaper? The locale has no place. This is all I have to ask. I have not forgotten these words that he and I said. This is what I have asked about, the fishhooks and the *Nupepa Kuokoa* and the *Au Okoa*, from volume 1 up until volume 17 of the month of March last. But since the ship was so late, the volumes of these last few weeks have not arrived. So we, the readers, should watch out for this generous work of the government for its people.

LEPROSY PATIENTS WORK TOGETHER
[KE HANA LAULIMA NEI NA MAI LEPERA]

This is the third of these sentiments that have been talked about above, and then that is all. There have been twenty-six people who are getting together to do this good work. The Farmers' Club [Hui Mahiai] has made nearly three or four acres where crops are growing. What we had planned for the most was sweet potatoes, watermelons, bananas, corn, cotton, and that sort of thing and this sort of thing. That is what we had planned to plant on the plains and on taro lands as well. I end here. I extend my affection to you all, from the one dwelling in the highest until those dwelling in the lowliest positions.

—J. N. Hōkūwelowelo. Waikolu, Moloka'i, APRIL 8, 1866.

Ka Nupepa Kuokoa. 26 MAY 1866. P. 2.
Ua Nele Na Lepera I Ke Kauka Ole. Leprosy Patients Left Without a Doctor.

A letter has come to our office, short in length, from J. N. Hōkūwelowelo, one of the leprosy patients [mai pake] living in Kalaupapa on Moloka'i, calling out asking where is the doctor for the leprosy patients [poe mai pake] living in Kalaupapa. They heard Dr. [Edward] Hoffman [Hopemana] saying that before they were taken to Moloka'i, there was a doctor on Moloka'i to treat the leprosy patients [mai pake]. But when they went to Moloka'i, they did not see any doctor for them there. They thought to search for this doctor in the mountains and if he was not found, they would go to Kalua'aha with the intention of meeting with the doctor. They say that the doctor was afraid of leprosy, so he ran and hid. They want the legislature to think of them, for their well-being when they are left without a doctor since they are nearly one hundred in number and two of them have died without treatment [make me ka lapaau ole ia]. And what does the legislature think about them, to just leave them or what?

Ka Nupepa Kuokoa. 26 MAY 1866. P. 4.

A. O. Forbes [A. O. Polepe: Rev. Anderson O. Forbes] described the living conditions of the leprosy patients [Mai-pake] in the districts [apana] of Waikolu, Kalawao, and Kalaupapa on Moloka'i. According to him he had a lot of compassion for them when he met with them. S. E. Bishop [S. E. Bihopa: Rev. Sereno Edwards Bishop] felt that this council needed to choose and determine the right person among them to encourage and strengthen what is needed among them since the leprosy patients [poe Mai-pake] are found within the borders of this council. The other churches have no right to choose and install anyone to encourage them in what is needed. The council heard the selection for lead delegates of the council to go to Honolulu to attend the "Conference of Hawaiian Churches" [Ahahui Euanelio Hawaii] this coming June. Those who were selected were W. P. Kahale, Esq., of Wailuku, Paulo of the church at Hālawa, Moloka'i, K. Kauka of Kā'anapali. This was ratified.

Ke Au Okoa. 1 OCTOBER 1866. P. 1.

Ka ike ana i na mai pake ma Waikolu ma Molokai. Seeing the leprosy patients in Waikolu on Moloka'i.

When I went to Moloka'i, I toured around Hālawa, and then went and arrived at Wailau. There is a large cliff standing there and most of the coast consists of rocky points all the way to Pelekunu, where there is a stormy harbor [he inoino ke awa pae malaila] that is good only when it's calm. It was helpful to go from Kawaelealanui paddling by canoe and arriving at Waikolu. When I got there, I saw the leprosy patients [mai pake] fishing. They were fishing with fishing poles on the beach and some were fishing from canoes with nets. Their faces were gnarled and cracked. We heard at Pelekunu that visitors do not often meet with them, so we did not talk with them, but we were filled with compassion at seeing them. So we continued on to the foreign manager [luna haole], Louis Leparp [Lepart], and he welcomed us warmly. We inquired after the number of leprosy patients [mai pake], and he told us that there were 116 living and 13 who had died. The people were good at farming sweet potatoes [uala] and harvesting tree fungus [pepeiao]. The leprosy patients [mai pake] told us that they were fortunate under the care of the government, which hands out clothes each month, along with blankets and other types of apparel. The government assisted with some horses to transport gear for them and on the horses they load the sacks of sweet potatoes, bundles of taro, bags of tree fungus, and drinking containers. They often say they no longer have any desire for their place of birth [aina hanau], but rather they prefer Waikolu and Kalawao. Their place is entirely enclosed, and the government is building houses. When we left, four houses were complete, or perhaps there were more. Furthermore, they are people who raise dogs. Dogs are the best thing there, and they have some of their own horses.

Maui's and Hawai'i's leprosy patients [mai pake] are very good at farming. Pahulu, from Waiākea in Hilo, is very strong at farming. Kahulanui and Kāne of Lāhaina have sweet potato gardens. The Honolulu leprosy patients [Honolulu poe mai pake] are very lazy [he palaualelo loa], like Honolulu people. The countenances of the leprosy patients [mai pake] living there are really bad and dark for some and shiny for others.

With aloha, S. W. Nā'ili'ili. Pūehuehu, Lāhaina, Maui.

» [The Board of Health appointed Louis Lepart as the first superintendent of the settlement. Pepeiao is a tree fungus that Hawaiians gathered as food. Prized as a delicacy by the Chinese, pepeiao was a commercial export in Hawai'i from the 1850s to the 1880s.]

Ka Nupepa Kuokoa. 19 JANUARY 1867. P. 2.
Ke Kuhina Kalaiaina. The Political Minister.

Last Tuesday, the Honorable F. W. Hutchinson [Ferdinand W. Hutchison] went to Moloka'i. He probably went to see the people who are afflicted with leprosy [mai lebera] living in Waikolu and Kalaupapa.

» [Dr. Ferdinand W. Hutchison was president of the Board of Health when the settlement was established.]

Ka Nupepa Kuokoa. 2 FEBRUARY 1867. P. 2.
Ke Kuhina Kalaiaina. The Political Minister.

One day last week, His Excellency, F. W. Hutchinson [Ferdinand W. Hutchison], came back from his tour where he went to see the leprosy patients [mai lepera] at Kalaupapa on Moloka'i.

Ka Nupepa Kuokoa. 23 FEBRUARY 1867. P. 2.
No na Lepera o Molokai. Regarding the Leprosy Patients on Moloka'i.

When we looked inside the newspaper of H. M. [Henry M. Whitney, editor] these past few weeks, we saw Dr. Bikinika's letter stating that he went and saw the leprosy hospital [Halemai Lepera] in Kalaupapa and he witnessed the problems of the leprosy patients [poe mai lepera] being without a treating doctor and without other things needed for living. Later we saw a letter in the same newspaper reporting that these serious problems of the leprosy patients [lepera] in Kalaupapa were real. This was unexpected, and then we saw that the letter was from R. W. Meyer of Moloka'i, who was reporting about the conditions of the leprosy patients [poe mai lepera] that confirmed that a crate of beef had overturned on the road, about which he stated, "The beef was very smelly, but the stench was not greater than the stench of what they ate, so this food was good enough for them."

And in the *Ke Au Okoa* last Monday, we saw again some words about the leprosy patients [poe mai lepera], stating that, "There are lots of problems that plagued us at this time. There are problems about the disease and food, food and clothing, and there are problems regarding the neglect of treatment. Do not think that anyone who should find themself among us will live. No, not at all." And so it is likely for these reports above that the political minister, Dr. Hutchison, went there to examine the problems of these people.

Ke Au Okoa. 17 OCTOBER 1867. P. 4.
Kaahele Ma Molokai. Helu 5. No Na Makani O Molokai & Ke Kai Koo. Tour of Moloka'i. Number 5. The Winds of Moloka'i and the High Seas.

Moloka'i is a windy island [with wind] continuously blowing from the east and from the northeast. Calm days are a rarity on Moloka'i, but it is calm in Kaunakakai and those areas until Punakou and those parts, where the Kioea and Ka'ao winds are found, which blow in the evenings and mornings. There is a strong wind that blows in the early afternoon called Moa'e. I can probably tell you about the names of some of the winds of Moloka'i in the mele of Kūapāka'a, combined with the winds of Maui, as found in that mele; for example:

There is an 'Ekepue wind in Wailau
There is a Pu'upilo wind in Pelekunu
There is a Kili'o'opu wind in Makaluahau
There is a Kōkīlae wind of Kalaupapa
There is Makakuapo wind of Nihoa.

THE LANDS OF THE WINDWARD SIDE OF MOLOKA'I
[NA AINA KOOLAU O MOLOKAI]

These are the names of the winds of Moloka'i, composed in the mele of Kūapāka'a, but there probably are other smaller winds as well. The Kona wind, however, is the one that destroys homes in the windward [Koolau] district of Moloka'i. Moloka'i is also an island of high seas when the winter months arrive until the time of the rising of the Makali'i constellation in the month of April, at which time the weather is more calm. This is a good time for visitors to come to the windward side [aina Koolau] of Moloka'i. In the six months [of summer] is the time to eat fish. If you go in the winter time, the sea is surrounded by cliffs and surges at Maka'ukiu at which time the natives of Hālawa eat 'ōhiki crabs from the beach [aeone] of Kāwili as well as the seaweed that the turtles eat to fatten their meat. Wailau, Pelekunu, and Waikolu are better, where the 'o'opu nōpili fish are found in the streams, but from Kalawao to Kalaupapa is best. In those places, the waves crash on wilted grass almost a hundred feet, more or less, in some places, and the yellow-backed 'a'ama crab that runs up on the wilted grass is the seafood that they catch and eat. The waves are dangerous, but fun for the children of Kalaupapa who know how to surf the waves that are well-known around the world.

THE MOUNTAINS OF MOLOKA'I [NA KUAHIWI HUI O MOLOKAI]

These are the high mountains of Moloka'i as called by name. Maunaloa at Kaluako'i, where Kalapāhoa [Kalaipāhoa] is found. It is probably gone now as a result of harvesting and quarrying as a sorcery god or a god to kill people when inserted into food. (This is why Moloka'i is called Moloka'i of the potent prayers [Moloka'i i ka pule o'o], from when the chiefs of Hawai'i came to war with the people of these islands all the way here to O'ahu, and with Kaua'i joining in.) Keōlewa is located between Kalaupapa and Waihānau in Makanalua. Kame'ekū is the mountain on the leeward side, where the spring, Keālia, is found. This is a spring that Pele dug, whose water travels all the way to Maui. 'Alae is located between Makanalua and Kalawao, Moa'ula is located between Kalawao and Waikolu, Ahumāuna is located between Waikolu and Pelekunu, 'Oloku'i is located between Pelekunu and Wailau, and inland of Pelekunu is Kaunu'ōhua. Kawainui is located between Wailua [Waialua] and Pāpala, Ka'ahakualua is located between Pāpala, Haka'a'ano, Pua'ahaunui, and Hālawa.

FLAT LANDS [AINA PALAHALAHA]

Kalaupapa is the flat land of Moloka'i, and the plain of Kai'olohia is another flat place situated between Mo'omomi and Pālā'au.

A GOOD PLACE FOR BEATING TAPA [WAHI KUKU KAPA MAIKAI]

In ancient times, Wailau and Pelekunu were where pa'ikukui and mahunali'i tapa would be beaten. In Haka'a'ano and Pua'ahaunui is where the pa'i'ula tapa would be beaten. The 'ahapi'i and kūmanomano tapa were known in Kalaupapa and those parts, and in this era, there is only one kind of tapa known, the cotton type of the white people [haole] that you buy.

—J. H. Kānepu'u. Pālolo. OCTOBER 8, 1867.

Ka Nupepa Kuokoa. 14 MARCH 1868. P. 2
No na Mai Lepera. Regarding the Leprosy Patients.

After having written on the subject of "The Leprosy Patients of Moloka'i," which was published in our paper last week, we heard through the graciousness of Dr. Hoffmann (Dr. D. Hoffmann) [Kauka Hopemana] that there were 325 people thought to have contracted leprosy who had arrived at the leprosy hospital [Halemai Lepera] in Kalihi since the beginning of last February. From among these people, one hundred were released, mostly for being diagnosed as not having a true case of leprosy. Seven of these were released and later returned. Four escaped and one returned. One hundred seventy-four of the leprosy patients [lepera] were sent to Waikolu, Moloka'i.

We thank very much the person who sent us the list of names of those who died of leprosy in Waikolu and we will be very appreciative if this person also sends us a list of the remainder of those who had died from the month of May of last year up until now. We continue to believe that he or she will continue to send us [information] regarding the dead and we shall print it.

The editors of the *Kuokoa* will reply regarding the terrible reasons for objecting to one of the totals reported by the *Ke Au Okoa* last week. We are always prepared to respond to theories and rationalizations, but we will not engage in lambasting and making disparaging comments as we do not entertain such actions. We leave it up to the national paper to do such things. These ministers are only seeking to broaden their columns into which harsh words have entered like those of a deranged person, but from here on out, they and their assistants will see the fruits of this type of activity, which tends to slip through in the realm of politics.

The *Ke Au Okoa* and *Hawaiian Gazette* are saying, "Everything is working smoothly in the government." But we can tell them that they are blowing wind and next time they will sow whirlwinds. We believe that there are people in the upcoming legislative session whose voices will be heard in support of the rights of the public who will also teach about the good things for ministers to learn with regards to the rights and powers of the people.

Ka Nupepa Kuokoa. 16 MAY 1868. P. 4.

Hookahi mai no Pukoo, Molokai nei, o Paeaina w., a hookahi hoi haole no ka malama o Dekemaba, 1867 laua. There is one patient from Pūko'o, here on Moloka'i, Ms. Pae'āina, and also one foreigner [haole]. Both came in the month of December 1867.

The total number of patients is 174, the patients who have been sent from Kalihi to join with the foreigner, but Ms. Pu'e'āina [Pae'āina] was released at Kalihi, and when she came back here to Moloka'i, she was discovered to have contracted the disease, so the police [makai] brought her to where the leprosy patients [mai lepera] reside. There were four new patients who were found among the population, and including this woman, the count is five. The total number of patients who have been brought in is 179, which is the total number altogether. In the month of April of 1867 until Feb. 29 of this year, 1868, the total number of deaths is 47, with 125 being the remainder and with 7 having been released. This is the true report to you. Please accept this readily and do not disregard us on the plains.

These are the helpers of the patients [kokua o na mai] who have also come by ships 1–22, 40 or more, but 4 have died and their names have been added to the list of patients as was reported in the ninth issue of last 29th of February, with some returning permanently, leaving 23, the total number of those residing. The patients live with hardship lacking food. It is almost this entire month that they have gone without eating [ai ole]. Farewell. This child of the people of Pali Ko'olau is going home as it is evening.

With aloha, H. K. K. Kalawao, MARCH 26, 1868.

III. FATHER DAMIEN (MAKUA DAMIANO) IN HAWAI'I: 1873 TO 1889

FATHER DAMIEN, SS.CC., was born on January 3, 1840, in Ninde, a hamlet of the principal village of Tremeloo, Belgium. He was named Joseph De Veuster and baptized the same day in Our Lady of Perpetual Help Church [Kerk van Onze-Lieve-Vrouw van Bijstand] in Tremeloo.

In 1859 he joined the Catholic order of the Congregation of the Sacred Hearts of Jesus and Mary, where he took the name Brother Damien. Along with other members of his religious congregation, he was sent to Hawai'i as a missionary in 1864 while still in training for the priesthood. During his first two months on O'ahu, he completed his training, and on May 21 Bishop Louis Maigret ordained him a Catholic priest in Our Lady of the Peace Cathedral in Honolulu.

Father Damien spent the next eight years as a missionary on Hawai'i island, serving in the districts of Puna, Kohala, and Hamakua. Fluent in Hawaiian, he dedicated himself to the needs of the Hawaiian people. During his time on Hawai'i island he saw many of his parishioners sent to Kalaupapa and heard stories of the harsh conditions at the settlement. In 1873, Bishop Maigret addressed the special needs at the leprosy settlement with his priests, and Father Damien volunteered to serve there. Accompanied by Bishop Maigret, Father Damien arrived at Kalaupapa on May 10, 1873, seven years after the first leprosy patients were transported to the peninsula.

The settlement then was in Kalawao, where there were two churches, Siloama Congregational Church and St. Philomena Catholic Church, which had been built in 1872 by Brother Bertrand of Honolulu. On Wednesday, May 13, 1873, the *Nuhou*, a newspaper published in Hawaiian and English, ran a short article in English on the arrival of Father Damien. Several days after it appeared, King Lunalilo sent a letter to the *Nuhou*, which was also written in English. Walter Murray Gibson, the editor, added an afterword. The king's letter is dated May 16, 1873, which is only ten days after Father

153

Damien's arrival. It shows how quickly word about him had spread and that he was already being acknowledged as a savior, not only by the Catholic minority of Hawai'i, but by the non-Catholic majority.

[The SS.CC. after Father Damien's name and other members of his congregation are the Latin initials for Sacrorum Cordium, or "of the Sacred Hearts." The letters are doubled to indicate that both words are plural, a convention of Latin abbreviations. The SS.CC. designation is only attached to the name of a professed Brother or Sister of the Congregation of the Sacred Hearts of Jesus and Mary.]

Nuhou. 13 MAY 1873. P. 3.
A Christian Hero.

We have often said that the poor outcast lepers of Molokai are without pastor or physician afforded an opportunity for the exercise of a noble Christian heroism, and we are happy to say that the hero has been found. When the *Kilauea* touched at Kalauwao [Kalawao] last Saturday, Monseigneur Maigret and Father Damien, a Belgian priest, went ashore. The venerable bishop addressed the lepers with many comforting words and introduced to them the good Father, who had volunteered to live with them and for them. Father Damien formed this resolution at the time, and was left ashore among the lepers without a home or a change of clothing, except such as the lepers had to offer. We care not what this man's theology may be, he surely is a Christian hero.

Thirty lepers were landed from the *Kilauea* at Kalauao [Kalawao] last Saturday, and eight doubtful leprous cases were brought to town. This leprosy is certainly the worst difficulty and the most important work with which the government has to grapple; and we doubt not it must be a severe task on the hands of the minister of the interior, who is esteemed as a humane and just man and one who has a tender regard for the native people.

Nuhou. 16 MAY 1873. P. 3.
Letter of His Majesty to the Lepers. Honolulu, April 20, 1873.
To My Friends at Kalaupapa:

By the hands of two members of the Board of Health, I send you these words. You all know that on account of the prevalence of this disease of leprosy in the nation, a division of land has been set apart for the isolation of those affected. This measure is for the good of the nation, and being a law, it must be executed. But it is indeed a sad thing to be thus separated from friends and loved ones; how else however are the laws to be executed?

I can only say to you that you shall receive all the benefits that the government can possibly bestow, and I trust that, in consultation with my advisers [*sic*], everything will be done for you, consistent with a regard for the good of the whole people. May the Almighty Father watch over, protect, and bless you, is the prayer of him whom the nation has chosen as its earthly head.

God preserve Hawaii nei. Love to you all. Lunalilo.

We hope His Majesty will remember the good priest who has gone voluntarily to minister unto His Majesty's afflicted people on Molokai. If this is not a "faithful minister of the Gospel," we don't think he is to be found in these islands.

Father Damien became the permanent pastor at St. Philomena Church and dedicated his life to serving the patients at the settlement. He lived there until his death on April 15, 1889. On Sunday, October 11, 2009, Father Damien was canonized by Pope Benedict XVI as Saint Damien, a saint in the Catholic Church.

In the Hawaiian-language newspaper articles that follow, Father Damien's name is spelled variously as Damiana, Damiano, Damien, Damieno, and Kamiana, although Damiano is used most often. The first article that follows was written while he was still a priest on Hawai'i island and documents some of his early activities as a young missionary. In 1870 he and other dignitaries attended an examination day for school children, which included students from the Catholic School of Wai'aka. In the second article, published in 1871, the writer presents an emotional defense of the skills of a kahuna lapaau, a Hawaiian medical expert, Isaiah Kahiko, who was also a Christian pastor. The writer concludes by saying that when Father Damien was sick, he asked for Pastor Kahiko's medical assistance and was cured.

The rest of the articles were written during the years Father Damien was at Kalaupapa, 1873 to 1889. Most of them mention his name, but those that don't provide information about the conditions at the settlement while he was there. The thirteen articles titled He Mau Hunahuna No Ke Kahua Mai Lepera O Kalawao A Me Kalaupapa (Some Tidbits about the Leprosy Settlement of Kalawao and Kalaupapa) were a series written by a patient at the settlement that ran before and after Father Damien's death. They are especially descriptive of everyday life at Kalaupapa.

Ka Nupepa Kuokoa. 29 JANUARY 1870. P. 5.
Hoike o na Kula Aupuni ma Kohala Hema, Hawaii. Report of the Government Schools in South Kohala, Hawai'i.
Dear *Kuokoa,* aloha.

As a result of a decision among schoolteachers of this district, the public schools hold exams in the last week of December. Two schools were to have exams at the same location, so I attended these exams.

Friday, the 3rd. Waikōloa's English school and the school at Wai'aka. S. H. Mahuka is the teacher at Waikōloa with his wife, Mrs. K. Mahuka, with twenty-nine students. Mrs. Lyons is the teacher of the English school, with twelve students. Kaia'ole is the teacher of Wai'aka, with fifteen students. On this exam day, the examination room was full of children and parents to observe the skill of the children. Also in attendance were District Judge F. Spencer, Esq., Mr. G. K. Lindsey, Rev. Damien [Damiano], Rev. Lyons, Z. Pa'akikī, W. Kealoha, and the public. After the prayer, the school of Waikōloa stood to read, and after that those of the Catholic School of Wai'aka stood, after which the English school stood, and they were shown appreciation. Their voices were nice and loud and the audience heard them well. There were two little girls of the English school who had just entered that school in the month of February who were good at reading. After this, each was shown a text and the knowledge of the children was demonstrated and the exam was ended on lesson 15 of math. They took a break at noon for a meal for the children there in the school building. The children proceeded in line and when the meal was done, they returned to the exam, where they reviewed the examination of the three schools, and there was no doubt regarding the children. There was a lot that took place that day. The children of the English schools sang together, as did the school of Wai'aka, and the school of Waikōloa sang lovely songs. There were speeches about the ali'i. It was a very festive day. The children were brave and alert. Should they become soldiers for Christ, this would be the greatest blessing. Since the time was short, the exam was ended that day. After this, I applauded loudly for the children and the parents of this district. Children and parents, awake and seek strenuously after knowledge and such things.

When this was done, the audience was excused with a prayer by Rev. Lyons [Laiana: Rev. Lorenzo Lyons].

—S. H. Mahuka, Waimea, Jan. 5, 1870. Superintendent.

Ka Nupepa Kuokoa. 25 NOVEMBER 1871. P. 4.
Kahuna Hawaii. Hawaiian pastor.
Dear *Nupepa Kuokoa.* Greetings.

This is the first time for us to shake hands [kuikui lima] traveling on the roadway that you are used to traveling among the churches and among all the Sabbath schools and schools and all true Christian families.

Isaiah Kahiko is a Hawaiian pastor [kahuna Hawaii]. For nearly twenty-six years he has been serving as a practitioner of medicine [oihana lapaau]. J. Kahiko is a member of the church. There have been many reports in the district [apana] of Kohala among those whom he has treated. He is appreciated for his steadfastness only in the truth. All the diseases of children and diagnoses have been sufficient to care for those who have young children.

He is appreciated for not adhering to idol worship [hoomanakii ole]. He has not found it necessary to partake of 'awa in observation of metaphysical practices, using black pigs and white chickens. We appreciate that he has not asked for dollars or cents. His greatest desire is to spread his knowledge as a kahuna. What he tends to is the work of treating sickness in seeing to the treatment of various kinds of sicknesses that cause paleness [haikea], consumption [wai-opua], cramps [haikala], unknown [kaikaiowi], unknown [kumu-pou], stomachache [nahu], headache [nalulu], swelling [pehu], neuritis [kalawa], obstipation [papaku], etc., etc., etc.

His contemplation on the types of medicines needed is expansive and long, as is his knowledge, accuracy, and honesty without deception. None of the afflicted is left wanting when they observe the prescription and directions. It is just as the white doctors [poe ili keokeo oihana kauka] do.

Those who have been treated by him when there were no laws are witnesses. This is how it was until the publishing of laws. He has continued to precribe remedies to the sick. At this time he is fearful, having been expelled by the constitution. He has held off [pale] those who have sent for [kii] him at night. They come secretly to send for him and urge [koi] him to treat their sicknesses.

It causes me worry that he treats those of other races as I believe it is not right that J. Kahiko treats white missionaries [Misionari ili keokeo]. However, as a doctor he will have to do so.

I forget when he treated Rev. D. [J.] Damien [Damiano], Catholic priest of Wai'āpuka. Rev. D. [J.] Damien sent for J. Kahiko to help treat him without concern. He agreed and his problems went away! There is knowledge among Hawaiians [Aia ia ike o Hawaii la]. Hawai'i of great seekers is full of it!

—C. Abs. Kahulanui.

Ka Nupepa Kuokoa. 9 AUGUST 1873. P. 2.
Na Mea Hou O Kalawao. News of Kalawao.
Dear *Kuokoa.* Please insert my letter wherever you have space.

With regards to the patients. [No na Mai.] The health of the patients is fine, probably due to the Kololio wind [same as Kokololio] that blows in from the ocean. The total number of patients these days has reached eight hundred, and since death approaches every day, it has decreased to below eight hundred. From that total number, there are six Chinese from China, ten part-whites [hapa haole], three whites [haole], thirty people of Lāhainaluna, three house representatives of years past, two consecrated pastors, and one from Kapunahou. Such lament!

Man killed by a pig. [Kanaka pau i ka puaa.] On Friday night of the 11th of last July, a pig threw up. It had eaten a man whose name was Kahula from Ho'okena, South Kona, Hawai'i, his homeland. This is how he died: His grandson, whose name is Nākapahau, buried him, believing that he had been interred, but it was not as it was said. The grave he dug was not deep enough, being only two feet deep. As a result, this man was eaten by the pig. Everything up to the shoulders was gone, including the arms. The body was left, but perhaps almost consumed had it not been seen. Officials have apprehended Nākapahau and jailed him for burial abuse of his grandfather.

The Store in Kalawao. [Ka Halekuai o Kalawao.] The Board of Health opened a clothing store of all sorts and is selling to those who have money. The prices of everything are reasonable, $1.25 for holokū, 75¢ for mu'umu'u. On the day the selling started profits reached $150.00. The money of the patients is lamented.

Loving Service. [Manawalea Aloha.] When the *Warwick* [Wawiki] arrived, Rev. Damien [Damiano] returned from Honolulu with donated clothes from the members of the Roman Catholic Church of Honolulu. There were men's clothes, women's, children's, shoes of all types. These were given to the poor among the Catholic parishioners and some to others in need among these people. How sad.

Regarding cooked taro and meat [No ka ai a me ka ia.]. The Board of Health continues to care for us, providing cooked taro [pai ai] and meat: twenty-four pounds of cooked taro, five pounds of beef [bipi] per patient a week.

Regarding Christian acts. [No na hana Karistiano.] The good works among this people continues to grow, including the Mormon faith [Hoomana Moremona], the Christian faith [Hoomana Karistiano], and the Roman Catholic faith [Hoomana Katolika Roma]. The lifestyle of the patients is safe and peaceful. No mudhen calls, no tattler wanders about, no owl hoots. [Aohe alae nana e kani, aohe ulili nana e holoholo, aohe pueo nana e ke'u.]

Regarding the Sabbath school. [No ke Kula Sabati.] J. H. Nāpela opened the Sabbath school inside Siloama, and the church was filled with those who went to see the expounding of Nāpela on the Bible. But upon observing it, some explanations were correct. The school was filled and then some.

With affection, D. W. Kalua.

» [The saying about the three birds in the next to the last paragraph is explained
in *'Ōlelo No'eau: Hawaiian Proverbs and Poetical Sayings*. It means, "There is
perfect peace."]

Ka Nuhou Hawaii. 27 JANUARY 1874. P. 4, and *Ko Hawaii Ponoi.* 28 JANUARY
1874. P. 4.
I Ka Lahui Hawaii No Kalawao Mai. To the Hawaiian Nation From Kalawao.
Dear *Ko Hawaii Ponoi.* Greetings.

Due to the amount of things contained in the *Nupepa Kuokoa* regarding
the way of life and regarding how the leprosy patients [Lepera] of Moloka'i are
being taken care of, and due to the amount of falsehoods that have been talked
about, therefore, I thought I should tell the whole truth about their way of life
and the way the Board of Health and its leaders care for those loving people
who have been segregated here due to leprosy [mai Lepera] so that the people
who care for these people may see how the patients [poe mai] living here are
praised.

Most of the people living here appreciate how well the Board of Health takes
care of them, those who are afflicted with leprosy. It is better than how the
previous board took care of them. The resident accommodations are fine and
the rations of rice have been increased. The rations of cooked taro [pai ai] and
fish remain the same, and the lifestyle of those afflicted is hopeful. And as the
lifestyle is good, the lifestyle is therefore comfortable and good, much better
for most of the people who live here than when they lived in their own places
of residence. There are churches here and they go about the work of improving
the lives of the people here with great care, led by the pastors of the Protestant
church under the direction of Rev. S. N. Kaholokahiki, who is dedicated to encouraging righteousness among the members of his sect. I am hopeful that the
fruits of his good seeds that he is growing will flourish here in this garden.

The Rev. J. Damien [Damieno], pastor of the Catholic Church, is very
dedicated in separating and planting the seeds of life among the members of
his church, and he is also dedicated to searching for everything that makes the
grieving lives of the patients comfortable in some places. He constantly goes
among the patients who are seen to be experiencing troubles in their lives,
giving hope to those who nearly depart for the face of Ha'ikū. The people are
very blessed to learn about the activities like this here. But just like the way of
life in countries around the world, so it is here. There are good people and bad
people among every nation, and so it is here. These are people who are afflicted
with jealousy and envy, fault finding and cursing, who are used to creating
falsehoods, and who constantly scold when having conversations. They do not
inquire after the truth or untruth about what they are talking about before ini-
tiating a conversation or before spreading such things among the public. Such
people as J. Nui and Keha'i, the Nuis want to spread thoughts without checking
into the truth of the matter being spread. The names, J. Nui and Keha'i, are
false names [inoa kapakapa]. These two have hidden their real names and they
point their hands here and there to disparage others with their words, whether
they are true or not. To enforce the laws here, it is completely prohibited to
be drunk or to deal with liquor. All sections of Chapter 42 of the Criminal
Code [Kanawai Hoopai Karaima] have been published and deal harshly with

lawbreakers. Some have been punished stringently who have broken the law, and there will truly be many who will test it. In measuring the punishment, the livelihood of those punished was also considered, whether they were in weak health and whether they were physically able to endure it. Therefore, it is not true that I have encouraged activities dealing with liquor inappropriately and incited a ruckus among my fellowmen who are enduring these hardships, and I ask the entire population to ask those in good standing who live among us to inquire of the church pastors, Rev. J. Damien [Damieno] and Rev. S. N. Kaholokahiki, and all good people living here as I have confidence in them, since, "Righteousness is strength, and strength is not righteousness." [O ka pono ka ikaika, aole o ka ikaika ka pono.]

When J. H. Nāpela was the superintendent for the leprosy patients [Luna o na Lepera], he ordered that animals be set free in the fields reserved for farming and planting crops, because he thought that the livelihood of the patients was not in caring for themselves, but rather with the Board of Health providing starch and meat to the leprosy patients [Lepera]. When I was set up as superintendent [luna], I did not follow after his lead in such things, but I directed that the crop fields be protected. I hired someone to care for the crop fields of the patients so that the patients would become interested in planting crops, such as sweet potato, melons, cabbage, sugar cane, bananas, taro, and other things of the like, and there is much farming being done at this time by patients. But for some evildoers who harbor jealousy and envy, they have gone and told some patients that farming is useless since all patients would be released in the next legislative session of the legislature of the government, among other silly things. Some people have abandoned farming as a result of such lies. We know well that those who are planting this kind of interest who also live among their family members, that they are people who would like to lay barren the dark green cliffs [pali hauliuli] of this group of islands by spreading their disease among the public, those who have more love for themselves than for their families and the entire population, and perhaps they would like the whole country to become likewise defiled everywhere with this disease that breaks the heart of the leprosy patient [Lepera]. I think that those who think to do such a thing to their families and the people are without compassion, and it is as if their hearts are without shame since patients of the thing known as Chinese disease [mai pake: leprosy] are despised by the healthy and yell at them, and they are ordered about by heartless people. I have heard that in China, they are incarcerated and not taken care of until they die. In Borabora [Tahiti], they are buried alive [he kanu ola ia]. In Sweden and Norway they are thrown into the sea, and last June or July I saw in the newspapers of San Francisco, California, that an award will be given in the amount of five hundred dollars ($500) for whoever shoots anyone who is said to have contracted leprosy who roams about San Francisco. But in the Christian nation of Hawai'i [Aupuni Kristiano o Hawaii], those who suffer from leprosy [mai lepera] are well taken care of and are provided with money to provide the patients [mai] with what they need to live comfortably here until the spirit returns to the Creator and the dust returns to the dust.

I am your obedient servant, William P. Ragsdale, Superintendent of the Leprosy Hospital [Luna o ka Halemai Lepera], Kalawao, Moloka'i, JANUARY 15, 1874.

Ka Nuhou Hawaii. 24 FEBRUARY 1874. P. 4.

Dear *Ka Nuhou Hawaii.* Greetings.

I am a patient [mai] living here on Moloka'i and I have read the incorrect reporting of W. P. (Wandering Bill) [Bila Auwana: William P. Ragsdale] in your paper of the 27th of January saying that we, the patients living here, are very appreciative of what a good job the Board of Health has been doing compared to the previous Board of Health. As I see it, since I am one of the first patients [mai mua], the Board of Health back then took care of things the same as this board, and what is strange [ano e] is the superintendents [luna]. The first superintendents watched over us well and taught us, but this particular super-intendent is mean and does not talk nicely. Foul language of the white people [olelo ino a ka haole] is always stuck in his mouth. This Wandering Bill has also spread the word that the accommodations are good. That is not correct. Only a few of the houses are clean, and it is those who live in these accommodations who have provided for themselves.

The portions of rice of this superintendent who says have been increased are the same as during the interim of J. H. Nāpela, which is three pounds a week. This Wandering Bill has said that most people living here are living bet-ter than at their own homes. Perhaps it is just this superintendent who knows this, but for us, this is not the case. If this superintendent is saying that I have caused more trouble to most patients, and that I have only taken care of a few, then his conscience [lunaikehala] along with the rest of us, should help him. He spoke of Rev. J. Damien [Damieno] that he is stalwart in going among the pa-tients to inquire about their problems and that is true. But that Rev. J. Damien has gone about his way is a result of his knowledge of the way the superinten-dent works, that he [the superintendent] stares threateningly and lords it over others.

It is not according to the orders of the entire world that people are detained from going about seeking what they need, but here this is done, and this is what we are taught by the Holy Bible: Ask and it shall be given, but here, if one goes and asks of Wandering Bill something to eat, he answers that one should die so that the people may live. This is amazing. So this Wandering Bill knows that his actions are not right in what he wrote in the paper so that the public would think that what he said is the truth and that he is harassed by us, the patients. The previous superintendents were not protested against and reported about. Isn't that due to how well they did their job? I believe so. This superintendent has also talked about how the people are farming now. That is true, but there are two big reasons why people are farming now. The first is that they fear that they will go hungry as they are always left without food by Wandering Bill. The second is that this is the best time to farm since the ground is moist with the rains of winter and since the ground is moist the crops that are planted will grow.

This superintendent has also said that those who are so inclined would like to lay desolate the dark green cliffs of this group of islands [pali uliuli o keia pae moku] by spreading this evil. I certainly do not believe that, like so many oth-ers here. I am one who showed compassion to the helpers [poe kokua] who are here among us, but when I saw the report of the doctor of the Board of Health in the *Kuokoa* paper of July 1873, my sorrow was lessened regarding these undiseased people [poe mai ole] who have joined us who have seen the patients and have been seen among them, the sick with the undiseased, and have not become afflicted.

We see this disgusting attitude of the white man [haole] toward these people who have been afflicted with the disease, and if those who are not afflicted are allowed to return home, where shall this Wandering Bill live? It is clear that his white brother-in-law will not allow him to live with him as he knows that he will be defiled. And since he is living high off of the requests of the Board of Health, he therefore strives to have the patients remain here with him. When he is annoyed at anyone, he denies them food and they will die. Then his problems of fearing that he will live here alone are over. This is why he seizes anyone near him to drown with him, sparing no one.

It continues even now. Until we meet again [a halawai hou kaua]. With great affection. Hu'ehu'e. Kalaupapa, Moloka'i, FEB. 10, 1874.

» [Bila Auwana, Wandering Bill, was a nickname for William P. Ragsdale. Hu'ehu'e, which means "to uncover or expose," was probably a pen name for the writer.]

Ka Lahui Hawaii. 25 MAY 1876. P. 4.
Na Mea Hou O Kalawao, Molokai. News from Kalawao, Moloka'i.
To the People of Hawai'i. Greetings.

1. Religious contention. This intense debate raged between Rev. Damien [Damiano], Catholic priest, and J. W. Hāhea of the Protestant religion, on the 18th of this month beginning at three o'clock and ending at four o'clock regarding these topics:

1. The true church
2. Peter
3. The body of Jesus, the true bread, according to Damien.

Regarding these subjects the fair-skinned child of France [keiki ili puakea o Farani] was completely off the mark and outside of the truth on the debate platform and was not able to expound on the heart of the established matters. Instead he veered off to talk about unrelated matters and grabbed a hold of his opponent, uttering insults, calling him a lying dog and other things. This is typical of the pope's religion. Shameful! These actions of the Catholic teacher are truly shameful in daring to contend with someone not of his standing. It would have been better for him to go and contend with S. N. Holokahiki and G. H. E. Keaui'a'ole. However, what is best is to humble oneself, to be patient, and to sit still.

2. The bonds of marriage broken. Mr. Kānekahuna, a Catholic, and Ms. Keaki, a Protestant, went before A. W. Pupulenui, the marriage commissioner. They obtained a permit, this permit was taken to Damien, and he married them. They remained together for about a year or more in the bonds of marriage. But in recent weeks this Catholic priest learned that the woman was not baptized into their religion, so he went to this woman and told her that their covenant of marriage was broken.

How amazing these actions of the Catholics [to say] whether one is married or not is dependent on the religion. However, it is the norm in Catholic countries to lift themselves up.

3. The livelihood of the patients. Most patients gossip about returning home as it is heard that the legislature will release them. As a result, some have abandoned farming and construction, so their labor is wasted and falls to others. The same thing is uttered by the mouths of everyone, that they will go home, and so on. Such talk flourishes regarding their dissatisfaction like withering kukui nuts that have no meat in them.

For what reasons would we return home? We have been brought as prisoners [pio] with the approval of the laws that we should live here until the dust returns to the dust as before.

The Committee of Thirteen recently sat down to discuss the merits of their appeal to the legislature. The members of this committee are among those who wish to return home.

4. Amazing pig. This pig was born three months ago and is in good health. It has its front legs and has one hind leg; its left leg. It does not have a right leg and it moves around on a push cart [kaa pahu]. It does have its thigh, however.

—J. P. Kalani. Kalawao, Moloka‘i, APR. 26, 1876.

» [Anti-Cathlolic sentiment was common in Hawai‘i during the 1800s. This article is an example of the religious clashes that occurred between Catholics and Protestants. Father Damien, as a Catholic priest and missionary, was a staunch defender of his faith.]

Ka Lahui Hawaii. 15 JUNE 1876. P. 1.
To *Ka Lahui Hawaii.* Greetings.

On the night of Saturday, the 18th, just passed, some people went to their canoe [waa], planning to go fishing, but it did not have its outrigger float [ama] and booms [iako]. As a result of their shock at their misfortune and in their anger at the perpetrator, not really knowing who the criminal was, they quit their idea to return home and sleep. When the sun rose the next day, Sunday, it was heard that Wandering Bill [Bila Auana: William Ragsdale] ordered the managers [poe luna liilii] to go and remove the outrigger floats and booms of all canoes for the following reasons:

1. Wandering Bill felt that patients would escape.
2. Wandering Bill was afraid he would be apprehended and mistreated at sea.

But these are things that are said to minimize the third reason, which is this: According to what some of his supervisors are saying, when the *Warwick* arrived, Mr. ‘Ōku‘u had boarded as he was engaged in some private venture in fishing, obtaining fish for the patients. ‘Ōku‘u said that on this voyage, Lili‘u went and got the royal [alii], Kekuaokalani, and that he would likely come again. Wandering Bill feared that the royal, Kekuaokalani, would be seated [again] in the legislature [Hale Ahaolelo]. He believed that he [Kekuaokalani] would not go without being questioned regarding the condition of the patients, whether they are being taken care of or not by the Board of Health, upon which the royal, Kekuaokalani, would tell all, that the Board of Health is inefficient. It feeds the patients sour salmon [kamano awaawa], even though a hundred cows come through. It is only when Wandering Bill [Bila Auwana] gets hungry does a cow get slaughtered for a hundred people, including patients. The legislature [Ahaolelo] would hear how the patients are given bad cooked taro [pai inoino], and if patients say that the food is bad, they are told that if they don't like it, they can leave it. Since there is a lack of food, they take it. They sort out the good parts, which are few, so food lasts only so many days. When it is gone, they eat only leftovers that week, until food is supplied again. There are a great many things that would be heard from the mouth of the royal, Kekuaokalani, regarding food, fish, clothing, housing, and living on the land. The royal, Kekuaokalani, is able to tell all with exactness. And since such things are not really known to Wandering Bill, he ordered his supervisors to do as reported above.

With gratitude, Daniel [Daniela] Ka'oka. Kalaupapa, Moloka'i, MAY 15, 1876.

» [Bila Auana/Auwana, "Wandering Bill," was the nickname of William Ragsdale, a Caucasian-Hawaiian lawyer who also served as an interpreter at the Hawaiian legislature. When he contracted leprosy in 1873, he volunteered to go to Kalaupapa. A controversial figure there, he served as superintendent at the settlement from the winter of 1873 until he died in 1877.

Kekuaokalani was the pen name of Peter Kā'eo, a cousin of Queen Emma. He was a member of the legislature in 1873 when he also contracted leprosy and was sent to Kalaupapa. During his three years there, Kā'eo wrote many letters to Queen Emma detailing the horrible treatment of the patients under Ragsdale's administration. In 1876, the Board of Health determined Kā'eo was free of the disease and discharged him from Kalaupapa. When he returned to Honolulu, he was reseated in the legislature. The letter writer, Daniel Ka'oka, suggests that William Ragsdale was afraid of what Peter Kā'eo would say to the legislature about the conditions at Kalaupapa during his three years there.]

Ka Lahui Hawaii. 22 JUNE 1876. P. 3.
Na Olelo Hooholo A Me Na Bila. Decisions and Bills.

The Honorable Mr. Halemanu led the first reading of a law to amend the law that was approved on the 23rd of June 1868, reviving the Board of Health of Hawai'i on each island to inform all appropriate people who use traditional practices of medicine [poe kupono e lapaau] as Hawaiian experts [ano kahuna Hawaii] that there would be a punishment placed upon deceivers and worshippers of the kahuna order [poe hoopunipuni a hoomanamana ma ke ano kahuna], as is seen among most who are involved in the practice at this time.

After discussing for a while, it was decided to have a second reading.

The Honorable Mr. Phillip [Pilipo] read the following rendering:

Decided—the President should select a committee of thirteen members, and select for Kaua'i two, for O'ahu three, for Maui and Moloka'i three, for Hawai'i three, and two nobles. This committee shall be sent to Kalaupapa and Kalawao, Moloka'i, to see the condition of the patients and advise the truth of the matter in a complaint from them. And three doctors shall be sent with them on this excursion. This decision is not to be obstructed by the members of the Board of Health and the members of the legislature [Ahaolelo]. Journalists [kakau moolelo] of the newspapers may go along if they want to. It is to be ordered by the minister of interior [Kuhina Kalaiana], and the agent of the steamship Kīlauea is to take text of that decision. Then the agent will advise when the ship will travel.

Ka Lahui Hawaii. 29 JUNE 1876. P. 2.
Na ko makou mea kakau ponoi. Kalawao, Molokai. Ka Huakai A Ke "Kilauea," Me Ke Komite He 13 O Ka Ahaolelo, No Ke Kahua Home o Ka Lahui Lepera—Na Hana A Ke Komite—Ke Ano O Ka Aina—Ke Kulana O Kolaila Mau Oiwi—A Me Na Hiona E Ae Ma Ka Makakai Ana A Na Hoa O Ka Papa-Pai, &c., &c. From our own reporter. Kalawao, Moloka'i. The Voyage of the *Kīlauea*, with the Committee of Thirteen of the Legislature, Regarding the Homestead Settlement of the Leprosy Nation—The Actions of the Committee—The Condition of the Land—The Condition of the Natives of That Place—And the Appearance of Various Things on the Excursion of the Members of the Publication Board, and etc., and etc.

Due to the request of the decision of Honorable Mr. G. W. Pilipo, it was approved by the lawmaking legislature of our nation [Ahaolelo kau kanawai o ko kakou nei Aupuni] on the 15th of June 1876. The horse-drawn carriage of the ocean [Lio-kakele o ka Moana] is readied for travel as a result of the kindness and generosity of the president of the Board of Health and the agent of the steamship of the town, the Noble, Honorable Mr. S. G. Wilder. This reporter of the natives of the newspaper, *Ka Lahui Hawaii,* received the honor of accompanying the members of the honorable house of the nation on the floor of the deck of the floating ark, the *Kīlauea.* There will be adequate time to witness a great lesson to demonstrate before the people the condition and appearance of our friends living under squalor and fear of the disease called leprosy [Lepera].

At nine o'clock, with minutes passing into the peacefulness of that Friday night on June 23, when the half moon nearly hid its beauty under the western horizon, and with the stars blinking lovingly in the sky from among the floating clouds on the canvas of space, that was when the queen of the Hawaiian ocean, the *Kīlauea,* left the dock and inched its way with its bow set toward the channel of Māmala. There was a large crowd gathered at the pier to bid their farewells, which joined together with our warm wishes. At that time the sea horse eased away and quickly passed the lighthouse [Hale Kukui] that leads in the night over the bay behind us. When I glanced over to look, it was as if the light was speeding inland, and that joy was not yet finished. The waves rustled along the sides, and I understood then in the channel of Māmala and uttered a few lines of a chant [mele] on a day that the monarch was seated. These are the lines:

Outside of Māmala, the sea spray blew,
I was drenched in the mist smearing the skin.

And at that time the engines of the gliding horse turned, allowing one to look back and see, "the wheel churns below," and that is when its nose took a breath in the sea of Ha'aluea. When I looked inland, it was as if the lights of the land retreated behind Waialua.

After the hustle and bustle on deck settled down, we went all over the deck to see how many colleagues came aboard to take on the sea on this wind-chilled voyage to Kalaupapa. We exchanged greetings with the president of the Board of Health, the royal, Wilder [Waila]; the director of the Committee of Thirteen at the time; and we had casual conversations with members of the committee, the Honorable Royal, P. Kanoa, Honorables Phillip [Pilipo], Māhoe, Nakaleka, Kauaʻi, Helekūnihi, Kalauokoa, Baranaba, Wana, Kamauoha, Nāukana, and Nāhaku. We met with some of our other excursion colleagues, the Royal, Smith, and Honorables Halstead, Lilikalani, Kahuila, and Nāʻili; the commissioner of France and his lady, Dr. Makipine, and a few others, and our members of the publication board, P. C. *Advertiser,* the *Hawaiian Gazette,* the *Kuokoa,* who are accompanied by a few others, and in total, there were about thirty or more people in the company.

While we were relaxing, sleeping, with "Puna and Kaʻū leaning upon each other," our ears were entertained listening to time-passing stories as the pastor Kahalaiʻa o Kūwaʻuwaʻu dreaming with a fan resting on our chests, and with the breeze carrying the dews that disappeared on the valleys of Kawaihoa and surrounding areas and wafting on the surface of the sea until it found us,

The *Kīlauea* makes its way and is gone,
Enjoying itself on the sea of Kaiwi,
The winds whip up from below.

At the point our voices went silent, we were surprised at the sounding of the bell (four bells) telling us that the hour hand on the clock face had reached the early hours of morning. A few minutes later everyone was silent and a feeling of dread spread across the deck as sleep had prevailed over the faces of the passengers envisioning dreamland, and this desolation invited me to look over. I was floored to observe that our friends were everywhere carrying their sleeping mats, with blankets rolled up, with the wings of the steadfastness of Niolopua covering over our colleagues who had been dragged to look with wonder at the communities of dreamland. At that time, it was as if I was in the midst of a desolate island since everyone was asleep except for the pilot with me as his second. As I observed the beauty of the movement of the ship, I was joined by the noise of snoring noses, with some rumbling and some whistling, and it was as if I was among the loving mountains of the Kona districts due to the kinds of singing tree snails [Pupukani oe] that were heard since the rumbling noises were the weazing snails. I slept for a bit and I was awakened again by the sight of the land being opened up in the light of dawn, which was when we were able to see the skin of the people. Our repose was shocked by the voice of the good attendant, Mr. Acosta, and his alert assistants, who asked, "Would you like a cup of coffee?" We were pleased with their generosity, and we accepted.

We saw the land some distance away and stretching out far to the left on the surface of the water, and the morning dews crept in and mingled with the cold, dampening mists of the cliffs. Kalāʻau Point [Lae o ka Kalaau] was off to the south of us, and ʻĪlio Point [Lae o ka Ilio] was straight ahead of us. When we arrived at Moʻomomi, we saw Kalaupapa lying at the face of the cliffs. At this place we faintly saw Lae Kapuʻupoʻi kissing the wisps of sea spray on the eastern side of Hālawa, and so, too, the headlands [makalae] of Wailau, the cliffs of

Pelekunu, and the small points [olaelae] of Kalawao, and the cluster of Hāʻupu (the islands in the sea) [Hui o Haupu (he mau moku iloko o ke kai)]. Kahio Point [Lae o Kahio] was drinking up the sea like a humpbacked camel in the cold. When I realized it, the ship, *Hoʻina* [poetic for "coming back"], was at the position it loved, and I uttered these lines:

Oh Hina! It is for you I long,
A love that lasts,
Your verdant cliffs,
A companion that loves the traveler,
And the cool breezes filled with dew,
That always bite at the skin.

As we were relaxing watching the cliffs, the ridges, the plains, and the points of land passing us by, our colleague cried out, "Here is Kalaupapa [eia o Kalaupapa]," and we turned in that direction and saw the houses set here and there on land. After a little while, the ship arrived at the harbor.

We boarded skiffs [waapa] and arrived onshore where we met with the many people huddled together. We shook hands with friends we knew from long ago who had disappeared from our view for years. (Here we can tell about how the gloves of some colleagues are slipped on, and to look at it is as if one puts on socks without shoes, the way we observed it.) We met with the many people who gathered there, Governor [Kiaaina] Ragsdale (Bila Auwana), our colleague we shook hands with first, and we met with a true friend of ours, a friend who met face to face with the ʻUkiu wind of Mt. Haleakalā in days passed, the police chief [makai nui] Crowningbourg (Bila ʻUlaʻula). When we uttered the words, "Aloha to you all!" [Aloha oukou a pau loa!], the echo of the chorus of voices reached us, "A-lo-ha!" showing us that their aloha was truly given to us. In looking at the type of terrain on land, it was good, not lacking great amounts of rain. The harbor was organized with a boardwalk, where the skiffs arrive and where the wings of the beautiful flag of Hawaiʻi wave proudly and wonderfully in the breezes. The appearance of the faces of the locals was disfigured for some, while others had the expression of true affections of love.

The governor was prepared, along with his second, the police chief, with horses. When we were all provisioned, we pranced along on the wide road headed straight ahead, with Kalawao being our objective on this excursion. It is about one mile away from the harbor. We arrived at the settlement home of the royal [alii] of the area.

Kekūokalani [Kekuaokalani], Peter Young Kāʻeo, was outside and was heard calling out to us in the usual way locals greet [leo aloha kamaaina], welcoming us with the words, "Come, come inside!" [He mai, e komo.] We accepted his generous greeting and visited with shaking hands. "Eat," [E paina] he said, but we were already fed onboard, and since we were in a bit of a hurry on the business of the committee, we asked him to let us leave to meet again upon our return. What we learned about the royal who lived on the land with the commoners [makaainana] is that all are well. We were a bit astonished. We did not forget the countenance on his face as he bid us a final farewell before he was bypassed [and told] to remain there. We thought at that time that there were not any real reasons for the necessity for health care. However, when we met with him, we were gratified as his previously morbid countenance was now handsome with a healthy, robust body, more so than he was before when he lived in the city. We nearly came to the conclusion that his sickness was over.

A few minutes after leaving his home, we observed the arrangement of the housing of the hospital and the people of Kalawao. This land is somewhat dry. On the north side are the high cliffs that dizzy the eyes to look at at a glance, with the voice of the waves calling out, battling with the rocky shore on the south side. When we were almost at where we determined to go, we caught the gentle, peaceful sound of horns and drums, and the breezes carried the sound to meet the cliffs as if they were returned there to entice the ears of the visitors. We were somewhat astonished, and when we inquired about this, we were told that it was the Horn Band [Band Puhi Ohe]! This was verified when we saw this when we arrived there, where we were met with happy faces and greetings with all of them. (To be continued.)

» [Another version of this trip to Kalaupapa by the Committee of Thirteen follows in the next article.]

Ka Nupepa Kuokoa. 1 JULY 1876. P. 2.
Na Hana o ka Ahaolelo. Business of the Legislature.

The legislature is moving very slowly in their debates. One point of discussion by one legislator will likely bring about contention later. Such is typical of debates between Hawaiian colleagues.

Last week Friday the legislature passed in the third reading the bill ratifying the Reciprocity Treaty with the United States [Kuikahi Panailike me Amerika Huipuia], which was met with a quick response that there were questions remaining. The representative of North Kona reaffirmed his displeasure with the proposal. Words of derision were heard from this representative at the foreign minister.

On the 20th of June, the bill to end the personal tax was considered in its second reading, and it was approved for the condensed version. This has been a bill that has been raised regularly in this session, but failed. Should this become law, the yearly income of the government would be reduced by $14,000 each year. A replacement for this deficit is being sought, now that this reserve has been shattered.

Last week was a week of major discussions at the legislature regarding the leprosy patients [mai lepera] and their complaints. Some are of the opinion that it is best that the leprosy patients [lepera], with their deformed hands and feet full of holes, should be extracted from Kalawao and returned to their homes. It was also discussed how the foreign doctors [kauka haole] are not able to cure the leprosy patients [lepera]. Kahui was brought into the legislature as an expert doctor in treating leprosy [kauka akamai i ka lapaau mai lepera] and he took with him some whom he had treated. Those only he treated. A Committee of Thirteen was appointed to travel to Moloka'i to examine the accusations of the leprosy patients [lepera] and to take them to Kahui.

On Friday night, the *Kīlauea* took the Committee of Thirteen to the troubled settlement [kahua o ka popilikia] along with a few others, for an expense of less than two hundred dollars. They arrived at seven o'clock in the morning on Saturday. The committee traveled the length and breadth of the settlement [ka loa'a i ka laula o ke kahua] for inspection, and according to the report of our writer published separately in today's paper, the findings can be seen.

Last Monday, the reports of the committee were considered before the majority and the minority of the house. At that time, the schoolmaster and some actions of the Board of Health were lambasted. The representative of Puna reported that vacation and additional pay was being paid to foreign schoolteachers [kumukula haole] of the union school in Hilo, but government Hawaiian-language day schools were not afforded vacation pay. They were only paid while school was in session. The superintendent was going back and forth, and this office was to be returned to the governors. We believe that the office is fine, but that it is people who should strike [olohani].

Ka huakai nana a na Komite 13 o ka Ahaolelo i na lepera. Kilauea no Kalawao. The inspection tour of the Committee of Thirteen of the legislature among the leprosy patients. Kilauea bound for Kalawao.

In accordance with the resolution of the house representative of North Kona, the select legislative committee was to be sent to Kalaupapa and Kalawao on Moloka'i, so the *Kīlauea* left Honolulu at nine o'clock at night on Friday [June 23] after waiting a few minutes for the Honorable G. W. Pilipo, the chairperson of the committee.

These are those who boarded the *Kīlauea* for Kalawao: the members of the committee, the royals, Waila [Wilder], Kanoa, Honorables G. W. Phillip [Pilipo], A. P. Kalaukoa, S. K. Māhoe, K. Kamauoha, E. Helekūnihi, J. A. Nāhaku, J. Nazareta, G. Barenabus [Barenaba], S. M. Nāukana, H. J. Wana, and J. Kaua'i. From our newspaper, A. C. Smith, G. Dole, John Sheldon, B. W. Kawainui, and other members of the legislature and other dignitaries from the city, and Dr. McKibbin and Kahui.

At the break of dawn on Saturday morning, we approached under Ka'īlio Point at the northwest [Lae o Kailio, ma ke Komohana Akau] of Moloka'i. After a few minutes of *Kīlauea*'s pitching, we safely passed the point, and we anchored at the point of the harbor [awa ku moku] of Kalaupapa at seven o'clock or soon after in the morning. At that time, the skiffs [waapa] were lowered, and we were transferred to shore. As we came into the temporary wooden pier, the Hawaiian flag was standing at the head of the wharf [uwapo], with the superintendent [luna nui], Wandering Bill [Bila Auwana: William Ragsdale], standing there in regalia, with his police chief [makai nui] William [Uilama] 'Ula'ula of Makawao.

We came ashore and shook hands with the two of them, and at that time, Wandering Bill instructed us to take our horses that were readied with saddles and were standing in the paddock. We quickly made our way over, got our horses, and waited for the last of our colleagues of the committee who were slow in disembarking off of their skiffs. Since they took so long, your newspaper reporter went over to the house of J. Komoikehuehu to see him. He took a while to arrive at the harbor to see what was happening and in brief, I left him in good physical health apart from some swelling in his face. With some starting and stopping of the horse along the way, I arrived at the home of Richard [Rikeke] of Kaua'i, saw him in good physical condition, and exchanged greetings as he sat at his glass door. From there, I went over to the rickety homes of the little town. As I looked at some people, they seemed not to be ill. Some had ears that were hanging down. When I inquired with some about returning home, they refused and wished not to return as they loved Kalawao. This is what these people felt. After meeting with them, it was the whip's turn, and I arrived at the home of the royal [ke lii], Kekuaokalani [Peter Kaeo]. There the members of the committee were assembled and were shaking hands warmly with him. Upon examining his condition and appearance it was as if the leprosy disease [mai lepera] had left him, as if he was back to his normal self with his stout stature.

There was a large gathering in Kalawao at eleven o'clock that afternoon [morning]. The committee left him to travel to Kalawao. As the horses pranced along, we found ourselves at the residence of the superintendent [luna], Wandering Bill, who was ready with his wife, Mrs. Hipua Wandering Bill, and she welcomed the committee graciously, along with your newspaper reporter. We had a pleasant talk with her, and we enjoyed ourselves. The committee ate some bananas, and when we were done with our meeting, we left that place to go and tour the infirmaries of the board. From there we went to the store of the board, where we stayed with the young royal of the land [opio alii o ka aina], G. W. Ke'eaumoku, who was the keeper of the store of the board. We shook hands with him and talked with him for a short while about the living conditions, and graciously, he thanked your reporter regarding the infirmaries, of which there were three situated in a triangle; two to the east, one to the north. There were thirty patients lying there. These were the weakest of all [mai nawaliwali loa] at those buildings.

Then we went over to the office of the superintendent and the pharmacy office. As we passed by these offices, we came across a horn and drum band [poe puhi ohe piula a me na pahu] playing under the direction of John Ka'ahaihanu. They were really good at playing. When we entered the veranda [lanai] of the building, there above the door were these words: "Welcome" [Aloha oukou] made of wāwae'iole moss by the great skill of the young royal, Ke'eaumoku. As you entered the pharmacy, bottles were inscribed with medicines. The name of the white person [haole] who ran that office was Ostrum. From there we entered the office of the superintendent and we saw technical books and handcuffs [kupee hao] for lawbreakers. The room was arranged nicely on the east side of the building, where cool sea breezes would waft in. In the comfort of the large room, we examined books and saw that statistics were managed well regarding the patients and the dead on a daily basis and more. After a number of minutes, we left that place and went to Waikolu to see our colleague, Enoka Kalauao, who isolated himself some miles away.

In the villages [kauhale] and on the roads we traveled, it was painful and sad to see Hawaiian nationals sitting on stone foundations, in doorways, and on the roadside, with distorted faces, their human countenance gone from their bodies. My pen cannot explain the state of difficulty and pain and pity incurred on my feelings for several minutes in our journey on the road all the way until we reached Waikolu, where our colleague, E. Kalauao, lived. When we arrived and shook hands with him, his wife was already there, who had been on the same ship as him. When we saw her face, the swelling as a result of leprosy was gone. The only disease that was noticeable was a rash and a blemish in her appearance. It was an indication of the kindness and generosity that she received. After all of the discussions and exchanges of greetings, the members of the committee dove headfirst [luu poo] into the stream. The coolness of the water was welcomed on this trip. When that was over, the committee met, and they settled on categories of sickness according to the level of severity. Sicknesses of category 1 were for those patients who could be sent home. Category 2 was for sicknesses that could be treated by Kahui. Category 3 was for sicknesses for which there was no cure.

Category 1, Mr. Enoka Kalauao, Ms. Kalakala, Mr. ʻŌpika, Kanoimalo. Category 2, Mr. Kaʻōiwinui, Mr. Papa. Category 3, Ms. Kaheanu, Ms. Kealoha. After this, the meeting was continued in Kalawao at twelve oʻclock noon. When the committee met to listen to the complaints of the leprosy patients [mai lepela], the Honorable Phillip sat as chair and the Honorable Māhoe was secretary.

The chair explained to the patients, "We are a committee appointed by the legislature and have been sent to inquire of you regarding your complaints that were sent to our house. Now, therefore, is the appropriate time for you to discuss with us regarding your complaints." The royal, Kekuaokalani, stood and raised a brief discussion apart from the complaints, and J. Komoikeehuehu added at length to this discussion: 1. This location [on Molokaʻi] was not suitable for us, the patients, as it was stormy at times, and incredibly hot at times. 2. This is not a contagious disease as some doctors allege, such as the ship's doctor. 3. Many helpers [kokua] for patients live in Kalawao and Kalaupapa. These are of other families. 4. The law of 1865 and 1870 should be abolished that segregates us to this place. 5. The meat and fish are not good. We are given salted salmon. 6. The man who arrives here without a helper [kokua] is as good as a dying dog who begs to be released to go home to his land of birth.

Wandering Bill and Wilder [Waila] spoke on behalf of the Board of Health. After the meeting was adjourned, a banquet was hosted for the lunch of the committee and other colleagues at the residence of the superintendent. After the luncheon, the committee met again at the home of the royal, Kekuaokalani, and the majority decided to return the royal that evening on the *Kīlauea*. When the royal was ready to go home according to the decision of the committee, S. G. Wilder, the agent of the Board of Health, protested, so the royal stayed back. The *Kīlauea* departed Kalawao at six oʻclock in the evening and reached Honolulu at twelve midnight. That is the brief report of this trip. Thanks should be given to the honorable representative of North Kona for including the secretary in the resolution. B. W. Kawainui. Reporter.

» [On Saturday, June 24, the Committee of Thirteen cleared Peter Kāʻeo (Kekuaokalani) to return home. They submitted their report to the legislature the following week, and Kāʻeo was allowed to leave Kalaupapa on July 4.]

Ka Lahui Hawaii. 6 JULY 1876. P. 3.

The bill for an act to change Section 9, Chapter 7 of the criminal law went through the second reading. It was moved to postpone. This was ratified.

The bill for an act to return the leprosy patients [mai lepera] of Kalawao [and] Kalaupapa to their own homes went through the second reading. It was moved that it be given to the board until the select committee who traveled to Molokaʻi to see the patients provides its report. This was agreed to.

The bill to amend the language of the agreement between masters and servants will go through its second reading. It was proposed to give this bill to the committee on bills of this nature.

Ka Nupepa Kuokoa. 8 JULY 1876. P. 2.
One of the royals [alii] of the legislature [Kekuaokalani: Peter Kāʻeo] has returned from where he was quarantined in Kalaupapa, Molokaʻi, and now he is among his own peers. He arrived last Tuesday [July 4] on the ship, the *Warwick* [Wauwiki], with Capt. John Bull [Keoni Bulu].

Ka Nupepa Kuokoa. 4 NOVEMBER 1876. P. 1.
Dear *Nupepa Kuokoa.* Greetings.
On the 22nd of Aug. 1876, I gave myself up to the government regarding the family-splitting disease [mai hookaawale ohana] with which I was afflicted, known as leprosy [mai lepera]. I abandoned views of my birthplace, and all of my family, and was taken to Honolulu and confined to the leprosy hospital [Halemai Lepera]. I stayed there for two weeks, after which I was brought all the way here to Kalawao on the 11th of September and was allowed out on the 15th.
As I observed the condition of this place and the appearance of everything, I saw that it was a good land with tall cliffs at the back of the place. The wind is strong. At times, it is chilly. Plants grow well here in Kalawao, but on the seaside of Kalaupapa and ʻIliopiʻi, it is very arid.
While living here in this place, it is stocked with food provided by the government, but my love for my family is greater than this, so I give my aloha here to my family. In your capacity as "Lookout" [Kilohana], please direct this message to all of them, hand-in-hand with my tears for my homeland. My stay here in this place, as we know, is a stay that is thought to be only due to my tribulations and sadness, which cause me to feel obligated to utter the following words from a chant [mele] that say, "My love rises up in me for the land of my birth." [Hu wale mai no ke aloha, O koʻu aina hanau.]
This is how my heart is continuously so disturbed for my love for my homeland and all of my family in body form. So, to my family in Maʻumaʻu, Hilo, and Mākuʻu in Puna Paia ʻAla, I send my aloha to you all. Here I am enduring a period of trouble and great sadness for the pains that beset my entire body. But if God has compassion to deliver me along with my many friends who are afflicted here in this compact government facility, then may the heavens be thanked, and may the Great Powerful One be thanked abundantly.
—W. S. Kipi. Kalawao, Molokaʻi.

Ka Lahui Hawaii. 23 NOVEMBER 1876. P. 3.
Haule I Ke Kai. Lost at Sea.
Dear *Ka Lahui Hawaii.* Greetings.
When the schooner, the *Warwick* [kuna Warwick], arrived at the leprosy colony [panalaau lepera] with supplies and seven leprosy patients [mai lepera], one leprosy patient [mai lepera] by the name of ʻAipalena fell into the sea, and in a matter of a few minutes, he died in the cold grave of the deep, dark ocean [lua kupapau anuanu o ka moana kai lipolipo]. This was a famous man, known across the islands for his great skill in horseback riding [holo lio] and lassoing

cattle [hoohei bipi]. It has been said that he was a real expert in that occupation, one to be feared. When he fell, the ship came to and a rope was tossed out along with a log, but he was not able to grab them as he was overcome with numbness from the cold, and as the ship got near, he passed.

On the 19th of this month at 3:30 is when he passed. He remains to be brought to the grave for which he has no love and for which he failed to return. There is only one thing that can be said, let the name of God be praised, the one who giveth and the one who taketh. With aloha. W. K. Wiki. Kalawao, Moloka'i, Nov. 20, 1876.

Ka Nupepa Kuokoa. 25 NOVEMBER 1876. P. 2.
Na Nuhou Kuloko. Local News.

On the last voyage of the schooner, the *Warwick* [Wawiki], to Kalawao from this harbor, one of its passengers jumped or fell, by the name of Aipelena ['Aipalena], who was afflicted with leprosy [lepera] and who was being taken to Kalawao.

Ka Lahui Hawaii. 7 DECEMBER 1876. P. 3.
Na Anoai. The News.

As the boat of Queen Kapi'olani sat outside of the wave break [kunana nalu: same as kulana nalu, the place where waves break] at Kalaupapa last week, unable to go ashore for the severity of the storm, hundreds of subjects [makaainana] were seen who were afflicted with leprosy [mai lepera] on the shore shouting hurrays [e huro mai ana] and singing. We were appreciative of their band who were singing happy songs. The superintendent [Luna] came to the shoreline and gave a speech on behalf of the subjects [makaainana] there. They regretted not seeing her, but were happy to know that their queen did not give up her hope to meet with them despite the big storm with its very large waves. They were ready with all that was needed, such as they were able to have on hand to welcome and host the royal visitor [malihini Roiala]. There was a veranda [lanai] that was decorated with foliage from the forest and prepared with the beautiful Hawaiian flag waving in the wind. What a pity for them. There were fifty cattle that were thrown out there [to swim ashore], with two having drowned in the storm.

Ka Lahui Hawaii. 7 DECEMBER 1876. P. 3.
Na Anoai. The News.

The *Kīlauea* towed the schooner *Warwick* [kuna Warwick] last Saturday night on its way to Kalawao, with some friends aboard who were afflicted with the supernatural disease known as leprosy [mai kupua he lepera] bound for Moloka'i. We were saddened to hear the crying of women and children who were denied their husbands and fathers by this terribly destructive disease that splits the family apart [mai luku weliweli a hookaawale ohana ana] and causes one to ask, "What will become of them from now on? Shall the women wander off and the children stray away to become bait for disaster? Shouldn't the government build suitable homes for them and shouldn't the government take care of them? And is it right to try to save the people in one way, but to harm them in another way?"

Ka Lahui Hawaii. 1 FEBRUARY 1877. P. 2.
No Kalawao, i Molokai. From Kalawao, Moloka'i.

On the evening of last Tuesday, the schooner *Warwick* [kuna Warwick] departed, followed by the *Kīlauea,* for the harbor of Kalaupapa, the settlement [kahua] of our friends who are afflicted with the terrifying disease known as leprosy [mai weliweli he lepera], at Kalawao, Moloka'i. On its deck, a few colleagues were also taken to the coffin of the living [lua kupapau o ke ola] as they came down with this dreadful disease [mai mainoino]. We met together with them face to face before leaving their friends behind in the leprosy hospital [haukapila lepera] on the west ['Ewa] side of the prison [Halewai]. What we saw there were sad countenances and lamenting and wailing among the men and women and among the parents and children and also among the friends. It was such a pitiful sight, such a sad and pathetic scene that one cannot wipe such things away from one's heart to look upon such scenes of outpourings of love.

How sad! How sad for parents whose countenances have been distorted by this accidental disaster of a disease, leaving one to mourn telling of the lives of the sick with so much pain, as children leave, the flesh of the loins gifted by our All Powerful Father [Makua Mana] that the heavens blessed with love in the hearts of living beings. Such pity for the children whose faces are drenched with tears of love, left to put their heads down to cry, seeing their parents being taken away from them forever, not by death, but by an unusual accident of this world. They will not ever see again the loving faces of their parents, never to hear again their comforting voices, and never to call out their names again, those who care and long for their well-being. Oh! It is like death itself! Yes! It is worse than the pitiful nature of death. Oh, who? Yes! Who is a parent who is without love for the young one of their loins, whom they cherished with eyes always alert day and night. And so, too, for the child to their parent? How pitiful! Pitiful indeed.

Such pity for husbands and wives. Such pity for their lives that they had enjoyed in peace, where love was sealed truly between them, where their days had been joined together as one river flowing gently throughout so many days all the way up until this accident, where their unshaken love was shattered and the life of the family split. How pitiful. It is so sad to see husbands mourning for the last time for their spouse [koolua], and so, too, wives who are deprived of the fathers of their lives, their husbands.

> Oh! Dear gracious powers of the heavens!
> Is Hawai'i so errant in your eyes?
> Is it true that you are angry with us?
> The love of yours, oh Redeemer?
> This life is yours, all of it
> And it is your will that will be done
> And this faith is in you
> May God save Hawai'i!

Ka Lahui Hawaii. 22 MARCH 1877. P. 2.
He welina aloha i ka Home. (He Leta Walohia). A warm greeting to my home. (A Sad Letter.)

Dear *Ka Lahui Hawaii*. Greetings.

With tears streaming down causing me dizziness, with belabored thoughts, with a heart filled with pain, and with hands trembling, quaking with sadness, and the point of the pen drinking up the black hue of ink to stain, so, too, I lay before you my show of love to all of you, those reading this.

Love to my birthplace [one hanau]: To "Puna of the rustling sea in the hala groves" [Puna kai nehe i ka ulu hala] from the border of Māwae to the "Lehua groves in Panaʻewa" [Ulu lehua i Panaewa], the work of love is cruel here, all the way to "Papalohi of ʻĀpua, the border at ʻOkiʻokiaho" [Papa-lohi o Apua, ka palena i Okiokiaho]. I am exhausted with love. I am drifting. Protect me.

It is Puna, my homeland [aina hanau], "Puna adorns itself in lei of hala and lehua, what those of that place usually adorn themselves with" [Lei no Puna i ka hala me ka lehua, o ko laila kahiko mau no ia]. The two spots are where I relax: Kaimū and Kaniumoe of Kalapana, together known as "Kalauonāone for the silent pili grass plains where no one lives at Kaunaloa" [Kalauonaone, mai ke kula-pili ano kanaka ole o Kaunaloa]. Where love lived was a long place, all the way to where the "Lehua moves toward the pāhoehoe lava fields of Kīkala" [Lehua nee i ka pahoehoe o Kikala], where love calls out unendingly, limping along, steadfast, traversing the way to ʻĀinaʻike [kee-keehi kulana o Ainaike], so, too, my love goes out to my birthplace; and this is what I call out:

"My thoughts of love are firm, etc.
To that birthplace of mine, etc."

Aloha to our friends: I am your friend living among the multitudes among us who have been dangerously enveloped by this disease so feared known as leprosy [mai i makau ia he lepera]. I send my greetings to you all, as the numbing cold of love, the friend that lingers inside me, goes out to my true friends out there from where the sun rises at Haʻaehaʻe to Kauaʻi of Manōkalanipō [mai ka la puka i Haehae a Kauai o Manokalanipo]. You are the fathers and mothers, the elder brothers and younger brothers, the sisters and children, and all friends; for you I utter these lines of a chant [mele],

"The entire form of the cliff of Hiʻilei wears a lei
Enjoying what love has to offer
Love that creates memories
Is found here."

I did not forget to extend my love to the true friends and colleagues, my many friends living in the "Seaspray Below" [Ehukai o Lalo: an epithet for Waialua, Oʻahu], where my love and I lived together along with our two children. That is where I lived knowing love, where the claws and jagged teeth of the bloodthirsty animals would roam [government officials who hunted for leprosy patients], and where they would toss the fragile bodies of travelers to the vicious lions of the city of Honolulu. These are those who decided, do not eat my flesh and do not drink my blood, but toss him to the grave of Kalawao [luakupapau o Kalawao], with the bones of his fellow men to pile up into a messy heap there. Not having dreamed ever before, I stepped onto the deck [papahele] of the schooner *Warwick,* the coffin that carries our friends back and forth to the grave at the colony of Kalawao [kuna Warwick, ka pahukupapau nana e auamo hele nei i na hoa'loha o kakou no ka luakupapau o ka Panalaau o Kalawao], leaving my friends in Puna [I am] "dragged by the current, dragged at Halaea" [ko nei ke au, ko i Halaea], and they, who are never to be seen again, are for whom I utter these lines of a chant [mele],

> "'Akuli is the flower of the plant in the water
> Floating in heaps at the edge of the pond with mirages
> Water that is held back in that place
> For that god of Mānā called Limaloa
> Causing my thoughts to haunt me!"

Aloha to the family: To my dear family living in the uplands of Kaueleau and at Keahialaka: my dad and my dear loving mom, here I am, your loving son, the first fruit of your loins, and to my younger siblings, brothers and sisters. There are nine of us who have emerged from the loins of our parents. Two have died, and there are seven of us left. And from us, the first four, ten rose buds (children) [pua rose (keiki)] have been born, two having died, with eight remaining. Your loving brother begs your patience in taking care of our parents who remain, as well as your husbands, as well as your younger siblings, "so that their lives on the land of Jehovah, our God, that he gave us may be long"; that we may continue our prayers asking that all trouble be taken away, and that you may flourish and sprout greatly, so that the motto [makia] of the government of Kalākaua may be established [Ho'oulu Lahui: increase the nation]. I ask with prayers to the heavens that you all may be delivered from the grasp of this terrifying disease [mai weliweli] with its cruel and dreadful effects that are unspeakable. I left my birthplace and the family on Monday, April 24, 1876, at Waialua in the Seaspray Below [Ehukai o Lalo], and on Wednesday, January 31, 1877, we left Waialua for Kalawao. You have heard that I am here, and you are filled with sadness lamenting forever. You forgive each other, and this causes me to utter,

> "How glorious are those who forgive
> Who forgive and are forgiven
> This life is one in which we are hunched over
> With hands rubbing at the chin
> With the lehua flowers of Mānā emerging
> Wandering off as the chin does!"

Love to my wife: This is the greatest gift that God has given all men in physical form. Fathers receive all kinds of love, and women receive heated love and a constricting love. My dear wife is the young bud of my love, as, "The eyes have hidden it and it is lost!" I am lost! Lost to Puna at a time of misjudging! Oh no! My dear love!

You and I are bound, brought together and bound with the golden chain of matrimony before God in the Protestant chapel of Waikapū in the Kololio [Kokololio] wind in the afternoon of the Sabbath, November 19, 1871, by Rev.

W. H. Kahoʻokaumaha. We were bound together in marriage for five years, two months, and twenty-three days, and the command of God remains with me here, saying, "What God had put together, let no man put asunder. Only death can separate you two." This is what God has locked firm, and yet it is broken.

What is more painful is my departure from the place I was new to (Waialua) [aina malihini (Waialua)] with the two little babies, one being able to walk and the other not yet able to crawl, and not able to help! I have come here, the father, the one whose job it is. Oh no! my dear children, as

"The Koʻolau side whips, and the loved ones are gone
The reviled flowers are heaped up at Wailua [Waialua]."

Hiding love that disappears, never to disappear, as told by the tears. This is what I lament, with moaning, as I utter the lines:

"Love will temper
How will it end?
It seals up and lightens our thoughts
I am cold hearing your voice."

And for these days in which we live, the clouds of burdens of sadness do not part from me regarding my birthplace [one-oiwi], my friends, my family, and my dear loved one. I go a long way to the breadth of Kalawao, where I am, never forgetting my love, and so I utter these lines,

"I go to the sandy fringes of Kalawao
A shell is laid before me
I put its lips to my ear
And hear what it has to say
From within its heart inset with pearls
A humble voice, so sad
As is it combined with words and tears together
Gently answering, 'It has passed.' "

Aloha to all of you. Ephraim Kanoe. Kawaluna, Kalawao, FEB. 20, 1877.
» [In this moving letter to his family, Ephraim Kanoe references Halaʻea, a powerful ocean current on the Kaʻu side of Ka Lae (South Point) on Hawaiʻi island, to describe what it means to be sent to Kalaupapa. According to *Place Names of Hawaii,* a canoe caught in the Halaʻea current would be dragged out to sea, never to be seen again.]

Ka Lahui Hawaii. 17 MAY 1877. P. 3.
He Panai I Ka Leta Walohia A. E. Kanoe. An Answer to the Sad Letter of A. E. Kanoe.
Dear *Ka Lahui Hawaii.* Greetings.

I perused and looked and saw in the 12th edition of your body the thoughts of the sad letter from Kawaluna, Molokaʻi, written by the one named Ephraim Kanoe.

With sad thoughts and a bereaved heart, and with tears streaming down,

I answer to give my greetings to that letter. As I saw those words there, along with the great loving message, the ponds of Kūlanihākoʻi [kiowai o Kulaniha-koi: mythical ponds in the sky that were the source of rain] quickly filled to the brim. It was as if they were with me, crying with me at that very moment, but when I turned and looked, I realized that I was taken by the currents of mis-judgment.

It is as if the walls of my home, Haleloa Home, were crying with me, along with the coconut trees that recline here in Kalapana [niu moe o Kalapana nei], where I lived for a long time, the birthplace [aina hanau] of your body. It is also as if the stone walls of Halāliʻi School House, where you and I were educated, were

Kissing me
In the calm waters
Filling up to capacity with petals

What have the moving lehua flowers done to you in the pāhoehoe lava fields of Kīkala where you were vigilant to remain close to the parents, the fam-ily, and the friends living here in our homeland [aina hanau], that you should go and be separated in a foreign place (Waialua), where the loveless claws dragged your body and tossed you to the grave, and so it is, you have been separated, and so, too, we have been separated.

I am he who has signed his name here, one of your kin, and I force my pen tip to drink the black stain of ink, as

I am troubled inside
Troubled with my thoughts

I have such great aloha for you, my dear child, who complains about all that has been taught and the things of God. My aloha is stirred up for you and can-not be satiated as you are not here, as you have been separated to somewhere else. What I have heard is that you were taken from Waialua to Honolulu, and what's more is that I heard that you died in Kalawao, but we have received con-firmation through your sad letter, and we are so overcome with sadness.

And so what has become of him? And so it is that you are separated and we are separated. We all spill tears, and we bear a sad burden of love that we carry. So this is our plea to God, that he would ease all of your thoughts of sadness, and that he would end all of our troubles.

I did not forget about you and what you did here, but it is all in vain. Had we still been living together here in our birthplace, then our cheeks would not be wet with tears.

Tears spill over
Not able to be held back
This is how love works
As it spills over

Here we are your parents and your younger brothers and sisters living here in our birthplace doing only one thing, wetting our eyelashes crying with love on the point of 'ōhi'a groves in Kaueleau, with our love going somewhere out to sea, but not finding you. So this then is the journey you have taken, leaving us behind, wherein:

> You have been invited to Kalawao
> To the boundary [anapuni] of the leprosy patients [mai lepera]
> The sickness that splits families [mai hookaawale ohana] and the lives of friends
> We are heaped up with disappointment on the shore
> Oh! I am so sorry, my dear son!

You are not a child, but you are a parent of my trouble, and I am the one extending my aloha to you, but you not so, as I know you withheld your love for your family at Kaueleau and Keahialaka, and how is it that I am the last of your mother and the entire family of yours living here in your birthplace extending greetings to you?

The love that works inside my heart is as if it is firmly established, with nothing that can break it. So if you see this, remember that I extend my greetings to you and that my family weeps with love for you, as does your wife who was left without a father with the children who are fatherless.

Grandpa (Kōnia) cries with love for you, as does your mother Mā'aha, also of your family. And it is as if in these last words that all of Puna in the fragrant walls of hala [Puna i ka paia aala] are also included in this sad greeting to you. Perhaps it is known well how much we feel for you with our love that has been thrown out from the grave (Kalawao) [luakupapau (Kalawao)].

With loving salutations to the typesetter boys of *Ka Lahui Hawaii,* along with the editor, with a firm handshake.

—S. Tito Pi'ihonua. Kalapana, Puna, Hawai'i, 1877.

» [In this moving response to the preceding letter by Ephraim Kanoe, the writer, S. Tito Pi'ihonua, references the "reclining coconut trees" of Kalapana (niu moe o Kalapana). In times past, young coconut trees were bent over and secured, forcing them to grow horizontally instead of vertically. Kalapana residents did this to commemorate visits of royalty to their village.]

Ka Lahui Hawaii. 31 MAY 1877. P. 3.
We have received word that William Charles Ke'eaumoku has been taken by death at the colony of leprosy patients [panalaau o na lepera] on Moloka'i, and we extend our sympathies to his companion [hoapili], his wife, and their children.

Ka Lahui Hawaii. 26 JULY 1877. P. 1.
Ka Mai Pake ma Hawaii nei. Leprosy here in Hawai'i.
This disease here in Hawai'i that is spreading throughout the island chain [pae aina] is a disease that could spell the end of this race [lahuikanaka] as the rumors have it. Before the years of 1864 and 1865, there were only a few people who had come down with this disease, and in those years, laws were passed to segregate those who are infected with the disease at Kalawao, Moloka'i. There is where those affected by the disease are taken. At the Evangelical Conference of the Islands [Ahaolelo Hui Euanelio o keia Pae Aina] here in Honolulu in 1873,

they decided to sign their names individually to bring a lawsuit against Mr. Holo, the minister of the interior [Kuhina Kalaiaina], at the time with regard to tossing out their sick, throwing them out, ejecting them according to the instructions of the Bible. This is what they did. Their protest was joined together with white doctors [kauka haole] saying that this is not a disease that warrants ejection and the tossing out of these people from among their peers who are not affected by the disease.

And since those years until today, people are still being taken over, and the people are increasing in number. So, too, the number of people being taken to Moloka'i is also increasing. One of these patients contracted syphilis [kaokao] from his parents, and a laborer on the sugar plantation came down with a severe disease as a result of his supervisors after being put to work in the rain and storm in the cold of the dews of the early morning hours of dawn. This person, therefore, contracted a blood disease with lumps as there was no one to offer massage to press out or walk on top of him. [Hawaiian massage, or lomilomi, may include walking carefully on the back of a patient as part of the massage therapy.] He was alone in his yearly cottage with no colleagues with him. There was a woman living with him, and she either left or who knows what?

So this is a reason for the nation to be vigilant, from the one sitting upon the throne to the lowliest farmer; that is, the health of the people. We encourage people to go and work on the sugar plantations, and yet there is a big burden remaining at Kalawao. You continue to pursue the ambition to obtain hundreds of thousands of pounds of sugar when the sugar cane matures, and on the first sign of problems, perhaps the tassels become clumped up and other problems that I described earlier, the problems become nothing, with only one thought remaining, that being the great valley that opens up at Kalawao, with its volcano lake [luapele kai] named Kauhakō.

Ka Lahui Hawaii. 13 DECEMBER 1877. P. 3.

Last Sunday afternoon, the Youth Organization of Kawaiaha'o [Aha Opio o Kawaiahao] raised funds for the new chapel [halepule hou: Kanaana Hou] in Kalaupapa, Moloka'i, and they obtained $15.

On the 27th of Nov. in Kalawao on Moloka'i, William P. Ragsdale died. He was the supervisor [Luna Nui] of the leprosy patients [mai lepera] there. We will publish his story later.

Ka Nupepa Kuokoa. 8 JUNE 1878. P. 1.
Huakai A Ke Komite 13 O Ka Ahaolelo I Ka Panalaau O Na Mai Lepera Ma Kalawao. Journey of the Legislative Committee of Thirteen to the Colony of the Leprosy Patients at Kalawao.
(By a writer from the *Kuokoa.*)

At five o'clock on Tuesday morning, I went up to the deck [oneki] and saw Kalaupapa below us and the flat settlement [kahua palahalaha] of Kalawao before us.

Mōkapu was out before us on the sea and 'Ōkala passed by to the side. The steep slope of Huelo was there in the calm, and the falls of Waiehu tumbled down the cliffs [of Waikolu]. That is where a loving memory came up in me as I remembered the waterfalls [wailele] of Waiānuenue and Akāka in Hilo.

The bow of the ship turned toward the island, and for a moment, the anchor clanged in the bay of Kalaupapa. It was six o'clock on Tuesday morning.

That is when we saw some people coming on horseback and some on foot, and not long after that the shoreline of the harbor was full of people.

After several unskillful attempts, the skiff [waapa] was launched and the committee left the deck of the *Kīlauea Hou* and reached the shore and met with colleagues D. Puna, J. K. Kahuila, P. W. Kaʻawa, J. H. Nāpela, and the new supervisor [luna nui] of the leprosy patients [mai lepera], W. K. Sumner, and other colleagues.

At seven o'clock and fifteen minutes that morning, the committee met at Kalaupapa. Before the start of the activities of the committee, the Hon. W. M. Gibson [Kipikona] offered a few words before the leprosy patients [mai lepera], stating: "Dear friends, we, the committee of the legislature, have come to see to the needs or not, pertaining to your living here. My heart is greatly saddened because of this affliction that is set upon this community. I have been chosen as a representative, but I did not consider much regarding the health of the people. We brought with us a few gifts for you from Queen Emma [Moiwahine Ema], including $100 and a few boxes of other gifts. And we have also come to extend our aloha to you." The patients [mai] gave a few shouts of hurray [huro].

Later, the Hon. W. O. Smith offered a few words: "Dear friends, that is what we came for, to understand your problems. Our greatest desire is to determine if it is possible to find a solution to these problems. We have, therefore, brought with us a few doctors."

After that was done, the committee sat and carried out its work. The patients laid some complaints before the committee, and the committee asked a number of questions of the patients regarding their complaints. The committee stayed for two hours inquiring of the patients. The committee finished its work at Kalaupapa and went on horseback to Kalawao.

Before starting their activities, a few delegates of the committee went on a tour of the flat settlement [kahua palahalaha] of Kalawao, and the Hons. J. Nāwahī, J. N. Kaiʻaikawa, and I went up to the source of the water line at Wailēʻia. From this pond [kiowai] is where the water enters the pipeline up against the cliff, where it is placed on posts until it reaches the flats of the land, and from there it goes underground until the square of the hospital at Kalawao. In my estimation it is almost a full mile in length.

After a brief rest there, we went back to the settlement work. When we got back, a great number of patients had gathered on the grounds of the hospital. At two o'clock in the afternoon on Tuesday, the committee sat again to perform its duties, after which time was given for photo taking [hana paikii] for the leprosy patients [mai lepera] by Mr. H. L. Chase at the direction of the committee. After the photos were taken, Mr. A. W. B. Nāhakualiʻi read a letter from the king to them. These are the greater points of the letter: "The committee is here to see you. Tell them all your troubles, etc." At four o'clock that evening, the committee finished its work for the day.

We quickly made our way once again to go and tour the stream of Waikolu, and we saw the taro patches [loi kalo] there. The dark water of that stream was flowing fine. The distance from Kalaupapa to Kalawao is two miles, and to Waikolu it is three miles. We turned and went back to Kalawao, and there we went to visit Kauhakō, a seawater pond [loko kai] between Kalaupapa and Kalawao. The locals there told us that if you have a rope eighty feet long and let it down into the lake, it will not reach the bottom. The water is green in appearance. When we left there it was dark, and we spent the night at the cottage of the Board of Health at Kalawao.

On Wednesday, the next day, May 29, at seven o'clock in the morning, the committee sat again to finish the rest of its duties and heard everything. The office records were examined and everyone great and small was interviewed. This is how the committee carried on its business until eleven o'clock in the morning. The committee finished its business and returned to Kalaupapa. In everything that I observed on this trip of the committee, there were three types of the patients: the first were those who were considered to be in good condition; the second were those who are considered to be partially afflicted; and the third were those who are seriously afflicted by the disease.

On observation, it is terrible to see our fellow subjects burdened with such awful effects of this degenerative disease. I have heard that there are probably fewer than seven hundred patients, but there are no fewer than fifty patients in good condition there.

At twelve o'clock in the afternoon was the last meeting in Kalaupapa, then they boarded the *Kīlauea Hou*. At one o'clock in the afternoon, they left Kalaupapa for Honolulu and at a half past six, the ship arrived at the pier [uwapo].

At the end of this report, and due to the graciousness of one of our colleagues, W. H. Kamoana, I provide this, a list of names of patients who died in Kalaupapa and Kalawao from the month of January all the way to May.

DEATHS AT KALAWAO. [IN 1878]

January 2, Lūkela of Honolulu, O'ahu.
   " 7, Ka'ili'ōpū of Lāhaina, Maui.
   " 10, Kelakika of Iwilei, S. O'ahu.
   " 10, Kamakauila of Hāmākua, H.
   " 13, Ka'oaka of Waialua, O'ahu.
   " 13, Kahalelā'au of Pelekunu, Moloka'i.
   " 14, 'Aikake, part-haole, of Honolulu, O'ahu.
   " 15, Nāwāhine of Kā'anapali, Maui.
   " 16, Kaluna of Haleali'i, S. O'ahu.
   " 27, Paukekohu of Kohala, Hawai'i.
   " 27, Kīnā of Ko'olaupoko, O'ahu.
   " 27, Keoni'ailama of Honolulu, O'ahu.
February 1, Keoni'āpiki of Honolulu, O'ahu.
   " 2, 'A'ā of Ka'ū, Hawai'i.
   " 7, Pelapela of Kāne'ohe, O'ahu.
   " 11, Pānui of Kona, Hawai'i.
   " 16, Kekāhili of Kailua, Hawai'i.
   " 19, Malaea of Ko'olau, O'ahu.
   " 22, Pōlea of 'Ewa, O'ahu.
   " 24, Nāpahu'ekolu of Mānoa, O'ahu.
   " 28, Nu'a of Waialua, O'ahu.
   " 28, Kanihi of Lāna'i.

March 3, Ke'o, part-haole of Waialua, O'ahu.
" 5, Helemauna of Kaupō, Maui.
" 9, Keawe of Lāna'i.
" 19, Ka'aikaula of Pu'unui, O'ahu.
" 19, John Honokoa of Honolulu, O'ahu.
" 22, Kahale of Hāmākua, Hawai'i.
" 23, Kalani of Honolulu, O'ahu.
" 26, Ho'opūhalu of Ka'ū, Hawai'i.
" 27, Kauluāhewa of Wailuku, Maui.
" 28, Mako'o of Kā'anapali, Maui.
" 31, 'Ālau of Honolulu, O'ahu.
" 31, Makua of Hāmākua, Hawai'i.
April 1, Ka'io of Kōloa, Kaua'i.
" 2, 'Ōpūnui of Wai'alae, O'ahu.
" 8, Iosepa Hanaloa of Waialua, O'ahu.
" 14, Ka'ili'ula'ula of Kahuku, O'ahu.
" 18, Ka'oi.
" 19, Kahula of Lāhaina, Maui.
" 19, Kalua.
" 21, S. W. [W. S.] Kipi of Hilo, Hawai'i.
" 23, Kahipono'ī of Honolulu, O'ahu.
" 28, Kamaka of Kaupō, Maui.
" 30, Kahaukomo of Lāna'i.
May 2, Kalakala of Hāna, Maui.
" 4, Kauhiahulu of Hāmākua, Hawai'i.
" 7, Nui.
" 9, 'Ūli'i of Honolulu, O'ahu.
" 15, Nāhulu of Waimea, Kaua'i.
" 17, Kīpaku of Honolulu, O'ahu.
" 20, Kimo of Pālolo, O'ahu.
" 20, Pāniki.
" 20, Kūkama.
" 25, Kupa of Mākila, Lāhaina, Maui
" 28, Moni.

The total number of deaths at Kalawao only is fifty-six in the span of five months.

DEATHS AT KALAUPAPA.

January 9, Kahololio.
" 12, Kaluna.
" 14, Ka'awa (male).
" 26, Kipela.
February 27, Kahoe.
March 3, Kahumoku.
April 20, Piko.
" 25, Kai'a.

May 11, Kopa.
  " 15, Ka'ilianu.
  " 19, Helekūnihi.
  " 19, Kalama.

The total number of deaths at Kalaupapa in the span of five months is
twelve, and the total number of deaths in Kalawao and Kalaupapa is sixty-
eight.

Ka Nupepa Kuokoa. 27 JULY 1878. P. 1.
Ka Make Ana O Ke Kiaaina Lepera. The Death of the Leprosy Governor.
Dear *Nupepa Kuokoa.* Greetings.
    What appears above is an expression of gratitude to William P. Ragsdale
(Bila Auwana) in the newspaper, the *Youths Companion* [a newspaper printed
in English], of the 27th of June 1878. And as we remember our very famous
orator [oretora], and as we now see that his fame has been appreciated by the
whites [ilikeokeo] in the millions, we therefore translate this article.
    W. P. Ragsdale (Wandering Bill) [Bila Auwana, a nickname], governor of the
leprosy settlement [Kiaaina o kahi noho o na lepera] on the island of Moloka'i
of the Hawaiian Islands [Hawaii Pae Aina], died last month in December.
He was a Hawaiian by birth, a son of a native Hawaiian woman with a white
American father. He was an attorney by occupation and was equally fluent in
English and Hawaiian, having a high command of both. He was the best of the
most famous orators in the entire country of Hawai'i. What he had contracted
was leprosy (elephantiasis), such an accident.
    He lived at his office building in Hilo, the capital of Hawai'i [island], on
some nights, whenever he would ponder greatly over a certain legal case. He
had an accident where the glass (chimney) on his lamp fell onto the table.
He forgot that the glass was very hot and grabbed it, not thinking it was hot. As
he jumped with fright he looked and did not see even a small burn.
    He shook it off and looked at his hand and saw that there was no indica-
tion of a burn on his hand. He tried to grab a hold of something later as he had
always done before and quickly realized that he had become an offering to the
terrifying disease of leprosy [mai weliweli o ka lepera], which was spreading
widely in warm climates.
    His concerns were confirmed by a doctor's knowledge, and he did not waste
any time in reporting the truth to the authorities of the government.
    But the police [makai] in the city were used to apprehending those who are
suspected of having leprosy, and Mr. Ragsdale, in his very famous position, was
not disturbed.
    Therefore, thinking for himself, he gave himself over as a living sacrifice to
the fearful disease [mohai ola na ka mai weliweli]. He was sent to Moloka'i and
installed as governor of the place where leprosy patients live [Kiaaina no kahi o
ka poe lepera], and it is in this capacity that he lived until his death.
    Due to his excellent work at his job, many changes were instituted, and as
a result of his gentle and gracious heart, he made himself comfortable in this
place where eight hundred individuals lived in sadness being afflicted with the

loveless disease [mai aloha ole], and for these reasons, he was loved as a father figure by these troubled people.

Below are the expressions of appreciation found in the English-language newspapers [nupepa haole] to our famous orator who proudly stepped forward to render orations in his day. Oh, he was a friend of wisdom. Although his body has died, his name remains for the people of this world to adore so that it may live on remaining famous among millions of souls.

—Raindrop. 'Ulupalakua, Maui.

» [The reference to elephantiasis in the second paragraph is from a Latin term formerly used for leprosy, *Elephantiasis graecorum*. Elephantiasis is an infection that causes extreme swelling in the arms and legs.]

Ko Hawaii Pae Aina. 30 DECEMBER 1882. P. 2.
Pane I Ka Haiolelo A Hon. A. F. Judd, Ma Ka Luakini O Kaumakapili. Response to the Speech by Hon. A. F. Judd at Kaumakapili Church.
Please allow for space in your column to accommodate this report of mine. Here it is:

I read the *Ko Hawaii Pae Aina* newspaper on the 16th of this month about the speech of Hon. A. F. Judd at Kaumakapili on the night of Dec. 1. I noticed a number of errors and untruths in his account of Hawaiian history [Moolelo Hawaii], which was skewed by American missionaries [Mikanere Amerika] and his appreciation of the king, who dealt cruelly with Catholic priests [Kahuna Katolika], along with their conspirators [poe kipi], as a result of his desire to coddle favor with those missionaries.

These errors and untruths are amazing and also sad, and so goes, too, for his admiration of the atrocious behavior when you think about it. This foreigner [haole] spoke in such a way to curry favor by speaking untruths about our Supreme Court justice, the one who clarifies the entirety of the law from beginning to end among the public.

His account that he selected is clearly off the mark because he compares Catholic priests to rebels of the country, rabble-rousers and alcoholics, and accomplices to sin. Are we to count among those great criminals Bishop Louis Maigret and the priest of Moloka'i, the Rev. Damien [Damiano], the one who was honored by King Kalākaua just last year, and all of the other Catholic priests who have given their lives for the betterment of this country without care and without seeking their own material benefit like their enemies have done?

And isn't the mistreatment of Catholic priests a grievous wrong that stains the history of Hawai'i, something that should not be recognized any more to cover good?

It is an untruth to be selective about Hawaiian history. The highly shameful actions of Ka'ahumanu and others along with some other Hawaiian chiefs are their own to answer for, and it is known by all that the American missionaries encouraged and urged the chiefs and commoners alike to expel the Catholic priests and threaten those who would consider converting to Catholicism and cause trouble to those who had already converted to cause them to abandon the Church.

These actions of the American missionaries are laughable. These men of the cross, which they revile, and because of this reviling they call Catholics idol worshipers and make cases against Catholic priests, those who truly love the cross, as if they would revive the idol worshiping ways of the ancient past.

Perhaps the hearing ears of those at Kaumakapili would be thrilled to hear about the great deeds of their ancestors and have taken courage once again in their hearts. It was not the fire of unity that the one who selected his history desired, but rather the fire of ancient cursing.

However, let the Most Powerful God be glorified. The time of ignorance and following after bigoted foreigners has passed. We live peacefully under the leadership of King Kalākaua.

—Catholic.

Ka Nupepa Kuokoa. 7 APRIL 1883. P. 2.
Pehea Keia? How about This?

During the past week, a person with leprosy [kanaka mai lepera] was sought on Kauaʻi, with the desire to take him to the place where those folks are being gathered. Kahalekumano is the name of that person, and Alapaʻi and Kume-heula are the policemen who went to get him. Kahalekumano ran because he was afraid of being taken to Kalawao. He was shot from behind by the police, and he was hit on the back of the neck. The bullet was taken out by the doctor, and it was seen that there was no great damage in his injury, and this Kumano was brought here to Honolulu. Here is what astonished us: What is going on with this kind of action, where sick people are being shot by the police? If Kumano was a robber, or a murderer, and the police came and shot him, that would not be so surprising. That one was a devastated man, afflicted by leprosy [mai lepera]; he was terrified of being taken to Kalawao, and ran, and was shot. What a shame.

The effort by the government to separate out the leprosy patients from among the healthy is absolutely correct; the government made a grave error in the brief [legislative] sessions that recently passed, because they neglected this issue. However, there is nothing correct in committing this action, which frightens and terrifies the patients and the public. The leprosy patients [mai lepera] are not sinners due to their illness, and it is entirely wrong to simply injure them, and terrify these troubled people. The leprosy patients are children of the government, not sinners. [He poe keiki na mai lepera na ke aupuni, aole he poe lawehala.] Quarantining them should be done comfortably, compassionately. The *Kuokoa* believes that the multitude of its readers are united in this opinion, and their compassion will assist those in trouble at all times. [Kahalekumano's grave is on the summit of Kauhakō crater. His headstone reads: A Monument for Kahalekumano. Born April 1, 1855. Died December 22, 1893.]

Ka Nupepa Kuokoa. 27 SEPTEMBER 1884. P. 2.
Na mai lepera i hoohuoiia. (Kakauia no ke Kuokoa.) The suspected leprosy patients. (Written for the *Kuokoa*.)

Here among the Hawaiian people [kanaka Hawaii] are some folks suspected of having leprosy; a great many of them are seen. And these infected people are living with those in good health, with those suspected not hesitating to meet with the healthy, and so it is with the healthy. There is nothing preventing these folks from soiling the homes of the people. They have eaten from the same bowl, bitten the meat from the same plate, chewed 'awa together, drunk together of the saliva that softened the 'awa, smoked with the same pipe, slept upon the mattresses with the beds and pillows, the sheets, blanket, and so on. Besides this is the drinking water, drinking together from the [same] glass, and meeting together without thinking that this is a malignant disease [mai aai] embracing the body parts from the time it is seen upon the one who did not have it before, but now has it. Not only these things, there are also some living in the defilement of men and women joining sinfully, adulterously, and through the usual thing of the Hawaiian people from the beginning of existence. And so, this disease is being perpetuated among the Hawaiian people and some folks from foreign lands. However, the writer is convinced that these are some of the causes that largely control this malignant disease [mai aai], Chinese disease [mai pake], and also royal disease [mai alii], upon these islands. And there are several other important causes that the writer has seen, and it is something inserted into the people.

The law of the government has appointed the government doctors, and they have given the idea to all people of this nation about injecting the arms of the men, women, children. I guess that the people have been injected with the rot of the varieties of terrible diseases, eating the flesh and entering the blood, and if I am not mistaken, the rot of the Chinese disease [mai pake]. In this past year of the Hebrew disease [mai hepera: smallpox], 1881, Dr. Peter [Pika] and the other doctors injected the arms of the Hawaiian people and some other folks, and the Caucasians [haole] were also injected. However, the Hawaiians and the Caucasians were not injected with the same pus [palahehe]. That of the Hawaiians was different from that of the Caucasians, and what was explained was that it was the difference of the swelling of the arms. That of the Caucasians was just fine, a little swelling but not a problem, but with that of the Hawaiians, it swelled malignantly until reaching the bone within. Several adults and children died, and the arms of some folks were abscessed with disfigurement. Is that what is right?

No. The terrible disease was inserted into the Hawaiian people. This is something helping the permanence of leprosy all across the land. It appears now that the disease has ravaged and contaminated the land all over, with no cleaning thing that can help, except for the generosity and the great love of the Heavenly Father, the one who holds all things within his power.

As for the Boards of Health that have been organized by the government, there have been many. They have worked for a long time, and the Boards of Health just keep changing. They are like farmers who are careless in removing a terrible weed and farm the wrong way. They have been placed as those watching over the health of the people. They have the power to take patients to Kaka'ako and Kalawao, Moloka'i. They have not properly carried out their great task. [Patients] are always being taken, yet the growth of the disease has not stopped at all. It grows now, because the leaves have been pulled off, but the trunks remain, the roots, the tap roots. In comparison with food crops, if the crops are covered by weeds, and the leaves are cut off in weeding, the weeds will grow again. If you go and look later, [the crops are] covered with weeds again. Such are the actions the Board of Health is taking. Money is gone, but the disease is not gone. An immense amount of money was spent, but no immense amount of people were cured. Alas! With concern for the life of the Hawaiians [Me ka minamina i ke ola o na Hawaii]. I will speak again later.

—Hoole-Pope [Protestant: a pen name. Hōʻole-Pope literally means "deny (the Catholic) pope."]

Ko Hawaii Pae Aina. 7 NOVEMBER 1885. P. 2.
Hou Pahi Mainoino Ma Kalaupapa. Vicious Stabbing in Kalaupapa.

Kanohooʻahu (male), Kaunulau (male), and Mahiki (male) were stabbed with a knife by Momona (male) between the hours of five and six oʻclock on the evening of Thursday, the 29th of October last. The first two individuals whose names appear above were stabbed in the abdomen with a knife and what was inside came out. They died on Sat., the 31st of Oct., and were buried on the first of this month at the cemetery at Papaloa [ilina o Papaloa] in Kalaupapa. Such a pity.

Regarding Mahiki, he continues, but his condition is unknown according to what Dr. Morrizts [Mouritz] told me.

This riot [haunaele] arose due to the daughters of Mr. Momona having been taken from him under the direction of Gibson [Kipikona], president of the Board of Health, to return the daughters to Kakaʻako. Therefore, Mr. Momona greatly loved his children, but what he did was ignorant.

Mr. Momona is in the jail [Halepaahao] at this time that I write this, and so far no court has arraigned him up until this moment.

Gibson and others are here at this time, having arrived aboard the *Hiiaka* yesterday. They will return this afternoon. I send this news quickly.

Yours truly, W. H. Kalā. Kalawao, NOVEMBER 3, 1885.

Ka Nupepa Kuokoa. 10 APRIL 1886. P. 3.
Mohai ia no ka Pono o ka Lehulehu. Sacrificed for the Sake of the People.

There has been news, which arrived in this office, revealing that Damien (Catholic priest) [Damiano (Kahunapule Kakolika)] is under the supervision of the Board of Health at this time. Herein is the report: On the 31st of last month [March], it was heard that Mr. P. N. Maʻilou, the secretary of the Board of Health in Kalawao, was interviewing Damien and was told that on the coast of Kalaupapa at five oʻclock in the evening on this day, Damien went home. This is when he was taken into the custody of the Board of Health as one to be counted among the patients [poe mai] as he had come down with the disease [mai]. He now remains under the authority of the quarantine. Is this true? If this is really the case, then do not linger where disease [mai] spreads. This paper cannot withhold its appreciation for the acts of love of this man in giving his life to rendering aid to those afflicted in Kalawao.

» [Father Damien was officially identified as a leprosy patient and placed under the authority of the Board of Health.]

Ka Nupepa Elele. 24 JULY 1886. P. 3.
Ke Komite A Ka Ahaolelo No Kalawao. The Committee of the Legislature for Kalawao.

At nine oʻclock on Friday night, July 16, 1886, the members of the committee met at the wharf of the *Likelike* [ship named for Miriam Likelike, sister of

Kalākaua and Liliʻuokalani] with the other colleagues of the legislature, along with the gentlemen who desired to see Kalawao, and in total, there were more than sixty. At a quarter past nine oʻclock, all delegates met together, and at 9:30 the engines of the *Aliiwahine* [Queen] turned. It made its way with the bow aimed directly for Kalaupapa.

The ocean was calm and there was no wind to whip up the surface of the water. The sea was like glass. The chiefess of the night was shedding her light in its fullness and it was beautiful and caused this writer to reminisce.

"It is so beautiful from Puna to Hilo
Kauanāhua finds fault at nothing"

While the *Aliiwahine* made its way, the delegates swayed from side to side, desiring to stop and disembark on land. At three oʻclock in the morning, Kaʻīlio Point [lae o Kailio] had passed us, the flat plains of Kaiolohia were before us, the sands of Keonelele spread wide, and there was Kaluakoʻi. Here the boat stopped for a short while, and at four oʻclock, the ship proceeded. At five oʻclock, the anchor was let go, and it was Kalaupapa. As we viewed the majestic beauty, the wood-framed houses stood stretched across the plain, and it was lovely to behold, such as this:

How beautiful Kaʻala, a pool of dew
The waters of Luakini are carried.

When it reached six oʻclock in the morning, the noble, S. G. Wilder [Waila], came over quickly, and with the committee ready, they were the first to disembark. As the committee arrived onshore, they met with friends afflicted with leprosy [mai] who were at the pier. Archways were erected with maile vines intertwined on them, and the roadway was adorned with verdure of the forest. At the entrance of the warehouse there was a large archway with letters clearly spelling out, "Aloha oukou" [Welcome].

When the committee entered the building, there was a multitude of people there to greet them. It was so lovely to see.

Later, the activities proceeded, and on the veranda [lanai] of the cottage of the Board of Health there gathered all of the patients with their colonel, B. N. Kamaʻe. Each of the delegates of the committee gave a short speech, and the Hon. J. K. Kaunamanō replied on behalf of the committee. This is accounted for here:

When the Hon. J. K. Kaunamanō introduced the committee and the honored delegates of the legislature to the crowd, while they were gathered on the floor of the veranda of the cottage of the Rev. Damien [Damiano], he said the following:

Dear people who love their Aliʻi, whose people are gathered together here, I introduce to you the committee that was selected by the law building legislature of the country you belong to, according to your wish and appeal that a committee be chosen, which has been sent to meet and talk with you.

Dear people who love our land, I present to you each member of the committee. This is the Hon. J. Kaʻuhane, the honorable legislator from Kaʻū, the land of the Hāʻao rain that flies inland of ʻAuʻaulele [ka aina nona ka ua Haao e lele ae la mauka o Auaulele].

This is the Hon. J. K. Nāhale, the honorable legislator from North Kona, the land about which these lines of the mele are sung:

> Kona of the sea where large clouds settle in the calm [O Kona kaiopua i
> ka lai]
> The billowing clouds of hīnano flowers, so calm [Opua hinano ua malie]

This is the Hon. E. K. Lilikalani, the honorable legislator of Honolulu, for which it is said, "Faces come together at Kou [Huhuhui aku na maka i Kou]." [Kou is a former name of Honolulu.]

I am also one of your legislators, and your appeals have reached us asking to select committees to investigate your problems, according to the Hon. A. P. Kāpaehaole.

The Hon. J. K. Kaunamanō stated in his speech, "Dear subjects of the king, my friends of the same heart of love.

As I was aboard the ship approaching the pier, I saw letters laid out on the archway at the dock saying, "Aloha oukou" [Welcome].

This is what Jesus taught his disciples, stating: In whatever house you first enter, say, "This house is loved." And if the child of love is there, he will welcome you.

Jesus also stated: Your love is what I desire, not sacrifice. And it is for this reason that I have come, as a torch and a light for the world, so all people would not remain in darkness, those who trust in me. And it is for this reason that we have come, to express our aloha without salt in our hands.

When this speech was over, J. P. Kamaʻe replied with the following words: "Dear honored committee, we continue to be grateful with aloha."

On this last occasion, the chair of the committee, the Hon. J. K. Kaunamanō, introduced to the crowd the other honored delegates standing on the veranda of the cottage of [Father] Damien.

Ka Nupepa Kuokoa. 31 JULY 1886. P. 2
Ke Panalaau o Kalawao. The Colony of Kalawao.
Dear *Nupepa Kuokoa.* Greetings. Please carry the news items listed below so that the public may read on your body the following:

1. In recent days, the patients have all become unified to expel W. M. Gibson [Kipikona], president of the Board of Health, from his office as president for several reasons having to do with problems and hardships that have befallen this colony.
2. When the committees of the legislature arrived on the 17th last, the problems were not yet resolved that they had been witnessing due to diversions and as a result of their having witnessed the terrifying home of the leprosy patients [home kaukaweli o na lepera] for the first time.
3. When Henry Waterhouse arrived here at Kalawao on the 17th of last month aboard the *Likelike,* he gifted money from his own pocket for the poor who numbered fifty or more, and this correspondent witnessed his act of purity.

4. The last voice of the patients that was heard in response to the honored delegates of the legislature and W. M. Gibson [Kipikona] while they were aboard the skiff [waapa] shoving off from the wharf of the *Likelike* with its bow set for Oʻahu was a loud din that filled the air with cheers. When all was quieted down, it was clear that the patients were saying, "Return, committee of the legislature and kick out W. M. Gibson and install S. G. Wilder as president of the Board of Health."

5. The food that our assistant superintendent [hope Luna Nui] prepared for the committee members of the legislature who arrived was not eaten. It consisted of pig roasted in the imu and delicious fish grilled. The reason the food was not eaten was due to fear of the leprosy patients [mai lepera], according to the word that was heard. [The committee members were afraid that leprosy patients had touched the food during its preparation.]

6. A few skinny cows were found recently on the plain of Kalaʻe by the committee, as this was a complaint of the leprosy patients [mai lepera] to the president of the Board of Health. This skinny cow that was wandering through the bushes was from the cold of the mountain of Olokuʻi. It was thought by all of the agents to do surveys before the arrival of the committee, and here is what we found.

7. Kupakeʻe and Damien [Damiano] were ordered by the president of the Board of Health to return to Kakaʻako under the care of Dr. Goto [Kauka Goto]. They returned, but what about these people who suffer the same plight? How amazing the magic that Gibson [Kipikona] pulls. Looking at the condition of the patients of this colony, we can see three stages:

   I.   The countenances of the people are healthy.
   II. One sees a few bumps in their appearance.
   III. You and I would be afraid to look at them.

Those who returned to Kakaʻako were of the Stage 1 and Stage 2 types. What all patients wish for is to have Dr. Goto sent here to Kalawao to conduct treatment, not like what this president did in unevenly shedding his light like the sun in Waiʻanae. This is what angers the patients.

Sincerely, J. A. Kahikina. Kalawao, JULY 20, 1886.

Ko Hawaii Pae Aina. 9 OCTOBER 1886. P. 4.
Na Make Ma Ke Panalaau o Kalawao Iloko o Ka M. H. 1885 Me 1886 E Nee Nei. Deaths in the Colony of Kalawao in the Year 1885 and Part of 1886.

Na Make I Ka A.D. 1885 (Koena mai ka Helu 28 mai). Deaths in AD 1885 (remaining from Edition 28).

Aug.	1	Kekolohe, Waiheʻe, Maui
	2	Paulo Kaluna, Hāmākua, Hawaiʻi
	6	Keliaka, Kāʻanapali, Maui
	20	Kahiamoe, Honolulu, Oʻahu
	23	Emelē, Honolulu, Oʻahu
	25	Hoʻomana, Hilo, Hawaiʻi
	27	Kaʻoihana, Wailuku, Maui

Sept.	11	Pulaika, Moanalua, Oʻahu
	12	Kumukahi, Hilo, Hawaiʻi
	13	John Nālau, Waiheʻe, Maui
	26	Kipi, Kalawao, Molokaʻi
	27	Kaʻōʻō, Honolulu, Oʻahu
Oct.	1	Akamu, Hāna, Maui
	3	Hoʻokano, ʻEwa, Oʻahu
	6	Kūhulukū, Hāna, Maui
	8	Kaʻenaokalani, Kohala, Hawaiʻi
	11	Kamana, Waimea, Kauaʻi
	15	Kamakeʻe, Hāna, Maui
	15	Hulēʻia, Waialua, Oʻahu
	20	Kanoʻonoʻo, Honolulu, Oʻahu
	21	Oliva, Kona, Hawaiʻi
	22	Kahue, Kaunakakai, Molokaʻi
	28	Kaʻaipohepohe, Hāna, Maui
Nov.	1	Nālole, Lāhaina, Maui
	1	Kaʻahanui, Honolulu, Oʻahu
	13	Marie, Kaupō, Maui
	15	Pāhole, Waikapū, Maui
	16	Pau, Kalawao, Molokaʻi
	17	Haʻehaʻe, Hāmākua, Maui
	21	Kaʻenaokalā, Waiheʻe, Maui
	24	Nāpua, Kohala, Hawaiʻi
	25	Waineʻe, Waikīkī, Oʻahu
	29	Pua, Kohala, Hawaiʻi
	30	Kalamau, Honolulu, Oʻahu
Dec.	2	Māhoe, Hilo, Hawaiʻi
	10	Kaʻenemi, Honolulu, Oʻahu
	10	Kalawaiʻa, Honolulu, Oʻahu
	11	Hiku, Hanapēpē, Kauaʻi
	14	Paʻaluhi, Kohala, Hawaiʻi
	17	Keliʻipupule, Honolulu, Hawaiʻi
	18	William Kapua, Wailuku, Maui
	27	Kanohoanu, Hāna, Maui
	30	Petero, Hāna, Maui
	30	Lino, Honolulu, Oʻahu
	31	Kahalewai, Honokōhau, Maui
	31	Kaiweo, Honolulu, Oʻahu

Na Make Iloko O Keia Makahiki. Deaths within this year [1886].

Jan.	3	Kānekoa, Lāhaina, Maui
	7	Haʻaleleʻia, Lāhaina, Maui
	20	Kahue Kamana, Waimea, Kauaʻi
	20	Kaulahuki, Waimea, Kauaʻi
	20	Lono, Kona, Hawaiʻi
	20	Kalua, Honuaʻula, Maui

	26	Manini, Mānoa, O'ahu
	29	Palaile, Kōloa, Kaua'i
	29	Kapela, Honolulu, O'ahu
	30	Mī'oi Thompson, Waialua, O'ahu
Feb.	5	Mālo'i, Lāhaina, Maui
	12	Kapuō, Olowalu, Maui
	12	Kini, Honolulu, O'ahu
	14	Līlia, Līhu'e, Kaua'i
	17	Kalehuamakanoe, Waialua, O'ahu
	25	Kamakahiki, Kalepolepo, Maui
Mar.	18	Uhai, Waikīkī, O'ahu
	24	Ka'aihue, Kona, Hawai'i
	24	Elena Maka'ike, Honolulu, O'ahu
	29	Malo, Lāhaina, Maui
Apr.	6	Kanaka'ole, Hāna, Maui
	11	Kaiākea, Lāhaina, Maui
	13	Ua, Honolulu, O'ahu
	13	'Ōpiopio, Hāmākua, Hawai'i
	19	Akona Pākē, Honolulu, O'ahu
	23	Barenapa, Kawaihae, Hawai'i
	25	Ha'aheo, Ko'olau, Kaua'i
May	4	Kanoholā, Honolulu, O'ahu
	7	Kamai, Hāna, Maui
	7	'Umi Deviki, Wai'anae, O'ahu
	8	Aku, Honolulu, O'ahu
	13	Kalo'ihā, Waiehu, Maui
	15	Po'oiki, Waimea, Kaua'i
	19	Kalā'aupuhipuhi, Kīlauea, Kaua'i
	21	Kāki'o, Wai'anae, O'ahu
	23	Nika, Wai'anae, O'ahu
	26	Lose, Honolulu, O'ahu
	28	Kamakolu, Makawao, Maui
	29	Kai, Wai'ōhinu, Ka'ū, Hawai'i
	30	Ka'ōme'o, Kā'anapali, Maui
June	2	Nāli'ikapu, Honua'ula, Maui
	7	Paulo, Makawao, Maui
	8	Keli'i'aukai, Laupāhoehoe, Hawai'i
	12	'Ī, Kohala, Hawai'i
	16	Kaluakini, Kalihi, O'ahu
	23	'Aui Pākē, Honolulu, O'ahu
July	2	Pi'ilani, Honolulu, O'ahu
	11	Iosepa, Hilo, Hawai'i
	19	'Alama, 'Ewa, O'ahu
	19	'Apela, Honolulu, O'ahu
	24	Kua'āina, Hilo, Hawai'i
	27	Kahule'ula, Waikīkī, O'ahu
	29	Kāne, Ka'ū, Hawai'i

	30	Kamaha, Wailuku, Maui
	31	Unele, Kapālama, Oʻahu
Aug.	1	Kiliona, Kohala, Hawaiʻi
	9	Samuel Kaukau, Waimea, Kauaʻi
	11	Paunini, Puna, Hawaiʻi
	11	Ahu Pākē, Waialua, Oʻahu
	16	Kalanui, ʻUalapuʻe, Molokaʻi
	25	S. P. Kahelenaue, Wailuku, Maui

With much aloha, P. K. Kalanilehua. Assistant Secretary.

Ka Nupepa Kuokoa. 26 FEBRUARY 1887. P. 2.
He Makana Nui i ko Kalawao. A Great Gift to the People of Kalawao.

By way of a news item offered in truthfulness, I send for your available columns these rather important thoughts that the Hawaiian people [lahui Hawaii] are not familiar with to pass before the crown of yours, Hawaiʻi, at the time of Kahikuonālani, for the benefit of those who gaze upon you, and this is the report:

When *Mokolii* arrived last week in Kalaupapa from Honolulu, she brought with her onboard her deck one hundred rolls or more of material of all sorts of colors worth six hundred dollars or more. These goods were sent under the name of U. Damien [U. Damiano], the Catholic priest here in Kalawao [kahuna pule Katolika o Kalawao nei], for the hearts full of Christian love from England as well as other loving souls who are thought to require covering for their destitute condition among all who have been blotched by leprosy here in Kalawao, as a "Gift of Love" [Makana Aloha].

But as Damien gave this gift, some received and others did not, with Damien saying, "You do not get clothes for not attending Catholic church services regularly. If you go, you receive, [but if] your lives are not in order, you do not get clothes."

This is where your correspondent witnessed the uneven distribution of the gift to some, and how wrong the unquestioned devotion of these people for ʻUmiāmaka Damien is, which is blemished inside. As this gift of aloha extends to these people under the Catholic religion, the spiritual civil rights of the patients to join the Catholic religion is deteriorated under these goods that disappear, being consumed by bugs. The spirit has gifts from God to grant to every living thing without cost. Did Peter not say to Simon the seer: "Your money is lost with you in death for your thinking that one can receive a gift from God with money." Acts 8:20.

Therefore, in my capacity as a true Catholic member, I am anchored in my belief in the peace of the day of Wailuku, Maui, that I am fully accustomed and familiar with the tenets of Catholicism, but today, I stand and return to the house of my parent, Protestantism [Hoole Pope], that which schooled my people, as I regret that my soul had been purchased with earthly treasures of this world, and I leave the Catholic religion on good terms. Should the Treatises on Redemption [Palapala Kalahala] by payment of the Catholics of Luther's day come out in the future, that should become my appeal.

My hope without regret is that you do not put aside this message that you were not familiar with, and that you would show this to the whole world. This is all I have here, but should the bird talk to the fish below, then the running grounds of Koʻiananā should be done away with by my seal.

Most sincerely, Petero Hōkūkano. St. Philomena [Pilemona], Kalawao.

» [In this letter to *Ka Nupepa Kuokoa* the writer is critical of Father Damien and states that he acted inappropriately toward non-Catholics. The writer also calls Father Damien "ʻUmiāmaka Damien," a reference to ʻUmiāmaka, a man who was known for deceiving others. In the two letters that follow, one to *Ko Hawaii Pae Aina* and one to *Ka Nupepa Elele*, members of St. Philomena Church refute the accusations against Father Damien.]

Ko Hawaii Pae Aina. 5 MARCH 1887. P. 3.
He Pane. A Response.
Dear *Ko Hawaii Pae Aina.* Greetings.

In the *Nupepa Kuokoa* of February 26 is where I saw the message of Petero Hōkūkano about what took place in regard to the gift of the spirit through Father Damien [Makua Damiano] at the colony [panalaau] here in Kalawao. What P. H. testified is untrue that the civil rights [pono kivila] of the Catholic religion would become defiled as a result of the gift that Kalawao received. His message was only an unrelated insult.

The gift was given to everyone of all religions and was donated by the Father with true aloha to all afflicted, apart from the wealthy who had no desire for the gray block-print material of mourning women and only pants to take.

It is due to this gift of aloha that the backs of men and women of all religions were covered here in this colony. Father Damien did not say that those people should go to the Catholic church in order to receive clothes. The only thing he did speak about is love for all afflicted as if they were his own children.

I fully regret that what I have to offer here is small, and I have not replied in full to this liar [kanaka hoopunipuni] who has not been seen here in Pilemona. Who is it?

With appreciation, Jos. I. Manuhoa. St. Philomena [Pilemona: Father Damien's church], Kalawao, MAR. 3, 1887.

Ka Nupepa Elele. 19 MARCH 1887. P. 2.
Ia Petero Hokukano. To Petero Hōkūkano.

P. Kahoʻopunipuni [literally, P. "The liar"] appeared in the *Kuokoa* of February 26 with slander and deceit about the gift passed on from the hand of Rev. Damien to be distributed among those afflicted with leprosy.

Here is the lie [hoopunipuni] of this P. Hōkūkano, when he said that he is a Catholic brethren belonging to the Bethel of St. Philomena [Pilemona]. This name is not real, and there is no Catholic brethren of St. Philomena [Pilemona] by that name. None, none at all.

Here is the truth: He is a brethren of the Protestant faith, and a mere Puritan brethren who abuses the Catholic faith. He has been in that denomination from his childhood until now, when he lies publicly. And because of an old enemy, he strayed to tell deceit, and to speak defeat of Father Damien [Damieno].

Therefore, due to this Petero Hōkūkano not saying his true nature outright,

and hiding under falsehood, thus truth falls away from what he reported in the *Kuokoa*.
    You will find me in the gentle Kiliʻoʻopu wind of Waikolu. Greetings soon.
    —St. Philomena [Pilemone]. Kalawao, MAR. 4, 1887.
» [Pilemona and Pilemone are both names for St. Philomena, Father Damien's church in Kalawao.]

Ka Nupepa Kuokoa. 16 JULY 1887. P. 2.
No Kalawao. About Kalawao.
    July 4, two o'clock. Activities begin.

1. Foot race among four little children, short distance, Keoki won.
2. Horse race among three horses, half-mile lap, won by the Kauaʻi boy, cash prize, $.50; (second run) $1.50 won by the Kauaʻi boy; (third run) two horses, won by the white boy [puakea].
3. A man who boasted of his strength this day had his lip bashed by another man. It would have been better for him to have sat still.
4. The lives of a few young babies were spared while they were being carried by some women. The horse was new, belonging to a boy named Dilahuka, whose umbilical cord was stolen by rats [piko pau i ka iole: a reference to the belief that a person became a chronic thief if his umbilical chord was stolen by a rat].
5. Canoe race [Heihei waa], two canoes sank [elua waa i poholo]. One canoe surfed [hookahi waʻa i paka].

    These are the events that were held in Kalaupapa. When I was done watching all these things, I returned home and arrived at my place at the stroke of five o'clock in the evening, at which time I went into the chapel when the service began. A boy named Ioba came in and went to talk with our Father, the Rev. Damien [Damiano], who was sitting near the altar. Upon hearing [the message] he suddenly turned and ran out. When he arrived at the scene of the accident, he saw Livai (male) lying dead. He carried Livai, calling out loud that the horse races are forbidden and that Livai had died. He carried Livai into the building where he lay at the moment. His body received no injuries, but his body was weak all over from pain. It was not sure if he was dead, but he was breathing.
    This was the cause of this tragedy. He had collided with a girl named Miss Kāne. This Livai was headed back to his stable on horseback and that girl came running at full speed on her horse when the two collided. The life of the girl was not in danger.
    What I first heard was that the girl tried to restrain the horse, but this was to no avail. So to you girls, do not try to ride foolishly like this.
    —B. M. Mokulehua.

Ka Nupepa Kuokoa. 16 JULY 1887. P. 2.
Haule Lio Ma Kalawao. Fall Off a Horse in Kalawao.
Dear *Nupepa Kuokoa.* Greetings
    I reported to the *Paeaina* regarding a fall from a horse here in Kalawao on the 4th of July [involving] Līwai (male) and Kāne (female). Līwai stayed at the

residence of J. Damien [Damiano] for almost three days without eating, after which he was taken to the residence of Eli Gorton, where he lay until the morning of Saturday, July 9, when he departed this life.

Upon the death of Līwai, a coroner's inquest [Aha Kolonelo] was convened with A. H. Kāneoaliʻi [Ambrose Kāneoaliʻi Hutchison], P. K. Kalanilehua, John Gaiser, Hanry C. Weight, Mr. Kahāʻulelio, P. Kiha, and J. Hanaloa as jurors. The verdict that was rendered was that there was no fault on the part of anyone and that his death was accidental.

The following Monday, the case of reckless riding was adjudicated and the following were penalized: Kāne (female) $3.00, ʻAʻane (female) $2.25, Bila (male) $2.24, B. Kaʻaialiʻi (male) fifty cents. These were small amounts of salt [paakai: a metaphor for fines]. It was the 4th of July here in Kalawao.

—Jos. ʻĪmaikalani.

Ke Alakai o Hawaii. 30 JUNE 1888. P. 6.
Ka Huakai Noii A Na Komite Ahaolelo I Ke Panalaau O Kalawao, Iune 24, 1888. Exploratory Journey of the Legislative Committee to the Colony of Kalawao, June 24, 1888.

At 4:30 a.m. there were the towns of Kalawao and Kalaupapa as dawn approached through the darkness. Your correspondent scrambled for a way to reach the harbor of Kalaupapa as quickly as possible.

On this ocean journey, there were five members of the newspaper business, whose names were: T. P. Spencer of the *Kuokoa;* S. P. Kanoa of the *Alakai;* Sam. Pua of the *Makaainana;* S. L. Kekūmanō and Geo. Kalāʻau of the *Paeaina.* They were all in good health on this ocean journey.

At 5:50, the west end of Kalaupapa was spotted where the land of Nihoa is, and at that time the *Likelike* entered the bay of Kalaupapa while the houses inland were laid out wide, which was lovely to see.

It was only a few short minutes in Kalaupapa when the party moved on to Kalawao and Waikolu. Most of the hard work fell onto the head of the committee to prepare the horses for the fellow riders. For your correspondent of the *Ke Alakai,* it had not been long that he had seized upon the honor of that duty. It is for this reason that this correspondent compliments him with these words, "The Jumping Shrimp of Kalaupapa" [Ka Opae Mahikihiki o Kalaupapa], and upon his back I set out with my traveling companions.

The chair of the committee entered the homes of the patients along with some of the members. It was at this time that the delegation split in two and headed for the water pipeline [paipu wai] of Waikolu. A few of the newspaper correspondents encountered some problems with their satchels.

The correspondent of the *Alakai* expressed his appreciation to the legislator of Waimea and Niʻihau and Dr. Meʻekapu. He reported on a wide range of medicines to cure this disease.

We made our way quickly to the food storage house [hale hoahu ai] of Waikolu. The path was in very sad condition to reach the storage house. Here there was some confusion about returning to Kalawao for a meeting of the committees, and they visited the hospital there first.

Father Damien [spelled in English] was questioned first by the committees regarding some children who were not afflicted with the disease whose parents had died, and one child whose parents had died.

The chair reported that there were twenty-seven children who were not afflicted with the disease, with three having been born in Kalawao and with twenty-four in other places.

After this, Dr. Kealoaliʻi was asked to have a look at one small child, as well as a second, and Dr. Meʻekapu also accompanied him. The two replied that their lives could be saved.

There is a bathhouse [hale auau] for the sick children, who bathe three times a day, and there is one treatment room [rumi haawi laau].

This is all that was done in Kalawao, at which time the final goodbyes were given to the patients [maʻi], and they made their way to the coast of Kalaupapa [kai o Kalaupapa].

It was here at Kalawao where I met with the younger sister of my wife, whose name is Susana Kahulikalā, along with her family, and my classmate of the Circling Rain [Ua Poaihala] of Kahaluʻu [Oʻahu], Peter Nāwaokele, and all the friends of that district who lived there in their pain. The final expression of aloha of your correspondent of the *Alakai* is laid in your wake.

At this time, the company progressed toward the coast of Kalaupapa, where they visited the cliff of Kauhakō [pali o Kauhako] where Pele had dug a home out for herself, and as she found it too shallow, she left that spot and moved on to Hawaiʻi.

On this hill [puu] is the grave [kupapau] of J. W. Nākuʻina and two others situated next to him. This is a beautiful spot to view for visitors since it is laid out clearly and splendidly with a good view of the farms of the patients [mala ai a na mai] to the southeast of the road with patches of clearings, [which are] the kuleana lands that had not become those of the government.

The company left that place for the coast of Kalaupapa as time was quickly moving on.

Ka Nupepa Kuokoa. 14 JULY 1888. P. 4.
Kuewa Hookahi I Ke Ala Me Ka Waimaka. One Wandering in the Street in Tears.
Dear Mr. Editor.

I ask for your kindness and patience to allow me some space in your body for a piece of my material that I put forth for all of the people of the two of us to commemorate.

The Puʻulena wind of Hilo has passed. It has sought out Papalauahi, so sad.

On the 19th of June last, in 1888, in the leprosy colony [Panalaau Maʻi Lepera] here in Kalawao, Molokaʻi, my younger sister, Miss Ceresia Pāniani, left me and went off on her own to that side of the pain of death. She left me to live on without a younger sister here in this land to wander in the streets alone with tears. Oh my dear younger sister!

She was taken away according to the authority of the government from the presence of our parents on the 2nd of Feb. 1888 due to the disease that pains the heart (leprosy) [mai hoehaeha puuwai (lepera)] from Upper Kawaihae, S. Kohala, Hawaiʻi, to that iron fence land [aina pahaohao: prison] of Kalawao, the final destination [pahuhopu], with hope that she would find rest, but now, not long afterwards, she had found comfort, but we all need to remember that we all have much more time.

This was a girl who had great trust in her parents. She was careful, obedient, and clever in all she did.

She worked to take care of the livelihood of the family and called out friends to come and she would welcome them, those of high stature and those of lowly stature; but now so that you among all her friends may hear, Miss Ceresia Pāniani passed away and has moved on to that dark place of Kāne, that pathway that can be sought and found.

Before this, I give my aloha to that homeland of ours. To the Nāulu Rain, I say, aloha to you all. L. S. Keaniani. Kalawao, JULY 5, 1888.

Ke Alakai O Hawaii. 10 AUGUST 1888. P. 2.
Ahaolelo o 1888. Legislature of 1888.
Reimbursement to Damien [Damiano] for duties [dute] addressing old sections of the Kalawao church, $103.

Ka Nupepa Kuokoa. 6 OCTOBER 1888. P. 2.
Kela me Keia. This and That [Miscellany].

Father Damien [Makua Damiana] of the leprosy settlement [kahua lepera] of Kalawao has been given a gift by the nuns [Virigini] from Immaculate Catherine School in San Francisco [kula Katarina Hemolele o Kapalakiko]. This is an act of love [hana aloha] that everyone should appreciate.

The shipping company of Wilder & Co. [Waila Ma] has received the contract for transporting leprosy patient attendants [ohua mai lepera] and cargo to the leprosy settlement [kahua mai lepera] of Kalawao for one year at $200 a month.

Ka Nupepa Kuokoa. 9 FEBRUARY 1889. P. 3.
He Mau Hunahuna No Ke Kahua Mai Lepera O Kalawao A Me Kalaupapa. Some Tidbits about the Leprosy Settlement of Kalawao and Kalaupapa.

Under this title, I am making a humble submission before your printing press, O Supreme Excellence of the Hawaiian Nation, O *Kuokoa,* so that your great multitude of friends may know of our life in this place where agony resides, as follows below:

1. The characteristics of the land and the features of its scenery. [Ke ano o ka aina a me kona mau hiohiona a ka nanaina.]
2. The types of people living here. [Na ano kanaka e noho nei.]
3. The medical condition of the patients. [Ke kulana mai o na mai.]
4. The homes being lived in. [Na home e noho ia nei.]
5. The sustenance provided by the Board of Health. [Na hanai ana a ka Papa Ola.]
6. How peace is maintained. [Ka hoomalu ana e maluhia ai.]
7. The helpers who aid the patients. [Na kokua e pono ai na mai.]
8. The three different religions. [Na hoomana like ole ekolu.]
9. The government doctors. [Na Kauka Aupuni.]
10. The various religious ministers. [Na kahunapule like ole.]
11. The supervisor and his assistant. [Ka luna nui me kona hope.]

Under these categories your storyteller [mea unuhi moolelo] will successively relate things that will make you joyous, that will stir compassion, and that will bring pain to the heart of the one reading this part of the story of this colony [Panalaau].

1. The characteristics of the land and the features of its scenery. [Ke ano o ka aina a me kona mau hiohiona o ka nanaina.]

It is a wide site [kahua akea] upon which all of the people of Hawai'i could live upon without filling it, flat [palahalaha] and wide in the middle but narrow on the east and west edges, with a large hill [ahua nui] in the middle that prevents the two towns from seeing each other, named "Kauhakō," which is a great crater [lua nui] dug by lava until it reached the sea, with a saltwater lake [loko kai] resting calm within it. The small shrimp [opae huna] is the creature swimming in it. Its depth makes it impossible to stand upon the bottom, being five fathoms; such was the report of the one who measured the depth, Mauliawa (male). On the upland side of this hill [puu] is the road that lies along the twisted stretch from Kalaupapa to Waikolu, which blocks it off, and along the edge is the water pipe [paipu wai].

Upland of the road rests a long field used for farming, and the seaward side is for livestock. On the sides of the road stand buildings, and in the middle of the land there are sometimes many or sometimes a few buildings to please the eyes of the traveler walking along the road, who will say, "It looks like a real town, like such-and-such."

There is a row of tall cliffs [kakai pali kiekie] to the south, and that is the mountainous part of this place. If you climb up, it will not take long before you encounter the fragrant leaves of the upland forest, the fragrant daughters of 'Aiwohikupua. Turn right around to see the land lying to the north with the ocean and the shores. I would not be wrong to make a comparison to part of my birthplace, Hāna of the small fish [Hana a ka i-a iki], the famous 'Āpuakea rain [ua apuakea], the love-snatching wind [makani kaili aloha] of Kīpahulu, and the stone-wall-hiding rain [ua pee papohaku] of Kaupō.

The low area is just like the shores of Haneo'o, and lower Nānu'alele until entering Punahoa. If compared to Kaua'i, it is like the shores from Wailua to Kapa'a, Keālia, Anahola, and Waliamanu. It is on the side from Pūahi onward, passing right on the ocean side of Kauhakō Crater [lua pele o Kauhako]. From there the cliffs rise high until Wailē'ia, the place where the pipe water [wai piula] pours out, and there is a cleft [owa] in the seaward part of Kalaupapa.

And at the place reserved for farming, it is suitable for crops. Sweet potato [uwala] is the main food planted by the strong patients [mai ikaika] and the patients' helpers [kokua]. If the effort is great enough to provide food for the patient and his helper for two or three months, then the patient's weekly allotment of cooked taro [pai ai] is made publicly available. This is called "staple food" [ai hanai]. After a month passes, cash is collected, and then some people see the face of some coins. The people who save up these bits of change into a large amount will receive what they desire, be it a horse, or a private house, or some other personal belongings. They will be well-supplied and comfortably situated, as if the money to acquire these supplies had come from outside.

However, the people who do not do this will live in clear poverty. Some people's means to supply their existence comes from outside, and some people receive their money from the actions of the Board of Health.

For the patient who does not work the land, it is a waste to exchange his cooked taro [pai ai] for cash.

This is a land of chilly air, somewhat like Kula on Maui at certain times, the final months of winter. In the months of May and August there is a heat that warms the skin of the patient, and sometimes the cold comes with the heat. That is what the locals teach the new patients [mai hou] when they arrive, to not travel far away from home every day until they are familiar with the weather of this land. The patient who heeds this rule of life will have a fine strength of constitution. For the one who does not listen and goes out into the cold and the heat, the illness will increase in severity to be worse than it was before. However, it is nothing to the new patients I have seen. This cold is nothing.

If you, the sightseer [mea makaikai], desire to see clearly the majesty of the two towns, climb up to the western edge of Kauhakō Crater [lua o puu Kauhakō]. Turn out and view the buildings of lower Kalaupapa like kōnane pebbles lined up on the kōnane board that Kamalālāwalu left from his days living here. Then turn toward Oʻahu of Kākuhihewa, which you, the reader of this story, will be stirred to express affection for:

"Like a white tapa cloth is the pili grass of Kohala
Small red Kaulu shrubs in the pili grass
The white buoy at the water's edge."

Then move up on the left edge of this crater and turn to the coming of the sun [east], and your gaze will first meet with the buildings of Māhulili, Polapola, Kawaluna, and Kalawao. Right in front will stand the homes of the people [hale kanaka]; the resting house [hale hooluolu] of Meyer [Maea: Rudolph W. Meyer], the supervisor [luna nui]; the medicine dispensary [hale haawi laau]; the actual hospital [haukapila] for the weak patients [mai nawaliwali]; the office [hale oihana kakau] of the Board of Health; the jail [hale paahao]; the store [halekuai] for all goods; the shop [hale lole bipi] for the leather clothing given to the patients; the storehouse [hale papaa] of the Board of Health; and the flagpoles [apahu hae] where the flags for the two existing funeral associations [hui hoolewa kupapau elua] wave in the lofty wind. You will be moved again to say to yourself, "Like a fine mat is the plain of Waikolupa" [Me he moena pawehe la ke kula o Waikolupa], as the buildings thread in both directions through the smooth plain.

(To be continued.)

» [This article is the first of a series written by a correspondent who was a patient at Kalaupapa. In his introduction he lists eleven topics that he intends to cover and eventually works his way through all of them. Each article is titled *He Mau Hunahuna No Ke Kahua Mai Lepera O Kalawao A Me Kalaupapa*.]

Ka Nupepa Kuokoa. 16 FEBRUARY 1889. P. 4.
He Mau Hunahuna No Ke Kahua Mai Lepera O Kalawao A Me Kalaupapa. Some Tidbits about the Leprosy Settlement of Kalawao and Kalaupapa.

When you turn again to face the south side of this hill [puu], you will see the wide expanse of the Waihānau river valley and the house of the assistant supervisor, and the house where the royal [alii] Peter [Pika] Kāʻeo lived during his days of tribulation, the first home I lived in during my days as a newcomer [malihini], and the house of Mr. Nāpela, a lawyer from Wailuku, Maui, and the houses of the patients [mai] and the local residents [kupa kamaaina] of this land.

And close to these houses there is a cliff famous in the mouths of the people of old that I have heard through their ancient chants [mele kahiko], the cliff of Kōloa [pali o Koloa]. It is not a real cliff. It is a place with a side of dirt on the edge of the constantly traveled road, and the part I have acquired is that which I am spreading forth with a sweet sound, like so:

How lovely is the cliff of Kōloa
The cliff turned toward Waihaneu [Waihanau], birthing [hānau]
How sad for one's fellow [hoahanau], returning with nothing along that
    long place.

2. The types of people living here. [Na ano kanaka e noho nei.]

There are eight types of people living here: True Hawaiians [Hawaii maoli], Caucasians [haole] and part Caucasians [hapa haole], Chinese [pake] and part Chinese [hapa pake], Spanish [paniolo], Gilbertese [lelewa], and Portuguese [pukiki]. For those last three types, there are two Spanish men, three Gilbertese men, and one Portuguese. The total for the majority, the remaining amount, is over a thousand. However, the true Hawaiians are the greatest number, and the other types of people are a smaller fraction. In the estimation of the storyteller, if men, women, and children are put together, there are less than one hundred.

3. The medical condition of the patients. [Ke kulana mai o na mai.]

The symptoms are not the same for everyone. Some have a light illness [mama mai], and some have it severely [koikoi loa], as follows:

The fingers bend down, and so it remains for all the places without the illness, and the eyelid is drawn down, but not the hands, or the entire body. The mouth is crooked, but not in all parts. There may be holes in the feet, or all over the body. For some, the hands are misshapen and the feet are maimed, although some portions of the body still have strength of movement. The people stricken by this symptom, from men to women and children, they have a few strong years, like some people who have lived ten or more years, and almost twenty for Mr. Kahului, who is still here tearing [uhae] cooked taro [pai]. He is the reason why this kind of symptom is called, "tearing cooked taro and beef for this colony" [he uhae pai ai a io bipi no ka Panalaau nei], if there is no other kind of condition of the illness.

Another symptom that some people have is that the top and the whole of the body becomes heavy, and afterwards the other parts become fragile and easily torn. If it is the hands then they are eaten until maimed, and if the feet then they are also chopped off, until all the toes are gone and only the sole remains, or else only the palm of the hand. These are the people who should be returned to the hospital. If the body is strong except for the injured parts, then he will fetch the cooked taro or beef, and carry these things with the stumps of the hands along with the teeth, if the person watching does not help him, and then he will stubbornly remain outside and not return to the hospital.

And as a gentleman who has been a resident of this place since before I arrived here, P. K. Kalanilehua, said to me,

"The average time that a patient of this kind lives is five years or fewer. For the strongest it is longer, but these people are rare." And other kinds of illness that affect some patients are blindness [makapo] as well as true diarrhea [hi maoli] and bloody diarrhea [hi koko]. It is said of these two kinds of diarrhea, "build the coffin" [o hana e ka pahu kupapau].

Stomach ache [nahu] is another illness, and constipation [lepo paa], chills [hui] all over the body, as well as numbness [maeele] in the hands and feet, along with heaviness and not feeling what is being done to them. If the hand and foot were being burned in a fire, the pain would not be felt; if cut by a knife or axe the pain would not be felt in the place cut. However, here is the bad part: the place burned by the fire will blister and become quite festered, and the place cut by the firewood axe will fester until it become a real problem. And if he puts on shoes and, say, gets on a horse, then if the shoe falls off he will not feel it until he gets to the place where he dismounts, and then he will see that his foot only has a sock and does not have a shoe on it.

Despite these painful symptoms [haawina ehaeha] that reign over the patient, he cannot simply sit and not fetch his allotment of starch and meat and other things on the days when these allotments arrive, or else he will be lacking. If he does not have someone to fetch his food and does not belong to the hospital or those of Damien [Damiano], or those of the Mothers of Mercy [makuahine o ke aloha] living in the house of the heart filled with compassion for our young women [Bishop Home], or one of the other organizations [where] there is an attendant to fetch these things, the one who is outside of these groups will fetch for himself, a sight that brings a painful feeling in the heart [alina ehaeha o ka naau].

(To be continued.)

Ka Nupepa Kuokoa. 2 MARCH 1889. P. 4.
He Mau Hunahuna No Ke Kahua Mai Lepera O Kalawao A Me Kalaupapa. Some Tidbits about the Leprosy Settlement of Kalawao and Kalaupapa.

4. The homes being lived in. [Na home e noho ia nei.]

There are four sections [mahele] where the patients live.
(A) Belonging privately to the patients. (E) Belonging to the Rev. Father Damien [Damiano]. (I) Belonging to the Board of Health. (O) Belonging to the Hon. Bishop [Bihopa].

(A) Some existing houses are privately owned by the patients, by means of the money obtained by them through the methods explained earlier.

From the staple food, working on the land, labor paid for by the Board of Health and income from outside, animals, pigs, and horses raised in here, and other sources of income.

The patient has complete authority over his personal house. The Board of Health has no right to insert a new patient to live with him without his permission and without its being someone related to him that he wants to live there.

If, however, he dies without a will [kauoha], and he has no relation living with him, such as a husband, wife, parent, child, or personal relation, then that house rolls into the hand of the Board of Health, along with other possessions such as horses or the furnishings within the house. But if he died with a will, then the relations outside and someone here that he chose will be made heirs, although only if the will is written. Oral wills [kauoha waha] are not well-regarded by the supervisor [luna nui] and his assistant.

If the heir is outside and wants to sell to the Board of Health or to someone else here, that can be done.

If the person named by the will is here, then whether he lives in the house or sells is up to him.

When the person owning a private house becomes ill and thinks that this might be his end, as the agony increases, then the desire grows to return to the hospital and be cared for by the doctor. If he lives and recovers, then he returns to his house. If he dies, then the doctor has the authority to order the attendant [kanaka] of this patient enclosure [pa mai] to bury him. If the deceased belonged to one of the two existing funeral groups [hui hoolewa kupapau elua], then he will be given a funeral with great dignity. The procession will travel with drums, horns, and waving banners. In my recollection, this is like the funerals of the town of Honolulu for the highest royalty and prominent people, and so it is done for all the deceased who are members of these groups, with no fee for this funeral.

If the deceased did not join these groups, he will be given a funeral with this honor beyond compare for a small fee that can be paid by a poor person, until he reaches the place to be buried.

If there is a desire to adorn the grave with coral [puna], that is for the person with a lot of money and who is survived by some helpers [kokua]. If that is not the case, then the grave will be covered with dirt.

However, if the ill person has some relations living in the private home, such as immediate family or friends bound by love, then they will not allow him to return to the hospital. He will remain in the house and the doctor will come to treat him. He might live or he might die.

Upon dying, all of the patients [mai] are allowed to receive a coffin [pahu kupapau] from the coffin-making shops [hale hana pahu] of the Board of Health for free. However, if a helper [kokua] dies, meaning someone who does not have leprosy, then his coffin must be paid for when it is fetched from the coffin-making shop of the Board of Health. The coffin-making shops that are operating belong to the leprosy patients [mai lepera]. A bereavement fee is paid by those living, to cover the coffin and the digging of the grave. If this is not possible for the family living with him, along with other honors that have a cost, due to lack of resources or lack of successor, then the grave will remain unmarked.

When the time comes, the coffin rides in a real hearse [kaa kupapau maoli], just like those of Honolulu, a carriage with four wheels and dipping black feather standards [kahili hooluu eleele] on top of the cab, which is pulled by the men of the group.

This is one of the greatest events [hana pookela] held in this colony [pana-laau].

The existing flagpoles [apahu hae] are like flagpoles for our government buildings at the sites of the heads of government and the counselors of various nations; that is entirely how they appear.

Those are what raise up these two groups. The heads of these groups are Mr. Kihe of Kaupō, Maui, and John [Ioane] Kalohi.

This act of dignifying and honoring the end of this life has become an act enthusiastically praised by all. If someone beloved is to die, his funeral will not be lacking.

(E)—Some of the houses lived in by the patients belong to the Rev. Father Damien.

(To be continued.)

» [Instead of A, B, C, and D, the writer uses the letters A, E, I, and O to list the four types of homes that patients live in. This is the order of the vowels in early Hawaiian grammar books, in which a, e, i, o, and u preceded the consonants.]

Ka Nupepa Kuokoa. 9 MARCH 1889. P. 4.
He Mau Hunahuna No Ke Kahua Mai Lepera O Kalawao A Me Kalaupapa. Some Tidbits about the Leprosy Settlement of Kalawao and Kalaupapa.

The majority of patients [mai] in his [Father Damien's] patient houses [hale mai] and under his care are young men and women, with a minority being fathers and mothers.

He has gathered this amount of patients by being truly vigilant when the patient ships [moku mai] arrive here. There is not one patient ship that he has not watched over. As soon as the assistant supervisor, Mr. A. Hutchinson [Ambrose Hutchison], has finished his count, then this one begins without delay to care for all the children who landed on this patient ship. They are fetched with carriages and horses to upper Kalawao, the place where his houses stand.

You, the one reading, know that this Rev. Father Damien [Damiano] is a priest of the Catholic religion [kahunapule o ka aoao Katolika], but he does not depend on that and only take the children of that faith with him. He supports children of all religions, and scorns no one. With an unwavering heart he reaches out to care for the children, like a hen keeping her chicks warm under her wings, and thusly he perseveres without payment.

In my experience with all the people who care for large families in this way, they are paid monthly and yearly. If he has been paid by the government, your storyteller has not seen it, so forgive me for my lack of knowledge about his payment for this great important work he bears upon his shoulders.

My guess is that this one will indeed receive a reward for first agreeing to sacrifice his good health, and now being stricken with this kind of disease. It will be the great reward in heaven that the Bible always teaches. The greater reward is in heaven, not the reward on this earth, a reward that is moth-eaten and rotten.

The personal belongings that the Board of Health gives to all the patients outside are also given to these children, and an attendant [kanaka] goes to fetch them under the guidance of this one. The children are properly provided with enough food and clothing, so the parents outside cannot complain that their child is lacking. This story is reporting that the children in this patient enclosure [pa mai] live cleanly, as I have seen, more so than the children outside of this enclosure. The boys and the girls are separated.

An attendant prepares the food, and the children just eat all the meals of the day.

If a child becomes ill, then the attendant brings food to the place of the ill one. If he becomes ill and dies, then the attendant, by order of Damien, will take him to be buried.

The houses where they sleep are large and long, and there are buildings for eating and for cooking as well.

(I.) The majority of the houses lived in by the patients belong to the Board of Health. [No ka Papa Ola ka hapanui o na hale e noho nei na mai.]

If there is a large house for the patients or if there is a small one, that is how the patients are housed, in all of the communities [kauhale].

For the patient who lives in these houses, he or they will supply themselves with all supplies when they first arrive, or they will truly be destitute and lacking. If a patient prepared beforehand for coming here and is living as a newcomer [malihini], then he is saved. If not, then there is a lot of blundering about to find the place that can meet these needs. However, if the pocket has some change, then it will soon be spent on all these needs. If you met someone outside before who already lives in the house you are living in, or you have a friend you landed with, or a cousin or parent or relative of your parents' generation who already lives here, then that is better because you have someone who will help you with the other needs, such as these needs as follows:

No mattress, no mat, pillow, iron pot, poi pounding board [papa kui ai], poi pounder [pohaku kui ai], firewood axe, and so forth.

If the patient lacks these things, he will become equipped in this way:

The new patients who have just landed are given vouchers [bila dala alualu] by the assistant supervisor or his secretary, to go and purchase from the existing store, the only store approved by the Board of Health for the patients to buy from. These vouchers are not allowed to be spent at other places.

At this time, you will make purchases with this voucher until the true value of this voucher is completely spent.

The one reading may wonder about this voucher simply given as a gift.

This gift is the set payment for the patient for the year from October of one year until the next October.

Before it was six dollars, and now ten dollars is the true value that the patient collects.

If the first steps upon the soil of this land begin on the first day of that month mentioned above, then the entire allotment will be received, but if the arrival comes later, then the allotment will be reduced as such until the year is complete. Such will it be until death, when this ongoing allotment to the patient will be finished.

That is the existence of the patients living outside of the houses of the Board of Health, but if you return to the actual hospital, then you will not meet with the needs described earlier.

You will only have food there at all times, and an attendant will prepare it.

(To be continued.)

Ka Nupepa Kuokoa. 23 MARCH 1889. P. 4.
He Mau Hunahuna No Ke Kahua Mai Lepera O Kalawao A Me Kalaupapa. Some Tidbits about the Leprosy Settlement of Kalawao and Kalaupapa.

If your prayer is not granted, Your Majesty, through us, the people living at this time, then maybe it will be for the people of the time after us, when we are already lying in the immeasurable belly of the earth, or your three prayers will be fulfilled, O royal ones, for the patients living their entire lives in this colony [panalaau]. Perhaps they will be fulfilled among the people, and this disease will never again be seen appearing upon a member of your beloved nation [lahui aloha].

Thus, the one who is writing this story knows of the great peace that the patients of this time will receive; and with the strength of your prayers as well as those of the truly devout of the Highest God, the patients will receive a feeling of ease, without weeping heavily from pain every day.

This story is not urging you all to pray in order to test our living God through prayer and the bending of the knees of the king of Hawai'i before Almighty God, along with the heir to the crown of Hawai'i and the queen and the devout, and then when the thing requested is not provided and the request does not draw nearer for a year or several years, then the mouth wrongly says that this is a God without power who does not heed the request of our royal chiefs, that we should all leave and find ourselves a new God.

This is not what this story is voicelessly calling for. Ask for the grace of God, and he will indeed provide guidance to the place where relief will be found by the entire nation of Hawai'i.

Please forgive me from this point on, and the gaze will turn upon the seventh section, in accordance with what was previously described in the sixth issue of this paper.

7. The helpers needed by the patients. [Na kokua e pono ai na mai.]

There are two main types of helpers [kokua nui] that are needed by the patients living here, and if these two things were missing, then good assistance to the one who has become extremely weak would be gone. Here they are below:

One: A horse [lio].
Two: An attendant [kanaka].

The horse is the quick path that speeds things up for the patients when they fetch starch and meat from Kalaupapa to Waikolu, or from Kalawao to Kalaupapa.

The distance is several miles, which the patients are unable to walk in order to fetch their food, and to fetch their own firewood, water (in the time when water was distant), and goods at the store.

These things are only made possible with a horse. The horse has been called a father and a mother for the patients living now.

The patients wondered greatly about these things in recent years, due to the rumors that the patients would be forbidden from raising horses, or there would be one horse for each patient.

If these rumors came to be true, the result is unknown. However, if the true rumors were gathered, then the patients would rise up in opposition with great and terrible action upon the superintendent and his assistant. That is truly what has been observed of the wild ideas emerging from the mouth, by the listener, that the terrible and wrong action will actually be performed. The rumor about maybe restricting horses to one per patient is being fulfilled, but luckily this idea was not expressed before the assembled patients rising to oppose the leaders of this colony [panalaau].

The suppression of the horses of the patients is a great consideration, such as the idea that the horses of the patients will eat all the weeds, and that the horses wandering around should be gotten rid of so the plains will become a place for the cattle that are desired to be raised. Perhaps the cattle will be for the patients, or maybe for the cattle owners raising them.

Whether the cattle belong to the patients or to some other rancher, it is not right to suppress and leave the patients lacking horses to ride upon this land, unless the Board of Health has ways of solving the problems of the patients that are the same as the horse, the tireless helper for the patients [kokua pauaho ole no na mai], the thing that the patients think greatly of as a father and a mother for this place. Would the heat of rage not truly burn in the patients if they were to be deprived of their mother and father? It would indeed.

The second helper [kokua] for the patients is the uninfected people [poe mai ole] who are permitted by the Board of Health to come here and help their specific patients. They are called "helpers" [kokua].

They work for their patients and for the Board of Health on every Monday each week, working one day each week at the place where it is desired to put the male helpers to work, as well as the females. Braiding cord [aho] was the work in earlier years. Cord for a fishing net [aho upena lawaia] is used for the Board of Health, and the patients eat the fish. At this time, their ongoing project is not clear.

The residents [kupa] and natives [kamaaina] also enter into this labor. Along with all of the helpers [kokua], they are subject to the rules of the existing Board of Health.

This past January, all the uninfected helpers [kokua mai ole] were counted, from the men to the women and the boys and girls, and there were 184: 83 men, 75 women, 11 boys, and 15 girls.

Thus, for the total of the boys and girls, they number at 26 who are in good health, without the blemishes of disease upon them. They are meeting with the patients by eating with them, sleeping with them, traveling with them, and living with them in the same house. Season after season they have been living together. They do not receive an allotment of starch and meat. There is just one bundle that the adult patients are supplied with, and that is not enough for the week.

So by removing this total of 26 youngsters living in good health, only the men and women remain. Some people make the ears of the government leaders ring and constantly remind them that we have good helpers, the progeny and descendants who will reproduce in accordance with the motto of the royal voice from upon the throne, which the nation will never forget, the motto [makia] of David [Davida] Kalākaua's kingdom [Hoʻoulu Lāhui: increase the nation].

Here are these roots with many sprouts [Eia keia mau kumulau la: women producing children], and the men. They must be considered quickly, so they do not wastefully enter the forest of 'O'opuloa [nahele o Oopuloa] and cause the progress of the people in growing themselves to limp along, because of this confused living with us.

(You must properly come, Your Majesty, and bring out this blood and the very bones of your people, to grow outside and have many offspring, so they are not also covered by this disease that reigns over these fine native folks.)

If this opinion above was quite rude to the dignity of His Majesty and his progeny, and it is thought that his royal station has been trampled upon by this call, then forgive the slave [kauwa] who is telling this story.

(To be continued.)

Ka Nupepa Kuokoa. 30 MARCH 1889. P. 4.
He Mau Hunahuna No Ke Kahua Mai Lepera O Kalawao A Me Kalaupapa. Some Tidbits about the Leprosy Settlement of Kalawao and Kalaupapa.

If it is thought to be a great task to bring the youngsters out, perhaps there should be independent homes for them at some unoccupied place in this colony [panalaau], to live without sleeping and eating in the same place as their infected parents. An uninfected adult would be set up there who could teach basic knowledge and manual trade skills, until they marry as husbands or wives, either as a part of that family or outside of it. Then they will stop living at that place.

When the government's money bags are full for this mission to propagate the nation [hooulu i ka lahui] in the [legislative] session of AD 1889, remember these seeds of this land that is close to being covered by blight and becoming rotten, putrid, and decayed, when these lei of yellow mamo bird feathers that adorn your crowned reign, O Royal King of Hawai'i, will disappear completely.

These male helpers [kokua kane] that have just been described possess enough strength to assist their personal patients and also help with the great labors of the Board of Health (which are paid for except for the single weekly work day that is not paid by the Board of Health), such as unloading cargo from the ships, working on the roads, working on fences, bringing cattle down the cliff trail [ala pali], slaughtering cattle, bringing food on a skiff from the rivers where the food is, attending to the cart that carries baggage with the help of strong patients [mai ikaika] who are paid by the board, and chopping firewood alongside the strong patients who do it for themselves, for the hospital, and for other patients who wish to buy firewood for themselves, for two and a half dollars per pile, or more to cover the fee of the cart attendant [kahu kaa] if the firewood is not for the actual hospital.

Half a dollar or more is the charge paid to the cart attendant for moving the patients' cargo beyond the hospital, according to the wishes of the patient, for firewood or other cargo.

These people are the ones who worked together to make the water pipe [paipu wai] that was recently laid down, for pay and for the single weekly work day of the Board of Health.

These labors and the other labors that the Board of Health undertakes that were not described here are carried out efficiently by the helpers.

The punishment for the helper who does not attend the single work day is to climb up the cliff [pii no i ka pali: i.e., leave by the pali trail] or go by ship and return to the land he came from. The full authority of his permit to come and live here until his patient dies is voided. You have no ground to stand on when breaking the rules of this land. Whether this person be great or humble, when the command of the supervisor to climb the cliff [pii i ka pali] strikes his ear, he climbs the cliff, with tears and mucus over leaving his patient, who will be weeping and trembling out of love for his helper.

However, if he stayed home for that work day due to a personal problem or for his patient, and the sheriff knows that it was a problem that prevented him from going to work, then he can stay home until the problem is resolved and this punishment will not be placed upon him.

On this single weekly work day you will be put to work on the public road that lies from Kalaupapa to Waikolu. All of you who pay the road tax should remember to request during this next legislative session that your road tax of two dollars be released. Those two dollars were fulfilled by the days that you worked on our road here. Is that wrong?

These are the great helpers of the patients as relates to this seventh section [mahele] of the story. The condition of the patients in past years was not like that of this current time, this time when the patient has these two helpers.

To quote the sheriff of this colony [panalaau], in his speech before the youth organization in Siloama Church [luakini o Siloama], this is what he said:

"To the Young People's Christian Endeavor Society of Siloama [Ahahui Opiopio Imi Pono Kristiano o Siloama], be hopeful and continue the righteous work that we do in the name of Jesus Christ, with sincere intent. Perhaps we will be graced by the heavens, and the wounds resting upon you will be eased, or we will all be released to return from this pit out to the place where we came from. Because when I see you now, O patients, the disease upon you has eased. It is not like before, when I came to this land in the year AD 1873.

"When I saw the patients, the ears were drawn down the shoulders. They were long and dangling like earrings, and the mouth and nose were disfigured and raised up. The mouth would be stretched open with the hand to thrust food in, and if they died, a fly would be the one crying, and the water buckets would ring all night and day. When fetching the cooked taro [pai ai], they could only walk while bearing the cooked taro upon the back. When the rain came, you could die from the numbing cold, and upon reaching the house you might die. The houses were filthy and smelled truly awful. You could not stay long in that place. In that time this house was being built by Pualewa [poetic for unfixed, always on the move]."

(To be continued)

Ka Nupepa Kuokoa. 6 APRIL 1889. P. 4.
He Mau Hunahuna No Ke Kahua Mai Lepera O Kalawao Me Kalaupapa. Some Tidbits about the Leprosy Settlement of Kalawao and Kalaupapa.

Thus, from the time when this church [Siloama] was established and God's will was done within it until now, the severity of the illness has changed and lessened. Now all of us who live here are the same, as if you are not ill people, due to the work of God's will. He has provided the blessings of this time and the needed helpers [kokua], which are the horses and the people allowed by the Board of Health to come here and aid their patients.

Some helpers [poe kokua] have lived on this land for a long time, for ten, twenty-five, or twenty-eight years. The native residents [kamaaina] have also lived with the patients, eaten with them, traveled with them, slept with them, and lived in their houses. They have not been stricken by this illness, and one who has contracted the disease is rare. They live with their own patient until the patient dies, and then live with another patient until that one dies, and so on until the present time. The blemishes of the disease are not upon them, although some helpers have died or become truly ill here.

Here are the names of those helpers who have lived here a long time, ten years or more, and almost twenty for some people. They have become residents [kupa a kamaaina] well-acquainted to this place, becoming natives of the land [kulaiwi hoi i ka aina] that outsiders are scared of due to the fear of being eaten by this disease. But to them, that nation-extinguishing scamp of Hawai'i [kupueu hoopio lahui o Hawaii nei] is not so hot.

Mr. C. Kopena, Mr. Kamakini, Mr. Kahā'ulelio, sheriff of this colony [ilamuku o keia Panalaau], Rev. I. Hanaloa, Mr. Auau, Mr. Li'ili'i, Mr. Kanuha, Mr. Manua, Mrs. Lilia Ila'i, Mrs. Hokela [Holt], Mr. Kalo'i'ele, and Mr. Kalili Paela, who recently passed away.

There are many more who have lived here for this long.

For some people who are living with their patients it has been less than ten years since they came here, but they also spent several years living together outside.

As for the names of some of the old native residents [kupa a kamaaina kahiko] of this land who have lived with the patients since the patients started living here until now, here are their names:

Mr. Simona Kahalehulu and his family, Mr. Kanakahelewale and his family, Mr. Kiliona and his nephew, Mr. Kalilikāne and his family, and R. W. Meyer.

After these named people, and some people living here whose names were not included here, have lived with, rubbed oil upon, and embraced the multitude of patients, where is the thing called a "contagious disease" [mai lele]?

So consider, O one who ponders, and carefully investigate the cause and the source for this kind of disease arriving, growing, and spreading widely here in Hawai'i.

If it indeed were a contagious disease, then this listing of names would have all been stricken by the illness, just like the other contagious diseases that have been seen here in Hawai'i.

8. The three different religions. [Na hoomana like ole ekolu.]

There are three existing religions in this land: The Protestant religion [hoomana Hoole Pope], called Calvinism [Kalavina], the Roman religion [hoomana Roma], who call themselves Catholics [Katolika], and the religion of latter days [hoomana o na la hope], Mormonism [Moremona].

There are two existing churches for the Protestant denomination: one in Kalawao named Siloama, and one in Kalaupapa, close to the harbor. They are well-built wooden buildings that can accommodate more than two hundred people each sitting on their own seats, with bell towers on the roofs, with well-made pulpits, and with lamps in the center and on the walls that cast out bright light to fully illuminate the entire building for meetings at night.

When I lived outside, I thought there were no churches here, and perhaps that is the mistaken assumption of other people, just like me. However, when I first arrived on this land, once I looked, those churches were standing there. I said to myself, "Here indeed are some temples [heiau] for worshipping the everlasting God."

On July 10, 1887, I arrived. It was a Tuesday, and the next Sabbath I went to properly see the goings-on. When I entered, there was a great crowd of patients and uninfected people filling the seats. The people who knew me shook my hand; the other people just looked at me, and some of them nodded their heads.

At that time those hours were for Sunday school, and the schoolmaster was sitting in the presiding chair. He was Solomona Kamahalo of Līhu'e, Kaua'i, who continues to be a leader and supporter for the church in Kalaupapa to this day.

The class teachers were being organized at that time when the crowd was gathered around and right then my name was called as a teacher for the class of adults with yellowed chins [the elderly] who had grown old, as white sugar cane, within the Bible. At that time this task was given to me. I said to myself, "How do these people know me, and know that I am a suitable teacher for the class that has eaten adult food, since they have never met me before? I am a complete stranger before this great gathering, with over twenty students in this adult class."

While we were conducting school, the Rev. Father J. Hanaloa, from Kalawao, came in. I was introduced by Mr. Pāpū to this angel of God that has been long placed by him in this place without scorn or fear of being bitten by this greatly feared disease.

This was the Sabbath at this church when he would lead the service, and when I first saw him, he appeared old and gray-haired, over eighty years of age. That was what he told me, but when he stood on the pulpit to speak, he was like a youngster right on top of the work of the Lord Jesus Christ.

At that time when he was giving his sermon, feelings of love swelled within me and my tears flowed for my old man whose white hair was like that of this one here, Rev. Daniela Puhi of Hāna, east Maui, who serves as the reverend for the church in Kīpahulu, Maui.

And on the Sabbath, the last day of July, I was given the task of leading the service, thanks to the kindness of the local ministers. I opened my speech before this full crowd with the Gospel written by John 20:19, in the last part, "Greetings to you," I presented the main ideas as I had thought of them, being these:

1. Love as relates to man.
2. The love of the Devil [Diabolo] that enters man.
3. The love of God.

And the ideas related to each of those three topics were also explored.

On the Sabbath, August 7, the Rev. Father J. Hanaloa performed the church service. On the Sabbath, the 14th, I went up to Kalawao to perform their service, having received the call through the secretary of the church, Mr. Unea. I fulfilled what I had spoken on the Sabbath, the 14th, when I went up, since the students in my class in Kalaupapa had not heard it.

When I and my native parents of this land, Mrs. and Mr. Nāihelua, entered Siloama Church, I was hosted by the one who had made the call earlier. Father Hanaloa did not come due to the weak state of his wife in those days. She only got worse and died, and now he lives alone without his companion.

While I was sitting, the Sunday school had not begun, and there were three people sitting close to the table, two men and one woman conversing together. There was one Native Hawaiian man [kanaka maoli], Mr. Unea, and one Caucasian [haole] named Clark [Kalaka], and one part-Caucasian woman [wahine hapahaole]. My eyes were upon them as I gazed and pondered: who among them was the Sunday school master? I guessed that it was one of the men, the Caucasian or the Hawaiian, since that is the usual thing at all of our places outside. However, it was the woman who eventually sat upon the Sunday schoolmaster chair, and the men were in charge of the classes for young men and young women.

At that time this woman opened with a hymn and quickly went back to play the organ. Then when the prayer was done, I said to myself, "Wow, all of the tasks are completely mastered by this woman. She sings, she plays the organ, and she leads the prayer, without any part of it going to a man."

After the singing and the prayer were done, the class teachers taught their students. I was in the class where Mr. Kahāʻulelio was also a student. It was in fact his wife who was leading the school. He was the schoolmaster before and then his wife took over. She was the woman the newcomer [malihini] was astonished by.

(To be continued.)

Ka Nupepa Kuokoa. 13 APRIL 1889. P. 4.
He Mau Hunahuna No Ke Kahua Mai Lepera O Kalawao A Me Kalaupapa. Some Tidbits about the Leprosy Settlement of Kalawao and Kalaupapa.

If you are staying there when you are weak, but you feel strong again and wish to return and live in the houses outside, that is your decision. When you tell the assistant supervisor that, you will leave from there. Then that patient enclosure [pa mai] is done taking care of you, and you will work for yourself, like what was reported earlier.

However, when you are living in the houses outside, and trouble appears again and death is near, and there is no one to take care of you, and perhaps it is unsuitable for the people living with you because of the terrible smell that cannot be endured until you die, and you have no personal possessions that cause the people living with you to hope to receive a benefit from you when you die, then a complaint against you will be brought before the assistant supervisor for you to be returned to the hospital, but you will not know and understand. You will be returned there without hearing about it. It will be known when you are carried and placed in the cart [kaa] of the Board of Health after the cart attendant [kahu kaa] is ordered by the supervisor, and then you will be taken with care to the hospital. Then this hospital will care well for you until you are left in a grave.

This hospital hides bones in the dirt [huna na iwi i ka lepo] for one without a helper, without relations or friends, and without personal possessions that earn the trust of housemates. This is a bad hiding place [wahi huna ino] that will not be carried abroad by the mouth of the one conversing, as is the constant nature of people.

And this building is a building where the weak people [poe nawaliwali] who return there are often placed. It is certainly better than staying in the houses outside when it is known that they cannot take care of themselves.

And this is a place that the patients always express affection for, with their helpers, when the anguish builds in them about returning there.

The existing houses of this time are beautiful and truly fine. The first shacks have all been cleaned away and moved to a different place. These are some new houses being lived in by the patients, with the separation of the strong patients [poe mai ikaika] and the weak patients [poe mai nawaliwali] who are near death.

This is a site that is feared by the patients, like the news heard outside in earlier days, due to the poor state of the patients living there. However, that was then, and now this story is reporting the truth, that this is a place of which I said to myself, this place is truly fine and comfortable. There is no work, just eat and turn the face upward.

There are many houses outside of the hospital that have been cleaned and reinforced with new shingles. But some houses are still in this filthy state. The job has not been completed, but they might all be made beautiful in the future, since this is a time of cleaning for all things.

There has been a great foul and terrible stench in the houses in past years, but at this time that stench is being fixed, since all the inhabited communities [kauhale] are supplied with pipe water [wai piula]. Before, there was no great desire to wash the floor of the house because the water was so far away. Only when some rain fell, then it would be washed. The bit of water they had would be kept for the throat and cooking food.

For the people who are not used to improvement and are somewhat messy, they will smell terrible, but the people who are neat and tidy will not have a terrible smell. When you enter, it is as if their houses are not inhabited by patients.

(O). The Hon. Bishop [Bihopa] owns a house lot [pa hale] full of fine houses inhabited by our young women [opio wahine] whom the nuns, the mothers of mercy [makuahine Virigine o ke aloha], are caring for patiently, just like their work in Kaka'ako. It is the same here. They will be blessed for [helping] the youngsters of this nation who have been injured in the body and in the heart.

(To be continued.)

Ko Hawaii Pae Aina. 4 MAY 1889. P. 2.

The Board of Health, by means of the president, sent to the bishop of Olba a letter of condolence [palapala hoalohaloha] for the death of Father Damien [Makua Damien], and the bishop gave a complimentary reply to the board for this condolence.

» [The articles in this section end with the death of Father Damien on April 15, 1889. The series called *He Mau Hunahuna No Ke Kahua Mai Lepera O Kalawao A Me Kalaupapa,* Some Tidbits about the Leprosy Settlement of Kalawao and Kalaupapa, continues in the next section about Mother Marianne.]

IV. MOTHER MARIANNE (MAKUAHINE MARIANA) IN HAWAI'I: 1888 TO 1918

MOTHER MARIANNE was born Barbara Koob, now officially "Cope," on January 23, 1838. She emigrated from Germany to the United States with her parents when she was two years old, and in 1862 she joined the Sisters of the Third Order of Saint Francis in Syracuse, New York. In 1877 she was elected by the sisters to be the superior general of the congregation and was re-elected for a second term in 1881. As the superior general, she was given the title of "Mother."

During Mother Marianne's second term, she received a request from the Hawaiian government asking for sisters to help care for leprosy patients in Hawai'i. She agreed to help and came personally with six sisters, arriving in Honolulu on November 8, 1883. There she took over management of the leprosy hospital in Kaka'ako. In 1888, a home for girls was built at Kalaupapa when Charles Bishop donated money for its construction. Mother Marianne and two sisters went to Kalaupapa on November 13, 1888, to run the Bishop Home for girls. She dedicated her life to serving the patients at the home and died there on August 9, 1918. On October 21, 2012, she was canonized by Pope Benedict XVI as Saint Marianne, a saint in the Catholic Church.

In Hawaiian-language newspaper articles about Mother Marianne (Makuahine Mariana), her name is spelled variously as Mariame, Mariana, Marianne, Mary Ann, and Mary Marianne. She was also called Sister Marianne (Kaikuahine Mariame).

In addition to kaikuahine (sister) and makuahine (mother), the Hawaiian-language newspapers also use the term virigine, a loan word for "virgin," to recognize female members of Catholic religious orders. While names such as "Virigine Maria" and "Virigine Makuahine" are translated literally as "Virgin Mary" and "Virgin Mother," the term "virigine" is more often translated as "nun," such as in Virigine Katolika, or "Catholic nun." While the Hawaiian-English dictionary uses "wilikina" for nun, "virigine" is usually the preferred term in the Hawaiian-language newspapers.

The two decades leading up to Mother Marianne's death in 1918 saw many changes in Hawai'i and at Kalaupapa. One of the biggest was the gradual transition from Hawaiian to English. It began with the overthrow of the Hawaiian Kingdom in 1893 and was followed by a law in 1896 mandating English as the language of instruction in all schools. This law ensured the decline of oral and written Hawaiian, a change that was reflected in the newspapers of the day, in the place names, and in the daily conversations of Hawai'i's residents. By the time of Mother Marianne's death, English was in use at Kalaupapa along with Hawaiian. Hawaiian-language newspapers, however, continued to be published until 1948.

The articles that follow begin after the death of Father Damien and continue in chronological order. Many of them include some mention of Mother Marianne. Those that don't were written during her lifetime at Kalaupapa and help to detail what conditions were like at the settlement for her and the patients.

Ka Nupepa Kuokoa. 15 SEPTEMBER 1888. P. 2.
Kela a me Keia. This and That [Miscellany].

Last Monday, Father Leonoro [Father Leonor Fouesnel, SS.CC.] boarded the steamer [mokuahi] *Mokolii* for Kalawao to meet with the priests [kahuna] there, and to observe the nature of the arrangements for the Nuns of Mercy [Virigine o ke aloha] there.

» [In the early years of Mother Marianne's Catholic order the sisters who worked at caring for the sick were called Sisters of Mercy. This writer called them Nuns of Mercy.]

Ka Nupepa Kuokoa. 4 MAY 1889. P. 1.
He Mau Hunahuna No Ke Kahua Mai Lepera O Kalawao Me Kalaupapa. Na Hanai A Ka Papa Ola I Na Mai. Some Tidbits about the Leprosy Settlement of Kalawao and Kalaupapa. What the Board of Health Provides to the Patients.

An equal allotment [haawina] of starch [ai] and meat [i-a] and other allotments are given to the adult patients, and some allotments are not given to the children, according to these directives as follows:

Twenty-one pounds of cooked taro [pai ai] for the week per patient, and seven pounds of beef. If cooked taro is rejected and crackers are desired, then eight and a half pounds are given. If not those two starches, and rice is the desired starch, then nine pounds are given per patient. If it's raw flour, twelve pounds.

For those last three starches, one pound of sugar is added to those things. These allotments of food are for one week. They are collected on Wednesday every week. However, the collection time for the cooked taro always changes, according to when it arrives on the skiff [waapa] or on the ships [moku].

Quite recently, though, the starch ceased to be brought on the skiff because of the many complaints by the patients about its landing at Waikolu, due to the distance, the poor quality of the road, and the other problems that struck. But when the skiff fetched the starch, it was enough for the patients to collect on the weekdays, and now with the ship, which lands at Kalaupapa, it is collected on the Sabbath day, with the ship arriving in the evening on the day of rest. The hungry one cannot travel on the holy day [la laahia], but the considerate people there wait until the sanctity is over.

Beef is the usual meat at all times. It is distributed on two days, Wednesday and Saturday. Ten or more cattle are slaughtered, and if that is not enough then salmon [kamano] is substituted. If there is a desire for salmon while there is plenty of beef, it can be obtained with permission from the head supervisor.

When fresh fish is brought, it is big-eyed scad [akule]. It is given to the patients at seven pounds per person, but only when it is seen that there is enough.

Cow's milk [waiu bipi] is another thing given out every morning if desired. The patient is the one who fetches it from the milking place [kahi uwi], one or two pints per person.

Another regular allotment for the patients is the monthly allotment: five pounds of salt, one or two [bars of] soap, four matches, one quart of oil, and the money voucher [bila alualu].

The four matches are not given to the children, and only the adults are given the money vouchers.

These allotments of oil, soap, and matches are not suitable and sufficient for the patients, and the people in the most trouble are the poor.

There are two supervisors who distribute these things with their assistants, and the Board of Health pays them a monthly salary. The exception is the money voucher, which the assistant head supervisor gives out. [It is effective] from the start of the year until the end, just like the details of the money allotment that were explained earlier. Also, the cow's milk has a different distribution supervisor, along with the milker [mea uwi waiu].

You, the one reading, must remember that none of these allotments mentioned above will be received unless the person has the metal number tag [helu mea kala].

This metal tag [mekala] is just like the metal tags of dogs. They have numbers from one to one hundred fixed upon them, in accordance with the number of patients residing and coming here.

This is the first gift given to you, the patient [mai], when you have just arrived at the land feared by all of us [aina i weli ia e kakou].

Right after your name is set down in the book of the assistant head supervisor, you are immediately commanded to fetch the metal tag, to quickly fetch it from his office above Kalawao. It is your starch and it is your meat until your days of living here are done. If you are lacking this thing, fetch it quickly to be supplied.

And if you have it, you will give this thing to the supervisor distributing starch and meat. If it has fallen and disappeared, you must quickly tell the assistant head supervisor, and he will give the order to the one who will again stamp your number that was lost with you also paying some coins to the one who stamps this metal tag.

At the places where starch and beef are distributed, there is a lot of trouble for the weak patients [mai nawaliwali], because of the shoving by the strong patient [poe mai ikaika] who wants to get his first. Each one is calling loudly, saying his tag number to be heard by the supervisors sitting inside the building. All the people are outside the small open door of the building to just report their tag number. It is given at the entrance.

Here is another problem at that place: If the time of distribution is during rainy days, then you will be buffeted by the rain from the house onwards. The Kiliʻoʻopu wind of Waikolu will stir forcefully with a numbing cold; the chilly water of the rivers will be carried by the wind; the wild waves of Kalaehala will break [e poi ana na nalu ahiu o Kalaehala], the ones that ransack [kuekaa] the road; the horse standing at the shore headland will be crushed; you will be buffeted by the Hoʻolehua and Kawaihānau winds, the two battling winds that cause the houses of Kalaupapa to fly about here and there; and upon reaching the distribution places you have become deathly ill from the numbing cold.

With this numbing chill you stand at the little doors calling your tag number, shivering with chattering molars, needing to receive it soon.

There is no sheltering part of the distribution center; the cold diminishes the patient until he returns home with that numbing chill, and warms up in a bed blanket. If he is cold and warms up and recovers, he will have nothing to say. If he rests and rests and the season changes to winter, and then suddenly he dies, there will be nothing to say. If he immediately dies, then this death is called by the native residents who have passed away "a wound blanket [he wili huluhulu]." You suppose he is resting, but suddenly the breath is completely gone.

However, these troublesome symptoms have not been seen in these current years; but in earlier years the storm and this pathetic death were seen.

With rain and wind the wound blanket death [make wili huluhulu] befalls the patients of this time. If personal helpers [kokua pili pono] for the patients have not been allowed to come by the Board of Health, there should be approval of enough for the rather frail patients, the patients for whom they would personally go and get their food, who have suffered this sudden disaster.

If, in spite of these difficulties, one goes and receives an allotment of cooked taro [pai ai], that is all good, but if it was all gone and one had to return the next day, the misfortune is multiplied.

That was the task when the skiff [waapa] brought the starch from the streams of Hālawa, Wailau, and Pelekunu. Now, that slipperiness [ano pakelokelo] is done and a steamship [mokuahi] brings it quickly.

(To be continued.)

Ka Nupepa Kuokoa. 11 MAY 1889. P. 3.
He Mau Hunahuna No Ke Kahua Mai Lepera O Kalawao Me Kalaupapa. Na Hanai A Ka Papa Ola I Na Mai. Some Tidbits about the Leprosy Settlement of Kalawao and Kalaupapa. What the Board of Health Provides to the Patients.

Sometimes there is trouble when the starch does not arrive due to the misfortunes that befall the skiff and the ship, and some people are unable to eat other starches, such as the starches previously mentioned. So then all the patients who want fresh taro [kalo maka] are summoned to the taro farm [mahiai loi] of C. Kopena in Waikolu, and they will pull [uhuki] it up with the uninfected people [poe mai ole], the helpers [kokua] of some patients who have come to live with their patients, and have become familiar, and been at ease, and become truly enraptured without a thought for the place of their birth, the homes with the multitude.

The patient with appendages will pull up his taro, while the one who needs help and the one with rotten flesh will wait for what is left over from the strong people when it is weighed by the supervisors and then inserted into a bag and weighed to provide thirty-five pounds per patient per week. Upon returning home, if possible he will cook it, then peel and pound it, and then sell it to other people for a quarter. If not in that way, then the other starches are fetched, as a filler for the time of no cooked taro [pai ai]. When the cooked taro arrives, then the collecting of these starches is over. The foreign starches and C. Kopena's taro patches [loi kalo] are only prepared for the problematic times when there is no taro for the patients.

That is how the Board of Health provides for the patients situated here, and as for the helpers [kokua] who came from the outside, it is in accordance with the compassion of the heart, weeping yearningly until the heart flutters. The ones who are greatly known as the open-hearted people, we have consumed their generosity until sated, and until some people among us simply lie in the earth.

And these patients are again asking, who else is open-hearted, should they arrive before you laden with gifts of love for the body and for spirits that mourn?

And due to the desire of some strong patients to increase the things that are inserted into the mouth, some patients, along with the helpers, have worked hard at fishing [lawaia]. They eat, give away, and also sell [the fish]. The women have gone to the shore for seaweed [limu], limpets [opihi], octopus spearing [ohee], and so forth.

In this work of the people knowledgeable in fishing, the face of the fish supplying the patient who offers some coins is greatly seen, but for the poor one, no fish peddled by the fishermen is eaten.

There are indeed many delicious fish [i-a ono] in this colony [panalaau] that refresh the throats of the patients. The doctors and others say that it is the great medicine [laau lapaau nui] to cure this illness. Fish and starch, eat until you lie on the ground [e ai a moe aku i ka honua].

6. The authority that keeps the peace. [Ka hoomalu ana e maluhia ai.]

This patient settlement [kahua mai] is controlled by rules that are simply spoken: the orders from the Board of Health to the agent Mr. R. W. Meyer, from him to his assistant residing here, Mr. Ambiode Hutchison Kanoealii [Ambrose Kanoeali'i Hutchison], and from him to the sheriff [ilamuku] of this colony and to the police officers [makai]. Mr. Kahā'ulelio is the sheriff of this colony. He bears the responsibility of protecting this patient settlement.

However, he does not keep order with the extreme heat that brought up a burning rage against the wrongdoer, which causes greater damage to the peace, like in the years previous, when the first sheriffs were there. Because of their wicked actions, one was ignorantly stabbed with a knife as per the bloody, merciless hand of the fat one in earlier incidents. Perhaps that is the case now, because, upon examining the desires of the patients, they truly become wild when the justice that is considered necessary is opposed. The one who is at fault surrenders and is locked in the jail [halepaahao] without much effort. If the crime warrants punishment by the head supervisor and his assistant, then there is punishment. If the crime deserves a warning then a warning is given. If the helpers [kokua] have committed the crime, their punishment is to climb up the cliff [pii i ka pali: i.e., leave by the pali trail] and return to the outside. If it is suitable for him to be warned, then he will be warned, like a mother to a child.

The head supervisors [luna nui] act as judge. The crimes that are suitable for the assistant head supervisor to deal with are his to deal with. For the serious cases that are unsuitable for the assistant supervisor, the head supervisor hears them, such as trials for robbery, assault, and anything relating to the property of the patients.

The criminal cases dealing with murder, grand theft, and trespassing by outsiders will be fully tried by our government courts of the outside, and these courts will make rulings in accordance with the established laws.

Some of the patients have greatly criticized this ruling by the supervisors in overseeing the trials concerning the patients. According to some, it would be fairer to have a real judge, so that the law is examined along with the case, and appoint some lawyers on the two sides to make arguments, in a court that is permanently established here, about the meaning of the law concerning the case being tried. Even if guilty, one could be saved by the cleverness of the lawyer, but might have already succumbed to punishment or have been spared.

This is a land completely forbidden [aina kapu loa] to outsiders who do not have the permit of entry provided by the Board of Health. For the one who tries to simply enter, with the idea that he has a patient or another reason to come in, he should not think that way or else he will soon have trouble.

There is no great and important person who can dare to simply enter and break the law of this colony [panalaau] without being ejected by the sheriff and the police through the order of the supervisor to climb up the cliff or go by ship. That is quite lucky for him; but if he is charged with trespassing, he will be punished.

Many people indeed have attempted to ignore and break the rules. Some have been ejected, and some are locked in the jail in here, to be tried by the true judge of this island. So do not try again, O friends on the outside, to come in, or else disaster will fall upon the one who does not hear and see that this is a forbidden land [aina kapu nei]. This is the report being given in this story, and it is the desire of the storyteller for you all to know about us, and us to know about you on the outside, and that is what I am requesting of your kindness. See and understand, the trouble is real that will fall upon the stubborn one who enters without the right of entry from the Board of Health. He will be thwarted, like the one being seen at this time.

The assistant head supervisor and the sheriff are working hard to search the baggage of the patients and the patient ships [moku mai]. The patients and the harbor watchman have been ordered to search for opium [opiuma], liquor [rama], and dynamite [giana-pauda: literally, "giant powder"]. Opium tins were found in boxes of poi, and the owner of these goods was fined with the growing dollars of the turkey [me na dala mahuahua a ka pelehu: a large amount].

These supervisors put in place by the Board of Health are not the only ones keeping the peace. There are also the ministers [kahunapule] and the truly devout [haipule] residing here, which are a great support on the side of peace to prevent the eruption of rioting and the restless desires that are growing. Not only them, but also the intelligent ones who treasure peace. They are pillars supporting the dignified status of the land at all times when it is inhabited.

Ka Nupepa Kuokoa. 18 MAY 1889. P. 2.
Kuu Pokii Aloha, Ua Hala. My Beloved Younger Sibling Has Passed.

Whereas, Almighty God has taken the precious breath of my beloved younger sibling John H. Kaalokai on April 26, 1889, in the Kalawao Colony [Panalaau o Kalawao]. He was born here in Honolulu on December 27, 1873, and he was a little over fifteen years old. Whereas, he was taken to the Kalawao Colony by the family-separating disease [mai hookaawale ohana] with good health of his body, and within just a few months the Lord took his soul. Whereas, we are the only fully developed fruit given by the Lord from the loins of J. H. Pāmaiʻaulu and Mrs. Iosepine ʻŌwela, there are six of us. Three have been taken on that same path of death, those being our youngest siblings. Three of us remained until our beloved younger sibling passed away, and only two of us remain in this dispirited world with our parents mourning for him in this earthly realm, as well as family, intimate friends, and beloved companions. Whereas, he died one week, and then the next week it was his father who was placed in that unfamiliar land [aina malihini] of the Rev. Damien [Damiano]. It could be said, "The parent goes, going together with his child in spirit." There is great sadness for us, the family living here, because before our sadness over his being taken had passed, that new sadness arrived. However, this sadness will be lightened by the Lord in Heaven. May the name of the Lord be praised, because he gives and he takes away. I am G. Haili.

Ka Nupepa Kuokoa. 18 MAY 1889. P. 3.
He Mau Hunahuna No Ke Kahua Mai Lepera O Kalawao Me Kalaupapa. Some Tidbits about the Leprosy Settlement of Kalawao and Kalaupapa.

The two Christian endeavor societies [hui imi pono kristiano] and the temperance societies [hui hoole waiona] existing these days below Kalaupapa and Kalawao are warming the peace in the heart and making it possible to say that this is a colony [panalaau] inhabited by Christian virtue, not the pain and the inhabitation of troubles like in previous years, when the thoughts of the patients were deceived into rising up against the first supervisors with dangerous weapons in their hands, and with a sword of words on their lips to show that the flesh and bones of the supervisors [the gists of the matters] were already in their mouths.

We are peaceful like calm, still water. If it bubbles up, then it crashes down to extinguish, since there are crests of water that extinguish and put out the burning of the fiery desire within the patients, like the ones described above.

There is nothing wrong if this story first puts out a call for all of the devout from Hawaiʻi to Niʻihau to make a request of the heavenly powers to unite in praying for the continuation of peace in the future, and for this illness to retreat back until it has been completely extinguished.

The devout are not the only ones that this story is inviting, since they are just some branches for the same great thing, the God of this earth, His Majesty Kaulilua David Kalākaua, king of his nation, being agonized, joining hands with Queen Kapiʻolani and Your Royal sister, Your Majesty, the heir to the crown of Hawaiʻi, Kamakaʻeha Liliʻuokalani.

Let our prayers sound as one, with you three at the head and your people behind. Perhaps the heavenly powers will be gracious through you, and rescue will be received by this portion of your people that is being overwhelmed by this disease that emaciates the nation until it is destroyed. The permanent motto [makia paa] of your kingdom is "Grow the Nation" [hooulu lahui].

Your Majesty, if you make a royal attempt, then the spread of this terrible disease over your people will be diminished. Turn and confer with God about us, this sum of over one thousand of your people constantly weeping in this pit [lua], while the God Jehovah is above, and then you, and we are your footrest, the citizens [makaainana] of your revered and sacred throne.

Ka Nupepa Kuokoa. 29 JUNE 1889. P. 4.
He Mau Hunahuna No Ke Kahua Mai Lepera O Kalawao Me Kalaupapa. Some Tidbits about the Leprosy Settlement of Kalawao and Kalaupapa.

This is a prayer [pule] and a chant of praise [kanaenae] to you, our Royal King [Kalākaua], until the fulfillment of your prayer with royal voice before the king of heaven, the one who placed you as a father for this nation that is filled with the black marks of mourning on the house doors.

Vigilance, alertness, and great consideration for the orphans [keiki makua ole] that land as newcomers [malihini] here.

Second: Preparation of large buildings for sleeping, eating, cooking food, tending to wounds, schooling, and praying.

Third: Increasing the helping hands, like the three new Catholic teachers [kumu pope] and the three nuns [virigine] living here.

With these three reasons, there will not be one child who wanders away from the Protestant denomination, like the news that outsiders are hearing. The Hawaiian board will build houses for the children on the Protestant side, because of the lack of children in this denomination. The children are rare indeed who live with their own parents that were born in here or came from the outside, who are encountered in our existing Calvinist churches.

In my estimation, there are not even forty children belonging to the parents from this denomination [Protestant] in that denomination [Catholic], which would bring the number of children to almost two hundred, of the children of all denominations.

Not only are the children of the poor [lopa] being nested here, there are also the children of the ministers who have been greatly guided and well educated on the side of the Gospel that points to Jesus, to pray and request of him in that name only, and everything will be received from the Father. However, it is being taught that in praying to Mary and the Apostles, they will pray to Jesus and then he will pray to the Father. It is being taught that Peter is the head of their church, and it is always taught at their Holy Communion [ahaaina] that the wafer is a true body of the lord, and the wine in the glasses and the little bottles by the priests praying at the altar is real blood.

If you, the ministers of the Protestant denomination, see that these guidances are correct, then so shall it be, but if they are incorrect in your teaching of the Gospel to your brethren and their children and yours, then how will it not be raised as a topic in the religious organizations here in Hawai'i?

9. The Government Doctors. [Na Kauka Aupuni.]

There are three doctors that the storyteller has clearly seen. They have these individual names, unless the English letters are incorrect in my spelling, and if incorrect then forgive me:

Here are their individual names: Dr. Mouritz, Dr. Peterson, Dr. Swift.

These doctors have not been installed by the government for treating and curing leprosy. Instead, they are someone to aid everyone living here, in the sense of the other illnesses that afflict the patients [mai] and the helpers [kokua mai].

Also, [they are] to examine the helpers to see if they have leprosy [mai lepera], and if they have it, they will be entered into the number of patients. Then they will receive allotments of starch and meat, and some other allotments, just like a leprosy patient [mea mai lepera] from the outside receiving the full allotment from the Board of Health. Then that helper will no longer be able to leave. He will live in that way until he dies here.

This is something where some helpers want to become patients. Enthusiasm and expedience is seen when the days arrive for the helpers to be examined by the doctor. One shows off his tinea splotches [pohaka kane] and ringworm [haukeuke] on the body, and disease [mai] on the skin, the thing that he had not dared to reveal to the doctors checking for illness while he was outside, yet here inside it is [like the old chant] a mark of pride from Hauaʻiliki, fostered, pelted by food until the stomach hurts.

As for the people who do not want to live here, they do not present their blemishes [kinaunau] on the skin, like the people wanting to expose all of their teeth or rough spots.

Ka Nupepa Kuokoa. 6 JULY 1889. P. 4.
He Mau Hunahuna No Ke Kahua Mai Lepera O Kalawao Me Kalaupapa. Some Tidbits about the Leprosy Settlement of Kalawao and Kalaupapa.

Concerning the first [two] names of the doctors [listed in the previous column], those two [Dr. Mouritz and Dr. Peterson] were quite cautious about entering the homes of the patients, and rather detached when caring for a body. However, the first doctor [Dr. Mouritz] was greatly admired by the patients for the fair way in which he gave out medicines to a patient, and we prized him greatly during the days he was with us. Concerning the last doctor [Dr. Swift], who is the doctor living here at this time, he has the full gratitude of the storyteller, and perhaps everyone here in the colony [panalaau]. With his completely strong body, the wind whistles [he goes at great speed], and it is a delight to meet with him; the features are pleasing and he does not avoid the stink and stand somewhere far away from the patient.

When he meets with the patient, he asks questions, and if there is a problem with the appendages, perhaps a puncture or rotting skin, he grasps it and feels it with his hands. If it is suitable to cut away the place where pain is felt, then it is cut, then washed with water, soap and a rag, and medicine is placed upon it. He has no hesitation in getting his hand stained with this disease that is greatly feared [mai e makau nui ia]. Some doctors are unable to get close to the leprosy patient, but he has no thought of scorning the patient.

He has suitable knowledge of the disease and the application of medicine and as a result, I clearly see myself through his insight, that I have a disease that makes it impossible to foresee the actions of this current year, and that I may pass on to the other side of the black river of death [muliwai eleele o ka make], where I would be unable to present this story.

However, the will of God was different, guiding me to the place where respite and ease would be received for this pain that I had for five years, a stomach ache that was truly painful in the stomach when it came, causing me to pass out. According to him, "The place of this pain of yours is known." However, the place where the stomach places food was about to rupture. If I had not been received by him and cared for with food that was suitable for a weak stomach, then the stomach would have ruptured and I would have died not long after. He said to me, "There is a great problem. Do not eat beef, do not eat hot things, and the food you will eat is cow's milk, fresh fish, and foods that are bland and soft, to not irritate the place where the stomach is damaged."

At that time, medicine from this doctor was taken with the food of milk, the food of younger days; that was the food that I ate sparingly, and then solid food sometimes, but milk for the majority of the time, and the pronouncement of this knowledgeable doctor was fulfilled.

In these current days, I have not met again with that stomach-harming friend of mine, who is stomach ache [Nahu].

And this doctor is carrying out his job with great energy, swiftly going to the dwellings and the actual patients of the hospital with the full strength of his body parts.

He is in two places every day. In the hours of the morning he is in Kalawao, and in the hours of the afternoon he is in Kalaupapa, greatly discharging his strength for his profession of healing the body, until that of the spirit remains for him. If he has completed both that of the body and that of the spirit, then there will not be another call for a caretaker [kahu] to come from a foreign land [Kahiki].

For the patient who properly carries out the instructions of the doctor, recovery will come quickly, not slowly. But for the patient who neglects the rules of the treatment, he can say that death will be the result.

As for Dr. Peterson, his work here did not progress much. His residency ended early without much time with us.

These are the reports concerning the government doctors who have resided in this colony, and we will move on to the tenth section of this story, about the religious ministers.

10. The various religious ministers. [Na kahunapule like ole.]

This section concerns the people who have been ordained, not the people perpetuating virtue and just giving speeches, such as the treasurers of the current church organizations, who constantly watch over the churches.

Just as there are various religions, so it is with ministers. However, there are two religions where it is known that there have been several ministers in those religions, being the Protestant faith and Catholicism.

In the Protestant faith there were several ministers before who lived here and who all died because they had leprosy when they came. It was not due to compassion for the souls of this land that Rev. Kaawa and Rev. Kahuila came here. They did their final work and then lay in the belly of the earth [opu o ka honua], along with some other ministers.

And concerning the Rev. J. Hanaloa, who serves as minister at this time, he did not come here for his job as minister and as a sacrifice for the masses. He came for his wife, who had the disease. If his wife had not gotten the disease, then this denomination would probably be lacking a minister. However, God was able to provide guidance to the place that allowed a minister to come here who did not have the disease and who was not frightened of coming here, like this one, and who would nourish the sheep of God in this land.

Due to his familiarity with living with patients, this disease became a shield for him. There is nothing that frightens him about meeting with the patients. Everyone is the same as if all are uninfected, or all are infected, including him, all mixed together, like mixing wild taro with cultivated taro [ka hui aku hui mai hui kalo i kanawao].

He is continuing to take care of the two churches, sharing the Sabbaths in how he carries them out all the time, from his time of strength of the body until his softness and old age, and forgetfulness sometimes.

The living he makes for the job he is doing comes from the Hawaiian Board and the donations made at the feast of the Lord, every quarter of the year. With this small allotment he has carried out the task for over ten years.

For the other ministers who had the disease and did the same job, it was not long before they were gone, while for the uninfected one, like this one, there has been a long time of carrying out the work. Due to this one's softness of old age and the separation between the two churches, his small strength has been unable to properly guide them, since the souls of the parish are multiplying. That is what he has complained [kaniuhu] about before Almighty God, for a strong minister to be sent to help him in this colony [panalaau].

And hopes are being raised for a call to be heard saying, "Here are the helpers coming, to feed the souls with the bread of eternal life with that eternal realm."

As for the Catholic faith, there are three priests in that religion, one in Kalaupapa and two in Kalawao. The second one has just died, namely the Rev. Damien [Damiano] who lived for many years in this colony [panalaau].

Ka Nupepa Kuokoa. 28 SEPTEMBER 1889. P. 3.
He Makua Hou. A New Father.
In one of the newspapers of Boston, this item below was published:

Rev. Valentine Franz [Rev. Valentin Franckx, SS.CC.] will be taking on the assignment of Father Damien [Damiana], who recently died on the leprosy island [mokupuni mai lepera] of Moloka'i, in the Hawaiian Islands [paemoku o Hawaii]. He will travel there on his mission of compassionate aid, so there will be a full three priests who have departed for the role of becoming a Father among those people who have been stricken with the wounds of the agonizing disease of leprosy [mai ehaeha o ka lepera].

Ka Nupepa Kuokoa. 26 OCTOBER 1889. P. 4.
Ka Haalele Ana I Ka Poli O Ka Makua A Me Ka Aina Hanau. Leaving the Bosom of the Parent and the Homeland.

I left my parent and the land of my birth in the famed cliffs in the mists of Honokōhau [na pali kaulana hoi i ka ohu o Honokohau], West Maui, and my face turned toward Honolulu, where it was directed that I be swept off to Kalawao, saying, "That one there has leprosy" [he mai lepera ko i ala].

I was born in Honokōhau, Maui, in the month of September, on the 12th, 1867, to Sam. L. Kalaola and Mrs. Keolamāhunehune Kamoku Kalaola. Therefore, that is the land of my birth [aina hanau], and this lei of jasmine flowers [lei pikake] that I love is for it:

Beloved land of my birth
My precious land
I love
Your streams
The ridges
The ever-green fields.

I was raised at Honokōhau until I grew, and when I turned six, I was sent by my parents to go to school. A. W. Kauahi was my teacher, and to all of you, my friends who suffered in the pursuit of education, I give my warmest greeting, and this maile vine lei [lei maile] that I wear:

Greetings to my friends
My classmates
It is time for me to go
A fond farewell
I will go singing
Put aside the lamentations
A fond farewell
Greetings to the fields
The ridges
My dear schoolhouse
A fond farewell
I leave for somewhere else
You will always have my gratitude
A fond farewell.

When I turned twelve, or so, at that school, I gained a little knowledge. After that, I was sent to the English school at Kaluaʻaha, and then later I was returned to the first school that I had gone to, and there I stayed until I grew up. In the year 1887, I returned to Kahikinui and my hands became completely deformed. On a day in this past September, my father was ordered by the deputy sheriff of Lāhaina to take me to be sent to Honolulu, and from Honolulu to Kalawao.

My father assented in accordance with his occupation, as a policeman of the Lāhaina district, though not happily, but with ill thoughts, thoughts about a lack of compassion and thoughts about a lack of friends. However, it was the right thing to do, for this was a person who had contracted this kind of disease, the disease called "the family-separating disease" [ka mai hookaawale ohana]. This lei ʻāhihi is for that disease:

You go to Kalawao
And you have the "Chinese disease" [maʻi Pake]
The disease scorned by the people
The brown-skinned and the white-skinned
Your companions change
There were many times together before
And you were with me, and I with you
One bite and we are severed.

On Friday evening, my father returned from Lāhaina and told me the news about my travel to Kalawao. He said to me his last thoughts, saying with words of grief, "You go, stand tall, go to this place that the law of the land has set aside for the people who have this kind of disease. This year God has put me into many difficulties, so do not forget my command to you, which is this: Do not forget God, our God who made the ocean, the cliffs, the rain, the heat of the sun, and so forth."

I went on Saturday, but there was no ship, and the salt returned to Waimea [hoi hou ka paakai i Waimea: i.e., I went home]. On Thursday of the next week, there again was no ship, and I waited in Lāhaina for a ship. At nine at night on Saturday, I boarded the steamship *Iwalani,* and this small expression of affection is for that ship:

The *Iwalani* turns back
To see the quiet calm of Kona
We are outside of Kailua
The Wiliʻāhiu wind blows
One push and we are in Honolulu
And I am at the hospital [hale maʻi] in Kalihi.

There were three of us from the same place, and at six in the morning on Sunday, we reached the pier at ʻĀinahou [in Honolulu Harbor]. We were received by the police and taken to Kalākaua Hale, and from there to Kalihi. We stayed there for a week, then swiftly came here to Kalawao. We now live in this friendless land [aina makamaka ole], the land set apart for us, and also the grave for our bodies.

Here I will conclude my journey, and to the editor my greeting and to the typesetting boys my goodbye.

I am Miss Sam. L. K. Kalaola. Kalawao, Molokaʻi.

Ahailono a ka Lahui. 8 FEBRUARY 1890. P. 3.
Ka Wahine I Aloha I Ka Poe Iloko O Ka Ehaeha A Me Na Palapu O Ka Mai Lepera! Ma Kona Alahele No Kalawao, Molokai.Ua hiki ae kekahi leta i ka Lunahooponopono o ka nupepa "Chronicle" ma Kapalakiko penei. The Woman Who Was Compassionate Toward the People in the Agony and the Wounds of Leprosy! On Her Way to Kalawao, Molokaʻi. A letter reached the editor of the newspaper *Chronicle* in San Francisco, as follows:

New York, Jan. 30. Among the ship passengers who just arrived aboard the ship *Bothnia* today from the East is Sister [kaikuahine] Rose Gertrude. She is on her way to Kalawao, Molokaʻi, the settlement of the leprosy patients [kahua o na mai Lepera], the place where the leprosy patients [mai lepera] are living in grief. She was born thirty-five years ago in Bath, England, and that was where she was raised into adulthood and also educated. She has quite wealthy parents.

This woman decided to become involved in charitable works, and she joined a charitable order, namely the Order of Saint Dominic. And while she was there, news arrived about the story of Father Damien [Damiana] while he was on Molokaʻi and his death, and due to this news there was a great deal of conversation among the ladies who worked under this Sister Gertrude. That was when she began to think about what she was going to do, and a bit later she decided to get up and leave the land of her birth, her parents, family, and friends and travel here to Hawaiʻi to live and die together with the leprosy patients [mai lepera] of Kalawao. There were many obstructions that appeared before her to detain her so that she would not travel here. However, the desire to be charitable to her fellow man was permanently branded within that woman. It could not be changed. Her desire to reside with and aid all the people living in the agony of the disease that is greatly feared [mai e makau loa ia] was permanently fixed, and she said, "I will live there for the remaining days of my life in this weak world."

This woman was seen in her room on board the ship *Bothnia*. She is a clearly beautiful woman, and she has a rather fearless aspect about her. There were many Catholic brethren gathered on the pier to meet with the visitor. She said to them, "I hope to reach Molokaʻi in the third week of February, and I will try to treat the patients with the medicine that I know grants salvation, and it is true that many friends have given me a multitude of gifts for the patients, and I will give them these gifts once I arrive there. And after I get there, I will buy a piano for the enjoyment of the patients. I believe that this is not my work, but the work of Almighty God, and I am seeing the signs of the progress of what I have chosen. I was urged by my father and my mother to give up my desire to come here, but when they saw that my mind was set and that my desire was the call of God, then their desire was overcome. I left my land with the compliments of Bishop Manning, and his last word to me was that he could not restrain me, since the thing I had chosen was indeed from Almighty God.

"Before I boarded the steamship in Liverpool, I received a letter from the Prince of Wales, giving congratulations for my journey. He was greatly pleased by my choice to travel to Hawaiʻi on this rather important mission of mine."

» [Sister Rose Gertrude was born Amy Fowler, the daughter of an English Episcopal minister. She converted to Catholicism and joined the Third Order of St. Dominic, where she took the name Sister Rose Gertrude. In this particular order she was free to live outside of a convent, to wear civilian clothes, and to travel alone in pursuit of a personal mission. When she heard the story of Father Damien, she decided to travel to Kalaupapa and devote the rest of her life to helping the leprosy patients. Her order approved this mission.

When Sister Rose Gertrude arrived in Honolulu in March 1890, the Board of Health denied her request to work at Kalaupapa, but offered her a position as a nurse at the Kalihi Hospital receiving station. She accepted but immediately found herself at odds with the two administrators there, who she believed were not acting in the best interests of the patients. She reported Charles Kahalehili and W. F. Reynolds to the Board of Health, which resulted in a legislative investigation and a report that recommended the dismissal of both men. She resigned in September 1890 after the report was completed.

During her brief stay at the Kalihi Hospital, Sister Rose Gertrude met Dr. Karl Lutz, a German physician. A specialist on the hospital's medical staff, he was looking for a cure for leprosy. After meeting Dr. Lutz, she left her religious order, and, as Amy Fowler, married him on April 21, 1891. The couple relocated to San Francisco in July 1892. This story generated national and international interest and was followed in many newspapers and magazines.]

Ka Nupepa Kuokoa. 15 FEBRUARY 1890. P. 4.
Ka Makua Rev. J. Hanaloa, Ua Hala. The Rev. Father J. Hanaloa, Deceased.

On January 21, at six in the evening, his last breath of this life was released, and the body was left for the dirt and the soul with God.

The total years in this life were eighty-five. Such was his telling in the days when strength was within him until there was pain in his throat, the illness that made his body waste away until he died.

Nāwaʻa was his father and Kawaimakaua was his mother, and Laupāhoehoe in Hilo was the place of his birth. That was where he was taught literacy when Bingham [Binamu] and company arrived here in Hawaiʻi.

Not long into his study, he knew it, and he became a teacher for others. Right after that he managed a store under Mr. Pitman [Pikimana], in Ohele, in Hilo, Hawaiʻi.

After that he went and lived in Waialua, Oʻahu, and studied the Bible with Mr. Emerson [Emekona] Sr. That was where he became skilled in biblical knowledge and helped to preach the Gospel there.

After that he worked with Orramel Gulick [Olomela Gulika] in managing a store in Honolulu. When that was done, he returned to Waialua and again preached with Emerson, and then managed another store with Samuel Emerson [Samuela Emekona] Jr.

At this time, the Church of Laupāhoehoe, the brethren of his birthplace, called for him to return and be a minister for them. He immediately complied, returning to that church and pushing forward in response to the calling voice.

He served as minister for that church for one year and he was ordained as a minister in 1868. At that time he was called by the Church of Kāʻanapali, Maui, and was installed as minister for that place in 1876 on February 10.

And on September 10, 1878, he moved here to Kalawao due to his wife's contracting leprosy, which is the family-separating disease [mai hookaawale ohana], the disease that agonizes the body [mai hoehaeha kino].

While he lived among the leprosy patients [lepera], he preached the Gospel until he was appointed as minister for the Protestant faith for this entire patient settlement [kahua mai]. He stood unshakingly in this work until his rest in peace.

And the sheep [hipa: i.e., church members] that he treated with kindness and always cherished are beset by grief. When affectionate memories of him arise, we wail tearfully [uwe] together, and the Lord will ease our sadness for the Father that lived into old age in the virtue of the Lord Jesus.

This is a story I personally heard from him, and what is being presented publicly in order that the works of this Father of spiritual virtue be known.

After the death of this Father, the two churches of this colony [Panalaau] entered into mourning with his younger siblings living here and his relations on the outside.

—A. Pua'aloa

Ka Nupepa Kuokoa. 14 FEBRUARY 1891. P. 4.
Na Pihe Kumakena Hue'a Ke Aloha Ka Makee Alii. Ike'a Ma Ka Waimaka I Ka hoohanini Mawaho. The Wails of Grief, Outpouring of Compassion, Affection for Royalty. Seen in the Tears Spilling Out.
To the Queen Dowager [Moiwahine Kanemake], Her Highness Kapi'olani:

Greetings to you. We, the patients at the leprosy quarantine station here in Kalihi [kahua hoomalu lepera o Kalihi nei], a number of your afflicted subjects [makaainana popilikia], we request your patience, your majesty, to permit us to join in bearing the sorrowful burdens and grieving agony of your heart [naau].

Due to the plucking of the precious life of King Kalākaua, your dearly beloved husband, in the distant land, without you seeing his final breath in this life. Thus, we are with you in grief. We ask Almighty God to lighten your sorrowful heart, and that he watch over you in peace.

We are with humility. The Patients. [Na Ma'i.]

By the grace of God, to Queen Lili'uokalani, of your Hawaiian Islands [Hawaii Pae Aina].

Greetings to you. Due to your predecessor on the throne, your dearly beloved brother, being taken by the callous hands of death in the land of gold [aina gula] on the soil of California.

Thus, a tragic burden has fallen upon you in agony, and so, this is what we request of your royal sacredness, for your highness to allow these pangs of grief to be shared by us, some of your afflicted subjects [makaainana ua popilikia] at the leprosy quarantine station here in Kalihi [kahua hoomalu lepera o Kalihi nei]. Thus, we are also in mourning with you, and so with humility and lamentation we call out to the heavenly powers to lighten your sorrowful heart, and to lengthen the life of the queen in peace upon these Hawaiian islands, the native sands [one oiwi] about which it was famously said, "The sovereignty of the land has persisted through righteousness." ["Ua mau ke ea o ka aina i ka pono."]

We are with humility. The Patients. [Na Ma'i.]

Ka Nupepa Kuokoa. 14 MARCH 1891. P. 3.
Kela me Keia. This and That.

The Board of Health had a meeting in recent days concerning the matter related to moving the buildings from the first leprosy quarantine station [kahua hoomalu lepera] in Kaka'ako to the new site in Kalihi. The Sisters of Mercy [kaikuahine o ke aloha] might be sent there. Get moving, Mr. Board of Health.

Ka Nupepa Kuokoa. 4 APRIL 1891. P. 2.
Ka Panalaau ma Molokai. The Colony on Moloka'i.
Greetings to you:

Please allow me some available space in your body for those words placed above, so that everyone living from Hawai'i to Ni'ihau may know the nature of the home that the kingdom has set aside for the people afflicted by the wounds of this disease that is causing immeasurable devastation to this race [lahuikanaka].

CONCERNING THE LAND. [NO KA AINA.]

Kalaupapa is the main town [Taona] here in the colony [Panalaau]. Numerous buildings stand everywhere along the streets, and this place truly resembles Honolulu. This is the place where the superintendent [Luna Nui] lives, and this is also the harbor for large ships at this time. The office, jail, warehouse, three churches, and three coffeehouses are here.

Here in this place is that home [Bishop Home] built by the noble [alii] with a hugely generous heart, the Hon. C. R. Bishop [Bihopa], with a total of seventy-four girls and women combined, under the protection and care of the nuns [Virigina] headed by Sister Marianne [Kaikuahine Mariame].

Kalawao is the second of the major towns [kulanakauhale] in this place. Here is the place where the doctor lives, here is the store of the Board of Health, and here is the place where the patients [ma'i] collect lamp oil, matches, washing soap, and salt, as well as crackers, sugar, bread, rice, and so forth, if the cooked taro ship [moku paiai] does not arrive.

CONCERNING THE ALLOTMENTS OF STARCH AND MEAT. [NO KA HAAWINA AI ME I'A.]

Every patient from big to small receives one portion of cooked taro [paiai] for the week, with seven pounds of beef [pipi] or salmon [kamano]. For some people, their food is at the store, and they collect everything they want. However, it cannot be over fifty cents, the same as the price of the cooked taro. Those are the people with the foreign foods [mea ai haole].

THE ALLOTMENT OF CLOTHING AND SO ON. [KA HAAWINA LOLE A PELA AKU.]

Every patient receives a voucher [bila waiwai] for the store of the Board of Health, five dollars ($5.00) every six months, beginning on April 1, the first half, until October 1, the last half. This is indeed the voucher [bila] with that famous name, "Loose Bill," [Bila Alualu] and with this voucher clothing and so forth are obtained. However, it is not received by children under fourteen years of age, and this is something that saddens the heart, looking at the children going about in poverty. Your writer does not know the reason for this deprivation.

There is no voucher for the Pauahi Home [Home Pauahi] and the Damien Home [Home Damiano] because the nuns [Virigina] actually care for them by always supplying the small necessities.

However, it is being heard that vouchers will be received by a great number of people this year. Such is the news heard in rumors.

THE NATURE OF THE PATIENTS. [KE ANO O NA MA'I.]

There is an incomparable strangeness [kupaianaha] to this disease in this land that is being lived in.

For many people among the patients who are brought here, upon coming here there is a great recovery until they seem uninfected. For others who are in good condition and come here, there is the greatest worsening of the disease. Some people stay the same.

However, looking at all kinds, there are no fingers, the feet are maimed, and the features of some people appear gruesome, while others have a terrifying appearance.

CONCERNING LIVING CONDITIONS. [NO KA NOHO ANA.]

The life of the patients is quite good here in the colony [Panalaau], and the care by the government is excellent. The patients are like millionaires: just sit, eat until stuffed, and sleep. This is better than the care from a parent and a family, because you obey the command of the parent, and with this you don't. There is one thing terrible about this separated existence, which is the longing for family, home, and friends.

THE GREAT NEED. [KA HEMAHEMA NUI.]

The great need that remains for us is that the Board of Health does not attempt to bring in treatments and suitable medicines for this disease rather than sitting and watching this thousand plus who are grieving on this side of the shores of Moloka'i, while unable to forget the many remembrances of love for family.

THE WICKED ACTS ARE ENDED AND THERE IS PEACE.
[PAU NA HANAINO A MALUHIA.]

After William Tell became the new superintendent [Luna Nuihou] for this colony [Panalaau], those kinds of naughty actions have not been seen at the beef distribution building, when the first one to bring a beer bottle or liquor bottle would be the one given the sweet beef, while the one without a bottle would receive the neck meat, which is the "lei" meat.

THE PIOUS WORKS PROGRESS. [HOLOMUA NA HANA HAIPULE.]

The pious works in this colony [Panalaau] have progressed among some folks, while other folks are sliding in the joys of this life. The folks who bear the serious afflictions of this incredibly horrible disease are living. In what I've become accustomed to from when we were brought here until now, three months and three days, among all of the deaths in this colony [Panalaau], the majority of the deaths were among all of the pious, and continue as such.

THE SCABIES DISEASE. [KA MA'I PUUPUU KUNA.]

That scabies disease is one of the greatly feared illnesses. It is itchy at the beginning, causing scratching continuously until the skin is raw. Then the skin begins to scab, the limbs and body become putrid; the god most feared of this kind of illness is water, and the patient does not bathe at all until dying. Those who endure and regularly clean the body receive relief. The Pauahi Home is a settlement that is greatly troubled, from the large to the small, all kinds of patients.

CONCERNING HORSES AND DOGS. [NO KA LIO ME KA ILIO.]

The patients are well supplied with horses, some having one, some two, some four, some five, some six, and some ten, and it is also a great help for the patients. As for dogs, there is probably no district in this group of islands [Paeaina] like this colony [Panalaau] for the number of dogs. I think this is the most in this group of islands, and there is an excessive amount of lice [uku], fleas [uku lele], and bedbugs [uku lio]. There is no house without lice in this place. The scratching goes on all night. And when the president, Mr. David Dayton, came he announced before the patients that all of the dogs should be put down for a suitable reason.

CONCERNING MONEY. [NO KE DALA.]

A great amount of money is coming in to the colony [Panalaau]. The Board of Health is paying over one thousand dollars for plantations [mahana] of every kind for one month. With one hundred dollars for those who provide their own food, they are the people who sell their allotments for two hundred dollars every month.

These things above are what I have reported to you, Mr. Editor, and the remainder will wait for later, another time.

With tingling love [Me ke aloha huihui], Jno. Kamanu. Kalaupapa, APRIL 1, 1891.

Ka Leo o ka Lahui. 29 APRIL 1891. P. 2.
Ka Huakai A Ka Moiwahine No Ka Panalaau O Kalaupapa A Me Kalawao. He 10 Hora ma ka Aina a he 16 Hora ma ka Moana me ka malie a me ke ola maikai. The Journey of the Queen to the Colony at Kalaupapa and Kalawao. Ten Hours on Land and Sixteen Hours on the Ocean, with calm and good health.

The steamship [mokuahi] *Likelike* left the pier [uwapo] at 10:00 p.m., April 26, 1891, the night of the Sabbath, carrying her majestic passengers: Queen Lili'uokalani and the Prince [Kūhiō]; Premier [Kuhina Nui] Samuel Parker; the members of the legislature, J. W. Pua, J. K. Ho'okano, L. W. P. Kāneahi, and J. Nāwahī; the commissioners for the nations of France and Portugal; Bishop Willis and Father Leonora [Father Leonor Fouesnel]; the gentlemen E. K. Lilikalani, Wm. Auld, Huntsman, S. W. Mahelona, and many other people; the attendants [ukali] of the queen and many ladies, with men, women, and children, and the military band [Puali Puhi Ohe]. The total number was almost 270.

The voyage on the ocean was calm that night, and we reached Kalaupapa at 7:00 a.m., April 27. There was much jostling on the ship due to the desire to board the skiff [waapa] early and go on land.

The shore was already full of people waiting, wanting to see their friends and relations. The mournful wails [leo uwe kumakena] of the citizens on shore and those on the ship were heard.

As we were nearing the pier, there were many people on shore calling the names of the friends that they saw and also calling to each other that they had friends coming ashore. There were many crying voices and a downpour of tears, like raindrops in winter.

The queen came ashore onto the land overcast by agony [aina a ka ehaeha e hoopoluluhi mai ana] at 8:00 a.m., and visited and was hosted at the place of the superintendent [Luna Nui], Wm. Tell. All of the people, perhaps as many as a thousand, assembled there and listened to the melodies of the band and the singing voices. And at 9:00 a.m., the royal oratory was begun by Premier

Samuel Parker. When he was done, Prince Kūhiō stood and gave his affectionate greeting to the citizens. After that, Hon. J. K. Hoʻokano, E. K. Lilikalani, and
Mr. Kekipi, and Kalana made speeches. Then D. K. Pa gave a speech of response from the side of the patients [maʻi]. When his speech was over, the son
of the Kanilehua Rain [Ua-kanilehua: epithet for Hilo], Hon. J. Nāwahī, came,
and without pausing for breath he laid forth some emotional words of admon-
ishment for our nation, insisting that it is necessary for young Hawaiians [opio
Hawaii] to immediately be sent to learn the medical profession [oihana lapaau]
in order to control the health of the nation. After this, Mr. Sam Mohakau gave a
response from the side of the patients [poe mai] for all of the speeches.

After the speeches were over, the queen went to view the "Pauahi Home,"
and at midday, the royal party traveled to Kalawao. They visited the home of
the nuns [poe Virigina] and rested there. That was where some youngsters sang
a few fine songs. When that was done, the royal party returned to Kalaupapa.
There was no speech there, and the people of that place did not assemble in
great numbers.

The royal party arrived in Kalaupapa at 2:00 p.m., and at the home of the
superintendent, the party had a meal. After that time, it pleased the queen to
prompt her premier to look after the suspected people, and perhaps ease the
contraction of leprosy [mai lepera]. There were a great number of little boys
and little girls who appeared in person before the premier, and their names
were set down in his journal.

At 4:00 p.m., the queen left Kalaupapa and went back aboard the deck of the
steamship *Likelike*. They left Kalaupapa at 5:00 p.m. and arrived here in Honolulu at 12:00 midnight.

The rather significant things that could be learned on this journey:

Concerning the amount of flat land [aina palahalaha] lying between the
shore of Kalaupapa to the west and the shore of Kalawao on the east side, and
below the line of cliffs [kakai pali], it has an area of about six square miles and
is inhabited by 1,507 people. There are 1,475 Native Hawaiians [poe Hawaii
maoli], 12 Caucasians [haole], and 20 Chinese [pake].

The total number of people who have leprosy [maʻi lepera] is 1,190: 1,158
Hawaiians, 20 Chinese, and 12 Caucasians.

As for the number of people living there who are not infected, they total
317. And the number of buildings is 327. There are 228 buildings in Kalaupapa,
22 between, and 177 in Kalawao.

Within this number, there are six churches: two for Protestantism, two for
Calvinism, and two for Mormonism. There is one shop and two teahouses
[hale inuti], one jail, and one hospital.

There are 700 horses running about this colony [Panalaau] that belong to
everyone, 314 cattle belonging to the Board of Health, and 200 dogs that belong
to certain people.

There appear to be equal numbers of children and youths being cared for
in the homes for boys and girls by the Catholic nuns [poe Virigina Katolika],
since there are eighty boys and eighty girls.

The air is chilled by the wind from the northeast, and the ridges and valleys
are dark green [lipolipo] in appearance; only the island [Mokupuni] of Oʻahu is
seen in calm times.

From Kalaupapa looking over the deep blue sea, it meets with the sky at a distant point.

These are the features of the land where our multitudes are living in the shady valley of death [awaawa malu o ka make], and for them we grieve with intensely sorrowful tears, despising the relationship that aggrieved the heart. Alas, what a pity.

Love for the Nation [Aloha Lahui].

—Mahina Mālamalama, on the deck of the *Likelike,* APRIL 27, 1891.

Ka Nupepa Kuokoa. 2 MAY 1891. P. 3.
Ka Huakai a ke Alii ka Moiwahine Liliuokalani no ka Panalaau o Kalawao. I ka Luna Hooponopono o ka "Pae Aina Puka La" J. U. Kawainui. The Journey of Her Majesty Queen Lili'uokalani to the Colony at Kalawao. To the Editor of the *Pae Aina Puka La,* J. U. Kawainui.

Greetings to you:

At ten o'clock last Sunday night, April 26, 1891, the steamship *Likelike* left the pier at 'Āinahou [in Honolulu Harbor] carrying on her deck the beloved and cherished Hawaiian to go see a portion of the nation that is in agony and profound anguish. Three hundred or fewer was the number of people that went on this journey. Here are the distinguished individuals that went:

Queen Lili'uokalani, Prince Keli'iana'ole [Kalaniana'ole], Premier [Kuhina Nui] Sam Parker, President [of the Board of Health] D. Dayton, the agent of the London Board of Health, Hon. J. Nāwahī, Hon. L. W. P. Kāneali'i, Hon. D. W. Pua, Hon. J. K. Ho'okano, E. Lilikalani, Hon. J. G. Hoapili, the French commissioner, the Portuguese commissioner, Mr. and Mrs. C. Clarke, Jos. Heleluhe, Mrs. Limaheihei, Mrs. Pamahoa Kalauli, Mr. and Mrs. S. M. Ka'aukai, Mrs. L. Keohokālole, A. Mahaulu, Bishop Wills [Willis], Father Leolono [Father Leonor Fouesnel], J. N. K. Keola, G. W. Kualaku, Tamara Moekapu, Mr. and Mrs. Auld and the girls, Mr. and Mrs. 'Ailau, Bandmaster Berger and thirty-one band students, two Caucasian women, Mrs. Makanoe and father, Mrs. Kuihelani, Māhoe, Malaea Ka'aipe'elua, Lala Kahelemauna, Mrs. Akau, and a multitude whose names I did not obtain.

The ocean was fine and the wind was light, although the wind was suitable to carry the cherished one to go ashore before her subjects in agony. The brilliance of the queen was casting out into the night with her beauty. The wheel of the younger princess *Likelike* was rolling along through the Kaiwi sea, the beloved sea [kai o Kaiwi ke kai aloha], like a child being carried in the embrace of friends in adversity, who cast their eyes over the crests of the sea to the realm of the land, with tears and grieving for the land of birth. At six o'clock Monday morning, April 27, 1891, we arrived at the harbor [awa] of Kalaupapa.

The point of the rear mast of the *Likelike* was displaying the crown flag [hae kalaunu], saying, "Here I am with a heart saddened for you all." The town [kulanakauhale] of Kalaupapa lay all before us, from the sea to the uplands. The row of cliffs curved out to the west of the town.

The shore was crowded with people at the harbor desiring to affectionately and tearfully embrace Her Majesty the Queen and the many others. Such was the case for Her Majesty the Queen and the many others with this same feeling.

The anchor of the ship was released. It was announced that several skiffs would first take the musicians until they were all ashore, then take the crowd with the queen. At this time I moved to travel with these skiffs, and this desire was actually fulfilled. Two skiffs carried the musicians. When they were about to land ashore, I saw the friends of that land and my beloved sweetheart sleeping in the sand of Papaloa [the writer's wife was buried in Papaloa cemetery].

I had left there on August 4, 1890, at 8:30 a.m., for eight months until we met again with affection. This fine gift came from above. To glorify is the thing to do.

At this time when we were being rowed to shore, the schooner *Robaloe,* belonging to Hon. D. Kahanu, was anchored in the harbor. On her deck were the captain and the sailors giving honors to the party of Her Majesty the Queen with a string of lights lit up on her deck. When we landed at the pier, the archways of the superintendent [luna nui] W. H. Tell were seen, made by the energies of the head carpenter B. Reid and the letter painter John Kamano, with these letters on the first archway: "Greetings to the Queen" [Aloha ka Moiwahine], adorned with the fragrant leaves of the upland forest by the committee members J. Kahāʻulelio and C. Kopena. That was the first archway at the head of the pier, and at the eastern corner of the storehouse was standing that archway with the words, "Strive for the summit" [Kulia i ka nuu: the queen's motto].

When the crown flag came down, it signaled the people shooting a gun salute for Her Majesty the Queen who were at Kiʻokiʻo, on the trail [alanui] going up to Kalaʻe, under the direction of the artillery commander John Gaiser, a German foreigner [haole Kelemania]. The voice of the dynamite cannon [pukuniahi kianapauda] sounded a reverberating crack at the base of the cliff. The cracking voice that was heard was greater than Kakaʻako's cannons, a twenty-one-gun salute that the patients affectionately extended to the queen.

When the queen reached land, the hearts of the distressed people were silent and still, due to the arrival of the queen before them like a dream that passes by when one is sleeping and then disappears, but upon waking from sleep, it did not. Such was the case with the features of the queen who loves her people. The skiff of Her Majesty the Queen landed, rowed by the three officers that traveled on the ship from Honolulu.

And when the queen came up and stepped ashore, the national anthem [mele lahui] was played by six musicians with two drummers from the United Heart Association of Kalawao [Hui Puuwai Lokahi o Kalawao] in a round building standing above the spring [punawai] called Lenalena (which is the spring where the friends lay bones to rest in the dirt of that unfamiliar land [aina malihini] with pity caused by stories that were heard before), under the direction of Chas. Manua Jr. [Opio]. There was a helper [kokua] and five boys stricken with this pitiful affliction, along with the loud, joyful voices of the land, and with the skiffs escorting the passengers to land.

No one could hold back their tears caused by great feelings of love. The royal tears were pouring out, and the prince was also welling up with tears. The tears of the premier and members of the Board of Health were tumbling down from seeing the native children of the Hawaiian Islands [Hawaii mau paemoku] suffering from pitiful afflictions. And when they were done playing, the Hawaiian band [Bana Hawaii] played, just like the things we are used to hearing. When that was over, the queen entered the first archway that I described earlier at the head of the pier with her attendants and traveled upon the pier as if it was a street, until reaching the storehouse of the Board of Health. When Her Majesty passed by the front of it, she arrived at the eastern corner, that second archway that was described earlier. That was where the carriage of the nuns [kaa pio o na Vilikina] was standing. Her Majesty the Queen, Prince Kalaniana'ole, and Premier S. Parker got in with J. Kahā'ulelio steering to the house of the superintendent, W. H. Tell. When Hawai'i's queen, who rules over the Hawaiian Islands [paeaina o Hawaii], arrived for the first time, the archway at the gate of the house of the superintendent greeted her with words drawn with paint. This was the third of the archways: "Greetings to you, Your Majesty" [Aloha oe, e Kalani]. Within this archway in front of the porch were the lights of the star Iwikauikaua and the fourth archway, which had the words as follows: "The Motto of your Kingdom, Virtue" [Ka makia o kou Aupuni, ka Pono]. Her Majesty the Queen entered the home of Superintendent W. H. Tell and his wife, who were hosting in the parlor of the home, inviting the queen to come in. This lordly party entered the shelter of the house with the traveling companions of the queen accompanying her to see firsthand the fate of the patients. The porch and parlor of that home were refreshed with decorations of forest leaves from the cliffs that wafted a strong fragrance to the nose of the ocean travelers, who could have no critiques of this land, and the wondrous sovereign who belongs to Hawai'i's rule from ancient days caught her breath. Hawai'i has known only male rulers; that is what we have known up until the seventh of the lords who have passed, and for the eighth lord of the Hawaiian Islands and the eight seas [na kai ewalu], we received a royal, a sacred, a female ruler. And in this incredibly remarkable time, her compassion led her to first go to see this portion of the people that are grieving and to share the motto of her crowned rule that we have fixed in our hearts. Virtue and doing right is the motto of her kingdom. Such was how the queen first grasped this path of travel to Kalawao that we are seeing, and the queen and the nation shall memorize this passage from the good book, which is, "What is the value if we receive everything but lose health and well-being?" [Heaha la ka waiwai ke loaa ia kakou na mea a pau a lilo aku ke ola?]

I am with humility, W. H. Kahumoku, Honolulu, APRIL 28, 1891. (To be continued.)

Ka Leo o ka Lahui. 5 MAY 1891. P. 2.
Ka Moiwahine No Ka Panalaau Ma'i O Kalaupapa. The Queen to the Patient Colony at Kalaupapa.
Mr. Editor. Greetings between us:

I present this shining news before your glory, O famed cannon [Pukuniahi kaulana], the mouthpiece of all persons desiring to speak before our multitude of friends.

Earlier, the news was received here in the colony [Panalaau] that Her Majesty the Queen would be arriving. The preparation meetings immediately took place in order to think of suitable honors to be presented before Her Majesty the Queen when she arrived.

During the fine deliberations, the overseers [luna] who would construct some archways and the bright red words that would be drawn upon these archways were decided upon. The committee members of the day were chosen: Kahāʻulelio and Kopena.

The business of that day was released, and the next morning, Sunday the 26th, the work began on the building of the archways. The number of archways was four: one archway at the steps of the pier, one beside the storehouse, and two at the home of W. H. Tell with forest leaves wrapped around them: the pāpalalai fern, the maile vine, and several other decorations from the mountains.

The one who drew the words on the archways was Manu, and here are the words: 1. "Greetings to the Queen" [Aloha i ka Moiwahine] 2. "Strive for the Summit" [Kulia i ka Nuu] [The wording for the third archway was left out of the article. It is: 3. "Greetings to you, Your Majesty" (Aloha oe, e Kalani)] 4. "Motto of Your Kingdom" [Makia o Kou Aupuni]. The words were correctly and skillfully created. In appearance they resembled a mirage of Mānā [Wai-Liʻula o Mana: on Kauaʻi].

The final activities that were prepared were a dynamite gun [pu kiana pauda] wrapped with lights, and three fire pits: one atop Kauhakō, one at Pūahi, and one at Pauʻaka. These fire pits were made with the belief that the ship would arrive at dawn, but in fact it arrived during the day.

That evening, the raindrops of the heavenly pool Kūlanihākoʻi gave a presentation through the release of its drenching raindrops. That drizzling rain continued until that night turned to day; and on the next morning, the 27th, the ship was sighted right off of ʻĪlio Point [Ka-lae-o-ka-Ilio]. In no time it had come quite near; and without even time to take a breath, the anchor was clattering down in the harbor at Kalaupapa.

To be continued.

Ka Leo o ka Lahui. 6 MAY 1891. P. 2.
Ka Moiwahine No Ka Panalaau Maʻi O Kalaupapa. (Hoomauia.) The Queen to the Patient Colony at Kalaupapa. (Continued.)

It appeared that the deck of the steamship [mokuahi] *Likelike* was crowded with passengers, full from front to back. After a few minutes, the skiffs [waapa] were set down, and the Hawaiian band [Bana Hawaii] was the first group that got on with their sweet-sounding instruments. The people after them were the relatives of the patients [ohana o ka poe maʻi], and the very last was Her Majesty the Queen and her premier [Kuhina Nui], Samuel Parker [Paka], and some attendants [ohua] of the queen.

As the queen's skiff neared, that was when the dynamite guns [pu kiana pauda] of the battery at Pūahi [Pakali o Puahi] sounded with a great booming, under the direction of John Gaiser [Kaika]. It sounded as if boulders were falling from the cliff, due to the rumbling, resembling a cannon.

When the queen reached the pier, a band from the dark green cliffs [pali hauliuli] of Kalawao played, and the royal affection had already been won by them when they first began to play and sing the national anthem [mele Lahui], "Hawaiʻi Ponoʻī." When the queen went up and entered the first archway, the musicians of the Hawaiian band played sweetly, as if you were the pheasant [Kolohala] in the calm night, due to the sweet sound grasping the heart.

While Her Majesty the Queen went to board the carriage, the band presented again for the second time, with a fluttering sound. It is indeed you, the yellow-faced 'i'iwi bird of the uplands of La'a [oia no oe o ka Iiwi maka polena o ka uka o Laa], resting. Everyone was invited to go up to hear everything uttered from the mouths of the queen's committee members and the words of the queen written on a piece of paper.

When all the patients had assembled, the oratory was begun by the marshal [Ilamuku] of the kingdom.

The Hon. Samuel Parker [Paka] was the one who began on the queen's side with thoughts written on a piece of paper. He read from start to finish. The thoughts were excellent. When his opening speech was over, Ho'okano stood and presented his greeting before the citizens; he gave a brief reply in his speech. The gist of his speech was to be patient and pray to the Lord, that there is a time in the future when this nation will receive salvation. When his speech was done, Kipi stood; their statements were of the same nature. In between was J. Nāwahī, the son of the Kanilehua Rain [ua Kanilehua] of Hilo Bay. I regret that I did not hear his honey voice.

After Her Majesty the Queen relaxed for a while, her party proceeded to the district [Apana] of Kalawao. When it had nearly struck two o'clock in the afternoon, the party left Kalawao and returned to Kalaupapa.

When it was about to strike three o'clock, the queen departed the colony to again see the town of Honolulu. When the queen boarded the skiff, the dynamite gun of the battery at Pau'aka sounded its final salute for the queen.

The queen went aboard the deck of the *Likelike;* she turned back and gazed upon her subjects residing in the land of agony [aina o ka ehaeha].

That is not the end, but these small bits of news are sufficient. It is better than nothing, and perhaps the completion is coming from your friends of the pen point. They will be the ones to give an account.

And I end my little thought; and with the typesetting boys my affection and with the fearless editor my final greeting.

I am with humility, E. M. Kaili Jr. [Opio]. Kalaupapa, Moloka'i, APR. 30, 1891.

Ka Nupepa Kuokoa. 9 MAY 1891. P. 1.
Ka Huakai a ke Alii ka Moiwahine Liliuokalani no ka Panalaau o Kalawao. The Journey of Her Majesty Queen Lili'uokalani to the Colony at Kalawao.

And the queen caught her breath in the home that was providing comfort. However, in her royal eyes it appeared that tears were ceaselessly pouring out due to pity. Outside of this location it was becoming "Kohala, crowded to the mouth with people [le-i Kohala, i ka nuku na kanaka]," because of the desire to hear the utterances of the royal voice that were being extended to them as a medicine for the veins that were being harmed by this affliction that Hawai'i is seeing.

Then, this presiding voice said, "O citizens, be still and listen." Such were the calls heard by your one who is recording this journey to that astonishing home that Hawai'i's multitudes desire to see, and they were truly fulfilled. At that time the voices of the crowd suddenly fell silent, listening to hear the medicine that will give hope and repel the pains that grasp the body of the citizens who are agonized. That was when the grandson of Parker of the Kīpu'upu'u

Rain of Waimea, the premier [Kuhina Nui: Samuel Parker] of the kingdom and a member of the Board of Health of Hawai'i, was seen standing and presenting with a loving heart:

"O subjects of the queen who have been afflicted, greetings to you all."
Voices struck the ear at this presentation, cheering, with heads bowed.

He read from a piece of paper the hopeful words of Her Majesty the Queen, and here they are: "All of us who have arrived here have sad thoughts for all of you, the people stricken by this terrible disease that separates the family, which has also separated you from your friends and loved ones, and the place of birth; this is the same terrible affliction that is laying waste to this beloved nation with endless misfortune. However, we have not been discouraged from making a powerful effort to seek out something that will reduce the wide spread of this illness. Concerning this desire, that is always anchored in the loving heart of our Queen Lili'uokalani, that is that thing that prompted her heart that cherishes the nation on behalf of this portion of her people in constant sorrow here, so that she and all of us came here in person to affectionately meet with you face to face."

Wm. Tell, the superintendent, presented before the crowd some brief thoughts that were nevertheless profoundly affectionate, followed by Mr. David Dayton, the president of the Board of Health.

Then a speech by Hon. E. K. Lilikalani, a marshal for the day, urging the friends to cast their eyes to God and rescue will be received, and explaining that this was the first-born [hiapo mua] of the queen who has been crowned, that Kalaupapa is the first of her visits, and so forth. [The term hiapo mua, or "first-born," is a poetic description of Kalaupapa as the first place she visited officially as queen.]

Then the Honorable J. K. Ho'okano, J. Kekipi, and J. Kalana [spoke]. On the side of the patients was D. K. Pa, who replied to these speeches. The reply was full of feeling. No tear was restrained upon hearing this voice from the patient pit of death [lua mai o ka make]. After his was the honorable one from the famous rain of Hilo, J. Nāwahī. When his was finished, Sam Kamohakau responded from the side of the patients.

The party of the queen pushed on to the Pauahi Home, in the carriage of the nuns [Vilikina], three of them, the queen, the prince, and the premier, steered by J. Kahā'ulelio. The traveling companions were on the horses that J. Kahā'ulelio supplied.

Upon arriving at this place mentioned above [Pauahi Home], leaves from the upland forest were growing as adornments for this home of the late royal, established by her husband [Charles R. Bishop] as a monument for this royal.

Upon entering the veranda [lanai] of the house of the nuns [hale o na Vilikina], the girls paraded out, and in front of the veranda they sang a song that had been composed about Queen Lili'uokalani. It was quite touching and painful to hear.

The features of the queen were displaying affection. When it was done, they gave their affectionate greeting to the queen, and the queen reciprocated with that same sentiment.

They returned to their fine and quite comfortable house that the government built.

The queen went in person to look at the sleeping quarters of the girls. When that was done, she again boarded the carriage to go to Kalawao, to the place where the nuns [Vilikina] care for boys, called the "Kalawao Boys Home" [Boys Home Kalawao]. And at the gate of that home, painted letters had been placed saying, "God Save the Queen" [E ola ka Moiwahine i ke Akua], festooned with leaves of the maile vine that had the fragrance of the forest.

The boys of this home appeared with Kalawao's citizens stricken with this affliction, and then the boys sang their affectionate prayer of praise to the queen. When the song was done, the boys gave their greeting with a bow, and the queen did so with that same sentiment. When this visit was over, the queen once again boarded the carriage to go to Kalaupapa.

As they passed the corner of a house belonging to Ape Kaaka who died in Kalihi [in Honolulu], and continued on to Māulili [Māhulili], the premier asked to see the leather shop [hale lole pipi] of the patients. He got on a horse and I became the guide who pointed out the things in that shop. When that was over, I took the premier all the way to Kauhakō Hill [puu o Kauhako], which has features just like Punchbowl [Puowaina: crater on Oʻahu]. However, this is quite high, while that is low; a horse is able to climb up without trouble.

I showed the place where the patients [mai] farm sweet potatoes [uala], which is the first level below, and after that place, the deep dark pool of seawater [lua kai uliuli a lipolipo] lay calmly before the eyes of the premier and the visitors being guided by me. After that, I turned the premier toward Kalaupapa and said, "This beauty lying before us and these buildings are the unforgettable monument of Kakina, the premier of the cleansing period, and how will you outdo that beauty in your term as premier?" The people accompanying the two of us inquired, and the premier replied quite humorously, "What will be the new thing I build? Some beautiful buildings before the patients are released." Then we all erupted in laughter at the humorous words of the premier.

I said to the patients accompanying us, "Hey, you are hearing the words of the premier. If he doesn't do it, then remind him that you will indeed be released."

I pointed out the grave of his father-in-law, and the tour was over. We returned to following after the queen. The queen went down to see Kapoli [Lizzie Kapoli Kamakau] and the two of us arrived there. There was affection and tears falling onto the cheeks of Kapoli, since the queen was a close friend of hers a long time ago. When that was done, we returned to the house of W. H. Tell for the queen and her traveling companions to have a meal. The band provided enjoyable melodies and there was great joy for the locals [kamaaina] as well as us. When these pleasures were done, it was three oʻclock and the whistle of the *Likelike* was sounding for us to return to prepare for the voyage home.

Between three and four oʻclock the queen prepared to return aboard the ship, while the premier went to see the prisoners [poe paahao] that were locked up by the jailer [luna paahao] T. E. Evens, who were arrested for possessing opium. There were eleven residing in the jail and two who died in the old church from the time of Hitchcock [Hikikoki]. A tall rock wall was built, ten feet high, as a jail to hold these people.

There is a different jail above the office of the Board of Health, and this building was converted into a jail. The premier said to the patients, "Be patient.

I will go back and deliberate with the board and give a report soon to your superintendent." The patients gave thanks to the premier with affection, and such was the response of the premier with his affection to them, before returning to the ship.

When the premier reached the pier, the skiff had arrived to return the royal party to the ship. They exchanged farewells with the locals, and that was when the gun salute from the patients was sounded by means of John Gaiser [Gaisa], the artillery commander for the colony [Panalaau].

Anguish [walohia] is the name of the harbor at Pau'aka, the harbor where cattle are unloaded, to the east of the harbor where the queen was returning to the ship.

At this point, the sum of those that were seen by us, the people who are currently living there, is being reported to you, and here is the breakdown: 12 Caucasians, 20 Chinese, 2 Gilbertese [Iewalewa], 1 Marquesan [Nuuhiwa], totaling 84; the remainder is 1,153. The sum of the helpers, men, women, and children [kokua kane wahine a me na keiki], is 317, and the total sum of patients and healthy people is 1,507. The corpses sleeping in the sand of that land nearly exceed 6,000. During the past twenty-six years, the horror, the terror of leprosy [mai lepera] has been boiling throughout the Hawaiian way of life. Forward, O queen [Imua e ka Lani], and reduce the overwhelming spread of the disease among your people, who are increasingly being lost to the disfigurement of leprosy.

When we were all aboard the ship, the hour hand had quietly moved to five o'clock. The people who boarded with us were a nun [Vilikina], a Catholic priest [kahuna Katolika], and Mrs. S. Waiwai'ole.

We departed Kalaupapa at six o'clock and reached the harbor at Kou [awa o Kou: Honolulu Harbor] at 12:30 in the early morning.

Ka Nupepa Kuokoa. 30 MAY 1891. P. 4.
Ka Mai Luku ma ke Panalaau o Molokai. The Epidemic in the Colony on Moloka'i.
Kalawao, May 21. Greetings to you:

On the Sabbath, May 10, we were all stricken with an epidemic of influenza [La Garipa], unable to care for one another, this being the four houses adjacent to ours. It was then understood that there is no house here in Kalawao that does not have this illness. Here we all are, weak, some people dying and some people recovering. All of the helpers [kokua] are sick, and the regular tasks are imperiled by the lack of people. The police [kaiko] are some other people who are all sick, as well as the helpers who carry the cargo from the ship [kokua nana e hoohikihiki mai i na ukana o ka moku], the people of the store [poe o ka halekuai], and the leather makers [poe lole pipi]. Some leprosy patients [poe mai lepera] from Kalaupapa are the people who make the leather, and such will probably be the case for the people who work on the ship [kanaka hana moku]. Because William Tell [Wiliama Tele], superintendent of the colony, has been stricken by this illness, John Gaiser has been appointed as assistant superintendent. On the last Sabbath, May 17, there were no worshippers in Siloama Church here in Kalawao, because no one came. There were three deaths last Sunday: Kalani, Manuia, and Kale Li'ili'i (female). The funeral organizations [hui hoolewa] did not come because all the members had the illness.

In Kalaupapa, many people have died, according to what has been heard. The coffins [pahu kupapau] that were previously built are being depleted. Alika Smith, the ship carpenter [kamana moku], passed away, and the same goes for Kealohapauʻole and Maʻemaʻe, the wife of Kupakeʻe Hoapili.

—J. K.

Ka Nupepa Kuokoa. 12 SEPTEMBER 1891. P. 2.
Palapala Hoalohaloha. Letter of Condolence.

To the Queen, Liliʻuokalani:

Dear mother: Due to the sad news that has spread over our association, since it pleased the Almighty to take the precious life of Prince [Keikialii] John Owen Domínis, which is the trouble that has settled over you, this grief has also settled over us, some of your subjects [makaainana] who have leprosy [mai lepera]. The pain that you have, we also have this pain. Therefore, in the name of the United Heart Association [Ahahui Puuwai Lokahi] of Kalawao, Molokaʻi:

Resolved: The leaders and all of the members of this association enter into grieving together with you; and

Also resolved: While you are in a state of grief and painful woe for the husband, we pray to Almighty God [Akua Mana Loa] for your grief to be permanently eased, and we shall allow his will to be done, not that of man.

We are with affection J. Kekuewa, Wm. Kaʻaiape, Jos. Kuaia, J. Kalua, P. S. Maunahui.

Kalawao, Molokaʻi, SEPT. 5, 1891.

Ka Nupepa Kuokoa. 13 FEBRUARY 1892. P. 2.
Na Anoai O Ka Panalaau O Kalaupapa. News From the Colony at Kalaupapa.

On the recent twenty-third day, the superintendent [Luna Nui] W. H. Tell received news that a cow belonging to the Board of Health had been killed by several people whose names were unknown. When this father [W. H. Tell] who cares for the weak people [poe nawaliwali], who total one thousand or more, heard this, the police [makai] were immediately called out. And when the police had assembled, that was when that hero [kaeaea] mounted his horse and lifted his arm up with his whip [uwepa] held in his hand. His arm pointed toward the place described in the news, the location where the cow had been killed. Quick as a flash, they arrived where the cow was. And upon seeing the truth of what had been said, it was finally understood, but the road by which the wrongdoer would be found was quite a mysterious thing, so this W. H. Tell stopped and looked. At that time he saw the various roads. One road ran to upper Makanalua, and he went that way for twelve feet. Then he returned and went on the road going up to Kauhakō Hill [puu o Kauhako], and went that way in the same manner as before. There were no tracks [meheu]. He then went down the road along the shore of 'Iliopiʻi; no tracks. On the fourth of the roads [alanui], which was the road going straight down to Papaloa, drops of blood were found lying on that road, and they were followed until they disappeared.

Then that detective [kiu] turned and said to the police, "The trail ends in lower Papaloa." That hero took another sniff and did not call out until reaching the town. All the buildings were searched, but no clue was found. Then he returned to his breezy home, took a short break, and said the words, "Before this day is over, the people who wrongfully killed the cow will be found." It was probably not ten minutes before word arrived that the people who had done wrong to the cow had been found. Then he remounted his horse, and when he arrived there and searched, he found two boxes, one full box and one partially full box. These people were hauled off to jail [halepaahao]. These people were all patients [poe mai]. Here are their individual names: Kini (male), Huailani (male), ʻIakopō (male), Kahananui (male), Kamai (male). On the 26th the court sat to examine the nature of their case, and the court found them guilty and gave the sentence of one year for each.

—J. N. Kamauoha, Kalaupapa, Molokaʻi, JAN. 27, 1892.

Ka Nupepa Elele. 26 MARCH 1892. P. 2.
No Makou Iho. Concerning Ourselves.

In a column of our paper for today, the story can be seen concerning the bishop of Olba [Bihopa o Oloba] and the famous deeds of his ancestors in the past century in several nations of central Europe. They were the ones to break and shatter the sanctity of idol worship [hana hoomanakii] in ancient times, and from within that generation came Father Herman [Halemano], the great bishop of Olba of the Hawaiian kingdom [Bihopa Nui Oloba o ke Aupuni Hawaii].

News was also received from one of our friends that the Honorary Cross of Kalākaua [Kea Hoohanohano o Kalakaua] that was given to him by the grace of Her Majesty, the living queen, while His Majesty King Kalākaua was on his trip around the world, was submitted before the queen with a request that she kindly send it to the head of the administration of the faith, Buse [Poo o ka Hooko Hana o ka Manaoio Buse: probably Father Marcellin Bousquet, superior general of the Congregation of the Sacred Hearts of Jesus and Mary], in the city of Paris. The queen displayed her virtue and great pleasure in submitting this Honorary Cross of the royal court of Hawaiʻi to that sacred place of faith.

Thoughts of His Majesty the late King Kalākaua were awakened. An Honorary Cross was given to Father Damien [Damiano] while he was living in the midst of the extremely terrifying disease of leprosy [mai weliweli loa o ka Lepera], on the island of Molokaʻi. When he died, this Honorary Cross was sent all the way to the administrator of the faith, Buse, in Paris [Hooko Hana o ka Manaoio Buse i Parisa] by permission of King Kalākaua. A grateful reply of great joy was received from the side of the teacher of the faith, Buse, with introductory words of everlasting love being said. This was the first Honorary Cross submitted into a sacred collection from a sovereign of this world, and Hawaiʻi received the great honor of submitting wishes for faith and peace to make steadfast the friendly meeting of the hearts of this nation from the Crown to the humblest person.

What we will say at this point is that we give our calls of gratitude to our mother of the nation [Makuahine o ka Lahui: Queen Liliʻuokalani] for graciously allowing the fulfillment of these friendly meetings, from the progressive actions of the land to the charitable congregations, and the peace that will build and make everlasting the Christian way of life for the salvation of the spiritual body.

Ka Nupepa Kuokoa. 16 JULY 1892. P. 3.
Huakai Makaikai No Molokai. Ke Komite Ahaolelo ma ke Kahua o na Ma'i. Kakau ia e W. C. Achi. (Koena mai kela pule mai.) Visit to Moloka'i. The Legislative Committee at the Patient Settlement. Written by W. C. Achi. (Continued from last week.)

From the superintendent [luna nui], the writer received accurate numbers of patients as of the third of July 1892, as follows. Men: 612 Native Hawaiians [kanaka maoli]; 45 part-Caucasians [hapa haole]; 26 Chinese; 4 English; 1 Irish; 5 Americans; 3 Portuguese; 3 Germans; 1 French foreigner; 1 Canadian; 1 Russian; 2 Gilbertese; 1 of another nationality; 705 total. Women: 414 Native Hawaiians; 30 part-Hawaiians [hapa] of all varieties; 2 Chinese. Total of 1,151. While the committee was staying at the house to see the girls cared for by the nuns [Virigina], they submitted a petition before the committee explaining several issues. The main issue was requesting that measures be attempted to prevent boys from mischievously entering into their home. The committee replied that they would consider this thing.

After the committee viewed the home for girls [home o na kaikamahine: Bishop Home], the committee and the newspaper writer traveled with the doctors and the other visitors on huge, beautiful horses provided by the patient helpers [kokua ma'i] from Kalawao. Upon examining the state of Kalawao, the number of houses there was less than the number of houses in Kalaupapa, and while Kalawao faces right into the wind on the side facing the northwest, Kalaupapa faces the southeast.

In Kalawao is the boys' school [kula o na keikikane], and they total 93. That school is overseen by Marianne [Mary Ann], a nun [Virigini], with two other ladies and one gentleman of the Catholic faith [Brother Dutton].

And while the committee and the visitors were there, the infected children sang some songs that inspired pity and awe, led by Mikaele Keli'ikoa, a young patient [ma'i] who was brought from Ho'okena, S. Kona, Hawai'i. The voices of the children projected well and had a joyous sound, while the voice of their leader sounded deeply among their many voices. The song "The Famous Patient of Hawai'i" [ka ma'i kaulana o Hawaii] was sung by them, the song that inspires pity and pain in the heart of the traveler. The greatest feelings of pity and anguish in the heart were from seeing the Hawaiian youngsters damaged by disease singing a song of love [mele aloha] composed by them, directly relating to the dire state they are in.

In the understanding of the writer, the problem that the boys have is the same as the problem that the girls have, which is that the children who are extremely ill [keiki ma'i loa] and the ones who have a weaker illness [poe ma'i lahilahi] are combined. This has caused the illness to spread widely among them.

After visiting that school for youngsters, part of the committee and the visitors went to see the beautiful valley of Waikolu. In Waikolu is the source of the water that was brought to Kalawao and Kalaupapa to take care of the water troubles of the patients. The planning was splendid and excellent by the water supervisor, Chas. B. Wilson, for the things concerning that water supply for the leprosy patients [ma'i lepera]. If there was something that could carry all that water of Waikolu to the fields of Kalawao and Kalaupapa, then food could soon be farmed there, enough to supply the patients [ma'i]. The water the patients drink in Kalawao and Kalaupapa from Waikolu is splendid and excellent water. The quality and excellence is greater than the drinking water in the city of Honolulu. There are many taro patches [loi] growing in Waikolu, planted by the patients and the helpers [kokua mai]. The harvest is divided into a fourth [hapaha] for the planter and half [hapalua] for the Board of Health; and that is one of their requests, that all the supplies be given to the one who labored. [The writer only accounts for three fourths of the harvest. Perhaps the amount for the planter should have been hapalua, or one half, instead of hapaha, one fourth.]

After the party returned from Waikolu, everyone was hosted for lunch at the home of Superintendent Wm. H. Tell. The party ate their fill of everything prepared by that energetic superintendent. And when asked directly by the writer, it was said that all the expenses for hosting the party were paid from the superintendent's personal funds. In the opinion of the writer, during visits by the committees of the legislature, all of these expenses should be paid out of an allotment from the government treasury.

After lunch, a brief presentation of speeches was held by several members of the committee and the other visitors before the patients. These gentlemen entered into this crowd of speakers: Chas. Wilcox, Hon. J. G. Hoapili, W. C. Achi, Hon. J. A. Akina, Hon. J. Kaluna, Hon. J. W. Bipikāne, and Mr. Lowela.

During Mr. Lowela's speech, he said these words: "In my examination of the illness affecting some of you, I can say that I can treat and cure it. I do not merely believe that you will be cured by me, but I have truly seen this thing. I have treated some people with this method in Honolulu, and I saw that they truly recovered."

After these speeches were done, everyone went to meet with friends in that troubled land [aina pilikia] until it was almost time to return on the steamship *Waialeale* to Honolulu. When it was almost that time, the harbor of Kalaupapa was jammed full with people, and at that time the visitors saw various patients of every kind. It was quite pitiful to see the friends that I had seen before. Their features had become quite different, until you could not know them, except for when they said their names and the places they had come from.

To look at it, one great problem among those people living in Kalaupapa and Kalawao is the lack of someone who treats the patients in the sense of treating leprosy [mai pake]. As for the doctor who lives there, he only gives medicine for minor illnesses [maʻi liilii], such as fever [fiva], headache [nalulu], and so forth.

Upon examining the state of the settlement of the leprosy patients [kahua o na maʻi lepera], it is a truly wide site [kahua akea maoli], and the crops of the patients are growing, which are banana [maia], sugar cane [ko], sweet potato [uala], gourd [ipu], and so on. The committee and the visitors ate the food of the people living in that settlement, the place that is called "the final grave of the Hawaiian people" [ka luakupapau hope loa o na kanaka Hawaii].

There is a multitude of cattle [bipi] roaming the patient settlement that belong to the Board of Health, and the patients always receive milk from the cows. There are separate people who do the milking. One member of a family being separated is truly pitiful, but if he arrives at that place and becomes accustomed to residing in that land, the way of life actually appears to be rather pleasant, except for not seeing family and friends. The way the writer sees it, it would be good for the public to have a yearly time to see the people separated from their families. There would probably be no problem in that, and it would become something to calm the angry thoughts among the public caused by their relatives being taken from their homes.

The writer for the combined *Kuokoa* and *Paeaina* gives great thanks to Wm. H. Tell, his wife, and the two girls for the assistance received in that unfamiliar land [aina malihini].

Ka Nupepa Kuokoa. 30 JULY 1892. P. 4.
Na Anoai O Ke Panalaau. News from the Colony.
Mr. Editor. Greetings to you:

Today a girl with leprosy named Fanny K. Harper will return to Honolulu aboard the *Mokolii,* to be re-examined by the doctors. If she is not infected, then she will be released, and if she is not released, then she will stay in Kalihi to be treated. Here is the dishonest thing about this action by the Board of Health: this is an act of favoritism, with the Board of Health knowing full well that the original doctors who confirmed this girl as a leprosy patient [lepera] are the same doctors as now. How about this return to be examined? I think that you are doubting, O reader. It is true, that is the case. The doctors did not have their glasses when this girl was first examined. Everyone is wondering about this business, and it is an action that will cause everyone to be dragged into unrest.

Last Monday night, the store of the Board of Health standing in Kalawao was entered, and some goods inside were taken [hului]. The thief was quickly found that night at the place close to the homes [kauhale], standing behind the place of superintendent Wm. H. Tell, by a man named Maewa, approximately between the hours of 12:00 and 1:00 a.m. The wrongdoer was returning home, and this Maewa was returning to his place. This Maewa wondered about this person traveling late at night with large bags carried in front and on his back. And when Maewa tried to ask where he had come from this dark night, the wrongdoer replied, "From Kalawao" and started to run quickly. This was when Mawae [Maewa] began to follow after him until the thief abandoned the bags in a deserted field. There was no building there. And when Maewa examined these bags, behold, there were some food tins, men's suits and many other goods, and the hat belonging to the wrongdoer was also inside these bags. The owner of the hat was known, the Chinese man Ah Fook. Everything that was stolen was returned to the store, and this energetic Ah Fook will probably be arrested.

This is the greatest time of drunkenness [ona] here in the colony [Panalaau], the thing about which the attendants of the superintendent always proclaim loudly with mouths choked by gibberish, "too much peace from weakness" [tomasi maluhia i ka malule], and perhaps there is peace, with the eyes bulging out. The drunkenness is from the superintendent [Luna Nui] to the people. The things that Mrs. Kekaulike declared are absolutely true, and such is also the case with that of Kapule and Hololani.

Last Tuesday, a great number of mackerel scad fish [opelu] came ashore here in Kalaupapa, in accordance with the nature of schooling fish. They were gathered by patients using lard tins to scoop them up. Some people were grabbing them with their hands. This is a completely new thing, with some people believing they will come ashore again in the near future.

Some idol worshippers [poe hoomanamana] are proclaiming that the ʻōpelu fish are a sign [hoailono] that W. H. Tell will be kept on as superintendent for two to four more years and will not be done this summer. Perhaps that is true, but here is the strange thing: Keliʻikoa, the head priest of W. H. Tell, said, "The god will not care, because my priestly knowledge is done." According to Keliʻikoa, "Here I am being treated by Dr. Richard Oliver. No hope is left. It is a waste of money to keep buying kava [awa] for idol worship." And he also said, "It would be better to return to Laeokahio [lae o ka hio]." What a pity!

Due to the alertness of your spy [kiu] who sniffs out news, several small bags were clearly found lying outside of the gate of W. H. Tell and inside the gate yesterday morning after the milk had been given to the patients.

Inside of these three bags were things for idol worship, like bundles of taro leaves [wa-hi luau], small stones [pohaku iliili], and other things for idolatry [mea hoomanamana].

Perhaps this is one of the things being done as a way to continue Mr. Tell's role as superintendent for this colony [Panalaau]. This is the epitome of ignorant acts.

The agent of the Board of Health reported that from the time Tell took over until the past 15th of July, not one weekly report from this colony has been correct, as well as many checks.

—Andrew Kauila Jr. Kalaupapa, JULY 22, 1892.

Ka Nupepa Kuokoa. 20 AUGUST 1892. P. 3.
He Halawai Kupanaha. A Strange Meeting.
Mr. Editor: Here I am again before you with rather important bits of news from here in the colony [Panalaau], and I swiftly send them to you for the benefit of the readers of the *Kuokoa.*

In these days when we are avoiding the hardships of this existence, your spy [kiu] was greatly blessed to truly see firsthand the strange acts [hana kupanaha] of our father, superintendent W. H. Tell, which will astonish you, O reader.

Several meetings were held by him and his trusted attendants in his house. The number of people in this assembly at that meeting was ten, counting your spy, including one ignorant, big-bellied government policeman who does not know how to write and read, two old men who are sorcerers of black magic [kahuna anaana], one from Waikolu and one from Kalaupapa, and some older cousins of the superintendent, as well as the superintendent and his wife, two girls, and two mangy dogs [ilio meeau] belonging to the old men.

The main business at this meeting was explaining the nature of the dream of the superintendent, and whether the aged ones could reveal the nature of that dream. Here is the nature of that dream, according to the superintendent:

"I received on the night of the 6th day of this month a strange thing in a dream, which was a great bull jabbing and tearing down the office until it was broken to bits. Then this bull began to come before me with its hooves all raking the ground until dust rose into the air. When it neared our gate, it began to chase me with great speed. Then I ran swiftly with this bull continuing to follow, wanting to gore me, until I climbed up the cliff here in Kalaupapa. I ran to escape in lower Kaunakakai. Then I cried out in fright, but oh! It was a dream."

And here the superintendent ceased speaking for two minutes, and then said, "Well, what do you two think of this dream?"

Moluhi stood and said, "This is not a very significant dream, although I see that you may be finished." That was also what the other kahuna said. Then the wife cried loudly and tears were falling on the cheeks; then everyone cried loudly. That weeping ended when one dog howled loudly and the other dog barked at me because I was watching through the window shutters. All of the crying voices fell silent. Then a thick set man as large as two came in. There were no fingers on his hands and his pants were held up by dirty ropes resembling those used for salted pork. He said, "Take heed, father. If you listen to what I say, then the problem will be over. These two need to immediately perform sorcery [anaana] until all of these people who are proclaiming about you in the newspaper are dead."

Then Moluhi said, "There is only one thing we all need to do: take off our clothes and go around the house five times. Then things will be a little better. You must never drink alcohol to excess, lest it be publicized again."

At this point I left the porch of the house and went home puzzled. There was another meeting last night, but nothing was done.

—Andrew [Analu] Kauila Jr.

Ka Leo o ka Lahui. 30 AUGUST 1892. P. 2.
Hoike a ke Komite Wae. E Pili Ana I Na Mai Lepera ma Molokai. Na Hoopii O Kela A Me Keia Ano. Report of the Select Committee. Concerning the Leprosy Patients on Molokaʻi. Petitions of Every Kind.

We thought that the petition for a money order office [Oihana Kikoo Dala Hale Leta] to be built at the post office [Hale leta] in Kalaupapa was a suitable request and that this thing would immediately be carried out.

Concerning the complaint about a woman. Upon examination it seems like there is another cause for this petition on this matter. One of the patients who was not suitable to go to the mountains was urged to go get firewood for them, since if they did not go they would not have any. It is necessary for this matter to be reformed now, and none of the feeble and elderly people should be expected to perform this arduous labor.

And on this same topic, we are finding out the truth, that the board charges the baker and manager of the coffee shop $16 per pile of hard firewood, and $6 to the patients.

The bakery [hale hana palaoa] that was built by a German, a patient, is greatly needed by everyone in that place. From this shop is supplied some baked bread of excellent quality with a price as cheap as that of Honolulu.

The reason for the high cost of the firewood is not known. The board has many work carts and oxen but we were told that the time when this equipment is utilized is very small. The proper utilization of them is something that would benefit the patients. We believe it is necessary to attempt, carefully and with great correction, O board, to grow trees in all suitable places close to the hospital settlement [Kahua Halemai]. We believe it is possible for firewood to be cultivated in a suitable location able to supply all the demand of the patient settlement [Kahua mai].

Concerning the submission of petitions and resolutions to the Board of

Health to be considered and acted upon, we want to report that we do not think it is something for the legislature to step back from, although there are also executive actions that should be submitted to the board.

THE BISHOP HOME FOR GIRLS AND BOYS.
[KA HOME BIHOPA NO NA KAIKAMAHINE A ME NA KEIKIKANE.]

We greatly desire to express deep gratitude to these immensely valuable places, and the priceless work that the Franciscan Sisters [Hoahanau Wahine Farancisca] and Mr. Joseph Dutton are doing.

A remembrance was prompted of the unpaid debt of the nation to Mother Marianne [Makuhine Marianne] and Sisters [Hoahanau Wahine] Leopoldina [Leopodina] and Elizabeth [Eliikapeka], in the Bishop Home for Girls, and Sisters Crescentia [Cresentia], Vincent, and Irene and Mr. Joseph Dutton at the Home for Boys [Home o na Keikikane], for their caring for the needs of the youngsters placed in their hands, with patience, wisdom, and souls filled with compassion.

If more places like this were built, and there were more pious people found who were suitable to care for these places, it would be something to bring endless blessings to the patient settlement [Kahua Mai].

We will also mention the tireless efforts of Father Wendelin [Father Wendelin Moellers, SS.CC.], the resident Catholic priest there. Besides these people, there are also the members of the Calvinist faith doing as much as they can. The talk concerning the varieties of worship and religious denominations has become a painful thing to hear, since we are all worshipping the same God and looking forward to the same Heaven, the place of respite and separation from all defilement. We appeal to the generosity of God for compassion and salvation. It seems as if this is an unsuitable place to hear a nasty opinion growing about this thing called religion.

WATER WORKS. [NA HANA WAI.]

A portion of the committee, accompanied by the president of the Board of Health, went to view the water supply from the patient settlement [Kahua Mai] with the desire to understand the actions being done to protect against a water shortage caused by an accident with the water pipes and to also consider increasing the distribution of the water by attaching more small water pipes.

During the tour of the water pipeline [lalani paipu-wai] from the community [kauhale] to the source of the water, a straight section was seen, one-eighth of a mile laid with large water piping, which could not go anywhere else, [except] at the base of a tall, jutting cliff, the place where the pipe would crack if falling rocks rolled into it, which could bring disaster to this laying of the pipes. Several weeks might pass before the pipes could be reconnected. Right after the water pipeline was laid, an event of this kind was seen, but since the laborers and the supplies to fix it were nearby, it was quickly rebuilt.

Besides the danger from rocks rolling down the cliff, here, too, is this frightening thing that will damage the water pipeline in this place. In times of rough seas, the breaking waves [ale poi] come straight up and strike right by the water's edge. That is when the ocean comes up and completely covers the pipeline, which disappears. Driftwood and rocks are hurled with great force against the base of the cliff at a height greater than where the pipe lies. Up until now this disaster has not happened to those [sections of] pipe, but it is not hard to imagine. It is not impossible at any time, and the water pipe will be broken in this place by the heavy things such as driftwood and rocks thrown on top of them by the force of the ocean.

To be continued.

» [The large diameter pipeline that carried water from Waikolu to Kalawao ran over a narrow boulder beach at the base of a high sea cliff. It was subject to constant damage from boulders falling from the cliff above and from boulders tossed onshore by heavy surf.]

Ka Nupepa Kuokoa. 24 SEPTEMBER 1892. P. 1.
He mea Maikai ke Aloha. Love is a good thing.

Here in the colony [panalaau], there are two entrances [puka], an entrance for the leprosy patients [lepera] and an entrance for the locals [kamaaina]. These doors are not the same. Door 1 [pani 1] is a door that is extremely difficult to open. Door 2 [pani 2] is the door that comes loose when it is opened. And this entrance is always open, night and day. At this entrance it has been seen that those outside come in, and those in here go out. At this entrance the helpers [kokua] have often been seen coming in to see their patients, and then returning, or living here. For the people who live here, they become locals. For the other entrance [door 1], the door is closed, unless there is a law [passed], which is stirring in the dirt. If it arises it will be a bitter thing.

This is the fourth, and it will soon be the fifth, year of my residence in this colony, and I have just seen the incredible number of helpers in this colony. All mixed up, mixing wild taro with cultivated [Hui aku hui mai, hui kalo i ka nawao]. The restriction is over. The land is free. You mix together, and what is being done? Whatever benefits yourselves. There is great intoxication here in the colony, that is what I am saying. The restriction is over, and the land is free. Drunkenness is not forbidden. The distiller of moonshine [puhi okolehao] is not arrested. The beer maker [hana bia] is not arrested. The maker of sweet potato kava [hana uala awaawa] is not arrested. The helpers coming in are not arrested. The leprosy patients [ma'i lepela] who go out and come back are not arrested. Here is the astonishing thing: T. S. Nāhinu was arrested. These trespassers were not arrested, these brewers of moonshine were not arrested. Kaluna was arrested and jailed, and he paid. The people who blew up fish [poe hoopahu i'a: people who fished by dropping dynamite into a school of fish] were arrested. The people who netted anchovies [nehu] on the Sabbath day were not arrested. What is our superintendent thinking, arresting some people and exempting others? Manuia is crooked, the ship is *Keokoi* [kapakahi manuia o Keokoi ka moku: someone is playing favorites].

—S. Hāla'i. Kawaluna, Kalawao, SEPT. 1, 1892.

Ka Nupepa Kuokoa. 21 JANUARY 1893. P. 1.
Hoike Kula Sabati ma Kalawao. Sunday School Exhibition in Kalawao.
Mr. Editor:

Last Christmas the catechism school of the students of J. K. Kalohi at the stone church of Damien [halepule pohaku o Damiano] had another exhibition.

Right after afternoon mass the church was completely filled with brethren and friends. Perhaps if there was no Sunday school at Kalaupapa, then Kalawao would have been filled to the brim with people on this day yearned for by my friends. The testing was begun. There were four classes with twenty-two children, and J. K. Kalohi was the teacher for all these classes.

The class had been taught from the old manual [Manuale kahiko], pages 122 and 138. The students spoke together with the same voice and easily answered the questions asked by the leader. After the group reading, the audience was asked if they had questions to give to this class about what they were taught. Some questions were given by several experts, and fitting answers to the questions were given by the students. The last question was the question that dizzied the thinking of the students of this class, but the teacher was permitted to fully explain all of the wrinkles. Here is the question:

In whose era was circumcision [okipoepoe] begun, and in which era was it ended?

In the time of Abraham, and it was ended when Jesus Christ died on the cross.

This is the reply given for these questions. When this class was done, the second class who was taught from pages 138 and 165 of the ancient manual [was questioned]. This class was quick to reply with answers until the end. Questions were given to the children by the audience, and they were answered.

When this class was done, the third class was questioned from pages 170 and 178 of this same book, concerning the Sacrament of the Eucharist, and the mastery of the lessons was just like the first class. The audience gave these questions below: Who was the sacrifice of the cross, and who was the priest who offered this sacrifice? Answer, Jesus was the sacrifice, and Jesus was the priest who offered it. What is the difference between the cross sacrifice and the altar sacrifice? And what is the similarity? For the cross sacrifice Jesus was injured and died, but for the altar sacrifice there is no injury and his blood does not flow. As for the similarity, Jesus was the cross sacrifice, and it is he at mass (altar). This is the answer that the children gave.

The fourth class was questioned from pages 32 and 42 of the ancient manual about the birth of the Lord, and the school lessons of that class were well learned. The audience was again asked for the last time, and several questions truly arose from the audience of which it was thought that they would be the bombs (questions) [pokapahu (Ninau)] to stump this class. However, that was not the case. The answers were told and that which was stuck was loosened. Here are some of these questions:

Who is the person who was told by the Holy Ghost that they would not die until knowing salvation? Who was the first prophet to see the birth of the Lord? Who was the first to prophesy the coming of salvation?

Here are the answers: 1. Simon [Simeona]. 2. Anna [Ana] was the prophet who first saw the Lord. 3. God was the one who first prophesied.

The one who asked the question expressed his appreciation, and the audience also expressed appreciation. This was the end of the school presentations, and Father L. L. Louis [Lui: Father Lambert Louis Conrardy] stood and encouraged the brethren and friends to imitate these fine acts, for it is God's desire that the right acts be done, not bad things.

This is the last thing seen by your writer before business was concluded, and I am also giving my congratulations. Continue, children, the command of the Lord. Here is his [command]: "The one who acts upon the desire of my father in heaven is my mother and my cousins." So forward, younger siblings, the payment is in heaven.

I am concluding my news report with a New Year's greeting to friends, and my greetings to the editor and the windmill-handed children of his office.

With affection, J. Kahale'iwa'iwa, Kalawao, DEC. 28, 1892.

Hawaii Holomua. 14 FEBRUARY 1893. P. 3.

In Kalaupapa, Moloka'i, on Thursday, the 2nd day of this month, Rev. D. K. Pa left this life, after over five hours of clinging to life. He left behind a close friend [hoapili], a wife, and three children.

Ka Nupepa Kuokoa. 12 AUGUST 1893. P. 4.
No ka Mai Lepera. Concerning Leprosy.
Mr. Editor:

For over thirty years leprosy [mai lepera] has decimated the Hawaiian people [lahui Hawaii]. During these long years the people have been dragged to Moloka'i, to live and age there until the time when death comes to cut short their agonies. Leprosy is a disease greatly feared [mai weliweli loa] by all nations that have been stricken with this kind of friendless disease [mai makamaka ole].

This disease is horrible in how it appears upon the people who have it. The disease causes disfigurements to the people who have it. When the signs of leprosy first appear upon someone, chills are already running all over his body, since his hour of leaving his family is nearing. He will go to live with people who are strangers [poe malihini] to him, under the care of the expenditures of the government that come without complaint.

This same feeling of grief is also spreading over the family. It is a sorrowful thing for the heart to realize that the one you love will be separated from you. For the love the mother has for her child that is being separated from her bosom forever, there is nothing that will comfort and console that. The mother has a true and tenacious love for her child, who is her burden and also her lei.

The falling tears of the mother that flow while her beloved child is undoing the support for their loving relationship are completely soaking the very root of her child's heart. As for the love of the father, it is profound, and something that sorrows the heart of the father. For the people whose children have been separated from them because of leprosy, they exclaim in unison: "Here we are, lamenting for our children." [Eia no makou ke uwe ae nei no ka makou keiki.] According to the length of years that their children have been isolated at the leprosy colony [Panalaau Lepera] of Moloka'i, such is the continual enlargement of the agony of their hearts for the children that have been taken.

And it is the same for the adults who have been taken with families remaining out here. The memories will not be forgotten. However, the thing that increases the agonies of desire is never again seeing the faces of the people you loved.

The people who are being isolated on Moloka'i, they are like dead people in how the faces disappear forever for the people living out here. It is exactly like death. Hope dies, freedom dies, and what is the value of this world that remains? It is a little better for the criminals imprisoned in Kāwā [jail in Honolulu], who are locked up for a few years, five or ten, and then appear again to meet with loved ones.

Being separated forever, from family, loved ones, and friends, that is the thing that increases the agonies of the people isolated in Kalawao. The agonies of the wounds on the body have lessened, and the agonies of the mind have grown to excess. It is something constantly emaciating the body.

There is no one who denies the tenacious love between the one going and those staying behind in grief. The one who lacks these feelings is not a man with the good mind that God has given him; he is an animal of the lowest order. The lowness and poverty of a man, or the blackness of his skin, are not things that take away these constant feelings that God has bestowed individually upon all people with good minds. This feeling has spread equally to all nations. However, it is a constant thing in this world that according to the prestige and wealth of a person, such is the amount of people who grieve for him, and in accordance with the lowly state and abject poverty of a person, such will be the weight of the burdens of scorn and disgust loaded upon him. The pure state of the soul of a man is not regarded if he has leprosy. That is appropriate during his lifetime.

However, the people know these agonies that constantly beset the people every second of their life, and yet, the Hawaiian people are the epitome of excessive stubbornness when it comes to mixed living. When a man is healthy, and these tragic symptoms have not appeared, the fixed rules of health are left in the corner. They are just useless rules, in their opinion. However, when the disease appears and the government begins to bring down its hand and take them to Moloka'i, that is when these thoughtless people begin to misbehave and resist the government. These wrongdoings are in vain. You have sought out your death, you have wasted yourself, and do not fault the government. If you had taken proper care of yourself and not mixed with the infected people like this, you would have continued to succeed.

I have my own relatives who are in Kalawao, and I strongly support the isolation of the infected people in a place where they will not mix with healthy people.

The Hawaiian people are the ones greatly afflicted by this disease. Thousands of them leave their bones on Moloka'i.

What is the reason for this great affliction of Hawaiians by this disease?

This is a rather significant question, and the knowledge and opinions of the wise doctors concerning the reasons are varied. Since I am not a doctor, some of the reasons that I have come up with may be mistakes:

1. Poverty [O ka ilihune].
2. Hawaiian kāhuna [O na kahuna Hawaii: priests of the ancient religion].
3. Not being taught the book of health [O kea o ole ia i ka buke ola kino].
4. Mixed living [O ka noho huikau].
5. Disobedience [O ka hookuli].
6. Unclean living [Nohona maemae ole].

At another time, I will explain causes 1, 2, 3, 5, and 6.

The fourth cause is what I will explain a little. Mixed living is an extremely foolish thing among Hawaiians. Do not get mad at me when I report the truth. Open your eyes, if you are blind.

People are not afraid of eating with, sleeping with, and fraternizing with people who have the disease. If warned about mixed living, they are rude, scornful, haughty, and so forth. If, however, they are afflicted, then they think on their disobedience, but the suitable time is over. It is much too late.

Dr. Trousseau (French) denies that leprosy [lepera] is a contagious disease [mai lele]. The knowledge of the doctors is not in agreement. Just as the doctors of this world do not have a medicine that cures leprosy, they also cannot decide whether leprosy is a contagious disease or a noncontagious disease [mai lele ole]. The French doctor denies that this is a contagious disease, and this is something that induces the people to mix. Leprosy is a rather strange disease. Some people who live together, eat together, and sleep together [with infected people] for several years will not get it. Yet for other people who just fraternize for a brief period, they catch it. For the children of the leprosy patients [poe lepera], some are infected and some are uninfected. This is quite an astonishing thing. So, the French doctor is not entirely correct. Would Father Damien [Damiano] have gotten leprosy if he had stayed in London, Paris, or Boston? God is the one who knows that. But not mixing with infected people is the best medicine. Those people are rarely afflicted. The disobedient people are the victims.

However, my guess is that if Damien had not come to live with the patients in Kalawao this way, he would not have contracted leprosy [mai lepera]. Leprosy [lepera] is indeed a contagious disease in my opinion. There are a great many contagious diseases, but what leprosy [lepera] does to a person's body is quite horrible, so it should be isolated, to protect the healthy people.

—Kaoaokalani.

Ka Nupepa Kuokoa. 2 DECEMBER 1893. P. 4.
Na Mea Hou Like Ole o ke Kahua Ma'i Lepera. Various News from the Leprosy Settlement.

Mr. Editor. Greetings to you:

Here I am with various bits of news from here in the leprosy settlement [kahua ma'i lepera], and your kindness will spread them before our news-loving multitudes.

On this past 31st day of October, the Japanese doctor [kauka Iapana] arrived here in the colony [Panalaau] with joyful features. In the hours of that evening, he met for the first time with his peer in the medical profession, the exuberant one from Japan, Dr. M. Goto. This was the very first time they had seen each other. The two of them stayed here for one week, and Dr. Goto first introduced him at the home for children, Damien Home [Damiano Home], meeting with the nuns [makuahine] and Jas. Dutton [Joseph Dutton] and Rev. L. L. Conrady [Rev. Lambert Louis Conrardy]. The next day, he was hosted at the home of respite, the place inhabited by the youngsters who have been affectionately named by the public "the youngsters of Lahainaluna Seminary."

Upon meeting with us, Dr. Goto invited us to be examined by this doctor, and we accepted the invitation of the open-hearted father.

When we were examined, there was thanks and joy, also thanking Dr. Goto for his skill in treating leprosy. And then someone was found to confirm the truth of the work of Dr. Goto, not because he was a perjurer due to the two of them being the same race, but because of his knowledge as a doctor. Thank you very much.

CONCERNING THE AGENT OF THE BOARD OF HEALTH.
[NO KA AGENA O KA PAPA OLA.]

During the first days of this month C. B. Reynold [Reynolds] came in person to the colony [Panalaau]. He came to examine the patient settlement [kahua maʻi] and the things relating to the new home for children. He saw everything first-hand, and the opening of the new store in Kalaupapa, and a lot more that this pen cannot simply go through.

CONCERNING THE STORE OF THE PATIENT SETTLEMENT.
[NO KA HALE KUAI O KE KAHUA MAʻI.]

The sale of the old store here in the colony [panalaau] was recently completed, which is the store standing in Kalawao, the building seen by all the crowds and the lives engulfed by the belly of the earth. This building was built many long years ago. The writer does not know the month, but it seems like it might have been after the period when William Ragsdale [Bila Auana] served as superin-tendent. There is great affection from the residents of this land, for whom is this small expression of affection:

"Poi made from the ʻape plant [ai ape] is not strained,
Pōkā [cannon ball] is in fiery destruction."

Such was the case for this old home. Pōkā struck, the hands of the ʻĀkōlea are destructive, abiding in Kalaupapa. It is much worse for those in the uplands who are frustrated, for whom is this small entertainment:

"No regard, it is only a Hilo grass,
A bothersome weed, eaten only by horses."

Kalawao has become Hilo grass, a bothersome weed.

CONCERNING THE FAMILIES OF BONY CATTLE BELONGING TO MEYER. [NO NA OHANA BIPI WIWI A MEYER.]

There is great grumbling by the patients about the leanness of the beef belong-ing to the agent of the colony [Panalaau], about how he brings his bony cattle and we are the ones who eat it. Maybe we are like dogs, maybe that is not right, maybe we should eat something clean, not like this. In earlier seasons, we had plump and fine cattle, but these days there are lean ones. That little song of old is fitting:

"A bony cow for Pīʻalu [sagging wrinkles].
Truly sagging, until only bones are left."

CONCERNING THE HOME OF DR. M. GOTO.
[NO KA HOME O DR. M. GOTO.]

Here are the children of Dr. Goto living in their home, everyone in fine and comfortable health, with features handsome in appearance. That was not the case in days past, when just a shadow was there, but these days the image of a person has returned. Luali'i and company have carved away until only fragments remain, thus the current poor condition, and it is the point of this small fascination:

"Luali'i simply carves Mana,
And upon seeing ugliness, leaves."
Such is the case for us, the fragments of leprosy.

We are fragments belonging to leprosy. We have the complete song by that boy who is lively in songwriting, Kaehu. Here are a few short lines that your writer has:

"What will happen to Hawai'i,
Leprosy is coming,
A disease scorned by the people,
Brown-skinned, white-skinned,
The hands point,
You go to Moloka'i,
Land of leprosy."

And there are a great many other expressions of affection in this song. This song by this boy is true, about how we are scorned. Yet this Dr. Goto, he does not scorn us. We have been felt by his hands. He is the doctor that will heal the people who are in distress. Indeed, respite will come to us, the people within the fiery pit of endless death [luahi o ka make mau loa: hell].

The number of us now at this home is thirty-six various kinds of people. For us, the first ones, we are approaching six months, and for the last ones one month, and their recovery is increasing these days. Great thanks was given to the heavenly powers for the swift aid in the time of affliction. The children of Dr. Goto have a small expression of affection. Here is how the loving goes:

The news arrives, Kalawao hears,
Recovery is coming,
Swimming in the long sea,
The swaying waves of Kaiwi.

—J. B. M. Kapule. Kalawao, Molakai [Moloka'i], NOV. 16, 1893.

Ka Makaainana. 29 JANUARY 1894. P. 7.
Hoopunipuni o S. W. Kawelo. Lie of S. W. Kawelo.
Mr. Editor:
    The idea expressed in the columns of your paper of the 8th day of this month by S. W. Kawelo, saying, "The annexationists tremble and sob," and so

forth, have no truth, except perhaps for J. A. Kanamu, the only person who has revealed himself to be an American. I report instead to you that from the mountains to the sea [mai ka uka a ke kai] here in the colony [panalaau], there is only one accord, unity [he hookahi wai o ka like]. And concerning J. P. Miau [Maiau], Kawelo is greatly mistaken. Miau [Maiau] strongly opposes annexation [hoohuiaina]. He is a true lover of royalty in all ways. From Kalawao to Kalaupapa, they only belong to Liliʻuokalani in every day of living on the soil of Hawaiʻi.

—Geo. Nākoʻokoʻo. Kalaupapa, JAN. 11, 1894.

» [The writer is voicing support for Queen Liliʻuokalani, who was deposed on January 17, 1893.]

Ka Leo o ka Lahui. 1 FEBRUARY 1894. P. 2.
Ka Nupepa Kuokoa. 3 FEBRUARY 1894. P. 2.
Olelo Hoolaha. Notice.
To the Title Holders in the Lands of Kalaupapa, Kalawao, Nihoa, and Waikolu, Molokaʻi.

We, the undersigned, have been appointed as commissioners under the law entitled "A Law empowering the Interior Minister to acquire and purchase, for the benefit of the Government, the Lands and Properties desired by the Board of Health, on the Island of Molokaʻi," approved on the 5th day of October, 1893.

And we declare that several meetings will be held for all persons who hold an allodial or other title to the lands in Kalaupapa, Kalawao, Nihoa, and Waikolu that are desired to be transferred to the Board of Health under the law mentioned above. Those title holders shall come to confirm their rights to these lands.

The first meeting will begin in Kalaupapa, Molokaʻi, on February 14, 1894, at ten o'clock in the morning. This meeting is for the people of Molokaʻi.

The second meeting will be held for the people living in other parts of this group of islands [Pae Aina] at the Kapuāiwa Hale in Honolulu, assembling on February 26, 1894, at ten o'clock in the morning.

Therefore, be watchful, lest your title soon be lost.

—Jos. S. Emerson, Robt. W. Andrews, Albert Trask, the commissioners.

Ka Makaainana. 5 FEBRUARY 1894. P. 1.
Ua Hala i ke Ala Hoi ole mai. Passed Away on the Path of No Return.
The newborn baby of Maria D. Waiwaiʻole passed away on the path of no return in Kalaupapa, on January 29, after only a few short months of breathing the air of this world. He was feeble and the skill of man could not save him from returning into the earth. He entered the sleep of summer and winter [ka moe kau moe hooilo: the sleep of death]. Our shared grief is with the mother. How sad for this precious flower bud [opuu makamae].

Ka Makaainana. 19 MARCH 1894. P. 3.
Na Anoai o Kalaupapa. News from Kalaupapa.
On the night of February 13th, the *Mokolii* arrived full of cargo. Upon her arrived the committee members who will decide the price of the lands belonging to the locals [kamaaina], who are J. S. Emerson [Emesona], R. W. Andrew, and Albert Trask. On the 14th they arrived at the location of the lands belong-

ing to the landowners to examine the quality and the state of the land, and to do the same with the buildings. At two o'clock in the afternoon they held a meeting at the place of S. Kahalehulu.

Here are the prices of the lands and the buildings that were decided by them. The land parcel of Lolo (male), nine acres, $90; that of Nakilani (male), in Nihoa, nineteen acres, $105; that of 'Aimoku (female) and her brother, in that same location, two parcels, $133; that of Kaliki junior (male), six acres, $65; that of Kaulukupa'a (female), a quarter acre, from the stone wall to the dirt, $25; that of J. I. Keoki, four acres, $20; for that of S. Kahalehulu, Kinimaka (female), Lono (female), and Walahia (male), theirs were deferred until the price is found out from Honolulu.

By this decision of the committee members the aforementioned prices have been set, and here is their statement to the landowners: "If they have a complaint, they must sue." What a pity for the natives of the land [kupa o ka aina] due to this law of simple robbery made by them [the committee members] and others.

The leaseholders [Na Poe Hoolimalima]. That of S. W. Kawelo, he has crops and the house, $275; that of Keaka (female), only a house, $80; the house of Ka'apela (female), $40; Kaehu Waiwai'ole's house, $70; that of Kalama (female) and Maoea (female), $20; for J. W. Kahalewai's house there was no decision, and it seems as if the Board of Health will simply take that house. These are the things concerning the titled lands.

On the night of the 14th, the musical boys of the Hawaiian band [Bana Hawaii] of Kalaupapa made a lively presentation, led by C. N. Kealakai, to entertain the committee members. During that time the chairman of the committee had great luck [laki nui] because he received the name of a shark kupua [mano kupua: a demigod]. This made a total of 101 shark kupua that he has found from Hawai'i to Ni'ihau. The reason for his luck was that he directly asked the crowd if they had heard the name of a shark kupua from Moloka'i, and the answer was yes. The name of that shark was Kānewa'ali'i [a reference to superintendent Ambrose Kānewa'ali'i Hutchison]. There was a burst of laughter.

On the 15th, they undertook the great labor of departing on the cliff trail [alanui pali], and on this return one of them got dizzy and rolled down the cliff until getting caught in a little stone pool. There were many [possible] places of injury, and R. W. Andrew [Anaru] was the one injured.

On the 21st the Chinese superintendent [Luna Nui Pake] of the food company that takes care of the food for the patients arrived because of the great number of official complaints about the food being spoiled. When he arrived, no food was seen that was spoiled. From him these uplifting words were received: "We shall be patient, the trouble is almost over. The queen will soon sit on the throne." Great joy was caused by his words, and three cheers [ekolu huro] were given for him.

—S. W. Kawelo. Kalaupapa, FEB. 22, 1894.

Ka Makaainana. 19 MARCH 1894. P. 8.
Kela A Me Keia. This and That.

Last Wednesday night the Board of Health held its regular weekly meeting. The deliberation was raised concerning Dr. Goto's continuation of his treatment for those stricken by leprosy [hana lapaau i na poe i loohia i ka mai lepera]. It was tabled until the following week. The people of Kalawao have strongly petitioned for his continuation in his treatment of them.

Ka Oiaio. 13 APRIL 1894. P. 4.
Na Leta. Letters.
Mr. Editor. Greetings to you:

Because I was thwarted by the editor of the newspaper *Hawaii Holomua,* I send this short letter to you concerning some rather significant things about Dr. M. Goto's treatment of the leprosy patients [maʻi lepera] here in the colony [Panalaau], and so forth. Since in my role as superintendent for the hospital of Dr. Goto here in Kalawao [Luna Nui no ka Haukipila o Kauka Goto ma Kalawao] I constantly see the skillful ministrations of Dr. Goto to the patients in that hospital, I decided that, for the good and the benefit of all persons, I should report all the true things about the job he is doing for the good of those afflicted by the serious symptoms of the disease greatly feared by those of the entire world [maʻi e kau nuiia nei ka weli e ko ke ao holookoa].

Here in this hospital are some people being treated with a truly serious case of leprosy affecting their bodies. In the first days of their admittance, their hands, bodies, and feet had become rotten and fragile, and they were truly weak due to the disfiguring consumption of leprosy. They all would have died if not for the skillful treatments they received from Dr. Goto. Today, they have recovered, strength returns to their bodies, and they eat the harvest from the sweet potato, cabbage, and onions that they themselves planted with their hands.

This is the tenth month of Dr. Goto's care for the patients of this hospital, and not one patient has died up to the day that I am writing this letter. For this reason the reader will see and verify the truth of what I am reporting before the public.

The patients being treated by Dr. Goto who properly followed the rules of taking medicine experience recovery. For the majority of the patients living in this colony [Panalaau], here they are, living and simply dying, without proper treatments being provided to them. This is the most tragic thing in my thoughts, how I see my fellow men of the same skin constantly dying due to this situation, since the founding of this colony. To my knowledge, concerning the average number of deaths here in the colony each month, ten is the lowest and over twenty is the highest.

My guess, due to the things I see, is that if all the patients of this colony were under Dr. Goto's care, then the deaths would probably not be so very overwhelming, like what is being seen these days. Due to the enthusiastic acclaim for Dr. Goto's treatment, I have been asked by the patients to create a petition [palapala hoopii] before the Board of Health to retain Dr. Goto in his position as doctor for the colony [kauka no ka Panalaau] for several more years, or perhaps as a permanent doctor [kauka noho paa].

Because of the joy of the children at the hospital of Dr. Goto [Haukapila o Kauka Goto] caused by them receiving respite and true strength of their bodies, they have composed this little song, as follows:

"This is lightning expressing affection
For the healing medicine of Dr. Goto [No ka laau ola a Kauka Goto]
The news has spread, the islands have heard
From Hawai'i to Ni'ihau
We are filled with joy
The helping deeds of Lili'ulani [Lili'uokalani]
Due to the searching until properly found
Magic medicine of Japan [Laau kaula a o Iapana]
That will cure the pains
Of merciless leprosy [O ka ma'i lepera hana lokoino]
Relief is received by your people
Grieving in sadness
We are eased, victorious
Salvation has arrived here in Kalawao
We shall all recover
And return to the native land
We call, you respond
Famous expert of Japan
The refrain shall be told
Lili'u is the living Hawaiian queen."

I greatly desire to tell my fellow men living in hiding due to the marks of leprosy to stand tall and come to this land. This is not a land of dying, this is a land for recovery [aohe keia he aina o ka make aku, he aina keia no ke ola]. In my understanding, it is as if this could be the land spoken of in the Great Book, Canaan [Kanaana], that was the place where milk and honey flowed [malaila kahi e kahe ana o ka waiu a me ka meli]. It is true, my dear friends, you will receive in this land the food of this kind when you desire it, as follows: cow's milk, taro, poi, sweet potato, rice, sugar, bread, crackers, salmon, beef, beef tripe, and such is also the case with soap, matches, kerosene, salt, and also so with clothing.

In the land of birth [aina hanau] the way of life is quite problematic, and in this land the way of life is successful in all aspects.

Due to frequent inducements by the patients not being treated by Dr. Goto, I have just made a petition to the Board of Health requesting that Dr. Goto be selected as a permanent doctor [kauka noho paa] here in the colony, and last Wednesday this action was carried out. In a few hours the total number of people who signed that petition reached 861, and it was sent to the president of the Board of Health.

That is just a little bit of news, until next time.

—Thos. K. Nākana'ela. Goto's Hospital. MARCH 30, 1894.

Ka Nupapa Kuokoa. 19 MAY 1894. P. 1.
Kia Hoomanao ma Molokai. Monument on Moloka'i.

We publish above [a drawing of] the monument, the statue built for Father Damien [Damiana], who died in Kalawao, Moloka'i, from the leprosy that afflicted him. A great sum of money was raised in London, and $500 was set aside for building this monument. This monument was brought here in the year 1893 and installed on September 12 of that year on Moloka'i by the provisional government [Aupuni Kuikawa].

» [This brief note accompanied a drawing that was captioned: Ke Kia Hoomanao O Damiano, or "The Monument of Damien." In 1891, Father Damien's friend, Edward Clifford, designed a red granite cross with the likeness of the priest cut into white marble. The monument was installed in Kalaupapa with inscriptions in English and Hawaiian, including the following: "Greater love hath no man than this, that a man lay down his life for his friends. John 15:13. Aole ko kekahi kanaka aloha i oi aku i keia, o ka waiho aku a kekahi i kona ola no kona mau hoaaloha. Ioane 15.13."]

Ka Nupepa Kuokoa. 26 MAY 1894. P. 4.
Huakai Makakai i ke Awawa o Waikolu. Expedition to Waikolu Valley.
Greetings to You:

Monday, May 14, the party of children was going straight along the path at the edge of the cliff until reaching the house facing the valley. We rested there, and at that time your writer took a full count of the amount of children on this expedition, over forty when including Father Conrady [Father Lambert Louis Conrardy] and the two supervisors, Keli'ikoa and Keola, and so it was over forty. When the break was over, we went upland. This valley is long. The locals said it is five miles in length from the shore to the great base [of the mountain at] the end of the valley. After about one-eighth of the valley, I sat down with six children, and as for the rest, they went up halfway along this river, not reaching the end.

This river is beautiful and truly excellent. It was inhabited by the locals of ancient times, since there are the laid stones of building foundations, and a great, vast number of taro patches [kaupapalo'i]. There I bathed in the skin-pinching water of Waikolu [wai iniki ili Waikolu]. I returned with the six children to the shore. My legs were quite sore. I rested there, exhausted, until the group returned at twelve o'clock noon. That was the place where we filled our sagging chests [satisfied our hunger], and once full [maona], we returned home, weary.

—H. K. Kealopali, Kalawao, Damien Home [Damiano Home], Moloka'i, MAY 16, 1894.

Ka Nupepa Kuokoa. 16 JUNE 1894. P. 4.
Na Anoai o ke Panalaau. News from the Colony.

Mr. Editor of the combined *Kuokoa* and *Ko Hawaii Pae Aina.* I have some small bits of news to be sent to you, to publish and report to the public, so that the multitudes of the land see the news of the land greatly feared [aina i kau nui] because of everyone afflicted by the wounds of leprosy, the disease that destroys so many people [ma'i lepera hookae a ka lehulehu], and it is this below.

On Friday evening or Saturday morning, Sam. L. Rosa fought intensely with Kiaipu. They kept rolling around, up and down, until Kiaipu was held down by S. L. Rosa. At that time it was seen that the upper part of Kiaipu's lip had come off. It appeared that S. L. Rosa might have bitten it off, since that part of Kiaipu's lip was not found. However, the reason for the fight was due to intoxication from beer, since that is the liquid to drink here in the colony during these

Pūahi days. Beer making goes from the lofty uplands of Kalawao all the way to Pūahi. There is one phrase in the mouth: "Root beer, root beer [ruke bia, ruke bia]." Due to the excessive quantity of beer, the shipment of sugar to the store of the Board of Health has been consumed within a single week. Twenty bags of sugar were not enough, and if it's not that [beer], it's root beer. This gives a topic to discuss in the sermons at the church that goes by the name New Canaan [Kanaana Hou], since not a single one of these preachers will discuss the Bible, but instead they constantly persist in telling the story of the beer drinkers who do not go to pray, as if the Bible is completely missing.

So when the town lacks beer, the beer factory of the colony was able to supply the town with this kind of root beer [Luka Bia].

Last Monday, June 4, Thos. K. Nathaniel opened a school for young children [kula no na keiki liiliii], and he got seven students, who are the children of the helpers [kokua] of the colony. A large law office [keena loio nui] for Mr. Abraham Kaoliko and Thos. K. Nathaniel [Nakanaela] also opened for all law-related matters.

On Thursday morning, June 5, Kahananui found Nakiaha dead. Kahananui told the news to Simona Kahalehulu, and he went to get some other people. When he found him, he had no clothes. He was in a cookhouse and a banana leaf was the thing covering him in front, with the man sitting doubled up and with a rope fixed around his neck and secured to the wall, and with his back turned toward the wall of the building. But the astonishing thing was, a coroner's inquest [aha koronero] was not convened to determine the cause of this strange death.

Rumors are going around these days that some amusements will be held on the upcoming 11th day of June [Kamehameha Day], such as horse racing, foot races, and so forth. Some new buildings will be built for the Bishop Home. Sincerely, Makaikiu [Māka'ikiu means "Spying-policeman," which may be a pen name]. Kalaupapa, June 7, 1894.

» [The references to root beer are to an alcoholic drink made from the roots of ti (ki) plants. In a report to the Board of Health in 1886, Father Damien noted that when he arrived in 1873, patients "passed their time drinking ki-root beer, home-made alcohol." Dr. Alfred Mouritz included this report in his book *The Path of the Destroyer.*]

Ka Makaainana. 22 OCTOBER 1894. P. 6.
Na Lono Hoohialaai mai ka Panalaau mai o ka Ehaeha. Delightful News from the Colony of Agony.

On September 12, the rose buds [opuu pua rose: poetic name for young girls] were released from the Pauahi Home to head along their path to the forested uplands of the waterfall of Wailē'ia in upper Kalawao. At 9:00 a.m. they left the Pauahi Home and marched along the path to the place mentioned above. The nuns [Makuahine Virigine] were also with them, from the young to the elderly. In the count by the experts of Dr. Goto [Kauka Goto], it seemed that there were approximately sixty of them. The distance from Kalaupapa to Kalawao is a little more than three miles. The nuns and the older women had great speed. They arrived at the Baldwin Home [Balauwina Home], the travelers caught their breath, and there they rested for a time until they went up to Wailē'ia.

This place is upland, a valley like Pauoa [in Honolulu] and such. The 'iwa birds [poetic name for the girls] safely arrived at that upland where fragrance resides. There they smelled the chilly air and the pandanus [hala] trees wafting their fragrance to the youths of the pleasant home of Pauahi. They strung some pandanus flowers, since Kahalaopuna had seen her descendants, and such was the case with Mailelauli'i and company. They had given their affectionate greeting to them, and the various leaves of the forest. While they were relaxing with them, the demigod [kupua] Kūlanihāko'i saw that it was hot, so he released a fine mist of rain [lelehune]. Those youngsters as well as the mothers [makuahine] were completely overcome by the heavy raindrops of the sudden shower. This small expression of affection was found:

Mana overflows with water from billowy clouds [Hoohanini Mana i ka wai opua]
Rippling in the uplands of Wailē'ia. [Hoaleale i ka uka o Waileia]

When the girls returned from the upland, they had been completely drenched by the misty droplets of that upland, but this had not been grieved over by those pretty ones. Those small drizzles of rain were nothing to the uplifted hearts.

On this same day, the youngsters [boys] of the Baldwin Home [Balauwina Home] set out. Their sightseeing trip was to Waikolu, and they always returned with Father Conrardy [Conorade: Father Lambert Louis Conrardy]. They set out before the nuns [Virigine] returned. One small youngster grumbled about his little pail being stepped on. Here was my joke, "Maybe it was the big, fat ulua fish that did it" [malia na ka ulua nui nepunepu], and laughter erupted.

On the 15th of the month, the doctor invited [his young patients], at the pleasure of the hospital, to travel with him to this place where the girls of the Pauahi Home had gone. His rascals accepted, since it was their pleasure, and your writer was another one on this journey. When lunch was over, we headed straight to that solitary upland. We met with the locals [kamaaina] of that upland, Mr. Kamakau and Manua, and took a little break for a time. These locals provided bunches of ripe bananas for Dr. Goto, and we gave thanks. We reached the place where the girls had been and that place passed behind us. We traveled far upland. The boys went to climb mountain apple trees [ohia] by the order of the doctor. We obtained many mountain apples [hua ohia], as well as candlenuts [hua kukui]. There was great admiration in seeing the forest leaves of the uplands, a pleasure to smell. We returned with ferns [palapalai] and ginger [awapuhi] leaves. We smelled the chilly air of that upland, the place where the patients pass the time pleasurably. It is a place often visited these days. The youngsters of the home of health returned to see the heart-snatching water of Japan [wai kaili puuwai o Iapana].

THE JUMBLED TRIALS OF THESE DAYS.
[NA HIHIA HUIKAU O KEIA MAU LA.]

In the final days of last month, Judge W. A. Kukamana arrived to try the cases of the leprosy patient settlement [kahua ma'i lepera], several trivial cases about the patients who went up the cliff of Kala'e to take cattle and sheep and were caught outright by the children of Maea. It was tried, and they received bags of salt [eke paakai: punishment]. The number of people being held is three. They are spending most of their time in dark deafness [Kulina Eleele: poetic phrase for jail]. Your spy [kiu] also heard that they will appeal, by means of their lawyer, Thos. K. Nathaniel [Nakanaela]. If the attorney general approves, then this case will go to the grand jury [Aha Kiure]. As for another boy, he secretly took the fabric of the Chinese and was indeed sprinkled, but not with a great amount of salt, just two partial bags (months).

SEVERAL BANISHED HELPERS. [MAU KOKUA I KIPAKUIA.]

During these same days, a female patient sued her male helper [kane kokua]. The name of this woman is Mrs. Wailua, versus Mr. David Pōʻai, her husband. The cause was her husband being lost to the great dark ulua fish [ulua nui palauli: a new love], and for this reason she became furious and departed from the leaf of the hau tree [lau o ka hau: home].

As the court sat to consider this case, the woman was questioned by the deputy sheriff of the patient settlement [kahua maʻi] and the lawyer of the defendant, the number two fire of Wailuku, W. K. Makakoa. The testimony of the woman and the other witnesses was excellent. The [defense] lawyer made a great effort, but his bait was viewed disfavorably and a skewed punishment was laid down, banishing this helper [kokua] from this land. The Pōʻai boy hastily departed for Honolulu and met with their daughters in the detention station [pa maʻi], who are Misses Annie and Maria Pōʻai. As for their mother, she will never again see the beloved lei that are children. Alas, what a pity! Such was also the case with another helper [kokua], S. W. Kalaeloa. His crime was refusing to work for the Board of Health, and he was banished [hookukeia]. Perhaps it was because he did not pledge allegiance to the republic government [Aupuni Repubalika].

The third of the helpers [kokua], E. J. Crawford (Ilai), was not banished. It was his desire to return to the land [he came from], since he lacked work. He was fired from the store. He lived a long time here in the colony [Panalaau], for many years after his patient. Here he is living without a problem. The wife and child are living here, probably without great trouble. If he gets work outside, then the well-being of his wife will be obtained.

To be continued.

Ka Makaainana. 29 OCTOBER 1894. P. 2.
Na Lono Hoohialaai mai ka Panalaau mai o ka Ehaeha. (Hoopau ana.) Delightful News from the Colony of Agony. (Completion.)
Policeman Assaults Chinese [Makai Pepehi Pake].

One night, in Kawaluna, here in Kalawao, the policeman C. Kopena and his wife went to the place of the Chinese named Akona and asked for beer [bia]. The Chinese gave it and all was well until the officer sat down. At that time this Kopena got up and assaulted the Chinese. The wife saw and ran to get some helpers [kokua]. Some other people saw, four of them, but they could not get him [Kopena] away until the helpers arrived. However, the Chinese got hit by the solid taro of Waikolu [kalopaa o Waikolu: received terrible blows].

But here is the astonishing thing: this policeman made an arrest for brewing beer [hana bia], possessing no document giving the order from the deputy sheriff, A. K. Hutchison, and yet he made the arrest. So the deputy sheriff is instructing him not to repeat those actions without being ordered.

To the policemen with certificates of appointment from the republic [abbreviation of Aupuni Repubalika, the republic government]: do not behave stupidly like this liquor-loving policeman who has bloodied his hands on the Chinese man. This policeman knows all the Chinese, and that thing [liquor] was easily obtained by him. In this action the superintendent was not grateful to him in simply arresting without a warrant. Do not do that again.

The next day, this Chinese appeared before the superintendent and made an official complaint about his injury by the policeman and the taking of small things that disappeared and have not been seen; based on these causes the Chinese made his complaint. According to the prognistication of your spy [kiu], this policeman will not be punished, because he is a nose hair [favorite] and mate [pili aoao] of the judge and the deputy sheriff. It is indeed possible to see the future.

CONCERNING THE DIFFERENT RELIGIONS.
[NO NA HOOMANA LIKE OLE.]

These days the Rev. S. [M.] C. Kealoha is always moving among the Calvinist brethren, searching exhaustively for the sheep [hipa: church members] living here in the patient settlement [kahua maʻi]. And in his search, indeed there are many. They are at the Bishop [Bihopa] and Baldwin [Balauwina] Homes, and here also at the Home of Health [Home o ke Ola]. At those homes, the Catholic faith has been brought in, for that is the desire of those people. On this day that I am writing, five children of Goto's hospital [Haukapila o Goto] have gone to Kalaupapa for an examination, and this Sunday they will enter to be baptized [bapetizo] as brethren.

The sheep who disappeared have been exhaustively searched for; perhaps they total a little over twenty. Such was not the case for Rev. S. Waiwaiʻole. He did not agree to go often to the place of the patients [maʻi]. Perhaps he was scared of getting leprosy [lepera], but such is not at all the case with this new shepherd [kahuhipa hou]. Thank you very much, continue forward with the work. Here too are some brethren returning to the Catholic faith [hoomana Katolika], going to teach at the catechism school [kula Kakekimo]. Thank you indeed. Such is indeed the case with the faith of the Latter-days [hoomana o na La Hope: Latter-day Saints]. If some turn to this religion, that is not a problem. It is up to the one who chooses. The path of righteousness is sought, perhaps meeting with the Lamb of God [Keikihipa a ke Akua], and success is found there.

CONCERNING THE NEW RESERVOIR. [NO KA LUAWAI HOU.]

The reservoir of the colony [Panalaau] is being dug again, being cleaned, and will perhaps be completed in the next few weeks, under the management of the agent of the Board of Health.

CONCERNING THE WATER THAT RELAXES THE BODY.
[NO KA WAI HOOMALULE KINO: LIQUOR.]

In these passing days the water that gives a strange quality to the body is appearing. These activities are arising due the patients [maʻi]. Most of those making bottles of beer [batala bia] are in Kalaupapa. When the children of Kalawao return, you will indeed see friends reeling on horses, with foreign words coming down in pidgin [e iho ana na olelo haole ma ke ano paiai]. Last Wednesday afternoon, some people returned and were right outside the hospital. One from that group did a dance [hula] for the song "Ipo Lei Manu" to every corner of the grounds. Laughter erupted from the companions. The amusements of the Hawaiians are not over. Perhaps it will only be when we are covered over with dirt.

—Lau 'Ōma'oma'o [Green Leaf: probably a pen name]. Kalawao, Moloka'i, OCT. 12, '94.

» [The transition from Hawaiian ('ōlelo Hawai'i) to English ('ōlelo haole) at Kalaupapa began after the overthrow of the Hawaiian monarchy in 1893. This article provides one example of pidgin English ('ōlelo pa'i'ai) in use then in everyday conversation.]

Ka Makaainana. 12 NOVEMBER 1894. P. 3.
Ko Kalaupapa Mau Mea Hou. Your Kalaupapa News.

Here in the colony [panalaau] is a fortune teller [kilokilo]. His vision is able to reveal the obscure secrets done in a hidden place, like the clarity of a looking glass [aniani kilohi]. And due to the vexed state of a patriotic Hawaiian [Hawaii aloha aina] caused by the fame of his name among those who witnessed his actions, he went before that fortune teller to seek word about the queen [Lili'uokalani]. The answer that was received was this: "Concerning the queen, it is almost her time to again sit upon the throne of the Hawaiian kingdom [Aupuni Hawaii], and the waving of the crown flag of Hawai'i in the gentle puff of wind will continue forever." When the patriotic Hawaiian and the entire crowd heard these words, they felt joyful hope, if indeed things truly come to pass in accordance with the fortune teller's prophecy [wanana].

Here in Kalaupapa are two croquet teams [hui koloke]. One is an old team and the other is a new team. The new team is named "Kīki'ipau" and the old team is "Ha'ikeau." The Kīki'ipau team boasts greatly about their skill, and such is also the case with the other team. There is much contention between these teams, and it has been rumored that they will compete one day in the future to snatch the honor of victory from the other.

—Linahome Vila. Kalaupapa, Moloka'i.

Ka Nupepa Kuokoa. 24 NOVEMBER 1894. P. 2.
Huakai a ka Papa Ola i ke Kahua Ma'i Lepera o Molokai. Visit of the Board of Health to the Leprosy Settlement of Moloka'i.

The Board of Health hired the steamship *Ke Au Hou* for the journey of the members of the board to officially see in person the state of the leprosy settlement [kahua ma'i lepera] on Moloka'i. And at nine o'clock at night on November 16, this brand-new steamship actually voyaged to the patient settlement [kahua ma'i].

Here are the members of the Board of Health who went on this journey: W. O. Smith, president; members F. R. Day, M.D., C. B. Wood, M.D., J. T. Waterhouse Jr., John Ena, T. F. Lansing, C. B. Reynolds, executive officer, and Mr. McVeigh, local supervisor for the Board of Health. Besides this was Interior Minister J. A. King, the government doctors Weddick, Raymond, McGettigan, and Murray, the consul for Great Britain A. G. S. Hawes, Bishop Willis, Rev. O. P. Emerson, Rev. J. Wai'ama'u, Rev. Father Leonore [Father Leonor Fouesnel], A. M. Brown, W. L. Wilcox, J. W. Girvin, W. N. Armstrong, Godfry Brown, C. D. Chase, Mrs. Bowen, Mrs. Clark, the Misses Jones, Ena, and Cook, and some other people.

When the brand-new steamship left from the wharf of the company, it traveled along to exit the harbor, and just below the lighthouse, its bow went off course, went into the sand and ran aground. The wheel attempted to turn backwards, but it did not get loose. The *Hilaka* [an alternate spelling of Hi'iaka] was sent to help, and with it pulling, they got free at a little after ten o'clock and traveled to Moloka'i after determining that no damage had been sustained by the steamship.

Sometime after four o'clock, in the predawn purple morning, after voyaging calmly, the lights on the shore of the colony [Panalaau] were seen glimmering, and not long after, the anchor was released. The passengers were fed in the predawn glow, and only when it was morning, perhaps seven o'clock, the party was carried from aboard the steamship to the shore.

Upon going ashore, people were swarming, and the band made a joyful display of playing songs. Among these swaying tunes was the song "God Save Queen Victoria," as an expression of affection to the consul for Great Britain, Hawes, since he was in the party. Superintendent Meyer and Deputy Sheriff Hitchcock [Hikikoki] had already arrived from Kala'e and were standing together at the harbor, ready to warmly embrace the visitors. Some folks scattered off to several places, the Revs. O. P. Emerson and J. Wai'ama'u to the place of Rev. M. C. Kealoha, and Bishop Willis to the place of the English mission [misiona Enelani]. There they received horses to go for a sightseeing ride in the colony [Panalaau] that belonged to agony before, but is now a land flowing with milk and honey [aina e kahe ana ka waiu a me ka meli].

The house of the superintendent was visited, and the Bishop Home for girls, the total being perhaps 107 at this time, under the Roman Catholic nuns [Virigini Katolika Roma], and it was found to be fine and simply clean. From there, the two brand-new round reservoirs [luawai poepoe hou loa] were examined that were just constructed at the high point between Kalaupapa and Kalawao; fifty feet is the diameter for one and thirty for the other, with the depth being ten feet for each. Stones were laid and plastered [hamo puna] in a truly solid way so as to lengthen the time they stand.

The place where the medical workers of Dr. Goto provide treatment to cure leprosy with the kind of medicine that he has bragged will provide a cure was examined. While the disease has indeed eased somewhat, recovery that is permanently successful has not been verified at this time. The amount of expenditures for this thing that is being tried have been excessive, but what is wrong [with spending money] for the search to find a little drop of recovery for the one who has that disease that has thwarted the medical knowledge of the entire world?

The clean and comfortable buildings of the Baldwin Home [Home Baluawina] for boys were visited and seen in person. They were built upon a site with three or four acres of land, below the foot of the mountain and suitable for the things desired. It was a gift presented by the generous heart of Mr. H. P. Baldwin [Balauwina] for a total of $5,000. Here is this house under the care of three nuns [Virigini Katolika], assisted by Mr. W. Dutton [Joseph Dutton].

Upon returning from Kalawao to Kalaupapa, the party visited and saw the Britannia Hall [Hale Beretania], a place for people to relax, and the new building built under the expenditures of Mr. G. N. Wilcox [Wilikoki].

The doctors of the Board of Health carefully examined several leprosy patients [maʻi lepera] that afternoon.

Right after, the party had a meal at the place of the Board of Health, made with food carried from aboard the steamship, with tunes also being played during the meal by the band of the leprosy settlement [kahua maʻi lepera]. The president of the Board of Health and the interior minister held a conference with the people holding land titles in Kalaupapa, which are the only lands that have not been transferred to the government. They are desired to be permanently transferred because these title holders have caused great problems for the work of the board by hosting the friends of the leprosy patients [maʻi lepera] at these properties, who come to simply break the rules. So a commissioner was appointed earlier to decide the true value of the few properties that remain. The government has just surveyed several land parcels in Kaluaʻaha [Molokaʻi], whose size are like that of the properties in Kalaupapa, and they have been provided for a land swap, with the board transporting for free these title owners and their baggage to the new place where they will be separated to. All these things were explained to the title holders with the display of pictures of the new land and also providing sixty days for them to consider and then respond. This giving of lands by the government is clearly understood to not be closed-fisted or stingy.

After three oʻclock in the evening, the party prepared to return aboard the steamship with the band again playing tunes until all the party had been carried.

Looking at the state of Kalaupapa today, it has a different quality from that of Kalaupapa in days past, in the fine quality of the arrangement of the houses, the cleanliness of the conditions and all the things that bring comfort to the quality of life for the patients [maʻi]. So they do not have ill thoughts and complain about not being properly cared for by the people filled with compassion and the exceedingly kind hearts of certain individuals that have again supplemented the comforts and fine things that make life enjoyable.

At four oʻclock in the evening, the anchor of the steamship was hauled up, and the bow turned toward Honolulu, where they arrived at nine oʻclock on Saturday night.

Ka Makaainana. 9 SEPTEMBER 1895. P. 6.
Ninau Kanawai No Kalawao. Legal Question concerning Kalawao.

Mr. Editor: On August 12, four women afflicted with leprosy [maʻi lepera] were arrested outside the boundaries that the law maintains for them, and on the 15th of that same month, one of those women was arrested again at that same place, due to the urge of love in her heart to go and see the one that she greatly desires, a man. The court of W. A. Kukamana sat to hear their case, under the charge of "leaving the leprosy settlement" [haalele i ke kahua maʻi lepera], and they were punished with $5 and $1 fines. As for the woman with two charges, her punishment was $10 and $5 fines. The two charges were entered into the same summons. And so I ask the honorable gentlemen of the republic [Aupuni Repubalika], "Was it correct to enter two charges into the same summons, since it was the same person?" If the action of the judge of the island of Moloka'i was correct, then excuse me for this thing. However, if it was not correct, then the government should teach him again about some matters.

I will not say that he has no knowledge of the law, but he is an obvious boot-lick [hoopilimeaai] to the superintendent of the colony [Luna Nui o ka Pana-laau]. There are a great many wise people here on Moloka'i, and so how was the man with a rather heavy head [poo ano kaumaha] placed in this position? This is not to belittle his name, but it is desired to clearly see the thing that was done, if he acted in accordance with his desire. It was suitable for Kānewa'ali'i to be placed as judge for that district. If he decides to punish, the back is smacked with the rise and fall of the pickaxe [hard labor] with no compassion in the staring eyes.

The reason these people left the patient settlement [kahua ma'i] was the great love for their men. The dark nights and steep trails [alanui nihinihi] of this burdensome land [aina hooluhi] became as nothing. Here they are working off their punishment in agony.

—S. K. Waipi'i. Kalaupapa, Moloka'i.

Ka Makaainana. 9 SEPTEMBER 1895. P. 8.
Kela A Me Keia. This and That.

On the warship *Olympia* [*Olimepia*], the wind instruments for the band [ohe o ka puali puhiohe] of the leprosy settlement of Kalaupapa [kahua ma'i lepera o Kalaupapa] arrived.

Ka Nupepa Kuokoa. 28 SEPTEMBER 1895. P. 3.
Ka Huakai i ke Panalaau o na Mai. Journey to the Colony of the Leprosy Patients.

On the journey that Rev. C. M. Hyde, D.D., undertook to the leprosy colony of Moloka'i [Panalaau Mai Lepera o Molokai] in this past month of August, he returned with several quite valuable memories from his visitation in person that we have brought forth below:

The lands of Kalaupapa and Kalawao were set aside by the Hawaiian king-dom [Aupuni Hawaii] in the year 1866 to accept leprosy patients [mai lepera], and there they would reign [nohoalii]. The size of these lands of Kalaupapa and Kalawao is about 3,800 acres.

Only a small part of the colony [Panalaau] is the place where buildings have been constructed, which is that part of the land that is a half-mile wide, lying along the base of the line of cliffs [laina pali]. Of these buildings, 178 are owned by the Board of Health and 231 are owned by the patients. They have been laid out with attention being paid to roads as well, unlike the usual nature of hu-man settlements. The nature of the house is the same as that of Honolulu and other places, with a veranda [lanai] in front, two rooms, and verandas in the back that have been enclosed with screens to get two more rooms. The major-ity of them have been plastered [hamo puna]. By the small yards surrounding the houses the nature of the one living in the house can be known. Someone's [yard] will be fine and attractive, someone else's will simply be left in an unin-teresting state, and that of another will seem as if it has not been cared for at all.

Some have flower gardens, fruit trees, and vines, making them seem like the people are accustomed to a state of cleanliness and pleasant appearance.

The lay of the land is a kind of half-circle joined to the wall of high cliffs [paia pali kiekie] that give shade. The spread seems to be two and a half miles from east to west, and perhaps that much from north to south. Bermuda grass [mānienie] grows upon the places not surrounded by yards, supplying the fine pasture land that supports the 758 head of cattle owned by the Board of Health and 694 horses and mules; within that number, the Board of Health owns 75.

Kalaupapa and Kalawao each have churches for the Protestant and Roman Catholic faiths, and there is one Mormon meeting house [hale halawai Moremona] in Kalaupapa. There are 145 brethren of the Protestant congregation in the two churches, but there are more than double that number of brethren who have not agreed to be released from their congregations. Eighty is the average number of people who regularly attend the Sunday school in Kalaupapa, and 125 people regularly attend the morning prayer service, and perhaps half of that number in Kalawao.

There are only 92 uninfected, able-bodied people living in the colony. There are 46 uninfected children living with their parents. There are 96 boys living in the Baldwin Home [Home Balawina] in Kalawao and 114 girls in the Pauahi Home [Home Pauahi]. The total number of patients at the time of this visit (August 1895) is 451 women and 619 men. Within this number, there are three British, four Germans, five Americans, seven Portuguese, 21 Chinese, and two of other ethnicities, and the rest are only Hawaiian.

There have been 4,904 patients brought to the colony from the beginning of the isolation on Moloka'i, over twenty-eight years, averaging 174 annually; 3,191 have died within that time, and 247 have been released for being uninfected.

The *Mokolii* is the steamship that regularly transports letter bags, food, and other cargo every week.

The leprosy patients [mai lepera] are given each week twenty-one pounds of cooked taro [paiai] (or eight and a half pounds of crackers and one pound of sugar, or nine pounds of rice, or twelve and one-fourth pounds of flour), a half pound of soap, one and one-fourth pounds of salt, one pack of matches, one half pint of kerosene, seven pounds of beef or five pounds of salmon, plus ten dollars per year given by the government for buying clothes, and so forth. The expenditures by the government are a truly large appropriation in the biannual appropriations bill. The annual expense according to what was seen in the appropriations bill submitted on March 31, 1894, is $88,210. The annual expense for one boy at the Baldwin Home is $69; that for one girl at the Pauahi Home is $78.

In the past two years fourteen outsiders who trespassed into the colony were caught and punished, and six leprosy patients [mea mai lepera] tried to escape. It is a great labor to forcefully keep the Hawaiians [poe kanaka] out of the settlement of the colony. Some of them are not infected people. They are people tired of working for themselves who tried to actually push themselves into being recorded in the number of the leprosy patients [poe mai lepera] in order to receive the food allotment that the government maintains every week.

The attempt by a patient to escape from the colony by sea has many dangers because here the land simply lies in the path of the northerly winds [makani akau], and sailing the channels to the other islands has many problems that one does not dare to challenge. The narrow trail [alanui olowi] going up the cliff is another of the paths that some do not dare to go on. The letter carrier and his horse bring the mail every Tuesday from Kaunakakai, and every Friday the letters being sent to the outside are taken from the colony. There is no problem with the trail that goes down below the cliff. The ridge of tall cliffs that stand in a line on northern Moloka'i do not have hard stone, but instead are dirt. A jagged trail has been carved out, three to six feet wide at the steep parts of the cliff, and it is continually worked on to keep it in good condition. However, you will soon be short of breath if you are on that narrow cliff trail and look down the cliff, two thousand feet from the top down to the bottom at the shore. Two years have passed since the letter carrier [hali leta] was on this cliff trail and a rock rolled down, hitting his head and killing him. In times of constant calm, there is no problem in coming down.

(To be continued.)

Ka Makaainana. 14 OCTOBER 1895. P. 8.
Kela A Me Keia. This and That.
The *Likelike* took fifty leprosy patients [ma'i lepera] to Moloka'i last Friday. The great majority of them were men.

Ka Makaainana. 23 DECEMBER 1895. P. 8.
Kalaupapa, Moloka'i, December 19, 11:00 a.m., Miss Lahapa Kiliona, younger sister of the wife of the deputy sheriff, A. Kauhi of the silent-voiced sea creature [ka Ia Hamauleo], left this life in her fifteenth year. The disease that separates families [ma'i hookaawale ohana: leprosy] took her to die in that unfamiliar land [aina malihini]. How pitiful for her!
» [The "silent-voiced sea creatures" were the oysters in Pearl Harbor. This poetic phrase was an epithet for the 'Ewa District of O'ahu.]

Ke Aloha Aina. 12 SEPTEMBER 1896. P. 7.
Na Palapala. Ka Leo Walohia O Na Ma'i Lepera. Letters. The Pitiful Call of the Leprosy Patients.
Mr. Editor. Greetings to you:
Please allow me some available column space of your newspaper. On August 21, the leprosy patients [ma'i lepera] chose a committee, W. K. Makakoa, J. A. Kamanu, and Josiah Haole, who will report to the Board of Health about the spoiled state of the cooked taro [pai ai] supplied to this leprosy settlement [Kahua Mai Lepera] from the Taro Farming Company [Hui Hana Mahiai Kalo] of Wailuku, Maui. There are two categories of color for the cooked taro. One part is fine, and the other is spoiled and foul-smelling, which we cannot eat, but perhaps those of Wailuku believe that our affliction and transformation into victims of leprosy [ma'i lepera] is a reason to feed us that foul-smelling cooked taro, the kind of food suitable for pigs, not for us. It is better for the leprosy patients [ma'i lepera] to be slaughtered than to have it happen by being fed bitter and foul-smelling food. It should be remembered that the government is paying the producer of the food with good money. The food producer should reciprocate with good food, and thus will the two sides become equal in

comparison. The committee submitted their response to the Board of Health, and what will they feed us so that we survive?

The premier [helu ekahi: number one] cooked taro that was supplied to this leprosy settlement [kahua maʻi lepera] two months ago was from some Hawaiians, A. P. Kapaehaole and M. Kāne, from Hālawa, Molokaʻi, and that was where my love swelled up for Hālawa, due to the sticky poi that settles nicely down the throat.

My greeting of deeply felt love to the typesetting boys for this spring of the summer. May Hawaiʻi live forever. [E ola o Hawaii a mau loa.]

Yours Truly, Jno. S. Kawailana. Papaloa, Kalaupapa, Molokaʻi, SEPTEMBER 4, 1896.

Ka Nupepa Kuokoa. 12 FEBRUARY 1897. P. 4.
Na Mea Hou O Ke Kahua Mai Lepera. News from the Leprosy Settlement.

Mr. Editor: I swiftly send to you our rather significant news of these days for the benefit of the friends and loved ones reading the Greatest Prize of the Hawaiian People [slogan of *Ka Nupepa Kuokoa*].

These are blustery days as the sea continually offers up praises at every place of this entire side of Molokaʻi, beginning on Friday of last week.

For those who have seen and are familiar with the harbor of Kalaupapa at the place where the anchors of ships are released, it is a place where enormous waves [nalu nunui] crash terribly these days. It has been six years since the last time I saw this kind of storm until this year, when it has just been seen again.

The winds also blow during this time of stormy seas, as if they have agreed to demolish or drown this paradise in the belly of the deep blue sea, and for the leprosy patients [mai lepera] to be left without the food from Maui and the other things from Honolulu. The darkening cloud of a food shortage and clear famine will strike if these two rascals continue to behave in that way for one or two more weeks.

The leprosy patients [mai lepera] greatly enjoy at this time the clothes and gifted hats that the Caucasian friends [hoaloha haole] of Honolulu sent, that this pen tip requested for the benefit of those who should be given aid. If the regular way of going about is just like the enjoyment of the gift, with steadfastness in acts of faith, then the sea will simply be still, and the wind calm, when the eyes glance upwards.

On Wednesday evening, the steamship *Mokolii* was seen by those of Kalawao steadfastly pushing through the storm until coming upon the eastern side of the islet of Mōkapu, which [on Oʻahu] is [also called] "Rabit Island" [*sic*] by those Caucasians [poe haole] who secretly unloaded the weapons of 1893. That is where it stayed anchored until that night turned to day. Yesterday morning it left that islet and went back, the bow toward Maui and then Honolulu. Usually if it is stormy everywhere, the ship can still deposit the food at Pāpio Point [Lae o Papio] at the harbor of Waikolu [awa o Waikolu], but during this storm, it was not possible; "Maui is indeed the best" [O Maui no e ka oi].

These days the patients are beginning to bathe in the new Japanese wooden bathhouse [hale auau laau Kepani] that the Board of Health just built for those in Kalaupapa. The bathtubs are beautiful, as well as are the laying of the pipes that heat the medicinal bathing salts. The thing that is criticized and often complained about is that this bathhouse has no place to sit. When clothing is removed and when the bathing is done, there is no place to put clothes, hats, and so forth within the walls of this bathhouse. People have often talked about this thing to me, and I have talked about this thing to the doctor, and it might be done.

There are three days when the men bathe each week, and three for the women, until this day when the coal has completely crumbled. These days have nothing until the harbor stops being stormy, and then coal will be received on the *Mokolii*.

The new beef distribution center [hale haawi pipi hou] here in Kalaupapa has been completed, a large and beautiful building, and if the beef distribution supervisor [Luna Haawi Pipi] cannot do something to end the shoving and the fighting of the patients, then tossing the money of the public for suitable buildings like this has been a complete waste, and the way everyone receives the meat allotment will still be terrible, receiving beef and salmon through shoving.

In the months of June and July, the construction of the new (Congregational) church here in Kalaupapa will begin. The anticipated cost for this bethel is $5,000, besides the suitable lumber and other things of the old church still standing. All of the devout from Hawai'i to Ni'ihau will be made joyful when they see this great work raised up under the direction of the Holy Ghost, of those stricken and burdened with the many wounds of leprosy, without the burdening of the congregations all across the Islands [Paeaina].

This very week I received a letter from Hon. H. P. Baldwin of Maui, about him giving me assistance for this great labor of our beloved Lord who was crucified on the cross.

I have spent a long time greatly desiring that this building be constructed, but my desire was obstructed by my friends due to error and the improper administration of these congregations by the ministers who have died and Rev. M. C. Kealoha, who was released to the place he went.

At this time when Rev. D. Ka'ai serves as minister, winter had ended, and here in the summer are the labors moving forward. For the things that remain, until next week.

With delight, J. A. Kamanu. Kalaupapa, Moloka'i. JAN. 29, 1897.

» [In paragraph six the writer notes that the name of the islet Mōkapu also appears on O'ahu. However, he says the Hawaiian name of Rabbit Island on windward O'ahu is Mōkapu, but the correct name of the island is Mānana. Mōkapu is the peninsula north of Mānana that forms one end of Kane'ohe Bay.

The incident he is referencing took place on Rabbit Island after the overthrow of Queen Lili'uokalani in 1893. Robert Wilcox and other royalists plotted to restore the queen to her throne, and their preparations included landing a secret shipment of arms and ammunition from San Francisco on Rabbit Island.]

Ka Makaainana. 1 MARCH 1897. P. 1.
Hoalohaloha no Iosia Haole. Letter of Condolence concerning Iosia [Josiah] Haole

It has often struck the ear,
The call for those of this world,

"You are dust from there
There you shall return"
Alas for our death!
Where will there be shelter?
Is there not a new life,
An everlasting life for us all?

—[By] Mrs. L. Kauwilaokalani, greatly beloved daughter of our brother in
the Lord Jesus Christ.

Papa Iosia Haole passed in the predawn purple morning [kakahiaka poni-
poni] of the Sabbath, February 14, at seven o'clock, from this agonizing land of
the colony [aina ehaeha aku o ka Panalaau], and from the presence of us, his
sisters, and the loved ones, his friends on this side of the black river of death
[muliwai eleele o ka Make].

Alas! Alas!! How tragic.

We are the Women's Christian Endeavor Society of the Congregation of
Kalaupapa [Hui Wahine Imi Pono Karistiano o ka Ekalesia o Kalaupapa],
Moloka'i, through our committee. And we have been afflicted by grief, by
sorrow, due to the passing of the soul, the companion of the body, from your
dearly beloved Papa, a strong worker with energy for the works of the Lord in
this congregation, working together with us until he passed away with unyield-
ing faith.

His work here is done, the burden is released, and dust returns to dust, and
the soul returns to the one who gave it. Such agonizing grief!

Those reasons, and many other reasons, have induced us to assemble, with
grief and mournful thoughts, to resolve these things below:

One. We enter together with you into sorrow and grief, sharing the burden
of agonies for your father who passed away with love;

Two. We ask the Heavenly Power to ease you;

Three. We pray to the Father of all Fathers to care for you, and guard you
with his loving protection, on the road that is best for your existence in this
world, and the good paths in his name.

May the protection of the Lord be with you. Affectionate greetings. We are
with humility Mrs. S. Pa'alua Ka'ai, Mrs. Lale Kainuwai, Mrs. Salome Kamakahiki. Done on this day of FEBRUARY 25, A.D. 1897.

Ka Makaainana. 22 MARCH 1897. P. 6.
Hoi ka Lepo i ka Lepo. Dust Returns to Dust.

Mrs. Rose Pi'ilani, from the Kūkalahale Rain of Honolulu, died here in
Kalaupapa on Friday, February 26. She suffered from chronic illness for a long
time, and the ailment that emaciated the body was in the heart. She was a
member of the Protestant church of Kalaupapa [Ekalesia Hoolepope o Kalau-
papa], a Sunday school teacher for the younger children of the Sunday school
of Kalaupapa [Na Pokii o ke Kula Sabati o Kalaupapa], and a member of the
Young People's Christian Endeavor Society of Kalaupapa [Ahahui Opio Imi
Pono Karistiano o Kalaupapa]. She sang for the last time with her brethren in
that final time of hers, and it was that song,

"My dear land of birth,
For you I sing."

After that, they all prayed three times. After the prayer, she slept. Her service was held at the YMCA of Kalaupapa on February 27, 10:00 a.m. The Rev. D. Kaʻai performed the service. The final speech was by the Sunday school master, the Rev. S. K. Kamakahiki, and then she was returned to lie within the cemetery of pale sand at Papaloa [ilina one puakea o Papaloa]. The Sunday school master performed the service there until dust covered dust. Simply sorrowful.

Between the hours of 8:00 and 9:00 p.m. on March 3, J. H. Kawainui died. He was from the ʻĀpaʻapaʻa wind of Kohala, from the hills ʻŌpili and Kalāhikiola that travel as a pair in the uplands. He was a wind-watching native of Kohala, the cherished land, from outer Kohala [Kohala-waho] to inner Kohala [Kohala-loko]. The bones of the travelers are left in the unfamiliar land of agony [waiho na iwi o kamahele i ka aina malihini a ka ehaeha]. The days of suffering from illness were not long, and then he went to the spirit land [aina uhane].

His multitudes simply grieve upon seeing this swift robbery of his life, residing in Kohala, the land and the district of Hawaiʻi spoken of in the riddle, "My father, Hāmākua; my leihala [lei of pandanus keys], Kohala. The soul passes, the companion of the body."

—Hoaʻloha [Friend: perhaps a pen name]. Kalaupapa, Molokaʻi, MARCH 4, 1897.

Ke Aloha Aina. 5 JUNE 1897. P. 1.
Ka Huakai Malihini I Ka Aina O Ka Ehaeha. Ike Kumaka i ka Nohoʻna o ka Aina i Weli Nuiia. Kakauia no Ke Aloha Aina. The Journey as Visitors to the Land of Agony. Seeing Firsthand the Way of Life in the Land that Is Greatly Feared. Written for *Ke Aloha Aina.*

Right after ten oʻclock at night on Thursday, May 27, the voyage of the Board of Health departed from the wharf where the *Iwa* [abbreviation of *Iwalani*] was anchored, with the companions on this voyage being the president of the Board, W. O. Smith [Kamika], the members N. B. Emerson [Emekona], C. A. Brown [Baraunu], and D. L. Keliʻipiʻo, the doctors aboard the warships [mokukaua] *Philadelphia, Marion,* and *Naniwa,* and the circle of newspaper writers, and there were only two writers from Hawaiian-language newspapers [nupepa Hawaii], which were those of *Ke Aloha Aina* and *Ke Aloha Aina Oiaio.*

When we departed from the harbor of Kou [awa o Kou: Honolulu Harbor], the ocean was still and completely calm, and suddenly the *Iwalani* was moving along calmly upon the surface of the ocean like a tub treading upon the swells of the sea. Thusly we traveled calmly until ʻĪlio Point [Kalae o ka Ilio] passed by us, when the voyage of the ship was finally intensified.

While the early light of dawn was glowing faintly, suddenly the white sea foam [kuakea] on the shore of Kalaupapa was seen with the wooden houses, and it looked like a real town. The mist was creeping upon the cliffs, the gentle movement like the rising of smoke.

At five oʻclock or so, the anchor clattered into the harbor of Kalaupapa, and that was when the harbor on shore was clearly seen, made white with sea foam by the waves [kuakea mai i na nalu], and the hesitant voice of the president of the Board of Health was clearly heard, saying how it was unsuitable to go ashore in the harbor.

At this time, the thoughts of everyone were made uncertain, waiting and not knowing whether we would go ashore or not. However, while I was sitting sullenly, I heard the call of the ship's officers and the rowers of the skiffs [poe hoe waapa] announcing that it was indeed possible to go ashore.

This was when the skiffs were seen being released on the side of the ship, and it was six o'clock in the morning. This was when the president of the Board of Health and four other people got on board to go and clearly examine the situation that would allow them to disembark onto land.

They floated straight onto shore in the harbor. This was when the melody of the silver flutes of the band of Kalaupapa was heard, like a voice of greeting calling to us, "Come ashore on land. There is no trouble in the harbor. The kindness of the heavens has given you permission." It was true. The skiff went ashore with true ease without anyone being soaked by the sea spray being sprinkled about at the base of the cliff.

And this was when the second skiff went out. With the final skiff I went ashore on land as I heard the tunes that the government band played here, made into a joyous sound by them that was also touching. I saw the wharf completely covered by people.

Upon going ashore on land, it pleased the president of the Board of Health, W. O. Smith, to introduce me before the superintendent, A. Hutchinson [Ambrose Hutchison], in my role as writer for the newspaper *Ke Aloha Aina,* and from there I went to the home of my Papa.

At this place I rested a little for a bit to eat the things prepared by the family within a short time.

When the sagging chest [hunger] had been completely sated, I and my dear Papa left his home on horses. Our journey went straight along behind the party of the Board of Health to the Pauahi Home, the place where there are seventy girls and fifty-four adult women living under the protection of the nuns [makuahine vilikina].

Their residence was divided into fourteen houses, ten to each house. In appearance, the state of their lifestyle was truly clean. These houses are quite low, with a length similar to schoolhouses.

At this place I felt compassion swell up within me, upon seeing the features of some for whom the severity of the disease affecting their bodies was too great to allow hope for their future recovery. The way that the destructive action of this disease has been portioned out upon us is extremely tragic.

For others, it was as if they were not infected, their features fine in appearance. Some of them were suitable to be released, and some others had a partial infection, and such was the status of infection for everyone in this Home of Pauahi [Home o Pauahi] cared for by the patient nuns [makuahine ahonui].

We went to take a look around in the yard of this home. It was beautiful and clean to see, with dark green plants adorning the interior of that yard.

When we were done visiting this place, with the mind entranced, we mounted the horses and our journey went straight along with the members of the Board of Health with Kalawao the goal. It was 8:45 in the morning.

Glancing about everywhere along the road, it was completely full of buildings. The cliff stood like nourishment for kites [lupe] on the southeastern side of our path to Kalawao, and the horses carried us gracefully as our minds were truly entranced.

At 9:20, we arrived in Kalawao at the home called the Baldwin Home [Balauwina Home], the place where there are 124 young boys, as well as adults not included in that number.

When we went into a room, we found 14 infected boys with brass horns. They played beautifully and their musical sounds were quite touching.

Their features had been expanded by the disease, but the astonishing thing was the excellence of their playing, under the direction of their young teacher, James Keohokalole. The president of the Board of Health gave some uplifting words to them, and those words can certainly be admired.

The only thing to be criticized is that the Board of Health does not set aside a different place for those with clean features to live, and the same for those whose condition is quite serious.

Perhaps the Board of Health will perform this work of compassion in the future. It is something for which their vigilance will be admired and not turn away the admiration of them, along with the searches for things that will provide respite to the troubled people there.

These boys have only been instructed in playing instruments for six months. They seem truly skilled, while their teacher was not actually taught by someone skilled, but just caught on quickly and thus gained proficiency.

We departed Kalawao for the famous hill [puu kaulana] Kauhakō, the location of that lake [luawai] that Pele dug. It has a depth of no less than eight hundred feet. We simply gazed at it, while also seeing the flat spread [kahela] of the land with an appearance that was truly beautiful.

We left that place and arrived at the place of J. T. Unea. We relaxed a bit there for a time and then went along to 'Īliopi'i, and from there to Papaloa, the place where we found the writer of *Ke Aloha Aina Oiaio* eating like a pig. His generosity spread forth, but because we were quite congested with the cargo of the food repository, we could not fill it again. We left him eating heartily of the rich food of Ka-Pu'ukolu [Kapu'ukolu on Kaua'i was famous for abundance].

We visited the leisure home for guests [home hooluana a ka malihini], examining and looking around that place. It was quite beautiful.

We left that place for Britannia Hall [Beritania Hale]. This is a place where the patients can pass the time, like the YMCA here in Honolulu, with some books to read, a place for billiards, and so forth. It is also a place set apart for times when there are concerts and so on.

And according to the words of the one who cares for that home, he made an invitation to us all: if you have spare books or newspapers, send them for the library of that home, and such is also the case for old newspapers. So please, friends, send them there.

We left that place for the place where patients were treated by Dr. Goto. This is two buildings. The building where the medicine is boiled is different, and the medicated water that has been heated is carried in pipes until it goes into six tubs of bath water [tabu wai auau].

Within one building are two rooms, and that is where these six tubs are, three tubs in each room. Here on the 'Ewa [west] side is the place where three tubs are, the place where those with an extremely severe illness bathe.

The temperature of the water is increased to 125 degrees, a heat that makes the entire body fragile, and probably the only reason they survive is because it is mixed with the medicated water.

These tubs are for the extremely ill [poe ma'i loa]. Sulfur [kukaepele] is mixed with the medicated water in one tub, and this is for the terribly ill. When they get in, they do not feel the heat. It is done that way until they feel the heat, and then they move to a different tub, and so it goes until they reach the tub for those with a quite mild illness. The days when the men and women bathe are separated.

For those with a mild illness, they bathe in a different room, and such is also true of those who are only a little bit infected. Their medicated water is heated to 75 degrees at the lowest. This is a great benefit received by the patients if the body is cared for properly, and a great disaster if care is not taken.

There is only one kind of medicine in this colony of agony [Panalaau o ka Ehaeha]. There is nothing beyond this that can be used for treatment, so the placement of another doctor in that place, doing nothing, is a consumption of the earnings of the government, more so than the president of the Hawaiian republic [Repubalika Hawaii], the one that I speak of, a waste of money by the government and a burden upon the people.

We departed from that place for the YMCA. This is a long building, and a place of leisure for the patients to read books in.

There are three kinds of religion in this place, and their strengths are equal. They are Catholicism, Mormonism, and Calvinism [ke Katolika, ka Moremona a me ke Kalavina].

There is a courthouse [hale hookolokolo] in this place, and I visited to see the nature of the work there, as well as the jail.

The number of patients in this leprosy settlement [kahua ma'i lepera] is 1,110, and besides them there are between 300 and 400 helpers [poe kokua] living there with their patients.

The Board of Health does a good job of providing food, clothing, and so forth, and the only thing that remains is the other medicines that can be used for treatment to provide long life. It is a land filled with joy, but this has become a thing of no significance to some, since they are remembering the loved ones that they left behind. For this reason, the steepness of the tall cliffs [nihinihi o na pali kiekie] became a mere trifle to them, as they escaped due to love of family.

One great blunder of the Board of Health is simply forcing patients into places not suitable for them to live, so that the manner of habitation is all mixed up, and some actions have arisen to bring unrest to the fine way of life of some people.

For those who own their own houses, they have no problem, since the Board of Health cannot simply insert patients into those places. This is the great problem for the patients being sent to Moloka'i, and there is a great need for the Board of Health to expand with new houses, so these people are not troubled.

We departed this place because John Unea invited us to his own house, the place where your writer ate heartily of the rich food of Ka-Puʻukolu. I ate until nauseated [lihaliha] of the foods prepared by the kindness of that native son [keiki kupa] of the Kanilehua Rain [Ua Kanilehua: an epithet for Hilo], and for him is my boundless gratitude.

And there I spent my final minutes looking upon the beloved features of my Papa, appearing before me until vanishing like a hallucination. It was several minutes of nausea [nalua] and agony of the mind, while the seconds of time constantly pushed forward in the wait for the sound of the bell of the *Iwalani*.

Right at four o'clock the first bell sounded, and that was indeed when we embraced for the last time with tears of true love for my father upon my cheeks, the thing that I could not guard against.

I shared a final handshake with the adopted family of my father and the friends of the unfamiliar land [aina malihini], and boarded the skiff to go to the deck of the *Iwalani*. At 5:30 we departed the harbor of Kalaupapa for Honolulu, and right at eleven o'clock at night we reached the wharf and went home.

Ke Aloha Aina. SEPTEMBER 18, 1897. P. 6.
Na Hoohiwahiwa La Hanau O Ka Moiwahine Liliuokalani Ma Ke Kahua Maʻi Lepera. The Festivities for the Birthday of Queen Liliʻuokalani in the Leprosy Settlement.

According to the announcement by the president of the Patriotic League of the Leprosy Settlement [Ahahui Aloha Aina o ke Kahua mai lepera], Mr. Robert M. Kaaoao, he had requested the kindness of several suitable gentlemen within the patient settlement, in discussing with him about holding festivities for the birthday of the queen that the people greatly adore. The president appointed them as committee members for requesting several kinds of assistance from the public, and their names are as follows:

Aluna Smith, L. B. Wahinalo, J. M. Spencer, J. Punilio, G. K. Kahelekukona, Job Kahiea, James Harvest, and Simon Kapaheʻe. With great energy, they completed the work with a unified desire and received olive leaves of love from the multitude of royalist [makaainana aloha alii] and patriotic [aloha aina] citizens in the amount of $52.35.

At their meeting held at the place of the president, Kalaupapa, careful consideration was made about the sufficient ability to hold a motherly feast [paina ai makuahine], but after the committee's deliberation, it was decided that this meal of light refreshments [paina o na mea ai mama] would be held, like drinking coffee at the coffeehouses [hale inu kope] of W. G. [F.] Feary in Kalaupapa and Roth Halt in Kalawao. It was truly carried out in that way on the day desired for this event, the 2nd day of September.

When the aforementioned day arrived, several events were also held in accordance with what is shown on the schedule of events of the day below, as follows:

Light Refreshments [Paina Mama]. 11:00 a.m. until 2:00 p.m.
Religious Service Thanking God [Halawai Haipule Hoalohaloha i ke Akua], by
the patriots, at 12:30 under the shelter of the veranda [lanai] where food is given, due to the refusal of the request by the president to the Protestant church of Kalaupapa to hold the Religious Service Thanking God celebrating the day of the One that the people love so deeply, which forced the

president to take this assembly under the shelter of this veranda. Here are the things done in this religious half hour.

Group Hymn: "E Hawai'i Ku'u One Hānau ē" [O Hawai'i My Beloved Land of Birth].

Prayer: Rev. S. K. Kamakahiki.

Group Hymn: "Ku'u 'Āina Hānau ē" [My Beloved Land of Birth].

Sermon Of The Day: Robert M. Kaaoao.

Closing Prayer: Elder president J. Punilio.

Hawai'i Pono'ī [Hawai'i's Own].

The Events of the Day. 1:00 p.m.

Canoe Race: Two canoes in this race, three paddlers, prize $3. Won by the canoe of Kalani Makini.

Swimming Race: Three people entered, prize $2.00. Won by Kalani Makini.

The Festivities on Land.

Small Horse Race: Six horses ran, prize $2.00. Won by John Bell.

Large Horse Race: Six horses ran, prize $2.50. Won by Dick, belonging to Keli'ikoa.

Donkey Race: Two donkeys ran, prize $2.00. Won by Jack, belonging to Pōmaika'i.

Foot Race: Five people ran, prize $2.00. Won by John Kilia.

Three-Legged Race: Four pairs ran, prize $2.00. Won by Jno. Kilia and Pūnohu.

Children's Race: Five kids ran, prize $2.00. Won by Miha'ai.

Wheelbarrow Race: Three people ran, prize $2.00. Won by Miha'ai.

Climbing a Greased Pole: $3.00 prize. Won by Kāne Kaluakini.

Apple Eating: Four people entered, prize $1. Won by Keoki.

Racing blindfolded, running straight to the pole, prize $2. [No winner listed.]

This was the conclusion of the day's events, and it was also held at the site of the festivities at sea and on land under the direction of the band, led by Prof. C. N. Kealakai.

On this day, a crowd of some hundreds assembled at those sites with great delight in seeing the festivities of the day under the management of the president R. M. Kaaoao and the aforementioned committee.

With great thanks for how the public maintained the dignity of the day quite peacefully. From men, women, and children, no actions breaking the peace of the public and the laws of the land were seen at all, all the way until all the events were concluded at a late hour of the evening, among the joyful cheering voices of the crowd.

At 7:30 that evening, a party was held at the place of the president by the committee of the day, with the instruments of the band sounding sweetly. The activities were concluded at 9:00 p.m., peacefully.

—Tho. K. Nakanaea [Nakanaela]. Kalaupapa, SEPT. 2, 1897.

Ke Aloha Aina. 18 FEBRUARY 1899. P. 1.

He Mau Kaikuahine No Ka Panalaau O Molokai. Sisters Going to the Colony of Moloka'i.

Syracuse, Jan. 26. Two sisters of the order of St. Francis [papa o St. Francis], Sister Flaviana and Sister Bonaventure, left this city tonight to join the leprosy colony [panalaau lepera] in the Hawaiian Islands [Paemoku o Hawaii]. Twelve Sisters of St. Francis have already left this city for the leprosy colony [panalaau lepera], and the order has made this work a rather significant branch of its missionary activities. It was the one that offered assistance, but this is truly a clear sacrifice of one's life. The family of one of them is in this city and that of the other is in Louisville, Ky. The hearts of their families have been pained, but no obstacles have been placed in their paths.

Ka Nupepa Kuokoa. 21 APRIL 1899. P. 2.

News was received here that Mother Marianne of the leprosy settlement [Virigine Marianne o ke Kahua Ma'i Lepera] on Moloka'i is extremely ill. There is no hope for her recovery.

» [Mother Marianne recovered and continued her work at Kalaupapa until her death in 1918.]

Ke Aloha Aina. 5 AUGUST 1899. P. 3.

Ka Huakai No Molokai. Ike Hou I Ke Kahua I Kau Ia Ka Weli. Maikai ka noho ana o na Ma'i. The Journey to Moloka'i. Seeing Once More the Settlement That Is Feared. The Lifestyle of the Patients Is Good.

At nine o'clock last Friday night, the members of the Board of Health, the newspaper writers, the relatives of patients and the visitors, totaling about 118, departed aboard the steamship *Malulani* and voyaged to the leprosy settlement that is feared [kahua ma'i i kau ia ka weli], Kalaupapa.

The ocean was calm during this journey of the Board of Health, and at 5:30 on Saturday morning the *Malulani* arrived in the harbor of Kalaupapa [awa o Kalaupapa]. At that time, the pier was filled with patients desiring to see their relatives arriving, and at that same time the sounding voices of the instruments of the musical boys [keiki puhiohe] of Kalaupapa burst out with an awe-inspiring sacredness.

The skiffs [waapa] were immediately released to ferry the relatives of the patients, and before the hour had struck six o'clock, behold, the lamenting voices were heard, carried by the gentle breezes, between the relatives that had arrived and the people afflicted with the wretched symptoms of disease.

The visitors were liberally released to go where they wanted to visit, and a great number went back to the homes of the patients to briefly visit with their loved ones. As for those who went with cameras, they were forbidden from photographing the features of the patients, but they were permitted to photograph the buildings, the mountain ridges, the harbor, and so forth, without being prevented by President Cooper [Kupa].

The first place that the members of the Board of Health visited was the Pauahi Home [Home Pauahi], the home of women afflicted by disease. Everything inside this home is clean, and they are under the care of the Marianne Mothers [makuahine Marianne]. The number of women living in this home is around 124, with 74 girls and 50 women at this place. The visitors were entertained by one girl who was skilled at playing piano.

After they were done visiting there, the party of visitors moved on to the home of the men, Baldwin Home [Balauwina Home] in Kalawao, under the care of Brother Dutton [Kaikunane Dutton]. The existing site of this home is fine and beautiful. There are 125 patients living within it. There the visitors were entertained by the tinkling tunes of the instruments of the young boys of that home, and because the visitors who went there were filled with joy for them, $9.50 was raised by the visitors and given to the father of that home.

There were many other places that the visitors went to see. Some folks went all the way to Waikolu, the location of the source of the water that supplies the leprosy settlement [kahua mai lepera]. At the rest house of Wm. Notley the travelers rested, with some folks becoming soaked by diving into the waters [luu wahi wai] of Waikolu.

In our full investigation of the condition of the lifestyle of the patients [ma'i], their lifestyle is good, and they have been supplied in all ways under the care of the Board of Health. Land is freely given to them for building private homes for them, with water being supplied. All the livestock that is desired to be raised is freely provided.

When everyone was ready to board the ship, Mr. W. O. Smith [Kamika] announced that the newspapers of Honolulu would be giving five prizes to those gardening in their yards. First prize $50, second $40, third $30, fourth $20, and fifth $10. These prizes will be awarded on October 1, 1900, with all those living in the patient settlement [kahua ma'i] allowed to compete equally for these prizes.

Smith also explained that five prizes will be given for those who make their yards tidy. These prizes will be awarded on April 1, 1900: to the tidiest one $25, second $20, third $15, fourth $10, and fifth $5. It is open to everyone in the colony [panalaau]. The committee members who will award the prizes are W. O. Smith and C. B. Reynolds of Honolulu, and W. Notley of Moloka'i.

At 3:30 the bell of the *Malulani* sounded, calling the passengers it had carried to return aboard the ship, and that was a time when tears again flowed between the relatives and the patients. At 4:15 in the afternoon the *Malulani* departed Kalaupapa and arrived back in Honolulu at 8:30 that night.

However, before the ship arrived at the entrance to Māmala Bay, Mr. John Kea stood on behalf of Cooper, the attorney general and also president of the Board of Health, and gave these brief statements, full of sweetness and greatly admired, before Hawai'i's Own [Hawaii Ponoi], which our pen points were unable to fully follow as he gave praise to the good works, which were uttered as follows:

"On behalf of the president of the Board of Health, he gives his great thanks to you all, with his saying that if he occupies the position he holds for a long time, he will indeed make every attempt to know each and every family and the adversity they face residing in that land of agony" [aina o ka ehaeha]. This was followed by calls of gratitude toward him from the entire crowd assembled aboard the ship.

Ke Aloha Aina. 29 DECEMBER 1900. P. 5.
Hookapu la Ka Waiona. Liquor Forbidden.

When the Board of Health met last Wednesday, full authority was given to Agent Reynolds to seize and destroy all liquor found within the boundaries of the leprosy settlement [palena o ke kahua maʻi lepera]. This is a fulfillment of a measure approved last week that banned alcohol or guns [e hookapu ana i ka waiona a i ole i ka pu] from being brought into the patient settlement [kahua maʻi], except in the form of medicine for the Board of Health. Reynolds reported that he had recently found a few bottles of gin, whiskey, and beer. A possible reason that this ban by the Board of Health arose is because of the many reports concerning the great amount of drunkenness [ona] in the patient settlement [kahua maʻi].

Home Rula Repubalika. 6 NOVEMBER 1901. P. 6.
Ka Papa Ola. The Board of Health.

In understanding this department of the government, it seems as if this is an independent government within the government, which has the same departments as the territorial government [aupuni Teritori], which are an executive power, a legislative power, and perhaps a judicial power.

This Board of Health is entirely capable of passing rules that are equal with, or perhaps greater than, the power of the laws that the legislature makes. With the rules that the Board of Health creates, the other government authorities are utterly unable to oppose them. This Board of Health is completely able to set laws for some people without that law applying to someone else.

Right before the legislature was in session last February, the Honorable F. W. Beckley, the representative of the Third District, requested approval for himself to go and meet with his constituents in that land of agony, the leprosy settlement [aina o ka ehaeha, ke kahua mai lepera], so that he could know their needs before the legislature met, but his request was denied. However, it seems that during those same days, a visiting Caucasian [haole malihini] asked to visit that settlement [kahua], and he was immediately approved.

The people are not unfamiliar with the many other actions by this small, astonishing government, so it would just be a waste for us to go on saying more about it. However, here we are lobbying the people to advise your spokesmen to pass a law toppling and destroying this Board of Health, burning it down and building a new Board of Health to be trusted by all the people. And to have its lawmaking power reduced, requiring approval by the public. Under the current law, these people have the power to collect us and bury us Hawaiians alive in that blowhole of agony [kanu ola aku ia kakou Hawaii ma kela lua puhi o ka ehaeha] in Kalaupapa. They have decided that absolutely no other doctors outside of their circle [aole loa e ae ia na kauka e ae mawaho o ko lakou pohai] will be allowed to treat those considered to be ill, so that their criticism will not be brought in.

It shows that they have no desire to say there is a cure for leprosy [maʻi lepera], since there are great piles of money that they consume every year. In our role as a mouthpiece for the public, this is what we report due to the knowledge gained during this last session of the legislature: there are a great number of our fellow natives in that colony [panalaau] who are not leprosy patients [mai lepera], but they are there living in good health. Due to that murderous law, arm vaccination, gonorrhea [maʻi pala] and its grandparent, scabies [mai kuna], have become widespread, and that is the reason they have gone to Molokaʻi as leprosy patients [maʻi lepera]. Alas for our death! Until we speak again. To be continued.

Ke Aloha Aina. 4 JANUARY 1902. P. 5.

Waiho Na Iwi I Ka Aina Malihini. The Bones Rest in the Unfamiliar Land.

Greetings. Please indulge me an available gap in your body, and you will be the one to embrace [my message] and carry it out to the four corners of the land [kihi eha o ka aina] and upon the shifting swells of the eight seas [ale hulilua o na kai ewalu], and from the rising of the sun at Haʻehaʻe to the setting at the pleasant base of Lehua [mai ka hikina a ka La i Haehae a ka welona i ka mole olu i Lehua], to be seen by the loved ones and friends of my beloved younger brother who has traveled far. Since on October 25, 1901, at 11:00 a.m., at the residence of Mr. Sam. Kalainaina in Hiʻilawe, Waipiʻo, Hāmākua, Hawaiʻi, it pleased Almighty God to take the precious life of my dear younger brother who was greatly loved, Damien [Damiano] K. Kauhi, after he was emaciated by tuberculosis [maʻi hokii] for more than ten years.

On October 21, he began vomiting blood, and then recovered. On the 25th he again began vomiting blood. He remained in this condition until his final breath made a solitary flight and silently glided upon the rainbow-hued trail of Kāne [ala koiula a Kane], and the water pool of the billowy cloud broke open.

The water drops of Kūlanihākoʻi [a mythical pond in the sky] poured down in a pelting of heavy rain. He has gone to a place of lying still. In the downpour of the water drops of Hiʻilawe [famous waterfall in Waipiʻo Valley]. Glowing brightly on the skin of the child. My beloved younger brother who has traveled far. Greetings, greetings, greetings of deep affection.

He was a native son of the Kohala districts; his place of birth was in the uplands of Niuliʻi, from within Mrs. Koleka Kanu and Barenaba Kauhi in the year 1863, Sept. 7. So he had thirty-eight years, two months, and thirteen days of his share of the joy and hardships of this life.

He was educated in the district school of Waiapuka under the leadership of Father Damien [Damiano] as principal, and from him he received the name he was known by, until he left in 1874. He entered the school of Joe M. Poepoe, administered by Father Fabim [Father Fabien Schauten]. In 1875 he left Kohala for the Kanilehua Rain [Kauakanilehua: an epithet for Hilo, Hawaiʻi], entered the school there run by Father Charles [Father Charles Pouzot], and in 1878 left Hilo for his birthplace. And he carried out every kind of work he could under C. F. Hart. He listened well to the commands of his masters.

In 1881 he married Miss Api Kahoʻokano, the oldest daughter of D. S. Kahoʻokano, and from them came four children, two children who have already died and two children who are living.

And after his wife died, he left his birthplace and came here to Waipiʻo. He found his companion for living in this unfamiliar land [aina malihini]. His heart was committed to his wife, until his bones rested in the bosom of the one he loved.

He left a wife with children and an older brother mourning for him. I give my thanks and blessings to the friends who assisted me, and who grieved with me until that sorrow was eased.

On the 26th his funeral service was held under the ministrations of the Rev. M. C. Kealoha, and he vanished forever.

With greetings of grief, T. N. Nāleilehua. Waipiʻo, Hāmākua, Hawaiʻi, DEC. 12, 1901.

» [While a student at Waiapuka school on Hawai'i island in the early 1870s, Damien Kauhi received his name from Father Damien, the school principal.]

Ke Aloha Aina. 25 MAY 1907. P. 6.
Haule Ka Manaolana. Haaleleia I Ke Anu A Hoohuli Mai La I Ke Kua. Hope Is Lost. Left in the Cold and the Back Is Turned.
To the newspaper *Ke Aloha Aina.* Greetings.

May it please your captain and your officers to lift up those phrases placed above, the title of this presentation of ideas.

May it be seen by our parents, grandparents, children, grandchildren, brothers, and sisters from the rising sun to the setting sun [mai ka La hiki a ka La komo] that we are here, left to weep in the cold, for these reasons:

1. The senators and representatives that we voted for, who won, look at us with disfavor.
2. The Health Committees that the Republicans put in due to our requests look at us with disfavor.
3. The Board of Genocide [Papa Pepehilahui] looks with disfavor at our request, which has the title Hope is Lost [Haule ka manaolana].

The writer is requesting of the people mentioned above that the Home Rule Democrats [Demokalaka me Home Rula] be our political party for this coming [election] season, since the billowy clouds are showing and the heavenly signs [kahoaka lani] are making clear that here is the salvation of the people and what is needed for the government in these parties combined.

These combined political parties will fetch your salvation, O people at the rising of the sun, and the requesting voices of these combined parties will be heeded. They are the salvation of the people and the wails of those who are agonized will lessen or even cease.

To our parents, children, grandchildren, older brothers and younger brothers, those who can vote, if you have love for us, then let the Home Rule Democrats [Demokalaka me Home Rula] be our political party in that season of 1908.

To my fellow patients residing from the headland extending in the sea of Pāpio to the multitude of sand dunes at Papaloa that make love to the rough breaking waves of 'Īliopi'i [lae oni i ke kai o Papio a hiki i na puuone kinikini o Papaloa e hooipo aku ana me ka nalu haki kakala o Iliopii], our hope is lost, our wishes will not be fulfilled.

Remember, my fellow patients [hoa ma'i], that day of campaign meetings. Deceptive tears flowed, teeth were shown in hypocritical smiles, and the talk was cunning like a fox, saying, "We love you, if you vote for us and we win, we will indeed go and strive to get what you need."

Where are those needed things? Have our requests been taken and tossed in the wastebasket? The thing that we did not command, for our senators to unite themselves with the Board of Genocide, that is what they have united with. No love indeed. The truth is that the cunning talk was for election day, and when they won, that talk was immediately forgotten. My companions in agony [hoa o ka ehaeha], we have seen the action of the Republican Party, and you have been left in the cold.

Therefore, the writer requests that if the Lord agrees to lengthen our days until that time, the Democrats and Home Rule combined will be our political party for this coming election season. Then you will receive a little of what you need, and our requests will be fulfilled. Therefore, a combined Democratic and Home Rule Club [Kalapu Demokalaka me Home Rula] will be established here in the patient settlement [Kahua Maʻi]. Everyone come join.

With gratitude, S. K. M. Nāhauowailēʻia. Kalawao, Molokaʻi, MAY 17, 1907.
» ["S. K. M." are the initials of S. K. Maialoha. His pen name was Nāhauowailēʻia, "the dews of Wailēʻia."]

Ke Aloha Aina. 14 SEPTEMBER 1907. P. 6.
Ku ke Kalapu Demokalaka ma Kalaupapa. The Democratic Club Appears in Kalau-papa.

Mr. Editor. Greetings to you:

During the meeting of the Democratic Club on August 31, 1907, S. K. Mai-aloha was elected as president, G. W. K. Palaualelo, vice president, Jno. T. Unea, secretary. Treasurer to come.

The aforementioned officers along with D. K. Kau and John Nāluaʻi are the Executive Committee. There are thirty-five members who are registered at this time, and many more remain. As soon as the rules and new revisions of the Central Committee of the Democratic Club are received, then business will move forward.

Yours truly, John Taylor Unea. Kalaupapa, SEPT. 7, 1907.

To the newspaper *Ke Aloha Aina,* the undying lamp for season after season [ipukukui pio ole i na kau a kau]. Greetings to you:

Please allow a little room for these small passengers placed above, and you will take them out to the shores and ridges [aekai a me na kualono] of the land we love.

On August 31, the Democratic Club appeared in the land of agony [aina o ka ehaeha], and the officers were elected.

To my fellow patients [hoa maʻi] from the chilly waters of Waikolu to the hot sun of Kalaupapa [wai huihui o Waikolu a hiki aku i ka la wela o Kalau-papa], wooing the children swimming in the sea of ʻIliopiʻi [e hooipo aku ana me na keiki aukai o Iliopii]:

Now is the time to arise, stand and go to have your names set down in the book of the secretary of the club.

My fellow patients, there is no other political party that will provide us with respite, equal rights, and future salvation, only the Democrats.

To my friends of the castle (Baldwin Home) of notched walls in Kalawao, march out to Kalaupapa, to the place of J. T. Unea, to have your names set down, to become soldiers for the day of battle that is approaching.

To the parents, grandparents, grandchildren, older brothers, younger brothers, and children who can vote, from Hawaiʻi Moku-o-Keawe [Island-of-Keawe] to Niʻihau, if you have love for us, join the Democratic Clubs in your districts.

You must select colonels (senators and representatives) who love the land, and love the people [aloha aina, a aloha Lahui]. Do not select crabs [papai] whose teeth are sharp but are empty inside.

This pen tip will continue to appeal to your love for us. The starch and meat, the coffee and tea, the crackers and the other supplies that the Board of Health feeds us are not things that will undo our burdens and the agonies of the disease, the love for you, our family.

Who will release this burden placed upon us? The writer believes that the Democrats will release it, since the leadership of the Republican Party is being indifferent to our distress with a heart that has no love for us.

Perhaps the reader will ask, "What is their lack of love?" Here it is: salvation has been withheld, the great salvation that cries out that it can heal, and more. At another time the writer will report more things relating to our club.

A member of the board, S. K. Maialoha. Kalawao, SEPT. 6, 1907.

Ke Aloha Aina. 23 NOVEMBER 1907. P. 5.
Ke Keikialii J K Kalanianaole Ma Ka Aina O Ka Ehaeha. Ka Mai Ke Aho I Ka Aina O Ka Ehaeha—Onou Pupuahuluia Na Palapala. Prince J. K. Kalaniana'ole in the Land of Agony. The Cord Connects to the Land of Agony—Documents Are Hurriedly Thrust [Upon Us].

To the magnetic lightning bolt [uwila makeneti], the newspaper *Aloha Aina.* Greetings between us:

May it please your captain and the typesetting boys of the printing press to send this out like lightning to the shores and ridges of our beloved land, and float it all the way out to the continents.

On Nov. 10, it was heard on the telephone [Telepona] that the prince was in Kaunakahakai [Kaunakakai] with Dr. W. J. Goodhue and passed the night in Kala'e. It was also reported that a citizens' meeting was being held in the patient settlement [halawai makaainana ma ke kahua ma'i nei].

On the 11th, the prince came down, piloted by J. D. McVeigh, Dr. Goodhue, Dr. Holman, Henry Meyer, and Mrs. Goodhue. After about three-fourths of the cliff had passed them by, they met with the government leaders of Kalawao County: J. K. Wai'ama'u [assistant superintendent], police captain Punilio, warden of the prison, J. K. Kainuwai, J. K. Alapa'i, Wm. Kameaaloha. The committee members: A. J. Kauhaihao, secretary; J. S. Wilmington; J. T. Unea; B. Palikapu; three committee members did not appear. The members of the Republican Party: R. M. Na'auao, P. Kiha, Una Alawa, Punohu.

J. D. McVeigh requested that J. S. Wilmington meet the prince. The writer did not hear the introductions, since he was in the stern of the canoe [i ka hope waa: at the end of the line], because it was a steep and sheer cliff. After the introductions, the procession continued until arriving at the roaring sands of Pūahi, that make a joyous sound [one kani o Puahi e uhene nei].

The workers of the patient settlement [limahana o ke kahua ma'i] were standing in a line. The prince gave his greeting and the workers gave three cheers. The procession continued again, and while the procession was travel-ing slowly, the prince was giving his greeting to the patients through speech and nods. Some folks gave their greeting, but some other folks just stood and stared, grinding their molars, like when they see the actions of the prince in the newspaper concerning the thing that was thought to be a salvation for the people.

They arrived at the home of the superintendent [Luna Nui] at approximately 11:00 a.m. After talking with the sailors, the captain was the partner for conversation. The police were sent to report that there would be a meeting at the Teerys Willie Park bandstand at 2:00 p.m., without the topic of the meeting being revealed.

This was just like what the president said, that it would be better to put up flyers, but this was by word of mouth. After 2:00 p.m., the band of Baldwin Home arrived, conducted by Pros. W. B. Lapilio, and they continued to provide songs that stirred the heart.

After it was past 1:30, a portion of the patients [maʻi] were seen going to the place that was assigned, but it was not all of the patients, because of the lack of interest in the prince. While the patients were waiting, the sound of the instruments of the band of Kalaupapa continued, sweet and soft. They went silent at a signal from Dr. Goodhue.

When the time came the prince was seen leaving the place of the superintendent accompanied by the committee members.

While the prince and the committee members went up the stairs to the bandstand, the band provided another heart-stirring tune. When the band was done, the chair of the committee, Wm. Notley, stood and called the meeting to order with commands of support: "Be silent, keep the peace and listen to the voice of the prince." The chair introduced the prince before the crowd.

The prince stood and gave his greeting [aloha]. The greeting was reciprocated. The prince shared his intentions. "I have come here to meet with you all. Those of Honolulu have heard of Walter's [Walaka] treatments, but we have not heard.

"My desire was to come here to ask you about the treatments of Walter [lapaau a Walaka]. Do you want them?" The patients called out, "Yes, we want them."

"If that is the case, then trust me. I am the delegate [to Congress] for the territory of Hawaiʻi. I will make a request in my capacity as a person of authority. In this, they will not deny me.

"The petition with 527 names from the patient settlement [kahua maʻi] is not a report on leprosy [maʻi lepera] being cured, and this document I have brought will be signed by your committee members, along with the contract between Walter and the patients." The prince clarified, "The documents were made in English [olelo Beretania] and translated by one of your committee members." The prince read the documents. 1. Petition. 2. Contract. After that J. S. Wilmington read them in Hawaiian. These two documents will be included here.

After the documents were read, the approval of the crowd was sought. Approved. The prince reported that he was one of the ten committee members selected for the ʻAʻala Park meeting: "What I hear is that they were working on political business and I abandoned them. Was rudeness by the citizens not the reason for leaving?" In his final statement he said, "I return to Honolulu on Wednesday, and on Thursday the board meets. If the Board of Health approves, then we will all benefit. If not, then only when the legislature meets, that is where the need will be fulfilled." In the first part of his speech, he could definitely do it, but in the latter part he pointed to the right belonging to Oniula, the genocidal board.

When the business was concluded, the committee members returned to the office to sign their names. In a statement by one of the committee members, there was not time to properly determine if the documents were correct or not before he hastily signed his name.

I have done enough with this.

—S. K. Maialoha. Kalawao, Moloka'i, NOV. 15, 1907.

» [The text of the document approved by the patients is on page two in this issue of *Ke Aloha Aina*.]

Ke Aloha Aina. 28 DECEMBER 1907. P. 2.
He Leo Kono. An Inviting Call.

The person is called to enter, to be fed until the mouth can take no more, here is the payment, the salvation of the people and the land.

To my dear undying lamp [Ipukukui pio ole], *Ke Aloha Aina*. Greetings between us:

Please allow some small, available space of your fragile body, and you shall carry this out like lightning. To my fellow patients who can vote, from the water of Waikolu that stings the skin to the smooth sand of Pūahi, which is caressed by the children who surf the rough waves of 'Īliopi'i [E o'u mau hoa ma'i i kupono i ke koho balota e noho ana mai ka wai hoeha ili o Waikolu a hiki aku i ke one wali o Puahi, i hooheno ia mai e na keiki heenalu kakala o Iliopii.].

Merry Christmas to us all [Aloha Karisimaka no kakou]. Those who remain, whose names have not been set down in the book of the secretary of the Democratic Club of the land of agony [aina o ka ehaeha], are invited to march over to the office of Secretary J. T. Unea, in Kalaupapa. Or else order the secretary or the president to appear in your glorious presence; those two are servants for you all.

Do not stand and wait. The heavenly signs [kahoaka lani] and cloud banks report that the Democratic president will win in this [election] season, and the Democratic Party is the party that will save the people and the land. And frustrate the predictions of the golden plovers [kolea birds: opportunistic foreigners] that appear in droves, that before fifty years have passed all the people of this race will be dead. So, the Democratic Party will be the political party that will crush this Board of Genocide [Papa pepehi Lahui] to a pulp in this coming [legislative] session.

And the writer requests of the friends from Hawai'i, island of Keawe, to Ni'ihau at the pleasant base of Lehua [island], that if you have love for us, then only the Democratic Party is the party that will release us, the people, from this coffin in which we are buried alive [pahu kupapau kanu ola ae], and the realm of land will again be seen. Onward and upward [Imua a iluna ae].

With gratitude, S. K. Maialoha. President of the Democratic Club. Kalawao, Moloka'i, DEC. 20, 1907.

Ka Nupepa Kuokoa. 19 JUNE 1908. P. 6.
Ka La 11 O Iune Ma Ke Kahua Ma'i. June 11 in the Patient Colony.

To the swift Messenger of the People, the *Nupepa Kuokoa*. Greetings to you:

From the time that the first light of dawn broke forth, the walls of the heavens were seen, unclouded, with the gentle blowing of the wind, a trade wind [Moa'e].

At 6:30, the procession of the women's [Horseback] Riding Skirt Society [Hui holo pa-u], whose president is Mrs. M. Notley, arrived in Kalawao upon their horses with embroidered red skirts [pa-u ulaula], yellow skirts [pa-u me-lemele], lavender [kaiina], and so forth.

At the head of the procession the star flag of America [Hoku o Amerika] flew proudly. The members of the society were adorned with the dark leaves of the upland forest, and royal purple flowers [pua poni moi] hanging around necks and off hats, and around like a sash.

When the procession returned to the home of the president of the society, the writer did not see that place. At 10:15 the procession continued on to Ka-lawao for the second time; each and every one traveled on their own and the procession was dispersed.

At 2:00 p.m. the baseball game between Good-Eye and Baldwin Home be-gan, and here is how it went: Good-Eye 16, Baldwin Home 14. [The original article includes scores for each inning.]

Many spectators came to the baseball field, between three and four hun-dred. At 3:30, the procession of the [Horseback] Riding Skirt Society arrived outside the baseball field. One part of the group was going around the park, and the other part was riding to 'Iliopi'i.

Several small parties were held by some folks at their homes, and some fes-tivities, and in the early evening, the horse riders were seen in the streets of the patient settlement [kahua ma'i], riding up and down.

With the typesetting boys and the editor my greeting of great affection.

Yours truly, S. K. M. Nāhauowailē'ia. Kalawao, Moloka'i, June 12, 1908.

» [On December 22, 1871, King Kamehameha V proclaimed June 11 a national holiday to honor Kamehameha I, the king who united the islands and estab-lished the Hawaiian nation. Hawai'i celebrated its first Kamehameha Day in 1872, and today June 11 is a state holiday.]

Ka Nupepa Kuokoa. 3 JULY 1908. P. 6.
Na Kauka O Na Mokukaua Ma Ke Kahua Ma'i. The Doctors of the Warships in the Pa-tient Settlement.

To the swift messenger, the *Nupepa Kuokoa.* Greetings. In the early morn-ing, 6:00 a.m., on June... [no date given], the *S. S. Maui* appeared with its visitors in the surging harbor of Kalaupapa, supported by the superintendent [Luna Nui] of the patient settlement [kahua ma'i], J. D. McVeigh.

They relaxed for a moment at the place of the superintendent while the carriages and horses were being prepared. When they were ready, the party headed straight to Kalawao, the place where the beautiful castles [Kakela nani] of the father government [Aupuni Makua] and the Baldwin Home stand.

And while the party was hurrying along, the traveling strangers were gazing at the land, the cliffs, the dark valleys, and the patients [ma'i] gathering along the road.

And when they returned from Kalawao, they visited the homes, the hos-pital, the medicine dispensaries [rumi haawi laau], the operating room [rumi oki], and the medicine preparation room [rumi hoohuihui laau], and they looked at some patients tossed to this land for the final breath of this life [aina no ke aho hope loa o keia ola ana]. Alas, how pitiful, and at 2:00 p.m. they boarded the *S. S. Maui* to go to Lāhaina, and while the party of visitors was traveling to Lāhaina, the superintendent went too. When the writer saw these doctors, they were pleasant and acted as gentlemen. Sorry, reader, the writer did not get the names of these doctors.

I have done enough here. The chilly wind of the land is gusting.

—S. K. M. Nāhauowailēʻia. Kalawao, Molokaʻi, JUNE 26, 1908.

Ka Nupepa Kuokoa. 4 SEPTEMBER 1908. P. 6.
Na Meahou O Ka Aina O Ka Ehaeha. News from Land of Agony.

To the news-reporting telegraph of the communities of Hawaiʻi, the *Nupepa Kuokoa.* Greetings. Would you please provide some small space of interest for the little bits of news from the land of agony?

THE BASEBALL TEAMS. [NA HUI KINIPOPO.]

There is much appreciation for baseball here in the patient settlement [kahua maʻi]. There are four baseball teams here in the patient colony: 1. Morning Star [Hoku Kakahiaka]; 2. Excellence [Kilohana]; 3. Baldwin Home; 4. Helpers [Kokua].

On August 15 the first team played with the last team. The feathers were scattered [puehu ka hulu: they won] by the last team by one run, and the team name "Helpers" was called. The members of that team are uninfected people.

On August 22, the Helpers team played again with Excellence. The wing feathers were scattered [puehu na hulu i ka pekekeu: they won] by Excellence by six runs; you have heard enough. From what the writer saw there were more men, women, and children at the church of the baseball folks [halepule o ka poe kinipopo], and at the house of God there were only a few.

My fellow patients, you should all go to church, bend the knees and look up toward the mountains, and from there our salvation will come.

BLOWN UP BY DYNAMITE. [PA-HUIA E KE KIANA PAUDA.]

On August 23, the workers for the lighthouse being built in Kalaupapa went to Nihoa, a place approximately one mile to the southwest of Kalaupapa, to shoot wild goats [kao ahiu]. There were seven of these mischief makers [poe hana kolohe] on the day of the Lord.

These folks shot and hit some goats. When they were all skinned, one of them went on to shoot more goats, but he did not shoot goats because he saw fish. In his breast [pocket] he had some dynamite [kiana pauda: giant powder]. He took it out and started to light it, and here is a short story that Dr. Goodhue told to the writer:

Kaaluea began to light the wick with a flame, and the smoke rose into his eyes. He was blinded and disoriented, and the dynamite was still held in his hand. But the flame burned and in a short time the dynamite blew up in his hand. Several people ran and saw the injury to this friend. His hand had flown off, and only the veins remained. These folks returned with the one who was injured, leaving the goats, their only desire to come here. [When they reached] the place where the injured one fainted, they carried him. An energetic return was made to Kalaupapa, where he went under the care of the doctors of the patient settlement [kahua maʻi]. His condition is improving.

This youngster is from Kaua'i, and he returns without a hand on his arm. It was reported to the writer that it was quite a regular activity for him at the place where they work. To ignore is death, to listen is life [he kuli ka make he lohe ke ola].

THE PATIENTS ARE WONDERING. [KE NUNE NEI NA MA'I.]

Because a portion of the patients [ma'i] saw in the newspapers that the food ration for the Caucasians [haole] will increase again, with a new home also being provided for them, the opinion arose among the patients that the supplies given to the Caucasians should be the same as the supplies for the Hawaiians [kanaka Hawaii], or other races, because:

1. The patients have seen that twenty pounds of cooked taro [pa'i ai] is not enough for a week. The patients requested during the past [legislative] session that the pounds of cooked taro be increased to twenty-five, but it was not approved. Such is the case for the pounds of meat, the lack is the same, and here is what the writer has seen.

If there are two, husband and wife, parent and child, a loved one, then one gets a bundle of food. One uses the number for the store, and that is how the patients get coffee and tea. And if there's just one, then one week is cooked taro, and the next week is to the store, and seventy cents is the true value of the stamped metal number [helu pa'i] at the store for the week. You see, readers, it is twenty pounds of cooked taro for two weeks, but it was probably done so that the appropriation of the legislature lasts, and how is that of the Caucasians is being increased again?

CONCERNING THE DEMOCRATIC PARTY. [NO KA AOAO DEMOKARATA.]

The Democratic Party is moving forward here in the patient settlement [kahua ma'i]; all the Republicans and Home Rule folks have signed up for the Democratic Club. Keep it going, my companions of the land of agony [Aina o ka Ehaeha]; let us try this party in this [election] season.

To the parents, children, and grandchildren who can vote, from the rising sun to the setting sun, if there is within your hearts love for us who grieve all night and day, the writer requests that you vote for the candidates of the Democratic Party and watch, examine, and recognize. Let there not be a Democrat coat over a Republican shirt.

THE FEDERAL BUILDINGS. [NA HALE O KA FEDERALA.]

The work on these buildings progresses. There is [a group of] three buildings, a building above and below, [a group of] four buildings, a single building, and two buildings that have been joined by the veranda [lanai] between them. They are grand in appearance, and it was reported to the writer that three more buildings remain [to be built]. The site has been planned and in the month of March 1909 they will be occupied. The instruments and supplies for the doctor's office [keena kauka] have arrived.

With the editor my greeting. S. K. Maialoha. Kalawao, Moloka'i, AUGUST 28, 1908.

» [When dynamite was introduced in Hawai'i, fishermen began using it for blast fishing. They would light a stick of the explosive and drop it into a school of fish. The concussion from the blast would stun or kill the fish, which then floated to the surface where they were easily netted. In 1872 the Hawaiian legislature passed a law prohibiting fishing with explosives, but it was difficult to enforce and the practice continued into the 1900s, resulting in injuries and fatalities to dynamite fishermen like Kaaluea.]

Ka Nupepa Kuokoa. 15 JANUARY 1909. P. 6.
Hoike I Ka Oiaio. Reporting the Truth.
To the editor and your boys of the printing press of the *Nupepa Kuokoa.* Greetings.

On December 24, 1908, at 8:15, two policemen [makai] came to my home and to the other houses of the patient settlement [Kahua Ma'i] to search for beer (Swipe) [pia (Suaipa)], since the Board of Health has an extremely strict rule that the one who makes something intoxicating, such as rum or other liquor, will be arrested and punished by law.

At the home of the writer, there were two gallons of punch made by me from lemons, rough lemons [kukane], and oranges, and mixed with sugar. The writer called it "wine" [waina], and also the blood of the one whose birthday it was [koko hoi o ka Mea nona ka la hanau], and the writer had made a drink to give to those visiting my home for Christmas [Karisimaka].

The policemen took the gallons, and at a place away from my home it was tasted. It was seen that it was sweet, not something bitter and intoxicating. The policemen met with their superior in the department, the sheriff of Kalawao County [Makai Nui o ke Kalana o Kalawao], and they discussed and decided that it was not an intoxicating beverage. The policeman said to me that the drink I had made was not liquor, and, "You are released." Because I am like Thomas [Koma: Doubting Thomas in the Bible], needing to see for myself, I went before his honor the sheriff, and his answer to me was just like what the policeman had said.

So, to my fellow patients from the chilly waters of Waikolu, to the smooth sand of Pūahi, caressing the waves breaking on the tip of 'Īliopi'i, the Hau trees of Wailē'ia [a play on the author's pen name] restrain the agitated swells of Kauoa [ale kupikipikio o Kauoa], that the Ulumano wind supports.

In what the writer has heard, a portion of the patients [ma'i] disapprove of my release, and place their disapproval upon the police and the sheriff. In order for you all to know, I publicly report in accordance with what is shown above. The writer hears that someone is petitioning the Board of Health. Take heed, friend or friends, cut it out or else the ship will stray onto the shore, and these words will be uttered: "The ship stops at Hā'ulepū, leaving squash over there, pumpkin over here." [Ku ka moku i haule pu, he pu ko o, he palaai koonei: All-fall-down.]

I have done enough here, S. K. M. Nāhauowailē'ia. Kalawao, Moloka'i, JANUARY 2, 1909.

Ka Nupepa Kuokoa. 9 APRIL 1909. P. 1.
Komite Ahaolelo No Molokai. Apo Ohaohaia na Hoa o ka Ahaolelo: Lohe i ka Makemake o na Ma'i Lepera. Legislative Committee to Moloka'i. The Members of the Legislature were Enthusiastically Embraced: Hearing the Desires of the Leprosy Patients.

At ten o'clock this past Saturday night, the members of the legislature, the doctors of the Board of Health, and some others, the total number reaching one hundred, boarded the steamship *Mauna Kea* to travel to the Kalawao colony [Panalaau o Kalawao], and at one o'clock that morning the ship stopped in the harbor [awa] of Kalaupapa. It remained anchored for part of the night, until a little after six in the morning, when everyone began going ashore.

Each and every side of the pier [uwapo] was already crowded with locals desiring to meet with their friends, and there were many among the patients who had come to see and affectionately greet their loved ones that had arrived. The band of the colony played, with large and small flags waving in the wispy breeze. It had truly become a holiday for the colony.

The breakfast for all the passengers was first completed on board the ship, and when the hour was about to strike seven, the first skiffs [waapa] landed ashore. The party of visitors stayed in Kalaupapa for an extremely short time, and then mounted horses and carriages to go to the town [kulanakauhale] of Kalawao.

A rather important place that most of them visited was the site of the new patient facilities of America [hale ma'i hou o ka Amerika: the U.S. Leprosy Investigation Station] in Kalawao. Eight hundred feet is the length of those buildings standing right at the base of the line of cliffs [kakaipali]. There are ten of those buildings. The medicine storehouses [hale waiho laau], the cooking houses [halekuke], the wash houses [haleholoi], the doctor houses [hale Kauka], and the offices [keenahana] have all been separated. It is believed that in those buildings the patients will be treated [to determine] if leprosy can be cured. Within these buildings, twenty patients can be treated at one time, and at that time the nature of this terrible disease that is spreading all around the world will be fully investigated.

» [The U. S. Leprosy Investigation Station in Kalawao opened in 1909 and closed in 1913.]

Dr. Goodhue and Wm. Mutch were the residents [kamaaina] who took the visitors around to sightsee in every part of those buildings, while explaining the nature and the reason for how those places would be used.

THE MEETING IN KALAWAO. [KA HALAWAI MA KALAWAO.]

At eight o'clock in the morning, a public meeting was called, and about fifty or sixty patients [poe ma'i] assembled at this meeting. Senator Coelho started to introduce the speakers within the meeting room [rumi halawai] of the Baldwin Home, and there the patients [ma'i] submitted their many petitions and the things they wanted, while hearing the opinions of the members of the legislature.

A. J. Kauhaihao, the schoolteacher of the Baldwin Home, was the speaker on behalf of the patients, and he submitted before the members of the legislature several things that the patients want done for them, similar to the petitions that were already sent to Honolulu. As he explained, a single patient cannot survive with the single bundle of cooked taro [paiai] that is given each week, and concerning the beef, the majority of the portion given to each patient is just bone.

There were many representatives and senators that answered on behalf of the legislature, with Senator Coelho introducing each of them.

The main idea of the statements on the part of the members of the legislature was that their real problems were understood and they were always ready to give assistance to them, as much as possible, in order to ease their burdens, which they were witnessing firsthand in all places. Those who were introduced to share their opinions before the patients were Representatives Douthitt, Representative Kamahu, Like, Kaniho, Kamanoulu, Kawewehi, and Carley; Senator Smith, Senator Fairchild. The last name of the representatives was the one who gave the patients the greeting from H. P. Baldwin to all the patients of the colony.

Many thanks were given to Senator Fairchild for his statement that he would do as much as he could to save the dollars of the public in all departments, in order for everything they desired to be fulfilled, and the calls of "Correct!" [pololei] came in unison from the assembly.

THE MEETING IN KALAUPAPA. [KA HALAWAI MA KALAUPAPA.]

Before the time for lunch, the visitors returned to Kalaupapa to the house of Superintendent [Luna Nui] McVeigh. A large meal was prepared in the yard, and there the honorable ones Coelho and Kealawaʻa gave speeches. After lunch, a meeting was held right in front of the bandstand [hale puhiohe], and there the many requests from the patients were heard, which were similar to the requests submitted in Kalawao.

VISITING THE BISHOP HOME. [MAKAIKAI ANA I KA HOME BIHOPA.]

After that meeting, most of the members went to the Bishop Home for girls, and there they saw the cruel symptoms of the disease among some of the little girls. Three of them sang the hymn [in English], "We sing this merry lay and bid you hearty welcome here this day," and all the members who had gone there were unable to suppress their feelings of pity and compassion. Because one of the honorable members was unable to endure his feelings, he immediately left that place and returned to the harbor. Those who went there expressed deep gratitude to Mother Marianne [makuahine Mariame], just like their gratitude to Dutton, the father of the Baldwin Home [makua o ka Home Baldwin].

» [A "lay," one of the words in the lyrics of the hymn, is a narrative poem meant to be sung.]

GRATITUDE FOR THE GOVERNMENT OFFICIALS. [MAHALO I NA LUNA AUPUNI.]

The patients have deep gratitude for Superintendent McVeigh, and the same goes for Dr. Goodhue, and it was requested before the honorable members that the two of them be well paid. Many expressions of gratitude were heard among the members of the legislature for Superintendent McVeigh, and it will be requested of the governor within a resolution [Olelo Hooholo] that he be appointed president of the Board of Health [Peresidena no ka Papa Ola]. The main desire is that he becomes the permanent superintendent in the patient settlement [Luna Nui nohopaa ma ke Kahua Maʻi].

MANY CHANGES SEEN. [NUI NA HANA HOU I IKEIA.]

Many changes have been undertaken for the patient colony [kahua maʻi] within the past two years. Many new houses have been built in place of the shacks, with verandas [lanai] going all around that are painted and clean in appearance with flower gardens surrounding the outside. The hospital in Kalaupapa is kept clean and is a great blessing to the multitude, and such is also the case with the steam-powered poi factory and the wash house [hale hana poi mahu me ka hale holoi]. They are kept clean.

The pipes for the water lines for the wash house are scattered out in pieces at the place where the pipes will lie, and the work just waits for an allotment of money for laying and connecting the pipes.

One of the requests submitted before the members of the legislature in Kalaupapa was for suitable progress to be made on the place where movies [kii onioni] will be shown to give value to the machine [mikini] that was sent there.

"I would be truly happy if there was someone here who could operate that machine," one girl said. That was a girl who left from Honolulu a short time ago, and she already saw movies in Honolulu. It was planned by one of the members of the legislature that the horses of the patients ridden by the members of the legislature should be paid for. According to him, "In Honolulu the payment for automobiles is five dollars an hour, and when we came here we rode on the horses of the patients without paying a cent."

MANY DOCTORS WENT TOO. [NUI NA KAUKA I HELE PU.]

Almost a dozen doctors went on that visit to the patient settlement [Kahua Ma'i], and among them were Drs. Sujimoto and Suzuki, the surgeons [Kauka kaha] of the Japanese warship [Mokukaua Kepani] that was accompanied by the British counselor [Kanikela Pelekani] R. G. E. Forster. Many joys and benefits were gained by the Japanese doctors on that visit.

At four o'clock in the afternoon, the visiting party left Kalaupapa. Everyone gathered at the pier, the band was playing, hands were waving, calls of farewell were given until they got on the ship. The ocean was calm, and before the hour had struck eight o'clock on Sunday evening, the *Mauna Kea* had reached the pier.

Ka Nupepa Kuokoa. 18 JUNE 1909. P. 7.
Hunahuna Mea Hou O Ka Aina O Ka Ehaeha. Bits of News from the Land of Agony.

To the *Nupepa Kuokoa.* Greetings. Here again is this small bundle of ours. Please endure to carry out to the shores, the ridges, the mountaintops of your beloved land, Hawai'i, the brief phrases placed above.

On May 22, the new water pipe with a length of approximately half a mile joined with the old water pipe. When the water of these pipes met, the old pipes that run from Waikolu to Kalaupapa were completely filled, and the writer saw that the water was gushing at several elbows [kui] of the pipes, ones that had not had a water source before. The writer remembered the song of that singing child of the land of agony upon the strings [kaula uwea] of the autoharp [pila hapa].

Beloved is the water of Waikolu, hold back [Komikomi],
That water that supplies the multitude, hold back,
Beloved is the water of Waikakulu, hold back,
That water gushing on the cliff, hold back,
Beloved is the water of Waimanu, hold back,

That water spraying on the cliff, hold back,
Beloved is the water of Waihānau, hold back,
That water up in the lofty heights, hold back,
To Kauhakō we go, hold back,
See the water of the crater, hold back,
We go there and see, hold back,
The hidden shrimp in the shallows, hold back.

The carpenters have finished constructing the buildings, which stand majestically and are companions to the mists [kehau] of Wailēʻia. The fences are done, the bridge [uwapo] on the river is done, and the pier for skiffs [uwapo pili waapa] is being built in Waikilu [Waikolu].

It was heard that next month, July, the patients will enter this hospital. It will be the time to see the beauty of electricity [uwila], since electricity was installed everywhere, in the residences, the offices, inside all the buildings and outside on the porches. The activity of the electricity reaches all the way to the grass field, and a lamp with four branches stands so that this grass field can be seen night and day. It has truly been made like a Caucasian place [kahi haole].

On the night of May 21, Liloa and Jack ran away, but while they were on the path to Makanalua, Jack had second thoughts. Jack returned to the place of the sheriff and told him everything. The police were immediately ordered to search, and three days later Sheriff J. K. Waiʻamaʻu received news that the miscreant was under the cluster of rocks at the shore of Pūahi.

The sheriff got him and took him to the jail, but a few days later he escaped again. The police searched again but did not find him. Then the sheriff found him again. The reason for his escape was asked, and the answer was that he was not well cared for with starch and meat. Secondly, he had great love for a petticoat (woman) [palekoki (wahine)]. Here is a short story told to the writer:

A few months ago, the trousers (man) [lolewawae (kane)] were living with the petticoat (woman) [palekoke (wahine)], and because of the excessive mistreatment of the petticoat by the trousers, the petticoat moved into the Pauahi Home [Home Pauahi]. However, a short time later, the trousers were passing along outside the enclosure [pa] of the home. When the petticoat saw him, love for her companion swelled up and she waved a handkerchief. The puffy clouds met up, and tumbled off to ʻAwalau [hui ae la na opua, a hina ae la i awalau].

And these puffy clouds (Liloa and Rose) kept doing it until one night, while the electric glow of the movie [uwila o ke kii onioni] was presenting wondrous acts, there was still light shining inside Pauahi Home. The police became suspicious because the light at the place of the movie was flickering. When the police investigated, they clearly found that part of the electricity was in Pauahi Home, "the electricity had flown to Kāneʻohe" [ua lele ka uwila i Kaneohe: a reference to the song "Kāneʻohe," which mentions electricity]. Liloa was arrested for entering the Pauahi Home to turn on the electricity. He was sentenced to six months imprisonment.

I have done enough at this time,
—S. K. M. Nāhauowailēʻia. Kalawao, Molokaʻi, JUNE 10, 1909.
» [This article has many examples of the colorful descriptions in the Hawaiian language. The writer, S. K. Maialoha, uses an interesting mix of old and new

terms to describe the events of the day and a poetic pen name, Nāhauowailēʻia, "the dews of Wailēʻia."]

Ka Nupepa Kuokoa. 24 JUNE 1910. P. 6.
Na Meahou O Ke Kahua Maʻi. News from the Patient Settlement.
To the newspaper *Kuokoa* and the boys who toss about the chilly metal letters, the patient editor. Greetings.

The assistant superintendent, J. K. Waiʻamaʻu, quit his job because of the lack of unity of the actions and opinions of his superior, and you [Waiʻamaʻu] were viewed disfavorably by the man.

It was reported to the writer that J. K. Waiʻamaʻu has served as assistant superintendent of the patient settlement [kahua maʻi] for fourteen years. He is a man knowledgeable in various skills, such as drawing blueprints, various kinds of painting, engineering metal works, and many more. A few days ago, one wheel of the poi mill broke [ua haki kekahi huila o ka wili ai]. The money-consuming Caucasian engineer [wiliki haole ai dala] said to send it to Honolulu, but with the knowledge of this man, after only a few hours of work it was fixed, and the milling of the poi is running properly.

This Waiʻamaʻu is a father to the patients and to the helpers [kokua]. His superior becomes quite angry at the patients and the helpers sometimes, but this man stood and defended on behalf of the patients and the helpers. Because of this great compassion the patients have created a fundraiser to get money for a gift or gifts.

After J. K. Waiʻamaʻu quit being the assistant superintendent, the superintendent, J. D. McVeigh, left his position as superintendent with the doctor, W. J. Goodhue. If this news is true, then this is a tsunami [kai hoee]. Everything will be soaked, no planted leaf will remain.

June 11th. [La 11 o Iune: Kamehameha Day holiday]

With the first light of morning broke forth on the day when the Conqueror of the Nation [Naʻi Aupuni] emerged from the loins of his mother, the walls of the heavens were cloudless and a gentle breeze was blowing from the northeast. Between nine and ten oʻclock, the procession of [horseback] skirt riders rode out [huakai holo pa-u], led by Mrs. Margaret [Makareta] Notley with the star flag [hae Hoku] waving and the skirts of various colors floating in the breeze.

The procession went all the way to Kalawao, and outside the federal enclosure they turned back toward Kalaupapa.

THE EVENTS OF THE NIGHT. [NA HANA O KA PO.]

A few days later, word spread throughout the patient settlement [kahua maʻi] that a sum of money had been set aside by Wm. Notley for movies, food, and coffee. At 7:00 p.m. the patients [maʻi] assembled, the seats were filled, and the crowd overflowed all the way outside. Before the movie was played, J. S. Wilmington spoke to the audience, explaining that the movies, the food, and the coffee all came from the open heart of Wm. Notley.

The events began with the band playing the national anthem [mele lahui]. After that, the movies played. While the movies were playing, the singing voices of the Papakailoi Club [Kalapu o Papakailoi], led by Jeo. Kaʻaiwela, sounded sweetly. Stewards were supplying bags of candy, peanuts, and oranges.

The humbug thing was that only the prominent people [kii maka nunui] were being provided these, with the ordinary folks [kii maka liilii] being left out.

Where the writer was sitting, it was clearly seen that the bags were unfairly given to the mature birds [manu hulu], with the fledglings [manu punua] being left out. The name of this biased steward [puuku hana kapakahi] is Mrs. Pelani Opulauoho. The bundles appeared, being carried by this one's friends, with nothing for some other folks, and some of those folks belonged to the Mormon faith [Hoomana Moremona].

Do not again give work to this unjust steward. When the events were almost done, the table was filled with those wanting to drink coffee. When the showing of the movies was over, everyone returned home. On the road, the writer heard some folks saying, "My pockets are full of bags of food," while another said, "I didn't get one bag." Someone else said, "Only because I asked someone else, I got my small orange." There were four stewards: Mrs. Punohu, Mrs. Like, Mrs. Ho'olapa, and Mrs. Pelani.

If all the stewards were biased in the same way, then the job should not be given to them again, but if it was as the writer witnessed, the other stewards were not at fault. An injustice was truly committed. To Wm. Notley goes great thanks.

To the patient friends [hoa ma'i], you should all cast your ballots for Wm. Notley. We are indebted to the generosity of this man. I have done enough here. Yours truly, Waihānau. Kalaupapa, JUNE 16, 1910.

Ke Aloha Aina. 21 JANUARY 1911. P. 1.
Na Virigine Katolika. The Catholic Nuns.

Hawai'i is truly blessed to have nuns [Virigine] to care for the children of the patients [keiki a ka poe ma'i] of Kalaupapa and Kalawao, living in the home for girls [home o na Kaikamahine] up in Kalihi. For almost twenty years these pure women with compassionate hearts have been doing this, yet absolutely no good deed has been done by Hawai'i for them. Here are these nuns [poe Virigine] living in temporary shacks that they maintain themselves with the help of a Japanese worker [Kepani lawelawe] that the government provided to carry out the most difficult tasks. There are over sixty children there, and the living conditions are unsuitable. How could the government treat them so uncaringly? The solons [Solona: lawmakers] should know about this thing. You must not be concerned that they are Catholics [Katolika] or else there will be no helpers [kokua]. Look at the good work that we, Hawai'i's own [kakou Hawaii], have scorned.

» [The writer is referencing Kapi'olani Home, an orphanage for girls whose parents were patients at Kalaupapa. Mother Marianne established the original home in Kakaako in 1885, but the Board of Health moved it to Kalihi Kai in 1891.]

Ke Au Hou. 22 MARCH 1911. P. 23.
Ka Huakai a na Hoa Ahaolelo no Molokai. The Journey of the Members of the Legislature to Moloka'i.

Right after 9:00 p.m. last Saturday night, the legislative committee left for Moloka'i on the *S. S. Maunakea* from the pier and emerged alongside the *Battleship Boe.* There it waited until 1:00 o'clock in the morning.

The number of people on this journey was fifty-five men and one woman

MOTHER MARIANNE: 1888 TO 1918

299

named Mrs. Pua. The ship arrived at Kalaupapa as the sun leapt above the line of cliffs [kakai pali], and the anchor was let go in the shelter of Kalaupapa. The three skiffs [waapa] of the ship carried the lawmaking travelers and the public ashore to climb onto the pier that was whitewashed with sea spray [huna kai].

With great honor, the band of the patient settlement [kahua maʻi] played for the lawmaking Solons. The party was hosted warmly by superintendent John McVeigh and the doctor of the colony [panalaau], W. J. Goodhue. In carriages and on horses the crowd was carried to Kalawao, to the Baldwin Home [Home Baluwina] for boys, about three miles away from the harbor [awapae]. The roads were not good on this journey. On the veranda [lanai] in front of that Baldwin Home, the multitude had gathered.

Senator Pali was introduced by Kilinawoti [Chillingworth] in the role of chairman for the committee, and he explained about the petitions submitted to the legislature for wine and light beer to be allowed within the colony [Panalaau]. As he reported, "Nothing has been done for these requests. Maybe more requests will come from you, but I will never choose to approve of this deadly poison being given to you." He continued, "I am glad to provide great assistance with your food, that gives you health, not with the thing that will kill you, and you should remember, you will never get from me that thing you desire, liquor [Rama]."

The chairman of the health committee of the lower house, J. H. Koni, was another who spoke, and his opinion was like that of Pali of the upper house, that the colony [Panalaau] will not get liquor.

THE SUBMITTED REQUESTS. [NA NOI I WAIHOIA MAI.]

From Moses Holi, a complaint that there is not enough [money for] clothing in the money provided, and he [also] explained that it costs $1.70 for a bag of flour bought there. When the meeting there ended, they left for Kalaupapa. When the party had gone about a mile, that was when thunder clapped, a sign [hoailona] saying that it would rain, and it was truly so, until they arrived at the place of the superintendent.

They visited the Bay View Home, and the Bishop Home [Bihopa Home], where girls from two to sixteen years old are cared for under the care of Mother Marianne [makuahine Mary Marianne] and two helpers [kokua]. There the piano was played by the girls in a duet, and that was how that time was passed joyfully. The mother answered all questions well, and according to her, everything has been supplied except for some rocking chairs [noho paipai]. The superintendent of the patient settlement [kahua maʻi] will supply them, dependent upon the legislature.

Twenty-five children are cared for there, aged from two days to two years, and when a child turns two, they are suitable to be returned to the Kalihi Home. At the place of the superintendent a Hawaiian meal was held, supplied with pumpkin pies and fish cooked in ti leaves [iʻa lawalu hoomoemoe i na lau la-i]. According to the writer for the morning newspaper, the baked dog [ilio kalua] was the most glorious and the poi ʻapiʻi [poi made from ʻapiʻi taro]. When this was over, Kilinawoti continued his work of asking questions, and the superintendent and the doctor answered.

And at the bandstand [kahi puhiohe] the big meeting was held. And the rather significant requests at that meeting were as follows:

1. Twenty-one pounds of poi per week.
2. The lack of the colony [panalaau] was approved; do not allow liquor.
3. A $3,000 hospital.
4. A $3,000 building for taking care of young children (babies) [keiki opiopio (bepe)].
5. Giving greetings to those of the other islands.

When the work was concluded, they got in the skiffs to go to the ship.

Ka Nupepa Kuokoa. 12 JULY 1912. P. 6.
Paina Hoomanao Ma Ka Aina O Ka Ehaeha. Remembrance Feast in the Land of Agony.

On June 28, 1:00 p.m., Mrs. Ellen Noholoa began a feast of remembrance for her beloved, and to mark a year passing since their separation, when they have not eaten and drank together at their dining table.

The wife who loved her husband laid out a feast completely filled with the rich foods of Kapuʻukolu [a place famous for abundance] for her to eat and drink with the loved ones of her husband, the grandchildren, the children, the sisters, and all the friends.

Before the aforementioned hour, the dining table and the room were covered with the adornments of the upland forest, the cool misty palai fern of Naihanau [Waihānau] and the fine-leafed kupukupu fern. The dining table was filled with various delicacies: sticky poi that settles nicely down the throat from Kalawao; sweet potato poi that was made sour [poi uala i hooawaawaia]; pig; chicken mixed with long rice [moa i huiia me ka laiki loloa]; octopus [hee] mixed with ʻalaʻalaʻula seaweed [also know as ʻaʻalaʻula or wawaeʻiole]; limpets [opihi] mixed with seaweed from the headland extending into the sea, Hoʻolehua; shellfish [pupu] found on the cliffs; the māhikihiki shrimp of Waikolu [opae mahikihiki o Waikolu]; the fragrant līpoa seaweed of Kaupokia-wa [lipoa aala o Kaupokiawa]; the famous kukui nuts of Kauhakō Crater [kukui kaulana o ka lua o Kauhako]; the bone fish that lie on the sands of Pūahi [na iʻa oio moe one o Puahi]; the manini fish that lie in pools in ʻĪliopiʻi [manini moe lua i Iliopii]; the sweet beverages; the soft pastries skillfully made by Willie Ka-leiheana; sweet potatoes baked [kaluaia] with the pig; sea urchin roe [iʻo wana]; kohu seaweed [limu kohu]; and so on.

In the count by the writer of the number of plates filled with each and every thing, except for the sweet beverages and the sweet potato, there were 156 plates, from big to small. The dining table was decorated.

When everything was ready, the diners were called and the writer was invited to appeal to the heavenly powers. When the prayer was finished, the forks went down, the spoons went up, Keonipulu [John Bull: a pun on "full"] arrived and Paohaka [Empty-cavern] departed. The feast was continued until 7:00 p.m. It was peaceful, without any rising seas [He maluhia aole wahi piipii kai: no one got angry].

—Nāhauowailēʻia. Kalawao, Molokaʻi, JULY 1, 1912.

» [In this article Nāhauowailēʻia, the pen name of S. K. Maialoha, lists the items on Mrs. Noholoaʻs dinner menu. Many of them are from the ocean on both the windward and leeward sides of the peninsula and show the rich diversity of seafood that was found at Kalaupapa.]

Ka Nupepa Kuokoa. 30 APRIL 1915. P. 4.

Na Mea Hou O Ke Kahua Maʻi. News From the Patient Settlement.

On March 31 and April 14, 1915, patients suspected of infection, thirty-two in number, were inspected. Several days after the members of the legislature came, the decision of the doctors was issued that sixteen people would be re- leased, those named below, and one of them would be permanently released, having no scar of infection upon him. He is Mr. Liloa Kuheleipo, and the other fifteen will go every three months to be inspected by the doctor of the Board of Health in each district where these folks are returning to again see the realm of land, alas! Here are their names:

Kaula Maikai, Liloa Kuheleipo from Nāhiku, Maui; Keliʻi Makakoa from Koʻolau, Oʻahu; Jno. Alawa from Kona, Hawaiʻi; Elia Kaʻaihua from Hilo, Hawaiʻi; Esther ʻUo from Kauaʻi; Lani Pahio, from Hilo, Hawaiʻi; Kaehu Brown, from Waikapū, Maui; Sam Kaluahine, from Waikīkī, Oʻahu; Wm. Kalimalu, from Lāhaina, Maui; D. N. Hoʻopilimeaʻai from Kīhei, Maui; J. K. Kahaleanu from Hilo, Hawaiʻi; Jno. Kealoha from Honolulu, Oʻahu; Mary Kapukana from Puna, Hawaiʻi; James Kimokeo, from Kona, Hawaiʻi; Marie Kahuila, Kīpahulu, Maui.

THE PETITIONS OF THE CAUCASIANS. [NA HOOPII A NA HAOLE.]

When the members of the legislature came, the Caucasians petitioned about the superintendent, and the answer was received: "We did not come here for trivial petitions. We came for the petitions concerning your problems." These Caucasians forcefully grabbed the club of Kekūokalani [Kekuaokalani], named Hoʻoleheleheki'i [disappointment].

News has reached the writer that it [their disappointment] has made the climb all the way to the place with the letter O in the Meridian line in London (Washington), and there the Steel Pen banana (petition) [maia Penikila (hoo-pii)] will ripen in its grumbling.

THE PROPERTY OF THE PATIENTS. [NA WAIWAI O NO MAʻI.]

The announcement has been placed about the property of the patients who die here in the patient settlement [kahua maʻi]. For the benefit of the relatives living outside, they are being told that for the friends who do not subscribe to the *Nupepa Kuokoa,* you should subscribe so that you always see the news from the patient settlement [Kahua Maʻi], and your rights, which the writer will con- tinue to report in his columns. It is the only newspaper where you will see it.

For the families, those to whom these relatives being described belong, go to the Board of Health in Honolulu and on the other islands inhabited by the agents of the Board of Health. For those who are rather confused, ask the writer. Thusly:

John Kekoi, Board of Health, N. Hilo, Hawaiʻi, $24.02; Liwai Haʻalelea, Kahaluʻu, S. Kona, Hawaiʻi, $27.32; Samuela Kuakaula, ʻAuwaiolimu, Honolulu, $5.50; Ah Siu, Wailuku, Maui, $330.31.

THE MEMBERS OF THE LEGISLATURE ARRIVE.
[HIKI MAI NA LALA AHAOLELO.]

At 6:00 a.m. the people described above were carried upon the broad chest of the Seafaring Woman [umauma lahalaha o ka wahine Aukai], the *S. S. Kinau,* anchoring and landing ashore amid stormy conditions in the surging harbor [awa haulani] of Kalaupapa. They affectionately met with the residents [kamaaina] of the land of agony [aina o ka ehaeha], some folks appearing a sad sight and some appearing a joyful sight. The visitors continually asked questions.

Between 9:00 and 10:00 a.m. the senators: Rev. B. S. Kiwini, Hon. Kula, the Representatives: Hon. Aiu, Hon. D. Kupihea, Hon. Lota, Hon. Goodness, Hon. R. J. K. Nāwahine, Duke Kahanamoku, Hon. Kawewehi, Hon. Coney, and many others whose names the writer does not have, all went up.

While the writer was conversing with some of the representatives, the writer arrived, and some folks had already finished sharing their thoughts. Some members of the legislature were returning, and some were going to visit the hospitals of the federal government, standing here in Kalawao. The governor, the former president of the Board of Health, shared some thoughts that were quite compassionate.

The discussions with the members of the legislature were not long. They reported that they would go back and fulfill the petitions of the patients, meaning the continuation of the fifty cents added on to the allotment voucher.

THE CONDITION OF THE PATIENTS. [KA NOHO ANA O NA MAʻI.]

The condition of the patients is good. Who does not have it good? The care is good, but the writer received news that we will be lacking starch and meat in the future, since the agreement with the Chinese [Pake] in Honolulu will be ended once this current contract expires.

The one who chooses the meat is not one permitted to choose, and the beef we eat is the beef of the patient settlement [kahua maʻi]. If that is over, what will be our meat and our starch? Might it be bread, rice, salted salmon and canned salmon, maybe the donkeys and horses that roam in the fields?

The writer received news from the superintendent that the farming by the patients in the farm plots of the patients will be ended. They will be planted with grass for the cattle to eat, and some cattle of the finest breed of the foreign lands will be raised. Perhaps when these cattle arrive, the suitable time will have passed, and new people will eat these cattle.

The keeping by patients of horses and donkeys in excess of one animal per each patient will be ended. The only great problem of the land at this time is that the land is covered by magnolia trees [mikinolia], cotton shrubs [mao], and kīkānia bushes, with great sums of money being spent to get rid of these plants that cover the land. Raising pigs and chickens are the things to enrich the patients. Raising these things might be how the patients get what they need in the future.

BUILDINGS RENOVATED. [HANA HOU IA NA HALE.]

The old buildings are being renovated. Several buildings in Kalaupapa have been finished, and here are these days passing gently. Kalawao's buildings are being renovated. The work on the buildings of Kalawao began with that old building in Kaukaopua, that house that Superintendent Meyers [Meyer] lived in before. The floors and the rotten beams have left and a new thing is being seen. The rot is not completely gone, but it is better. Here in these days at the house of Mr. Moke Holi, a house close to the house of the writer, there are new shingles and new purlin. The bad thing has gone and the good thing has come. Such is the case with several boards, until it is finished, moving on to the house of the writer, and so on. This is probably not a completely new thing, and the writer reports seeing the first folks who came out for the things that were done, since the superintendent said that the buildings here in Kalawao would not be renovated.

Ka Nupepa Kuokoa. 15 OCTOBER 1915. P. 5.
Na Itamu O Ke Kahua Maʻi. [News] Items from the Patient Settlement.

On September 6, 1915, the young big-eyed scad [hahalalu: juvenile akule fish] were surrounded [with a net] by the Fishing Society of Kalaupapa [Hui Lawaia o Kalaupapa], which is the organization in which Geo. Kanikau serves as supervisor [lunanui] and Mr. Manuel [Manuela] Soares and Henry Kalawaiʻa serve as head fishermen [poo lawaia], at this time.

The total was 2,343 pounds, which was one-fourth [of the catch]. Three-fourths of the fish were released. The allotment for each patient was one-fourth of a gunny sack [eke huluhulu]. A completely full skiff [waapa], which was not weighed, was set apart and divided among those who had labored and the people of the society. This is the largest encirclement of fish seen here in the patient settlement [kahua maʻi]. The fish remain, not netted. The patients who hang fish to dry have a full load.

NARROWLY AVOIDED FATALITY. [PAKELE MAI POINO KE OLA.]

On the evening of September 16, Kealawaiʻole fell down the cliff in front of the medicine dispensary [hale haawi laau] of the Board of Health, which is twenty-four feet high. Here is the story reported to the writer:

On the aforementioned evening, he and his wife came down for the movie, and on Damien Street [alanui Damiana], at the place where the store of Kimo Hawe stands, an "internal problem" [pilikia kuloko] came to Kealawaiʻole. He went to deal with the problem at the aforementioned place. When that problem was over, he started to return. The wife heard a groan while she was nearing that place. She ran to peer down and saw that the husband was lying below. She went down a different way, lifted him, and saw that his head was punctured and blood was flowing. Meanwhile there was a person coming near who the writer heard was drooping over the water of Pāʻieʻie [ua luhe no i ka wai o Paieie: drunk].

The wife called to Kawaipua to come down and help, and the two of them lifted but could not pick him up. The wife went up again to get help. She found Geo. Kahoakapu, and they went to the movie theater and told the policeman. The policeman came along with the crowd and lifted up the injured man. The assistant doctor arrived, and he was returned to the surgical hospital [haukapila oki]. His arm was broken in two places.

On the 26th the writer went in person to see the one who was injured, and as the writer observed, the bone was not broken. It seemed cracked, since the part that was thought to be broken was not raised. Some pieces of wood were joined [to the arm: a splint]. If it is Hawaiian wood [laau Hawaii], then the wood will restore the bones that are broken and cracked. He continues to moan in pain.

TRULY SEEING THE LAND WHERE MILK AND HONEY FLOW. [IKE MAOLI I KA AINA E KAHE ANA KA WAIU AME KA MELI.]

On the ship of September 23, the schoolmate of the writer, J. W. Haau, stepped as a visitor upon the land greatly feared [aina i kau nui ia ka weli], but these expectations were mistaken. On the 25th the writer met with my dear companion in seeking wisdom from the Boarding School of Hilo [Kula Hanai o Hilo], that building of increasing knowledge that was patiently inhabited by us. From the time we were separated until meeting up again, forty-five years and five months had passed.

THE CONDITION OF THE PATIENTS. [KA NOHO ANA O NA MAʻI.]

The condition of the patients is good. Those patients with pain in their hands, in the feet, in the throat, are being operated upon by our patient doctor. The blood spurting into his eyes is nothing, seeming like a true father for the patients.

Through the patient work of this doctor, a long life is regained for some folks! The most serious illness seen in the patient settlement [kahua maʻi] is the pain that prevents breathing, but in the skillful search of the doctor, this problem has been ended, because the throat is cut into and a pipe is inserted there. Upon coughing the stubborn mucus comes out, the mucus that causes the pain and prevents breathing. Great is the wisdom. Many of these people are now living.

As for those whose feet and hands are amputated [oki], they live in the surgical hospital [haukapila oki], being well cared for. There are separate nurses for the night and the day. There are beds, sheets, mosquito nets, and bells to call if something is wanted. Everything is splendid. The dormitories, the cafeteria, everything is pleasant. The writer went to visit and this was seen clearly.

THE PIOUS COME TO PRAY WITH THE PATIENTS. [KOMO NA HAIPULE E PULE ME NA MAʻI.]

For several Sabbaths the writer entered the surgical hospital, and for several weeks he clearly saw the manner in which the meeting is held. The Mormons joined in with that prayer service. There were no Catholics in the prayer service where the writer sat. The Calvinist faith is the one doing that superior work of glory.

After the meeting at the surgical hospital was over, I went on to the Bay View Home. The writer gives his great thanks to those raising up that superior work of glory, and here are their names: J. K. Kainuwai, Sam Lovell, J. K. Kawaiwai, Lui Luaiwi, Mrs. Mary Baker, Mrs. Sela [Ringer], Alohikea of Hawaiʻi. Move forward to the final goal! [Nee aku imua a ka pahu hopu!]

SUNDAY SCHOOL EXHIBITION. [HOIKE KULA SABATI.]

The writer did not receive a paper describing the activities of the day, but here is the gist. On the 26th, at 10:00 a.m., the activities of the Sunday school exhibition were opened, beginning with group singing. That class from Kalawao finished with their hymns on the Day of Adoration.

[Then] the schools of Kalaupapa, the school of the Bay View Home, blind folks, and the last was a school class from the surgical hospital, they were three led by J. Kanikau from ʻEwa, Oʻahu. The activities of this class were full of joy. Seven dollars [$7] were raised.

Yours truly, Waikakulu. Kalawao, OCT. 1, 1915.

» [Waikakulu, the name of a freshwater pool, was another pen name of S. K. Maialoha. He also used Nāhauowailēʻia.]

Ka Nupepa Kuokoa. 5 NOVEMBER 1915. P. 3.
Paina Hoomanao. Feast of Remembrance.

On October 23, 1915, Mr. Nāuahi and Dick Lāhaina created a feast of remembrance [papaaina hoomanao] for Mrs. Puarose, for the fulfillment of one year of Puarose's resting in the sleep of summer and winter [death], on a dining table filled with sticky taro poi [poi kalo uouo] from Waikolu, fat pigs from Kalawao and Kalaupapa, beef liver [ake bipi], limpets [opihi] that move [nee] along the smooth stones [paala] of Mokio, desserts, soda water, shrimp [opae mahikihiki] from Waikolu, the ferns [hoio] that lie in the cold, and much more.

People were invited to go and appear together on the night of the one who rests, and also folks from outside. There was eating, there was drinking, and there was still a great deal of food so the remainder was distributed to the workers [poe lima hana] and others as well.

Ka Nupepa Kuokoa. 22 SEPTEMBER 1916. P. 4.
Na Meahou O Ke Kahua Maʻi. News from the Patient Settlement.

A fish pond [lokoiʻa] was opened here in the settlement by our doctor with a heart that loves the people. This fish pond is in ʻĪliopiʻi, in the place constantly flooded by freshwater in the times when the water levels rise, reaching a depth of six or seven feet. It is encircled by a stone wall [pa pohaku], and water to supply this pond is being dug for. If the water is not sufficient, then a windmill [ena makani] will be made to pull in ocean water for filling this pond, with the power of money.

In days of old, it was the power of the command of the chiefs [alii] or the lesser chiefs [konohiki], or else the menehune [mythical race of little people], that created the ponds, the temples, but in this era it is silver and gold that create them.

This pond will be filled with various fish and various seaweeds [limu]. The writer met with the owner of this pond, and he asked what the suitable fish were. The writer replied, "milkfish [awa], mullet (young) [amaama (puaia)], and the brown-bellied baby mullet [pua amaama opu lepo]." Those who are able to supply milkfish and young mullet, write directly to him (W. J. Goodhue, M.D.), or to the writer.

DESTRUCTIVE FIRE IN THE PATIENT SETTLEMENT.
[PAUAHI MA KE KAHUA MAʻI.]

On September 2, 4:00 p.m., fire spread at the Bay View Home in an accident. Here is a story obtained by the writer:

At that aforementioned time, the fire leapt from the chimney to the side in front of the building, onto the shingles, and began to burn. Due to the great amount of wind, the burning of the fire spread widely.

In this home there are many blind people [makapo], as well as infirm people [poe nawaliwali] left in bed. The strong folks [poe ikaika] took them out until the helpers [kokua] arrived.

The possessions of some folks were removed, but the majority were lost. The money of some folks was obtained, and that of others was lost. Some clothing was on the skin of some folks, and other folks had taken it all off. Some folks who were in the bathroom [rumi auau] only had underwear.

Compassionate people [poe aloha] raised money, and clothing was bought for those in need. The [sewing] machines in the patient settlement [kahua maʻi] were brought to the veranda [lanai] of the medicine dispensary, and there the clothing was given.

The superintendent was greatly alarmed by this disaster, since the new houses are not ready. Due to this lack of houses, the troubled people [poe pilikia] were returned to the surgical hospital, to the Bishop Home and the Baldwin Home, and the houses outside. However, it was lucky that no life was lost.

The Mormon faith [hoomana Mamona] is arising to hold a concert, and it will be held on the evening of September 16.

THE PATIENTS CONTINUE TO EAT FISH. [AI IʻA MAU NA MAʻI.]

For three weeks the patient settlement [kahua maʻi] has been supplied with the fat mullet fish [amaama momona] from the pond in Kūpeke on Molokaʻi. The total weight reached around six thousand pounds, approximately, at ten cents per pound. The water of the tender young coconut gurgles on and on [U-li no ka wai o ka niu haohao].

INTENSE SUN THESE DAYS. [NUI KA LA I KEIA MAU LA.]

The sun is intense these days. The plains [kula] now seem as if they have been burned by fire. The animals roam about, needing many water troughs. The people sweat excessively. The crops are drying up, needing a water hose, and the amount of water is shrinking. That is enough for you and me.

Nāhauowailēʻia. Kalaupapa, SEPT. 15, 1916.

Ka Nupepa Kuokoa. 8 DECEMBER 1916. P. 5.
La Kanakolu O Novemaba Ma Ke Kahua Maʻi. The 30th of November in the Patient Settlement.

On the morning of November 30 there was a fine calm. The wind was gently blowing from the north and bringing a chill. Early that morning, the American flags [hae Amerika] were raised on all the flagpoles in the patient settlement [kahua maʻi], totaling eleven, with the exception of two flagpoles, that of the Society of Knights [Hui Naika: Knights of Columbus] and the house of the assisting doctor who returned outside.

Time passed until it was half past nine, when the bells of the churches, Calvinist, Catholic, and Mormon [kalawina, Kakolika, Mamona], sounded with a powerful ringing, calling the pious to go to those temples, bend the knees, and look toward the mountains. From there shall be obtained the necessary things in accordance with the proclamation of the day that was commanded.

On the morning of the aforementioned day, the doors were opened, and everything inside was seen, which was this: the walls of the building [hale], the ceiling above, the floor, the risers the chairs stand on, the projection room [rumi o ka mikini hoolele], room for the helpers [rumi o na kokua maʻi], the room of the superintendent with the doctor and with the family.

They had been painted with reddish paint mixed with varnish. It was beautiful in appearance. At the place where the activities would be performed, there was a cloth painted with various colors, with the forest, the mountain, the mist spreading over the peaks of the mountain, and the base of the mountain, and many other things.

The most impressive thing was that the screens can change. If there is a robber, or a thief, the screens will change, and you will see policemen grasping the knobs of the doors, continually entering in every room. If there is a tableau, there is a different scene of beauty. There are between two and four options for the screens.

On the ceiling above there are eight lights with covers, preventing pain to the eyes of those with eyes that hurt. The strength of the light is such that a pin could be seen. The walls of the building were adorned with American flag bunting, and at the doorposts were little lights of various colors.

It was reported to the writer that there are three hundred individual seats, and several other chairs, but when the people came in, there were not enough seats. When the time progressed again to just after twelve oʻclock, some small cannons were sounded, since a portion of the patients had arrived.

When the building was opened, the superintendent explained the reason that this beautiful building is standing. Here is the story obtained by the writer:

Some people gathered to consider building a new movie theater [hale kii onioni hou], since the hut where festivities are held is narrow. A committee of five members was chosen. They decided to meet with the superintendent. When the committee went, the superintendent was surprised, because he thought that the patients were hungry, or the taro was overripe, the salmon was bad, or the beef was lean.

When the reason for their appearance was properly explained, everything that the committee had planned was reported. The superintendent immediately approved it to be done quickly and done by the committees among the patients. Several hundred dollars were obtained. When the superintendent went out to meet with the governor, the governor made the theater his responsibility. As for the furnishings inside, another fundraiser was held that raised a full $1,000. When the kids with little bags from Kauaʻi (the Wilcoxes [Wilikoki]) received the news, the two of them unfolded their hands and gave a piano, their gift, played by electricity. There were many other uplifting thoughts from the superintendent.

Everyone went to eat on the long tables outside of the theater, held on the veranda [lanai]. Electric lights were put in. The feast was filled with poi that slides nicely down the throat from Kalawao, pork wrapped in ti leaves and mixed with taro leaves [luau], salmon, octopus [hee], the fat mullet fish [amaama] from the ponds of Molokaʻi, onions, pork baked in an earth oven [imu], and much more. The place where the pork wrapped in ti leaves was obtained was from the pigs that the Board of Health brought for the meat allotments of the patients. The pigs baked in earth ovens were from the superintendent and some others. The dining tables became full. When the first folks were done, they went inside, and the remaining festivities were continued until 5:00 p.m., when there was a break.

Between 6:00 and 7:00 p.m. the patients [ma'i] came again. While the electric light was showing its beauty, all the seats on the prepared risers were filled with patients, but the patients were still coming. The long wooden benches from the veranda where the meal was served were fetched and placed in the area kept clear for dancing and other festivities, which was most of the building, and then there was no place to dance [hulahula]. Not everyone was inside. Some folks crowded on the verandas, in the doorway, and the windows, and when it was over, the events were begun. While the festivities were held, peanuts, candy, and so forth were given out. This year the folks who gave out the aforementioned things were men. In past years it was only women.

Right at ten o'clock, an ice cream social [papaaina aihau] was opened. At twelve o'clock the festivities were ended, but they were not completely over because the movie was postponed to the night of Friday, Dec. 1.

The writer gives many thanks to Mr. Kameaaloha, the head manager of the housewarming party [paina komo hale]. You were quite attentive to taking care of the food, since this is the writer's thirteenth year in the patient settlement [kahua ma'i], and no one was seen returning home with boxes, gunny sacks, or book bags. In your vigilance the people of this kind were all found. In years past, that was the news of the writer, but this year only a small bundle was taken back.

Forgive me, reader of the *Kuokoa,* for not reporting on the dancing tunes [leo hulahula] because they were not reported to the writer. What the writer saw was twirling all around the room with no one to do the calling, and two places made available for standing in the open. Mrs. Elena Pilima hosted the building of the Board of Health, and Mrs. Lizzie Manuwa had the shoreward taro terraces [Papakailoi]. Because some folks could not get enough delight on Friday, the 1st, there was dancing from the morning until 4:00 p.m. Please excuse, reader, if there is a fault in this report.

Yours truly, S. K. M. Waikakulu. Kalaupapa, DEC. 1, 1916.

» [Waikakulu, the name of a freshwater pool, was another pen name of S. K. Maialoha. He also used Nāhauowailē'ia.]

Ka Nupepa Kuokoa. 18 OCTOBER 1918. P. 8.
Kuu Pokii Aloha Ua Hala. My Beloved Younger Sibling Has Passed.
Mr. Editor of the *Nupepa Kuokoa.* Greetings to you:

Please allow me some small, available space in your columns for my bundle, which is that title placed above, to be seen by the parents, older siblings, younger siblings, children, and all of our relatives who reside from the rising sun at Kumukahi to the setting of the sun at Lehua [mai ka la puka ma Kumukahi a ka welona a ka la i Lehua].

Whereas, in the early morning of Tuesday, Oct. 1, 1918, it pleased God to take the spirit of my beloved younger sister, Mrs. Koleka Anderson, and separate it from the body, and leave an earthly body for me to grieve over with the family.

Mrs. Koleka Anderson was born from the loins of Kuhaulua (male) and Makaweli (female) in Kanahena, Honua'ula, Maui. Twenty-nine years of her breathing the chilly air of this life has passed, filled with disasters.

In her youth, she was educated at the day school of 'Ulupalakua. She was a girl who obeyed the commands of our parents, and our parents became an important thing to her. When she grew up, she married Mr. Anderson, and they lived in happiness until the death of her husband. Right after those days my beloved younger sister returned and lived with me, her older sibling, and with our children, in Wailuku, Maui. How beloved is that place where the two of us lived!

On June 1, 1916, the hands of the Board of Health seized and took away my beloved younger sister from my presence, to the detention station [pamaʻi] of Kalihi, and there she lived for six months. After that time, she was taken away to the patient settlement [kahua maʻi] of Kalaupapa and lived in the Bishop Home [Bihopa Home], under the care of the nuns [makuahine vilikina].

While she lived there, she became a brethren of the Protestant Congregation of Kalaupapa in the time of Rev. D. Kaʻai, the minister, and she appeared there until her death. On August 24, 1918, she left the Bishop Home with her infirmity and went to live with the older cousin of our mother, Mrs. K. Kalaʻau. Due to the immensity of my love for my dear younger sister, I sent a letter to [superintendent] J. D. McVeigh to allow me to go there as a helper [kokua] for my dear younger sister. I received the response that I should go to see my dear younger sister at the house for helpers [hale kokua]. When I arrived and stayed at the house for helpers, I met with Dr. W. J. Goodhue and requested of his kindness to telegraph McVeigh for me to become a helper for my dear younger sister. He consented, and on the evening of Friday, Sept. 27, 1918, the response of the Board of Health was received, allowing me to go be a helper for my beloved younger sister.

Thus, I departed from the house for helpers, and went to live with my dear younger sister for only three days, until she left me and her mother, living in grief and sorrow for her.

At 3:00 p.m., October 1, her earthly body was borne to the church of Kaanaana Hou for the holding of her prayer service by the Rev. D. P. Mahihila. Her prayer service was held with the solemnity of the uplifting words to me and all the friends who gathered to see her for the last time. When the prayer service was over, her earthly body was taken and laid to rest in the graveyard in Papaloa [pa ilina ma Papaloa].

Thus, I give my many thanks to her friends that came to see the earthly body with their gifts of flowers for adorning the body, and the same as well for all the other friends who gathered to accompany the procession. How tragic!

I also give my deepest thanks to Superintendent [Lunanui] McVeigh and Dr. Wm. J. Goodhue, and to Father W. [D.] P. Mahihila goes my greatest thanks for his words of honey that nourished me and the entire assembly.

So please take my thanks, and Almighty God shall ease the sorrows placed upon me and all of you. With all of these things reported above, I end here, with greetings to the typesetting boys of your printing press.

—Mrs. Mary Kahiko. Kalaupapa, OCT. 8, 1918.

Ka Nupepa Kuokoa. 29 NOVEMBER 1918. P. 4.
He Hoalohaloha No Mrs. Hokela Holt. A Condolence concerning Mrs. Hokela Holt.

The heavens, my dear home where I will be always at ease,
Brief, impermanent is my residence here;
Why complain when there is a multitude of,
Pains, burdens, sorrows!

With sorrowful thoughts and falling tears and a grieving heart of compassion, Mrs. H. Holt left her husband and us, the family. Mrs. H. Holt departed on Nov. 12, 1918, at 6:00 a.m., and that [passage] of the Great Book [Buke Nui] is fulfilled, dust returns to dust and the spirit to the one who made it [Nui e hoi ka lepo i ka lepo a o ka uhane i ka mea nana i hana].

The halo light of Hulēʻia has gone out and wearily staggered off to the cliff of Kēʻē, perhaps relaxing with Lohiʻauipo in Hāʻena, vanished, gone out, resting for all time. Our hearing of your voice is over. You rest in the sleep of summer and spring [moe kau moe hooilo: death]. How sorrowful!

O fog [uhiwai] of Waikolu, your dampening of the lovely cheeks of Mrs. H. Holt has ended. O waterfall [wailele] of Waimanu, her gazing upon your hidden cascades is over; O pandanus [hala] trees of Wailēʻia, she will never wear your lei again; O sea spray [ekukai] of Kaupokiawa, your dampening of her lovely cheeks has ended; vanished, taken out of sight by the Koʻolauwahine breeze; the house where love would visit is now chilly; such grief!

With these pitiful tears we share with you, the husband deprived of a wife; and God shall ease our grieving hearts.

With you, Mr. Editor, our greeting of deep affection, and with the typesetting boys of your printing press our love.

We are the grieving family.

—Geo. W. Kahaʻiʻeuanelio, Mrs. Kahaʻiʻeuanelio, Mrs. Kahawai, Jas. Hatchie, Kalani Akana. Kalaupapa, Molokaʻi, NOV. 18, 1918.

Kanikau

KANIKAU, OR DIRGES, are one of the hidden gems in the Hawaiian-language newspapers. Prior to the introduction of the printed word, composing these poetic chants to honor the memory of a loved one was a common practice, so composing kanikau for publication in the 1800s offered a new way to express this important Hawaiian tradition. Today, kanikau are treasuries of language, history, genealogies, and cultural knowledge, especially place names.

While most of the kanikau that follow were written for someone who was a patient at Kalaupapa, several were composed for people who lived there before the arrival of the first patients in 1866. One of these, which is especially valuable for its place names, is from the September 8, 1877, edition of *Ka Nupepa Kuokoa,* a kanikau for a woman named Kaumiokalani. She was born at Kalaupapa, moved away, but later returned and raised seven of her fourteen children there until she left for good in 1860. Kaumiokalani was well versed in traditional Hawaiian culture, including place names. She knew that the land division of Polapola, or "Borabora," in Kalawao was named for one of her ancestors and passed this family history and more on to her children. They in turn included information from their mother in her kanikau.

Kanikau often take the form of a trip that goes past places familiar to the deceased. For patients whose lives ended at Kalaupapa, kanikau reconnected them to their family and former lives through the places they once knew. Family members and friends would often collaborate on the text with each person contributing a verse. This practice is evident in many of the kanikau that follow, the first of which was written in 1864 and the last in 1924.

Hawaiian words or phrases in brackets in the translations are from the original text in the Hawaiian-language newspapers. They were inserted by the author for readers and researchers who have an interest in the Hawaiian

313

language that was in use at Kalaupapa and elsewhere in the 1800s and early 1900s. They also include spelling corrections. Comments in brackets in the translations or after them were inserted to provide additional information about people or places. Words or phrases in parentheses were inserted by the writer of the original text.

Ka Nupepa Kuokoa. 3 SEPTEMBER 1864. P. 4.
He Inoa No H. [Heneri] W. Auld. A Name Chant for H. [Henry] W. Auld.

Answer me Uwilakūlani, the eldest to whom this name belongs
You the first born of Kimo, Uwinihepa is your mother,
Maunaloa is beautiful, the mountain of Molokaʻi,
As it peers down upon the lehua blossoms of Kūkalia
Passionately absorbed with the sighing seas of Kaiolohia
Plotting with the seas of Kaiehu
To make Lehuamakanoe a distraction for me,
As you gaze down upon the beauty of Kaʻawaloa
With the sands of Manawaanu laid out like a kōnane board,
The constant bucking by the sea of Hālō,
Constantly breathing in the fragrance of Kahalakomo
That lingers with you beyond the cliffs of Nihoa
Upon the Hikioe wind
It brings a rain, proudly upon the cliffs
Proddingly revealing the plant of Nānāhoa, entering Puʻulua,
A steadfast affair of love,
Strongly rooted are the pandanus trees of Māpuana by the sea,
Firmly embraced by the Nāulu rain,
I long to see the buds of the ʻŌhiʻa,

The beckoning sway of the Koaiʻe, throbbingly pushes upon the plain,
Prodded by the Hoʻolua wind like a probing tongue,
In a sudden downpour where all barriers are removed
Pounding hard against the Puʻuhehi [Puʻuhahi] plain
A wayward trampling of the rain upon the trees
No edge of Waihānau remains untouched,
Chasing the birds, who rest in the forest
You have gone all the way to Linohau,
Painfully smitten by the pandanus trees of Kepa,
Without a cushion of pandanus trees at Waikolu,
For you to massage, resist, draw in, to lap up the Kiliʻoʻopu wind
Swift is the rough sea of Mōkapu
That proudly carries off Huelo in the wind
Amid the swirling seas of Papapaiki,
Rubbed firmly by Kamalinoāmoʻo,
And constantly slipping back and forth by Pāʻūonuʻakea,
When gazing across at the calmness of Nuʻuhiwa,
The ti of Koaʻea are perfectly beautiful.
Answer me, Uwilakūlani, the eldest by this name

Majestic Hāʻupu, perched on the sea,
The flock of Hano afloat, floating in the wind
The knees of Kana are suspended, suspended in the waters,
The waters of Waiehu hang, hanging against the cliff,
Continuously swirled around, by the Kiliʻoʻopu wind.

» [The last two lines describe Waiehu as a "hanging" waterfall (lewa ka wai o Waiehu). In English hanging waterfalls are also called "upside-down" falls. They occur when the water flow in a falls is light and wind gusting up the face of the cliff is strong enough to suspend the falling water and turn it into mist (ehu a ka makani).]

Ka Nupepa Kuokoa. 12 NOVEMBER 1864. P. 1.
He inoa no Marie. A name chant in honor of Marie.

Child of Māhoe
Darling of ours
Hear this
Oh, leaf of the palapalai fern
Dwelling in the shade of the kukui trees
In the calm of Hauola
You and I live
Off of the rain that steps on the cliffs
The cliff of ʻAlele
The sea flies past
In the presence of Kahio
The dream that has come to me
Finding me here
In the love of my companion
Prodding in the uplands
The uplands of ʻAhuli
I turn and look
At the beauty of Kōloa
There is no length in the plains
To the nose of my horse
Cuddling together, the two of us
In the cold of Kiʻinui
The mind is set upon
Desiring to see
The plains of Pāpaʻalā
It is my lucky day
When I reside among the ʻakuli flowers
I make a noise
Like the noise of birds
The noise that says to me
The lehua flower
That there are two of us
Who faced the cold

KANIKAU

315

The cold of the dews
Mōkapu is clearly visible
'Ōkala is dignified
The leaves are jagged
And its flowers are fragrant
My flower that I ponder
—By T. Māhoe. Kalaupapa, Moloka'i, NOV. 2, 1864.

Ke Au Okoa. 2 JUNE 1870. P. 4.
Kanikau Aloha no Kamakahukilani Kekumuhinu. Loving Lament for Kamakahukilani
Kekumuhinu.

A lament, a love for you, Kamaka
The blossom of Alaka'i incessantly weeps
Waiola Kelautila is the birth mother
My love for my beloved child of the plains of Kalaupapa
You are indeed a native child of this home land
We are connected through the plains of Kanomanō
I search and turn to face the east
Pu'uohōkū appears before me in the misted wind
Your unseen body vanishes from our sight
Kīkīpua mountain appears, Malelewa'a steps out
The pandanus tree that sways in the sea as Keiu weeps
Lovingly abiding at Waiehu, those proud waters
Upon the staff your ensign is hoisted
Mokumana inquires, whose voice is this?
The child of Alaka'i Waiola Kelautila
Weepingly searching for her firstborn
The Kahuna speaks out, of the peace of Moi
But there may not be any, perhaps at Kahikikū
Perhaps at Kahikimoe, perhaps places unseen
A token of love this song is for you Kekumuhinu,
Indeed Kamakahukilani.
—By Kelaukila Kawaiola (female).
» [This verse ends with references to Kahikimoe, the horizon, and Kahikikū, the
sky just above the horizon.]

Love for you is in this song, Kamaka
A love for my beloved younger one, indeed my companion,
Of this place without friends
My only true friend, in the good intentions of the foreigners
Who saw that we needed to be there
Our love is divided, you embraced my hand
And left this world to be with the parents
Love for you, my hand-holding friend
Knowledge seeking friend, entering Mana'olana
In the safety of Nīoi, I am grieving
My pandanus flower is gone, now at Punaakanoe

In the sweet lands, wafting with the fragrance,
You delight there, in the mounting lehua blossoms of the birds,
Love for you in this song, Kekumuhinu,
Indeed Kamakahukilani.
—By Rebeta (female)

A wailing call of grief of Hoʻokano, a rearing parent
My beloved, you are my sweet child, my beach-going companion
The sea of Wailoi, the waters of Wailēʻia,
You are perhaps swimming, in the arms of Hanakaulani,
You delight in the rocking chair,
In the glowing window, with Kaiue your rearing parent
With Kamohola the swift, you have swiftly gone,
Gone without caring to turn and come back
To the embrace of parents
A lament of love for you Kekumuhinu,
Kamakahukilani indeed.
—By Kahoʻokano.

A wailing call of grief of Hāmau, a rearing parent
You are my beloved child that I no longer see
I ask you, where have you gone?
Our precious child caressed by the parents
Who carried you, who fed you,
Love for you my beloved child of the visiting fish
In your native land the akule fish is in the sea
The hinana fish are in the uplands, alas my child
My dear companion who enjoyed watching water surfacing
At the base of the cliffs, there perhaps you are,
At the long upland grove, frolicking and relaxing
With your twin ancestors of Kamauoha
In the protection of the Neleau, we have lost
You to Kelupoka, o flower at Alakaʻi
I proclaim the name of your father
Kūlana at Maui, a surfer of waves
Gotten from within Kawelewele
For whom is this fallen mamo flower
A grieving song of affection for you Kekumuhinu
Indeed Kamakahukilani.
—By Hāmau (female)

A wailing call of grief from Mikiholo, a rearing parent
My beloved first child of the birth land
Of my time of abundance in this district
Love for my child of the fragrant cliffs
Shaking the pandanus flowers of the cliffs that are impassable by foot
The coastline in the sea spray of your beloved land
From my ancestors forth, comes my ability to love

Amid the salt-laced misting rains upon the sea
You have shown a great measure of love as you two have departed
Your existence in the world with your older sister Leleahikulani
A grievous song of aloha for you Kekumuhinu
Indeed Kamakahukilani.
—By Maka'imi

A wailing call of grief of Keomolewa, your brother
My darling sister of the windward cliffs
Expansive is my love for you my departed
I am left alone with our parents
You have gone along the path only you can travel
There is but one thing that consumes me
My love and grief for you my young one
I have affection for the plains of Kōloa
The lonely plain that quakes because of you
At one time there were many men upon horses at Keki'inui
From the heights of 'Alae I turn and look
Love for the islets that swim in the sea
Love for Huelo, 'Ōkala, and Mōkapu
A lament of love, for you Kekumuhinu
Indeed Kamakahukilani.
—By Keomolewa

A wailing call of grief by Ka'iama indeed your brother
My darling sister, from the clinging heights
Of Pu'ukapae I turn upland
The waters of 'Aimanu [Waimanu] weep
For you Kekumuhinu, indeed Kamakahukilani
You were just here in Wailē'ia
Ensconced in the fragrance wafting with love
For you regent, the chilled fragrance surrounds
Entwined delicately
With the pandanus of Kepeno, a lei for the visitor
An adornment for the sands of your birth
We arrive at our home
At Makaluahau
This lament of aloha, for you Kekumuhinu
Indeed Kamakahukilani.
—By Kaiama

A wailing call of grief by Mareka [Mareko], your brother
My darling sister of the roaring seas
The wintry sea that resounds against the cliffs
The waves reaching upland, the Kili'o'opu wind reaching for shore
The Ke'eleawa'a fills the uplands
We are completely consumed with this thing called love
Indeed a significant love of Kaunu'ohua

Reaching high above the windward cliffs
That is how such love makes its way to you
You were perhaps just here in the sun at Kumukahi
At Haʻehaʻe in the east, such a strong affection for you wells up
The one who has disappeared from us
This is my lament of love for you, Kekumuhinu
Indeed Kamakahukilani.
—By Mareko Kaukemi

A wailing call of grief by Kaha, your grandparent
The adult who sought healing, alas my precious grandchild
On the path held in the hand in your short time
We dwell here in this unfamiliar land
You have gone, separated from me
I can no longer see you my grandchild,
You have succumbed to the sickness; come back here
Among my whole family to find a cure
I have abandoned the assembly of priests established by the council
We shall all search for the life of my beloved grandchild
Hidden by the physical ailments of your flesh
But I see that the sickness only afflicts you on the outside
In the clouds that move back and forth, the beauty returns
Your mothers we shall turn back
If the powerful father allows it
We shall be blessed.
This is my lament of love for you, Kekumuhinu
Indeed Kamakahukilani.
—By Kaha of Nīnole, Waialua, Molokaʻi, MARCH 25, 1870.

Ka Nupepa Kuokoa. 24 MAY 1873. P. 1.
Make I Alohaia. Death of a Loved One.
This is a story about M. Kahoʻoukunui, the one who went down the path of
no return [ala hoi ole mai]. She was born in Waikolu on the island of Molokaʻi
on the 10th of April 1852. The number of days she spent on this earth is
twenty-one years and eleven days, and she went the way of the world, the final
goal of all the world. In her eighteenth year she got married to S. Kaholokula of
Kalaʻe. They were together for only three years and then she left her companion
and went to the house of no companions [hale kokoolua ole]. During her life
on this earth she was known to be a kind woman who took care of her husband
and was not objectionable or combative. She was not quick to talk, she took
care of her family, those older and younger than her, her grandparents and
parents. She was a parent to all, kind in entertaining guests. Most women are
not like this woman, like Kahoʻoukunui. So we have composed a few lines of a
poetic lament [mele kanikau] and here it is below.

KANIKAU

319

Kanikau aloha no M. Kaukunui. A loving lament for M. Kaukunui.
My dear wife of the island of Molokaʻinuiahina
The island tall on the surface of the sea

Like a crown flag waving on the sea of Kaiwi
In the expanse of Lae'ahi in the calm
In the sea of Ka'ena spraying upward.
Oh, my dear wife, my dear companion in the struggle
Companion in times of strife in the works of the body
My dear wife from the dark green cliffs of the windward side
From the Ko'iawe rain on the cliffs
Drenching the leaves of the ginger
From the cold uplands of Kīao
How I love the uplands that cause the skin to tingle in the cold where we
    lived.
Oh, my dear wife who awakes in the middle of the night
Of the long nights of winter
My dear wife from the Kili'o'opu winds of Makaluahoa [Makaluahau]
From the humid uplands of 'Ahina
From the fresh waters we swam in at Moa'ula
From the multitudes at Ka'aiea
From the loud-voiced sea at Pōhakuloa
Calling out to the base of the cliffs
From the scent of the līpoa seaweed at the sea of Kepeno.
Oh my dear wife, my dear friend
Close companion of the places we traveled
My dear wife from the hot day at Māhulili
From the turmoil that causes one to cry out at Kalawao
From the kualau rain on the ocean
From the two-sided cliff of the land
How I love the plain of Kōloa when we traveled there.
Oh, my dear wife, how I suffer an endless loss
My beloved lei that never fades for all time
My dear wife from the humid slopes of Pu'upāne'ene'e
We would go to the shade of the kukui grove
The beautiful fragrance of the forest would blow our way
The fragrance of the kupukupu ferns on the cliff
With the scent of the maile vines in the forest
Where we would rest atop Kilohana
There is where we would rest from stiffness
Where the eyes would turn to look east
Where the cool Malanai wind would blow our way gently
And the cool gentle Mālualua wind of the windward side.
Oh, my dear wife, my dear traveling companion of the hot plain of Kalaeloa
The long plain where you and I would go
My dear companion from the sticky heat on the day of the Makali'i stars
Comforting to rest in the shade of the valley
I clamor inside myself, troubled with love
Perhaps you there at Hi'ikua telling the news
As a beautiful lei of the evening.
Oh, my dear wife, my dear companion with whom I cuddle in the cold
That chilly upland, cold and damp

A fire was our blanket to keep us warm.
My dear wife from the cold upland of Maunahui
You have gone and entered the chilling waters in vain
On that lonely, desolate upland
Populated with the voices of birds
With the voices of the kāhuli snails crying out on the leaves of the ʻakolea
    ferns.
Oh, my dear wife, my dear traveling companion of the seas and oceans
Cuddling companion among the lauʻawa flowers of the forest.
My dear wife from the Keʻalapupukahia wind on Molokaʻi
From the whispering sea of Kapalaoa
From the sinking sand of Kawaʻaloa
From the cool slope of Keonelele
How I love the top of Moʻohalaʻia shimmering in the sun
How I love Kāʻā and Kanaha spreading out
How I love the plain of Kaiolohia shimmering in the heat of the sun
How I love the extreme calm of the birds.
Oh, my dear wife, my dear traveling companion of that place of no food
Companion who looked at the bays of Piʻilani
My dear wife from the wet wind of the bow of the canoe
From the rainbow-hued rain of the ocean
From the cold moving rain of the mountain
The dews dampen the tender young leaves of the ʻōhiʻa trees
How I love my dear wife, my close companion in the rain and sun
The cold and the damp, dizzying tribulation
I turn and you are not there
I grasp at your body lying in state in vain
Until your love comes to me, I cry
Oh, my dear wife.
—Holokula. Waikolu, Molokaʻi, APR. 25, 1863 [1873].

Ka Nupepa Kuokoa. 23 DECEMBER 1876. P. 4.
Make i aloha nuiia. The death of a loved one.
Dear *Nupepa Kuokoa*. Greetings.

Will you please, along with your directors, allow me to give a full account of a sad event that happened to me and all of the family of the deceased.

On the 7th of December, 1876 last, at 7:20 in the evening, the unkind hands of death came to take my wedded husband, Mr. Kālaimanō, to take him away, and on the 8th at two oʻclock in the morning, his body was carried away and laid in that place where all the living are laid to rest.

He left me, his wedded wife, and parents, as well as his younger siblings of the same clan [poepoe hookahi], as well as all the family [ohana], mourning on this side of the rag-filled pit that knows no love [lua-pihawelu a ke aloha ole].

He was born in Kamaʻole, Kula, Maui, in 1849. He was joined together with me in the gold bonds of marriage on the 9th of March in the year 1863. We lived together comfortably and well in those years with love abounding all the way up until the time he was taken to Kalawao, Molokaʻi, on the 9th of July in the year 1873. He was stricken with the family-splitting disease [mai hookaawale ohana]. As I had so much love for him, I searched for him in this place for two years. And on the 11th of June 1875, he was returned here to the royal city [Honolulu] to see the Board of Health. His countenance was fine, not affected by that sort of disease, except for illness with his breathing. This was his problem. He was beset with this sickness for five days all the way until his last breath left his life.

He died in the twenty-seventh year or more of his life. It was in the thirteenth year, the eighth month, and twenty-eighth day of our long life together under the covenant of marriage when he left me.

He took care of his wife, parents, and younger siblings. He saw and called out to everyone to come and visit him at our residence, as he did to all people of all races.

And as I love him so, as do our families, therefore, we have composed a lament [kanikau] for him, which we show below:

Kanikau aloha keia nou e Kalaimano. A loving lament for you, Kālaimanō.
My dear husband of the coconut leaf shredding wind of Honuakaha
From the shade of the house at Kaukaweli
A house with a voice of great tears where you and I lived
My father of this fatherless place
The responsible one, the one who would point out dangers
Who knew so well the Heavenly Lords of ours
My dear husband, my endless loss.

My dear husband in the hot sun of the salt flats
Where you and I would visit inland and onshore
My dear husband of the murmuring sea of Kalia
From the front looking down the bow of the ship
We are now separated and you have gone
I am left to caress what we have left
Oh, my dear husband, my lei that never falls
I mourn for you for I have lost you, Kālaimanō
My dear husband of the place without friends
There is only one friend, and that is the Board of Health
You are in trouble and I come swimming after you
You and I live in an unfamiliar land
That place with high cliffs carrying our loads on our back
How I love the long plains of Pūhahi
Where you and I would go
Carrying a load of firewood on our back
My dear husband from the days where we were dizzy from hunger
We survived by eating leaves that flew past us in the forest.

My dear husband from the cold breeze of Kalawao
From the muggy slopes of Pūokapae
From the cold water that stings the skin in Waikolu
My dear husband is probably atop Kauhakō
Listening to the rustling of the kukui leaves

The love of my husband points toward Waihānau
The fragrant forest of ginger
How I love the plains of Makanalua with its bands of horses
There are two burdens that I carry in my heart
I spill my tears
I cry for the inseparable nature of our bond
You have just left me, leaving me behind.
—Mrs. Becky Kālaimanō
» [This kanikau has additional verses not included here that identify place names on Hawai'i island and O'ahu.]

Ka Nupepa Kuokoa. 8 SEPTEMBER 1877. P. 1.
He Makua I Aloha Nuiia. A Parent Greatly Loved.

It pleased the heavens to take our mother who was greatly loved in the early morning of the 13th of July 1877 here in Waiho'olana in Mānoa. We miss her dearly. We warded off the final enemy of the world with strong medicine [lapaau kupaoa ana], but such was not the plan of the creator.

Kaumiokalani was born at the time of the first great plague [kau Okuu mua] in Kapuna in Kalama'ula, Kona, Moloka'i. Her father was Malamakūhi'ona, a man of 'Ewa, and her mother was Nāwai of Maui and Moloka'i, her birthplace [ewe]. She was a descendant of Ha'eha'eahuakāka'alaneo, and a descendant of Borabora on the other side. It is after her Borabora ancestor that the name of the place in Kalawao is called "Borabora," which is its name until this very day, so she is a daughter of royal lineage of all these places. Kalama'ula is where they lived mostly until she got married to the descendant of 'Ewanui'alaakona, Malamakūhi'ona, and they had a child named Kupihea Kaumiokalani.

However, in her childhood days, she was taught the duties of women, and when she blossomed, she married H. Hukilani. They lived together well. They had two children during the time of Liholiho Kamehameha II. At that time she was taught literacy, and since she did so well, she was made a schoolteacher [kumu kula]. At the time of Kamehameha III is when the last of her children was born. She had seven children in Kalama'ula, and she went to live in Ko'olau in Kalaupapa. She had seven more children there, and so she had fourteen children altogether. Ten of these were boys and four were girls. The strength of her health was rather amazing, and the world would be so beautiful if all women were like that. Of greatest importance to this woman was that her children be knowledgeable, so she sent some of her children to the college [Kulanui] at Lāhainaluna.

In 1860, her husband left her to live as a single mother with children, and in that year she left Moloka'i and came back to the sands of Kākuhihewa [O'ahu]. She lived for a little while in the city and then returned to "The beauty of Mānoa" [Ka ui o Manoa], where she lived for many years. She passed some of the time in Lāhaina and Hawai'i with the royal, 'Akahi, and here in Mānoa is where she last lived to retire and rest her body. In her eightieth year of life on this earth, she left us to live parentless.

She was a woman who was taught the songs and chants of the royals of the old days and she had memorized the days, years, and months according to the Western system and the Hawaiian system. She was a calendar for those who inquired of her. She did not forget those things. For these reasons she invoked tears to fall on our cheeks, and because of our great love for her, we composed a lament [kanikau] for her, which is this:

» [The original kanikau that was included in this September 8, 1877, article was revised by Kaumiokalani's family, resubmitted to *Ka Nupepa Kuokoa*, and appeared in the September 22, 1877, edition of the paper. The revision is the version that follows.]

He makua i aloha nuiia. (Kanikau pololei o Kaumiokalani.)
A parent greatly loved. (A true lament of Kaumiokalani.)

This is a lament for you, Kaumiokalani
My dear mother from the land of your birth at Kalaupapa
From the inside waves at 'Īliopi'i
From the long slopes of Pu'upāne'ene'e
There is nowhere on that cliff that you and I did not travel
We drank the water of Wai'alalā
The water that our ancestors drank
The soul drank the water of Kāne
In your lifetime you lived with the Powerful Father above
With Jesus Christ the savior of all
Our lives are from him along with our blessings
The one who lengthens our lives
Our loftiness and our eternal victory
This is a memory of love for you.
—N. H. Po'ookalani

This is a loving lament for Kaumiokalani
My dear mother whom I love so much
Who did not slip away so gently in the morning
Your smile is what I see on your lifeless body
You and I are two who lived in the calm of Moloka'i
Suddenly I have a great burden I carry
Love that rules over my entire body
Your body is what I cherish and your spirit has gone
How I love the soul, the companion of the body
Put together by us in the uplands of Papakailo'i
That comfortable home of ours where we lived
In the grove of kou trees and the leaves of pandanus trees
The parent has passed on, the one whom I love
I miss you for all time
You are there in the eternal kingdom
We remain grieving you.

How I miss and love you
My dear mother in the waters of Waikolu
From the high cliffs of Keanakua
From the rain that creeps over the cliff at Kalawao

From the steep face of Polapola
The land where our ancestors lived
Where we loved the inland of Maulili [Māhulili]
I ache in my heart, and I am filled with your love
How I love Kōloa in the face that turns at Waihānau
You were born in the month of Ka'elo
The parent passes by and is atop Pū'uwa'u
Watching the mirage of the land
You saw the amazing waters of Kauhakō
I am dragged, being tugged by love
How I love Kanomanō in the pathway on the plains
Those plains where we lived
Where we relaxed in the comfort of the bowl.

How I miss and love you
My dear mother in the waters of the Nāulu breeze
In the patches of haokea taro in Ki'ikolu
There were three sharp points on the shore before God
The points of Ho'olehua, Kāhili, and 'Īliopi'i
I climb and rest at the top
Your love is my throne
Love is a continuous chief of mine
How I love the waves of Kai'a and Kanaloa
Pūōhāhā and Pua'ō are joined together
I am filled with light inside with the light of your love
How I love Lenalena, the waters enjoyed by visitors
How I love Pu'uhahi in the sands of Pikoone
How I love the 'ōhi'a trees of Ki'oki'o and 'Ōhi'a
The lehua flowers of 'Ili'ilika'a gather together
The blessings of love are released and I cherish them
All of love is with my chief as it comes to me.

How I miss and love you
My dear mother at the top of Kala'e
From the 'Alahou wind of Kalama'ula
Adorning itself with lehua flowers of Kahana
The two are measured together with Kaiolohia
Desiring the land of birth
The coolness of the Lawelawemālie wind
Your love is what I take gently
Filling the coffers fully
Love is a great treasure to me that I care for
How I love the sands of Kamiloloa where you would go
I love Kaunakakai where you lived
I love the fish you ate that would strike the leg
Moloka'i of Hina, recount the stories
Oh Mom, come back to me.

How I miss and love you
My dear mother in the calm of Honolulu
From the hustle and bustle of the city
From the crowds of the pier
I embrace your love that is not ended
I love Kulaokahua where you and I would go
How I love Puʻuomānoa where you and I would rest
I love Pukaomaʻomaʻo where we would sleep
You and I would sleep together at the gate
You and I lived together at home
I love Mānoa in the torrential Kuahine rain
The place where you and I lived as residents
And became accustomed to living there
That is where you lived as a royal
A favorite of the children
A favorite in the days of youth
You are quickly exhausted
Living together with the children
And you are now with the ancestors
How I miss and love you.
—S. K. K. Hukilani. Waihoʻolana, Mānoa, SEPT. 1, 1877.

Ko Hawaii Pae Aina. 22 JUNE 1878. P. 1.
He Kino Uhane Ua Hala, Ua Moe I Ka Moe Kau Moe Hooilo. Kanikau he aloha no Kahaukomo. A Soul Lost, Asleep for All Time. A lament of love for Kahaukomo.

My dear daughter of the hot days at Mānele
Oh, my dear daughter
My love wells up inside me
At the double-sided cliffs of Kalaupapa
How I love that place where you lived
Where we endured hardship
How I love the steps up to Kōloa
How I love the valley of Waihānau
How I love the seashore at Kauhakō
How I love the descent at Māhulili
I love Polapola with all its people
I love the climb at Kawaluna
I love that cliff where waves crash at Waikolu
How I love that place where you lived
And there at Kalawao rest your bones
Living in the cold of the Koʻolau district
Oh my dear daughter.
—J. H. Kahiamoe

Ko Hawaii Pae Aina. 20 JULY 1878. P. 4.
He Himeni Kanikau: A Song of Lament:

1. A spirit, an expression of love
For you, Moeikaʻuhane
You have gone
The way of no return.
Chorus: Oh! An expression of love for my companion
My dear companion in the cold
I lived with sadness
Saddened because of you.

2. I love the upland of Waimanu
That place where you and I would go
Where the leaves of the kukui trees would sway
I imagine that it is your body.

3. How I love the water of Wailēʻia
Where you and I would be together
On the days when those above would come down
Where you and I were.

4. I love the water of Waikolu
Where you and I would hold each other
In the bitter cold
In the cold Kiliʻoʻopu wind

5. I love the sands of Hoʻolehua
Where you and I lived
We lived with hardship
In that place without food

6. I love the bell of Siloama
As it would call us
Where are you, Moeikaʻuhane?
You and I were well with the spirit.

7. I love the calm of Kawaluna
Where you and I lived
I live alone
You have gone, my dear lady.

8. You have probably gone to heaven
With the legions of angels
With our Father of Everlasting Power
In the Paradise of Eden.
—E. Kailiʻapaʻiʻole. Kawaluna, Molokaʻi, JULY 8, 1878.

Ko Hawaii Pae Aina. 30 AUGUST 1879. P. 4.
[*Kanikau no Emalia Makapoepoe. Ua hanau ia oia ma Kalawao i Molokai.*] [A lament for
Emalia Makapoepoe. She was born in Kalawao on Molokaʻi.]

My dear wife of the calm of ʻĪliopiʻi
And the long sands of Hoʻolehua
How I love the harbor of Kalaupapa
And the cold uplands of Kauhakō
That place where you and I were together
—J. Kāʻilimaʻi. Kapuʻukolo, Honolulu, AUGUST 18, 1879.

Ko Hawaii Pae Aina. 14 OCTOBER 1882. P. 4.
He Niua I Ke Aloha Welawela I Kuu Lei Momi Ua Hala. Dizzy With Heated Love for My
Pearl Necklace Who Has Passed.

The tight bond between us is shattered
The bonds that bind us are torn
My love is heaped up like a bundle of gold
I wander with tears streaming down.
Aloha, my dear wife, my love, the burden of my tears drenches my very
soul.

Dear *Ko Hawaii Pae Aina.* Greetings.

Please insert this headline that you see above in a space on your delicate
body so that the families of the deceased still living in the homeland of the
drenching rain [ualoku] at Hanalei, Kauaʻi, may see regarding the elder sibling
of Lopailani, child of Līwaimakaina.

Mrs. Luka died on the 17th of August 1882 in Kalawao, Molokaʻi. She was a
woman greatly loved, and as you loved her dearly, I composed a loving lament
[kanikau aloha] for her, which appears below:

A loving lament for you, Luka
My dear wife from the hot plains of Kawaluna
That place where she and I were together in love.
I send out my love for my wife of the Waiʻōpua wind
Carrying the sweet fragrance of the nēnē grass down to Pilemena
The soul is hot, my dear wife living in the mountains
Cavorting with Lāʻieikawai
With the woman who strings lehua flower lei at Paliuli
I am dark inside me, bitten by love
My heart shakes within me like an affliction
Oh, my wife, my dear companion.

My dear wife of the slopes of Puʻuokapae
You have left me, your companion and husband
You have gone the way where no friends are found
Your body lies in a cold house
Lying still in the cold
My heart is torn apart and I am pained inside
My dear wife at the source of the faucet water
From the fragrant pandanus tree grove of Wailēʻia
How I love that place where you and I went

Where we dove headfirst into the water of Waikakulu
That water of my dear love that I shall never forget
Until your love comes to me, I shall weep.

My dear wife from the nose of the horse
Gathering as she goes at Kalaehala
The soul has passed on, the companion of the body
Oh, my dear wife of the cold nights of the dews
You are not a woman, you are a parent
You are a companion of the ocean pathway
Where you and I traveled is an ocean pathway
My companion who endured harsh words
That were uttered here and there
Your love is my close companion of my body
Living in a friendless land
I have only one companion, my health
Oh, my dear wife, my loving companion.

My dear wife from the twisting Kiliʻoʻopu wind
Perhaps you have drunk of the puddles of water of the lehua blossoms that
    the birds drink
Your love is a lehua blossom that has come to me
The burden is heaped up on my eyelashes
My tears and nose flow
You have gone like a shadow of a cloud passing by
My dear companion of the day filled with people at Waikolu
You and I rest in the calm of Poʻaʻiwa
How I love that taro patch where you and I worked
Where you, my love, and I worked hard
With my dear wife of the clouds that hang over Kawailoa
The severing of your love endures for a long time
Cutting up my heart into pieces
How I love the woman, my traveling companion of the valley.

My dear wife from where the royals come in the uplands
Your love is a chief to me that I wear as a lei
A golden necklace that never falls for all time
Finally love has left me
I send my aloha to Siloama
Where she, my dear wife, and I were counted
Among the members of righteousness of the Lord
Until the prayers were uttered for my love and I
Oh, my dear wife, my dear companion.

My dear wife of the gathering of food provided by the Board of Health
From the struggling fish in the hand
How I love Polapola, filled with crowds of people
Where my love and I relaxed

Where we were together in the chilling cold
My heart runs cold that you have passed on
You have gone the way of no return
Oh, my dear wife, my dear companion in the cold.

My dear wife from the slopes of Maulili [Māhulili]
From the dust-sweeping wind of Pōhakuloa
The leaves of the kupukupu fern are laid down
I love the hot days of the hot plains of Kōloa
The plain where she, my love, and I went.

My dear wife from the bitter rain of the mountain
Creeping along above Waihānau
There is a large pond, where the rain clouds burst
Your love is a chief to me that I cherish
The house that you go to is not right
You leave on a journey where there is no love
Until your love comes, I weep
I extend my love to my dear wife who has passed on
You have gone on a journey without friends
I remain to mourn your love unceasingly
Like a rain cloud that has arrived
Oh, my dear wife, my dear companion.

My dear wife from the slopes of Makanalua
There were two great tasks that trouble my thoughts
I mourn and grieve for you
My dear wife from the sea spray of Puʻuhahi
Like a fire, the love of my dear sweetheart who comes to me
The soul of my wife comes to me
Stirring me to awake
We two awake with my love
Oh, my dear love, how I pain forever for you
—G. D. Kaiʻaiʻa. Kalawaluna [Kawaluna], Kalawao, Molokaʻi, SEPTEMBER 27, 1882.

Ko Hawaii Pae Aina. 23 DECEMBER 1882. P. 4.
Kuu Minamina Pau Ole Ua Hala. My Unending Grief for This Passing.

A lament of love for you, Nohola
My dear young sibling from the long plains of Kawaluna
How I love that place where you and I went
My dear young sibling from the cold waters of Analoa
From the hala grove of Wailāʻia [Wailēʻia]
From the long plain of Kalawao
From the busy noise of Polapola
How I love the hot plain of Māhulili
The loving one of the siblings who is no longer

I look and see the plain of Kōloa
I have such great love for the plain of Papakailoʻi
My dear younger sibling of the harbor of Lenalena
From the fresh water mixing in the sea
My dear younger sibling of the humid slope of Puʻupāneʻeneʻe
I look and see the plain of Kalaʻe.

Ka Nupepa Kuokoa. 6 MARCH 1886. P. 3.
He Mele Kanikau No Loke. A Song of Lament for Loke.

A lament of love
For you, Loke
I cry, telling of past events
Of the nest of the father
How I love my feather lei
My unwavering companion
My companion with whom I shared the peace of home
The still of the evening
Until your love arrives
I shall cry
My dear daughter
From the Kualau rain
That creeps as it progresses
On the ocean side of Hoʻolehua
Your love is a lehua blossom
That I wear as a lei
A hand spread open wide on the pili grass
Standing proudly in the calm at Kaupokiʻawa
The house with no roof
Where you and I lived.

A lament, an expression of love
For you, Loke
I cry, telling of past events
A mother tells
Of my love for my daughter
Of the calm of Kalaupapa
That place where you and I lived
With your younger siblings
Life was taken there
In the waters of Lenalena
Life turns toward the cliffs
To the ascending trail of the visitor
Where I search to see
The kukui trees of Hāʻupu
My thoughts reflect
On my love for you.

A lament of love
For you, Loke
I cry, mourning
Agnes, your mother
How I love my child
And the shade of the kukui grove of Hauola
Where you and I relaxed
In the lushness of the cliffs
The plains are calm at Papaloa
Effortless for horses to travel
Carrying love
The slopes of Kōloa
No distance of the plains is too great
The top of Māhulili
Infused with the scent of lauaʻe ferns
Your voice is gentle as it replies
We arrive at the presence of the Father
Seeking the justice of the Lord
This is what I love
The bond with the parent.

Ko Hawaii Pae Aina. 25 DECEMBER 1886. P. 4.
[*Kanikau No William Kalua*] [Lament for William Kalua]

How I love *Mokolii,* the ship of love that I sat on
You and I endured the cold of the Kaiwi Channel
Our thoughts rested on seeing the beauty of Molokaʻi
With Kaʻīlio Point extending ahead on the sea
We enter the harbor of Kalaupapa with sails unfurled
We behold the beauty of the Koʻolau cliffs
How I love my living companion Kanoealiʻi, my precious child in the calm
    of Polapola
The parent of many in this land
I love Makanalua with its face turning toward Waihānau
The home of my dear child where we lived in the time of trouble
My thoughts are troubled that my dear feather lei has passed
He has left me to lament for him
Perhaps you are with the all-powerful Father
Dwelling in the Paradise of that life
Oh, my sorrow, my unending love for you.
—Mrs. Mikahala Nāhiʻelua.

Ko Hawaii Pae Aina. 25 MAY 1889. P. 4.
Owau Ka Ka Ke Aloha I Luaiele Ua Kuewa I Ke Ala Me Ka Waimaka. I Am the One for
Whom Love Has Dissipated, I Have Wandered Down the Tearful Path.
To my beloved *Paeaina.* Greetings between us:
    If it is agreeable to you and your helmsmen, please insert in some vacant

space of your columns those words placed above, so that they may be seen by the many friends of my lei [poetic term for "child"] who live from the rising sun at Kumukahi to the sunset at Lehua, and all the way to the lagoons of Niʻihau of the Mikioi wind [mai ka la hiki ae i Kumukahi, a ka welona i Lehua a hala loa aku i na kuaau o Niihau o ka mikioi].

Keoni Nuʻuhiwa, my lei, was born on Sept. 5, 1887, in Kawela, Hāmākua, Hawaiʻi, to Emalia Nuʻuhiwa and Mr. Nuʻuhiwa, and his last breath was taken on Apr. 11, 1889, in Laupāhoehoe, Hilo, Hawaiʻi. Due to the immensity of my love and heartache for him, I have composed a brief chant of eulogy and affection [kanaenae aloha]. This is it.

Kanikau aloha no Keoni Nuuhiwa kuu keiki.
A loving lament for Keoni Nuʻuhiwa, my son.

The umbilical cord is cut, we are separated
The power of the trinity takes you, you are gone
I am in a state of grief and sorrow
Tears flow until the bed is soaked
Like the heavenly pool of water, Kūlanihākoʻi
My beloved son from the cool forest of Kamomoku
From the house laden by the upland mists
Rest and listen to the singing of the land shells
As if they are saying that we have awoken
Greetings to Makahikilua and Kawela
The place where my beloved son was born
My beloved son from the food blown about by the wind
From the day of dizziness when endured
There are two of us, the parents
All of you, the children
The pandanus grove of Makamaka was dear to us
The loving voice of the ocean on the cliffs was experienced
The falling rain is above, we are below
The blanketless night is warmed by the children
My beloved son from the crowds of Honokaʻa
From the double confusion of that place when experienced
You live with your ancestors, we two are separate
But the golden chain of love has come undone
Separation was not desired
The motion of the ship's bow in Kawaihae harbor
I have just seen the power of the government
In the merciless hands without compassion
Saying, "You are going to Kalawao"
The place that the Board of Health desired
A patient parent without voice
There is no need, it has been well supplied
One great thing of the thoughts
A desire in the night, yearning in the day

My beloved lei have I desired, and you have come loose
You had only just begun, and you passed away
Alas for my beloved son, my endless sorrow.
—Mr. Nuʻuhiwa. Kalawao, Molokaʻi.

Ka Nupepa Kuokoa. 12 MARCH 1892. P. 4.
Kuu Lei Gula Ua Hala Ua Wehe I Ka Pili Hooko-o Ia Loko. My Golden Necklace Has
Passed, Undoing the Connection That Supported the House.

On Tuesday, Feb. 16, 1892, at eleven o'clock in the morning, the unfeeling
hands of death came to snatch the living breath of Mariana Kalakini. She was
born in Kalawao, Molokaʻi, on February 14, 1891, to Sam Qui and Kikilia.
One year of her breathing the air of this world had passed. And because of
the great quantity of love I have for her, I have composed a chant of eulogy
[kanaenae] to be seen by her grandparents living in the birthplace, and all of
the family.

My beloved daughter from the lamenting crowd of Kalawao
From the double confusion of Polapola
Greetings to that place where the two of us lived
We lived in that unfamiliar place
Life depending on the bow of a ship
    Alas for my daughter
    My beloved daughter
My beloved daughter from the rise of Māhulili
From the pandanus grove of Pōhakuloa
Long has been the search for you, my beloved lei
What I am looking for this very day
Perhaps you are speaking with Hiku
With the women who reside in the uplands
    Alas for my daughter
    My beloved daughter
My beloved daughter from the hot plain of Kōloa
From the turning face at Waihānau
Your love is like a birth when it appears
Until your love appears I shall weep
    Alas for my daughter
    My beloved daughter
—Mrs. Kikilia Makaliʻiliʻi.

A loving lament for you, Kalakini
My beloved daughter from the sea spray of Pūahi
Your love is as hot as fire when it appears
Until your love appears I shall weep
My beloved daughter from the double confusion of Kalaupapa
Greetings to this place where the two of us traveled
Seeking the virtue of the Lord
    Alas for my daughter
    My beloved daughter

My beloved daughter from the lamenting crowd of Kanaana
We listen to the sound of the bell
Calling out, "Be prepared!"
Alas for my daughter
My beloved daughter.

Lament For Mariana Kalakini.

A lament of love
For you, Kalakini
For you is this 'ilihia flower
Being embraced
    O my lei, my beloved lei
    My darling
    Return, let us return
    Embrace your beloved
How shall it be ended
This heavy burden
It will not be ended
Because, it is a baggage of sorrow
So much pity
The parent of this beloved child
The connection has come undone
Separated from the parent.

A lament of love
For you, Kalakini
Perhaps the soul is yours
That has quietly passed on
    Perhaps the soul
    Is in the deep green uplands of Waihānau
    Effortlessly stringing a lei
    An 'āhihi flower lei for the woman
The woman is adorned in the uplands
Making love with the lehua flower
The mind yearns to be there
To be a companion residing in those uplands
    The soul will reside, listening
    To the sound of the 'I'iwipolena bird
    The mind is ensnared
    By the desire to be a companion residing in those uplands.

A lament of love
For you, Kalakini
You have abandoned
The great baggage of love
    You went alone
    On the path of no return

You have abandoned
The connection to the parent
Kulia wails and recounts
Alas for my beloved lei
My beloved burden has passed
With the Almighty Father
    God is praised
    And there is peace on earth
    He indeed gives
    He indeed takes.
—Mrs. Julia I. Keoki.

A Name Chant for Kalakini.

The bud of the lehua flower is simply beautiful
Growing lush in the forest
The woman is adorned
For Kalakini in the sacred place
    This flower is simply fragrant
    Causing a tingle when smelled
    I sniff and continue
Making a regal lei for my body
A fond remembrance appears
Carried by the fragrant breeze
An adorning lei for the body
For Kalakini in the sacred place
Call out your name
Lehua petals in the forest
If it is the beautiful flower
It is indeed Kalakini in the sacred place.

A Lei for Kalakini.

Your famous lei, Kalakini
Is in the calm of Kalaupapa
You have a lei, famous
Heard of by the flock of birds
Your love is freely given when it appears
Upon being invited to march away
There is no gift in my hand
I have an offering that shall be seen
One great thing on the mind
Your day of joy has arrived
You are a beautiful, cherished blossom for Kulia
And constantly thought of, a favorite
    Make an offering of your attractive lei
    Kalakini indeed in the lofty place

Your famous lei, Kalakini
Is in the calm of Wailēʻia
Being rubbed by the palai fern
The fragrant forest of those uplands
Is just like the lemon-scented Verbena
The strong perfume late at night
Living there, you will hear
The loving voices of parents
You are a cherished blossom of Kikilia
And a darling of Akamukoi
Make an offering of your attractive lei
    Kalakini indeed in the sacred place.

Greetings to the watery place of Waikolu
Bathwater of my darling
The beloved one is caressed at the chest
The first fruit of this land
Friendless, unfamiliar land
One finger on the hands
Five great things in the mind
Like a cut diamond glittering
    Make an offering of your attractive lei
    Kalakini indeed in the sacred place.
—Mrs. Kikilia Makaliʻiliʻi. Kalaupapa, MAR. 3, 1892.

Ka Oiaio. 31 AUGUST 1894. P. 2.
He Hoomanao Kanikau No Mrs. Akiu M. Kealakai I Hala. A Dirge of Remembrance for
the Late Mrs. Akiu M. Kealakai.

Mrs. Akiu M. Kealakai was born from the loins of Mr. Hon. P. Hāʻupu in
Honoliʻi, Hilo, Hawaiʻi, Oct. 17, 1871. We were married by Rev. J. Waiʻamaʻu,
Nov. 14, 1885. She died in Kalaupapa, Molokaʻi, Aug. 9, 1894. She was a woman
who loved her family and loved her husband. She never had a blemish, from
the time she was married until her departure from her husband, younger
brothers, grandmother, and a large family that are lamenting after her. Due to
the immensity of my love for her, I have composed a dirge of remembrance
[kanikau hoomanao] for her.

My beloved wife from the calm of Honokaʻupu
From the stifling heat of the town
Love reminds me that you are no more
My darling is no more
My lei that honors and eases the body
That I shall wear as a remembrance
The house has become lonely, you have passed
Leaving me, a baggage of love
It is the only baggage in my chest
That I alone will bear upon my back

Alas for my darling, O my beloved wife
My beloved wife from the cliffs of Nuʻuanu
Sprinkling the full extent of the cliffs
I will bring a little ease
To my heart that is simply adrift
You have gone, the companion of the home
That home of ours, residing in the upland
The hair is wet, the skin is dampened
On the relentless ascents of the trail
You, O Sun, the one who owns the heavens
Call forth and host my beloved wife
Alas for the sorrow, O my beloved wife
My beloved wife from the bow of the *Mokolii*
With the swells of the Kaiwi and Pailolo channels
That is the path where we will meet
May the love that flutters the heart always persevere
I arrive at Kaunakahakai [Kaunakakai]
Remember the sight of you
The tranquil sea is calling me
Here is your lei, being snatched
I go to Kalaʻe, in the dust of the wind
Heaped up at Apuakalamaʻula
Alas for my grief, O my beloved wife
My beloved wife from the cliff of Kalaupapa
That cliff muddied by the rain
It is a path you have traveled for the first time
I will endure after you
You go indeed, the joyful-voiced ʻŌʻō bird
Lest the sight be dizzying, let the gaze be shielded
Perhaps you will meet with our child
Of the land where agony resided
We simply go without shelter
Without a roof to provide warmth
Alas for my beloved wife, O my beloved wife
My beloved wife from the sandy shore of Papaloa
From the rest house of the Board of Health
Greetings to the uplands of Puhai [Pūahi]
That place where we live
Greetings to the great and the many
The multitude of friends from that land
Greetings also to my dear younger brother
That the two of us bear together
To my ancestors from the upland to the shore
Cherish my beloved
To the great Father in Heaven
Embrace her in your Paradise
—M. A. Kealakai. Honolulu, AUG. 28, 1894.

Ke Aloha Aina. 16 JANUARY 1897. P. 5.
Kuu Lei Hala Ua Haule Iho Nei Ka Pua I Wailuanui. My Dear Pandanus Lei Has Fallen,
the Flower in Wailuanui.
Mr. Editor. Greetings to you:

Because I have received cherished memories of my dear unforgettable lei, a
husband, for whom is that title placed above.

> Two things happen within me,
> Desire and yearning, overwhelming, loved ones are in Puna,
> Arriving, disappearing,
> My beloved golden necklace has fallen,
> The three-stranded ropes of love have been severed,
> My endless love for my dear husband,
> For my beloved companion of this land where agony resides,
> Vanished, hidden are the eyes in the invisible beyond of Kāne,
> Having departed from me, from the companion, a wife.

Mr. Peter Kamakaionaona Ka'aikapu was born in Wailuanui, Ko'olau, Maui,
in AD 1856. He was forty years old when he passed away. He lived a long time
here in the colony [Panalaau], a little over thirteen years, becoming a native
[kupa] well acquainted to this land. He was not a leprosy patient [ma'i lepera].
He was a helper [kokua]. That was the reason he lived in this land. He came to
assist his first patient, and when his first patient died, he joined with me in AD
1889. We spent seven years and nine months living together, and due to the
immensity of my love for my dear husband, I have composed an affectionate
chant of eulogy [kanaenae aloha] for him, to be seen by his many friends living
in the homeland [aina kulaiwi]. It is this below:

> This is a dirge [kanikau], an expression of love for you, Kamakaionaona,
> My dear husband from the Kili'o'opu wind of Waikolu,
> Greetings to that place where we travel,
> My dear husband in the pandanus grove of Wailē'ia,
> We turn to look up at the top of Moa'ula,
> Greetings to you, the husband, the companion,
> The companion for huddling against the cold and the chill,
> My night is chilly, you have gone, the husband,
> I grasp your corpse in vain,
> How shall I find you,
> Alas my dear husband, my endless love to you.
> This is a dirge, an expression of love for you, Kamakaionaona,
> My dear husband in the tumult of Kalawao,
> From the double confusion at being led by the horse's nose,
> From the childish food of this land,
> Densely populated with the companions in agony,
> I was injured with the unintended pain of love,
> Antagonizing, what can make it stop,
> The love that I embrace is a great thing,
> Floods cannot drown it,

Until your love appears I will weep,
Alas for my dear husband,
My dear husband in the quiet calm of Polapola,
Of that home of ours crowded with the fragrance of flowers,
Alas for my dear husband, my endless sorrow for you.

I am sincerely, Mrs. Mahina Kaluna. Polapola, Kalawao, JAN. 5, 1897.

Ke Aloha Aina. 30 JANUARY 1897. P. 6.
He Kanikau No Kamakaionaona. He Kanikau he Aloha keia nou no e Kamakionaona. A
Dirge for Kamakaionaona. This Is a Dirge, an Expression of Affection for you, Ka-
makaionaona.

My dear son from the crowds of Kalaupapa,
From the double confusion at the nose of the horse,
Breaking in masses on the shore of Papaloa,
Where the gaiety will appear,
Until your love appears I shall weep,
Alas for my dear son,
My dear son from the Kulaʻihale wind of Waihānau,
From the hot plains of Kōloa,
Greetings to those plains where my dear son traveled,
Life desiring the bow of a ship,
My dear son from the exhausting labor of the Board of Health.

» [The remaining lines in this kanikau for Peter Kamakaionaona Kaʻaikapu are
unreadable.]

Ke Aloha Aina. 26 JUNE 1897. P. 3.
Kuu Lei Aloha He Kane Ua Haalele Mai Iaʻu I Ka Hoapili He Wahine. My Dear Beloved Lei,
a Husband, Has Left Me, the Companion, a Wife.
Mr. Editor. Greetings to you:
   I ask that you and your workers endure my little bundle of olive leaves shining before you, and you shall send it out like lightning before our news-loving
friends for whom is that title placed above.
   My dear beloved, a husband, my dear companion of quiet talk in the long
nights of winter and the hot days of summer, my beloved golden necklace has
passed, has vanished, and I grope in vain for the spirit. Alas for my dear companion, a husband.
   Paulo Keliʻiluahine was born in Pālolo, Oʻahu, in the year 1877. He was
twenty years old when he passed away. He died on May 26, 1897, in Kalawao,
Molokaʻi. His long illness lasted for many days. Recovery was sought in many
ways, but no respite was found. Due to the immensity of my love for my beloved husband, I have composed a short chant of eulogy [kanaenae] for him,
below.

This is a dirge [kanikau], an expression of love for you, Paulo Keliʻiluahine,
My beloved husband from the double confusion of Kalawao,

In the house-overturning wind of this land,
My beloved husband with the childish food of the land,
Densely populated with the companions in agony,
Alas for my beloved husband,
My love for you is endless,
My beloved husband on the hot plains of Kōloa,
From the turning face at Waihānau,
I move toward you, my beloved companion, a husband,
How shall I find you,
Alas for my beloved husband,
My dear companion of quiet talk in the night when laid to rest,
Companion for huddling against the cold and chill,
My night is chilly, you have gone, the husband,
The companion who dispels loneliness in a lonely place,
My beloved husband who endured the little thing that we have,
Borne equally by us in the rain and the sun,
Alas for my endless love for you,
My husband in the tumult of Kalaupapa,
Greetings to the place where we travel,
From the double confusion at being led by a horse's nose,
Alas for my beloved husband,
My grief for you is endless.

I end here. With the typesetting boys my greeting.
—Elikapeka Kauaheahe.

Ke Aloha Aina. 15 JANUARY 1898. P. 7.
Kuu Ipo Aloha Ua Hala Iho Nei, Ua Wehe I Ka Pili Hookoo Ia Loko. My Beloved Sweet-
heart Has Passed, the Connection Supporting the Heart Has Come Undone.
Mr. Editor. Greetings to you:

If it pleases you and your workers concerning my small bundle of olive
leaves placed above are to be seen by our beloved multitudes who reside from
the rising sun at Haʻehaʻe to the pleasant base of Lehua [mai ka la puka i Haehae
a ka mole olu aku o Lehua].

My dear beloved has passed, my beloved companion of quiet talk in days
past, who is my dear, greatly beloved husband, Mr. Aprahama Pihi, a native and
a resident of the land of the famous rain, "Kanilehua" [a rain of Hilo], and the
forest bower fragrant with pandanus, Puna [Paia ala i ka hala o Puna], and the
land of the Hāʻao rain [aina Ua Haao: famous rain of ʻAuʻaulele, Kaʻū]; that is
the birthplace of my beloved husband who has left me, the companion, a wife,
wailing in grief at the edge of the grave. Alas! Simply pitiful. Aprahama Pihi
was born in Puʻuʻeo, Hilo, Hawaiʻi on Jan. 5, AD 1872, to E. P. Hoʻoʻai (male)
and Lilia Palapala (female). They had seven children, five girls and two boys,
and two of them have followed the footprints of their parents, and five are left
grieving on this side, four girls and one boy.

He was educated at the Boarding School of Hilo [kula Hanai o Hilo], under
the administration of Rev. W. R. Oleson [Olesona] as principal. When he was
done at that school, he then entered the Kamehameha School in AD 1893. He

was at that school for one year. Then because he knew he had contracted this disease that separates families [mai hookaawale ohana: leprosy], he asked the principal, Rev. W. R. Oleson, to dismiss him. He returned to Wailuku, Maui, the place where his mother was living with his new father, Rev. S. Kapu. He stayed with his parents until he was ensnared by the family separation. The parent and his little ones are separate. And he was isolated in this friendless land [aina makamaka ole] in AD 1895. The amount of his years in this world was twenty-four years, eleven months, and thirteen days, until he released his final breath.

We were married on December 24, 1896, by Rev. D. Ka'ai at the place of Beni Li in Kalaupapa. Our year of marriage was not complete when he passed away.

He died on December 14, 1897, and on the 15th his earthly body was borne to the graveyard in Papaloa [ilina o Papaloa], seaward of Kalaupapa. The Angel Society [hui Anela] and the Honorific Society of Latter Days [hui Hoohano-hano o na la hope], for which P. Kiha serves as president, honored his earthly body under the direction of the band of Kalaupapa led by D. [C.] Kealakai.

And the Angel Society was in front of the hearse [kaa kupapau] with the band, and the Honorific Society [hui Hoohanohano] and the family were behind the hearse. He was a member of these societies.

The procession traveled from Kalawao to Kalaupapa. In the YMCA a religious service was held for his earthly body, and from there to his grave-home [hale lua]. Due to the immensity of my love for my beloved husband I have composed an affectionate chant of eulogy [kanaenae aloha] for him, which is this below:

This is a dirge of love,
For you, Aperahama Pihi,
My beloved husband in the double confusion of Kalawao,
The land where agony resides,
Here I am, injured with the unintended pain of love,
Groping in vain for the spirit,
How shall I find you,
Alas for my husband,
My endless love is for you,
My beloved husband in the pandanus grove of Wailē'ia,
Of that lonely, uninhabited place where the two of us traveled,
We dispelled loneliness with the call of birds,
With the 'I'iwi bird living in the forest of that upland,
Alas for my beloved husband,
My endless love is for you,
My beloved husband in the calm of the Bladwin [Baldwin] Home,
That sacred, revered home where my beloved husband lived,
Where the long day was endured,
Life being dependent on the sounding of the bell,
Alas for my beloved husband,
My endless sorrow is for you,
My beloved husband atop Kawaluna,
Greetings to those places where the two of us live with my beloved husband,
My beloved husband in the house without crowds,

Only one crowd,
The companions of agony,
Alas for my beloved husband,
My endless love is for you,

I end here with my greeting to the typesetting boys.
—Mrs. Hattie Pihi.

Ke Aloha Aina. 17 DECEMBER 1898. P. 8.
Kuu Lei Rose Ua Nalo. My Beloved Lei of Roses Has Vanished.
Mr. Editor. Greetings to you.

Please insert, in some available space of our cherished one, my small bundle, which is this below.

On Nov. 28, 1898, the hands of death came and took the breath of my dear, beloved wife, Mrs. Lepekaka'ahumanu. At 11:25 at night, she released her final breath and left me and our grandchildren grieving on this side of the grave.

Lepekaka'ahumanu was born in Puna of the forest bowers made fragrant by pandanus [Puna paia ala i ka hala], from the loins of Kela and his wife. In AD 1886, she contracted leprosy. In 1887, she came here. In 1894, she became president of the Charitable Society [Hui Manawale'a]. I worked hard for her recovery in all manner of ways, until she simply passed away, and because of the immense size of my grief for my beloved wife, I have composed a chant of eulogy [kanaenae] for her, tearfully:

A dirge, an expression of affection [He kanikau, he aloha],

For you, Lepekaka'ahumanu,
Who has just passed,
Along the path of no return,
The two of us remain,
With our burden,
Alas my endless love for you,
My beloved wife from the upland of Pōhakuloa,
Greetings to that place where we were together,
We sat, listening to the call of the birds,
The eyes turn,
Gazing at Kalaemilo,
Adorned,
By the spray of the sea,
Alas my love for you,
My beloved wife striving for the virtue of the Lord,
Greetings to the voice that replies,
You and I shall uplift virtue,
Greetings to your lei, a grandchild,
Our child,
Alas my love for you,
An everlasting light [ipukukui pio ole]
In its actions upon me,

Alas my grief for you,
O Papaloa,
Have you seen Lepekaka'ahumanu,
Yes, she is at 'Īliopi'i,
Relaxing in the sea spray,
The surging swells of the ocean,
Greetings, greetings to that place where we traveled,
That lonesome, uninhabited plain of Ho'olehua,
Have you seen Lepekaka'ahumanu,
Yes, she is at Makanoni,
With the stone-eating woman,
Alas my love for you,
When antagonized by love,
How can it be ended.
I am tearfully,
Maneaulani.

A dirge, an expression of affection [He kanikau, he aloha],
For you, grandmother Lepekaka'ahumanu,
Who has just gone,
On the path of no return,
Gliding out there along the far reaches,
Where have you passed to,
Greetings to your voice, grandmother Lepeka.
I am your grandson,
Keoki Kalauwao.

And for the accuracy of this I give my greeting to the editor and to the typesetting boys my expression of affection.
I am tearfully, Manueaulani. Kalaupapa, DEC. 9, 1898.

Ke Aloha Aina. 1 APRIL 1899. P. 7.
Kuu Mea Aloha Ua Hala. My Dear Beloved Has Passed.
To the editor of the newspaper *Ke Aloha Aina*. Greetings to you:
Please insert [this] in some available space of your columns, in order that
the multitudes and our friends living in the Kanilehua Rain [ua Kanilehua:
poetic name for Hilo] may see it.
At 4:00 p.m. on March 8, 1899, my greatly beloved grandson, Kaleimoku,
departed from this life. He was born in Pu'u'eo, Hilo, Hawai'i, from the loins of
Kueka'a (male) and Kalakoili (female), and due to my great grief for my beloved
grandson, I have composed a small dirge [kanikau] for him.

A dirge, an expression of affection for you, Kaleimoku,
My beloved grandson from the Lanipili Rain of Hilo,
The famous rain of the land, the birthplace of the grandmother,
My beloved grandson from the crowds of Punahoa,
The soft-shelled pāpā crab of Wailuku,
My beloved grandson from the tall rise of 'Ama'u'ula,

Greetings to that place where we were together, my beloved grandson,
Kīlauea calls for us to return, evening has come,
Perhaps you are speaking at ʻĀwehi with the woman stringing flowers of the
    land,
The widespread lehua flower, the cherished food of birds,
My beloved grandson from the creeping rain of Panaʻewa,
Drenching the bud of the lehua flower,
My beloved grandson from the sweltering sun of Kamakaiki,
Greetings to that place where we were together, my beloved grandson,
Perhaps you are speaking atop Haʻaheo,
Or bathing in the water of Honoliʻi,
Your love is a chief that I shall wear as a lei, a thing for the heart to crave,
My beloved grandson from the palace in the sea,
A hope arises to see the beauty of Molokaʻi,
The land where the crowd gathers, the friends of this land,
That you might say at Waikoliʻi, to go on and drink the water of Wailoa,
Turning to gaze upon Hāʻupu, that hill moving at the shore, my beloved
    grandson,
Wailēʻia resides in the uplands, Waimanu perfumes the cliffs,
Greetings to the mist resting above, perhaps you are speaking there, my
    beloved grandson,
I am antagonized by endless love of a grandson,
My beloved grandson from the softly sounding sea of Pauʻaka,
Love is quite clear when it arrives, gently surging,
You are valuable to me as a lei, an unforgettable lei around the neck from
    my beloved grandson.

I am with sorrow, Mrs. Kaʻaluʻalu Paʻahao. Pauʻaka, Kalaupapa, Molokaʻi.

Ke Aloha Aina. 19 AUGUST 1899. P. 3.
Kuu Opuu Rose Ua Mae. My Beloved Rose Bud Has Wilted.
Mr. Editor. Greetings to you:
    Please insert into some available space of our newspaper the words placed
above, and it will be the one to carry the news to the four corners of the land
[kihi eha o ka aina], to be seen by all of the multitudes of my beloved rose bud
that passed on the path of no return, living in the Kanilehua Rain [Ua Kanile-
hua] of Hilo.
    Mary Nohinohiana was born in Puʻuʻeo-uka, Hilo, on January 13, 1883,
from the loins of Mr. and Mrs. W. P. Kalohe. She entered the leprosy settlement
[kahua maʻi lepera] on Molokaʻi on May 9, 1889, and died on July 21, 1899, in
Kalaupapa, Molokaʻi. And because of how immense our love is, the two of us
have composed a small chant [mele] for her.

    This is a dirge [kanikau], an expression of affection for you, Mary Nohino-
        hiana,
    A wailing chant of remembrance [uwe helu] by me, Kealualu,
    Alas for my beloved daughter,
    My beloved friend of this unfamiliar land,

My beloved companion in the sea spray of Pau'aka,
From the breaking waves of Pua'ō,
Beloved are the broad plains of Papaloa,
Beloved is that place where we would be together,
We were close with the cold wind, a Ho'olehua,
My beloved daughter from the crowds of Kalaupapa,
My beloved daughter from the bow of the ship that is life,
We survive on the uncommon food of the foreigner,
You are an adornment for the parent, a unique lei of mamo bird feathers,
A wailing chant of remembrance by me, Mary,
Alas for my beloved daughter,
My beloved companion in following and carrying out the work of God,
My beloved daughter from the shelter of the house called Homelani,
Beloved is that home where I and my beloved daughter live,
You go on the path of no return,
I remain, mourning and grieving for you,
My beloved daughter, my dear beloved has passed.

—Composed by Mrs. Kealualu, Mrs. Mary Keaka.

This is a dirge, an expression of affection for you, Mary Nohinohiana,
A grieving lament [uwe haalipo] by me, Kahalepouli,
Alas for my beloved older sister,
My beloved friend of this land of agony,
My heart has been injured by the unintended pain of love,
Beloved are you who has passed on alone,
My beloved older sister from the sweltering sun of Makanalua,
Beloved are the broad plains of Kōloa,
Beloved is that place where we roamed,
Enduring together the cold wind, a Kili'o'opu,
Quite beloved is the top of Māhulili,
And then we see the beauty of Mōkapu,
Waikolu appears beautifully in the calm,
We go there and see the waters of Wailoa [Kawailoa],
Beloved is the unfamiliar place where we roamed,
This is a dirge, an expression of love for you, Mary Nohinohiana,
An affectionate lament by me, Williams,
Alas for my beloved sister,
My beloved companion of the sea of Nāpuka,
Your voice emerges pitifully,
Take heed, you two, my younger siblings,
Your voice is beloved when expressing,
That all of you share your affection,
This is my final hour,
You must all remain hopeful,
My beloved sister, my dear beloved has passed.

—Composed by Lukia Kahalepouli and Williams.

Ka Nupepa Kuokoa. 16 OCTOBER 1924. P. 5.

Kuu Wahine Aloha Ua Hala. My Beloved Wife Has Passed.

To Mr. Editor of the *Nupepa Kuokoa,* Solomon Hanohano. Greetings to you:

Please provide some small available space in the favorite of the people, so that it may disperse to the eight seas [na kai ewalu] with that bundle placed above, to be seen by the multitudes of my beloved wife, Mrs. Hattie K. Nihipali, living from Hawai'i, island of Keawe, to Ni'ihau, base of Lehua [mai Hawaii Moku o Keawe, ahiki loa aku i Niihau Mole o Lehua], because it pleased almighty God to take the living breath of my dear wife, who was greatly loved, from our home, in Hau'ula, at 1:50 a.m. on Wednesday, Sept. 24, 1924, and left the body lying motionless before me, the children, the grandchildren, her older siblings, her younger siblings, and the entire family. Alas!

My beloved wife was born from the loins of her mother, Mrs. Pau'ole Kailua and Mr. Māhoe Lau'ahi, in Kalawao, Moloka'i, on July 14, 1861. Thus she was sixty-three years old before dust returned to dust, the spirit to God, since he gives, and he takes away. How sorrowful!

We were married by Rev. Samuel Paulo, minister of Hālawa, Moloka'i, in Waialua, on August 14, 1880, and so we spent forty-four years in purity.

Beloved are the lines of cliffs [kakai pali] of that homeland of ours. Beloved also are the three waters [na wai ekolu], Wailē'ia, Waikakulu, and Waihānau. Beloved are those waters where you bathe. Beloved is Leinaopapio, towing along Huelo and 'Ōkala. Beloved is Ka Lae o Kahio extending out into the sea. Beloved is Kalaemilo, that place that you traverse with your multitude. Beloved is the sea of Papaloa and the fresh water mixing with the ocean water of Lenalena, that swirling water that opens and closes.

Beloved is the summit of Kauhakō [luna o Kauhako]. Job's words are fulfilled, that the person born of woman has only a portion of days, filled with troubles.

Beloved is the cliff trail [ala pali] of Kukuiohāpu'u, that place where you trudged along, the rain and wind above, you marching below. Beloved is the plain of Kala'e red with dirt, the water of Wai'alalā, that lofty water with the acidic soil. Moomoni [Mo'omomi] and Kaiolohia, never again will the two of you see her, Mrs. Hattie K. Nihipali. She has passed, vanished on the path of no return [ala hoi ole mai].

O Ka Lae o Kalā'au, Haleolono perched above, beloved is that place where you traveled with your papa, Simon Kahalehulu. Punakou, Lae o 'Īloli above Kīlauea, those places have indeed been traveled by you. Pālā'auone where the birds of Kama'ipu'upā [Kama'ipu'upa'a] run about on salt beds [alialia], Kalama'ula piled with dirt, the two of you will never again see my dear beloved, a wife.

O peaceful Kaunakakai of the bird, a Kioea; beloved is that place where she met with that grandparent [tūtū] of hers, Ki'eki'e. Never will you see her again, the light has gone out, the house is dark, and the golden three-strand chain of the covenant of marriage has broken. Death shall part you, and it is indeed the third part of a person's life: 1. birth, 2. marriage, 3. death; and when these three things meet, dust is the final inheritance.

The long sands of Kamiloloa, there is the kicked fish [i'a ka wawae] of Hīlia, the place where my beloved wife enjoyed eating the fish that eats leaves of that land of ours, with some simply prepared sweet potato [uala], sustenance for the day. Pakuhiwa, Kawela, made fragrant by the flower of Kaihuanu, Keonekū'ino darkening my thoughts, since my beloved wife has passed, my dear beloved.

O Kamalō, you will never again see Mrs. H. K. Nihipali. Keawanui, 'Ōhi'a, Manawa, 'Ualapu'e, never again will she tread upon your soil. Kalua'aha, she will not see your holy walls again. Mapulehu, the three Pūko'o, she will never again see your green pastures. Kūpeke, Ahaina, your ridges. Honomuni arm-in-arm [kuikui lima], the place where my dear beloved relaxed with the parents, the grandparents. Beloved is that place where we met in the days when we first arrived.

She was a native [kupa], a local [kamaaina] for all of Moloka'i. She lived at Hālawaiki. She was familiar with the kukui trees of Lanikāula [kukui o Lanikaula], with the swells [ale] of Pu'upo'i, with Mokuho'oniki extending into the sea like a bird.

And so, my beloved wife was generous, welcoming, hospitable to all from high to humble, and open-hearted; and her family and her children, her grandchildren, were important to her, until she simply passed on to that faint world.

We had eleven children; five are living with me, only males; one male passed before with five girls, and she followed on that trail.

So, Moloka'i was her land of birth [onehanau], and O'ahu of Kākuhihewa was her adopted land [aina hookama].

We left Moloka'i on September 26, 1881, for this reason: our dear parents were confused by the god, since the god of the people of Moloka'i had been burned by fire, and our parents thought that it would be found in Lā'ie. My beloved wife was lured into going to visit and then return to that land of ours, except deceit was the thing done to my beloved wife, and she stayed and became a native local [kupa kamaaina] in these Ko'olau [windward] districts.

Upon arriving in Lā'ie, indeed, there was a god of baptism, but not like the Moloka'i god, which touches the heavens, poisonous. She lived in Lā'ie for about ten years, then went to Kaluanui and lived there for over five years. Some land was obtained in Hau'ula, and I rejoined my beloved wife, becoming a native and local [kupa a kamaaina] of this proud land and carrying it upon my back.

My dear beloved and I traveled all around O'ahu, the town of Honolulu searched by us from the sea to the uplands, from this edge to that edge. Pu'unui, that place where we relaxed with my younger sibling, the children, we will never again see her. She has passed, vanished on the dark path of Kāne [ala polikua a Kane], perhaps with Hiki stringing lei of lehua flowers in the forest, as a lei for the election day.

Kapālama was loved by us, experiencing the 'Ōlauniu wind [makani o Launiu] of that place. Beloved are the markets of the town, that place where we walked for the needs of the body. Beloved is Pauahi Street, the intersection of automobiles [otomobile], the place where we mixed with the children of China and Japan. We were together in these Ko'olau districts, in the time of horse carriages. That need passed, then trucks [kaa kalaka] came, we were there. That passed, then automobiles came, until you rested in the sleep of summer and winter [death]. Beloved is our house, Halealoha. You would greet the high and the humble, the tall and the broad, you would simply greet everyone.

Beloved is 'Ewa with the silent voice sea creatures [I'a Hamau Leo: oysters], the place where our older sibling lives. It was simply traveled by us, and to Waialua to the place of those parents of ours, Peter Kailio and Mrs. Pulewia P. Kailio. Beloved are those two mountainous places where we relaxed and listened to the voice of the sea of Pua'ena. Beloved is Kahuku, the land floating in the sea [aina lewa i ke kai]. Lā'ie, the wings of birds. Kaipapa'u of teeth-gnashing 'ōpule fish. Kao'o and Waikulama, those blessings having been patiently gained by us, and you are without and I am also without. Alas!

So, your good deeds toward me are an unforgettable monument for you, forever. I give my limitless thanks to everyone who stood watch with me in my hours of sorrow and sadness, and the same to all those who gave their gifts of flowers [makana pua] upon the body of my greatly loved wife. Love to her older siblings Mr. and Mrs. Kapanookalani for taking their younger sister to the grave, and our beloved child, W. A. Kanakanui, for taking the important things that will comfort the body, and those who dug her grave and took her and followed her on her final journey, blessed by Mr. Kapanookalani here at home, and by I. K. Palea at her grave. The body was released in the beloved soil of Lanakila [the cemetery of Lanakila Church in Hau'ula].

Please accept my limitless thanks for each of you all, and God will bless all of us. Amen.

I end here with great thanks to the editor, and to the typesetting boys of your printing press my unending affection.

With thanks. I am sincerely, Sam M. Nihipali, With the Family. Hau'ula, Ko'olaupoko, OCT. 1, 1924.

Interviews

When the University of Hawaiʻi Press published my first book, *Beaches of Oʻahu*, in 1977, I began researching my second, *Beaches of Maui County*. I spent two years, 1978 and 1979, visiting the four islands in Maui County: Maui, Molokaʻi, Lānaʻi, and Kahoʻolawe. I walked the beaches on each island, including Kahoʻolawe, which at that time was under the jurisdiction of the U.S. Navy. I requested permission to visit the island on April 20, 1979, and the U.S. Navy approved my request. I gathered additional information for the beaches on all four islands by interviewing residents, especially kupuna, who knew the areas well, and I submitted my manuscript to the University of Hawaiʻi Press. They published *Beaches of Maui County* in 1980.

During the course of my research on Molokaʻi, I visited Kalaupapa three times, in February and May of 1978 and in August of 1979. I wanted to learn as much as I could about its beaches before I went, so I interviewed several residents of the settlement who were living on Oʻahu. Mary Duarte from Hāna, Maui, was sent to Kalaupapa on December 19, 1932, and Sanford Smith from Kapaʻa, Kauaʻi, on October 7, 1936, but in 1977 both of them were staying at Hale Mōhalu in Pearl City so they could receive dialysis treatment at St. Francis Hospital in Honolulu. I visited them twice at Hale Mōhalu, where they were cordial and generous with their information. At that time, in addition to working for the Honolulu Fire Department, I was taking classes at the University of Hawaiʻi at Mānoa for a degree in Hawaiian Studies. One of my classmates in the program was Elroy Makia Malo, another resident of Kalaupapa, so I interviewed him, too, once at UH and then again at Hale Mōhalu with Mary and Sanford.

After my interviews with Mary, Sanford, and Makia, I was ready to visit Kalaupapa, so Mary put me in touch with her sister, Rachael Nākoa, who still lived there. Rachael sponsored me for each of my three trips to the settlement, meeting me each time at the bottom of the pali after my walk down

351

the trail from Palaʻau. I stayed in the Kōkua House. During the course of those visits, I met Charles Busby, the superintendent at the settlement, and the following residents: John Cambra, John and Lucy Kaona, Rose Lelepali, Edward Marks, Teetai Pili, and Meli Watanuki. In addition to providing me with information about Kalaupapa, they told me that Elmer Wilson, a former superintendent, lived Topside at Hoʻolehua. I interviewed him at his home in May 1978. All these individuals contributed to what I know about Kalaupapa, including its beaches and place names.

The interviews that follow are from the journals I kept during my field trips to Maui County in 1978 and 1979. The place name information is exactly as I wrote it, which did not include any diacritical marks in the Hawaiian words or place names.

Sanford Smith and Mary Duarte. Interview at Hale Mohalu, Pearl City, Oahu. September 28, 1977.

Wharf. Good swimming.

Boat House. The beach near the graveyard. It was named for an old boat house for canoes. The last old canoe there was owned by a man named Hamakua.

Black Sands. The beach at the bottom of the pali. It experiences seasonal accretion and erosion, but the other beaches don't.

Hoolehua. The beach to the rear of the lighthouse. No swimming, only fishing. Residents mostly pole fish and throw net. Paul Harada is the main fisherman now. Points in this area are named after residents, such as Kamahana Point and John Davis Point. Plenty paakai [salt] in this area during the summer. Opihi [limpets], too, but commercial fishermen come and raid their opihi. They anchor offshore and swim in.

Iliopii. A young man named Sylvester used to surf there. His last name was Apiki, but he was hanai [adopted], so now it's Paalua. He's an ex-patient, so he moved to Oahu.

Waikolu Valley. Opae, hihiwai, oopu, and prawns in the stream. White ginger with orange throat and white ginger with red throat that Hashimoto found are there, but he didn't show anyone where the patch is. Also maile. Axis deer come close looking for water.

Topside. The rest of Molokai to all the Kalaupapa residents.

Waihanau. The "mystery" valley. When you call, your voice always sounds like it's coming from far inside even if the caller is outside the valley. Old Hawaiians always said never call, only whistle.

Kikania. Bush with red berries, which grows all over. The berries are popular for making lei at the settlement. [Kikania is the Hawaiian spelling of "zizania."]

Waialeia. Everyone pronounces the name as "Waileia." Valley good for pig hunting. Supposedly there was an old trail down into the valley from Topside.

Mikilua. A crater down on the makai side of Kauhako.

Elroy Makia Malo. Interview November 1977 at the University of Hawai'i–
Mānoa.

Black Sand. Beach beneath the pali. Fine sand. Erodes during the winter.
Area called Puahi.
Boat House. Beach where you can get wet. Not really deep enough to
swim. Most of the swimming is done at the wharf. He and his friend,
Sylvester, learned to bodysurf at Keaau on Oahu. The residents of
Hale Mohalu would go to Makua to swim (they called it Hale Mohalu
Beach), and sometimes on the way back, they would stop at Keaau
Beach Park and bodysurf. Later, they bodysurfed at Kalaupapa at
Iliopii.
Kalawao. Used to have a black sand beach, but the 1946 tsunami washed it
away.

Sanford Smith, Mary Duarte, and Elroy Makia Malo. Interview January
2, 1978, at Hale Mohalu, Pearl City, Oahu.

Puahi. Hawaiian name of Black Sand Beach. Site of the old dump. Stream
that comes out there used to run past Kauhako Crater and flood the
town. It was diverted before Sanford and Mary's time. Can't cross it
after heavy rains. Two other small streams are in the same shoreline
area.
Old Ladys' Cave. Makia said the story of the cave, Ananaluahine, is in
Molokai: A Site Survey by Catherine Summers [This name is spelled
Ananaluawahine in *Molokai: A Site Survey*]. The people hiding in the
cave were massacred.
Bird Cave. Close to Old Ladys' Cave. Birds, terns, nest there.

Points and shoreline areas named after people:

Spud's. Ocean View Pavilion area where "Spud" Spatois (not sure of
spelling) had a house. The 1946 tsunami wiped out his house. The
pavilion was built when Bill Malo, Makia's brother, was president of the
Lions Club and initiated the project.
Shinsato Point. Said to be an old canoe landing. Good fishing, flat reef.
Miyoshi Point. Near the airport.
Kamahana Point. David Kamahana had a beach house there.
John Davis Point. He drowned there.
Nenue Point. Probably Kalae o Kahio. Ernest Hoohuli had a beach house
nearby. Near the airport.
Mormon Pond. Directly opposite Waileia Valley. Natural tidal pool where
the Mormons baptized their converts.
Kahili. Beach marked on the map. Makia knew the name from an old chant
composed by one of the old-timers. Site of a heiau.
Papaloa. Beach area near the graveyard. Where the settlement proper starts
at the cattle guard.
Pauaka. Place name at Papaloa. Makia said the "pau" maybe pa'u [pa'u'u],

a growing stage of ulua, like the word papio. He heard fishermen there [at Kalaupapa] use the term, but hadn't heard it anywhere else.

Kaahemo. Old dispensary, now the Visitors' Quarters. Sanford said an underground cave there had an underwater entrance near shore. A resident named Paulo found the entrance while diving and said the cave had been used as a burial site, but the entrance collapsed before he could show anyone else. Visitors hear noises at night, perhaps water washing in the lava tube cave.

Mary got these Kalaupapa place names from David Kupele, a Kalaupapa resident, who visited Hale Mohalu before this interview.

1. Nihoa (Makia said this is the flat area between Kalaupapa and Moo-momi.)
2. Kahola Pele
3. Pohaku Mana (A stone in the ocean. All three of them thought the name should be Pohaku Manu.)
4. Ana Puka
5. Hoolehua
6. Kapalaola
7. Kamahana
8. Kapukiawa
9. Kukui
10. Makalii
11. Lei Hala

John Cambra. Interview February 14, 1978, at his beach house at Papaloa, Kalaupapa.

Kamahana Point, Jack Miyoshi Point, John Davis Point, and Shinsato Point are all named after patients. John showed me David K. Kamahana's grave, which is in the cemetery in front of his house. He said David had a beach house at the point that is named for him that he bought from Dr. Goodhue. Some people know it as Jack Sing Point for Jack Sing, who had the house after David. The other three points are named for patients who died while fishing at those spots.

Pohaku Ilio. A flat, shiny stone in front of his beach house. It's connected somehow to Iliopii Beach, which is the next beach over.

Laupapa. The name of the area where the wharf is now. There used to be a leaf-shaped papa [reef] there. The wharf is named for P. O. Dawson, who was with the Board of Health. He was loved by everyone.

Pohaku Manu. Big rock on the beach before you go up the pali trail.

Pohaku Noho. Big rock that looks like a chair near one of the cattle guards.

Monkey's Point. Named for a Korean man who was washed off the rocks and drowned while he was fishing about 1926 or 27. His nickname was "Monkey." The point is also known as High Rock and Nenue Point.

S.S. *Kaala.* Steamship that went aground in 1932. Part of the boat is still visible above the surface of the ocean. Some years after the grounding, several of the crew members came to Kalaupapa as patients. They said the night they went aground, they were guiding on a red light they thought was the navigation light marking the wharf. It turned out to be a red light on a beach house at Iliopii Beach where a late night party was going on.

Waikolu. John came to Kalaupapa on January 13, 1924, and stayed in the old Baldwin Home until it closed. That same year there was a severe landslide between Waileia and Waikolu that they heard from the home. The landslide destroyed a section of the pipe from Waikolu that ran over the boulders at the foot of the pali between the two valleys. The pipe brought fresh water to Kalawao, and when it was damaged the boys at Baldwin Home had to help with the repairs by carrying the replacement pipe. John said it took over twenty of them to carry one length of the nine-hundred-pound section of pipe.

Waileia. One of the Hawaiian residents had a big canoe that he kept at Waileia. When he wanted to go fishing, he would get some of the boys from Baldwin Home to help him carry the canoe across the rocks and down to the water. Then they would go out to the lobster cave at Mokapu [island].

John Cambra and Teetai Pili. Interview February 15, 1978, while riding in John's truck and following the shoreline of the peninsula.

Hoolehua. July and August are the best months for salt. Get it by the bags.

Mormon beach house. Steps and concrete side walls were standing alone alongside the dirt road.

Kaliko's place. Next ruins past the Mormon beach house.

Kapalawa. Lava area from here on.

John Davis Point. 1948 or 49, he was washed off the rocks and drowned while fishing for ahole.

Kamahana Point. Just past John Davis Point. Only the walls of his beach house were left. The beach house standing nearby was built by Elmer Wilson, who was superintendent from about 1947 to 1974. He retired and lives Topside. Tree Kamemoto owns the place now.

Shinsato Point. Near the dump area for abandoned cars. Safest of all the exposed points on this shore.

Makalii. Area before the old wharf.

Baldwin Home. The rock structure that is still standing was part of the kitchen.

John and Lucy Kaona. Interview at their home in Kalaupapa. May 30, 1978. I returned to Kalaupapa for a final visit on Monday, May 29. Rachel met me at the bottom of the trail, took me to the Kokua House, then loaned me her car to do my research. Driving through the village, I spotted a beautiful glass ball shrine in Edward Mark's back yard. When I stopped to take a picture, he came out and gave me one of the small ones and a small glazed clay-mold statue of Father Damien that he sells to the tourists. He told me he'd found the glass balls at Hoolehua.

» [Japanese fishing floats made of glass that wash up on Hawaiʻi's beaches are commonly called "glass balls" by local residents.]

That evening Lucy and John Kaona invited me to dinner in their home, where the main course was spiny lobster, slipper lobster, and 7-11 crab, all from the waters offshore. John doesn't have any fingers, so he amused us by opening the pull-tabs on his beer cans with his teeth.

The next day, May 30, I had breakfast with John Cambra. I'd seen him the day before, and he'd invited me to come to his beach house in the morning. He made me a six-egg omelet with a generous helping of his wonderful lobster-potato salad. Then I drove out to Hoolehua to look for glass balls, but only found a lot of bottles. John and Lucy had invited me to their home for lunch, which was fish: nenue and lai. When I was ready to go, Lucy gave me a lei of orange kikania berries that she had made and then she and John explained its significance. They said that kikania [*Solanum aculeatissimum*] was a special plant to the residents, and that they considered the berries to be the "flowers" of Kalaupapa. They explained that the kikania thrives in arid areas and that it's a symbol of the resiliency of the residents who were sent to a desolate place but who thrived in spite of their hardships. They said they don't make the lei often, only for special occasions.

Elmer Wilson. Interview at his home in Hoolehua, May 31, 1978. He is a retired superintendent at Kalaupapa who is now the minister of the church in Halawa. He has always been interested in traditional Hawaiian culture, speaks Hawaiian, and talked to the old-time residents of Kalaupapa. He gathered the shoreline place names that are on the wall map at police headquarters, which I copied in February.

Ke One Nee o Awahua. Literally, "the sliding sands of Awahua." Awahua is someone's name. This is the correct name of the black sand beach.
Nihoa. The plateau beyond Awahua toward Moomomi.
Puwahi. Name of a place and a point, and possibly a heiau.
Pikoone. Also the name of a place, but he never located it exactly.
P. O. Dawson Wharf. He was superintendent for the Board of Hospitals and Settlement under Harry Kleugel.
Papaloa. Not only the name of the beach and the cemetery, but also the area inland of the cemetery. The old-timers said this was the garden area of the settlement in the 1920s, where they grew watermelons.
Ocean View Pavilion. The concrete slab is the foundation of Spud Patua's (perhaps Patuwa) home. He was married to a resident and ran the laundry. He wasn't assigned a home in the settlement, so he used the beach house there as his home. When the 1946 tsunami took out his home, he was given a house in the settlement. When the laundry was moved to Hale Mohalu on Oahu, he left. Ocean View was built about 1952.
Iliopi. He pronounces the "pi" as a single, long "i" and said it literally

means, the "stingy dog." Beach and area inland. Formerly a village site. Can still see many old walls. Hadn't heard of Pohaku Ilio at Papaloa.

Kahili. Beach named for a woman, Kahiliopua, a chiefess from Iliopi. She moved to the airport area and only had female retainers. If someone wanted a wife or helper, a kokoolua, she acted as an intermediary. She conducted her affairs at Kanohopohaku o Kahiliopua, the chair rock near the airport gate. One went to her with gifts, "Hele no a lako."

» [The article that follows mentions Kāhiliʻōpua, the woman Elmer Wilson associated with the place name Kahili.

Ka Nupepa Kuokoa. 12 NOVEMBER 1864. P. 4.
Ko Molokai Alii Ame Kona Mau Akua. Molokaʻi's Aliʻi and Gods.

La'i is the paramount ali'i of Moloka'i who had seven gods, and these are the names of his gods: Kahuilaokalani, Kālaipāhoa, Kapowahine, Kauhuhuakua, Kāhiliʻōpua, Kaʻalaeʻahina, and Makakūikalani, and under these gods are the commoners, and the role of their gods was to announce information to all aliʻi and people, and this is how the people of ancient times grew.]

Hoolehua. Turtles laid their eggs at Hoolehua Nui, where it was easy for them to come in over the rocks, even when the surf was big. They usually went to the east corner of the beach. Plenty of salt from Hoolehua to the airport.

Pali Trail. His wife, Abigail, was a nurse. When the patients had babies, she carried them up the trail when they were several weeks old and accompanied them to Honolulu.

George McClain. He wrote the song "My Sweet Sweetie" about 1915 or 16. It tells the story about his girlfriend at Kalaupapa. He compares her to the rainbows that sometimes can be seen looking toward Ilio Point. Someone else copyrighted the song.

» [*My Sweet Sweetie* is now regarded as a traditional song. The words with a translation by Mary Pukui are as follows.

Kuʻu ʻohu lei anuenue	My adornment, a rainbow lei
Koʻiaweawe nei i ke pili	Lies spreading over the pili grass
ʻO ka pai a ka makani Kiu	When lifted by the Kiu wind
Ka ʻiniki ʻana iho welawela	One feels a sharp pinch.
Hui:	Chorus:
Hoʻi mai kaua e pili	Come, let us be together
My sweet sweetie	My sweet sweetie
ʻAʻohe pili hemoʻole i kau	Never more to be separated through the seasons
My sweet sweetie.	My sweet sweetie.]

Waikolu. Sometimes a black sand beach accretes there to Kalaekiloia, but not often. He recalls seeing it in 1946, 51, 68, and 69.

Kauhako. Means "intestines."

Laupapa. Reef on the north side of the breakwater.

Kaala. He heard there was a party onboard the ship. When they were
coming up from Ilio Light, they were guiding on Kalaupapa Light and
ran aground.

Baldwin Home. There's a big bucket there that he had built to carry the
sand and concrete to build the water intake at Waikolu. They fattened
cattle in Waikolu, slaughtered and butchered them there, then used a
D7 [bulldozer] and the bucket to bring the meat out.

References

Andrews, Lorrin. *A Dictionary of the Hawaiian Language*. Honolulu: Island Heritage Publishing, 2003.

Brocker, James H. *The Lands of Father Damien*. Hong Kong: James H. Brocker, 1997.

Bunson, Maggie. *Faith in Paradise*. Boston: Daughters of St. Paul, 1977.

Catholic Mission Press. *Mission Catholique des Iles Sandwich, Eglises, chapelles, du Vacariat Apostolique des Iles Sandwich*. Honolulu: Imprimerie de la Mission Catholique, Janvier 1875.

Chapin, Helen. *Guide to Newspapers of Hawai'i 1834 to 2000*. Honolulu: Hawaiian Historical Society, 2000.

Chung, H. L. *The Sweet Potato in Hawaii*. Hawaii Agricultural Experiment Station, U.S. Department of Agriculture. Bulletin No. 50. Washington, D.C.: Government Printing Office, 1923.

Clark, John. *Beaches of Maui County*. Honolulu: University of Hawai'i Press, 1980.

———. *Hawaiian Surfing: Traditions from the Past*. Honolulu: University of Hawai'i Press, 2011.

Damon, Ethel. *Siloama: The Church of the Healing Spring*. Honolulu: The Hawaiian Board of Missions, 1948.

Daws, Gavin. *Holy Man: Father Damien of Molokai*. New York: Harper & Row, 1973.

Fornander, Abraham, and John F. G. Stokes. *An Account of the Polynesian Race: Its Origins and Migrations, and the Ancient History of the Hawaiian People to the Times of Kamehameha I*. Honolulu: Mutual Publishing, 1996.

Franciscan Spirit: Saint Marianne Cope Commemorative Edition. Volume 2.4 (Spring 2013).

Gibson, Walter M. "Report of the President of the Board of Health to the Legislative Assembly of 1886 on Leprosy." Reprint from the collections of the University of California Libraries.

Gonschor, Lorenz, and Kamanamaikalani Beamer. "Toward an Inventory of Ahupua'a in the Hawaiian Kingdom: A Survey of 19th and Early 20th Century Cartographic and Archival Records." Unpublished manuscript.

Green, Linda W. *Exile in Paradise: The Isolation of Hawai'i's Leprosy Victims and*

Development of Kalaupapa Settlement, 1865 to the Present. Historic
Resource Study. Denver, Colo.: National Park Service Northwest Planning
Branch, 1985.

Griffin, Claire McCaffery. "Craftsmen in Kalihi: The Story and Style of the Kalihi
Catholic Orphanage." *American Studies* 690 (Fall 94), April 29, 1996.
University of Hawai'i–Mānoa.

Holy Bible. American Revision Committee. New York: Thomas Nelson & Sons,
1901.

Hutchison, Ambrose K. "In Memoria of Reverend Father Damien J. De Veuster and
Other Priests Who Have Labored in the Leper Settlement of Kalawao,
Molokai." Unpublished manuscript handwritten in 1931 together with a
copy of the manuscript transcripted by Father Paul Macken, SS.CC., in
1998. Damien Collection (Damiaan Vandaag), Louvain, Belgium.

Inglis, Kerri A. "'Cure the dread disease': 19th Century Attempts to Treat Leprosy
in the Hawaiian Islands." *Hawaiian Journal of History* 43 (2009).

————. *Ma'i Lepera: Disease and Displacement in Nineteenth-Century Hawai'i.*
Honolulu: University of Hawai'i Press, 2013.

Ka Baibala Hemolele. New York: American Bible Society, 1966.

Ka 'Ohana O Kalaupapa. *Adjourned With a Prayer: The Minutes of Siloama &*
Kanaana Hou Churches, Kalawao & Kalaupapa, Molokai, 1866–1928.
Honolulu: Ka 'Ohana O Kalaupapa, 2011.

Kanahele, George, and John Berger. *Hawaiian Music and Musicians.* Honolulu:
Mutual Publishing, LLC, 2012.

King, Robert K. "Districts in the Hawaiian Islands." Reprinted from University of
Hawai'i Research Publication No. 11, and revised to June 30, 1942.

Law, Anwei Skinsnes. *Kalaupapa: A Collective Memory.* Honolulu: University of
Hawai'i Press, 2012.

Law, Anwei Skinsnes, and Valerie Monson. *Ili Nā Ho'omana'o o Kalaupapa: Casting*
Remembrances of Kalaupapa. Waipahu, Hawai'i: Pacific Historic Parks,
2012.

Lycayan, Emalia, Virginia Nizo, and Elama Kanahele. *Aloha Niihau.* Honolulu:
Island Heritage Publishing, 2007.

Macdonald, Gordon A., Agatin T. Abbott, and Frank L. Peterson. *Volcanoes in the*
Sea: The Geology of Hawai'i. 2nd ed. Honolulu: University of Hawai'i
Press, 1983.

Malo, David. *Hawaiian Antiquities.* Bishop Museum Special Publication 2, 2nd ed.
Honolulu: Honolulu Star Bulletin, 1951.

Malo, Makia, with Pamela Young. *My Name Is Makia: A Memoir of Kalaupapa.*
Honolulu: Watermark Publishing, 2011.

Moblo, Pennie. "Defamation by Disease: Leprosy, Myth and Ideology in Nineteenth
Century Hawai'i." PhD dissertation, University of Hawai'i, 1996.

————. "Ethnic Intercession: Leadership at Kalaupapa Leprosy Colony, 1871–1887."
Pacific Studies 22, no. 2 (June 1999): 27–69.

————. "Leprosy as Colonial Metaphor: Segregation in late Nineteenth-Century
Hawai'i." Hamilton Library, Hawaiian Collection, University of Hawai'i:
Graduate Paper, 1995.

————. "Leprosy, Politics, and the Rise of Hawaii's Reform Party." *Journal of Pacific*
History 34, no. 1 (1999): 75–89.

Monsarrat, Marcus D. "Molokai: Local Names and Station Marks." Unpublished
copy of survey notes. Honolulu, 1884.

Moran, Michelle T. *Colonizing Leprosy: Imperialism and the Politics of Public Health*
in the United States. Chapel Hill: University of North Carolina Press,
2007.

Mouritz, Arthur Albert St. M. *The Path of the Destroyer: A History of Leprosy in the*
Hawaiian Islands, and Thirty Years of Research Into the Means by Which It
Has Been Spread. Honolulu: Honolulu Star Bulletin, Ltd., 1916.

Pukui, Mary Kawena. *'Ōlelo No'eau: Hawaiian Proverbs and Poetical Sayings.*

Bernice P. Bishop Museum Special Publication No. 71. Honolulu: Bishop Museum Press, 1983.

Pukui, Mary Kawena, and Samuel H. Elbert. *Hawaiian Dictionary.* Honolulu: University of Hawai'i Press, 1971.

Reesman, Jeanne Campbell, Sara S. Hodson, and Philip Adam. *Jack London, Photographer.* Athens: University of Georgia Press, 2010.

Remy, M. Jules. *L'ile de Molokai avant la Leprosarie. Journal de M. Jules Remy, Naturaliste-voyaguer du Museum.* Arcis-sur-aube, France: Imprimerie Leon Fremont, 1893. Translated by Mildred M. Knowlton. Typed copies at Bishop Museum and Kalaupapa National Historical Park.

Richardson, Janine. " 'None of Them Came For Me': The Kapi'olani Home for Girls, 1885–1938." *Hawaiian Journal of History* 42 (2008): 1–26.

Shallenberger, Robert. *Hawaiian Birds of the Sea: Nā Manu Kai.* Honolulu: University of Hawai'i Press, 2010.

Sigall, Bob. *The Companies We Keep 3.* Honolulu: Small Business Hawaii, 2010.

Silva, Noenoe K., and Pualeilani Fernandez. "Mai Ka 'Āina O Ka 'Eha'eha Mai: Testimonies of Hansen's Disease Patients in Hawai'i, 1866–1897." *The Hawaiian Journal of History* 40 (2006): 75–97.

Soehren, Lloyd. Catalog of Hawai'i Place Names. Database and webpages maintained by the University of Hawai'i at Mānoa Library.

Stewart, Frank. *Almost Heaven.* Honolulu: University of Hawai'i Press, 2012.

Summers, Catherine. *Molokai: A Site Survey.* Pacific Anthropological Records, Number 14. Honolulu: Bernice P. Bishop Museum, Department of Anthropology, 1971.

Thomas, Mifflin. *Schooner from Windward: Two Centuries of Hawaiian Interisland Shipping.* Honolulu: University of Hawai'i Press, 1983.

"United States Leprosy Station Sites in Waikolu, Kalawao and Makanalua, Molokai as Selected by U.S. Surgeon-General Walter Wyman, P.H. & M.H.S." Survey and plan compiled by George F. Wright, June 1905. On file in Hawai'i State Survey Division as Registered Map 1728.

Wood, K. R. "Vegetation Descriptions of Kuka'iwa'a Peninsula and the Three Islets of Huelo, Mokapu and Okala, Kalaupapa, Moloka'i, Hawai'i." Special Report Prepared for Kalaupapa National Historic Park. National Tropical Botanical Garden, Department of Conservation, Kalaheo, Kaua'i, 2008.

Yzendoorn, Father Reginald, SS.CC. *History of the Catholic Mission in the Hawaiian Islands.* Honolulu: Honolulu Star Bulletin, Ltd., 1927.

Index

Names in the index are spelled the way they appear in the Hawaiian-language newspapers, which is without diacritical marks.

Kainuwai, J. K., 28, 43, 287, 305; Lale, 274; S. K., 74

Kaiolohia, Molokai, 188, 314, 321, 325, 347

Kaiue, 316; D. W., 119

Kaiwi (channel between Molokai and Oahu), 31, 63, 137, 165, 234, 256, 320, 332, 338

Kakaako Hospital, Honolulu, Oahu, 9, 16, 17, 123, 144, 145, 186, 187, 190, 213, 214, 229

Kala, W. H., 187

Kalaau, George, 196; K., 14, 310

Kalae, Molokai, 25, 31, 35, 55, 78, 100, 111, 114, 115, 190, 235, 263, 267, 287, 319, 325, 331, 338, 347

Kalaea, 28, 31. *Also* Kalaeaa, 28, 31

Kalaehala, Waikolu, 217

Kalaekiloia, 65, 357

Kalaeloa, 31, 32, 320; S. W., 264

Kalaemilo, 28, 31, 68, 343, 347

Kalahikiola, Kohala, Hawaii island, 135, 275

Kalahili, 116

Kalaimano, Becky, 323

Kalakala, 169

Kalakaua, King, 14, 15, 175, 184, 185, 188, 207, 220, 221, 229, 243

Kalakini, Mariana, 334

Kalakoili, 344

Kalama, 183, 258; Waha, 31

Kalamaula, Molokai, 79, 113, 114, 323, 325, 347

Kalana, J., 233, 239

Kalani, J. P., 162

Kalanianaole, J. K., 233. *Also* Keliianaole, 233, 236, 237

Kalanilehua, P. K., 193, 196, 202

Kalaola, Sam. L. K., 225, 226

Kalapana, Hawaii island, 73, 174, 177, 178

Kalauao, Enoka, 169, 170

Kalaukoa, A. P., 167

Kalauli, A., 61, 86, 121; Emelia Namaielua, 61; Pamahoa, 234

Kalaupapa, 32–35

Kalaupapa lighthouse. *See* Hale Ipukukui

Kalaupapa National Historical Park, xi, xii (map), xiii, xvi

Kalauwao, Keoki, 344

Kalawao, 36–40

Kalawaia, Henry, 302

Kalawaiakanoa, Samuela, 72

Kalawaiaopuna, Samuela Maalo, 72

Kalei, 124; Sam, 63

Kaleiheana, Willie, 49, 301

Kaleihua, Mary

Kaleimoku, 344

Kalepa, 22; M., 8

Kalepo, S., 38

Kalihi Hospital, Honolulu, Oahu, 5, 6, 11, 123–125, 128–131, 146, 151, 152, 227–229, 240, 246, 299

Kalilikane, 210

Kaliki, 258

Kalohe, W. P., 345

Kalohi, J. K., 94, 204, 250, 251

Kalu, 2

Kalua, 182, 191; Adam, 97; D. W., 157; Eliza Hakuaikawai Kahula, 83; J., 241; William Kalikolani, 84, 332

Kaluaaha, Molokai, 111–114, 117, 121, 148, 225, 268, 348

Kaluaihakoko, Maui, 125

Kaluakoi, Molokai, 31, 100, 102, 150, 188

Kaluna, 26, 27, 181, 182, 250; J., 245; Maliana, 340; Paulo, 190

Kamae, N. B., 17

Kamai, 192, 243; Kimo, 39

Kamaipelekane, E. P., 67, 118

Kamaka, 182; H., 38; J. N., 98

Kamakahiki, Rev. S. K., 42, 44, 74

Kamakaiki, Hilo, Hawaii island, 345

Kamakau, 101, 263; Lizzie Kapoli, 240; Samuel K., 36, 80

Kamakea, J. K., 40

Kamakee, 116, 191

Kamakele, 62

Kamakini, 210

Kamala, 62

Kamalalawalu, 58, 200

Kamalinoamoo, 314

Kamalo, Molokai, 78, 348

Kamano, 71; John, 235

Kamanoni, Molokai, 126

Kamanu, J. A., 8, 43, 73, 232, 271, 273

Kamauoha, 165, 317; J. N., 243; K., 167

Kamealoha, 309. *Also* Kameaaloha, William, 287

Kameeku, Molokai, 102

Kamehameha I, 50, 290; II, 79, 323; III, 79, 323; IV, 32, 112, 117; V, 50, 123, 290

Kamehameha Day, 50, 262, 290, 298

Kamehameha School (Kula o Kamehameha), 341

Kamohakau, Sam, 239

Kamomoku, 333

Kanaana, 41, 125, 260

Kanaana Hou Church, 7, 10, 40, 43, 73, 179, 262, 335. *Also* Kanaanahou, 40, 42, 43

Kanaha, 321

Kanakahelewale, 210

Kanakaokai, 126

Kanakaole, 68, 81; J. S., 137; W. H., 94

Kanalu, 104; George, 19; W., 94, 98, 99

Kanamu, J. A., 257

About the Author

JOHN R. K. CLARK is a former lifeguard and a retired deputy fire chief of the Honolulu Fire Department. He is the author of ten books about Hawai'i's beaches, surf spots, and shoreline place names published by the University of Hawai'i Press.

About the Translators

IĀSONA ELLINWOOD holds an MA in Hawaiian from the University of Hawai'i–Mānoa. Besides his work as a translator, he is also an educator and a regular contributor to *Abstract* magazine.

KEAO NESMITH, PhD, is an applied linguist and researcher who is fluent in Hawaiian, having been taught the language by his grandmother and by having grown up among native speakers of Kaua'i and Ni'ihau. A native of Kaua'i, Keao has also lived in New Zealand and Tahiti, where he taught the Hawaiian language at universities in both places in addition to teaching for nearly twenty years at universities in Hawai'i. He works as a cultural consultant, author, teacher, and teacher trainer, as well as a translator of foreign texts into Hawaiian.